Creating Tomorrow's Organizations

Creating Tomorrow's Organizations
A Handbook for Future Research in Organizational Behavior

Edited by

Cary L. Cooper
*Manchester School of Management, University of
Manchester Institute of Science and Technology, UK*
and
Susan E. Jackson
*Stern School of Business Administration,
New York University, USA*

JOHN WILEY & SONS
Chichester · New York · Weinheim · Brisbane · Singapore · Toronto

Other Wiley Editorial Offices

John Wiley & Sons, Inc., 605 Third Avenue,
New York, NY 10158-0012, USA

WILEY-VCH Verlags GmbH,
Pappelallee 3, D-69469 Weinheim, Germany

Jacaranda Wiley Ltd, 33 Park Road, Milton,
Queensland 4064, Australia

John Wiley & Sons (Asia) Pte Ltd, 2 Clementi Loop #02-01,
Jin Xing Distripark, Singapore 129809

John Wiley & Sons (Canada) Ltd, 22 Worcester Road,
Rexdale, Ontario M9W 1L1, Canada

Library of Congress Cataloging-in-Publication Data

Creating tomorrow's organizations: a handbook for future research in organizational
behavior/edited by Cary L. Cooper and Susan E. Jackson.
p.   cm.
Includes bibliographical references and index.
ISBN 0-471-97239-8 (cloth)
1. Organizational behavior—Research—Planning.   I. Cooper, Cary L.
II. Jackson, Susan E.
HD58.7.C73 1997
658—dc21   96-53015
CIP

British Library Cataloguing in Publication Data

A catalogue record for this book is available from the British Library

ISBN 0-471-97239-8

Typeset in 10/12pt Times by Best-set Typesetter Ltd., Hong Kong
Printed and bound in Great Britain by Bookcraft (Bath) Ltd
This book is printed on acid-free paper responsibly manufactured from sustainable forestation,
for which at least two trees are planted for each one used for paper production.

Contents

About the Editors

Cary L. Cooper, *Manchester School of Management, University of Manchester Institute of Science and Technology, PO Box 88, Manchester M60 1QD, UK*

Cary L. Cooper is currently Professor of Organizational Psychology at the Manchester School of Management (UMIST) and Pro-Vice-Chancellor of the University of Manchester Institute of Science and Technology. Professor Cooper is the author of over 80 books (on stress, women at work, and industrial and organizational psychology), has written over 250 articles for academic journals, and is a frequent contributor to national newspapers, TV and radio. Founding President of the British Academy of Management, he is currently Editor-in-Chief of the *Journal of Organizational Behavior*, and a Fellow of the British Psychological Society, Royal Society of Arts and The Royal Society of Medicine.

Susan E. Jackson, *Department of Management, Stern School of Business, New York University, Tisch Hall, 40 West 4th Street, Suite 7-14, New York, NY 10012, USA*

Susan E. Jackson received her PhD in organizational psychology from the University of California at Berkeley in 1982 and is now Professor of Management at New York University's Stern School of Business. Her primary areas of expertise are organizational behavior and the strategic management of human resources; special interests include workforce diversity, management team staffing and development, and the design of human resource management systems to support business imperatives. She has published over 100 articles on these and other topics, as well as four books. In addition to her university activities, Professor Jackson serves on the Board of Governors for the Center for Creative Leadership (Greensboro, NC, USA), and is actively involved in numerous professional associations, including the Society for Industrial and Organizational Psychology, and the Academy of Management, where she has served as President of the Organizational Behavior Division and as Editor of the *Academy of Management Review*.

Contributors

Eric Abrahamson, *Graduate School of Business, Columbia University, 3022 Broadway, New York, NY 10027, USA*

Chris Argyris, *Graduate School of Business, Administration, Harvard University, Soldiers Field, Boston, MA 02163, USA*

Julian Barling, *School of Business, Queen's University, Kingston, Ontario, Canada K7L 3N6*

Robert J. Bies, *School of Business, Georgetown University, DC 20057, USA*

John P. Briscoe, *School of Management, Boston University, 621 Commonwealth Avenue, Boston, MA 02215, USA*

Larry D. Browning, *College of Communication, University of Texas at Austin, Austin, TX 78712, USA*

Jean Carletta, *Human Communication Research Centre, University of Edinburgh, Edinburgh EH8 9LW, UK*

Sue Cartwright, *Manchester School of Management, University of Manchester Institute of Science and Technology, PO Box 88, Manchester M60 1QD UK*

Georgia T. Chao, *Department of Management, Michigan State University, East Lansing, MI 48824, USA*

Taylor Cox Jr, *University of Michigan Business School, 701 Taplan Street, Ann Arbor, MI 48109-1234, USA*

Dan R. Dalton, *Graduate School of Business, Indiana University, Bloomington, IN 47405, USA*

James W. Dean, *CBA, University of Cincinnati, PO Box 210165, Cincinnati, OH 45221, USA*

P. Christopher Earley, *Graduate School of Management, University of California, Irvine, CA 92717, USA*

Karin B. Evans, *Bell Atlantic, 600 East Main Street, 6th Floor, Richmond, VA 23219, USA*

Daniel C. Feldman, *College of Business Administration, Department of Management, University of South Carolina, Columbia, SC 29208, USA*

Michael Frese, *Faculty of Psychology, University of Amsterdam, Roetersstraat 15, NL-1018 WB Amsterdam, The Netherlands*

Simon Garrod, *Human Communication Research Centre and Department of Psychology, University of Glasgow Glasgow, UK*

Barbara A. Gutek, *Department of Management and Policy, University of Arizona, McClelland Hall 405, Tucson, AZ 85721, USA*

Douglas T. Hall, *School of Management, Boston University, 621 Commonwealth Avenue, Boston, MA 02215, USA*

Herminia Ibarra, *Graduate School of Business Administration, Harvard University, Soldiers Field, Boston, MA 02163, USA*

Boris Kabanoff, *Queensland University of Technology, PO Box 2434, Brisbane, Queensland 4001, Australia*

Kathy E. Kram, *School of Management, Boston University, 621 Commonwealth Avenue, Boston, MA 02215, USA*

Edward E. Lawler III, *Center for Effective Organizations, School of Business Administration, University of Southern California Los Angeles, CA 90089-1421, USA*

Gerald E. Ledford Jr, *Center for Effective Organizations, School of Business Administration, University of Southern California, Los Angeles, CA 90089-1421, USA*

E.A. Locke, *College of Business & Management, University of Maryland, College Park, MD 29742, USA*

Allan M. Mohrman Jr, *Center for Effective Organizations, School of Business Administration, University of Southern California, Los Angeles, CA 90089-1421, USA*

Susan Albers Mohrman, *Center for Effective Organizations, School of Business Administration, University of Southern California, Los Angeles, CA 90089-1421, USA*

Nigel Nicholson, *Centre for Organisational Research, London Business School, Sussex Place, Regent's Park, London NW1 1SA, UK*

Dennis W. Organ, *School of Business, Indiana University, Bloomington, IN 47408, USA*

Edward Ottensmeyer, *Clark University,Worcester, MA, USA*

Jone L. Pearce, *Graduate School of Management, University of California at Irvine, Irvine, CA 92717-3125 USA*

James Campbell Quick, *Department of Management, University of Texas at Arlington, Box 19467, Arlington, TX 76019-0467, USA*

Anat Rafaeli, *School of Business Administration, Hebrew University of Jerusalem, Mt Scopus, Jerusalem, Israel*

Rafael Ramirez, *CBA, University of Cincinnati, PO Box 210165, Cincinnati, OH 45221, USA*

Amy E. Randel, *Graduate School of Management, University of California, Irvine, CA 92717, USA*

Randall S. Schuler, *Department of Management, Stern School of Business, New York University, Tisch Hall, 40 West Fourth Street, Suite 7–11, New York, NY 10012, USA*

Henry P. Sims Jr, *University of Maryland Van Munching Hall, College Park, MD 20742, USA*

Sim B. Sitkin, *Fuqua School of Business, Duke University, Durham, NC 27708-0120, USA*

Lynn Smith-Lovin, *Department of Sociology, University of Arizona, Tucson, AZ 85721, USA*

Deidre Sorensen, *School of Business, Queen's University, Kingston, Ontario, Canada K7L 3N6*

Kathleen M. Sutcliffe, *University of Michigan Business School, 701 Tappan, Ann Arbor, MI 48109-1234, USA*

Ramakrishnan Tenkasi, *Center for Effective Organizations, School of Business Administration, University of Southern California, Los Angeles, CA 90089-1421, USA*

Linda Klebe Treviño, *Pennsylvania State University, 416 Beam BAB, University Park, PA 16802, USA*

Rosalie L. Tung, *Faculty of Business Administration, Simon Fraser University, Burnaby British Columbia, Canada V5A 1S6*

Michael A. West, *Institute of Work Psychology, University of Sheffield, Sheffield S10 2TN, UK*

James C. Wimbush, *Graduate School of Business, Indiana University, Bloomington, IN 47405, USA*

Introduction

Cary L. Cooper
Manchester School of Management, UMIST, Manchester, UK
and
Susan E. Jackson
Stern School of Business, New York University, USA

The 1980s, in most developed countries, was described as the decade of the "enterprise culture", with people working longer and harder to achieve individual success and material rewards. We had globalization, privatization, process re-engineering, mergers and acquisitions, strategic alliances, joint ventures and the like, transforming workplaces into hot-house, free market environments. In the short term, this entrepreneurial period improved economic competitiveness in international markets in the countries that embraced it. But as strains began to appear, the concept of "burnout" joined "junk bonds", "software packages" and "e-mail" in the modern business vocabulary (Cooper, 1996; Van der Spiegel, 1995). Nevertheless, *work* was carried out essentially the same way as before; it was still business as usual in large or growing medium-sized organizations in US Inc., UK plc, Germany GmbH, and so on.

By the end of the '80s and into the early '90s, a major restructuring of work as we have known it since the industrial revolution was beginning to take place. The early years of the decade were dominated by the effects of recession and efforts to get out of it. Organizations throughout the Western world, and even further afield, dramatically "downsized", "delayed", "flattened", and "rightsized". Whatever euphemism you care to use, the hard reality experienced by many was job loss and wrenching change. Now many organizations are smaller, with fewer people doing more and feeling much less secure. New technology, rather than being our savior, has added the burden of information overload as well as accelerating the pace of work at a greater speed of response (e.g. faxes, e-mails) becomes the standard business expectation. And, at the same time, as more and more companies adopt a global perspective, organizations and the individuals

Creating Tomorrow's Organizations. Edited by C.L. Cooper and S.E. Jackson.
© 1997 John Wiley & Sons Ltd.

they employ are finding that success in the global arena requires fundamental changes in organizational structures as well as individual competencies. Just as organizations are redesigning to be more flexible and adaptive, individuals are expected to be open to continual change and life-long learning. Workers will be expected to diagnose their abilities, know where to get appropriate training in deficient skills, know how to network, be able to market themselves to organizations professionally, and tolerate ambiguity and insecurity.

As more organizations experiment with "outsourcing", "market-testing" (in the case of the public sector), "interim management" and the like, many more of us will be selling our services to organizations on a freelance or short-term contract basis. We are creating a corporate culture of blue collar, white collar, managerial and professional temps—in a phrase, a "contingent workforce". In the UK, for example, more than one in eight workers is self-employed; part-time and short-term contracts are growing faster than permanent full-time work. The number of men in part-time jobs has nearly doubled in the past decade, while the number of people employed by firms of more than 500 employees has slumped to just over one-third of the employed population. Similar trends are occurring around the globe (Paoli-Pelvey, 1993).

In predicting the look of future organizations, many experts argue that most organizations will have only a small core of full-time, permanent employees, working from a conventional office. They will buy most of the skills they need on a contract basis, either from individuals working at home and linked to the company by computers and modems (teleworking), or by hiring people on short-term contracts to do specific jobs or carry out specific projects. In this way companies will be able to maintain the flexibility they need to cope with a rapidly changing world (Handy, 1994; Makin, Cooper & Cox, 1996).

Much of this change is already happening. For example, a recent survey found that 13% of UK companies already allow some employees to work from home. British Telecom claims that there are already more than 2.5 million people working from home on a full- or part-time basis in the UK, and that this figure is expected to rise to 4 million in 1998. In the US, studies of contingent work arrangements reveal that a majority of firms now fill clerical jobs with contingent labor, and about one-third use contingent workers to staff production, technical and professional positions. Although the reasons for using contingent workers differ by industry and country, the global trend is clearly toward loosening the ties between employees and employers (Conference Board, 1995).

How will these changes affect individual careers? Obviously far fewer (if any) people will have careers for life. Steady-state and linear careers may virtually disappear, to be replaced by spiral, and probably to a greater extent, transitory careers. To think in terms of traditional career stages may soon be meaningless. As Handy (1994) has suggested, we shall have to change the whole way we think about work and having a job. He gives the following illustration:

> There were two people in my house the other morning. My friend was saying: "It's terrible—there are no jobs any more for people like me, it's disgusting, civilization

is crumbling". And then the plumber who was there to fix the pipes said: "Oh God, it is terrible, I've got so many jobs on this week I can't cope". Interesting use of the word job. I said to my kids when they left college: "Don't get a job". "Horror!" they said, "Dad wants us to go on the dole". "No", I said, "Don't get a job, get a customer. Because if you can do something or make something which people are prepared to pay money for, you will be confident for the rest of your life".

In other words, we may be moving back to a view of *work* nearer to that which existed before the industrial revolution, where the individual thinks of himself or herself as a tradesperson or craft worker with a skill to sell. Apart from the traditional trades and crafts, these skills will include the older professions (such as law and accounting), as well as new ones, such as computer programming and information technology skills. Furthermore, as was true in earlier times, work may often be conducted from home. In contrast to earlier times, however, now sophisticated information technologies will support vast networks of employees who work together as members of a virtual organization.

Concurrent with these trends in the nature of work are changes in demographics of the workforce. Economic need, smaller families and a shift to more egalitarian gender attitudes have created societies in which more and more women are employed in full-time jobs. Furthermore, the cracks appearing in the "glass ceiling" indicate that now many women are advancing into higher-level jobs that demand full mental, physical and emotional attention (Tomaskovic-Devey, Kalleberg & Marsden, 1996). Thus, growing numbers of women and men are highly committed to their work and also committed to involvement in family and life beyond work. With two out of three families being two-earner or dual-career families, and with more work being conducted out of the home, the question of who plays what role in the family, and the conflicts surrounding work and domestic space, may upset an already delicate work–home balance.

In summary, the nature of work and organizations is changing as a consequence of globalization, cross-national alliances, privatization, outsourcing, information technology and the contingent workforce. Consequently, we believe, the research questions addressed by those of us who study work and organizations should also begin to change. As we approach the new millennium, the challenge for those of us working in the field of organizational behavior is to change as rapidly as the organizations and people we study. What new research questions are raised by the changing nature of work? And how should we go about conducting our research in the future?

To address these points, we invited some of the leading scholars in organizational behavior (OB) to provide their ideas about new types of research of particular relevance in these turbulent times. Their charge was to creatively consider the future and set the agenda for OB research for the beginning of the next century. Out of this exercise emerged essays on a wide range of topics. We then categorized these essays into the five broad topic domains, which are the basis for the five sections of this volume:

- OB in a multinational or global environment.
- OB reaching beyond traditional boundaries.
- New forms and new processes for organizing.
- Future careers.
- New methods and constructs in future OB research.

We hope you find the many ideas presented in these chapters to be both stimulating and energizing. Most importantly, we hope that reading this volume causes you to ask new questions and explore new phenomena as you plan and conduct research in the twenty-first Century.

REFERENCES

Conference Board (1995). *HR Executive Review: Contingent Employment.* New York: The Conference Board.

Cooper, C.L. (1996). Hot under the collar. *Times Higher Education Supplement,* June 21, p. 15.

Handy, C.B. (1994). *The Empty Raincoat.* London: Hutchinson.

Makin, P., Cooper, C.L. & Cox, C. (1996). *Organizations and the Psychological Contract.* Leicester: British Psychological Society.

Paoli-Pelvey, C. (1993). Working time. In R. Blanpain & C. Engels (eds), *Comparative Labour Law and Industrial Relations in Industrialized Market Economies,* pp. 395–421. Amsterdam: Kluwer.

Tomaskovic-Devey, D., Kalleberg, A.L. & Marsden, P.V. (1996). Organizational patterns of gender segregation. In A.L. Kalleberg, D. Knoke, P.V. Marsden & J.L. Spaeth (eds), *Organizations in America,* pp. 276–301. Thousand Oaks, CA: Sage.

Van der Spiegel, J. (1995). New information technologies and changes in work. In A. Howard (ed), *The Changing Nature of Work,* pp. 97–138. San Francisco: Jossey-Bass.

Part I

Organizational Behavior in a Multinational/ Global Environment

Chapter 1

The Multicultural Organization Revisited

Taylor Cox Jr
University of Michigan Business School, Ann Arbor, MI, USA
and
Rosalie L. Tung
Simon Fraser University, Burnaby, Canada

INTRODUCTION

Five years ago, in writing about high performance organizations of the future, Cox (1991, p. 34) argued that: "Organizations will be increasingly heterogeneous [on dimensions of cultural significance such as gender, race and nationality]. . . . To capitalize on the benefits and minimize the costs of diversity, organizations of the '90s must be quite different from the typical organization of the past". Cox referred to the new organization form that was needed to respond effectively to the changed environment as "The Multicultural Organization".

Today, as we look toward the twenty-first century, we believe that these statements have not only been borne out by developments in the early 1990s, but it is even more clear that new forms of organization are needed to address the changes taking place in the workforce and marketplace worldwide. While the multicultural organization still seems an apt label for this new form of organization, the earlier description was framed for use with a practitioner audience. As a result, limited attention was given to existing and proposed theoretical and empirical research related to the model. Therefore, in this paper we offer an update and revision on this earlier thinking, with the objective of stimulating well-focused theory and research on multiculturalism as a critical competency for the effective functioning of organizations in the future.

Creating Tomorrow's Organizations. Edited by C.L. Cooper and S.E. Jackson.
© 1997 John Wiley & Sons Ltd.

In this chapter, "multicultural organizations" refers to those entities which effectively include and leverage human resources that are diverse on identity dimensions which have cultural significance. Previous theory and research have shown that these identity dimensions include nationality (e.g. Tung, 1984; 1988a), gender (e.g. Tannen, 1990; Gilligan, 1982), racio-ethnicity (e.g. Bell, 1990; Kochman, 1981), work specialization (e.g. Hambrick & Mason, 1984; Trice & Beyer, 1993; Barnett, 1994), age (Rhodes, 1983) and religion (Mamman, 1995) among others. Used as a label for human capacity, multicultural competence can be analyzed on multiple levels of analysis. While Cox's earlier model focused on the macro level of analysis, we propose that achievement of the multicultural form of organization requires the combination of certain contextual conditions (macro level of analysis) and specific competencies at the individual member level (micro level of analysis). After a brief discussion of why we are convinced that this subject deserves high priority in the research agenda of the organization sciences, the balance of the chapter will explain more specifically our view of multiculturalism along these two levels of analysis.

Why Multiculturalism?

As already indicated, the purpose of the multicultural organization is to respond to increasing cultural heterogeneity among critical constituencies of organizations, especially employees, customers and suppliers. A variety of high impact business trends are converging to create this growing diversity in critical constituencies, and as a result, make understanding and managing diversity central to organization effectiveness (Tung, 1995; Cox, 1993). Four such trends are: (a) the increasing formation of global strategic alliances; (b) the increasing globalization of the workforce and of markets for products and services; (c) the emergence of the network structure; and (d) the increasing diversity of gender and racio-ethnic background in labor and consumer markets. Each of these trends is briefly explained below.

Formation of Global Strategic Alliances

There is a growing realization among companies that in order to compete effectively in the twenty-first century, it is often necessary to form joint ventures with other organizations, sometimes including competitors, for the purpose of new product development, production and/or marketing. Beginning in the mid-1980s, industry giants such as IBM, Boeing, Nippon Telephone & Telegraph (NTT) and Philips, which were once adverse to such arrangements, have been quietly entering into cooperative alliances across international boundaries. While many of these strategic alliances will unite partners whose cultures are significantly different from one another, research has shown that such differences are often the source of failure in international business ventures. For example, the failure rate among American expatriates can be as high as 40% (Tung, 1988b; Copeland & Griggs, 1985). Likewise, in a recent study in which managers from different nationalities were asked to identify the most and least preferred partners (by nationality) for mergers and acquisitions, the findings showed that most respondents preferred those who were most culturally similar to themselves. For example, the British respondents most preferred Americans, and vice versa. The least preferred partner for the British, French, German and American respondents were the Japanese. The reasons given were "incompatible language, and incompatible understanding" (Cartright, Cooper & Jordan, 1995).

Globalization

Here we use "globalization" to refer to the dual trends of increasing diversity of nationality in the workforces of organizations and in their product service markets. Johnston (1991) has coined the term "Global Workforce 2000" to refer to the growing migration of workers from the less developed countries to the industrialized economies. This trend in turn has been spurred by two other developments: (a) the easing of barriers to immigration and emigration in many countries; and, (b) the overall aging of the population in the industrialized countries. In addition to global workforces, organizations also increasingly sell to global markets. In the USA a large percentage of firms, including familiar names like IBM, Exxon, Coca-Cola, Dow-Chemical and Digital Equipment, derive more than half their revenues from overseas markets. This trend is now also extending to service companies like Citicorp, which has reported that more than 50% of its revenues have come from non-USA markets in recent years (*Forbes*, 1992).

Emergence of the Network Structure

In the quest for greater organizational efficiency and higher performance, a new organizational form has begun to emerge in the early 1990s—the network structure (Charan, 1991). Network structures are intended to overcome the inefficiencies associated with traditional organizational forms by spanning: (a) hierarchical levels (to break away from the vertical, status-driven boundaries of the past); (b) interunit divisions (breaking functional, business unit and other horizontal boundaries driven by specialization, expertise and socialization); and (c) barriers between internal and external organizations, which breaks the boundary between components in the distribution chain (Prahalad, 1995). In 1991, Jack Welch, CEO of General Electric, coined the term "boundaryless" to refer to his goal of reducing the number of layers between the president's office and product divisions from nine to four, and then ultimately to one. The reduced resource slack which results from organizational downsizing associated with "boundarylessness" means that maximum contribution from all organizational members becomes even more crucial. Not having the old slack makes a previously "not good" situation of under-utilization now criminal. Organizational survival may be at stake if we cannot get full contribution from all members in today's "leaner" workforce.

The network structure also implies that work in organizations is increasingly being done in work teams composed of people from different functional areas and across geographic boundaries (Bassin, 1988; Levine, 1987; Raudsepp, 1988). This requires greater understanding of other disciplines, and again calls for a capacity to work with people from different cultural backgrounds.

Increasing Diversity of Gender and Racio-Ethnic Background

The workforce in many nations of the world is becoming increasingly more diverse on gender, race and nationality (Fullerton, 1987; Johnston, 1991). For example, in the USA roughly 45% of all net additions to the labor force in this decade will be non-White (half of them first-generation immigrants, mostly from Asian and Latin countries), and almost two-thirds will be female. These trends go beyond the USA. For example, by the year 2000, an estimated 20% of Canada's population will be composed of visible minorities (*Bergman, 1994*), 5% of the population of The Netherlands (de Vries, 1992) and 8–10% of the population in France are ethnic minorities (Horwitz & Forman, 1990). There are also substantial and growing non-Caucasian segments of the workforce in many parts of Italy and Germany. Moreover, the increases in representation of women in the workforce in the next decade will be greater in much of Europe, and in many of the developing nations of the world, than it will be in the USA. (Johnston, 1991).

Behind these workforce facts are some rather startling world population demographics. Virtually none of the traditional industrial powers of the world have a fertility rate that is great enough to replace their existing population. This means that growth of the labor forces in these nations, including that of the USA, must come from immigration or from increasing labor-force participation by groups that are presently under-represented (Johnston, 1991).

These four trends led Tung (1995) to assert that the distinction between effective practice of management in international vs. domestic assignments is becoming less clear-cut. Since more and more domestic assignments involve frequent, if not daily, interactions with people from different "cultural" backgrounds, the skills traditionally required only of international managers on expatriate assignments will increasingly be required of employees working in their home countries. Thus, we argue that organizations seeking to remain competitive in a world changing along the cited dimensions must be transformed to a multicultural model. In the remainder of the paper we discuss the characteristics and competencies that we believe define the multicultural form of organization. In the process, we cite examples of previous research which is pertinent to our conclusions and suggest needed avenues for future work.

MULTICULTURALISM AS ORGANIZATIONAL CONTEXT

In the earlier article, Cox (1991) characterized organizations as either monolithic, plural or multicultural on the basis of conceptual profiling of the organization's climate along the following six dimensions:

1. Form of acculturation.
2. Degree of structural integration.
3. Degree of integration in informal networks.
4. Degree of cultural bias (personal and institutional).
5. Identity group differences in organizational identification.
6. Extent of "diversity"-related inter-group conflict.

Subsequent developments in both the academic realm and the world of practice have generally confirmed the viability of these dimensions as descriptors of context relevant to workforce diversity. However, the inclusion of the organization identification concept in item (5) above has proven to be problematic for several reasons. First, there is much confusion about the definition of the concept itself (Ashforth & Mael, 1989) and the most frequently used definition (the degree to which a person defines himself/herself in terms of characteristics of his/ her organization) is not the same as the connotation intended in the multicultural organization model (Mael & Ashforth, 1995; Dutton, Dukerich & Harquail, 1994). Second, and perhaps most important, there is concern over whether this factor is best treated as context or as an individual outcome measure. Cox operationalized the concept as a measure of differences in likelihood-to-stay and in employment satisfaction for people of different identity groups (e.g. Cox & Finley, 1995). Certainly, organizational units may be characterized on the basis of the extent to which there is a gap in measures of "identification" between people of specified identity groups, but the cognitions and behaviors themselves (intent to stay and satisfaction) are more clearly understood as outcomes of the interaction of individual characteristics and organization context. For these reasons, we chose to exclude the organization identification factor from this update on the multicultural organization model. Although the remaining five dimensions are not necessarily exhaustive, we believe they are useful as a framework for discussing the context for multiculturalism. Here, we want to discuss these dimensions with more depth and with greater attention to the academic literature, focusing on exemplary research and our learnings from other sources which have occurred in the last 5 years.

Acculturation

Tung (1993) argued that acculturation is a dimension common to managing cross-national and intra-national diversity, and is therefore a generic factor in understanding cultural diversity. Following Berry (1980) and Rieger & Wong-Rieger (1991, p. 2), we define acculturation as "the process by which group members from one cultural background adapt to the culture of a different group". Berry (1980) identified two determinants of the mode of acculturation: cultural preservation and partner attractiveness. Rieger & Wong-Rieger (1991) utilized these two dimensions to derive a four-cell typology of acculturation which was applied to structuring and strategy formulation in international firms: (a) integration; (b) separation; (c) assimilation; (d) deculturation. This four-cell typology can be applied to the process of acculturation between expatriates and host country nationals in an international context and among members of cultural subgroups within a given nation.

Based on an analysis of data collected in *Fortune Magazine*'s survey on corporate reputation, the Gordon Group Inc. concluded that "companies with well-respected employee practices scored highest on critical measures of long-term corporate performance, including the utilization of capital and total returns on investment". "Well-respected employee practices" refer to "workplace practices which enhance opportunities for workers at all levels within organizations to participate in the decision-making process and share information about the workings of that organization. These practices . . . [provide] greater opportunities for minorities and women who may have previously been denied access to such chances" (Glass Ceiling Commission, 1995, p. 27). Thus, we hypothesize that the acculturation mode labeled "integration" (where the organizational member desires to preserve his/her own culture and at the same time is attracted to the partner's culture) represents the optimal form of acculturation, as positive elements from the various cultures or subcultures are combined to bring about an efficient deployment of resources and materials. Conversely, we hypothesize that "separation" (where the organizational member desires to preserve his/her own culture and disdains the partner's culture) is the most dysfunctional mode of acculturation. Under separation, each group disdains the culture or subculture of the other group and hence is incapable of working with the other with the maximum effectiveness. Between the two extremes lie assimilation and deculturation. Under assimilation, the members of the subordinate group unilaterally adapt their behavioral norms and patterns to those of the dominant group. Under deculturation, on the other hand, each group retains its distinct sets of norms and behaviors, with no attempt to synthesize or integrate the two or more sets of value systems and operational patterns. Deculturation is not conducive to efficient organizational functioning (Berry, 1992).

These modes of acculturation have been used in conceptual work and case analyses addressing the cultural dynamics of mergers and acquisitions (e.g. Nahavandi & Malekzadeh, 1988; Malekzadeh & Nahavandi, 1990). Moreover, Cox & Finley-Nickelson (1991) provide a theoretical framework for application of these acculturation modes to intra-organizational cultural diversity. They argue that a set of six factors across three levels of analysis (individual, inter-group and organizational) combine to determine which mode of acculturation will be manifested in a particular organization. They offer 18 specific theoretical propositions which predict modes of acculturation, given specified levels of the six determining factors. For example, assimilation is predicted to be the dominant mode of acculturation under the following conditions:

1. Culture identity structures among members of minority groups are monocultural majority (i.e. members of demographically different minority groups identify "culturally" with the majority culture and not their micro-culture group).
2. The amount of overlap in norm systems between the groups is high.
3. Norms systems between the groups are highly complementary.
4. The knowledge of specific cultural norms of the other group tends to be high for members of social–cultural minority groups but low for members of the cultural majority.
5. The degree to which the organization values diversity is low.
6. The organizational culture identity structure is characterized by high pressure for conformity for both pivotal (core) and peripheral (non-core) values and norms.

Despite the conceptual work that has been published on modes of acculturation, we are not aware of any published empirical research to date which examines the relationship between a specific mode of acculturation and organizational effectiveness. At the individual level of analysis, the limited empirical work on acculturation and personal outcomes has mainly focused on stress and mental health. For example, in a comparative study of acculturative stress of 1197 individuals from a variety of cultural groups in Canada (native peoples, immigrants from Korea, refugees from Vietnam, and sojourners from Malaysia and China) over a 15-year period (1969–1985), Berry et al. (1987) found that native people who preferred integration experienced significantly lower levels of stress, while those who favored separation were prone to greater stress.

While Berry's longitudinal and cross-sectional studies of various cultural groups in Canada have shed light on the level of acculturative stress experienced by immigrants and sojourners from different ethnic backgrounds, future research should test the relationship between modes of acculturation and financial and non-financial measures of organizational effectiveness. Anecdotal data to date suggest that there is indeed a relationship. Tung (1987) referred to a case example in which an American expatriate who was sent as marketing manager to Japan lost 98% of his company's market share to a major European food competitor in the course of his 18-month assignment in that country. This devastating outcome was attributed to this individual's inability to cope with the stresses and strains associated with living and working in a society which is very different from the one he was accustomed to. Future research examining the relationship between modes of acculturation and organizational performance should utilize samples of people who have a permanent commitment to remaining in a country (immigrants and refugees) *vis-à-vis* those who are there for a shorter period of time (sojourners such as expatriates and foreign students). Such studies are, by nature, complex and time-consuming. However, they are much needed in light of the growing diversity in the workplace.

Structural Integration

Structural integration essentially refers to proportional representation of people from different cultural groups in a single organization (Cox, 1991). However, a critical dimension of the concept is the distribution of identities along several key dimensions of organization structure: ". . . to get a proper understanding of structural integration it is important to look beyond organization-wide profile data, and examine cultural mix by function, level and individual work group" (Cox, 1991, p. 36).

Thus, it is argued that identity distribution, or group proportions, is one central dimension of context for assessing multiculturalism. This claim is supported by an extensive body of work on organizational demography (see Tsui, Egan & Xin, 1995, for an excellent review) as well as research from the field of sociology on minority-group density and tokenism. Seminal work in the latter category includes the classic studies of Kanter (1977a,b), Blalock (1967) and Blau (1977). More recent research has continued to show that the proportions of an identity group in the total social system, as well as proportions in the most powerful positions within the system, are important contextual factors for understanding effects of cultural diversity on organizational behavior. For example, in a study of university faculty, Tolbert, Andrews & Simons (1996) found that the probability of hiring women was affected by both the proportion of women already in the workgroup (inverse relationship) and the proportion of women in higher level positions (positive relationship).

This research highlights one of the most perplexing research challenges for work on the structural integration dimension, namely resolving the tension between the benefits to minority-group members of having a critical mass of their identity in the work-group (perhaps best articulated by Kanter, 1977a, b) and the possibility of loss of support for further work-group integration, on the part of majority-identity members, which may accompany such increases in "minority" representation. A related dilemma is that increased diversity on dimensions like gender and race has been shown, at least in the case of unmanaged diversity, to increase negative outcomes such as employer attraction, job satisfaction and absenteeism among White men (Tsui, Egan & O'Reilly, 1992).

The critical empirical question which remains unresolved at this juncture is: under what circumstances can proportionate representation of "minority" groups be increased in a work-based social system without engendering a reduction of support for further changes in identity mix and negative affective response among members of the traditional cultural majority group?

In the cross-national arena, Tung (1993) has pointed out that issues of structural integration are perhaps becoming less critical because of the trend toward using host country nationals throughout the organization structure in multinational firms. Still, she cautions that the managing diversity issues are nevertheless salient in the interface between the headquarters personnel and the subsidiary operations in various countries. Additionally, there is still some question of whether or not host country nationals have a legitimate opportunity for promotion to the highest levels of the corporate governance coalition. For example as recently as the early 1990s, survey research suggested that only a small percentage of US firms had diversity of nationality on their boards of directors (Glass Ceiling Commission, 1995). Thus, the fundamental issue of diversity of representation across structural dimensions of function and level is highly relevant for managing diversity in multinational firms.

Furthermore, in light of the need for managers to develop a global orientation in order to deal with the challenges of international competition and cooperation, many companies have found that an effective way to foster this mentality is to use international assignments for career development of fast or elite trackers. Tung (1988b) has referred to these as the new breed of expatriates, where international assignments are used for grooming them for senior management positions rather than merely filling overseas positions. In a 1989 survey of US executives about the requisites of the CEO for the year 2000, the consensus of opinion was: The person "must have a multi-environment, multi-country, multi-functional, maybe even multi-company, multi-industry experience" (*Wall Street Journal*, February 27, 1989).

Informal Integration

Informal integration is the extent to which social and informal communication networks are open to and equally effective for all organization members. Previous research has shown that: (a) access to informal networks of organizations and to informal career support processes such as mentoring are important to career outcomes of workers (e.g. Ibarra, 1993; Dalton, 1959; Whitely, Dougherty & Dreher, 1991; Turban & Dougherty, 1994); and (b) that worker identities such as gender and racio-ethnicity have at least some effects on such access or on effectiveness of networks and mentoring (e.g. Dreher & Cox, 1996; Ibarra, 1995; Rose-Ragins, 1989).

Still, answers to even some of the most basic questions remain unresolved. For example, despite numerous studies it is not clear whether or not gender or racio-ethnic identity have any substantial effects on basic access to a mentor. Some research indicates barriers and lower access to mentoring for racio-ethnic minority men and/or for women (e.g. Cox & Nkomo, 1991; Noe, 1988; Ragins & Cotton, 1991), while other research shows no such effects (e.g. Dreher & Ash, 1990; Scandura & Rose-Ragins, 1993, Turban & Dougherty, 1994).

Recently researchers have sought to resolve this confusion by focusing more on cross-identity issues of mentors and protegés. For example, Thomas (1993) has shown that successful cross-race mentoring relationships are more likely to form if mentor and protegé have similar preferences (denial, suppression, or open discussion) for treatment of their racial difference. Also, Dreher & Cox's study (1996) of MBA alumni, using a sample of Hispanics, Blacks, Whites and Asians, produced no main effects of gender or racio-ethnic identity on access to a mentor. However, they found that White women and racial minority men and women had lower access to mentors who were White and male. Thus a relational demography (Tsui & O'Reilly, 1989) approach to this area of work may be more fruitful than simple main effects of protege identity.

Recent field experience suggests that another area which is deserving of attention is the investigation of access differences among people in the gender/racio-ethnic majority group. In Japan and South Korea, for example, many management personnel in large corporations and governmental ministries have graduated from the same universities. In North America, there is some indication that critical informal networks, especially at higher organization levels, are not easily penetrated by anyone except a narrowly defined group of people who share not only gender and race but also socio-economic class, attendance at the same schools, similar hobbies and a variety of similar characteristics. Examples of this include Useem's work on the corporate elite (Useem & Karabel, 1986; Useem, 1984) and the work of Whitely, Dougherty & Dreher (1991) on the moderating effect of protégé socio-economic status on the mentoring–career success relationship. Are organizationally-relevant social "inner circles" so narrowly defined so as to exclude all but a handful of very similar people, and if so, how important are these networks to career effects? Especially critical is a better understanding of how strong a link exists between access to informal networks and job-performance optimization among organization members. Still another set of critical questions has to do with whether or not it is feasible for organizations to open up these networks and how they should go about doing so.

Cultural Bias

According to Cox (1991), cultural bias incorporates the attitudinal form of prejudice and the behavioral form of discrimination. Further, these operate on two levels, personal and institutional. The potential for personal discrimination is illustrated in the popular myth that women will not be accepted as business partners in male-dominated societies; hence the reluctance of US multinationals to consider women for expatriate assignments (Adler, 1984; Moran, Stahl & Boyer, undated). This is a major factor in low representation of women among US expatriates. More recently, Florkowski & Fogel (1995) showed that perceived host ethnocentrism can be an important determinant of expatriate adjustment. Future research should examine how ethnocentrism in a cross-national setting or cultural bias in an intra-national setting can affect: (a) the levels of representation of people in different types of organizations and at various organizational levels; (b) the ease or difficulty of acculturation; and (c) the decision to terminate an assignment. In the past, it was generally assumed that the ease of acculturation was positively correlated with the decision to remain in an international assignment. Research underway by Caligiuri & Tung (1996) suggests that this may not be the case. The female expatriates in a large US multinational organization reported more problems of cross-cultural adjustment in countries that score high on masculinity, thus supporting Florkowski & Fogel's (1995) hypothesis, that perceived host country ethnocentrism is an important determinant of expatriate adjustment. However, despite this difficulty, these women chose to continue in the international assignment in such masculine countries. In other words, the women expatriates chose to "tough it out".

Institutionalized discrimination occurs when cultural preference patterns become embedded in the way organizations are managed so as to inadvertently create barriers to full participation by members from cultural backgrounds that differ from the traditional majority group (Cox, 1993). Many existing principles of organization and management, which were developed in a context where professional/managerial ranks were occupied primarily by White males of the same national origin, and even of similar educational background, may not be optimally effective for the complexities and dynamics of managing, planning and organizing for an increasingly diverse workforce. For example, Hofstede (1980) has shown that significant differences exist across cultures among the dimensions of individualism–collectivism, uncertainty–avoidance, power–distance, and masculinity–femininity. A highly individualistic culture, such as the UK, values functional specialization, compartmentalization of activities, and rewards based on individual efforts. A collectivist culture, on the other hand, such as Japan, emphasizes cross-functional rotation, reaching out, and teamwork. Group-based rewards are the norm. Thus, policies and practices which were based on individualism, such as individual contributor bonuses, ranking systems of appraisal and commission-based compensation for salespeople, may inadvertently disadvantage members from collectivist-cultural backgrounds. Even the simplest preference patterns may lead to institutionalized barriers to inclusion. For example, despite the increasing number of Americans who work for US subsidiaries of Japanese firms (an estimated 400 000), the senior management positions in these organizations are essentially staffed by Japanese expatriates. A prominent contributor to this is the use of Japanese as the language of communication between corporate headquarters and its subsidiaries. Since very few Americans are proficient in the Japanese language, this preference essentially excludes them from promotion to top-level jobs.

As suggested by Cox (1991), a multicultural organization should have made demonstrably significant progress in minimizing at least the behavioral forms of cultural bias. Moreover, examples of how institutional cultural bias is manifested in organizations have been identified in the literature (e.g. see Cox, 1993; Loden & Rosener, 1991). However, we believe that an even broader range of cultural norms which do not, on the surface, appear to be related to diversity, need to be included in future research if we are to get a more complete understanding of institutional barriers to cultural diversity. Specifically, by focusing on bias, another dimension of institutional barriers gets overlooked, namely norms which do not necessarily discriminate against particular identity groups *per se* but which

Table 1.1 Cultural content items relevant to assessment of multiculturalism

Item	Traditional Organization	Multicultural Organization
Risk-taking	Risk-averse	Supportive
Handling of dissenting views/ opinions	Squashes dissent	Welcomes dissent
Communications	Closed	Open
Status consciousness	Hierarchical	Egalitarian
Valuing of people	Low priority	High priority
Flexibility	Low priority	High priority
Logical processes[1]	Linear	Spiral and linear
Beliefs	One truth	Many truths
Pattern of interaction	Competitive	Cooperative

Linear logic refers to Greek Aristotelian logic characterized by deduction and induction. Spiral logic, in contrast to linear logic, is circuitous. People who use spiral logic may be able to see relationships between systems and concepts which are not readily apparent to those who espouse linear logic, and *vice versa*.

work against divergent thought and behavior more generally. Cox (1993) argues that the specific culture content of organizations is important in evaluating the effectiveness of organizations for managing diversity in the workforce. He offers some examples of norms which distinguish the content of the "anti-diversity" (e.g. quick to evaluate, risk adverse) and the "pro-diversity" (e.g. flexible, deferred evaluation) culture. We would like to take this approach a step further by suggesting that a subset of cultural content items taken from research on organization culture and cross-national culture (e.g. Rousseau, 1990; Maruyama, 1992) are particularly relevant for distinguishing multicultural organizations from the more traditional organizational forms which they might replace. Our thoughts about this are summarized in Table 1.1.

We submit that these dimensions of organization context are related to the ability or organizational capacity to manage and leverage diversity in much the same way that specific dimensions of personality are related to the personal capacity of individuals to tolerate and value diversity (a subject to be addressed further in the next section of this paper). In a time when teamwork, individual empowerment, creativity and innovation are being emphasized as imperatives for competitive success, the characteristics shown here as typical of traditional organizations are dysfunctional for all workers. What makes them relevant to workforce diversity is that the potential for each of these cultural factors to hinder contribution is exacerbated for members of cultural minority groups. For example, a culture which values conformity, and hence habitually squashes dissent, may inhibit the generation of new ideas which differ from approaches of the past. As a group, members from cultural traditions different from the historical majority group are more likely to hold such dissenting views. In addition, because the status of "minority" members in groups is often marginalized, it may be more risky for them to raise dissenting opinions than for persons who feel more secure in their membership. Therefore, the impact of this norm, while negative for the vast majority of workers, is expected to be especially severe for members of cultural minority groups.

Similarly, in a closed-communications environment all workers will be affected, but when there are culture-related obstacles to communication (such as language differences and differences in communication styles) the adverse effect of this norm is expected to be intensified. Research has shown that significant language and communication style differences indeed do exist on the basis of various identity-group factors, including nationality (Hall, 1976; Ting-Toomey, 1985), gender (e.g. Tannen, 1990; Glass, 1992) and racio-ethnicity (e.g. Kochman, 1981). Similarly people from high-context cultures, such as East Asians, may avoid direct confrontation, while members of low-context cultures (the historical majority group in the USA) may perceive this trait as indecisiveness, and hence a weakness.

The contents of Table 1.1 may be reorganized into hypothesis statements about the relationship between the noted dimensions of culture and various indicators of success for creating and leveraging workforce diversity. This type of research has been hindered by the necessity of very detailed data from a multi-organizational sample and by typical barriers to research at the organization level of analysis, such as non-comparability of industry, financial strength or other potentially confounding factors.

Inter-group Conflict

Conflict is an overt expression of tension between two or more parties with divergent interests (Rummell, 1976). Here we are concerned especially with conflict in which: (a) the parties are members of distinct social–cultural groups; and (b) the conflict is directly or indirectly related to the group identities of the parties (Cox, 1993, p. 137). While conflict *per se* is not always dysfunctional, and may even be needed for optimal effectiveness of groups (Moorhead & Griffin, 1989), it seems to us that several forms of inter-group conflict which are common in diverse workgroups are distinctly dysfunctional. Previous theory and research suggests that conflict can increase (e.g. Cox, 1993) and cohesiveness decline (e.g. Tsui, Egan & O'Reilly, 1992) as groups become more diverse.

While inter-group conflict is often overt, it can also be covert. Many people, for example, feel uncomfortable talking about race relations and issues (Finley, 1996). Caucasians may fear that their remarks may be interpreted as racist, while racial minorities may avoid the subject for fear of being alleged as "oversensitive". Anecdotal data have shown that this can generate a lot of mistrust, hurt and resentment (Cose, 1993).

In addition, there is considerable evidence that members of the cultural majority group may display "backlash" behaviors when organizations invest heavily in change processes related to diversity. Both of these forms of conflict can be destructive to organizational performance. Thus, another contextual difference between traditional organizations and multicultural organizations is that these forms of inter-group conflict are common in the former but absent or minimized in the latter.

Since the potential for destructive inter-group conflict in diverse groups is fairly well established in the literature, perhaps the most pressing research need in this area is: "what can be done to counteract identity-related inter-group conflict and reduced cohesiveness in diverse groups or, conversely, to harness these dynamics to enhance performance outcomes of diverse groups?".

MULTICULTURALISM AS AN INDIVIDUAL COMPETENCY

We now turn our attention to the micro level of analysis. The challenge that we face is illustrated by the following example from Lipp & Clark (in press): Smith, an American employee with the US subsidiary of a Japanese company, received from his Japanese boss, Yamamoto, a performance rating of 4 on a 5-point scale. Smith has been with the company for 2 years. Dissatisfied with this rating, Smith approached Yamamoto to ask for critical feedback and specific information on how he can improve his performance. Yamamoto explained that he received a good performance rating but would not elaborate on specific areas where the employee could improve. Each party was disturbed by the action of the other. Why? From Smith's perspective, he wanted to get a "feel of where he stands" among his peer group. He perceived Yamamoto as ineffective, a slavedriver, and one who could not give an honest feedback to his employee. From the American's perspective, honesty was paramount. The Japanese manager, on the other hand, perceived the American employee as immature because he demanded constant feedback. In his opinion, an employee should know what his manager thinks of him "by the way he is treated". From the Japanese perspective, the purpose of a written performance appraisal is to make the person feel good and to motivate him or her to strive for excellence (the principle of *keizan*). To the Japanese employer, harmony and the ability to understand implicit messages were paramount.

The above episode illustrates the hidden cost of ignoring the effects of diversity on the effectiveness of individual performance in today's organizations. Countless episodes like these highlight the urgency of our quest to understand the personal qualities, skills and abilities which distinguish people who are highly effective at working in, and leading, culturally diverse groups from those who are not effective.

As a step in that direction, we set forth the premise that competence for managing diversity is best understood as a constellation of specialized knowledge, skills and abilities which must become embedded in the day-to-day activi-

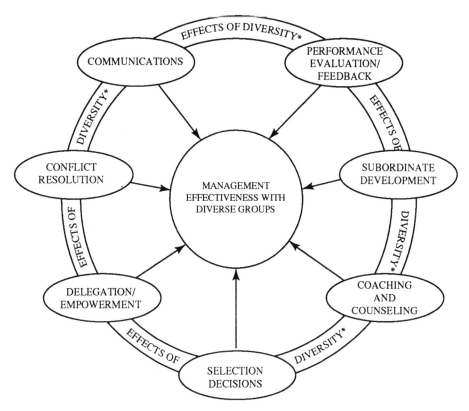

Figure 1.1 A framework for understanding managerial competency for leading diverse groups. Figure adapted from one first used by Taylor Cox Jr in a presentation to the Human Resource Partnership, University of Michigan, September, 1992

ties and responsibilities of leaders. This premise has led to the development of the analytical framework shown in Figure 1.1.

In the context of a diverse workforce, the definition of managerial competence must be expanded to embrace the many ways in which cultural diversity affects work behavior and human performance. We contend that the performance of each of the activities shown in Figure 1.1 is changed quite substantially by these effects. While detailed attention to all seven dimensions is beyond the scope of this paper, we will illustrate the framework by the examples of communication and performance appraisal.

Communication

Miscommunication can arise when the message intended by the sender fails to resemble the message perceived by the receiver. This gap between intention and perception can stem from the different fields of experience of the sender and the receiver, including the meanings/interpretation assigned to specific words and the encoding/decoding of messages on either side (Howell, 1982; Ronen, 1986). These different fields of experience are largely culture-based. For example, members of high-context cultures (such as Japan, Latin and Mediterranean countries) flourish on implicit messages, whereas members of low-context societies (such as the USA and northern European countries) insist on directness. An estimated 70% of the world's population is high-context (Hall, 1976). As a second example, Tannen (1990, 1995) has shown that communication between USA-born men and women is also "cross-cultural".

Building on the five-stage model of communication competency developed by Howell (1982) and Ting-Toomey (1992), Tung (1993) has applied it to the process of cross-national and intra-national communication. The five levels of communication competency are: unconscious incompetence, conscious incompetence, conscious competence, unconscious competence, and unconscious super-competence. Unconscious incompetence, on one end of the continuum, may stem from ignorance, i.e. a member of one group may unintentionally insult members of another without being aware that he/she has done so. An example of unconscious incompetence in the intra-national setting is billionaire Ross Perot's referring to African-Americans as "you people" in his 1992 US presidential campaign. Perot insulted his audience without being consciously aware that the phrase, "you people", can be construed as racist. An example of unconscious incompetence in the cross-national context is referring to Korea as the "second Japan". While the sender may think it is a compliment, the receiver (an ethnic Korean) may be insulted by the comparison in light of the brutality and hardships imposed by the Japanese upon the Koreans during the 40-year Japanese occupation of Korea.

With unconscious super-competence, on the other end of the continuum, the person becomes truly bicultural and bilingual (in the cross-national context) and moves with spontaneity between one set of cultural norms and another. The goal of managing cross-national and intra-national diversity is to attain level 3 (conscious competence) and, hopefully, levels 4 (unconscious competence) and 5 (unconscious super-competence).

Future research must add to our knowledge of cultural differences in communication styles and explore methods of detecting and responding to identity-based barriers to communication. For example, Finley's research (1996) on the straight-talk process indicates that it may be a promising technique for improving communications between members of different culture–identity groups.

Performance Appraisal

As illustrated by the performance appraisal anecdote given earlier in the chapter, Western cultures tend to assess an individual on discrete dimensions. Hence Mr Smith's request for specific areas in which he can make improvement. In many East Asian cultures, on the other hand, people tend to adopt a holistic perspective, i.e. the person's total performance is considered rather than specific dimensions or attributes (Tung, 1994). Furthermore, the individual's performance is not assessed within a specific time-frame of 6 months or a year, but rather from a longer-term perspective.

These differences in attitude toward performance appraisal are reflected in the different reward structures practiced in the USA vs. Japan. In the USA, the merit system stems from the principle of equity. The Japanese system, on the other hand, is tied to the cultural emphasis on age and seniority (Lipp & Clark, in press).

An additional example of the effects of identity differences and culture on performance appraisal occurs in research on modesty bias. Many managers rely heavily on self-evaluations done by subordinates in developing formal ratings of performance (Northcraft & Neale, 1990); however, due partly to cultural diversity, people vary greatly in the extent to which they are comfortable giving visibility to their own accomplishments (Cox, 1993). For example, in a study of 982 leader–subordinate dyads of US and Taiwanese national origin, Farh, Dobbins & Cheng (1991) found that a modesty bias influenced the ratings for the Chinese workers and was a factor behind the lower self-ratings made by the Chinese workers compared to their US counterparts. They conclude that "it is clear that the use of self-ratings by multinational firms may be biased against Chinese employees". Since research on acculturation indicates that cultural norms from a root culture often survive for many generations, this research is applicable to US-Americans of Chinese ancestry as well as native-born Chinese.

A subsequent study by Yu & Murphy (1993) claimed to cast doubt on a culture-based explanation for the lower self-ratings by the Chinese found by Farh, Dobbins & Cheng (1991). However, the latter authors' results (i.e. that workers tended to give themselves higher ratings than their supervisors in a separate sample of just Chinese workers) did not compare the Chinese worker data to a Western sample, and thus could not draw conclusions about the extent to which people from the two backgrounds differ on facility to use self-ratings to the greatest personal advantage.

Another example of diversity effects on performance appraisal processes is the work of Greenhaus & Parasuraman (1993) on manager attributions for performance ratings. In a study of 1648 managers, they found that for high-potential managers, the performance of women was less likely to be attributed to ability than the performance of men, and that the performance of Black managers was less likely to be attributed to ability or effort and more likely to be attributed to help from others than the performance of White managers.

As a final example, in a study of 125 first-level managers in a public utility, Cox & Nkomo (1986) found that social behavior factors (e.g. perceived friendliness, perceived range of interests and perceived open-mindedness) were significant predictors of overall job performance ratings for Black managers, but not for White managers. They concluded that performance criteria impact differentially on ratings based on race of the ratee, and that Black managers appear to be assessed on a broader set of criteria.

Something to be noted about the cited research is that the effects go beyond simple main effects of identity on mean ratings. Even when mean ratings between culture groups are the same, modesty effects on self-evaluation input, differential attributions of the cause of the performance, or differential criteria in the development of global ratings may be operating. Managers working with diverse groups need to have knowledge of these possible effects on the process of rating performance. Only then will they be able to adjust their own behavior and be qualified to do a thorough assessment of the effectiveness of their appraisal-related behavior.

Future research should identify the specific areas along which cultures converge and diverge. Where there is divergence, it should go beyond the mere identification of such differences and seek to unravel why such differences exist. For example, based on analysis of popular ancient works in East Asia, Tung (1994) has identified twelve principles which govern the East Asian mindset in its approach to the formulation and implementation of business strategies, including competition and collaboration. This type of work gives a deeper understanding of the sources and manifestations of differences. Such knowledge can facilitate more effective interaction between groups from different cultural groups.

The application of the model presented in Figure 1.1 requires that managers follow a three-step process to competence: (a) managers must become knowledgeable about the ways in which diversity influences the execution of these core activities of managerial work; (b) selection and development of managers should give attention to the possession of this knowledge; and (c) managers must learn behaviors and create feedback mechanisms which allow them to translate the cognitive insights of item (a) into observable differences in how they do their work.

For example, if we return to the illustration of the Japanese manager that introduced this segment, Mr Yamamoto might adjust his behavior by altering the process to include a written explanation of suggestions for improving on the current rating even though, from his point of view (which is strongly influenced by his cultural background), such detailed explanations should not be necessary. It is only when the manager decides to change his future behavior, in this case by changing the level of detail on the forms or what he does in the feedback session, that the learning he obtained about the impact of culture will begin to improve his effectiveness as a leader.

CONCLUSION

In order to respond effectively to a changing environment, organizations of the future must be "multicultural". We have offered specifics on competencies that must be developed in order to meet the challenges posed by cultural diversity, and cited some exemplary research that is pertinent to these competencies. We have also identified some critical gaps in the existing body of research. More aggressively addressing these gaps should be a high priority in the research agenda of scholars and practitioners worldwide as we approach the twenty-first century.

REFERENCES

Adler, N.J. (1984). Women do not want international careers: and other myths about international management. *Organizational Dynamics*, **13**, 6.

Ashforth, B.E. & Mael F. (1989). Social identity theory and the organization. *Academy of Management Review*, **14**, 20–39.

Barnett J.J. (1994). Understanding Group Effects Within Organizations: a Study of Group Attitudes and Behaviors of Engineers and Scientists. Doctoral dissertation, The Fielding Institute, Santa Catalina, CA.

Bassin, M. (1988). Teamwork at General Foods: new and improved. *Personnel Journal*, **67**, 62–70.

Bell, E.L. (1990). The bicultural life experience of career-oriented Black women. *Journal of Organizational Behavior*, **11**, 459–77.

Bergman, B. (1994). Points of contention: myths and facts about immigration. *Maclean's*, **February 7**, 35.

Berry, J.W. (1992). Acculturation and adaptation in a new society. *International Migration Review*, **30**, 69–85.

Berry, J.W. (1980). Social and cultural change. In H.C. Triandis & R.W. Brislin (eds), *Handbook of Cross-cultural Psychology* (pp. 211–79). Boston, MA: Allyn & Bacon.

Berry, J.W., Kim, U., Minde, T. & Mok, D. (1987). Comparative studies of acculturative stress. *International Migrant Review*, **21**(2), 491–511.

Blalock, H. Jr (1967). *Toward a Theory of Minority-group Relations*. New York: Wiley.

Blau, P.M. (1977). A macrosociological theory of social structure. *American Journal of Sociology*, **83**, 26–54.

Caligiuri, P. & Tung, R.L. (1996). Female expatriates' adjustment and performance in masculine and feminine countries. Working paper, Simon Fraser University: Vancouver.

Cartwright, S., Cooper, C.L. & Jordan, J. (1995). Managerial preferences in international merger and acquisition partners. *Journal of Strategic Change*, **4**, 263–9.

Charan, R. (1991). How networks reshape organizations—for results. *Harvard Business Review*, September–October, 104–15.

Copeland, L. & Griggs, L. (1985). *Going International*. New York: Random House.

Cose, E. (1993). *The Rage of a Privileged Class*. London: Harper Collins.

Cox, T.H. Jr (1993). *Cultural Diversity in Organizations: Theory, Research & Practice*. San Francisco: Berrett Koehler.

Cox, T.H. Jr (1991). *The Multicultural Organization. The Executive*, **5**(3), 45–56.

Cox, T.H. Jr & Finley, J. (1995). An analysis of work specialization and organization level as dimensions of workforce diversity. In M.M. Chemers, S. Oskamp & M.A. Costanzo (eds), *Diversity in Organizations* (pp. 62–90). Thousand Oaks, CA: Sage.

Cox, T.H. Jr & Finley-Nickelson, J. (1991). Models of acculturation for intraorganizational cultural diversity. *Canadian Journal of Administrative Sciences*, **8**(2), 90–100.

Cox, T.H. Jr & Nkomo, S.M. (1991). A race and gender group analysis of the early career experience of MBAs. *Work and Occupations*, **18**(4), 431–46.

Cox, T.H. Jr & Nkomo, S.M. (1986). Differential appraisal criteria based on race of the ratee. *Group and Organizational Studies*, **11**, 101–19.

Dalton, M. (1959). *Men who Manage*. New York: Wiley.

de Vries, S. (1992). *Working in Multi-ethnic Groups: the Performance and Well-being of Minority and Majority workers*. Amsterdam: Gouda Quint bu-Arnhem.

Dreher, G.F. & Cox T.H. (1996). Race, gender and opportunity: a study of compensation attainment and the establishment of mentoring relationships, *Journal of Applied Psychology*, **81**(3), 297–308.

Dreher, G.F. & Ash, R.A. (1990). A comparative study of mentoring among men and women in managerial, professional and technical positions. *Journal of Applied Psychology*, **75**, 539–46.

Dutton, J.E., Dukerich, J.M. & Harquail, C.V. (1994). Organizational images and member identification. *Administrative Science Quarterly*, **39**, 239–63.

Farh, J.L., Dobbins, G.H. & Cheng, B.S. (1991). Cultural relativity in action: a comparison of self-ratings made by Chinese and U.S. workers. *Personnel Psychology, Inc.*, **44**, 129–45.

Federal Glass Ceiling Commission (1995). A solid investment: making full use of the nation's human capital. *Recommendations of the Glass Ceiling Commission*. Washington, DC: US Government Printing Office.

Federal Glass Ceiling Commission (1995). *Good for Business: Making Full use of the Nation's Human Capital*. Washington, DC: US Government Printing Office.

Finley, J.A. (1996). Communication double binds: the Catch 22 of conversations about racial issues in organizations. Doctoral Dissertation, University of Michigan, Ann Arbor, MI.

Florkowski, G.W. & Fogel, D.S. (1995). Perceived host ethnocentrism as a determinant of expatriate adjustment and organizations commitment. Paper presented at the National Meetings of the Academy of Management, Vancouver.

Forbes, July 20, 1992.

Fullerton, H.N. (1987). Labor force projections: 1986–2000. *Monthly Labor Review*, **September**, 19–29.

Gilligan, C. (1982). *In a Different Voice: Psychological Theory and Women's Development*. Cambridge: Harvard University Press.

Glass, L.G. (1992). *He Says, She Says: Closing the Communication Gap Between the Sexes*. New York: G.P. Putnam's Sons.

Greenhaus, J.H. & Parasuraman, S. (1993). Job performance attributions and career advancement prospects: an examination of gender and race effects. *Organizational Behavior and Human Decision Processes*, **55**, 273–97.

Hall, E.T. (1976). *Beyond Culture*. New York: Doubleday.

Hambrick, D.C. & Mason, P.A. (1984). Upper echelons: the organization as a reflection of its top managers. *Academy of Management Review*, **9**, 193–206.

Hofstede, G. (1980). Motivation, leadership and organization: do American theories apply abroad? *Organizational Dynamics*, **9**, 43–62.

Horwitz, T. & Forman, C. (1990). Clashing cultures. *The Wall Street Journal*, 14 August, A1.

Howell, W.S. (1982). *The Empathic Communicator*. Prospect Heights, IL: Waveland.

Ibarra, H. (1995). Race, opportunity and diversity of social circles in managerial networks. *Academy of Management Journal*, **38**(3), 673–703.

Ibarra, H. (1993). Personal networks of women and minorities in management. *Academy of Management Review*, **18**(1), 56–87.

Johnston, W.B. (1991). Global workforce 2000: the new world labor market. *Harvard Business Review*, **69**(2), 115–27.

Kanter, R.M. (1977a). Some effects of proportions on group life: skewed sex ratios and responses to token women. *American Journal of Sociology*, **82**(5), 965–90.

Kanter, R.M. (1977b). *Men and Women of the Corporation*. New York: Basic Books.

Kochman, T. (1981). *Black and White: Styles in Conflict*. Chicago: University of Chicago Press.

Levine, M. (1987). Making group collaboration work. *Production and Inventory Management*, **28**, 31–3.

Lipp, D. & Clarke (in press). *Kiki: Dangers and Opportunities—the Crisis Facing U.S.-based Japanese Companies.* Chicago, IL: Intercultural Press.

Loden, M. & Rosener, J.B. (1991). *Workforce America! Managing Employee Diversity as a Vital Resource.* Homewood, IL: Business One Irwin.

Mael F.A. & Ashforth, B.E. (1995). Loyal from day one: biodata, organizational identification, and turnover among newcomers. *Personnel Psychology*, **48**, 309–33.

Malekzadeh, A. & Nahavandi, A. (1990). Making mergers work by managing cultures. *Journal of Business Strategy*, **11**, 55–7.

Mamman, A. (1995). Employee intercultural effectiveness in a multicultural workplace: theoretical propositions, strategies and directions for future research. *International Journal of Human Resource Management*, **6**(3), 528–52.

Maruyama, M. (1992). Changing dimensions in international business. *Academy of Management Executive*, **6**(3), 88–96.

Moorhead, G. & Griffin, R.W. (1989). *Organizational Behavior.* Boston, MA: Houghton Mifflin Co.

Moran, Stahl & Boyer (undated, c. 1987). *Status of American Female Expatriate Employees Survey Results.* Boulder, CO: Moran, Stahl & Boyer.

Nahavandi, A. & Malekzadeh, A. (1988). Acculturation in mergers and acquisitions. *Academy of Management Review*, **13**(1), 79–90.

Noe, R.A. (1988). An investigation of the determinants of successful assigned mentoring relationships. *Personnel Psychology*, **41**, 457–79.

Northcraft, G. & Neale, M. (1990). *Organizational Behavior: a Management Challenge.* Chicago: Dryden.

Prahalad, C.K. (1995). Foreword to R. Ashkenas, P. Ulrich, T. Jick & S. Kerr, *The Boundaryless Organization* (pp. xiii–xvii). San Francisco, CA: Jossey-Bass.

Ragins, B.R. & Cotton, J.L. (1991). Easier said than done: gender differences in perceived barriers to gaining a mentor. *Academy of Management Journal*, **34**(4), 939–51.

Raudsepp, E. (1988). Put teamwork in work teams. *Chemical Engineering*, **95**(10), 113–14.

Rhodes, S.R. (1983). Age-related differences in work attitudes and behavior: a review and conceptual analysis. *Psychological Bulletin*, **93**(2), 328–67.

Rieger F. & Wong-Rieger, D. (1991). The application of acculturation theory to structuring and strategy formulation in the international firm. Paper presented at the Strategic Management Society Annual Meetings.

Ronen, S. (1986). *Comparative and Multinational Management.* New York: Wiley.

Rose-Ragins, T.B. (1989). Barriers to mentoring: the female manager's dilemma. *Human Relations*, **42**, 1–22.

Rousseau, D.A. (1990). Assessing organizational culture: the case for multiple methods. In B. Schneider (ed), *Organizational Climate and Culture* (pp. 153–92). San Francisco, CA: Jossey-Bass.

Rummell, R.J. (1976). *Understanding Conflict and War.* New York: Wiley.

Scandura, T.A. & Rose-Ragins, B. (1993). The effects of sex and gender-role orientation on mentorship in male-dominated occupations. *Journal of Vocational Behavior*, **43**, 251–65.

Tannen, D. (1995). *Talking from 9 to 5.* New York: Avon Books.

Tannen, D. (1990). *You Just Don't Understand: Men and Women in Conversation.* New York: Ballatine.

Thomas, D.A. (1993). Racial dynamics in cross-race developmental relationships. *Administrative Science Quarterly*, **38**, 169–94.

Ting-Toomey, S. (1992). Cross-cultural face negotiation: an analytical overview. Paper presented at the Pacific Region Forum, Simon Fraser University, Vancouver, April 14.

Ting-Toomey, S. (1985). Toward a theory of conflict and culture. In W. Gudykunst, L. Steward & S. Ting-Toomey (eds), *Communication, Culture and Organizational Processes* (pp. 71–86). Beverly Hills, CA: Sage.

Tolbert, P.S., Andrews, A.O. & Simons, T. (1996). The effects of group proportions on group dynamics. In S.E. Jackson & M. Ruderman (eds), *Diversity in Work Teams: Research Paradigms for a Changing Workplace* (pp. 131–60). Washington, DC: American Psychological Association.

Trice, H.M. & Beyer, J.M. (1993). *The Cultures of Work Organizations*. Englewood Cliffs, NJ: Prentice-Hall.

Tsui, A.S., Egan, T.D. & Xin, K.R. (1995). Diversity in organizations: lessons from demography research. In M. Chemers, M. Costanzo & S. Oskamp (eds), *Diversity in Organizations: New Perspectives for a Changing Workplace* (pp. 191–219). Thousand Oaks, CA: Sage.

Tsui, A.S., Egan, T.D. & O'Reilly, C.A. III (1992). Being different: relational demography and organizational attachment. *Administrative Science Quarterly*, **37**, 549–79.

Tsui, A.S. & O'Reilly, C.A. (1989). Beyond simple demographic effects: the importance of relational demography in superior–subordinate dyads. *Academy of Management Journal*, **32**(2), 402–23.

Tung, R.L. (1995). Wanted: A person for all seasons': an examination of managerial skills and core competencies for the 21st century. Paper presented at the Academy of Management meetings, Vancouver, August 6–9.

Tung, R.L. (1994). Strategic management thought in East Asia. *Organizational Dynamics*, **22**(1).

Tung, R.L. (1993). Managing cross-national and intra-national diversity. *Human Resource Management*, **23**(4), 461–77.

Tung, R.L. (1988a). Toward a conceptual paradigm of international business negotiations. *Advances in International Comparative Management*, **3**, 203–19.

Tung, R.L. (1988b). *The New Expatriates: Managing Human Resources Abroad*. Cambridge, MA: Ballenger.

Tung, R.L. (1987). Expatriate assignments: enhancing success and minimizing failure. *Academy of Management Executive*, **1**(2), 117–25.

Tung, R.L. (1984). *Business Negotiations with the Japanese*. Lexington, MA: Lexington Books.

Turban D.B. & Dougherty, T.W. (1994). Role of protegé personality in receipt of mentoring and career success. *Academy of Management Journal*, **37**, 688–702.

Useem, M. & Karabel, J. (1986). Pathways to top corporate management. *American Sociological Review*, **51**, 184–200.

Useem, M. (1984). *The Inner Circle: Large Corporations and the Rise of Business Political Activity in the US and UK*. New York: Oxford University Press.

Wall Street Journal, February 27, 1989.

Whitely, W., Dougherty, T.W. & Dreher, G.F. (1991). Relationship of career mentoring and socioeconomic origin to managers' and professionals' early career progress. *Academy of Management Journal*, **34**(2), 331–51.

Yu, J. & Murphy, K.R. (1993). Modesty bias in self-ratings of performance: a test of the cultural relativity hypothesis. *Personnel Psychology, Inc.*, **46**, 357–63.

Chapter 2

The Political and Economic Context of Organizational Behavior

Jone L. Pearce
University of California, Irvine, CA, USA

Organizational behavior has developed into a particularly non-contextual applied social science. It is clear to any observer that organizational behaviors tend to differ across societies, yet discussions of these differences typically document variations in organizational practices and cultures, which are descriptive without being explanatory. These accounts do not address why organizational practices and behavior differ in different societal contexts and so cannot be used to, among other things, predict change. Here ideas drawn from comparative institutions theories are applied in an effort to better understand organizational behavior in the organizations of relatively more traditional societies, and the circumstances under which organizations are likely to adopt comparatively more modern practices.

This approach relies on unpacking that classic of organization theory, bureaucracy, in order to gain insight into organizational changes in response to changing demands. This unpacking relies on the work of scholars from anthropology, sociology, political science, history and economics who long have debated the evolution and effects of different social institutions. Several prominent theories of comparative institutions that have sought to explain why different organizational practices have evolved (cf. Jacoby, 1985; North, 1990; Zucker, 1986) and how it is that new organizational forms and practices are or are not adopted (cf. Fallers, 1965; Walder, 1986; Putnam, 1993). These theories can offer us real insights into organizational behavior once we are willing to abandon the limiting conception of bureaucracy which has become dominant in the field of organizational behavior.

Creating Tomorrow's Organizations. Edited by C.L. Cooper and S.E. Jackson.
© 1997 John Wiley & Sons Ltd.

CULTURAL VALUES AND THE ADOPTION OF FOREIGN PRACTICES

Much of the application of cross-cultural psychology to organizational behavior describes how different cultural values affect employees (c.f. Adler, 1991; Hofstede, 1980a). Yet, the psychological approach to cultural differences has nothing to say about which practices developed under other values systems will be adopted, and which stoutly resisted. Since we observe that organizations do adopt foreign practices, we wanted to identify those circumstances in which "cultural comfort" may be overridden.

The first step was to develop a systematic measure of organizational practices reflecting different values. While there are numerous essays suggesting that certain practices reflect a cultural feature in their natal societies, these are rather more *post hoc* accounts of why certain practices were resisted (or distorted in their application) than explanations of which foreign practices would be adopted which opposed, and why. However, such explanations are available from the comparative institutions theorists, who have long analyzed the adoption and modification of "modern" organizational practices in "traditional" societies.

The distinction between "traditional" and "modern" forms of social organization began with modern social science itself (Comte [1832–1840] 1855; Toennies [1887] 1957). Because these have been central concepts in the comparative institutions work of so many disciplines, these societal-level forms of social organization have been called by many different names. Weber (1947) distinguished the rational-legal authority of bureaucracy from traditional authority; Riggs (1964), substantive bureaucracy from formalistic bureaucracy; Fallers (1965), modern bureaucracy from Bantu bureaucracy; Putnam (1993), civic communities from patron-clientelism; and Coleman (1993), purposive organization from primordial social organization. Modern societies are characterized by organizations purposely constructed around offices (not persons) which use rules, supervision and incentives by designated agents for social control; this collection of organizational features dominant in modern societies will be summarized as "intentionally universalistic" organizational practices. By contrast, in traditional societies social organization develops through birth ties and social control depends more completely on status, reputation and moral force; this set of organizational practices are referred to as "particularism" here. Of course, today all societies (and most large organizations) contain mixtures of both universalistic and particularistic practices. Yet the difference in degree is an important one.

Universalistic organizational practices were first described in detail by Weber and labeled "bureaucracies". Weber described both the objectives of bureaucracies (i.e. that they are intentionally goal-oriented, rule-constrained, using impersonal merit-based staffing) and a particular mechanism for achieving those objectives (e.g. offices arranged in a hierarchical order, selection based on objectively determined credentials, strict separation of office and person, and job security and pensions for incumbents, etc.). As both Clegg (1990) and Perrow

(1979) note, in the field of organizational behavior the term bureaucracy, unfortunately, has become focused only on Weber's nineteenth century means and dissociated from the objectives these means were designed to achieve (which are rarely criticized). While this serves the purpose of scholars such as Mintzberg (1979), who needed to give a familiar label to a kind of rigid, formalistic organizational type in order to distinguish it from alternatives, this practice has tended to draw attention away from Weber's original focus on the intended purposes of bureaucratic organizations.

A shift in attention back to the objectives of bureaucracy provides a fruitful basis for understanding cross-national differences in organizational practices. This is so because the degree to which organizations are intentionally universalistic affects a whole host of organizational practices and participant reactions. For example, intentionally universalistic organizations would establish procedures intended to constrain office holders to hire, reward and promote based on the contribution an employee can and does make to organizational goal achievement. Such employees would be expected to dispute such decisions or obtain organizational rewards by making claims that they have a better idea for reaching such goals. By contrast, in particularistic settings those with the power to hire, reward and fire would be expected to do so based on the employee's personal characteristics (e.g. that she is the daughter of a friend, or is personally loyal to the power wielder, or is deserving of more money because of family circumstances). Disputes and attempts to get ahead in these settings would be based on claims of greater personal need or loyalty. This separation of objectives and means of Weber's rational-legal bureaucracy is especially important in analyzing organizations in traditional societies, many of which have organizations adopting the bureaucratic means of formalism and hierarchy harnessed to particularistic ends.

One of the best descriptions of how a traditional societal context alters the use of imported modern bureaucratic practices is an analysis by Fallers (1965) of what he called "Bantu bureaucracy". In his study of the African Soga people (in today's Uganda) during the colonial period in the mid-twentieth century, Fallers discovered what he described as a conflict arising from an incompatibility between the Soga's traditional particularistic practices and the European-imposed bureaucracy. Whereas the former, based on lineage and chiefdoms, is particularistic, the latter is universalistic. The incompatible objectives of these two types of organization resulted in interpersonal conflicts and instability in administration. For example, universalistic colonial rules dictated that employees should be selected based on merit, yet tribal chiefs also had strong moral obligations to distribute resources to kin and loyal dependents. Fallers (1965) indicated that universalistic meritocratic organizational practices were adopted only nominally.

This pattern is also reported by Putnam (1993), who contrasted the evolution of new regional governments in the relatively more universalistic northern Italian regions with the ways in which the more particularistic southern Italian regions constructed these mandated organizations. Despite the same formal national requirements for these new regional governments, the different societies in the north and the south resulted in the development of quite different organizations. The north had a long experience with civic participation, whereas in the south there was more vertical dependence on powerful patrons and more amoral familialism, which Putnam characterized as "clientelism". Putnam found that in the north the new regional governments had active citizen involvement and were more effective, while the new regional governments of the south were ineffective because captured by local autocrats. As Walder's (1986) and Putnam's (1993) research indicates, the more universalistic organizational forms of modern societies often have been altered to fit the prevailing system of particularistic relations in more traditional societies. Just as modern societies contain many organizations dominated by particularistic practice (e.g. nepotism), some organizations in more traditional societies have adopted some universalistic practices. These organizational variations within traditional societies provide an opportunity to test ideas about why foreign practices may or may not be adopted. My colleague, Khalid Al-Aiban, and I thought we could identify one area in which we could make predictions about such adoptions (Al-Aiban & Pearce, 1993).

We tested Bozeman's (1987) argument that governmental organizations would be more likely to adopt organizational practices reflective of their national cultures than would businesses. This is because governmental organizations are both (a) viewed by members of society as entities which should reflect their core societal values; and (b) monopoly providers of services experiencing less pressure for efficiency than many businesses seeking profits in competitive environments. Following existing cross-cultural research, we expected cross-national differences in business' organizational practices, but we proposed that there would be significant differences between businesses and governments within each culture, consistent with the value preferences of their members. This test in a sample of Saudi Arabian and American businesses and governmental agencies also provided an opportunity to develop measures of organizational practices we expected to be found in traditional societies, which could be contrasted with the available measures of bureaucracy.

Since most of the Saudi managers who would provide the data were well aware of prevailing Western views on the inferiority and "primitiveness" of traditional Saudi organizational practices, we tried to develop measures which were descriptive and non-evaluative in order to avoid, as much as possible, priming the Saudis to report what they thought would be socially desirable to researchers. We did successfully develop scales with good reliability and discriminant validity. The initial scales piloted in this Saudi–American sample were subsequently refined and developed in the larger Lithuanian and Hungarian studies described below (Pearce, Branyiczki & Bigley, 1997; Pearce, Bigley & Branyiczki, 1997). The two scales were called "meritocratic practices" (reflecting a key feature of universalistic practices found in modern societies) and "clientelist practices" (representing particularistic organizational practices more characteristic of traditional societies). Examples of clientelist items are "'Connection' or 'who you know' is more important than job performance in getting ahead here", and "It really is standard practice in this organization to use one's position to help friends or family".

While Saudi managers in both business and government organizations reported significantly higher use of clientelist practices in their organizations than did the Americans, the Saudi business managers also reported significantly less clientelist practices than did their government-organization counterparts. These results held even when controlling for amount of time respondents had spent working with Westerners (i.e. "learning" could not account for the differences).

Saudi cultural values emphasizing the primacy of obligations to family affected organizational practices in predictable ways, and the effects were more pronounced in those organizations expected to reflect those values. In these governmental organizations managers were resistant to adopting universalistic practices, despite the fact that most respondents were instructed in the "best practices" of Western schools of business and public administration. In contrast, top managers in the profit-seeking business in Saudi Arabia faced different incentives—less responsibility to reflect their society's values and more interest in reaping the benefits of purposeful profit-seeking. This study demonstrated that those who control organizations would adopt different foreign practices in response to their own incentives, and suggested we could learn more about employees' attitudes and behavior in particularistic organizations.

BUREAUCRACY AND PROCEDURAL JUSTICE

While there has been a long-standing critique of the ethnocentrism of theories of organization (c.f. Hofstede, 1980b), we wondered whether, ethnocentric or not, would practices designed to foster universalism characteristic of bureaucratic organizations be as well received by employees from traditional societies who have little experience with and no expectation of such practices? Procedural justice, as a well-established concept reflecting universalism, was chosen to explore this question.

Much of the research in the area of procedural justice has focused on organizational rules and policies as antecedents of fairness perceptions, which in turn are posited to affect employee attitudes and behavior (e.g. Folger, 1977; Tyler, 1987). Many of the organizational factors that have been linked to employee perceptions of procedural justice (e.g. voice, bias suppression) reflect the meritocratic principles of universalism and impersonal decision-making that Weber (1947) associated with bureaucracy. Particular procedural characteristics which have been shown to foster perceptions of justice, such as formal mechanisms for voice and public criteria for evaluation (e.g. Thibaut & Kelley, 1975; Leventhal, 1980), long have been considered surrogates for bureaucratization by scholars of institutional development (cf. Jacoby, 1985). Further, it is undeniably ethnocentric. Certainly, echoes of American cultural influences are apparent in the study of procedural justice in organizations. The litigiousness and overabundance of lawyers in the USA has long been noted and decried. Nevertheless, ethnocentric to American preoccupations with legalisms, procedural justice concerns also reflect intentionally universalistic organizational practice.

This idea was tested in one of the more interesting examples of societies dominated by particularistic organizational practices—communist and immediately post-communist organizations. Walder (1986) described what he called the "neo-traditionalism" of the workplace in the People's Republic of China. He suggests that all communist states rely on neo-traditionalism, a system characterized by:

> . . . dependence, deference, and particularism . . . in contrast with the more familiar modern forms of industrial authority that are notable for their relative impersonality and anonymity, the relative political and economic independence of workers from management, and the resulting prominence of group conflict, bargaining, contract, and the relatively tight bureaucratic restriction of personal discretion of immediate supervisors (p. 10).

In communist neo-traditionalism, the workplace was the focal point for the delivery of goods and services not available from other sources, the party tried to eliminate all competing informal political organizations of employees, and the discretion of supervisors was relatively unrestrained by enforceable regulations. Despite these organizations' use of bureaucratic "means"—such as formalism—particularism was necessary for political control. In order to maintain this control, wide discretion was delegated to managers and party officials who then had the latitude to exercise it as they saw fit (Pearce, 1991; Pearce & Branyiczki, 1996; Voslensky, 1984).

My colleagues, Imre Branyiczki and Gregory Bigley, and I proposed that employees would concur with our assessments that the neo-traditional workplaces of newly post-communist Lithuania would be more clientelistic and less meritocratic than the modernist American ones. Yet, despite this difference, employees' reactions would be mediated by the organization's use of meritocratic practices—that is, meritocratic practices would have similar positive effects on employee perceptions of procedural justice in the neo-traditional societies, despite employees' lack of experience with them (Pearce, Bigley & Branyiczki, 1997).

Using self-report questionnaire data from managerial and professional employees in American and Lithuanian electronics companies we found that, indeed, Lithuanian employees reported significantly less use of meritocratic practices by their employers and that meritocratic practices mediated the relationship between society and perceptions of procedural justice. Further, we found that procedural justice was positively associated with employee commitment, even when controlling for society. As predicted, just procedures were as positively associated with employee attitudes, such as commitment, in societies having little expectation of them as they were employees in those in which had come to expect them as a right. This reflects an important distinction between employees' accommodation to a bad situation and their embrace of it.

These results shed a new light on the reports of the distortions of universalistic practices reported by Riggs (1964), Walder (1986), Putnam (1993) and others. In each of these cases resistance consisted of elites' rejection of the constraints universalistic organizational practices would place on them (in their positions of authority). Historians note that managers have rarely chosen to constrain themselves with procedural niceties. Jacoby (1985) described the evolution of professional personnel policies and the specialists who developed and enforced them as an attempt to pre-empt worker-protective legislation and trade union organizing in the USA. Trade unions and professional personnel specialists worked to bureaucratize the personnel systems in organizations as the best defense against the arbitrary supervisory actions which were threatening great political costs. Workers in democratic polities have some means to protect themselves from arbitrary actions, and they often seek to do so by imposing bureaucratic procedures of objective assessments of merit and due process guarantees on their employers (Jacoby, 1985). Thus, just as elites may have incentives to adopt those foreign practices which they find useful (as the Saudi business managers did), so local elites may resist those which constrain them.

BUREAUCRACY AND TRUST

Just as the field of organizational behavior has developed an extensive understanding of employee attitudes and behavior in intendedly universalistic bureaucracies, these early results suggested that a better understanding of cross-national collaborations may be served by more developed theories of organizational behavior in traditional societies. A reading of comparative institutions scholars indicated that organizations in traditional and neo-traditional societies are characterized by a pervasive distrust; because trust is so central to organizational behavior and reactions to organizational change, this seemed a useful place to begin.

Trust has been addressed by theorists from a wide range of economic, social and psychological sciences and so an unfortunate consequence has been that the numerous definitions of trust, developed for different purposes, have little in common. For example, some economists defined trust as a form of implicit contracting (Arrow, 1974); sociologists such as Schutz (1967) considered it to be "the taken for granted world in common" that makes social life possible; alternatively, the psychologist Rotter (1967) defined trust as the generalized expectation of an individual that the promise or statement of another individual is reliable. Although specific definitions of trust vary considerably, especially when viewed across social science disciplines, one general idea emerges in most discussions of the topic: trust is a belief that another or others do not intend to harm you.

Comparative institutions theorists have argued that one reason bureaucratization developed was that it could produce trust when the scale and
scope of economic interdependence overwhelmed particularistic relationships
(cf. Zucker, 1986). Bureaucracy fosters trust by providing explicit rules to govern
responsibilities and relationships. Employees who understand the rules under
which they are all governed have less to fear from others, vital when those others
are distant or foreign. In support of this idea, several studies have demonstrated
a positive relationship between procedural justice (i.e., modernist practices) and
supervisory trust (summarized in Tyler, 1987).

Consistent with this argument, I and my colleagues found, in a large sample of
US and Hungarian employees in manufacturing and service industries (sampled
just as communism was falling), that the Hungarians reported significantly more
distrust of their organizations than did comparable American employees (Pearce,
Branyiczki & Bakacsi, 1994). We found that employees working in these neo-
traditionalist organizations also reported that they were significantly more anx-
ious, that their employers were more unfair, and that their co-workers were less
trustworthy than did the American employees. This finding was supported in a
replication of the earlier Hungarian results, in which we found significantly lower
trust in peers among employees from diverse industries in two neo-traditionalist
societies—Lithuania and Hungary—compared to employees from a sample of
companies in the modernist USA (Pearce, Branyiczki & Bigley, 1997; Pearce,
Bigley & Branyiczki, 1997).

That employees would distrust the employers who distribute rewards based on
particularistic criteria may be expected. However, the suggestion that employees
in these neo-traditional workplaces would also distrust their peers is less intuitively obvious. Yet, Gambetta (1988) has eloquently described how the
unpredictability of clientelism fosters such distrust. This distrust leads, in turn, to
a retreat to the only available protection—dependence on a powerful patron.
Particularistic practices can be capricious, and so it is hard for peers to know
where they stand with one another. Because the criteria for rewards are unclear,
no one knows whether or not they have done enough or whether someone else
has done more. Since power in traditionalist societies is based more on connections than on office, even peers can pose a threat. Peers may be well-connected
themselves; and even if they are not particularly well-connected, one can never
be sure that they will not seek to ingratiate themselves to the powerful by
denouncing or informing on you (Haraszti, 1977; Pearce, 1991; Walder, 1986).
Without universalistic organizational practices trust must be constructed with
particular others, one contact at a time.

Just as the excessive impersonalism to which universalism is subject can foster
employee alienation (Crozier, 1964) and infantilism (Argyris, 1957), so excessive
particularism can foster distrust. Such distrust can have a powerful effect on
organizational behavior. Rotter (1967) has demonstrated that distrusting individuals are more likely to lie, cheat and steal, and our own observations have
supported this claim (Pearce, Branyiczki & Bigley, 1997).

COPING WITH SYSTEMIC DISTRUST

How do managers and employees who must live with the distrust fostered by the particularistic practices characteristic of traditional societies get work done? Organized activity does take place in such societies, and so we wondered whether some of the business practices labeled as the result of cultural differences (but left unanalyzed) may reflect individuals' strategies to cope with the distrust engendered when particularistic organizational practices are dominant in societies with extensive economic interdependence. While managers in traditional societies may adopt some modernist practices in the domains they control, they would still find themselves in larger networks of organizational and governmental relations on which they can not impose their preferences. My colleague Katherine Xin and I proposed that one reason executives seek out "good connections" and cultivate close personal relationships with the powerful is to obtain resources or protection not otherwise available in their societies (Xin & Pearce, 1996).

Such personal connections seem especially important to executives in traditional societies without the stable legal and regulatory environment that allows for impersonal business dealings (Redding, 1990; Zucker, 1986). For example, without an impartial judiciary, executives are reluctant to develop business relationships with those they do not personally trust. We drew on the work of Redding (1990), Putnam (1993), and Nee (1992; 1989) to develop hypotheses about which executives in the People's Republic of China would find personal relationships with business connections critical to their success and invest more in their cultivation.

Redding (1990, p. 56) observed that *guanxi* networks of personal relationships among the Overseas Chinese are useful in the regulation of transactions in the absence of state institutions for that purpose. We proposed that managers in China would cultivate personal connections to substitute for institutional stability of established rule-of-law characteristic of modern societies (see Boisot, 1986; Riggs, 1964; Walder, 1986). We tested this idea by proposing that while the weak rule of law in China is problematic for all who do business there, such unreliability would prove particularly burdensome for private businesses.

Nee (1992) has classified present-day Chinese organizations into three types: state-owned, privately-owned, and collective-hybrids (which typically are owned by local governments and produce products for competitive markets). Private companies are especially vulnerable in a country with uncertain property rights because the potential for interference from party and governmental officials is great. Because Chinese private companies do not have the institutional protection of local-government or state ownership, they are more vulnerable to extortion and arbitrary attacks by the powerful (Nee, 1992). We took Nee's insights as a point of departure and hypothesized that Chinese private-company executives would not await their fates passively. Rather, they would draw on the practices traditionally available to Chinese business people and would create their own protection via particularistic trust—*guanxi*—as a substitute for their counter-parts' formal structural protection of state and local government ownership. That is, they would cultivate relationships of personal obligation among the powerful in order to obtain protection from possible expropriation or extortion.

Using data collected from structured interviews with executives from a wide variety of industries, we found that *guanxi* relationships for private-sector execu-tives were more important to them and consisted of relationships of deeper trust than those of the collective-hybrid or state-owned company executives. Further, if *guanxi* was more important to those with the greatest need for a substitute for the trust produced by more reliable universalistic practices, we expected this to be reflected in the ways these executives characterized their relationships. In particular, their use of good personal connections as protection was found to be reflected in greater reliance on these connections as a defense against threats and a greater reliance on connections in government. Rather than reporting the usefulness of connections in obtaining customers or market information, or se-curing credit, as executives in more modern societies might, Chinese private-company executives reported needing connections to help them face fundamental threats, such as expropriation and extortion due to weak rule-of-law (Redding, 1990; Yang, 1994).

Thus, business practices, such as building particularistic relationships with one another before doing business, which have been described as characteristic of the business cultures in traditional and neo-traditional societies, can be seen as practical responses to the uncertainty of organizing there. Rather than treating this difference in organizational behavior as if it were an unexamined property of different cultures, it is more productively viewed as an adaptation to the difficulty in establishing trust in the absence of modernist bureaucracy.

PLACING ORGANIZATIONAL BEHAVIOR IN CONTEXT

This work has provided several examples of the value of placing organizational behavior in its political and economic context. The work of comparative institu-tions theorists has provided the basis for explanations for the adoption of foreign organizational practices and has suggested insight into organizational behavior in organizations dominated by particularism.

First, we have learned something about why some foreign organizational practices may be adopted while others are resisted. Those organizations more centrally concerned with representing and promulgating their society's cultural values were more resistant to the importation of organizational practices based on alien values. This work has identified just one setting—governmental agen-cies—in which societal values take precedence over efficiency considerations; future research might profitably explore other organizations (e.g. schools) or circumstances (e.g. government protection from competitive pressures) in which this might also be the case.

Second, hypotheses based on unpacking bureaucratic objectives from Weber's bureaucratic means have been useful in predicting the reactions to specific practices. Employees have responded positively to the foreign organizational practices of bureaucracy when those practices are personally beneficial. While members of the same national culture may hold similar values and share experiences with similar ways of organizing, they do not all benefit equally from their culturally-based organizational practices. This is illustrated by the finding that practices characteristic of modern societies which serve to constrain elites received the same positive responses from employees, regardless of past experiences. Heretofore, cross-cultural descriptions treated all members of a society as undifferentiated (except as possible members of subcultures), whereas this work suggests that others are as pluralistic in their interests as are Westerners. Those who speak for their (or others') natal cultures have their own positional interests and theories of organizational behavior which can articulate and explain those points-of-view that offer great promise.

Finally, to provide a contrast to the extensive documentation of organizational behavior in intendedly universalistic organizations, participants' attitudinal and behavioral reactions to particularistic organizational practices have been analyzed. Despite the obvious importance of particularism, its impact on organizational behavior has not received much attention. As an initial step, it has been found that particularism was associated with distrust—not only of authorities but of co-workers as well. Further, reliance on building a network of personal connections can be placed into its theoretical context—as a strategy for coping with systematically fostered distrust. That is, intentionally universalistic practices, despite their own costs, produce something quite valuable—participant trust. This has rather important implications for organizational behavior, ones that had been hidden as long as bureaucracy was seen only as a particular kind of means, rather than as an attempt to achieve goals by reliance on merit and an organizational version of rule-of-law. While these ideas have been applied to cross-national comparisons here, they are not confined there. If this analysis is accurate, particularistic organizational practices should foster general participant distrust, no matter what the societal context.

In conclusion, although this line of research has suggested several insights, it remains a risky area for empirical research. Theories of comparative institutions and individuals' organizational behavior operate at very different levels of analysis, which leads to serious concerns about the validity of any observed relationships. Although correlates have been discovered between societal-level phenomena, organizational practices, and employee attitudes, eliminating all of the alternative explanations is never possible. Consequently, one cannot be sure that the causal arguments presented here are complete. In addition, as a practical matter, it is more difficult to obtain samples of societies than to obtain samples of employees. Yet, ours is an empirical field and, love it or hate it, credibility rests on the ability to hold our arguments up to empirical refutation. It seems that only by providing measures and statistical tests do our colleagues take our work seriously enough to criticize it, and to collect their own data proving it wrong.

Further, as Staw (1995) suggested, studies wherein there is the greatest distance between independent and dependent variables, while controversial, are the potential "jackpots of social science".

Acknowledgments

The author wishes to thank Greg Bigley, Chris Earley and Sue Jackson for their comments on earlier drafts.

REFERENCES

Adler, N. (1991). *International Dimensions of Organizational Behavior*, 2nd edn. Belmont, CA: Wadsworth.

Al-Aiban, K. & Pearce, J.L. (1993). The influence of values on management practices: a test in two countries. *International Studies of Management and Organization*, **23**, 35–52.

Argyris, C. (1957). *Personality and Organization*. New York: Harper and Row.

Arrow, K.J. (1974). *The Limits of Organization*. New York: W.W. Norton.

Boisot, M.H. (1986). Markets and hierarchies in a cultural perspective. *Organization Studies*, **7**, 135–58

Bozeman, B. (1987). *All Organizations are Public*. San Francisco, CA: Jossey-Bass.

Clegg, S.R. (1990). *Modern Organizations: Organization Studies in the Postmodern World*. London: Sage.

Coleman, J.S. (1993). The rational reconstruction of society. *American Sociological Review*, **58**, 1–15.

Comte, A. ([1832–1840] 1855). *Cours de Philosophie Positive* (The Positive Philosophy), translated by H. Martineau. New York: C. Blanchard.

Crozier, M. (1964). *The Bureaucratic Phenomenon*. Chicago: University of Chicago Press.

Fallers, L.A. (1965). *Bantu Bureaucracy*. Chicago: University of Chicago Press.

Folger, R. (1977). Distributive and procedural justice: combined impact of "voice" and improvement on experienced inequity. *Journal of Personality and Social Psychology*, **35**, 108–19.

Gambetta, D. (1988). Mafia: the price of distrust. In D. Gambetta (ed), *Trust* (pp. 158–210). New York: Basil Blackwell.

Haraszti, M. (1977). *A Worker in a Worker's State*. New York: Penguin.

Hofstede, G. (1980a). *Culture's Consequences: International Differences in Work-related Values*. Beverly Hills, CA: Sage.

Hofstede, G. (1980b). Motivation, leadership, and organization: do American theories apply abroad? *Organizational Dynamics*, 42–63.

Jacoby, S.M. (1985). *Employing Bureaucracy: Managers, Unions and the Transformation of Work in American Industry, 1900–1945*. New York: Columbia University Press.

Leventhal, G.S. (1980). What should be done with equity theory? New approaches to the study of fairness in social relationships. In K.J. Gergen, M.S. Greenberg & R.H. Willis (eds), *Social Exchange Theory*. New York: Wiley.

Mintzberg, H. (1979). *The Structuring of Organizations*. Englewood Cliffs, NJ: Prentice-Hall.

Nee, V. (1989). A theory of market transition: from redistribution to markets in state socialism. *American Sociological Review*, **54**, 663–81.

Nee, V. (1992). Organizational dynamics of market transition: hybrid firms, property rights, and mixed economy in China. *Administrative Science Quarterly*, **31**, 1–27.

North, D.C. (1990). *Institutions, Institutional Change and Economic Performance*. New York: Cambridge University Press.

Pearce, J.L. (1991). From socialism to capitalism: the effects of Hungarian human resources practices. *Academy of Management Executive*, **5**, 75–88.

Pearce, J.L. & Branyiczki, I. (1996). Legitimacy: an analysis of three Hungarian–Western collaborations. In P.W. Beamish & P. Killing (eds), *Cooperative Strategies: European Perspectives* (pp. 298–319). San Francisco, CA: New Lexington Press.

Pearce, J.L., Bigley, G.A. & Branyiczki, I. (1997). Procedural justice as modernism: placing industrial/organizational psychology in context. *Applied Psychology: An International Review*, 46.

Pearce, J.L., Branyiczki, I. & Bakacsi, G. (1994). Person-based reward systems: a theory of organizational reward practices in reform-communist organizations. *Journal of Organizational Behavior*, **15**, 261–82.

Pearce, J.L., Branyiczki, I. & Bigley, G.A. (1997). Insufficient bureancracy: Trust and commitment in particularistic organizations. GSM Working Paper. Graduate School of Management; University of California at Irvine.

Perrow, C. (1979). *Complex Organizations*, 2nd edn. Glenview, IL: Scott, Foresman.

Putnam, R.D. (1993). *Making Democracy Work*. Princeton, NJ: Princeton University Press.

Redding, S.G. (1990). *The Spirit of Chinese Capitalism*. New York: Walter de Gruyter.

Riggs, F.W. (1964). *Administration in Developing Countries*. Boston, MA: Houghton Mifflin.

Rotter, J.B. (1967). A new scale for the measurement of interpersonal trust. *Journal of Personality*, **35**, 651–65.

Schutz, A. (1967). *A Phenomenology of the Social World*. Evanston, IL: Northwestern University Press.

Staw, B.M. (1995). Repairs on the road to relevance and rigor. In L.L. Cummings & P.J. Frost (eds), *Publishing in Organizational Sciences* (pp. 85–97). Thousand Oaks, CA: Sage.

Thibaut, J. & Kelley, H.H. (1975). *Procedural Justice: a Psychological Analysis*. Hillsdale, NJ: Erlbaum.

Toennies, F. ([1887] 1957). *Community and Society*, translated by C.P. Loomis. East Lansing, MI: Michigan State University Press.

Tyler, T.R. (1987). Procedural justice research. *Social Justice Research*, **1**, 41–6.

Voslensky, M. (1984). *Nomenklatura: the Soviet Ruling Class*. Garden City, NY: Doubleday.

Walder, A.G. (1986). *Communist Neo-traditionalism: Work and Authority in Chinese Industry*. Berkeley, CA: University of California Press.

Weber, M. (1947). In A.M. Henderson & T. Parsons (trans. and eds), *The Theory of Social and Economic Organization*. New York: Oxford University Press.

Xin, K. & Pearce, J.L. (1996). *Guanxi*: Good connections as substitutes for institutional support. *Academy of Management Journal*, **34**, 1641–58.

Yang, M.M. (1994). *Gifts, Favors & Banquets*. Ithaca, NY: Cornell University Press.

Zucker, L.G. (1986). Production of trust: institutional sources of economic structure, 1840–1920. *Research in Organizational Behavior*, **8**, 53–112.

Chapter 3

Organizational Socialization in Multinational Corporations: The Role of Implicit Learning

Georgia T. Chao
Michigan State University, East Lansing, MI, USA

Realities of a global marketplace have inspired many organizations to initiate or expand their international operations. Multinational corporations (MNCs) face a variety of challenges as they start up new ventures in foreign countries. Foremost among these challenges is the management of human resources from a different culture and the integration of these people in an organization's existing work force. Cross-cultural interactions bring forth theoretical considerations regarding how individuals perceive others who are different from them, how attitudes toward other cultures are developed, and how these attitudes affect behaviors toward individuals from different cultures. In addition, cross-cultural interactions in organizations bring forth practical considerations regarding how individuals adjust to a specific job or work role, and adjust to a multinational organizational environment in general. Together, theoretical and practical considerations should be integrated to guide organizational interventions designed to facilitate work adjustment.

The focus of this chapter is to integrate two streams of theory and study that can illuminate future research on individual work adjustment within an international organizational context. First, organizational socialization theory and research directly examine individual work adjustment and provide a foundation for future study. Second, implicit learning theory describes how much of our knowledge can be absorbed and shaped at a non-conscious level. The role that implicit

Creating Tomorrow's Organizations. Edited by C.L. Cooper and S.E. Jackson.
© 1997 John Wiley & Sons Ltd.

learning plays in organizational socialization can stimulate new theory and research that would increase our understanding of cross-cultural interactions as well as aiding the success of multinational corporations.

ORGANIZATIONAL SOCIALIZATION IN MULTINATIONAL CORPORATIONS

Organizational socialization pertains to the work adjustment process as an individual enters a new organization or experiences major job changes within his/her organization (Van Maanen, 1976). An excellent review of organizational socialization is provided by Fisher (1986) and will not be reiterated here. However, since that review, more empirical research has been published that supports basic tenets of socialization theory. For example, how well an individual "fits in" or "learns the ropes" in the organization is an important predictor of that person's job satisfaction, organizational commitment and salary growth (Chao et al., 1994). Although there is a growing body of empirical research on organizational socialization, very little of the research examines socialization issues within an international context. One exception is a study by Black (1992), who surveyed American expatriates in the Pacific Rim. He found significant relationships between socialization tactics and a manager's likelihood toward role innovation.

Although the problems of American expatriates have been well documented (Tung, 1981), underlying reasons to explain why expatriates experience difficulty adjusting to a foreign environment remain relatively unexplored. Adjustment problems may stem from prejudices against a foreign group, ethnocentrism or inflexibility. Many attitudes that hinder adjustment have non-conscious roots that would be difficult to identify and research. An examination of implicit learning theory and how it affects organizational socialization is presented to explore these non-conscious roots and to identify future avenues of research.

IMPLICIT LEARNING THEORY

Although philosophers and psychologists have long speculated about the unconscious and its effect on behavior, the study of implicit learning has a relatively short history, with most of the empirical research conducted within the past 30 years (Reber, 1993). Reber defines implicit learning as "the acquisition of knowledge that takes place largely independently of conscious attempts to learn, and largely in the absence of explicit knowledge about what was acquired" (Reber, 1993; p. 5). Researchers in this area have used various terminology to describe processes that are not conscious. Since the term "unconscious" includes popular conceptions associated with sleep or trauma (e.g. a blow to the head knocked him unconscious) as well as wakeful states of conscious unawareness, the term "non-conscious" will be used here to denote a physical state of consciousness but a lack of conscious awareness. The non-conscious component of implicit learning plays a critical role in two respects. First, the learning process itself is generally non-conscious, so the individual is unaware that learning has occurred. Second, since the individual is unaware of knowledge that was implicitly learned, that person is non-conscious that such knowledge would influence the individual's attitudes or behaviors and is generally unable to consciously retrieve or articulate this knowledge.

Empirical research examining implicit learning generally began with Reber's laboratory studies on artificial grammar learning. Subjects memorized strings of letters that could not be pronounced, but the set of strings conformed to arbitrary rules. New stimuli were then shown and subjects were required to discriminate between strings that conformed to the artificial rules of grammar and those that did not. Although subjects could not articulate what the grammatical rules were, their identification of grammatical and non-grammatical strings significantly exceeded chance predictions. Thus, subject performance indicated they had some knowledge about the grammatical rules even though they could not articulate them.

Additional research has been conducted using a variety of laboratory tasks such as anticipating changing probabilities of flashing lights (Reber & Millward, 1971), achieving production goals in a simulated plant (Berry & Broadbent, 1984) and locating targets in a matrix (Lewicki, Czyzewska & Hoffman, 1987). Excellent reviews of this literature are presented by Reber (1993) and by Berry & Dienes (1993). Although the scope of implicit learning theory is too broad to cover in this chapter, a few elements are highlighted for their relevance to socialization in a multicultural context.

Primacy of Implicit Learning

Lewicki, Hill & Czyzewska (1992) describe the ubiquity of non-conscious acquisition of information. They assert that non-conscious learning is faster and processes more information than consciously controlled cognition. A review of the research showed that subjects' non-conscious ability to discover and use rules regarding stimuli co-variation was significantly better than their ability to consciously identify this information. By removing the requirement that the individual be attentive or be motivated to learn in implicit learning, it is easy to see how implicit learning becomes the default learning option when all methods of explicit learning are not operating. Thus, implicit learning may occur regardless of whether explicit learning is taking place—making implicit learning the primary learning process.

Characteristics of Implicit Learning

Berry & Dienes (1993) describe four characteristics of implicit learning: (a) specificity of transfer; (b) association with incidental learning conditions; (c) sense of intuition; and (d) robustness against time, psychological disorder and interference with other mental activities. The specificity of transfer characteristic recognizes that implicitly learned knowledge is context-bound. Co-variations among stimuli observed in a subject's environment may have limited transferability to new stimuli. Thus, association of a specific trait with a particular type of people—for example, Chinese are frugal—may generalize to other Asians but not to Europeans. The lack of general transferability may explain why conscious access of this knowledge is difficult. Subjects in many implicit learning studies were unaware that they learned anything and were unable to articulate any rules, even when they were informed about the nature of the study or were offered large rewards for rule identification (Lewicki, 1986). Without articulating rules about stimuli co-variations, the probability of generalizing that rule to completely different situations is likely to be small, hence the lack of general transferability.

The second characteristic, association with incidental learning conditions, is described by Wagner & Sternberg (1985) when they postulate that tacit knowledge is not directly taught. There is no intention to learn anything specific during implicit learning, thus there is no need to structure a direct learning experience. Without any structure of learning objectives, the knowledge acquired through implicit learning is less manipulable by others. Furthermore, initial encoding algorithms that are used to establish links between stimuli may be based on observations that are not representative of true stimuli covariation. The resulting interpretations would lead to illogical biases or irrational preferences that may be resistant to corrective attempts.

The third characteristic, sense of intuition, describes how subjects report a strong feeling that is not based on conscious reasoning when explaining their decisions or behaviors that are influenced by implicit learning. Reber (1989) describes intuition as a cognitive state providing an inexplicable sense of what is right or wrong that helps an individual make decisions or engage in a particular course of action. In his artificial grammar studies, Reber's (1989) subjects typically reported an intuitive sense for grammatical and non-grammatical strings of letters, but could not provide reasons to support or explain their intuitions. Reliance on this sense of intuition eliminates rational analysis, results in faster reaction times, and may avoid performance degradations under stress conditions (see Masters, 1992).

Finally, implicit learning is characterized by robustness to time, psychological disorders and secondary tasks. Reviews by Reber (1993) and by Berry & Dienes (1993) found evidence to support that subjects use implicitly learned knowledge long after explicit knowledge is lost. In addition, their reviews of research on neuropsychological patients indicated that people who suffered from amnesia, clinical depression, brain damage and other serious psychological and/or neurological disorders were able to implicitly learn information they were unable to explicitly master. Finally, subjects who were distracted on secondary tasks showed little interference in their ability to implicitly learn (Winter, Uleman & Cunniff, 1985).

Tacit Knowledge

For this chapter, knowledge gained through implicit learning will be referred to as tacit knowledge. Reber (1993) traces the origins of the term "tacit knowledge" to the social philosopher, Michael Polanyi, and defined it as "knowledge whose origins and essential epistemic contents were simply not part of one's ordinary consciousness" (p. 12). Although the defining characteristic of tacit knowledge is that it is largely non-conscious and cannot be articulated or openly expressed, Wagner & Sternberg (1985) assert that tacit knowledge may be accessible to conscious awareness. These two perspectives can be resolved when one considers that conscious and non-conscious states describe ends of a continuum and not mutually exclusive categories. Berry & Dienes (1993) acknowledge that implicit learning and tacit knowledge have some conscious components, but the larger non-conscious aspects are what characterizes these constructs. Thus, the more conscious components of tacit knowledge are analogous to the visible portion of a floating iceberg—a relatively small part that gives little clue to the much larger part of the iceberg that is hidden below the water.

The emphasis on non-conscious aspects of tacit knowledge is important because it highlights implicit learning processes and presents a challenge for researchers who want to measure it in field settings. There may be a tendency for some academics to downplay the non-conscious aspects of tacit knowledge and to emphasize conscious, verbalized aspects. The term "tacit knowledge" has been used to describe more explicit knowledge bases, such as procedural knowledge (Sternberg et al., 1995), job knowledge (Schmidt & Hunter, 1993) and even strategic knowledge that is a form of verbal knowledge (Kraiger, Ford & Salas, 1993). Such usage dilutes the original definition of "tacit knowledge" with a strong conscious component and will only serve to confuse subsequent researchers.

The elements of implicit learning were described to set a foundation for integrating implicit learning with organizational socialization. Specific areas for this integration are discussed in the next section.

ORGANIZATIONAL SOCIALIZATION AND IMPLICIT LEARNING IN MULTICULTURAL CONTEXTS

Organizational socialization has been described as an ubiquitous process that individuals undergo as they change organizational positions or as their current positions evolve (Van Maanen, 1976, 1984). Like implicit learning, organizational socialization pervades many activities and it is not obvious when these experiences result in information acquisition that subsequently affects work adjustment.

The first two characteristics of implicit learning—a context-bound characteristic and a focus on incidental learning events—are also descriptive of organizational socialization (Louis, 1990). Organizational socialization is context-bound. Chao et al. (1994) describe six content areas that individuals must learn in order to be well socialized. These areas are: *performance proficiency*—learning how to perform the job; *language*—learning organizational and professional jargon and acronyms; *people*—learning how to get along with other organizational members; *politics*—learning about who has power; *organizational goals and values*—learning what the organization strives for; and *history*—learning about the organization's and work group's past. All of these content areas are bound to an individual's position and organization. Mastery in any area may have limited generalizability if the individual changes jobs or organizations.

Within a MNC, these content areas are enlarged to include cross-cultural features. For example, *language* concerns will include basic language skills needed for expatriates and host nationals to communicate with one another, as well as more specialized nomenclature. Less obvious, but perhaps more important, would be the expanded areas of *people* and *politics*, where new interactive roles may be required to develop positive relationships with people from a different culture.

Lewicki (1986) has shown how social-behavioral reactions may be shaped by non-conscious information acquisition. Results from his research program found even a single exposure of stimuli covariation could influence subjects' subsequent reactions to a similar stimulus. Within a MNC, it is likely that socialization content areas that embody social-behavioral reactions would be influenced by implicit learning and the resulting tacit knowledge. Thus, of the six content areas described by Chao et al. (1994), *people* and *politics* are most likely to be affected by implicit learning, since these areas involve social judgments and interactions. Likewise, *performance proficiency* has procedural knowledge components that can be shaped by implicit learning. Learning about the *organizational goals and values* may be explicit if the organization has a strong culture, or it may be more implicit if goals and values are not well specified, not well communicated, or there is a perceived gap between what is espoused and what is practiced. Finally, explicit declarative knowledge regarding *history* and formal training of *language* may decrease the role implicit learning has on these content areas, relative to the other areas.

Much of organizational socialization occurs in informal ways through unstructured learning experiences (Chao, 1997). Socialization is often associated with incidental learning conditions that were not planned or intended to teach specific lessons. Ostroff & Kozlowski (1992) investigated how newcomers acquired information in four socialization content areas: task, role, group and organization. Newcomers reported that most of the socialization information they learned was acquired by watching others. Other important sources involved direct interactions with a newcomer's supervisor or co-workers. To a great extent, reliance upon observation necessitates reliance on incidental learning conditions, since most people do not control the events they observe. Thus, information relevant to organizational socialization is likely to be acquired through incidental observation and much of this information may be tacit knowledge.

Within a MNC, the number of new stimuli covariations would increase as an individual encounters new ways of perceiving, judging and reacting to organizational behavior in a different culture. Expatriates adjusting to a new role within a foreign environment are exposed to a variety of incidental learning conditions that are likely to shape their attitudes and behaviors in non-conscious ways.

The third characteristic of implicit learning, a strong sense of intuition, is less directly tied with organizational socialization than the previously two discussed characteristics. Subjects report that they base their decisions on a sense of intuition in implicit learning experiments (Berry & Dienes, 1993). Intuitive decision-making has not been a prominent feature in the organizational socialization literature. However, theoretical papers on organizational socialization (Louis, 1980; Van Maanen, 1976) describe subjective feelings of "fitting in" or "learning the ropes" that may be difficult for individuals to articulate. Thus, both organizational socialization and implicit learning have subjective components that are difficult to verbalize.

Lastly, the robustness characteristic of implicit learning has no obvious counterpart in socialization theory. However, Louis (1980) describes how anticipatory socialization knowledge sets up expectations regarding early job experiences. These expectations help newcomers interpret or make sense of their experiences, especially surprising ones. The expectations themselves may be conscious or non-conscious and an individual may experience role ambiguity if these expectations are unmet and unknown. Engagement in a variety of job activities can yield a wealth of information that can be used to minimize role ambiguity. Thus, socialization information-seeking, particularly at the non-conscious level, could be robust to other tasks.

In addition, Van Maanen (1984) describes chains of socialization whereby socialization in one role may facilitate socialization in subsequent roles. Tacit knowledge gained in one socialization context may serve as a knowledge base to interpret new information. Like implicit learning, this tacit knowledge may be robust to time.

An Illustrative Example

A study by Chao & Sun (in press) interviewed 22 expatriates and 22 local Chinese people working in the People's Republic of China, to examine cultural factors and identify training needs that would facilitate interactions between these groups. The most commonly identified training need, for both expatriates and Chinese, was a better understanding of how culture affects work behavior. Although formal training programs were believed to help, many interviewees thought on-the-job interactions, i.e. organizational socialization, would be more effective. Specific content areas for better socialization included: general cultural awareness of Chinese or Western business practices, language instruction, and realistic expectations of work in a MNC operating in China. Thus, organizational socialization would be a powerful tool in improving multinational organizational relationships.

One specific training need for expatriates was only identified by the Chinese sample. They suggested that some attitudinal training was needed to improve expatriate interactions with Chinese personnel. Several of the Chinese remarked that some expatriates projected an ethnocentric attitude and behaved as if they were superior to the Chinese. This belief was mentioned with regard to a number of expatriates with various Eastern and Western nationalities, but attitudes of superiority were more frequently mentioned with regard to overseas-Chinese expatriates (e.g. Singapore, Hong Kong, Taiwan and Chinese-American expatriates). Furthermore, the Chinese believed these attitudes interfered with an expatriate's work adjustment and particularly the ability to work well with local Chinese employees. Interestingly, the expatriate-interviewees with Chinese ethnicity believed that they were better adjusted to the Chinese work environment than their Western counterparts because they were either more fluent in Chinese, more knowledgeable about the Chinese culture, or could better identify with the Chinese.

Perhaps the most parsimonious reason for the Chinese discrepancy between overseas-Chinese and Western expatriate attitudes is that there are true differences between Caucasian expatriates and overseas-Chinese expatriates. However, given the primacy of implicit learning, explanations for this discrepancy are also speculated to be related to tacit knowledge. From everyday experiences, local Chinese develop a body of tacit knowledge regarding appropriate and inappropriate attitudes and behaviors for Chinese people. Different attitudes and behaviors of Caucasian expatriates may be more acceptable to the Chinese than the same attitudes and behaviors from overseas-Chinese expatriates, because the tacit knowledge of what is appropriate and inappropriate generalizes to overseas-Chinese expatriates but not to Caucasian expatriates. Thus, differences between the local Chinese and overseas-Chinese expatriates are less likely to be accepted by the local Chinese. Additionally, the overseas-Chinese expatriates developed a tacit knowledge base that includes Western business practices. Their everyday attitudes and behaviors are likely to be manifested without conscious awareness of these Western influences and it may be difficult to articulate the extent to which their behavior is representative of their Chinese cultural heritage or to Western culture.

The expatriates and local Chinese responded to a hypothetical situation involving an expatriate manager who assigned a large amount of work to a Chinese employee (Chao & Sun, 1996). The expatriate asked the Chinese if he would be able to complete the work in time, to which the Chinese responded that he would "do his best". Interviewees were asked how they would interpret the Chinese's response. The majority of the expatriates interpreted "do his best" as an affirmation that the work would be completed on time. However, almost all of the Chinese interpreted the response as a face-saving answer that strongly suggested the work would not be completed on time.

One explanation for the group difference lies in the culturally-based interpretations of "do my best". Since most of the expatriates were Americans and the USA is culturally stereotyped as being high on an achievement dimension (Hofstede, 1980), "do my best" is likely to be interpreted with achievement connotations. It is speculated here that "doing one's best" covaries with accomplishment for Americans and they would generalize this interpretation for Chinese workers. Conversely, the Chinese often use indirect ways to communicate negative outcomes and the phrase "do my best" is speculated to covary with these situations. Hence, cultural interpretations are based on how a particular phrase is generally used in past situations. Whether this knowledge is primarily explicit or tacit is currently unknown; however, the different interpretations are certain to hinder effective cross-cultural interactions.

Findings from the above study have been presented to illustrate how tacit knowledge may influence cross-cultural interactions and subsequent work adjustment. This example also illustrates the difficulty in identifying implicit learning effects and tacit knowledge in a field setting. If knowledge is easily specified by experimenters, there may be a strong probability that the knowledge is explicit for subjects as well. Furthermore, the non-conscious acquisition of information would, by definition, be difficult for subjects to express to researchers. However, if one accepts the primacy of implicit learning, it must be considered in research that focuses on learning and adjustment in new environments. Although a strong logical argument is made for the role of implicit learning in organizational socialization, its study will pose a considerable challenge for research.

FUTURE RESEARCH DIRECTIONS AND CHALLENGES

All of the current research in organizational socialization is based upon explicit learning. Current socialization theory, research designs and research methods examine how the individual consciously learns about the job and organization and how the individual consciously adapts to his/her role. Explicit learning is assumed to be the mode of learning when the research is focused on the organization's perspective (e.g. examining socialization tactics; see Jones, 1986) or from the individual's perspective (e.g. examining newcomer expectations, see Major et al., 1995).

Despite this exclusive attention on explicit learning and explicit knowledge, implicit learning and tacit knowledge are very likely to have profound influences on a newcomer's interpretation and sense-making of organizational behavior. The prominence of implicit learning and tacit knowledge may be even more dramatic when the newcomer's interpretive schemata are operating in a multicultural context. Two areas of future research are described to illustrate how implicit learning theory can be studied within organizational socialization.

Extending Laboratory Research in Organizational Behavior

Research on implicit learning has been exclusively laboratory studies examining subject performance in a variety of artificial learning situations. Many of these studies were quite creative in their tests of implicit learning, but required subject responses that were unique in order to rule out explicit knowledge effects (e.g. identifying color after-images following social influence on the identification of colored stimuli; see Moscovici & Personnaz, 1980). Some of the laboratory studies on social judgments have more direct implications for organizational socialization, yet these studies lack an organizational context. Results showed people can non-consciously detect covariations between computerized facial features and personality characteristics (Hill et al., 1990) and that people automatically make personality trait inferences when they encode behavior (Winter, Uleman & Cunniff, 1985). These studies can help future researchers understand how people make social judgments of others from a different culture.

The research challenge is to extend these laboratory studies to include organizational behavior. Berry & Broadbent (1984, 1988) demonstrated how subjects implicitly learned to reach production targets in a simulated sugar production factory; however, their subjects responded individually to a computer task. Cannon-Bowers, Salas & Converse (1990) proposed that shared mental models among team members would be positively associated with team effectiveness. If each team member had a common understanding of the mental models required for teamwork and task performance, an implicit coordination strategy would emerge to maximize team effectiveness. An example of an implicit coordination strategy would be a basketball player throwing a blind pass to a team-mate who would be in a better position to score. Although the player did not explicitly know a team-mate would be in position to receive the blind pass, knowledge about the team dynamics and the specific circumstances of the play would facilitate an implicit strategy for the pass.

Laboratory research on team performance may be designed to manipulate some information implicitly and to investigate the effects of this information on subject performance and satisfaction. For example, as part of an orientation to the team task, subjects may view videotapes of other teams performing. These tapes would contain team players modeling an organizational behavior that is characteristic of a particular culture, but not essential to team performance. Effects of the manipulation may be measured under various conditions that encourage or discourage the target behavior. Results would demonstrate how organizational behaviors may be implicitly learned and manipulated to affect individual and team performance.

Within an organizational socialization context, exposing subjects to information that characterizes a strong organizational culture may foster tacit knowledge and effect a mental model regarding the organization's goals and values. Chatman & Barsade (1995) ran subjects through an organizational simulation and explicitly manipulated the organization's culture to reinforce individualist or collectivist values. They found a significant interaction between a subject's personal individualist/collectivist orientation and the organization's culture on subject behavior during the simulation. The extent to which the culture was implicitly learned is unknown, but certain interactions could be designed for subject observation that could reinforce a specific culture. This manipulation can also include other content areas of organizational socialization which may facilitate work adjustment.

Laboratory research examining group adjustment in a variety of demographically diverse groups could be designed to examine socialization within a multicultural context. Training sessions before group interaction could be designed explicitly to acquaint the subject with the group task, orientate subjects toward a common mental model for teamwork, and allow subjects to implicitly learn specific culture–behavior covariations. Although the researcher must guard against alternative explanations for subject behavior (e.g. prior knowledge of a specific culture–behavior link), the subject's ability to articulate the stimuli covariation and his/her behavior in the group, can provide valuable data regarding implicit learning and multicultural group adjustment.

Emotional Interpretation of Events

Mesquita & Frijda (1992) reviewed the literature on cultural differences in emotions and identified several cross-cultural similarities and differences. Although there are universal emotional reactions (e.g. sadness is aroused with the loss of a loved one), there are also cultural differences in emotional interpretations of situations, behavioral expressions of an emotion, and in defining socially desirable and undesirable behavior. Given these cultural differences, tacit knowledge regarding appropriate emotional reactions is not only contextually bound to the situations in which it is acquired, but it is also culturally bound. The extent to which emotional reactions are part of the sense-making process in organizational socialization would be a second area for future research.

Culturally different emotional interpretations of organizational behavior most likely operate at a non-conscious level. Although the literature reviewed by Mesquita & Frijda (1992) did not involve organizational behaviors, they found evidence that people from different cultures would identify different emotions in an ambiguous situation. Interactions among multicultural personnel with different interpretive schemata may hinder the development of a coherent organizational culture and socialization of that culture. Furthermore, these different emotional interpretations of organizational behavior are likely to exacerbate problems associated with interpersonal conflict. Here, the research challenge will be to measure these cultural differences and demonstrate their impact on work adjustment.

Qualitative research on the emotional interpretations of common business situations may help identify cultural differences. In turn, this information can be used to train people in other cultures on the emotional interpretations of a target culture. Subjects could be exposed to a variety of situations, along with the most likely emotional interpretation and expressions of a target culture. This exposure of culturally different stimulus–response situations may enhance learning of these stimuli covariations. Although explanations for a particular emotional interpretation may be largely implicit, the identification of the emotion can be made explicit and can help trainees reproduce an implicit map for these emotional interpretations. Within a training context that requires trainees to play a role in comman business situations, the map can help trainees to identify culturally appropriate responses.

Emotional reactions to work situations are everyday occurrences that provide a number of incidental learning situations for organizational socialization. The extent to which these reactions are shaped by an individual's culture and how tacit knowledge of these reactions can help people interact with others from a different culture, remain to be researched. Results of such research can advance cross-cultural psychology and also have practical applications for managers charged with the responsibilities of staffing MNCs with international personnel, socializing organizational newcomers, or building cohesive work teams.

Other Research Directions

Jackson, Stone & Alvarez (1993) describe a number of research propositions that could be tested when an individual joins an established group. They draw the analogy that such a newcomer is like anyone entering a foreign culture—the adjustment will be easier when the newcomer is demographically similar to others in the group. Research on relational demography and management practices of diversity in the workplace (see Jackson & Associates, 1992) can serve as a framework for future socialization research in MNCs. However, much of that research assumes a dominant culture of a majority group, and minority groups operating within this dominant culture. Such conditions may not be applicable to all MNCs or international joint ventures.

The integration of implicit learning theory with organizational socialization elicits a number of research directions that are too numerous to cover in a single chapter. A sample of these research questions include:

1. Under what conditions would tacit knowledge facilitate/hinder the application of explicitly acquired information?
2. Are there cultural emotional differences in reaction to specific socialization tactics? For example, would newcomers from collectivistic cultures be more accepting of divestiture socialization tactics that are designed to strip away individualism?
3. Can formal socialization practices or training programs counteract tacit knowledge that reflects cultural prejudices and negative social behaviors?
4. Can organizations shape emotional reactions of their employees?
5. How does prior exposure to cultural stereotypes build links between nationality and traits that become tacit knowledge? How does this tacit knowledge

interfere with efforts to learn about real people and to interact with them at a personal level?

6. Are there cultural sets of tacit knowledge (e.g. concept of *face*, ethnocentrism, masculine managers/leaders, etc.) shaping work behaviors that may not be in the best interests of MNCs?

Research that address these questions would yield a rich database that would advance socialization theory beyond its current constraints of explicit learning and unicultural investigations.

SUMMARY

The purpose of this chapter has been to integrate two separate research areas: organizational socialization and implicit learning, and to stimulate new research directions. The globalization of many business corporations has opened new avenues in which organizational socialization and implicit learning may be applied and studied. From a cognitive psychology perspective, the types of stimuli covariations that are implicitly learned by individuals observing business practices in a different culture are currently unknown. Nonetheless, the tacit knowledge gained by these observations are believed to profoundly affect the individual's social judgments, attitude formations and subsequent behavior. How this knowledge shapes the individual's socialization into a multicultural organization is also currently unknown. However, based on the current research presented here, implicit learning is a ubiquitous process that pervades an individual's organizational socialization. In order to understand better how and what an individual learns as he/she adjusts to a new position, it is imperative that research should address all modes of learning, especially the primary, implicit acquisition of information.

REFERENCES

Berry, D.C. & Broadbent, D.E. (1984). On the relationship between task performance and associated verbalizable knowledge. *Quarterly Journal of Experimental Psychology*, **36A**, 209–31.

Berry, D.C. & Broadbent, D.E. (1988). Interactive tasks and the implicit–explicit distinction. *British Journal of Psychology*, **79**, 251–72.

Berry, D.C. & Dienes, Z. (1993). *Implicit Learning: Theoretical and Empirical Issues*. Hove, Sussex: Erlbaum.

Black, J.S. (1992). Socializing American expatriate managers overseas. *Group & Organization Management*, **17**, 171–92.

Cannon-Bowers, J.A., Salas, E. & Converse, S.A. (1990). Cognitive psychology and team training: training shared mental models of complex systems. *Human Factors Society Bulletin*, **33**(12), 1–4.

Chao, G.T. (1997). Unstructured training and development: the role of organizational socialization. In J.K. Ford, S.W.J. Kozlowski, K. Kraiger, E. Salas & M.S. Teachout (eds), *Improving Training Effectiveness in Work Organizations* (pp. 129–51). Mahwah, NJ: Erlbaum.

Chao, G.T., O'Leary-Kelly, A.M., Wolf, S., Klein, H.J. & Gardner, P.D. (1994). Organizational socialization: its content and consequences. *Journal of Applied Psychology*, **79**, 730–43.

Chao, G.T. & Sun, Y.J. (in press). Training needs for expatriate adjustment in the People's Republic of China. In Z. Aycan (ed.), *Expatriate Management: Theory and Research*. Greenwich, CT: JAI Press.

Chatman, J. & Barsade, S.G. (1995). Personality, organizational culture, and cooperation: evidence from a business simulation. *Administrative Science Quarterly*, **40**, 423–43.

Fisher, C.D. (1986). Organizational socialization: an integrative review. *Research in Personnel and Human Resource Management*, **4**, 101–45.

Hill, T., Lewicki, P., Czyzewska, M. & Schuller, G. (1990). The role of learned inferential encoding rules in the perception of faces: effects of non-conscious self-perpetuation of a bias. *Journal of Experimental Social Psychology*, **26**, 350–71.

Hofstede, G. (1980). *Culture's Consequences: International Differences in Work-related Values*. Beverly Hills, CA: Sage.

Jackson, S.E. & Associates (1992). *Diversity in the Workplace: Human Resources Initiatives*. New York: Guilford.

Jackson, S.E., Stone, V.K. & Alvarez, E.B. (1993). Socialization amidst diversity: the impact of demographics on work team oldtimers and newcomers. In B.M. Staw & L.L. Cummings (eds), *Research in Organizational Behavior* (pp. 45–109). Greenwich, CT: JAI Press.

Jones, G.R. (1986). Socialization tactics, self-efficacy, and newcomers' adjustments to organizations. *Academy of Management Journal*, **29**, 262–279.

Kraiger, K., Ford, J.K. & Salas, E. (1993). Application of cognitive, skill-based, and affective theories of learning outcomes to new methods of training evaluation. *Journal of Applied Psychology*, **78**, 311–28.

Lewicki, P. (1986). *Non-conscious Social Information Processing*, Orlando, FL: Academic Press.

Lewicki, P., Czyzewska, M. & Hoffman, H. (1987). Unconscious acquisition of complex procedural knowledge. *Journal of Experimental Psychology: Learning, Memory, and Cognition*, **13**, 523–30.

Lewicki, P., Hill, T. & Czyzewska, M. (1992). Non-conscious acquisition of information. *American Psychologist*, **47**, 796–801.

Louis, M.R. (1980). Surprise and sense making: what newcomers experience in entering unfamiliar organizational settings. *Administrative Science Quarterly*, **25**, 226–51.

Louis, M.R. (1990). Acculturation in the workplace: newcomers as lay ethnographers. In B. Schneider (ed.), *Organizational Climate and Culture* (pp. 85–129). San Francisco, CA: Jossey-Bass.

Major, D.A., Kozlowski, S.W.J., Chao, G.T. & Gardner, P.D. (1995). A longitudinal investigation of newcomer expectations, early socialization outcomes, and the moderating effects of role development factors. *Journal of Applied Psychology*, **80**, 418–31.

Masters, R.S.W. (1992). Knowledge, knerves and know-how: the role of explicit vs. implicit knowledge of a complex motor skill under pressure. *British Journal of Psychology*, **83**, 343–58.

Mesquita, B. & Frijda, N.H. (1992). Cultural variations in emotions: a review. *Psychological Bulletin*, **112**, 179–204.

Moscovici, S. & Personnaz, B. (1980). Studies in social influence. *Journal of Experimental Social Psychology*, **16**, 270–82.

Ostroff, C. & Kozlowski, S.W.J. (1992). Organizational socialization as a learning process: the role of information acquisition. *Personnel Psychology*, **45**, 849–74.

Reber, A.S. (1989). Implicit learning and tacit knowledge. *Journal of Experimental Psychology: General*, **118**, 219–35.

Reber, A.S. (1993). *Implicit Learning and Tacit Knowledge: an Essay on the Cognitive Unconscious.* New York: Oxford University Press.

Reber, A.S. & Millward, R.B. (1971). Event tracking in probability learning. *American Journal of Psychology*, **84**, 85–99.

Schmidt, F.L. & Hunter, J.E. (1993). Tacit knowledge, practical intelligence, general mental ability, and job knowledge. *Current Directions in Psychological Science*, **2**, 8–9.

Sternberg, R.J., Wagner, R.K., Williams, W.M. & Horvath, J.A. (1995). Testing common sense. *American Psychologist*, **50**, 912–27.

Tung, R.L. (1981). Selection and training of personnel for overseas assignments. *Columbia Journal of World Business*, **16**, 68–78.

Van Maanen, J. (1976). Breaking in: socialization to work. In R. Dubin (ed.), *Handbook of Work, Organization, and Society* (pp. 67–130). Chicago: Rand McNally.

Van Maanen, J. (1984). Doing new things in old ways: the chains of socialization. In J.L. Bess (ed.), *College and University Organization: Insights from the Behavioral Sciences* (pp. 211–47). New York: New York University Press.

Wagner, R.K. & Sternberg, R.J. (1985). Practical intelligence in real-world pursuits: the role of tacit knowledge. *Journal of Personality and Social Psychology*, **49**, 436–58.

Winter, L., Uleman, J.S. & Cunniff, C. (1985). How automatic are social judgements? *Journal of Personality and Social Psychology*, **49**, 904–17.

Chapter 4

Culture without Borders: An Individual-Level Approach to Cross-Cultural Research in Organizational Behavior

P. Christopher Earley
London Business School, London, UK
and
Amy E. Randel
University of California, Irvine, CA, USA

The field of cross-cultural and inter-cultural organizational behavior has witnessed a rapid expansion of research consistent with the exponential growth of international businesses, trans-global companies, etc. With this rapid growth, there are a number of fundamental issues that have arisen that must be explored for further research progress to be made in the field. A primary issue in this literature concerns the nature of the construct of culture and its role in empirical research. Although this is an existing debate in many fields including anthropology, psychology and sociology, it remains a critical issue for cross-cultural organizational behavior (OB) because of the diversity represented in the field. The purpose of this chapter is to provide a brief overview of existing approaches and a general typology with which to classify them, and to propose the adoption of a specific form that is argued to be highly useful in advancing micro-level theory in organizations. This preferred form is an individual-level representation of "culture" in which societal, social and individual differences influences on values, beliefs, and behavior are manifested through an individual actor's psychological profile.

Creating Tomorrow's Organizations. Edited by C.L. Cooper and S.E. Jackson.
© 1997 John Wiley & Sons Ltd.

OVERVIEW OF CULTURE AS A CONSTRUCT FOR INVESTIGATION

Culture has been defined in a number of ways. An oft-cited definition is Kluckhohn's assessment, which stated:

> Culture consists in patterned ways of thinking, feeling and reacting, acquired and transmitted mainly by symbols, constituting the distinctive achievements of human groups, including their embodiments in artifacts; the essential core of culture consists of traditional (e.g. historically derived and selected) ideas and especially their attached values (1954, pp. 85–6).

Herskovits (1955, p. 305) defined culture as the human-made part of the environment, whereas Triandis (1972) and Osgood (1974) define it as the subjective part of the human-made environment. The subjective aspects of culture include social events, beliefs, attitudes, norms and values, and shared roles. Definitions vary from very limited and focused, such as Shweder & LeVine's (1984) view that culture is a set of shared meaning systems, to a broad, all-encompassing view that it is the human-made aspect of the environment (e.g. Herskovits). Other definitions include Skinner's (1953) view that culture is a complex series of reinforcement contingencies moderated by particular schedules of reward, and Schein's (1985) view that at the core of culture are the untested assumptions of how and why to behave. Hofstede (1980) defines culture as a set of mental programs that control an individual's responses in a given context, and Parsons & Shils (1951) view culture as a shared characteristic of a high-level social system.

There are many influences of culture on institutional and organizational levels of behavior. Culture shapes the types of organizations that evolve and the nature of social structures as they grow and adapt (Hofstede, 1980). Societies shape their collectivities and social aggregates according to the rules implied by culture. Culture is sometimes viewed in terms of antecedents such as time, language and locality variables, as well as historical and ecological commonalities.

Rohner (1984, p. 119) states, ". . . we define culture as *the totality of equivalent and complementary learned meanings maintained by a human population, or by identifiable segments of a population, and transmitted from one generation to the next*" [italics in the original]. While Rohner states that the multi-generation transmission aspect of his definition may have exceptions, he concludes that the "equivalent and complementary learned meanings" are of critical importance. By this, he means that these meanings are not universally shared by an entire society, neither are they precisely shared. In other words, any two individuals from a given culture may hold slightly different meanings for the same event or construct, and these two individuals may have shared meanings with other parties in the society but not with one another. As Rohner argues:

> It is probable that no single individual ever knows the totality of equivalent and complementary learned meanings that define the "culture" of a given population,

and it is therefore unlikely that the person is able to activate, at any given moment, the full range of meanings that define the "culture" of his or her people. But complementary meanings free one from the necessity of having to know all of one's "culture". For example, most persons do not need to know how to behave as a physician or shaman if they are ill, only how to behave properly as a patient (p. 122).

He defines the concepts of social system and society as well in describing culture. A social system refers to the behavioral interactions of a multiple individuals who exist within a culturally organized population, whereas a society is defined as ". . . the largest unit of a territorially bounded, multigenerational population, recruited largely through sexual reproduction, and organized around a common culture and a common social system" (p. 131). While we agree with many aspects of Rohner's presentation, there is an important limitation in his conclusion that the psychological assessment of culture is "untenable" and misguided. He has mistaken the view of culture from an individual-level perspective as being an extension of personality.

What is useful from Rohner's definitions of society, social system and culture is that it is possible to separate the various effects of these constructs on individuals' actions and behavior through the clarification of the concepts. For example, Rohner cites White's analogy of American football in describing the relationship of culture to social system. The point is that knowing the rules (culture) of football does not enable an observer to anticipate or predict the next play that will be made during a game (social system, or resulting behaviors). Cultural knowledge allows the observer to judge the appropriateness or legitimacy of a given "play" but not to predict the content of the play. However, this distinction is not nearly so clear-cut as Rohner assumes. Again, we will draw upon the football metaphor in making our point. If we have an intimate knowledge of the rules and functioning of football, then knowledge of the given play in the context of the current game's status will enable me to predict (albeit, with probabilistic accuracy) the next play to be run. If the score is tied at 20–20, and Team A has the ball on the defense's 30-yard line with 8 seconds left in the game, we can predict with high certainty that the next play for Team A will be a field goal attempt. If, however, the ball is on the defense's 40-yard line under the same conditions, we can predict that the play will be a long pass. Thus, culture is not merely knowing the "rules" *per se*, it implies a knowledge of the inter-relatedness of those rules along with "typical" or normative functioning of the rules. As a result, behavior of specific individuals, and their personal beliefs and values, can be predicted from culture.

Another contentious split concerning concepts of culture is presented and evaluated in a recent book by Joanne Martin (1992). She presents a characterization of three general forms of organization culture, namely integration, differentiation and fragmentation. Briefly, an integration view posits culture as shared meanings held in common. The differentiation view points out that there exist subgroups within any given organization that probably differ in their shared meanings from one another. Finally, a fragmentation perspective suggests that culture is a differential network of meanings that are inter-related and reciprocally related but ill-defined and inconsistent. Our interpretation of these perspectives is that they can be thought of using a factorial design having two factors. The integration view is a main effects perspective, whereas the differentiation perspective is captured by an interaction term. Finally, the fragmentation view is best thought of as some form of within-cell variance, or individual differences. Using this analogy, it becomes clearer that culture is not simply a monolithic construct capturing all of the minds within a given society. It is Rohner's idea of complementary, but incompletely shared, meaning systems.

This discussion is consistent with recent work proposed by Brett et al. (in press) who propose the "N-way" form of cultural research. According to this approach, Brett et al. suggest that a useful cultural paradigm for conducting research is one in which multiple researchers from varying cultural backgrounds work in a team in order to conduct sophisticated emic–etic research. There are a number of important features of their conceptualization and recommendations concerning culture. First, they recommend a team of diverse researchers who share a common view of research styles to collaborate. The purpose of this team is to ensure that research questions asked are comparably meaningful in the various cultures to be studied. Second, the team jointly develops a research question but with local (emic) operationalizations of the construct. Third, their approach provides for convergence and divergence of constructs within specific process models. They do so by incorporating relationships and constructs that are both etic and emic. To the extent that emic constructs diverge and etic constructs converge, their approach provides unique strength in conducting cross-cultural work. Ultimately, they define culture as a collage of characteristics including dimensions such as individualism–collectivism, power differentials, economic orientation, etc. Further, these dimensions may be overlapping as well as discrete, and their relationship to one another may differ as a function of a particular culture. For example, the correlation of power distance to individualism might be strong in a given culture but weak in another. Although their collage complicates matters quite a bit, it has the strength of providing a union among cultural dimensions to capture interactive effects much like the fragmentation perspective described by Martin (1992).

CLASSIFICATION OF APPROACHES AND STYLES

These various approaches to culture and research can be classified into four forms using a typology proposed by Earley & Singh (1995). These four forms include: *unitary*, or an emic-style emphasizing the thorough understanding of a single culture on its own terms; *gestalt*, or relationships among variables are examined as they occur across different cultural systems, and constructs and hypothesized relationships are derived from general principles rather than the systems themselves; *reduced form*, or an emphasis on breaking down a system into component parts in order to understand better the functioning of processes within the system; and *hybrid form*, which refers to an approach that utilizes aspects of both a gestalt and a reduced perspective. In the hybrid form, research questions are studied in order to identify important aspects of the systems, and hypothesized relationships are derived across systems and they are not necessarily unique to a given system.

Using this categorization scheme, it is possible to classify various approaches described by researchers concerning cross-cultural OB. For example, Rohner's approach falls into the unitary form, as does much of the work in anthropology and as does Martin's fragmentation form. Brett et al.'s preferred approach (N-way, Type III hypotheses), recent calls by Triandis (personal conversation) and others would fall into a hybrid form. Increasingly, there appears to be a movement (a healthy movement in our view) in conceptualizing culture as a complex construct accessible through multiple methods. It is this conceptualization that we suggest provides new and important opportunities for research.

However, approaches using a hybrid form as posed in the existing literature face some serious limitations. For instance, Brett et al. (in press) argue that culture is best viewed as a collage having multiple, potentially interactive, elements. Further, the relationships among these elements may differ as a function of a particular culture. This suggests that conducting cross-cultural research is extremely troublesome. For example, it means that a given research question might be addressed using two very different methods of assessment in two different cultures. How can we understand if null findings represent true similarities (i.e. universals) or poor/inaccurate instrumentation? Brett et al. suggest that by examining patterns of similarities and differences based on a theoretical model it is possible to determine true vs. apparent differences. Although we agree in principle that their complex form may possibly provide such answers to culture's complexity, actually using their approach is problematic; there is an alternative approach that simplifies this process while clarifying the theoretical linkage of culture to action. This alternative style focuses on specifying a strong theoretical model underlying connections of culture to substantive process variables. Our approach has the strength of prediction—a limitation to other models that lack such precision.

So what, then, constitutes culture, social system and society? In our usage, we define culture as individual-level manifestations of shared meaning systems which are learned from other members of the society. This learning process can occur through a number of outlets including child-rearing practices, peer transmission, media, etc., and it is an ongoing occurrence having decreasingly less impact as a function of maturation. A social system refers to those roles and positions existing in a society, including the pattern and nature of interactions. While resulting behavior is an important outcome from a social system, we differ from Rohner in as much as we view behavior as an outcome from a social system and not the system itself. A social system refers, then, to the connections and inter-relationships among societal members, and these relationships are shaped and guided by culture. However, the distinction between culture and social system is not one of "rules of the game" vs. "plays"; rather, it is the distinction of meaning and significance vs. structured relations void of individual personality.

In this sense, culture captures the meanings and personal significance of behavior for people, whereas the social system is the arena in which these meanings and significance are given direction and structure in which to manifest themselves. Our metaphor is one of an artist having a certain concept she wishes to capture (culture), who then uses a particular medium (e.g. painting vs. sculpture) with which to express the concept. What is important with this metaphor is that the concept of culture is dependent on the medium; that is to say, the concept of romance expressed in oils is not identical to romance expressed in marble or charcoal. More concretely, understanding the importance of culture in OB requires a complete understanding of the specific process being described and how it relates to specific aspects of culture.

EXAMINING CULTURE FROM AN INDIVIDUAL LEVEL OF ANALYSIS

An individual-level analysis can be thought of as the local manifestation of cultural values, beliefs and behavioral content within an individual. We view culture as a specific set of beliefs, values and behavioral dispositions that are shared loosely by individuals having a common geographic and resource base, as represented by individual-level phenomena. In other words, culture is defined as *the psychological manifestation of incompletely shared and understood meanings of the environment, social relationships, patterns of behavior, norms of conduct, etc.* Contrary to most views of culture, we advocate that culture is best thought of as a psychological experience of individuals and not a collective phenomenon, group characteristic, or the like. Our argument is based on prediction and utility and not simply research tradition. That is to say, the focus of interest in micro-OB is the prediction and explanation of individual and group-level behavior, and our approach creates the most direct connection of culture to behavior. As we describe later in the chapter, this added precision provides a concrete way of connecting culture to individual action.

Although our approach is only now being used increasingly by OB researchers, its conceptual origins can be traced to the subjective culture work of scholars such as Osgood (1964) and Triandis (1972). The approach used by a number of intercultural researchers has been bases on the argument that culture is an enacted phenomenon tied to the collective perceptions and interpretations of people within a society, or subjective culture. Triandis (1972, p. 4) defined subjective culture as: ". . . a cultural group's characteristic way of perceiving the man-made part of its environment. The perception of rules and the group's norms, roles, and values are aspects of subjective culture". His model concerns itself with the way people in different cultures perceive their social environment as well as the impact of environmental factors on these processes. Perhaps the most notable aspect of Triandis's model is its breadth in trying to assess the relations among environment, social environment, values, and psychological process. The determinants of action in Triandis's model are an individual's behavioral intentions and habits. Patterns of action are a function of behavioral intentions which are influenced by subjective culture. It is the link of subjective culture to behavioral intentions that provides an explicit relation that is lacking in value-based models. In a subjective culture approach, values influence behavioral intentions through an individual's affective states as well as cognitive structures (although values are reciprocally determined by cognitive structures). Patterns of action and behavioral intentions resemble other information-processing models, although many of the details concerning roles, norms and tasks remain as unspecified antecedents in these other models. Triandis adds non-volitional antecedents of action not typically incorporated in others' models as well. Habits, he argues, represent the impact of repeated feedback concerning particular actions. In associative cultures, linguistic cues often convey rank among people and these nuances of language are enacted habitually. Likewise, social behavior and proto-col, such as social distances, reflect habit rather than cognition. Anyone coming from a culture that uses a large social distance knows how uncomfortable it can be to interact with someone "face-to-face" who is from a small social distance culture.

While an individual's cognitions, values, etc. capture "culture", they capture individuals' unique experiences as well. Thus, an assessment of cultural values or beliefs through an individual level of analysis is contaminated by "culture" and "personality". While this point is discussed from a methodological view in forums (e.g. Earley, 1994; Earley & Mosakowski, 1996; Lachman, Nedd & Hinings, 1994; Leung & Bond, 1989), it is important to note that our representation of culture is at the individual level (and it is possible to separate these components conceptu-ally as we discuss). It is this approach that we firmly believe well enable research-ers to understand better (and detect) the true influence and significance of "culture" in organizational functioning.

This conceptualization is useful for several reasons. One can use a hierarchical, cognitive structure of a person-in-society as a way of describing affective re-sponses to culturally-relevant situations (Lord & Kernan, 1987). A hierarchical structure aids us in understanding why merely altering specific expectations may not be sufficient in integrating culture and work practices. Second, this approach provides a consistent means of integrating cultural-level influences with indi-vidual-level actions. A recurring theme in anthropology suggests that culture refers to shared knowledge and meaning systems (D'Andrade, 1984). Therefore, culture can be viewed as a hierarchical structure of beliefs and values, shared among individuals having a common background, that shapes action.

What then, does an individual-level approach to culture provide in the ad-vancement of cross-cultural organization behavior? By matching the level of culture to associated constructs at an individual level it is possible to develop specific, process models of organization behavior within, or across, particular nations or cultures. For example, it is possible to examine significant moderating influences between work context and social behavior directly attributable to cultural values, norms and beliefs. Rather then arguing that the relation of X → Y is significant in country A but not in country B, it is possible to test whether or not the magnitude of the relation of X → Y varies as a linear function of some moderating characteristic Z (cultural value or belief). Of course, an individual-level measure of cultural characteristic Z reflects both "shared meaning" and "unique experience". Conceptually, this suggests that an individual-level assessment of culture is interdependent with individual differences, personality, etc. (This bisection is misleading in as much as the shared meaning is not necessarily "shared", as we argued earlier. In this sense, it might be better to discuss three components: fully-shared meaning, e.g. denotative linguistic elements; imperfectly-shared meaning, e.g. Rohner's patient vs. Shaman; and idiosyncratic experience, e.g. personal history. We might add that the sequencing of one's personal history may add a further degree of idiosyncrasy.) We will discuss in this chapter some empirical and analytic methods that have been used and that might be used to account for such contamination. Empirically, such "contamination" greatly enhances an ability to predict specific outcomes (particularly behavioral outcomes) because more antecedents of the outcome are explained.

APPLYING AN INDIVIDUAL-LEVEL ANALYSIS TO OB

How, then, can the individual-level approach to cross-cultural organizational behavior be utilized? Conceptualizing ways in which to operationalize an individual-level representation of culture while tackling OB research questions requires a balance to be struck in accounting for differences and similarities among both individual and shared beliefs. In other words, both intra-cultural and inter-cultural sources of variation on constructs of interest should be considered in order to attain the greatest level of precision in the conclusions drawn concerning culture and behavior. Numerous approaches based on an individual-level representation of culture have been adopted, although there is ample room for further research in this area that refines existing approaches and develops new ways of putting the individual back into cross-cultural OB.

One approach to this problem is to analyze scores on a cultural dimension based on levels of extremity. In this way, individuals with high or low values of a cultural dimension are examined solely on the basis of their response scores, rather than on geographical location, such as the country in which they live. For instance, Earley (1993) utilized this approach in hierarchical regression analyses that tested the relative performance of individualists and collectivists working alone, in an ingroup context, and in an outgroup context among Chinese, Israeli and American subjects. In order to interpret significant interaction terms, the subjects were separated into groups of individualists and collectivists using the criterion of where their scores fell with respect to the median score on the individualism–collectivism scale. While a country-level approach, for example, might assume that all Chinese subjects were collectivists on the basis of the mean score for subjects from that country, the individual-level approach illustrated here allowed for the possibility that a Chinese subject could be strongly individualist despite socialization experiences encouraging collectivistic behavior. This approach is consistent with Rohner's argument that culture is loosely and incompletely shared. Country effects can be tested for in this approach by including a dummy-coded variable representing the subjects' country of origin in the regression analyses. Earley found that country of origin did not explain additional variance in performance once other variables in the model, including individualism–collectivism, were included in the regression equation.

A method related to the regression technique that offers a way of conceptualizing intracultural and intercultural differences and similarities is cluster analysis (Ronen & Shenkar, 1985). Clusters are defined by both intra-cluster similarity and inter-cluster differences; observations in one cluster must be more similar to one another than to observations external to that cluster (Punj & Stewart, 1983). Cluster analysis is inductive and purely data-driven in the sense that clusters are not derived from assumptions, such as individuals' countries of origin, but rather from the data collected for each individual (or aggregated at the country level) included in a sample. An advantage of this technique over the median-split approach is that multiple groups, such as high, medium and low clusters on individualism–collectivism, may be identified. However, cluster analysis has been criticized for the somewhat arbitrary way in which cluster boundaries are identified (Punj & Stewart, 1983; Cattell, 1978). Factor identification in exploratory factor analysis is often critiqued on similar grounds (Pedhazur & Schmelkin, 1991), although arguably cluster analysis attempts to address both the convergence and the divergence of observations, while exploratory factor analysis focuses primarily on the convergence of observations. The use of cluster analysis with factor analysis may provide additional confidence in identified clusters. Although it appears that cluster analysis methods have not been applied to the individual-level approach to cross-cultural OB to date, this method is suggestive of how procedures new to the individual-level approach might be adopted or developed.

Smallest space analysis (SSA) is another method that relies upon a linkage between the physical location of data points in multidimensional space and conceptual significance. Schwartz & Bilsky (1987) utilized SSA with subjects from Israel and Germany to investigate the criteria that individuals used when ranking the importance of values. Schwartz & Bilsky calculated correlations from subjects' value rankings on the Rokeach Values Survey and analyzed the resulting correlation matrix with the Guttman–Lingoes Smallest Space Analysis multidimensional scaling analysis technique. When partition lines were drawn separating the data points on the basis of *a priori* theoretical value domains, the resulting regions and the values contained within each region could be interpreted. In SSA, an analysis of the data groupings is based not on distinct data clusters, as in cluster analysis, but rather on the basis of substantive theory. Like cluster analysis, the similarities and differences among data points in SSA are interpreted by use of distances in multidimensional space; points that are close together in space are interpreted as more conceptually similar than points that are further apart. Using a comparison across country samples, Schwartz & Bilsky found that the partitions they imposed had applicability in both their Israeli and German samples.

Another method that has been used in an individual-level approach to cross-cultural OB has been proposed (Earley, 1994; Earley & Mosakowski, 1996; Leung & Bond, 1989; Leung, 1989). Using this approach, individuals are assigned the mean value of their culture on a dimension. Then, the difference between the individual's score on the cultural dimension and the mean value of their culture is calculated. The mean value is interpreted as the extent to which a cultural value is shared within a country, while the difference score signifies the contribution to a dimension by each individual apart from that which is accounted for by country. This approach was utilized by Earley (1994) to differentiate country and individual differences in individualism–collectivism. A problem inherent in using this difference-score approach is that difference scores often demonstrate low reliability (Cohen & Cohen, 1975). If the variables used to calculate the difference scores are intercorrelated or unreliable, reliability problems are amplified to a greater extent.

A question to be considered with the difference-score approach is whether the mean score from which it is derived truly captures what is shared among individuals in a country. This is a question posed not only by the difference-score approach, but also from international and cross-cultural research in general. Despite the frequent usage of mean country scores in international research, it seems possible that mean scores result from computational and conceptual convenience, rather than being significant in their own right. The over-interpretation of mean country scores is particularly problematic when mean scores on a given dimension are assigned to individuals in a country, based on the averaged responses of different individuals measured at an earlier point in time or in a different study. Even when the level of analysis of interest involves an aggregation of individuals' behaviors, we argue that it is inappropriate to assign cultural scores (e.g. Hofstede, 1980) *a priori* to individuals or groups. For example, Roth (1995) examined the extent to which the relationship between brand image strategy and a product's market share was moderated by regional socio-economic and cultural variables, by assigning the values that Hofstede obtained for power distance, uncertainty avoidance and individualism to regions within countries without specifically measuring those dimensions in the geographic area of interest. The relevance of the these three cultural dimensions cannot be assumed without explicitly measuring them. Once individual responses to measures of cultural dimensions are collected, the meaning attached to mean scores and derivations of such scores must be carefully considered.

The individual-level approach to cross-cultural OB is not without limitations. The rejection of hypotheses involving an individual-level conception of culture does not rule out the possibility that culture may impact the relationship in question. The cultural dimension being measured may have been misspecified or measured inadequately; the interaction among several cultural dimensions also may not have been taken into account (Triandis, 1995; Earley & Mosakowski,

1996). Furthermore, close attention should be paid to measurement issues while representing culture at the level of the individual.

Because an individual-level approach to culture strives to capture both intracultural and intercultural differences, it is most effective when the measurement instruments utilized are strong with respect to construct validity and reliability. Such qualities are expected of measurement instruments in all research; however, high validity and reliability standards are especially important to obtaining the measurement precision required in capturing intracultural as well as intercultural differences. Contributions are made to cross-cultural research when insight is gained into how and why differences exist across cultures, rather than when cross-cultural differences are merely identified (Earley & Singh, 1995). To accurately account for how and why cross-cultural differences exist, construct validity is essential in order to be certain that a variable claimed to be the cause of a difference between cultures cannot be mistaken for a different causal explanation (Cook & Campbell, 1979). We discussed earlier the importance of reliability in the use of difference scores; however, reliability concerns also are of importance with an individual-level approach more generally. Group means, by nature, have an advantage over individual scores in terms of reliability, although aggregating individual scores results in a lower number of degrees of freedom (Cook & Campbell, 1979). Measurement instruments with high reliability increase the certainty with which conclusions can be made using the individual-level approach.

Another argument for the necessity of measurement precision in conjunction with the individual-level approach builds on Rohner's (1984, p. 121) assertion that "probably no two individuals ever hold precisely identical meanings (such as beliefs, values, norms) with respect to any phenomenon". A literal interpretation of this argument suggests that individuals who respond with identical scores on a scale may not hold equivalent beliefs with respect to an underlying construct. Extremely specific items, perhaps supplemented with open-ended written or interview questions, may improve the accuracy of conclusions drawn from measurement items utilized in an individual-level approach to cross-cultural OB. In fact, an advantage of an individual-level approach is that it enables a researcher to collect time-intensive data from interviews, observations, etc. If participants in a cross-cultural research endeavor speak different languages, issues pertaining to the translation of measurement instruments increase the attention that must be allocated to identifying items that might be construed in multiple ways (Brislin, 1980).

INSIGHTS FROM EXISTING STUDIES USING AN INDIVIDUAL-LEVEL APPROACH

In this section, we re-examine several studies using an individual-level approach in order to illustrate the advantages of this perspective. Additional insights might be gained by applying an individual-level perspective to studies that have utilized alternative approaches. For example, Hofstede et al. (1990) measured organizational culture by aggregating individual responses within an organizational unit and comparing the resulting aggregated variable across units. Hofstede et al. justify their usage of mean scores with the rationale that organizational cultures are derived from organizational units rather than from individuals. Although there is merit to analyses performed at the aggregate level, we may have gained an increased understanding of organizational culture by including individual-level analyses. Hofstede et al. characterize organizational culture as a social construction, which Berger & Luckmann (1967) imply to be a phenomenon that can benefit from an individual-level interpretation, due to the imprecise correlation among meanings assigned by different individuals. Hofstede et al. found that the variability of values across organizational units was much less than that of practices; patterns of variability underlying this finding might have been uncovered by the usage of an individual-level approach. The authors offer a *post hoc* explanation for their practices-over-values finding by suggesting that the values of organizations' leaders, but not of other organizational members, influences practices. By further differentiating among organizational members, their conclusion may have been modified or strengthened.

Hofstede, Bond & Luk (1993) reanalyzed the data from Hofstede et al. (1990) at the individual level, resulting in quite different findings. While Hofstede et al.'s (1990) analysis at an aggregate level indicated that practices were able to explain more variance than values, Hofstede, Bond & Luk's (1993) individual-level analysis found that values had more explanatory power than practices. Hofstede, Bond & Luk (1993) interpret this difference in findings as suggesting that values are a domain closer to individuals than units, whereas practices are better distinguished at the unit level. Through the inclusion of an individual-level analysis, we are able to learn more from this data than we were able to learn when only an aggregate-level analysis was conducted.

In a country-level analysis, Shane (1994) argued that differences among nations concerning trust determine firms' preferences for direct foreign investment or for licensing agreements. Using Hofstede's (1980) power distance index and the Chinese Culture Connection's integration index as proxies for national-level trust, Shane found that licensing was preferred over direct foreign investment in countries with high levels of trust. Several aspects of this paper may have benefited from the inclusion of an individual-level approach. For instance, the R^2 values of regressions based on cultural variables were low, which may have been due to trust levels that varied within each country as well as between countries. Foreign investment reflects national policies as well as the proclivities of particular firm actors, and a country-level assessment will fail to capture these firm-specific tendencies. An increase in explanatory power would be expected if one was to account for the differing trust levels held by those responsible for strategy decisions in the firms represented. Accounting for trust values at a lower level of analysis than the national level also might lend further clarification to the conclusion that the USA is a high-trust country, which runs counter to literature indicating otherwise.

In another example, Agarwal (1993) tests a model in India that has been supported in the USA. The model posits that formalization (e.g. rule observation and job codification) leads to high role stressors (role ambiguity and role conflict), which in turn lead to high work alienation and low organizational commitment. Based on the notions that role stress occurs when a salesperson's desire for autonomy conflicts with a formalized work environment and that power distance and individualism–collectivism relate to a person's desire for autonomy, Agarwal tests the model in India and the USA, countries that Hofstede (1980) found to differ widely on those two cultural dimensions. The relationships included in the model were found to be stronger overall in the USA than in India, but it was not possible to explain fully the observed pattern of relationships with the cross-national approach utilized. By assuming that two distinct groups exist based on their country of origin and that all respondents within each country group assume the cultural dimension values found by Hofstede, it is difficult to interpret why a particular pattern of relationships among the variables was observed. An individual-level approach applied to this study, for instance, would have been able to test the possibility that power distance and/or individualism–collectivism in fact were not strongly influential in the model.

CONCLUDING REMARKS

As suggested by the plentiful calls that more research on cross-cultural OB be conducted (e.g. Adler, 1983; Erez & Earley, 1993), this area is ripe with possibilities for the development of research programs on topics throughout the field of OB. The applicability of theories across cultures concerning topics such as motivation (Adler, 1991), leadership (Misumi, 1985) and training effectiveness (Earley, 1994) have been questioned; however, topics within OB that have not been thoroughly examined in a cross-cultural context are far too numerous to list here. By addressing OB topics in a cross-cultural setting, the strength and generalizability of our theories increase as we become more able to predict behavior among people throughout the world. The increasingly global nature of the business environment today indicates the urgency of the need for such research. Our argument here has been that an effective, accurate approach to cross-cultural OB research is at the individual level.

Our purpose in this chapter has been to argue for a new conceptualization and operationalization of "culture". We suggest that while the romance of culture as a grand concept capturing the complexity of society and life is tempting, this conceptualization is both limiting and misleading in OB. An individual-level manifestation of culture provides precision in measurement, and it allows researchers to build detailed and predictive models that lend themselves to empirical assessment.

REFERENCES

Adler, N.J. (1991). Cross-cultural motivation. In R.M. Steers & L.W. Porter (eds), *Motivation and Work Behavior*, 5th edn. New York: McGraw-Hill.

Adler, N.J. (1983). Cross-cultural management research: the ostrich and the trend. *Academy of Management Review*, **8**(2), 226–32.

Agarwal, S. (1993). Influence of formalization on role stress, organizational commitment, and work alienation of salespersons: a cross-national comparative study. *Journal of International Business Studies*, **24**(4), 715–39.

Berger, P.L. & Luckmann, T. (1967). *The Social Construction of Reality*. New York: Doubleday.

Brett, J.M., Tinsley, C.H., Janssens, M., Barsness, Z.I. & Lytle, A.H. (in press). New approaches to the study of culture in I/O psychology. To appear in P.C. Earley & M. Erez (eds), *New Perspectives on International Industrial/Organizational Psychology*. San Francisco: Jossey-Bass.

Brislin, R.W. (1980). Translation and content analysis of oral and written materials. In H. Triandis (ed), *Handbook of Cross-cultural Psychology*, vol. 2 (pp. 389–444). Boston, MA: Allyn and Bacon.

Cattell, R.B. (1978). *The Scientific Use of Factor Analysis in the Behavioral and Life Sciences*. New York: Plenum.

Cohen, J. & Cohen, P. (1975). *Applied Multiple Regression/Correlation Analysis for the Behavioral Sciences*. Hillsdale, NJ: Erlbaum.

Cook, T.D. & Campbell, D.T. (1979). *Quasi-experimentation: Design and Analysis Issues for Field Settings*. Boston, MA: Houghton Mifflin.

D'Andrade, R. (1984). Cultural meaning systems. In R.A. Shweder & R.A. LeVine (eds), *Culture Theory: Essays on Mind, Self, and Emotion* (pp. 65–129). New York: Cambridge University Press.

Earley, P.C. (1994). Self or group? Cultural effects of training on self-efficacy and performance. *Administrative Science Quarterly*, **39**, 89–117.

Earley, P.C. (1993). East meets West meets Mideast: further explorations of collectivistic and individualistic work groups. *Academy of Management Journal*, **36**(2), 319–48.

Earley, P.C. & Mosakowski, E. (1996). Experimental international management research. In B.J. Punnett & O. Shenkar (eds), *Handbook for International Management Research*. Cambridge, MA: Blackwell.

Earley, P.C. & Singh, H. (1995). International and intercultural management research: what's next? *Academy of Management Journal*, **38**(2), 327–40.

Erez, M. & Earley, P.C. (1993). *Culture, Self-identity, and Work*. New York: Oxford University Press.

Herskovits, M.J. (1995). *Cultural Anthropology*. New York: Knopf.

Hofstede, G. (1980). *Culture's Consequences: International Differences in Work-related Values*. Newbury Park, CA: Sage.

Hofstede, G., Bond, M.H. & Luk, C. (1993). Individual perceptions of organizational cultures: a methodological treatise on levels of analysis. *Organization Studies*, **14**(4), 483–503.

Hofstede, G., Neuijen, B., Ohayv, D.D. & Sanders, G. (1990). Measuring organizational cultures: a qualitative and quantitative study across twenty cases. *Administrative Science Quarterly*, **35**, 286–316.

Kluckhohn, C. (1954). *Culture and Behavior*. New York: Free Press.

Lachman, R., Nedd, A & Hinings, B. (1994). Analyzing cross-national management and organizations: a theoretical framework. *Management Science*, **40**, 40–55.

Leung, K. (1989). Cross-cultural differences: individual-level and cultural-level analysis. *International Journal of Psychology*, **24**, 703–19.

Leung, K. & Bond, M.H. (1989). On the empirical identification of dimensions for cross-cultural comparisons. *Journal of Cross-Cultural Psychology*, **20**(2), 133–51.

Lord, R.G. & Kernan, M.C. (1987). Scripts as determinants of purposeful behavior in organizations. *Academy of Management Review*, **12**, 265–77.

Martin, J. (1992). *Cultures in Organizations: Three Perspectives*. New York: Oxford University Press.

Misumi, J. (1985). *The Behavioral Science of Leadership: an Interdisciplinary Japanese Research Program*. Ann Arbor: University of Michigan Press.

Osgood, C.E. (1964). Semantic differential technique in the comparative study of cultures. *American Anthropologist*, **66**, 171–200.

Osgood, C.E. (1974). Probing subjective cultures: Parts 1, 2. *Journal of Communication*, **24**, 21–34 and 82–100.

Parsons, T. & Shils, E.A. (1951). *Toward a General Theory of Action*. Cambridge, MA: Harvard University Press.

Pedhazur, E.J. & Schmelkin, L.P. (1991). *Measurement, Design, and Analysis: An Integrated Approach*. Hillsdale, NJ: Erlbaum.

Punj, G. & Stewart, D.W. (1983). Cluster analysis in marketing research: review and suggestions for application. *Journal of Marketing Research*, **20**, 134–48.

Rohner, R.R. (1984). Toward a conception of culture for cross-cultural psychology. *Journal of Cross-cultural Psychology*, **15**(2), 111–38.

Ronen, S. & Shenkar, O. (1985). Clustering countries on attitudinal dimensions: a review and synthesis. *Academy of Management Review*, **10**(3), 435–54.

Roth, M.S. (1995). The effects of culture and socioeconomics on the performance of global brand image strategies. *Journal of Marketing Research*, **32**(2), 163–75.

Schein, E.H. (1985). *Organizational Culture and Leadership: a Dynamic View*. San Francisco, CA: Jossey-Bass.

Schwartz, S.H. & Bilsky, W. (1987). Toward a universal psychological structure of human values. *Journal of Personality and Social Psychology*, **53**(3), 550–62.

Shane, S. (1994). The effect of national culture on the choice between licensing and direct foreign investment. *Strategic Management Journal*, **15**, 627–42.

Shweder, R.A. & LeVine, R.A. (1984). *Culture Theory: Essays on Mind, Self, and Emotion*. New York: Cambridge University Press.

Skinner, B.F. (1953). *Science and Human Behavior*. New York: Macmillan.

Triandis, H.C. (1995). Culture: theoretical and methodological issues. *Handbook of Industrial and Organizational Psychology*, vol. 4, 2nd edn. Palo Alto, CA: Consulting Psychologists Press.

Triandis, H.C. (1972). *The Analysis of Subjective Culture*. New York: Wiley.

Chapter 5

Prime Movers: The Traits of Great Business Leaders

Edwin A. Locke
University of Maryland, College Park, MD, USA

> If you ask me to name the proudest distinction of Americans, I would choose—
> because it contains all the others—the fact that they were the people who created
> the phrase "to *make* money". No other language or nation had ever used
> these words before; men had always thought of wealth as a static quantity—to be
> seized, begged, inherited, shared, looted or obtained as a favor. Americans were the
> first to understand that wealth has to be created (Rand, 1957/1992, *Atlas Shrugged*,
> p. 386).

In the nineteenth century, wealth was created in America at a rate and on a scale
unprecedented in the history of the world. The economic achievements of the
nineteenth century were a product of the age of the Enlightenment which had
reached its zenith in the previous century (Peikoff, 1982). The Enlightenment
was made possible by three momentous discoveries—all originating in the Western world. These three pillars of Western culture—pillars which modern "multi-
culturalists" have tried desperately not to let anyone discover—were reason,
science and individual rights. Greek thought began to free men from domination
by superstition and supernaturalism (Hamilton, 1942). Aristotle, for example,
showed that knowledge is gained through the observation of reality and the use
of logic. It was the re-discovery of Greek (especially Aristotelian) thought in the
West that ushered in the Renaissance. From post-Renaissance scientists such as
Bacon, Kepler, Newton and Galileo, we learned that the world is governed by
natural laws which are discoverable through observation, reason and experiment.
Modern science and technology began to free men from the vicissitudes of
nature. From philosopher John Locke (1986/1690), we learned that all men
possess inalienable rights—the rights to life, liberty, property (i.e. the right to
earn property) and the pursuit of happiness. The concept of individual rights

Creating Tomorrow's Organizations. Edited by C.L. Cooper and S.E. Jackson.
© 1997 John Wiley & Sons Ltd.

began to free men from the tyranny of other men or, more specifically, from tyrannical governments.

As the Industrial Revolution and capitalism progressed, physical drudgery was gradually replaced by machinery, prayer by purposeful action and looting by production and trade. The principle of individual rights allowed men to act freely on their own judgment and to keep the wealth they had earned. The result was a stunning increase in the standard of living and in population growth.

Based on my research, I consider it a great historical injustice that the wealth creators of the late eighteenth century were popularly called, and are still called, "robber barons". Folsom (1991) has pointed out that the real robber barons were not the true market entrepreneurs who earned their wealth (e.g. Morgan, Rockefeller, Vanderbilt), but the "political entrepreneurs" who got their money through political pull, i.e. through favors and subsidies from the government. Robert Fulton, for example, although an innovator in the steamboat business, was able to make money thanks to a monopoly on steamboat traffic granted to him by the state of New York. When the monopoly was struck down, Thomas Gibbons and Cornelius Vanderbilt put their own more efficient steamboats into service, drastically reduced passenger rates and put Fulton out of business. In the railroad industry there were endless scandals, mostly caused by federal subsidies which rewarded political entrepreneurs for building poor-quality track along ill-conceived routes. In contrast, James J. Hill built the Great Northern Railroad without any government subsidies, and this was the only major railroad never to go bankrupt (Rand, 1967). Hill, Morgan, Rockefeller, Vanderbilt and many others were not robber barons but wealth barons. The money-makers were creators, men who, through the brilliance of their vision and the force of their own energy, moved civilization forward. They were and are what Ayn Rand (1957/1992) called "prime movers".

My thesis is that the prime movers, the creators of great wealth in a free (and even semi-free) economy, possess special qualities, which I will call traits (see Locke et al., 1991, Chapter 2, for an earlier discussion). To claim that these qualities or traits were the cause of their achievements is not to claim that such qualities are the only causal factor involved. A key political pre-condition of the creation of wealth is freedom (i.e. individual rights). However, within a free (or even semi-free) society, not everyone is equally capable. Some are able to earn much more than others. Overwhelmingly, most creators of wealth did not inherit much wealth (e.g. to use as seed money); they made their own (Folsom, 1991). (Banker and financier J.P. Morgan was one of the few who was born to wealth, but he created far more than he inherited.) But what were and are these creators made of?

I developed inductively the list of traits presented below, based on my own research and through the research of students in an MBA elective that I have taught twice, entitled "Business Heroes in Fact and Fiction". (Some of these traits, of course, have been identified by other writers, especially those who have studied entrepreneurship.) The course begins with Ayn Rand's (1957/1992) epic novel *Atlas Shrugged*, which glorifies the industrialist, and follows with books about nineteenth- and twentieth-century wealth creators. (I use the terms industrialist, entrepreneur and wealth creator more or less interchangeably in this chapter. The industrialists in question all promoted enormous growth even if they did not start their own firms.) The list of traits generated from the study of *Atlas Shrugged* and those identified (independently) from the study of from books about real entrepreneurs were remarkably similar. Nor did I observe any notable differences between the traits of the nineteenth- and twentieth-century industrialists.

It must be emphasized that when discussing the traits in question, I am referring to the motives, premises and methods of thinking which guided the entrepreneurs' actual business achievements, not to their professed philosophies—which sometimes had little connection to the philosophies they practiced—or to their activities outside of work. For example, some great business leaders were quite religious (e.g. Mary Kay), but none of them made money by praying rather than acting on their rational judgment, by using faith instead of reason, or by sacrificing themselves to their competitors. Others were opposed to (organized) religion (e.g. Carnegie). Some were adulterous (e.g. Morgan), and others were dedicated family men (e.g. Rockefeller.) Some had contemptible viewpoints on certain issues (e.g. Henry Ford's virulent anti-Semitism). Some eagerly sought publicity (e.g. Ford); others avoided it at all costs (e.g. Rockefeller). Some were philosophically muddled (e.g. Carnegie); others were disinterested in wider issues; and still others were clear and insightful thinkers (e.g. James J. Hill). None were serious philosophical thinkers. But when it came to business—they were all business.

I have categorized the traits into three groups: those pertaining mainly to cognition (cognitive ability, methods of thinking); those pertaining mainly to motivation (values and actions); and those pertaining to attitudes toward employees (hiring and rewarding of subordinates).

COGNITION

Reality Focus

In *Atlas Shrugged* the heroes are intransigent with respect to their perception of reality. Facts are facts. A is A. In contrast, the villains focus on everything except reality: they characteristically indulge in evasions, rationalizations, unidentified emotions, out-of-context wishes, delusions, etc. There are examples of this contrast between villains and heroes throughout the novel. Here are two examples. In Part 1, Chapter 1, Dagny Taggart is arguing with Jim Taggart about ordering Rearden metal, a brilliant new discovery, in order to make desperately needed rails:

Jim: "You haven't given me a chance to form an opinion."
Dagny: "I don't give a damn about your opinion . . . Just say yes or no."

"That's a preposterous, high-handed, arbitrary way of—"

"Yes or no?"

"That's the trouble with you. You always make it 'Yes' or 'No'. Things are never absolute like that. Nothing is absolute."

"Metal rails are. Whether we get them or not is" (Rand, 1957/1992, p. 29).

On the other side of the same coin, at the end of John Galt's world-shaking speech, which passionately defended a revolutionary moral code, the morality of egoism, Head of State Mr Thompson says, "It wasn't real, was it?" (Rand, 1957/1992, p. 984).

Focusing on reality is implicit in any business achievement (or any achievement in any field), but it is especially striking when a business leader identifies the principle explicitly. Consider Jack Welch, the CEO of General Electric Co. Since Welch took over as CEO in 1980, the value of GE stock has increased over 500%. This represents an increase in market value of about $100 billion! What made it possible? One cause, I am convinced, is the consistent application of one of his six rules: "Face reality as it is, not as it was or as you wish. . . . facing reality is crucial in life, not just in business. You have to see the world in the purest, clearest way possible, or you can't make decisions on a rational basis" (Tichy & Sherman, 1993, pp. 12–13).

Compare Welch to the former CEOs of GM and IBM. Under these leaders both companies had been steadily deteriorating. Customer service and quality had been slipping. Market share had been eroding. Key employees had been leaving. New products had been slow to market and non-competitive. And all the time the CEOs kept saying that things were going to improve, that the needed steps were going to be taken, and that recovery was just around the corner. (One autombile executive told a friend not to invest in a Toyota dealership, because the US auto industry was going to destroy them.) Yet nothing fundamental, in fact, was done until the increasingly enormous losses threatened bankruptcy, and the CEOs were fired. These companies lacked business heroes to bring them toward recovery. They lost billions of dollars in wealth, because their leaders refused to face reality. Under new leaders, both companies are now coming back to life.

Honesty

The villains in *Atlas Shrugged*, in contrast to the heroes, show dishonesty of every kind, from stock swindles to denials of the virtually self-evident (e.g. that Taggart Transcontinental Railroad cannot survive without profits) to evasions of obvious cause–effect relationships (e.g. that increasing economic controls were causing increasing poverty).

The need for honesty in business in the real world is readily apparent (Locke & Woiceshyn, 1995). A successful businessman has to be honest in his assessment of the market and of his financial resources, in his judgment of the relative attractiveness of his products and of the capabilities of his employees, and in his treatment of suppliers, lenders and customers. (Faking reality, of course, must be distinguished from honest ignorance of relevant facts). Andrew Carnegie, one of the greatest steel magnates in business history, an amasser of a $500 million fortune, had it right when he said, "I have never known a concern to make a decided success that did not do good, honest work" (Hacker, 1968, p. 354). Carnegie was quick to fire executives who did not live up to the standards of honesty by which he lived. (In at least one instance, involving his treatment of Henry Clay Frick, he may not have lived up to his own principle; Wall, 1989.)

General Electric CEO Jack Welch made it clear to GE executives that only "100% ethical behavior" would be tolerated. He would ask them, "Can you look in the mirror every day and feel proud of what you are doing?" (Tichy & Sherman, 1993, pp. 113–114). GE has had a few scandals since Welch took over, but these seem to have been in spite of, not because of, his leadership. Furthermore, when unethical actions were detected, the problems were addressed forthrightly and aggressively.

Another aspect of honesty is to acknowledge failure. For example, early in the history of Nucor Corporation, when it was still called Nuclear Corporation of America and was on the verge of bankruptcy, furious stockholders at the annual meeting demanded to know why the company was doing so badly. "It's a rotten company, what can I say?" (Preston, 1991, p. 73), answered CEO Ken Iverson, with the kind of candor virtually never seen at such meetings. Iverson, of course, went on to make Nucor the most valuable steel company in the USA and the stockholders rich.

Independence and Self-confidence

I have combined these two traits because they are reciprocally related. Using one's independent judgment promotes self-confidence and confidence encourages independence. These traits markedly differentiate heroes from villains in *Atlas Shrugged*. One example occurs in Chapter 3, Part 1, which is concerned with Dagny Taggart's childhood. "She was 12 years old when she told Eddie Willers that she would run the railroad when they grew up. She was fifteen when it occurred to her for the first time that women did not run railroads and that people might object. To hell with that, she thought—and never worried about it again" (Rand, 1957/1992, pp. 54–55). A later example occurs in Chapter 8, Part 1, before the first run of the John Galt Line which was built from a radically new steel substitute, Rearden metal. A reporter says to Dagny, "Tell me, Miss Taggart, what's going to support a seven-thousand-ton train on a three-thousand-ton bridge?" Dagny answers, "My judgment" (Rand, 1957/1992, p. 223).

From the real world of business let me introduce Mary Kay Ash, founder of Mary Kay Cosmetics and arguably the most successful female entrepreneur that America has ever seen. When she was about to open Mary Kay, after many years of outstanding performance in the retail business (and many years of being blocked from advancement due to being a woman), her husband, who was also to be her business partner, died. Her lawyer told her to abandon the business at once, citing all the cosmetics companies that had gone bankrupt recently; her accountant told her to abandon her commission system, claiming it would bankrupt the company; and financial experts criticized her credit policies. She ignored them all in favor of her own judgment (Ash, 1981a). Today the company has sales of close to $2 billion a year and is very profitable (Ash, 1995).

Virtually all business heroes have gone against the crowd when earning their fortunes, if only because they were breaking new ground. Ken Iverson of Nucor "bet the company" on more than one occasion by sinking a fortune into new, unproved steel-making technologies (Preston, 1991). In one case he bought a new machine from West Germany which would make a strip of steel in one continuous operation. To place this problem in context, steelmen had been trying to do this since 1856, that is, for over 130 years, without success!

Going back to the eighteenth century, consider James J. Hill, builder of the Great Northern Railroad, and Cornelius Vanderbilt, and entrepreneur in the steamboat industry and builder of the New York Central Railroad system (Rand, 1967). In both industries it was normal for competitors to ask for and receive either government-backed monopoly power to prevent competition and/or subsidies to promote the business. As noted, Hill's was the only major railroad built without government subsidies and the only one that did not go bankrupt. Vanderbilt put the subsidized Robert Fulton out of the steamboat business on the Hudson River. One biographer wrote of Vanderbilt, "he was absolutely unconciliatory; he didn't care what people thought about him" (Smith, 1927, p. 34). Similarly, John D. Rockefeller, founder of Standard Oil, who received more abuse in the press than perhaps any other nineteenth-century entrepreneur, paid no attention to it. In another example of confidence in his own judgment, he told his skeptical board of directors that he would invest his own money in the purchase of some oil fields containing oil which was too sulfurous to refine, because he was convinced that a method could be found to remove the sulfur; and he was right (Folsom, 1991, p. 90).

Let me stress that independence does not preclude borrowing business ideas from others. What is required is an independent judgment as to the validity and usefulness of the ideas of others. We all know of the "NIH" (Not Invented Here) syndrome, a premise held by many stagnant businesses—stagnant because they refuse to adopt any idea they did not discover themselves. Such a false view of independence is clearly suicidal in the business world. Sam Walton (1992), founder of Wal-Mart, was an obsessive borrower of merchandising ideas based on his observations of other retail chains.

Active Mind

Ayn Rand observed many times that the conceptual faculty is not (properly) passive but active. To quote from John Galt's speech: "*man is a being of volitional consciousness. Reason does not work automatically"* (Rand, 1957/1992, p. 930); and later, "All thinking is a process of identification and integration" (p. 934). The heroes in *Atlas Shrugged* use their minds to their fullest capacity; the villains do everything possible to evade the responsibility of thought.

Under capitalism there is constant change, as existing businesses are besieged by competitors who try to develop better products and services and by entrepreneurs who enter the market with bold new ideas. This process is now occurring on a global scale. The businessman who remains passive and tries to live off past success is doomed to fail. Success in the free market requires a continuously active mind; and the greater the scope, size and complexity of the business, the more thinking is required. The focus must be on constant innovation and improvement in everything one does.

One of my heroes in this realm is the late Sam Walton. In a period of 30 years, between 1960 and 1990, Wal-Mart sales increased from $1.4 million to $26 billion and profits from about $100 000 to $1 billion. In 1992, the year Walton died, sales exceeded $50 billion. This achievement is all the more remarkable in that Walton began with nothing. Here are some examples of how Sam Walton thought (from Walton, 1992):

> I never could leave well enough alone, and, in fact, I think my constant fiddling and meddling with the status quo may have been one of my biggest contributions to the later success of Wal-Mart (p. 27).

> . . . in business, I have always been driven to buck the system, to innovate, to take things beyond where they've been (p. 47).

> It's almost embarrassing to admit this, but it's true: there hasn't been a day in my adult life when I haven't spent some time thinking about merchandising (p. 56).

In his search for new ideas, Walton would even visit the stores of K-Mart, his main competitor, during family vacations! This policy was not a breech of the virtue of independence; rather it was the sign of an active mind.

One of the more amusing examples of an active mind was recounted by Henry J. Kaiser's employee, Joe Reis. (Kaiser was a pioneer in steel, aluminum and other industries.) They were sharing a room together on a train and, about two in the morning, Reis was awakened by Kaiser repeatedly asking, in a progressively louder voice, "Reis, are you awake?" This eventually woke up Reis. There followed a long discussion of what to do in the next day's meeting. This was not the last time that Kaiser, who needed very little sleep, woke Reis up to discuss business (Heiner, 1991, p. 48).

As CEO of Coca-Cola since 1981, Robert Goizueta has achieved a stunning increase in shareholder value. As of 1994, Coca-Cola was the number one company in the USA, in terms of market value added (MVA; Morris, 1995). Early in 1980, when he was COO, he turned business planning meetings into such relentless question-asking sessions that they became known as the Spanish Inquisition. The knowledge he acquired enabled him to later lead a brilliantly successful reorganization of the company.

Observers of Bill Gates have always been astonished at the voluminous amount of reading he does, not only in the computer software field but also in physics and biology. He is described as a massively parallel thinker with extraordinary bandwidth (quoted in Wallace & Erickson, 1992, p. 339).

Moving back to the nineteenth century, Cyrus McCormick perfected and sold the mechanical reaper used to harvest wheat. Unlike his competitors, McCormick made constant improvements in every aspect of the business. This included: the use of interchangeable parts on an assembly line, constant addition of new features to the reaper, the provision of outstanding customer service, and arrangement of financing and credit for farmers who wanted to purchase a reaper. These innovations helped him to outdistance all rivals (Gunderson, 1989, pp. 93–94).

Constant improvement is a result of constant thought.

Competence (Ability)

Focusing on reality, being honest and independent and being mentally active are crucial requirements for business success, but they are not sufficient. Successful businessmen, and especially the creators of great fortunes, must also be competent, that is, must possess ability, especially cognitive ability (intelligence). *Atlas Shrugged* is one of the few novels ever to explicitly glorify human ability and to show the causal link between ability and human survival. Ragnar Danneskjold, talking to Hank Rearden, says ". . . my only love, the only value I care to live for, is that which has never been loved by the world, has never won recognition or friends or defenders: human ability. That is the love I am serving— and if I should lose my life, to what better purpose could I give it?" (Rand, 1957/ 1992, p. 537).

Business heroes have not necessarily been intellectual geniuses, but they have been intelligent enough to understand thoroughly the products they were making and the markets in which they were working. In many cases prime movers were especially competent in mathematics (e.g. J.P. Morgan). They have had the capacity to observe a number of concretes and form valid generalizations. An example is Sam Walton (1992) who, after visiting a number of stores around the country, concluded that discount merchandising would be the wave of the future. Another example is Bill Gates, who was himself a pioneer in software development and grasped the value of software sooner than and far more thoroughly than other people in the computer field.

A second aspect of intelligence is the capacity to grasp causal connections. An example is Cyrus McCormick's insight that if he spent more money on customer service in the short run, he would gain more customers and therefore make greater profits in the long run (Gunderson, 1989).

A third aspect of intelligence is the capacity to look at overwhelming complexity and formulate out of the chaos a few simple principles to guide action. Roberto Goizueta, for example, formulated this idea: "You borrow money at a certain rate and invest it at a higher rate and pocket the difference. It is simple. It is the essence of banking" (Morris, 1995, p. 88). Jack Welch stressed the need for every GE business to be number one or number two in its industry. A third aspect of intelligence is the ability to project the future based on knowledge of present trends (cf. Rockefeller). This brings us to the next trait: vision.

Vision

During President George Bush's administration there were numerous references to what his staff, semi-contemptuously, called "the vision thing". This expression confessed two things: that they did not take the issue of vision seriously, and that they (and Bush) didn't have one—which is one reason why Bush lost the next election.

A key aspect of vision is seeing the future trend of an industry—not what products are selling now but what will sell in the future, not how manufacturers are making things now but how they will make them in the next decade, not what services exist now but what services people would buy if they were offered.

All business heroes with whom I am familiar were visionary. Take John D. Rockefeller of Standard Oil. When everyone else was drilling frantically for oil, he saw that the real profit would be made in oil refining. He also saw that he would make more money by lowering the price of oil through continuous reduction in costs. At one point he controlled 90% of the American refining market. He also saw the value of marketing, of international sales and of pipelines. John Archbold, one of the directors of Standard Oil and later to become president of Standard Oil of New Jersey, said of Rockefeller, "In business we all try to look ahead as far as possible. Some of us think we are pretty able. But Rockefeller always sees a little further ahead than any of us—and then he sees around the corner" (Folsom, 1991, p. 93).

Cornelius Vanderbilt, after making a fortune in the steamship business, saw that the key to success in the railroad business was to consolidate local and competing lines into an integrated system. The result was the N.Y. Central and an even bigger fortune.

James J. Hill envisioned a transcontinental railroad and built it after a terrible struggle (Martin, 1991). Cornelius Vanderbilt saw the possibilities inherent in steamships and later in integrated railroad systems (Folsom, 1991). Walt Disney foresaw the mass appeal of animated cartoons and feature films, synchronized sound, Technicolor and theme parks. Thomas J. Watson Jr brought IBM into the age of electronic computing even when the company was making record profits from its punch-card machines (Watson & Petre, 1990). Ross Perot saw that software systems and data-processing services would become a huge growth industry (Mason, 1990). Bill Gates recognized that computer software would become more important than hardware. He also refused to scuttle Windows™ after one of his top executives urged that the project be killed. Windows™ became the biggest-selling software product ever (Wallace & Erickson, 1992).

Vision is often misunderstood. The great business leader does not necessarily possess a detailed, long-term, fixed plan envisioned at the outset of his career. Rather, the leader sees a promising direction and pursues it, one step ahead of everyone else, and continually refines it as he learns from experience. Henry Ford is a case in point. After a number of false starts, he saw the value of an inexpensive, mass-market automobile that would sell to the middle class at the time when all the other manufacturers viewed the car as a luxury product to be sold to the wealthy. His Model T was a smashing success and totally dominated the market for many years. Roberto Goizueta, after the problems encountered in introducing New Coke, grasped the significance of customer loyalty to the Coke brand and used this knowledge to help the marketing effort take off (Morris, 1995).

Nor is a given vision, once formulated, good forever. Henry Ford's loss of vision, specifically his refusal to grasp that the model T could not last forever, nearly bankrupted the company. Steve Jobs, a brilliant visionary with respect to the PC, later lost his way and was eventually forced out of the company. He is now CEO of another very successful high-technology company.

MOTIVATION

Egoistic Passion for the Work

Ayn Rand demonstrated in *Atlas Shrugged* that the act of earning money was morally virtuous and that love of money represented love of productive achievement. I want to stress that love of money *alone* is not sufficient to motivate a person to maximum, long-term effort. I believe, as Ayn Rand did, that you need to love the means by which you make the money, too—that is, you must love the work itself. My reason is a simple one. Working only for money is insufficiently selfish. You only get paid once or twice a month. Depositing the check takes about one minute. To feel pleasure for 2 minutes a month is not a very exciting prospect, especially if you are bored to death or disgusted for at least 160 hours each month. All the heroes in *Atlas Shrugged* had a passionate love for their work—this was especially stressed in the character of Dagny Taggart. Dagny's greatest conflict was whether or not to leave Atlantis. When she decides to leave she says, "If you want to know the one reason that's taking me back, I'll tell you: I cannot bring myself to abandon to destruction all the greatness of the world, all that which was mine and yours, which was made by us and is still ours by right . . ." (Rand, 1957/1992, p. 744). Later Francisco says to her, "Dagny, all . . . of us are in love—with the same thing, no matter what its forms. Don't wonder why you feel no breach among us. You'll be one of us, so long as you'll remain in love with your rails and your engines—and they'll lead you back to us, no matter how many times you lose your way. The only man never to be redeemed is the man without passion" (p. 745).

In the same way, real prime movers are passionately in love with their work. Sam Walton said that merchandising, "has been an absolute passion of mine. It is what I enjoy doing as much as anything in the business" (Walton, 1992, p. 57). Listen to Ken Iverson of Nucor Corp.: "Hot metal has a fascination all of its own. . . . There is a fascination about melting a metal and pouring it into a shape. A hot metal man has to feel that fascination. That's why he works around hot metal" (Preston, 1991, p. 8). Bill Gates expected his people to be "hard core', which meant working long hours, including weekends, even at the expense of family life. For many years he refused to marry, because he was so totally wedded to his work (Wallace & Erickson, 1992).

Walt Disney's passion was in some ways the most remarkable of all. His father was a cruel, tyrannical, Christian fundamentalist and socialist. True to socialist principles, he made his two sons, Roy and Walt, work grueling hours delivering newspapers and then took the money they earned away from them under false pretenses. So Walt took on a secret job at a candy store and started a bootleg paper delivery operation in order to earn money for himself. He used the money to pay for night art classes, also taken in secret (Stavrou, 1993).

Mary Kay Ash says, "I derive my keenest enjoyment from my work and because I feel this way, I often work in preference to indulging what others might call fun. My work is fun, and I feel very fortunate to be able to derive so much pleasure from it" (Ash, 1981b, p. 135).

Passion means that you can get angry when things do not go well. Many great business leaders lose their tempers from time to time, not necessarily because they want to intimidate anyone but because they care so much. Passion is their source of energy. Both Welch and Goizueta agree that energy is the number one requirement of a successful leader in today's economic environment (Morris, 1995).

In her article "The Money-Making Personality" Ayn Rand summed up the issue beautifully: "Behind his usually grim, expressionless face, the Money-Maker is committed to his work with the passion of a lover, the fire of a crusader, the dedication of a saint and the endurance of a martyr" (Rand, 1983, p. 4).

Commitment to Action

One of the important sub-themes in *Atlas Shrugged* is mind–body integration and its converse, the mind–body dichotomy. Henry Rearden represents an honest version of the mind–body dichotomy; he initially fails to see the contradiction between the principles by which he runs his business life and those by which he lives his personal life.

Some specific expressions of the mind–body dichotomy in *Atlas Shrugged* are reason vs. emotion, the spiritual vs. the material, theory vs. practice, and thought vs. action. The form I am concerned with here is the relationship between thought and action. Business heroes are great thinkers, at least when it comes to the world of business. Thinking, however, is not sufficient if one's goal is to create wealth. One must also act on the basis of one's thinking. Let's start with a quote from Chapter 8, Part 1, of *Atlas Shrugged* concerning Dagny Taggart's approach to the issue: "First, the vision—then the physical shape to express it. First, the thought—then the purposeful motion down the straight line of a single track to a chosen goal. Could one have any meaning without the other? Wasn't it evil to wish without moving, or to move without aim?" (Rand, 1957/1992, p. 226). This is an example of total mind–body integration in the business context. It is very characteristic of creators of great wealth.

One of my heroes in this realm is Ken Iverson of Nucor who, as noted, "bet the company" more than once on unproved new technology. When Iverson bought the continuous steelmaking machine from a German manufacturer, no one had ever bought such a machine and not one full roll of steel had ever been made from it, even in the manufacturer's own tests. But after studying the machine the Nucor staff decided that it would work and they bought it. It consisted of one million parts and cost $70 million. This amount would be refunded if it did not work, but the cost of the one-million-square-foot facility that was to house it, which cost far more than the machine, would not. The plant was designed while it was being built, an enormous risk. Many of the workmen had never done construction of any kind. During this period the big steel companies were spending thousands of dollars doing analyses of why the new machine would not work, why the project would cost far more than anticipated and why, if Nucor did build it as planned, they would not make a profit from it. Iverson went ahead and built it. "As a manager," said Iverson, "you have to make decisions. If you don't make decisions, you are going nowhere and doing nothing" (Preston, 1991, p. 88).

Sam Walton said, "I've always had a strong bias toward action—a trait that has been a big part of the Wal-Mart story" (Walton, 1992, p. 12). One of his strategies was to open a new store whenever he made sufficient profits from the previous store. In some years Wal-Mart grew at the rate of three stores a week. This meant that he was perpetually in debt but also perpetually growing In business there is often a fine line between growth and over-extension of one's resources. When Mary Kay Ash awoke each day, her first action was to make an action agenda for the day, usually consisting of six important tasks to be accomplished. The same technique was used by Charles Schawab, Andrew Carnegie's protégé, who re-built Bethlehem Steel into a highly profitable enterprise. Henry J. Kaiser made the following statement, which is very characteristic of the philosophy of prime movers, "It is always good to get on high ground and see the vision. But I can never escape the urge to do something about it" (Heiner, 1991, p. 21).

Ambition

Ayn Rand defined ambition as, "the systematic pursuit of achievement and of constant improvement in respect to one's goal" (Binswanger, 1986, p. 12). In *Atlas Shrugged*, Francisco d'Anconia represents the pinnacle of ambition in the realm of business. In Chapter 5, Part 1, he says, "In his lifetime, every one of my ancestors raised the production of d'Anconia Copper by about ten per cent. I intend to raise it by one hundred" (Rand, 1957/1992, p. 94).

Real-life business heroes are just as passionately ambitious as those in *Atlas Shrugged*. Sam Walton said, "I have been overblessed with drive and ambition from the time I hit the ground" (Walton, 1992, p. 11). Early in his career he decided that, "I wanted my little Newport store to be the best, most profitable variety store in Arkansas within five years" (p. 22). Later on, his wife Helen had this to say about him, "I kept saying, 'Sam, we're making a good living. Why go out, why expand so much more?'... After the seventeenth store, though, I realized there wasn't going to be any stopping it" (p. 78).

Personal ambition is expressed in the level of responsibility and expertise one aspires to and acts to achieve. Jack Welch stated in 1973 that he wanted to be CEO of General Electric; by 1980, he had made it. Welch was equally ambitious for GE once he took over. He set extraordinarily ambitious goals for the company. Welch calls this "raising the bar'. "The standard of performance we use is: *to be as good as the best in the world*" (Tichy & Sherman, 1993, pp. 187, 246). GE Vice-President Steve Kerr calls Welch's stretch targets "Looney tunes stuff that he has no right to ask... [but the employees] get so energized.... they are damned well going to help him do whatever he asks" (Morris, 1995, p. 94).

Effort and Tenacity

Effort and tenacity (or persistence) are implicit in traits such as commitment to action, an active mind, passion and ambition, but I have listed them separately for purpose of emphasis. In *Atlas Shrugged* (1957/1992) industrialist Henry Rearden spent 10 years and overcame countless failures before he perfected Rearden metal. Things are no easier for real-life wealth creators. Business heroes are enormously hard-working and expect the same from key subordinates. Further, they redouble their efforts in the face of failures and setbacks.

American Steel (Preston, 1991) specifically describes 20–30 major failures in the attempt by Nucor to get the new continuous-steelmaking machine operational and refers to many others. But finally they got it working and made tremendous profits from the steel it produced. The company later built a second profitable facility just like the first, and they are constantly upgrading the technology in all of their plants.

Failure does not discourage prime movers. Listen to David Glass's description of the opening of one of the earliest Wal-Mart stores: "It was the worst retail store I had ever seen. Sam had brought a couple of trucks of watermelons in and stacked them on the sidewalk. He had a donkey ride out in the parking lot. It was about 115 degrees, and the watermelons began to pop, and the donkey began to do what donkeys do, and it all mixed together and ran all over the parking lot. And when you went inside the store, the mess just continued, having been tracked in all over the floor. He was a nice fellow, but I wrote him off" (Walton, 1992, pp. 45–6). David Glass is now CEO of Wal-Mart. Sam Walton admitted later that Glass had come on a bad day, but Sam, who was often described as relentless, never let any setback stop him.

Stewart Alsop describes Bill Gates this way: "Gates is tenacious. That is what's scary. . . . Bill always comes back, like Chinese water torture. . . . People are scared of Microsoft because they are so persistent" (Wallace & Erickson, p. 400). His first Windows™ program took 7 years to develop and suffered from cost overruns, delays, lawsuits and widespread skepticism, even from within the company. Gates's typical workweek is 70–90 hours long (Manes & Andrews, 1993).

Mary Kay Ash often worked 16–18 hour days. Mistakes do not bother her. "I've told my consultants and sales directors countless times," she says, "if we ever decide to compare knees, you're going to find that I have fallen down and gotten up so many times in my life" (Ash, 1981a, p. 11). Walt Disney, due to making foolish contracts, lost the rights to a number of his early productions, but he always bounced back with new and even more brilliant creations.

ATTITUDE TOWARDS EMPLOYEES

Respect for Ability

The whole of *Atlas Shrugged* is based on profound love of ability on the part of the heroes (and the author). Dagny Taggart shows her appreciation of human ability, including her own, in Chapter 3, Part 1: "Studying mathematics, she felt, quite simply and at once: 'How great that men have done this' and 'How wonderful that I am so good at it'" (Rand, 1957/1992, p. 54). Later, Andrew Stockton says, "To me—the foulest man on earth, more contemptible than a criminal, is the employer who rejects men for being too good" (p. 670).

Business leaders must have followers, or else they cannot be leaders. It is of crucial significance whom they pick to work for them. Since no leader can run a business of any size without help, hiring people of ability is essential to success.

First, however, the leaders have to find them. Billionaire Ross Perot stressed the importance of selection as much as any business hero I have studied. He used to give prospective employees long questionnaires to fill out, followed by grueling interviews. He also used to raid other companies in order to hire away their top talent—including IBM, which he had left when they cut his sales bonuses because he was making too much money! Recruits were told frankly what to expect if they went to work for Electronic Data Systems (EDS)—14-hour days, weeks away from home, sleeping, at times, on cots at the office. At one point, only 1 out of 70 applicants to EDS was hired (Mason, 1990).

Bill Gates observed in his dealings with IBM that they hired some good people and some not so good people. Microsoft, he claimed, hired only good people, using rigorous selection procedures. He frequently hires top people away from competitors. Microsoft also follows a policy of constantly winnowing out the least able employees (Wallace & Erickson, 1992). Nucor hired people who were good enough to actually take control of a factory after it was built and run it themselves. Ken Iverson wanted people who could think for themselves even if they had no previous experience with steel. Nucor plant manager, Keith Busse, expressed the philosophy as follows, "What better ways is there to learn [than on the job]. The mind's a powerful thing" (Preston, 1991, p. 16). Sam Walton was continually nosing around other competitors' stores, looking for talent. David Glass, the present CEO, was hired away from another company.

John D. Rockefeller attracted top talent by paying above-market wages. Said one observer about Andrew Carnegie, "He exceeded any man I ever knew in his ability to pick a man from one place and put him in another with maximum advantage" (Hacker, 1968, p. 358). Carnegie himself said that, "I am sure I never could have [been successful] without my partners, of whom I had thirty-two, the brightest and cleverest young fellows in the world" (p. 358). Pierre DuPont actually used to buy other companies solely in order to get the most able people in these companies to work for him. Perhaps his greatest achievement in spotting talent was his promotion of Alfred P. Sloan, first to operations vice president and then to president of General Motors. Sloan was arguably the greatest CEO GM ever had.

Another aspect of respect for ability that should not be overlooked is the willingness of the great business leader to allow subordinates to disagree with him. The principle here is that even the most brilliant leader is not omniscient. If he has hired very bright people, it is very likely that some will know more than he does about specific issues. Jack Welch loves no-holds-barred debates among top executives before important decisions are made in order to insure that every issue has been addressed thoroughly. Like Bill Gates, he greatly respects people who are willing to stand up to him if they can make a good case for their position. Nucor is famous for its heated arguments amongst the top executives; hot metal men may not be suave, but they do get to the bottom of every issue.

Great business leaders do not allow subordinates to reject their vision; disagreement is allowed only within the context of a common vision and common principles (e.g. integrity). Any other policy would produce organizational chaos.

Commitment to Justice: Rewarding Merit

The virtue of justice requires that other men be judged objectively, according to rational standards and be treated accordingly. Justice was the virtue that Hank Rearden in *Atlas Shrugged* practiced in his work, but, through ignorance, did not practice in his personal life—until he grasped the nature of his error. The whole of *Atlas Shrugged*, is, among other things, a play on justice on a global scale. When the world rejects the men of mind, it collapses.

Business heroes are not only great admirers and judges of ability, they are typically generous about rewarding it. Sam Walton introduced profit-sharing, incentive bonuses and discount stock purchase plans for his employees. Many of his executives are millionaires. Microsoft pays lower than normal salaries but backs them up with lucrative stock options. It is estimated that 2000 Microsoft employees are now millionaires. Mary Kay has one of the most elaborate reward and recognition systems of any company in the world. The rewards range from ribbons, pins and merchandise to incentive pay and pink Cadillacs. Mary Kay was considered crazy for offering her saleswomen generous commissions, but they ended up selling so much that they made her rich. Pierre DuPont gave high salaries and stock bonuses to the top executives at both GM and DuPont, resulting in tremendous loyalty to these organizations. Nucor makes extensive use of profit-sharing bonuses at every level of the organization; some of the profits go into retirement plans consisting partly of Nucor stock. Thus everyone in the company prospers if the company does well. At Coca-Cola even lower-level managers who help create wealth for the shareholders can become millionaires.

There is what I call a "success-triad" in dealing with employees that has been used over and over by business heroes. Its three parts are (1) hire extremely talented, motivated people; (2) demand and expect extraordinarily high performance from them while giving them very high responsibility; and (3) reward them generously for success.

CONCLUSION

In an insightful observation, Mary Kay Ash (1995, p. 151) said, "There are three types of people in the world: those who make things happen, those who watch things happen, and those who wonder what happened'. Prime movers are neither thinkers without motion nor actors without thought. They are thinkers who act. They are not looters but creators of wealth. They move civilization forward by the tremendous force of their energy and ability. In an insightful observation, James J. Hill (Martin, 1991, p. 557) wrote:

> Nations, like men, are travelers. Each one of them moves, through history, toward what we call progress and a new life, or toward decay and death. As it is the first concern of every man to know that he is achieving something, advancing in material wealth, industrial power, intellectual strength and moral purpose, so it is vital to a nation to know that its years are milestones along the way of progress.

The fundamental causes of national progress are: reason, science, individual rights (including the egoist morality on which this concept is based; Rand, 1964)—and prime movers.

This does not mean that men of lesser ability and drive contribute nothing. As noted earlier, prime movers depend on and utilize people who possess less vision, ability and drive than themselves but who, nevertheless, are highly capable in some respect(s) and who work to their fullest capacity. Sometimes, of course, those who begin as followers are more capable than their leaders and ultimately outshine their previous bosses. Even people of lesser ability and ambition can be successful entrepreneurs, even if on a smaller scale than the great wealth creators. Shopkeepers and small-scale manufacturers may not have the ability and tenacity of a Rockefeller, but they still create wealth.

Let me stress that the twelve traits noted above are not sufficient to guarantee business success. I have not addressed at all the issue of business strategies, which are a crucial element of business leadership. There are certain strategies that I believe are timeless. Among these are: low cost, high quality, outstanding customer service, fast response time and innovation. Those who are able, mentally active and tenacious, of course, are more likely to discover viable business strategies and to implement them effectively than those who are not.

A relevant question to ask about the foregoing list is: are these traits only applicable to the USA in the nineteenth and twentieth centuries, or are they timeless and universal? I would argue that they are timeless and universal. The reason is that *the task requirements for earning money are the same everywhere and in every time period*. The successful businessman has to look at the economic, market and technological facts relevant to his time and place objectively; he cannot deal with reality if he tries to fake it. He cannot create something new unless he thinks independently and is confident of his own judgment. He cannot originate or evaluate money-making ideas without an active mind. He cannot know what to do without vision and cannot implement the vision without ability. He cannot sustain effort unless he loves what is he doing. He cannot move ahead without ambition and cannot overcome the inevitable setbacks and obstacles without effort and tenacity. He cannot achieve any large-scale objective without hiring competent subordinates and cannot retain them unless they feel justly rewarded for their efforts.

What implications does this list of traits have for work in the next millenium? I can think of two. One is selection, and, as a corollary of this, early identification (see below). The other pertains to education and training. If people know what traits are required to become prime movers, and want to become prime movers, they can work to develop these qualities insofar they are readily modifiable. Obviously some, such as honesty and effort, are more in the person's direct volitional control than others, such as ability and vision. Certain traits may be especially difficult to change in adulthood (e.g. self-confidence, ambition). Others may be a matter of finding a proper match between the person and the work (e.g. passion).

Despite the above arguments and the evidence gathered to date, my list of traits is not necessarily complete. There are many problems inherent in the process of inferring traits (e.g. what type of evidence is to be considered and from what sources?). Inferring the degree of a given trait possessed by an individual is also difficult. Furthermore, I have not studied business leaders and entrepreneurs from other countries or from other time periods, although a preliminary study of eighteenth-century English businessman Josiah Wedgwood, a producer of pottery and porcelain (which is still sold today), reveals many traits found on my list (Reilly, 1992). Clearly more studies of non-US business magnates would be useful.

Observe that I did not mention competitiveness as a trait of prime movers. It is true that many wealth creators are highly competitive—Sam Walton, Jack Welch and Bill Gates are cases in point. However, the essential elements of this trait are implicit in those that I have mentioned, e.g. focus on reality, vision, active mind, tenacity, ambition. A businessman who does not understand what his competitors are doing and does not strive to do better in order to get customers' business will obviously not succeed. Given these other traits, however, adding competitiveness to the list seems unnecessary.

I can suggest a number of interesting questions that could be addressed in future research:

1. What methods could be used to infer the quantity of a trait possessed by a deceased business leader based on biographical and autobiographical material? Can trait measurements of such people be made reliably? House, Spangler & Woycke (1991) were able to do this for US Presidents.
2. How well can these traits be measured in existing business leaders (e.g. assessment centers, tests, interviews, peer ratings)? Howard & Bray (1988) found that intelligence and ambition, measured by tests and interviews, were the best predictors of advancement of AT&T managers over a 25-year period.
3. Could such traits be measured early in a person's career as a way of identifying "prime mover" potential? Howard & Bray's results suggest that they could, but their dependent variable was promotion rather than wealth creation.
4. Would quantitative analysis support 12 distinct traits, or could they be grouped into a smaller number without loss of important information? My prediction is that they can be combined into a smaller number.
5. Do the traits operate independently (e.g. in additive fashion) or are there interactions between them? I have one prediction here: I think dishonesty negates all a person's other virtues in that it divorces a person from reality in principle (Locke & Woiceshyn, 1995). A complicating factor, however, is that people are not always consistent in their honesty or dishonesty.
6. Do the same traits produce wealth creation in all cultures? I would say yes, although there may be culture-specific traits as well.
7. Do prime movers and (lower-level) managers and differ in their traits only in degree, or are there more fundamental differences? I would predict big difference in degree on some traits (e.g. ability, ambition). In the case of vision, on the other hand, some managers may not have any at all.

One final issue requires discussion. One can readily observe that, despite their brilliant achievements, most wealth creators, especially the most successful, have not been and are not now admired for what they have done. Many have been and are passionately hated and not just by their less successful competitors. It is almost an axiom of wealth-making that the more one earns, the more enemies one makes. John D. Rockefeller, the first man ever to earn a billion dollars but who would never talk to the press, was one of the most reviled men of his time. His sin: total domination, through his own ability, of the oil market—which involved putting less competent competitors out of business, including one of his own brothers who refused to work with him (Collier & Horowitz, 1976). Once, when it was learned that Rockefeller had donated $100000 to the Congregationalist Church, the eminent Congregationalist, Rev. Washington Gladden said indignantly:

> Is this clean money? Can any man, can any institution, knowing its origins, touch it without being defiled? [This money was made] by methods as heartless, as cynically iniquitous as any that were employed by the Roman plunderers or robber barons of the Dark Ages. In the cool brutality with which properties are wrecked, securities destroyed, and people by the hundreds robbed of their little [savings, assets], all to build up the fortunes of the multi-millionaires, we have an appalling revelation of the kind of monster that a human being may become (Collier & Horowitz, 1976, p. 3).

This was said about the man who almost single-handedly developed the US oil industry and made the USA a world power in oil. One of the actions he was most hated for was getting rebates (quantity discounts) from the railroads that transported his oil—an intelligent business practice. (P.S. The Congregationalists kept the money!)

Cornelius Vanderbilt was criticized because, "There was in him nothing of that will to public service, which moved [people] . . . to sacrifice their energies and wealth to the attainment of an ideal [the ideal apparently being self-sacrifice]" (Smith, 1927, p. 41).

J.P. Morgan's reward for risking his fortune in order to save the US government from bankruptcy was a Congressional investigation (Allen, 1949)—for the sin of making a small profit as his reward. He was not treated any better when later he saved New York City from collapse. Morgan, by the way, helped turn the USA into the world's leading financial power. Andrew Carnegie was reviled after an ugly court battle with one of his partners revealed how much money he had made from being the low-cost steel producer.

Things have not changed much in this century. Michael Milken, the greatest financial genius since J.P. Morgan, was made the subject of a vicious government vendetta for the sin of making too much money and helping to restructure the US economy. The chief US prosecutor, in addition to greatly resenting Milken's fortune, was planning to run for public office (which he later did, successfully) and was well aware of the public relations value of attacking the rich. After being convinced that the government, despite having almost no case, was going to get him no matter what he did, Milken pleaded guilty to some technical violations (which had never been crimes), paid an enormous fine bearing no relationship to his alleged financial misdeeds, and was sentenced, in a behind-the-scenes betrayal, to 10 years in prison, of which he served two before being released (Fischel, 1995). He was also barred from the securities industry for life.

Bill Gates has been treated somewhat better, so far, but the more successful he has become, the more his competitors run to the government complaining of unfair competition. Gates is beginning to see the handwriting on the wall: "I've developed a new view that being successful is not a fun thing sometimes. There is just a phenomenon where people don't like a company as successful as ours" (Wallace & Erickson, 1992, p. 377).

What is the cause of this hatred of the great wealth creators? The conventional explanation has always been that they did not earn the money but got it through deceit, manipulation and theft (i.e. that they were robber barons). But this is only a rationalization. Even Gates's (better) competitors admit that he earned his market dominance (e.g. Wallace & Erickson, 1992, p. 381). Similarly, Milken earned his money; there was no credible evidence of any fraud on his part (Fischel, 1995). The same goes for many nineteenth-century industrialists.

The real reason for hatred of wealth creators is neither economic nor political but moral. Consider the following excerpt from an article in *Newsweek* (itself quoting novelist John Steinbeck), cited in Wallace and Erickson (1992, p. 401):

> The things we admire in men, kindness and generosity, openness, honesty, under-standing and feeling are the concomitants of failure in our system. And those traits we detest, sharpness, greed, acquisitiveness, meanness, egotism and self-interest are the traits of success. And while men admire the quality of the first they love the produce of the second.

Ignoring the false package-dealing (e.g. honesty and failure, meanness and success), consider the second part of the quote. Sharpness (i.e. intelligence), greed (i.e. the desire for money), and self-interest produce wealth, and yet we detest the people who produce it. Why? First, they are detested because they are competent and successful! Superficially, the motive for this hatred is envy, but Rand (1975) has identified the deepest reason: it is hatred of the good for being the good, hatred for values and value achievement as such.

Secondly, such men are hated because, regardless of their professed philoso-phies, they are egoistic. According to conventional morality, it is considered an axiom that egoism is immoral and that self-sacrifice (altruism) is moral; but Ayn Rand (1957/1992) has shown that just the opposite is true. The purpose of a moral code, that is, a code of values, is to enable men to live successfully on earth. The good is that which promotes man's life and the evil is that which negates it. "It is only the concept of 'Life' that makes the concept of 'Value' possible" (Rand, 1964, p. 17). Since the purpose of a moral code is to further man's life and since the ultimate standard of any code of moral values is life, it would be a contradic-tion to assert that morality entails self-sacrifice. Egoism asserts that each indi-vidual is an end in himself, not a means to the ends of others, and that he should be the beneficiary of his own actions. Egoism is the moral base of the concept of individual rights (Peikoff, 1991).

The concept of egoism, in itself, does not tell one how to act. To live successfully, one needs moral virtues. Since man's mind is his basic means of survival, reason must be his highest virtue. The other key virtues, e.g. independ-ence, honesty, productiveness, are derivatives of rationality. (For a discussion of why honesty is in the businessman's selfish interest, see Locke & Woiceshyn, 1995.)

Rather than being despised because they are egoists, business heroes should be revered for it (assuming they are rational egoists). It is their egos, along with their rational judgment, which make their achievements possible. Great wealth creators have not been evil. Rather they have been condemned by a wrong moral code. This tragic error was corrected in *Atlas Shrugged*. To quote from Galt's speech (Rand, 1957/1992, p. 967):

> I have called out on strike the kind of martyrs who had never deserted you before. I have given them the weapon they had lacked: the knowledge of their own moral value. I have taught them that the world is ours, whenever we choose to claim it, by virtue and grace of the fact that ours is the Morality of Life. They, the great victims who had produced all the wonders of humanity's brief summer, they, the industrialists, the conquerors of matter, had not discovered the nature of their right. They had known that theirs was the power. I taught them that theirs was the glory.

Acknowledgments

The author is indebted to Ken G. Smith for his helpful comments on this chapter and to Donna Montrezza for her outstanding editing.

REFERENCES

Allen, F.L. (1949). *The Great Pierpont Morgan.* New York: Harper & Row.
Ash, M.K. (1981a). *Mary Kay.* New York: Harper & Row.
Ash, M.K. (1981b). *Mary Kay on People Management.* New York: Warner.
Ash, M.K. (1995). *Mary Kay.* Rocklin, CA: Prima.
Binswanger, H. (1986). *Ayn Rand Lexicon.* New York: New American Library.
Collier, P. & Horowitz, D. (1976). *The Rockefellers.* New York: Holt, Rinehart & Winston.
Fischel, D. (1995). *Payback: The Conspiracy to Destroy Michael Milken and His Financial Revolution.* New York: Harper Collins.
Folsom, B.W. (1991). *The Myth of the Robber Barons.* Herndon, VA: YAF.
Gunderson, G. (1989). *The Wealth Creators.* New York: Dutton.
Hacker, L.M. (1968). *The World of Andrew Carnegie.* New York: J.B. Lippincott.
Hamilton, E. (1942). *The Greek Way.* New York: Mentor (New American Library).
Heiner, A.P. (1991). *Henry J. Kaiser: Western Colossus.* San Francisco, CA: Halo Books.
House, R.J., Spangler, D. & Woycke, J. (1991). Personality and charisma in the U.S. Presidency. *Administrative Science Quarterly*, **36**, 364–96.
Howard, A. & Bray, D. (1988). *Managerial Lives in Transition.* New York: Guilford.
Locke, J. (1986). *The Second Treatise on Civil Government.* Buffalo, NY: Prometheus Books. Originally published in 1690.
Locke, E.A. & Associates (1991). *The Essence of Leadership.* New York: Lexington (Macmillan).
Locke, E.A. & Woiceshyn, J. (1995). Why businessmen should be honest: the argument from rational egoism. *Journal of Organizational Behavior*, **16**, 405–14.
Manes, S. & Andrews, P. (1993). *Gates.* New York: Doubleday.
Mason, T. (1990). *Perot: An Unauthorized Biography.* Homewood, IL: Irwin.
Martin, A. (1991). *James J. Hill & the Opening of the Northwest.* St. Paul, MN: Minnesota Historical Society Press.
Morris, B. (1995). The wealth builders. *Fortune*, December 11, 80–94 (The unauthored article "A conversation with Roberto Goizueta and Jack Welch" which follows, pp. 96–102, is treated as part of this reference).

Peikoff, L. (1982). *The Ominous Parallels*. New York: Stein & Day.

Peikoff, L. (1991). *Objectivism: The Philosophy of Ayn Rand*. New York: Dutton.

Preston, R. (1991). *American Steel*. New York: Prentice Hall.

Rand, A. (1957). *Atlas Shrugged*. New York: Signet (New American Library; all quotations are from the 1992, Signet, 35th anniversary edition, 52nd [or later] printing).

Rand, A. (1964). *The Virtue of Selfishness*. New York: Signet.

Rand, A. (1967). Notes on the history of American free enterprise. In A. Rand (ed.), *Capitalism: The Unknown Ideal*. New York: Signet.

Rand, A. (1975). The age of envy. In A. Rand (ed.), *The Anti-industrial Revolution*. New York: Signet.

Rand, A. (1983). The money-making personality. *The Objectivist Forum*, **4**(1), 1–9.

Reilly, R. (1996). *Josiah Wedgwood*. London: Macmillan.

Smith, A.D.H. (1927). *Commodore Vanderbilt: an Epic of American Achievement*. New York: R.M. McBride.

Stavrou, M.A. (1993). Walter Elias Disney. Unpublished paper, College of Business & Management, University of Maryland, College Park, MD.

Tichy, N.M. & Sherman, S. (1993). *Control Your Destiny or Someone Else Will*. New York: Doubleday.

Wall, J.F. (1989). *Andrew Carnegie*. Pittsburgh: University of Pittsburgh Press.

Wallace, J. & Erickson, J. (1992). *Hard Drive*. New York: Wiley.

Walton, S. (1992). *Made in America*. New York: Doubleday.

Watson, T.J. Jr & Petre, P. (1990). *Father, Son & Co*. New York: Bantam.

Part II

Organizational Behavior Reaching beyond Traditional Boundaries

Chapter 6

A Strategic Perspective for Organizational Behavior

Randall S. Schuler
New York University, USA

In this chapter a presentation is made of a strategic perspective for organizational behavior (OB). This presentation is based upon the premise that the field can gain a greater understanding of the impact of traditional OB variables if put into a larger context, one that systematically incorporates a broad set of contextual variables with a broader set of outcome variables. Combining the traditional perspective of OB with the strategic perspective of OB may offer the field a greater ability to systematically incorporate more relevant variables and explain more variance in outcomes relevant to multiple stakeholders of organizations.

Central to the strategic perspective of OB are the strategic tasks that are common across organizations. Together, these tasks are the essence of organizations. Their character and detail for each organization result as a consequence of its contextual variables and its unique stakeholders. Together, these contextual variables and the unique stakeholders force a need for the organization to attend to its strategic tasks. The organization does this through its strategic tools. These tools are the variables of long-time interest to traditional OB researchers. When applied within the strategic perspective for OB, these variables become strategic tools.

The remainder of this chapter is devoted to presenting the strategic perspective for OB. It begins by discussing the multiple stakeholder perspective, one upon which the entire strategic perspective for OB rests. Next, the contextual variables and the strategic tasks of this perspective are discussed. Following this the strategic tools and their application to the strategic tasks and relevance to the strategic outcomes are described. The chapter concludes with a section on the implications of a strategic perspective for OB. Here implications for research in OB are presented along with a brief set of theoretically-based propositions.

Creating Tomorrow's Organizations. Edited by C.L. Cooper and S.E. Jackson.

A STRATEGIC PERSPECTIVE FOR OB

Multiple Stakeholder Perspective

As we move into the twenty-first century, organizations will increasingly confront realities and needs that result from attempting to satisfy a wide array of diverse and multiple stakeholders (Tsui, 1990). Stakeholders are the institutions and people who influence and are influenced by how well organizations are managed. They include the organization itself, stockholders and investors, customers, employees and society. This increasingly large and more diverse set of stakeholders is a major part of the realities and demands of the twenty-first century for many organizations. Because this group of stakeholders is growing so powerful, their concerns and their outcomes of most interest are becoming "organizational" outcomes and, given that attainment of these is the essence of organizational effectiveness, they are regarded as "strategic" outcomes. These strategic outcomes relevant to each stakeholder are shown in Table 6.1. When organizational success is defined as effectively serving stakeholders, their concerns define a firm's fundamental, and hence "strategic", outcomes around which business objectives are shaped and established and to which substantial resources are committed. Providing further character and specificity to these outcomes are the contextual variables.

Table 6.1   Stakeholders in the strategic perspective for OB

Stakeholders	Strategic outcomes
Customers	Quality service
	Quality products
	Speed and responsiveness
	Low cost
	Innovation
The organization	Productivity
	Profits
	Survival
Stockholders/investors	Shareholder return
	Return on sales
	Return on assets
	Return on investments
Employees	Fair treatment
	Satisfaction
	Empowerment
	Employability
	Safety and health
Society	Legal compliance
	Social responsibility
	Ethical management practices

Adapted from Schuler & Jackson (1996), with permission.

CONTEXTUAL VARIABLES

There are two major sets of contextual variables that play an important role in the strategic perspective for OB. The first encompasses the internal environment, the qualities and characteristics of the organization itself, referred to here as the "business strategy set". Each set impacts the other and together they help shape the specific qualities and characteristics of the organization's strategic outcomes.

Business Strategy

At risk of oversimplification of a rather complex area, business strategy variables address several areas of organization that impact the nature of the strategic tasks. These areas include: type of competitive strategy, values/assumptions/characteristics of top management, financial and output targets, product or service, location, and processes of production/delivery.

Competitive Strategy

Competitive strategies are important in the strategic perspective for OB because they impact behaviors needed from employees. Descriptions of competitive strategy by Porter (1980) and Schuler & Jackson (1987) suggest that the types of behaviors needed from employees differ with three types of strategies: cost reduction, quality enhancement and innovation (Treacey & Wiersema, 1995). Knowing these relationships is important, but it is also critical to add that getting each of these behaviors requires a different sets of OB tools or, in the terms of Schuler & Jackson (1987), different stimuli and reinforcers.

Values/Assumptions/Characteristics of Top Management

The decisions and directives of top management often determine what the organization does and how it is done. The values of top management are reflected in these decisions and directives. The assumptions that top managers make about the environment relevant to the organization and about the people in the organization (e.g. as characterized by Miles & Creed, 1995, as managerial philosophies) also play a significant role in what the organization does and how it manages its people. Other characteristics of top management that play a major role in a strategic perspective for OB include how top managers perceive and interpret the environment and the cause–effect relationships they assign to what they see (Jackson & Dutton, 1988).

Financial and Output Targets

The targets or goals established have an important role to play in the level of effectiveness at which the organization needs to operate. The higher the level, the more efficiently and effectively all the resources of the organization need to be utilized. This in turn necessitates that strategic tasks be done more effectively than ever. Although increasing either target requires greater effectiveness, it is likely that each has its unique impact and requirements in a strategic perspective for OB. From this perspective, greater output targets may imply that individuals have to be more productive, while greater financial targets may require that individuals, if not being more productive, may need to be willing to work for less compensation.

Product or Service

Whether the organization's business centers around producing a physical product or delivering an intangible service does matter in some respects (Schneider, Wheeler & Cox, 1992). Individual behavior may be more difficult to appraise if it occurs during the course of a brief 5-minute interchange between a customer and a service employee. How can the organization tell for sure if the employee was smiling, friendly and flexible with the customer? Who is able and willing to provide this information? Alternatively, an employee producing a welding machine can be appraised by judging the final output—its features, its reliability and its appearance—with minimal difficulty (Bowen, 1996). Of course, if teamwork and cooperation are important in making a welding machine, the appraisal process may become more complex.

Location

The location of the organization determines several aspects of the organizational context, particularly the national culture, labor market, unionization and the legal, social and political features (Schuler, Dowling & DeCieri, 1993). These all have their unique impact, as described in the section below on organizational context.

Processes of Production/Delivery

The method of production/delivery that is selected has always been a major decision for organizations. It has also had a major impact on the variables in a strategic perspective for OB. The methods of production/delivery can be variously described from assembly line to batch to craft or one-of-a-kind. These can influence the nature of the work processes, the nature of the design of jobs, whether work is organized around individuals or groups, and how units within the organization are differentiated and integrated (Woodward, 1965).

Organizational Context

This broader organizational context includes: industry characteristics; labor markets; legal, social and political conditions; technology; national culture; size; representation; and the extent of globalization.

Industry Characteristics

The term "industry" refers to a distinct group of productive or profit-making enterprises, such as manufacturing or services. Bowen & Schneider (1988) described three characteristics that distinguish the activities of services from manufacturing organizations. First, a service is generally intangible. Second, in services, the customer and employee usually collaborate in the service production-and-delivery process. Third, in services, production and consumption are usually simultaneous. Because customers play a central role in services, they can be thought of as partial employees, whose behavior *vis-à-vis* the organization needs to be managed (Bowen, 1986; Mills & Morris, 1986). Differences in the nature of manufacturing and services appear to have implications for selection, training, compensation, stress management, use of temporary workers and the development and maintenance of appropriate organizational climates and cultures (see Davis-Blake & Uzzi, 1993; Jackson & Schuler, 1995; Jackson, 1984; Terpstra & Rozell, 1993).

Labor Market Conditions

Labor market conditions can be characterized along several dimensions including unemployment levels, labor market structure and labor diversity. Unemployment levels and labor market structures have long been recognized as important macro-economic variables, whereas the importance of labor diversity has been recognized more recently.

Unemployment levels are relevant in a strategic perspective for OB because of their potential impact on employee motivation, selection and compensation. For example, the relationship between job satisfaction and employee turnover has been found to be moderated by the level of unemployment (Carsten & Spector, 1987). Labor market structures are also relevant in a strategic perspective for OB because they help shape the quality and quantity of the labor force available to organizations. An insufficient external labor market may stimulate an organization to create its own "internal" labor market, which in turn gives rise to such activities as training and internal promotion (Osterman, 1992). The more recent phenomenon of greater labor force diversity is a result and recognition of the increased number of individuals from distinct categories, including older workers, minority groups of various ethnic and religious backgrounds, and more occupational groups welcoming females in increasing numbers (Johnson & Packer, 1987). These characteristics of workforce diversity are critical in a strategic perspective for OB through their impact on the creation and use of work teams, individual motivation, selection, socialization and organizational culture (e.g. see Jackson & Whitney, 1995).

Legal, Social, and Political Environments

Within the USA, many aspects of strategic OB are affected by the legal and regulatory environment (Begin, 1991). In the process of attending to the legal environment, the field also responds to the social and political environments that give rise to and shape the promulgation, interpretation and enforcement of acts of Congress, executive orders and tax codes. As US corporations expand their operations abroad, however, they face additional legal concerns. For example, in European countries, organizations are obliged to set aside specific sums of money for formal training (Brewster & Hegewisch, 1994). In many European countries, employee welfare and unionization have greater legal and social support than they do in the USA.

Technology

Technology refers to a system's processes for transforming inputs into usable outputs. These processes can vary along many dimensions, including the degree of continuity in the production system (e.g. Woodward, 1965), the types and levels of knowledge required by the system (Hulin & Roznowski, 1985), the degree to which tasks are routinized and predictable (Perrow, 1967) and the linkages and interdependencies among tasks and people (Thompson, 1967). The impact of technology on the group dynamics within organizations has long been recognized (Burns & Stalker, 1961).

National Culture

The globalization of national economies and the evolution of multinational enterprises have resulted in increased awareness and documentation of the differences in how human resources are managed among countries (Brewster & Hegewisch, 1994; Towers Perrin, 1992). Because countries often have unique cultures (i.e. values, norms and customs) it is widely presumed that multinational enterprises must understand the culture(s) of the region(s) in which they operate in order to manage organizational behavior effectively (Hofstede, 1993).

In addition to national culture, industry and organizational cultures have also been shown to have an impact on organizational behavior. Research suggests that these various forms of culture can represent significant variables of constraint as well as opportunity on an organization's ability to gain competitive advantage and increase effectiveness (Chatman & Jehn, 1994; Denison & Mishra, 1995).

Size

Considerable evidence shows that organizational behavior varies systematically with organization size. Specifically, compared to smaller organizations, larger ones are more likely to (a) use more sophisticated staffing (Terpstra & Rozell, 1993) and training and development (Saari et al., 1988) procedures, and have more highly developed internal labor markets (Baron, Davis-Blake & Bielby, 1986; see also Ferris, Buckley & Allen, 1992); and (b) pay their employees more (Mellow, 1982), but also put more pay at risk through the use of bonuses and long-term incentives (Gerhart & Milkovich, 1990). Compared to larger organizations, smaller ones are more likely to have higher levels of employee satisfaction (Cummings & Berger, 1979; Kotter, 1995).

Representation

In the USA, employees represented by unions have received wages estimated to be up to 33% greater than those not represented by unions. Represented employees typically have better and safer working conditions. Formal representation offers the promise of fair treatment; establishes policies and procedures for handling wage and working condition grievances; provides for job security; and secures health and retirement benefits (Freeman & Medoff, 1984; Jackson, Schuler & Rivero, 1989; Kochan, Batt & Dyer, 1992; Youngblood, Trevino & Favio, 1992; Greenberg, 1990). In addition to helping represented employees, unions have probably motivated employers without represented employees to provide many of these same benefits (Foulkes, 1980).

Globalization

Faced with unprecedented levels of foreign competition at home and abroad, firms are beginning to recognize how important it is to find and nurture the human resources required to implement global strategies. As we move into the twenty-first century, more and more companies will see opportunities that can be seized only by adopting a global perspective, and the question of how best to staff and manage such organizations will become more pressing. Apparently, many companies underestimate the complexities involved in international operations, and poor management of human resources is responsible for many business failures in the international arena:

> The primary causes of failure in multinational ventures stem from a lack of understanding of the essential differences in managing human resources, at all levels, in foreign environments. Certain management philosophies and techniques have proven successful in the domestic environment: their application in a foreign environment too often leads to frustration, failure and underachievement. These "human" considerations are as important as the financial and marketing criteria upon which so many decisions to undertake multinational ventures depends (Huey, 1994).

All these contextual variables are central to a strategic perspective for OB because they all can shape and impact the strategic outcomes of OB, as shown in Figure 6.1. This influence of the contextual variables on the strategic outcomes is through the strategic tasks of organizations.

Strategic Tasks of Organizations

While organizations and their environments do vary in terms of their products/ services, location and many other dimensions, organizations have in common several strategic tasks, i.e. tasks that are essential in influencing the success of the organization as defined by the multiple stakeholders. Because of the extremely competitive and global environment of the twenty-first century, these tasks need to be performed more skillfully and effectively than ever. This can be facilitated by strategic OB. The six strategic tasks include: *cohesion, coordination, commitment, communication, competencies* and *consistency* (Beer, 1995).

Cohesion: Vision, Values, and Sense of Purpose

Vision and values give meaning and an overall sense of direction to where the organization is going. Equally important, they describe what means and processes are legitimate for attaining its overarching vision and goals (Zucker, 1987). In essence, a sense of purpose is attained through thoughtful and deliberate analysis of what the organization stands for and where it wants to go and why. Thus, as a result of the vision, values and sense of purpose, cohesion can exist among the individuals and units within and for the organization. Another result is an increased level of certainty and a diminished level of individual stress (Quick, 1992).

Coordination: Connection, Cooperation and Balance

In the attainment of the vision, values, direction and goals, organizations need to deploy and mobilize resources as efficiently and effectively as possible. Decisions need to be made as to how these resources are deployed and differentiated. Decisions then need to be made as to how these same resources are to be mobilized to work together to the advantage of the entire organization. This process of deployment and mobilization involves attaining the cooperation of the differentiated parts of the organization and seeking a balance in power and influence among them (Lawrence & Lorsch, 1967).

Commitment: Focus, Motivation and Energy

One of the important resources organizations need to involve in the success of the business strategy are the people. Maximizing the contributions from each individual and each group is critically important in an organization's ability to satisfy its multiple stakeholders at world class standards of performance. This means that everyone needs to be highly energized, motivated and focused on their essential roles and tasks in the organization. The vision and values of the organization can provide the focus. This set of vision and values, along with the appropriate reward structures, can also enhance employee motivation to help attain the strategic outcomes. Coupled with concern for the health and safety of individuals, the vision and values can provide the needed physical and mental energy for employees more effectively to attain the strategic outcomes (Lawler, Mohrman & Ledford, 1992).

Communication: Horizontal and Vertical Information Flows

Assisting in the first three strategic tasks are the flows of information and communication throughout the organization. For units that are spread across the organization and globe, horizontal communication is needed to mobilize and integrate their otherwise separate efforts (Davenport, 1993). Organizational learning takes place through this horizontal information flow (Slocum, McGill & Lei, 1994). Communication up and down in the organization is also necessary to ensure that the vision, values, purpose and direction are known and shared by all (Kotter, 1995).

Competencies: Skills, Abilities and Behaviors

For the organization to make maximum use of its human resources, individuals need to have the appropriate and necessary skills, abilities and behaviors. In the strategic perspective for OB, these skills, abilities and behaviors of the workforce are shaped initially by the characteristics of the business strategy. These characteristics manifest their influence through a variety of means, but especially through the shaping of the work processes, job design, customer demands and the nature of the competitive forces (Schneider & Bowen, 1995a,b).

As organizations prepare to enter the twenty-first century they are already witnessing a major shift in required competencies at both managerial and non-managerial levels (Bartlett & Ghoshal, 1992). The non-managerial employees increasingly will be hired for organizational roles rather than the traditional jobs. As a result, they are being expected to demonstrate competencies of flexibility, problem-solving, self-management and continuous learning. The managerial employees are being expected to shift from being managers to being leaders (Kotter, 1990).

Consistency: Alignment with Business Strategy and Strategic Tools

The sixth critical strategic task is the alignment of the business strategy characteristics with all the strategic tools. These tools, the essence of traditional organizational behavior, need to be carried out based upon analysis of the needs of the business, as determined by the characteristics of the business strategy, as set in the particular organizational context.

It is because of these six strategic tasks that we can form an integrative, strategic perspective for strategic organizational behavior. As illustrated in Figure 6.1, these six strategic tasks are the essence of, and are common to, all organizations. The characteristics of the business strategy and organizational context shape the nature and qualities of the six strategic tasks in each organization. The contextual variables and the stakeholders, together with the strategic tasks, give life and meaning to organizations and at the same time create a need

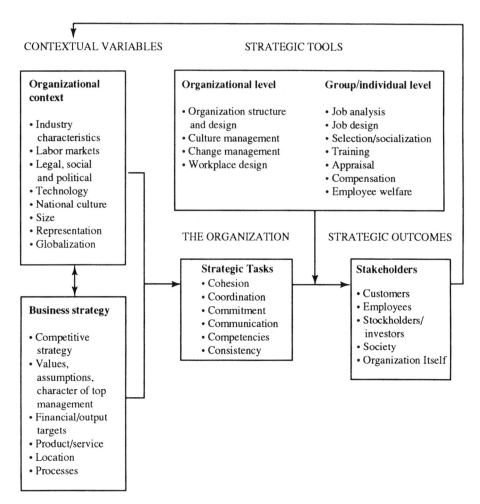

Figure 6.1   Integrative framework in the strategic perspective for OB

for action and implementation. The formulation and application of the strategic tools, shown in Figure 6.1, provide for this action and implementation in order to attain the strategic outcomes, i.e. the concerns of the stakeholders. These strategic tools are described below.

Strategic Outcomes

Completing this strategic and integrative framework of OB are the strategic outcomes, the purposes against which the success of the implementation of strategic tools is determined. Consistent with the earlier reference to the stakeholder model, strategic outcomes consist of those conditions relevant to a wide and perhaps diverse group of constituents—customers, employees, stock-holders/investors, society, partners, and the organization itself (Tsui, 1990).

STRATEGIC TOOLS

The strategic tools are those traditional OB practices and knowledge used to address the realities and needs of twenty-first century organizations as defined by the multiple stakeholders and shaped through the contextual variables. As strategic tools, OB practices and knowledge serve to successfully accomplish the strategic tasks of organization. Although all organizations face the six strategic tasks, each organization is unique. Consequently, its business strategy, organizational context and stakeholder concerns need to be systematically analyzed and characterized, because they create a set of requirements and needs for coordinated action and implementation across the strategic tools unique to each organization. Thus the business strategy, organizational context, and stakeholder concerns shape the implications for the strategic tools of organizational behavior. The implication here is that the traditional OB practices offer many alternatives to the researcher and practitioner in successfully accomplishing the strategic tasks of organizations. The strategic perspective of OB suggests that some of these alternatives may result in greater organizational effectiveness, i.e. the attainment of the strategic outcomes, than others. While this "contingency-like" thinking is not new to OB (e.g. contingency theory in organizational design, Lawrence & Lorsch, 1967; or path–goal theory in leadership, House, 1971), the argument for systematically coordinating across strategic tools to manage six strategic tasks in the service of multiple stakeholders is.

Organizational-Level Strategic Tools

As shown in Figure 6.1, these strategic tools are categorized by levels of analysis frequently used in OB: organizational and group/individual (Hellriegel, Slocum & Woodman, 1995). Included at the organizational level are the traditional OB practices and knowledge, including organization structure and design, culture management, change management, and workplace design. Perhaps newer to this set is workplace design. Workplace design includes decisions as to the nature of the work flow, the nature of the technology to be used, whether or not work is done by individuals or teams, and the nature of the relationships between the individuals or teams.

Group/Individual Strategic Tools

Included at the group/individual level of analysis are traditional OB practices and knowledge including: job design, socialization, training (learning), appraisal, compensation (reinforcement). Perhaps somewhat newer to this set are job analysis and selection. The inclusion of these newer variables, however, is entirely consistent with the realities and demands on organizations in the twenty-first century and the strategic perspective for OB. Employee welfare includes the traditional OB areas of stress, satisfaction and quality of work life.

Application of the Strategic Tools

To successfully accomplish the six strategic tasks of organizations, the strategic tools have to be applied in a diagnostic, systematic and coordinated manner. For the purposes of brief exposition, an example using one strategic task, *consistency*, is illustrated. By no means is even this one example meant to be exhaustive, neither is it meant to describe exactly how the other strategic tasks needs to be managed. Each is unique, consequently there is the need to be disgnostic and systematic in deciding how each strategic task is to be managed.

The strategic task of *consistency* calls for the alignment of all strategic tools with the business strategy as detailed in Figure 6.1. For illustrative purposes here, business strategy is based on a competitive strategy of innovation. For just this one part of the business strategy, the implications for the strategic tools are several. For example, job design may reflect characteristics of enrichment; job analysis will need to describe the job requirements and skills needed that emphasize risk-taking and uncertainty; selection will need to focus on selection tests that help predict one's propensity for risking-taking and the ability to perform under conditions of uncertainty; performance appraisal will need to have dimensions of performance that measure performance under risk and uncertainty; compensation will need to be contingent upon performance under risking-taking and uncertainty (and consequently may have long-term and short-term performance criteria); the structure and design of the organization will reflect greater openness and less formality; the management of the culture will also reflect informality, tolerance for risk-taking and error-making and the spirit of innovation; the management of change will reflect the importance of continual change and organizational learning; and workplace design will reflect open boundaries and the legitmacy of cross-functional teams and regular infusions of new employees with new ideas (Porter, 1985; Schuler & Jackson, 1987; Treacy & Wiersema, 1995).

This abbreviated version of one example using one strategic task hopefully begins to offer insight into the amount of diagnosis, systematic analysis and multiple-tool coordination required to successfully manage the several strategic tasks of organizations with a relatively complete set of strategic tools, in order to attain the strategic outcomes of the multiple stakeholders.

IMPLICATIONS OF A STRATEGIC PERSPECTIVE FOR OB

The strategic perspective for OB argues for considering the contextual variables of organizations and the concerns of multiple stakeholders when studying OB. A reason for proposing this perspective is the premise that this represents the reality of organizations in the twenty-first century. Given this, the strategic perspective for OB can explain more variance in the strategic outcomes of organizations. Another major premise for this framework is that organizational behavior is carried out differently in different organizations, and some of this difference is explained by an organization's unique contextual variables. These in turn give specificity to the generic strategic tasks of organizations. It is, then, through the strategic tools of OB that these strategic tasks can be managed to result in successful attainment of the strategic outcomes. Thus, the use of the strategic perspective for OB requires a systematic and contingent approach. The result of this conceptualization of strategic OB, as depicted in Figure 6.1, are several implications for the field of organizational behavior.

Multiple Levels of Analysis/Research

Looking at OB in this strategic context has several implications. First, it implies that discussions of traditional OB topics such as motivation should take place at multiple levels of analysis: one level is the traditional, more micro aspects of individuals and groups. The second is the broader macro level, with aspects such as organization structure and design. The third is the meso or middle level, the intersection of these macro and micro levels. This is largely consistent with House & Rousseau (1993) and others who have argued for the efficacy of studying organizational behavior across levels of analysis. Their meso argument has been that a great deal of organizational behavior can be understood better by analyses that are informed by micro and macro organizational behavior perspectives concurrently.

What is being proposed here for strategic OB continues this "meso perspective" by encouraging researchers to consider micro, meso and macro as three levels of analysis in their investigations. In other words, strategic tools are found at all three levels. The implications for action for an organization's business strategy, organizational context and strategic outcomes, shown in Figure 6.1, reflect the strategic tasks and the use of strategic tools at three rather than two levels of analyses.

Incorporation under Broader Constructs

Secondly, the strategic perspective implies that discussions of traditional OB tools should take place under broader constructs. Discussions of motivation may take place under a more general construct called "employee commitment", which includes focus and energy as well as motivation. For example, if the organization is pursuing a competitive strategy of quality, it needs to have individuals motivated to work cooperatively in teams to continually improve the process and product/service (Lawler, Mohrman & Ledford, 1992). If an organization is in a service industry, it needs to have the individuals motivated and focused on reacting to the customer (Schuler, 1996). In either scenario, because the environment is so intensely competitive, the individuals need to be highly energized to contribute 100% to the organization. Thus, with the use of broader constructs more variance in strategic outcomes might be explained.

Additional Constructs

A third implication of the strategic approach is that some topics should receive more extensive treatment in OB. For example, employee commitment is certainly an important aspect of individual/team performance, but is only half of the traditional equation explaining performance. Ability is the other half that is often treated, in OB, under career development and learning. Ability could be more extensively discussed under the construct of employee competencies. Using competencies invokes the consideration of employee behaviors. Thus, while employees need to have skills and abilities to perform the technical aspects of their jobs, increasingly individuals are also expected to perform organizational roles that require specific behaviors. For example, an employee may need to have the technical knowledge to take a customer's order to buy 1000 shares of stock, but increasing competition demands that this employee also be friendly, flexible and fast in this transaction (Schneider & Bowen, 1995a). The strategic perspective for OB encourages inclusion with these additional constructs to possibly help explain more variance in the strategic outcomes.

Utilization of Multiple Theoretical Frameworks

A fourth implication is that several theoretical frameworks can be used in studying the perspective of strategic OB. While the above discussion may suggest that a contingency theory framework is the main one being suggested, in fact it is quite the contrary. At this point, the use of multiple frameworks is likely to be more fruitful, both in encouraging more researchers to investigate strategic OB and in explaining more variance in the multiple outcomes that organizations of the twenty-first century need to reach. Borrowing from strategy, organizational theory and especially strategic human resource management (Barney, 1991; Wright, McMahan & McWilliams, 1994; Jackson & Schuler, 1995), there are several theoretical frameworks that can be used to generate testable propositions in a strategic perspective for OB.

Behavioral Theory

Strategic OB tools such as compensation, socialization and performance appraisal are an organization's primary means for sending information through the organization that can signal and support desired behaviors. These tools are effective when they communicate consistent expectations and evaluate performances in ways that are congruent with the system's behavioral requirements (e.g. see Frederickson, 1986). Schuler & Jackson (1987) developed a typology of human resource practices around Porter's competitive strategies, based on the assumption that these strategies have different behavioral requirements. Consequently, organizations need to examine their strategies and determine their implications for employee behaviors. Then compensation, socialization and appraisal practices can be selected. The practices identified included selection, performance appraisal, training and compensation, activities that are treated here as fundamental levers for strategic organizational behavior. Hypotheses for how variations in these practices relate to Porter's competitive strategies were based on behavioral theory, an application of reinforcement theory (Hellriegel, Slocum & Woodman, 1995). Using behavioral theory, strategic organization behavior can incorporate aspects of the business strategy with different variations of traditional OB topics such as compensation, socialization and appraisal.

Proposition 1: Organizations with different business strategy characteristics will utilize different strategic tools. For example, organizations that have a competitive strategy based on innovation will likely choose job design and compensation qualities that motivate and reward creative behaviors.

Institutional Theory

A behavioral theory perspective assumes individuals respond to stimuli and reinforcement in determining which behaviors to perform. Similarly, institutional theory views organizations as social entities that seek approval for their performances in socially constructed environments. Organizations conform to gain legitimacy and acceptance, which facilitate survival (Meyer & Rowan, 1977; Zucker, 1977). Because multiple constituencies control needed resources, legitimacy and acceptance are sought from the many stakeholders shown in Table 6.1.

Research on institutionalization (Zucker, 1987) focuses on pressures emanating from the internal and external environments. Internally, institutionalization arises out of formalized structures and processes, as well as informal or emergent group and organization processes. Forces in the external environment include those related to the state (e.g. laws and regulations), the professions (e.g. licensure and certification) and other organizations—especially those within the same industrial sector.

Proposition 2: The organizational context will have a significant impact on an organization's utilization of strategic tools. For example, organizations in the same legal, social and political environments will likely utilize many of the same strategic tools, whereas organizations in different legal, social and political environments will likely not utilize many of the same strategic tools.

Resource Dependence Theory

Like institutional theory, resource dependence theory focuses on the relationship between an organization and its constituencies. However, resource dependence theory emphasizes resource exchanges as the central feature of these relationships, rather than concerns about social acceptability and legitimacy (Pfeffer & Cohen, 1984). According to this perspective, groups and organizations gain power over each other by controlling valued resources. Consequently, change or alignment in strategic tasks based on an analysis of an organization's contextual variables, strategic tools and strategic outcomes may not occur.

> *Proposition 3*: Groups and organizations will not reflect an alignment of strategic tasks, contextual variables and strategic tools, despite its relevance for organizational stakeholders, if the process of alignment means reduced resources and therefore reduced power for some groups.

Human Capital Theory

In the economics literature, human capital refers to the productive capabilities of people (Becker, 1964). Competencies have economic value to an organization because they enable to be productive and adaptable; thus, people constitute the organization's human capital. In human capital theory, contextual variables such as labor market conditions, unions, business strategies and technology are important because they can affect the costs associated with alternative approaches to using strategic OB tools to increase the value of the organization's human capital and the value of the anticipated returns, such as productivity gains (e.g. see Russell, Colella & Bobko, 1993). Consequently, the nature of the contextual variables will impact the utilization of strategic tools.

> *Proposition 4*: Where external labor markets are full of highly competent and committed work applicants, organizations will be likely to utilize selection rather than training in their attempts to have a highly productive work force.

Transaction Cost Theory

Transaction cost economics assumes that business enterprises choose governance structures that economize transaction costs associated with establishing, monitoring, evaluating and enforcing agreed exchanges (Williamson, 1979, 1981). Predictions about the form of the governance structure an enterprise will use incorporate two behavioral assumptions: bounded rationality and opportunism. These assumptions mean that the central problem to be solved by organizations is how to design governance structures that take advantage of bounded rationality, while safeguarding against opportunism by individuals and groups. The interests of the organization as stakeholder will take on primary importance in studying the strategic perspective for OB using transaction cost theory.

> *Proposition 5*: Strategic OB tools, such as socialization and organizational structure and design, will be utilized to motivate and manage employees with minimum cost and maximum control to the organization.

Agency Theory

Agency theory focuses attention on the contracts between a party (i.e. the principal) who delegates work to another (i.e. the agent) (Jensen & Meckling, 1976). Agency relations are problematic to the degree that (a) the principal and agent have conflicting goals; and (b) it is difficult or expensive for the principal to monitor the agent's performance (Eisenhardt, 1989). Agency theory appears to be particularly useful for understanding executive and managerial compensation practices, which are viewed as a means for aligning the interests of the multiple stakeholders, e.g. owners of a firm (i.e. principals) with the managers in whom they vest control (i.e. agents). Recent efforts by companies to extend stock ownership to non-managerial workers can be interpreted as having the same motivation and impact.

> *Proposition 6*: Programs that enable managerial and non-managerial employees to become stockholders will be attempts to align the interests of the organization as stakeholder with those of the employees as stakeholder.

SUMMARY AND CONCLUSION

Organizations of the twenty-first century will be facing environments far more complex, global, competitive and volatile than ever before. We can expect these conditions to bring challenge and excitement to us in our study and understanding of organizational behavior. While our traditional approaches and tools in studying OB remain the cornerstones, they can be complemented by a strategic perspective for OB. This strategic perspective encourages the OB researcher to systematically incorporate a broader perspective in understanding how and why OB operates in organizations through combining the traditional perspective for OB with the strategic perspective for OB.

In this chapter we have presented the outline of a perspective that helps the researcher incorporate variables from the organization's external environment and characteristics of the organization's business strategy in our study of OB. The rationale for the inclusion of these variables and a description of their importance is through "strategic tasks" facing all organizations.

Because the realities of the twenty-first century demand more accountability and value of the organizations we study, the strategic perspective for OB offered here includes the strategic outcomes of concern to a multiple set of stakeholders. It is against the concerns of these multiple stakeholders that work in strategic OB will be evaluated. Testable research propositions are very much a part of the strategic perspective for OB. To facilitate the generation and examination of propositions, several theoretical frameworks were briefly described that can fit this strategic perspective for OB. A few examples of propositions derived from these perspectives were offered as possible starting points.

Without much doubt, doing research in strategic OB is likely to prove as demanding as is the task of making organizations effective in the twenty-first century. But for both academics studying organizational behavior and practitioners managing organizations, the new realities offer excitement and rewards to those who are successful.

In addition to the challenges arising from the realities and needs of multiple stakeholders, organizations will need to meet these challenges in an intensively competitive, global environment. Consequently, organizations will need to be managed more effectively than ever before (Hamel & Prahalad, 1994; Kanter, 1994). Strategic OB is about providing knowledge, insights and frameworks for managing organizations in these new realities as effectively as possible.

REFERENCES

Barney, J. (1991). Firm resources and sustained competitive advantage. *Journal of Management*, **17**, 99–120.

Baron, J.N., Davis-Blake, A. & Bielby, W. (1986). The structure of opportunity: how promotion ladders vary within and among organizations. *Administrative Science Quarterly*, **31**, 248–73.

Bartlett, C.A. & Ghoshal, S. (1992). What is a global manager? *Harvard Business Review*, **September–October**, 131.

Becker, G.S. (1964). *Human Capital*. New York: National Bureau of Economic Resources.

Beer, M. (1995). Personal conversation with author, October 7th, discussing his model of organizational behavior using many of these aspects of the strategic tasks.

Begin, J.P. (1991). *Strategic Employment Policy*. Englewood Cliffs, NJ: Prentice-Hall.

Bowen, D.E. (1986). Managing customers as human resources in service organizations. *Human Resource Management*, **25**, 371–83.

Bowen, D.E. (1996). Market-focused HRM in service organizations: satisfying internal and external customers. *Journal of Market-focused Management*, **January**.

Bowen, D.E. & Schneider, B. (1988). Services marketing and management: implications for organizational behavior. *Research in Organizational Behavior*, **10**, 43–80.

Brewster, C. & Hegewisch, A. (eds) (1994). *Policy and Practice in European Human Resource Management*. London: Routledge.

Burns, T. & Stalker, G. (1961). *The Management of Innovation*. London: Tavistock.

Carsten, J.M. & Spector, P.E. (1987). Unemployment, job satisfaction, and employee turnover: a meta-analytic test of the Muchinsky Model. *Journal of Applied Psychology*, **72**, 374–81.

Chatman, J.A. & Jehn, K.A. (1994) Assessing the relationship between industry characteristics and organizational culture: How different can they be? *Academy of Management Journal*, **37**, 522–53.

Cummings, L.L. & Berger, C. (1979). Organizational structure, attitudes and behaviors. In L.L. Cummings & B. Staw (eds), *Research in Organizational Behavior*, **1**, 169–208.

Davenport, T.H. (1993). *Process Innovation: Re-engineering Work Through Information Technology*. Boston, MA: Harvard Business School Press.

Davis-Blake, A. & Uzzi, B. (1993). Determinants of employment externalization: a study of temporary workers and independent contractors. *Administrative Science Quarterly*, **38**, 195–223.

Denison, D.R. & Mishra, A.K. (1995). Toward a theory of organizational culture and effectiveness. *Organization Science*, **6**, 204–23.

Eisenhardt, K.M. (1989). Agency theory: an assessment and review. *Academy of Management Review*, **14**, 57–74.

Ferris, G.R., Buckley, M.R. & Allen, G.M. (1992). Promotion systems in organizations. *Human Resource Planning*, **15**, 47–68.

Foulkes, F. (1980). *Personnel Practice in Non-union Firms*. Englewood Cliffs, NJ: Prentice-Hall.

Frederickson, N. (1986). Toward a broader conception of human intelligence. *American Psychological Review*, **41**, 445–52.

Freeman, R.B. & Medoff, J.L. (1984). *What Do Unions Do?* New York: Basic Books.

Gerhart, B. & Milkovich, G.T. (1990). Organizational differences in managerial compensation and financial performance. *Academy of Management Journal*, **33**, 663–91.

Greenberg, J. (1990). Looking fair vs. being fair: managing impressions of organizational justice. In B.M. Staw & L.L. Cummings (eds), *Research in Organizational Behavior*, vol. 12 (pp. 111–57). Greenwich: JAI Press.

Hamel, G. & Prahalad, C.K. (1994). *Competing for the Future*. Boston, MA: Harvard Business School Press.

Hellriegel, D., Slocum, J.W. Jr & Woodman, R. (1995). *Organizational Behavior*, 7th edn. St Paul: West Publishing.

Hofstede, G. (1993). Cultural constraints in management theories. *Academy of Management Executive*, **7**, 81–94.

House, R.J. (1971). A path–goal theory of leader effectiveness. *Administrative Science Quarterly*, **16**, 321–38.

House, R.J. & Rousseau, D. (1993). On the bifurcation of OB, or if it ain't Meso it ain't OB. Working paper, University of Pennsylvania.

Huey, J. (1994). The new post-heroic leadership. *Fortune*, **February 21**, 42–50.

Hulin, C.L. & Roznowski, M. (1985). Organizational technologies: effects on organizations' characteristics and individuals' responses. *Research in Organizational Behavior*, **7**, 39–85.

Jackson, S.E. (1984). Organizational practices for preventing burnout. In A.S. Sethi & R.S. Schuler (eds), *Handbook of Organizational Stress Coping Strategies* (pp. 89–111). Cambridge, MA: Ballinger.

Jackson, S.E. & Dutton, J.E. (1988). Discerning threats and opportunities. *Administrative Science Quarterly*, **33**, 370–87.

Jackson, S.E. & Schuler, R.S. (1995). Understanding human resource management in the context of organizations and their environments. *Annual Review of Psychology*, **46**, 237–64.

Jackson, S.E., Schuler, R.S. & Rivero, J.C. (1989). Organizational characteristics as predictors of personnel practices. *Personnel Psychology*, **42**, 123–57.

Jackson, S.E. & Whitney, K.E. (1995). Understanding the dynamics of diversity in decision-making teams. In R.A. Guzzo, E. Salas & Associates (eds), *Team Decision-making Effectiveness in Organizations* (pp. 204–61). San Francisco, CA: Jossey-Bass.

Jensen, M. & Meckling, W. (1976). Theory of the firm: managerial behavior, agency costs, and ownership structure. *Journal of Finance and Economics*, **3**, 305–60.

Johnston, W.B. & Packer, A.E. (1987). *Workforce 2000: Work and Workers For the 21st Century*. Washington, DC: US Department of Labor.

Kanter, R.M. (1994). Change in the global economy: an interview. *European Management Journal*, **March**, 1–9.

Kochan, T.A., Batt, R. & Dyer, L. (1992). International human resource studies: a framework for future research in research frontiers. In D. Lewin, O.S. Mitchell & P.D. Sherer (eds), *Industrial Relations and Human Resources* (pp. 147–67). Madison, WI: Industrial Relations Research Association.

Kotter, J.P. (1990). *A Force For Change*. New York: Free Press.

Kotter, J.P. (1995). Leading change: why transformation efforts fail. *Harvard Business Review*, **March–April**, 59–67.

Lawler, E.E. III, Mohrman, S.A. & Ledford, G.E. (1992). *Employee Involvement and*

Total Quality Management: Practices and Results in Fortune 1000 Companies. San Francisco, CA: Jossey-Bass.

Lawrence, P.R. & Lorsch, J.W. (1967). Differentiation and integration in complex organizations. *Administrative Science Quarterly*, **12**, 1–47.

Mellow, W. (1982). Employer size and wages. *Review of Economic Statistics*, **64**, 495–501.

Meyer, J.W. & Rowan, B. (1977). Institutionalized organizations: formal structure as myth and ceremony. *American Journal of Sociology*, **83**, 340–63.

Miles, R.E. & Creed, W.E.D. (1995). Organizational forms and managerial philosophies: a description and analytical review. *Research in Organizational Behavior*, **17**, 222–72.

Mills, P.K. & Morris, J.H. (1986). Clients as "partial" employees of service organizations: role development in client participation. *Academy of Management Review*, **11**, 726–35.

Osterman, P.O. (1992). Internal labor markets in a changing environment: models and evidence. In D. Lewin, O.S. Mitchell & P.D. Sherer (eds), *Research Frontiers in Industrial Relations and Human Resources* (pp. 273–308). Madison, WI: Industrial Relations Research Association.

Perrow, C. (1967). A framework for the comparative analysis of organizations. *American Sociological Review*, **32**, 194–208.

Pfeffer, J. & Cohen, Y. (1984). Determinants of internal labor markets in organizations. *Administrative Science Quarterly*, **29**, 550–72.

Porter, M.E. (1980). *Competitive Strategy: Techniques for Analyzing Industries and Competitors*. New York: Free Press.

Porter, M.E. (1985). *Competitive Advantage: Creating and Sustaining Superior Performance*. New York: Free Press.

Quick, J.C. (1992). Crafting an organizational culture: Herb's hand at Southwest Airlines. *Organizational Dynamics*, **Autumn**, 45–56.

Russell, C.J., Colella, A. & Bobko, P. (1993). Expanding the context of utility: the strategic impact of personnel selection. *Personnel Psychology*, **46**, 781–801.

Saari, L.M., Johnson, T.R., McLaughlin, S.D. & Zimmerle, D.M. (1988). A survey of management training and education practices in US companies. *Personnel Psychology*, **41**, 731–43.

Schneider, B., Wheeler, J.K. & Cox, J.F. (1992). A passion for service: using content analysis to explicate service climate themes. *Journal of Applied Psychology*, **77**, 705–16.

Schneider, B. & Bowen, D.E. (1995a). *Winning the Service Game*. Boston, MA: Harvard Business School Press.

Schneider, B. & Bowen, D.E. (1995b). The service organization: human resources management is crucial. *Organizational Dynamics*, **Fall**, 39–52.

Schuler, R.S. (1996). Market-focused management: human resource management implications. *Journal of Market-focused Management*, **1**, 13–29.

Schuler, R.S. & Jackson, S.E. (1996). *Human Resource Management: Positioning for the Twenty-first Century*, 6th edn. St Paul: West Publishing Co., p. 8.

Schuler, R.S. & Jackson, S.E. (1987). Linking competitive strategy and human resource management practices. *Academy of Management Executive*, **3**, 207-19.

Schuler, R.S., Dowling, P. & De Cieri, H. (1993). An integrative framework of strategic international human resource management. *International Journal of Human Resource Management*, **December**, 717–64.

Slocum, J.W. Jr, McGill, M. & Lei, D.T. (1994). The new learning strategy: anytime, anything, anywhere. *Organizational Dynamics*, **Autumn**, 33–48.

Terpstra, D.E. & Rozell, E.J. (1993). The relationship of staffing practices to organizational level measures of performance. *Personnel Psychology*, **46**, 27–48.

Thompson, J.D. (1967). *Organizations in Action*. New York: McGraw-Hill.

Towers Perrin (1992). *Priorities for Competitive Advantage*. New York: Towers Perrin.

Treacy, M. & Wiersema, F. (1995). *The Discipline of Market Leaders: Choose Your Customers, Narrow Your Focus, Dominate Your Market*. New York: Addison-Wesley.

Tsui, A.S. (1990). A multiple-constituency model of effectiveness: an empirical examination at the human resource subunit level. *Administrative Science Quarterly*, **35**, 458–83.

Williamson, O.E. (1979). Transaction-cost economics: the governance of contractual relations. *Journal of Law and Economics*, **22**(2), 233–61.

Williamson, O.E. (1981). The modern corporation: origins, evolution, attributes. *Journal of Economic Literature*, **19**, 1537–68.

Woodward, J. (1965). *Industrial Organization: Theory and Practice*. London: Oxford University Press.

Wright, P.M., McMahan, G.C. & McWilliams, A. (1994). Human resources and sustained competitive advantage: a resource-based perspective. *International Journal of Human Resource Management*, **5**(2), 299–324.

Youngblood, S.A., Trevino, L.K. & Favio, M. (1992). Reactions to unjust dismissal and third-party dispute resolution: a justice framework. *Employee Responsibilities and Rights Journal*, **5**(4), 283–307.

Zucker, L.G. (1977). The role of institutionalization in cultural persistence. *American Sociological Review*, **42**, 726–43.

Zucker, L.G. (1987). Institutional theories of organization. *Annual Review of Sociology*, **13**, 443–64.

Chapter 7

What is an Organization? Who are the Members?

Anat Rafaeli
Hebrew University of Jerusalem, Israel

An implicit assumption embedded in essentially all writing about organizations is that there exists something that can be called "an organization". By implication, the assumption is that this organization has members, who can be distinguished from non-members. This assumption is evident, for example when a distinction is drawn between an organization and it's environment. To illustrate, Lawrence & Lorsch's (1967) classic analysis of the interplay between organizations and their environments posited that organizations are open systems, with a free flow of various resources across organizational boundaries. The implication is that a clear distinction exists between what is inside and outside an organization. In this vein, Jones, Moore & Snyder (1988) use the label *Inside Organizations* for a collection of essays that talk about symbolic behavior in organizations.

In other words, an implicit assumption in organizational studies is of some kind of a boundary between an organization and its environment, so that individuals can either be within this boundary, in which case they are assumed to be members of the organization, or outside of the boundary, which makes them non-members. Working on the boundary itself are individuals who, as Tushman (1977) explains, perform "boundary-spanning roles" (see also Adams, 1976; Friedman & Podolny, 1992):

> Special boundary roles evolve in the organization's communication network to fulfill the essential function of linking the organization's internal network to external sources of information (Tushman, 1977, p. 587).

But when we talk about an organization, or about organizational members, who are we really talking about? How can we define or identify organizational membership? Can we easily distinguish members from non-members? These are

Creating Tomorrow's Organizations. Edited by C.L. Cooper and S.E. Jackson.

the questions that this essay raises, and begins to address. I begin by outlining and illustrating the complexity of the question. Next I review some provisional answers, which I believe are apparent in the organizational studies literature. What will become obvious from this review is that membership is abstract, with multiple, sometimes overlapping, but at other times competing dimensions. Building on this complexity, in the final part of the essay I suggest some implications for research of organizational behavior.

THE QUESTION

A dictionary entry of the term "organization" provides three different definitions: (a) the act or process of organizing or being organized; (b) the condition or manner of being organized; (c) an administrative and functional structure, or the personnel of such a structure (*Webster's Seventh New Collegiate Dictionary*, 1971). These multiple definitions begin to capture the wealth of ways in which the construct can be defined and interpreted. At least the first two definitions do not connote an inherent beginning and end, or distinct boundaries. The idea of "a structure" embedded in the third definition is the only one that connotes inherent boundaries.

From a research perspective these three definitions only begin to scrape the surface of the questions addressed here: "What is an organization?" and, more specifically, "who are its members?" That organizations hold an administrative and functional structure is not new to organizational scholars. But how can one identify "the members of this structure"? Are these only the people physically in the structure? But then what about customers, vendors or patients? And what about sales representatives, recruiters, labor negotiators or telecommuters who are not physically in a plant? An alternative definition of membership may be people paid by the organization. But then what about suppliers or vendors? And what about volunteers: are they really not members?

In the study of organizational behavior the term "organization" is typically defined as "a structured social system consisting of groups and individuals working together to meet some agreed-on objectives" (Greenberg & Baron, 1995, p. 11). This definition highlights the fact that organizations comprise multiple parts and people, which need to be integrated into larger, interconnected wholes. Still unspecified, however, is how the whole is divided into parts, or how the (human) elements are identified as belonging to the whole. In an attempt to address this question, we may turn to the concept of "a member", which is defined in *Webster's Seventh New Collegiate Dictionary* (1971) as either (a) "one of the individuals composing a group", or (b) "a constituent part of a whole".[1]

Interestingly, these definitions view membership as defined by the collective

---

[1] The Webster's definition includes other possibilities, such as "a body part or organ" or "one of the elements of a mathematical set" but these were not thought to be relevant to this essay.

with which the individual is associated. Obviously, this does not help solve the current dilemma since it creates a tautology—membership is defined by the group in which one is a member. Moreover, as role theory showed, individuals belong to multiple groups and collectives, allowing for multiple memberships of the same individual (Katz & Kahn, 1973). When does individual membership move from one group to another? How is the salience of membership navigated by individuals and organizations? In other words, the notion of a "boundary" between one group and another is challenged by the fact that the same individual can be a member of the two groups.

What does this mean to organizational life or organizational theory? Consider your local grocery store. Cashiers and other employees working in the store are obviously members of the store organization. But what happens when they physically leave the store, either to go home, or on store business? Do they remain members in both cases? To a similar extent? What if they take a leave of absence or if they are on sick leave? What if they retire or take a different job? What if they go on strike, and walk a picket line outside the store? Are they still members? Are they ever relieved of this membership? And what if they are retained by a temporary employment agency, as opposed to by the store itself: at some level such temporary employees are assumed to be members of the temporary agency, but does that make them non-members of the store? If we transfer this example from a grocery store to a software development firm, a law firm, or a bio-technology new venture, these questions become even more complex.

As noted by Pfeffer & Baron (1988), variations in the temporal and administrative relationships between employers and employees are increasingly popular. Yet, at some level, a temporary employee working full-time in a store may be more strongly associated with the store than a permanent employee working only two days a week. Of some conceptual help here is the literature on group membership. Arrow & McGrath (1995), for example, distinguish between "standing" and "acting" group membership, suggesting that group membership may comprise people who are not physically active on a particular component of the group task, yet are viewed by themselves or others as members of the group. Similarly, organizational membership may comprise various shades, depending on particular aspects of the relationship between the member and other members.

The dilemma regarding membership is even more complicated when organizational constituents who are not employees are considered. To illustrate, consider the customers of the store. They may not be paid by the store, but they do pay money to the store, and they are physically present and active in the store. From a contractual perspective, they may also be viewed as members, in that they are active contributors to the store's production process. In many cases customers perform physical work essential for store performance by taking items off shelves, putting them into carts, or pushing the carts around. Without these activities, the store would not survive.

Even without physical activity, only customers' behavior drives store operations. It is a customer call to L. L. Bean that sets the phone order operation going, and only a patient's coming to the hospital justifies the existence of the hospital. If the assumption is that members are defined by the production of a common goal, obviously both employees and clients or customers need to be included as members. Popular slogans, such as Burger King's "We Do It YOUR Way" or Mary Kay's "The Customer is Our Inspiration" suggest not only that customers are members, but that they are valued and important members. In this vein, Bowen (1986, p. 371) wrote about "Managing Customers as Human Resources", and Mills & Morris (1986, p. 726) refer to "Clients as Partial Employees of Service Organizations". These scholars suggest that management of members should not be limited to salaried employees, but should include customers.

What about the suppliers to this store? Suppliers are paid by the store to bring products into the store facility. Employees hired by suppliers often work within the aisles of the store, unpacking merchandise, pricing or shelving; others interact directly with customers, while serving product samples or promoting sales. Are these individuals "members" of the organization? Are they more or less "members" than a customer or a former employee? Similarly, what about employees of an advertising agency retained to develop a promotion campaign for, or to monitor the service delivery of the store. These people are likely to spend some time in the store, observing customers and learning about the object they need to promote, acting as "mystery shoppers", or running focus groups. Are these individuals not at all "members" of the said organization?

In short, a random person strolling into this grocery store will have a difficult time discerning the different "members" suggested above. While instinctively many random observers, and perhaps even organizational scholars, might refer only to employees as "members", the complexity of the issue of membership should not be overlooked. Modern organizations comprise diverse types of relationships with different individuals. The concept of "membership" is not as easily or clearly articulated as may appear at first, and may be construed in different ways. Theories in organizational behavior may embrace assumptions about particular membership relations. These assumptions should be both stated and examined.

The goal of this chapter is to take a closer look at the construct of organizational membership. The initial assertion is that this construct should be conceptualized as a variable, which means that membership is a matter of degree. Individuals can be members to a greater or a lesser degree, depending on the particular perspective or the particular framework one adopts. A second assertion, therefore, is that there are different ways in which memberships can be defined. Moving between definitions may change the extent of membership of the same individual. The assumption embedded in much of the organizational literature—that membership is a dichotomy typified by "all or none" qualities— is therefore simplistic because it overlooks the variety of ways in which membership can be defined, and the range of values that each definition can comprise.

In the following pages I offer a summary of various ways in which membership has been implied or assumed by organizational students and scholars. What will

become obvious from this review is both that there are multiple ways of constru-
ing membership, and that each of these constructions implies a range of values
rather than a dichotomy.

SOME POSSIBLE ANSWERS

A scanning of research in and of organizational behaviors reveals that different
studies adopt different implicit assumptions about organizational membership.
Scholars do not state the perspective they take because they consider it to be
obvious; yet different perspectives are conceptually and operationally distinct.
The only assumption common to all perspectives is that organizations and memberships are patterns of relationships. Perspectives differ in how these relationships are defined: according to physical or temporal interactions, legal or
psychological contracts, participation in a common production process, or sharing cultural norms and values.

Organizations and Membership as Physical
or Temporal Relationships

To most people the concept of "organization" and the question "what is an
organization" connotes some physical and geographical boundaries. Students
probed about "What is IBM?" refer to the company headquarters or the various
company offices around the world, and the people who work either in headquarters or in the one of the other offices. The underlying (and typically unstated)
idea here is that membership in an organization is defined by physically being
together, seeing and interacting with each other. Thus, Oldham, Cummings &
Zhou (1995, p. 1) write about *The Spatial Configuration of Organizations*, and
Gagliardi (1990) discusses corporate architecture as a representation of the corporate culture. Pfeffer (1982, p. 260) explicitly notes:

> Organizations are, in many instances, physical entities. They have offices, buildings,
> factories, furniture, and some degree of physical dispersion or concentration.

By implication, if organizations are physical structures, then organizational
members are the people operating within these structures. Interestingly, however, research in marketing has also examined the implications of open space and
other variants of physical arrangements on customer behavior (cf. Bitner, 1992;
Everett, Pieters & Titus, 1994). Since customers spend time inside organizational
structures, they should also be viewed as "members". Furthermore, as noted
above, a large and growing number of formal employees do not operate within
the physical organizational structure: sales people, recruiters, labor negotiators,
service technicians or public relations officers. As noted by Pfeffer & Baron
(1988, p. 257), "workers may be only weakly connected to the organization in

terms of physical location". With the advent of information technology, member-ship can be established and maintained through various electronic media: organi-zational duties can be performed from a home, a remote cottage, or a self-maintained office (cf. Rheingold, 1994; Shamir & Solomon, 1985).

According to the simple physical definition of membership, such production arrangements would not be considered organizations, and participants may not be considered members. A variety of scholars echo Rheingold's (1994, p. 34) assertion that computerized technologies build a new kind of place, generating "virtual" rather than physical communities. One implication is that the extensive organizational literature on traditional concepts such as job satisfaction, job involvement, organizational commitment, or even job enrichment needs to be re-examined under the non-physical definition of membership (Simons, 1994).

In a similar vein, it appears difficult if not impossible to define membership in organizations that operate in nature. Arnould & Price (1993), for example, studied river rafters as service provides, and Cohen (1989) studied trekkers in Thailand. Both reported distinct organizational patterns. Similarly, Marks & Mirvis (1981) describe environmental influences on the performance of members of a baseball team that within one season traveled to 60 different locations, in addition to playing 49 home games. These groups operated in a physical context that is either variant (in the case of baseball teams) or non-existent (in the case of trekkers and river rafters). Yet there appears to be consensus that they are organizational members. Is it the case that the individuals employed in these settings do not belong to an organization? How should their membership be defined?

A related issue is the distance between an organization's physical location and an employee's residence. Formally, employees may be members no matter where they live. But employees living further away from the organization's physical core will by necessity be more constrained in their relationship to the organization. They are less likely to come to work at odd hours (evening or weekends), they may be more constrained to formal working hours due to commuting or carpool arrangements, and they may be less committed to the organization because of these constraints (cf. Koslowsky, Kluger & Reich, 1995). One plausible implication is that long commutes decrease the degree of membership in the organization.

A focus on interaction, rather than physical location of employment, as the core issue of membership does not alleviate the dilemma. Studies of service employees reveal, for example, that most interactions are with customers rather than with managers or co-workers (cf. Rafaeli, 1989a; Mars & Nicod, 1984). A typical service person spends most of his/her time in interaction with clients, rather than with managers or co-workers. Similarly, teachers and doctors spend far more of their time with students and patients, respectively.

Another group whose membership remains unclear are volunteers. Volun-teers often operate within the physical boundary of the organization but are somehow assumed to be different from employees. Some authors automatically assume them to be non-members. Perhaps a more appropriate conception is that they are members "to a lesser degree?" Cheng (1996), for example, describes how volunteers in a civilian auxiliary Civil Air Patrol unit view themselves as members of the United States Air Force.

In short, a physical definition of membership leaves a lot of open questions. Some alternative conceptions that may help resolve these questions are considered next.

Organizations and Membership as Contractual Relationships

A second conception that can be labeled "classic" assumes that financial obligations and responsibilities define organizational membership. From a financial perspective, a firm is a "nexus of a set of contracting relationships among individuals" (Jensen & Meckling, 1976, p. 311). In this perspective, members are individuals paid by the organization for their participation in organizational activities. Hence, in addition to employees, vendors, suppliers and contractors can also be argued to be members.

It has also been argued that the psychological contract between employers and employees is a more apt (or at least an alternative) explanatory mechanism of membership than the financial or legal contract (Rousseau & Parks, 1993). However, psychological contracts are based on psychological attachment, which can exist among many parties, not just employees and employers, and can range in strength, suggesting varying degrees of membership. Both sets of contractual relations therefore leave open questions about the relative membership status of various groups.

First, employees who have retired, taken a sabbatical, maternity leave or other form of paid leave of absence, should also be considered members of the firm, since there typically is some form of contractual relationship between them. Both financial obligations and psychological attachment connect these people to their organization. Similarly, customers, who have obvious, although highly variant, contracts with the firm, should also be considered organizational members. At some level the contracts with customers are as important as, if not more important than, the contracts with employees. Similarly, employees of vendors, suppliers and contractors are also financially and psychologically committed to the firm. Are they not members?

On the other hand, individuals being interviewed for employment, who have not yet established formal contractual relations, are contractually non-members. Yet, there are reports that individuals feel an affinity to a firm in which they applied for employment (Baumeister & Leary, 1995; Rafaeli, 1996). Furthermore, Shanteau & Harrison (1991) eloquently illustrated that individuals tend to remain committed to an employment course of action even if they are not constrained by a formal contract, and have more lucrative offers elsewhere. In this study, subjects viewed an initial interaction with an organization as a more important source of bonding than either a formal contract or financial incentives.

Similarly, alumni of many colleges and universities typically view themselves as continuing to be a part of the institution long after they graduate. To some extent this construction of partial membership of alumni is reinforced by fund-raising offices seeking to encourage financial support. Notwithstanding, there are no contractual relationships that bond alumni to the college and university. The interesting question that emerges is, therefore, are alumni not members? Alternatively, perhaps alumni are merely members in a different way than current students or faculty.

In a similar vein, volunteers who are not paid and hold no financial or other commitment to an organization, should not be construed as members. Yet it is obvious that they feel some level of commitment, and descriptions exist of how the level of loyalty of volunteers exceeds that of paid employees (see Deci, 1980). Available analyses of psychological contracts do not take such relations into account. In short, the definition of membership according to contractual relationships embodies an inherent assumption of a dichotomy, according to which a contract either exists or does not. Yet obviously, psychological contracts and the various forms of attachment described above cannot be viewed as dichotomous.

Organization and Membership as Hierarchical Relationships

A third perspective on membership is based on the traditional bureaucratic model, which views the hierarchy as the key to building and governing organizations and to designating relationships among members. Building on Weber's (1947) work, Schein (1980, p. 11) for example, notes that "organizations coordinate their various functions through some kind of hierarchy or authority", and Leflaive (1996, p. 17) explicitly defines and discusses organizations as "Structures of Domination". In this perspective, organizations are enacted by hierarchical authority relations mandated by senior managers. Membership is established by accepting employment in a firm, and is defined by appearance on the same hierarchical organizational chart. Individuals without a designated place on the organizational chart should therefore not be viewed as members.

Several problems emerge with this conceptualization. First, as noted by Pfeffer & Baron (1988, p. 257) "employers are increasingly externalizing a buffer against a core or permanent work force". Externalization involves relying on various alternatives to the traditional employee–employer arrangements. A typical version of externalizing is relying on other firms that will do a part of the organization's tasks. Special firms can act as a mediator between the organization and the task by performing various functions such as recruiting, selection or training. Thus, individuals performing tasks in one organization may be hired, selected, trained and retained by another organization. To illustrate, data entry tasks for many insurance companies is done by individuals recruited, screened and trained by data entry contractors.

This process of externalization yields a confusion regarding hierarchically controlled members. The work performed by "externalized" employees is often for one master, who is not hierarchically superior to the employee. Performance can be monitored by technology, or by people who are not members of the hierarchy (e.g. customers, vendors, consultants). The former notion of organizational hierarchy is peripheral. Membership may alternatively be defined according to decision jurisdiction regarding salary, bonuses, promotion or retention, but different combinations of these functions are plausible: an individual may be retained by one firm, paid by another and evaluated by a third. In which firm is he or she a member?

In this vein, large corporations, with various companies (such as Johnson & Johnson, see Anonymous, 1993) have recently introduced a concept of "Shared Services Recruiting" according to which service functions such as payroll, recruiting or selection are performed by one central operation for various otherwise distinct production facilities. From an administrative and hierarchical perspective, members of the shared service operation are not subordinate to the same hierarchy as members of the other parts of the company. In a sense, they may be viewed as members in a totally different organization. Alternatively, their membership in the production facility could be argued to be "of a lesser degree" than that of core employees of the facility.

A second problem regarding a hierarchical definition of membership emerges with respect to members of professional or occupational groups employed in organizations. One defining attribute of a profession is a formally accepted code, which acts as a superior standard and governs behavior (Abbott, 1988; Trice, 1993). When professionals are employed by organizations not headed by others of their own profession, however, they may be hierarchically subordinate to members of the organization but professionally subordinate to the professional code of conduct. This is clearly the case with doctors, lawyers, psychologists and accountants employed by a wide range of organizations. These people are likely to sense membership with their professional association just as much, if not more than, with the organization that pays their salary. Gouldner (1957) noted that the membership of such professionals may be more "cosmopolitan" (or loyal to the profession) than "local" (or loyal to the organization). Again, the implication is that membership varies among different organizational members.

A third problem is that similar hierarchical relations may imply varying psychological attachment among members of the same organization. Rousseau & Parks (1993) argue that employees can perceive employment relationships to be more or less transactional or relational. Transactional relationships are argued to be more economic, extrinsic, static and narrow than relational relationships. By extension, transactional employment contracts appear to imply a more limited form of membership than relational contracts. Hence, defining membership as a function of hierarchical relations overlooks the psychological dynamics that can strengthen or weaken membership.

The situation is even more complicated if the distinction between different types of relationship that organizational leaders can form with their followers is considered. In an extensive and impressive research stream on transformational leadership (Avolio & Bass, 1988; Bass & Avolio, 1995) leadership has been argued to be an influence process that goes beyond transactions based on hierarchical relations. What is material here is that transformational leaders are asserted to change the nature of the relations between individuals and organizations. Administrative, hierarchical definitions of the organization are therefore only a point of departure for member definition: some people are likely to become *members to greater degree* by virtue of leader behavior.

In short, observing membership as a product of administrative, hierarchical relations reveals complications, in that people who appear to be equal (because they are formally employed by the same organization) may be very different in terms of their membership in the organization.

Organization and Membership as a Production Relationship

A fourth, manufacturing or production perspective views organizations as entities that produce particular goods. Defining membership as participation in the process of producing the goods is, however, deceivingly simplistic. A first problem with this perspective is again posed by the growing segment of service delivery, and the role of customers in this industry. This is because two unique aspects of service production are that "services are produced while they are consumed", and that "customers participate in the production process" (Bowen & Schneider, 1988; Chase & Erickson, 1988).

In manufacturing settings, customer considerations are also increasingly considered fundamental to organizational design and process. To illustrate, Lele (1986) talked about the influence of service on product strategy, bringing to bear the idea that the separation between production and customer contact hampers production processes. Hence, customers are participants in a production process as well.

Furthermore, modern production processes are based on a composition of several components (which are typically produced by sub-contractors); the composite is the organization's final product. In this production strategy, who are the individual members? Are employees of a sub-contractor not "members" of the organization that puts its name on the final product?

Organization and Membership as a Cultural Relationship

Students of organizational socialization and organizational culture might suggest that membership can best be defined according to common experiences shared by organizational members, and the norms of behavior that emerge from these experiences: Building on Morgan (1986), it may be that from an organizational behavior perspective, organizations should be construed as cultures that serve to shape the social reality of their members. This would be consistent with assertions that leadership in and of organizations can be viewed as the management of meaning (Smirchich & Morgan, 1982) or the management of ambiguity (Pfeffer, 1977). In part, that membership is so abstract, may be an explanation for the intriguing assertion made by Meindel, Ehrlich & Dukerich (1985) that organizational leadership is only a romantic attribution, rather than an objective reality.

This is a very attractive perspective for organizational behavior scholars who believe in the importance of a healthy and stimulating organizational culture. However, such a definition does not alleviate the problem. Many of the problems mentioned above apply here as well. More importantly, this perspective is limited in that the core defining concept of culture is itself unclear: there is no consensus about what culture means (Gordon, 1991; Smirchich, 1983). Hence, the perspective that a shared culture defines organizations and their members uses an ambiguous and ill-defined term for the definition of another ambiguous and ill-defined term.

Furthermore, as Gordon (1991) states, organizations in a similar industry tend to share cultural forms and attributes. Individuals employed in similar industries are therefore suggested by this perspective to be members of the same organization. The broad foundations of institutional theory (Dimaggio & Powell, 1983) would suggest that individuals employed in the same industry or institution are likely to share socialization practices and cultural norms, yielding shared membership. Hence, the distinction between employees or individual members of different organizations in the same organizational field are not obtained by this perspective. To illustrate, the values of a car sales person or a nurse typically do not reveal the particular agency or hospital in which he/she works. But does that mean that the distinction between membership in the two agencies or hospitals is immaterial? Individuals are likely to feel and to be perceived as a "member" of the organization in which they work, even though they may share cultural norms and standards with other organizations (see also Dutton & Dukerich, 1991). Such membership distinctions are overlooked by this perspective.

In short, none of the perspectives suggested offer a simple resolution to the definition of membership. In some cases too many people are included within a definition. In other cases, the definition excludes important individuals.

SUMMARY AND IMPLICATIONS

The self-evident implication of this essay is that organizations, organizational boundaries, and organizational members are abstract rather than concrete notions. These notions can be defined in different ways; the definition adopted will selectively include or exclude different groups of people. However, it is first important to clarify that no one perspective is either right or wrong. There is no one best or accurate definition of an organization or of membership. Rather, each perspective bears different implications for the people viewed as members, and for the managerial practices that will promote organizational goals.

The various definitions of membership are not mutually exclusive: most relations can be typified according to most of the proposed membership perspectives. Different perspectives, however, may yield different degrees of membership with respect to the same set of relations. The concept of membership, therefore, is a prism with many facets. To illustrate, a college professor may be more of a member according to the physical definition of membership, but less of a member according to the hierarchical definition. Within the physical perspective, college professors may not be homogeneous in the degree of their membership. Some professors stay at home to read and write rather than coming into their campus university office. Such behavior limits their endorsement of a physical definition of membership. Thus, some professors are members to a greater extent than others, if one judges by their physical membership. Physical messages about membership may predict other important aspects of individual behavior in an organization. It could be, for example, that deciding not to come in (or reducing the extent of physical membership) is associated with a lower commitment to organizational citizenship (Organ, 1990).

Membership in some organizations may be more clearly defined than in others, due to cultural crystallization (Martin, 1992) or identity formulation (Albert & Whetten, 1985). A distilled, non-fragmented organizational culture and identity may serve to clarify the social identity of organizational members, enhancing the sense of membership. To illustrate, when Hewlett-Packard employees are socialized to operate in the "H-P way" the organization helps define both the identity of the organization and the boundaries of its membership. The great effort Disney places on training and socializing members to dress and act is an attempt to highly distinguish the organization, through the rites, rituals and symbols, from other organizations. When there is shared agreement among organizational members about core values and norms that distinguish an organization from similar organizations, the concept of membership may be more distilled.

An analysis of membership also suggests that organizational theorists should examine the notions of "core" vs. "peripheral" members. Different perspectives appear to make different groups of people closer to, or further from, the core of organizational performance. To illustrate, secretaries sitting at the desk in the corporate headquarters, or employees working the production line, appear to be "core" according to the physical and hierarchical perspectives. However, with a poor quality work ethic, such employees may maintain a very limited membership from a contractual or production perspective. Ethnographic evidence, such as Hamper's (1991) description of the GM production line, vividly illustrates this tension between the various perspectives. In contrast, customers may be core according to the physical perspective but peripheral according to the hierarchical perspective, while shareholders may be core according to the contractual perspective, but peripheral according to the physical or hierarchical perspective.

This complexity suggests that it may be most accurate to define and describe membership as a profile rather than a dichotomy. Descriptions of relationships between individuals and organizations may be best described according to the pattern of relations in the different perspectives. For example, an individual may be high on physical membership, medium on hierarchical membership, and low on production membership. In this case, additional research is essential on the implications of different patterns of membership for various dependent variables such as job satisfaction, job and organizational involvement, or turnover.

Such profiles, however, may themselves be dynamic, because membership relations may be a matter of salience, similar to the concept of social identity. At different points in time, different perspectives may be more or less appropriate for the same set of organization–member relations. Students of social identity have argued that individuals navigate among multiple identities, with particular identities being more or less salient at different times according to various contextual constraints or demands (Ashforth & Mael, 1989; Tajfel & Turner, 1985). The present analysis contributes to the stream of research on social identity by highlighting various mechanisms that may define and articulate individuals' organizational identity. Organizational identity is suggested here to be a matter of degree or saliency, rather than a dichotomy. To illustrate, a production worker's contractual construction of membership may be high as long as the employment contract is intact. Once a labor dispute emerges, however, this form of membership is severely weakened.

By implication, the multiple perspectives on membership suggest that the construct of "boundary-spanning" is more complex than previously recognized. As summarized by Tushman (1977), there are likely to be many boundaries in organizations, and consequently many boundary role positions. What this analysis challenges, however, is Tushman's (1977, p. 589) assertion that organizations have one distinct "external boundary". The different perspectives reviewed here imply multiple plausible external boundaries. Each of these boundaries leaves different sets of people closer to, or further away from the core of the organization, and a different set of people sitting on the boundary.

Indeed, a review of research on boundary-spanning positions finds a wide set of roles to be represented, including sales clerks (Rafaeli, 1989b; Singh, Goolsby & Rhoads, 1994; Sutton & Rafaeli, 1988), police interrogators and bill collectors (Rafaeli & Sutton, 1991), departmental spokesmen (Organ, 1971), college professors (Schneider et al., 1994), professional employees (Keller & Holland, 1975), physicians (Freidson, 1960), purchasing agents, (Spekman, 1979), gatekeepers and opinion leaders (Tushman, 1977), industrial products managers (Lysonski & Woodside, 1989) and management negotiators (Perry & Angle, 1979).

The alternative perspectives about membership discussed here help explain how such a diversity of organizational roles can be included in one construct of boundary-spanning roles. A question this essay raises, however, is to what extent studies of roles that assume one set of boundaries can be generalized to roles defined by other boundaries. Are the dynamics of a physical definition of membership similar to those of a hierarchical or contractual definition? Most likely not. Future research needs to consider these differences, and their implications for research on both boundary-spanning and other elements of organizational theory research.

An additional implication of the multiple perspectives raised here is that researchers and managers should pay attention to the implicit definition of membership that they engage. Morgan (1986) notes that the images and metaphors individuals hold of organizations are likely to influence the research questions they explore, and the theories and explanations of organizational life that they develop. The analysis offered here builds on Morgan's argument, in that it asks not "what is" (an organization) but "where does it begin and who does it comprise". In this vein, it is essential to examine whether different definitions of membership attenuate theoretical or empirical findings. Assumptions about membership may be embedded into existing theories, in which case the theory may require changes in order to apply to alternative definitions of membership.

Finally, the complexity of defining organizational membership implies the importance of creating a shared language, or collective, cohesive and distinctive mind-sets among constituents. One helpful suggestion to resolve the membership issue may be that the focus should shift from rational, verbal, definitions to tacit, emergent, largely symbolic and typically socially constructed definitions of organization and membership. Weick & Roberts' (1993) analysis suggests that organizations may be tacitly defined by their members according to the collective and heedful inter-relating that emerges in the course of operation.

This is corroborated by Sutton & Rafaeli's (1988) findings that employees and customers tacitly and quickly agree about norms of behavior according to contextual elements such as busyness of the context. In this study, the formal organizational members according to the physical and production definition (i.e. both employees and customers) challenged prescriptions attempted by a hierarchical conception of membership (i.e. rules of behavior designed by management). The emergent standards of behavior are argued by Sutton & Rafaeli (1988) to contribute to the accomplishment of organizational goals more than the hierarchically prescribed standards.

Similarly, Rafaeli et al. (1997) suggest that employees use organizational dress to facilitate navigation through multiple forms of defining organizational membership. The secretaries in this study were cognizant of competing demands from members of the different environments with which they interacted (e.g. students, faculty, corporate representatives and executives in a university business school setting). Employees assumed that these multiple constituents should determine their own (the secretaries') behaviors. That only some of these constituents were formal employees of the organization was not an important distinction to subjects in this study. Dress, it appears, was the symbolic vehicle engaged by the secretaries for attending to the multiple constituents. Hence, when confused about their membership, employees turn to a socially constructed but tacitly espoused form of symbolic behavior.

CONCLUSION

Weick's (1976, p. 1) analysis of organizations as "loosely coupled systems" argued that "organizational elements are often tied together frequently and loosely". Weick's focus was on the interdependence and inter-relationships among the elements that together comprise "an organization". The analysis presented in this chapter extends Weick's argument to suggest that the concept of organization is, in itself, loosely coupled and laxly defined. Membership in organizations is both a matter of degree and a matter of perspective or definition. It may be more emotional than rational, challenging typical conceptions in organizational scholarship. Future organizational behavior theory and research should be cautious, to consider the implicitly embraced definition of membership and its implications.

REFERENCES

Abbott, A. (1988). *The System of Professions: an Essay on the Division of Expert Labor.* Chicago: University of Chicago Press.

Adams, J.S. (1976). The structure and dynamics of behavior in organizational boundary roles. In M.D. Dunnette (ed.), *Handbook of Industrial and Organizational Psychology.* Chicago: Rand McNally College Publishing.

Albert, S. & Whetten, D.A. (1985). Organizational identity. In L.L. Cummings & B.M. Staw (eds), *Research in Organizational Behavior*, vol. 7 (pp. 263–295). Greenwich, CT: JAI Press.

Anonymous (1993). Johnson & Johnson cuts 3000 jobs worldwide. *Chemical Marketing Reporter*, 5 (August 16).

Arnould, E.J. & Price, L.L. (1993). "River magic": hedonic consumption and the extended service encounter. *Journal of Consumer Research*, 20, 24–45.

Arrow, H. & McGrath, J.E. (1995). Membership dynamics in groups at work: a theoretical framework. *Research in Organizational Behavior*, 17, 373–411.

Ashforth, B.E. & Mael, F. (1989). Social identity theory and the organization. *Academy of Management Review*, 14(1), 20–39.

Avolio, B.J. & Bass, B.M. (1988). Transformational leadership, charisma and beyond. In J.G. Hunt, H.R. Baliga, H.P. Dachler & C.A. Scriesheim (eds), *Emerging Leadership Vistas*. Lexington, MA: Heath.

Bass, B.M. & Avolio, B.J. (1995). Transformational leadership: a response to critics. In M.M. Chemers & R. Aman (eds), *Leadership Theory and Research*. New York: Academic Press.

Baumeister, R.F. & Leary, M.R. (1995). The need to belong: desire for interpersonal attachments as fundamental human motivation. *Psychological Bulletin*, 117(3), 497–529.

Bitner, M.J. (1992). Servicescapes: the impact of the physical surroundings on customers and employees. *Journal of Marketing*, 56, 57–71.

Bowen, D.E. & Schneider, B. (1988). Services marketing and management: implications for organizational behavior. In B.M. Staw & L.L. Cummings (eds), *Research in Organizational Behavior*, vol. 10. Greenwich, CT: JAI Press.

Bowen, D.E. (1986). Managing customers as human resources in service organizations. *Human Resources Management*, 25, 371–84.

Chase, R.B. & Erickson, W.J. (1988). The service factory. *Academy of Management Executive*, **2**, 191–6.

Cheng, C. (1996) Uniform, symbols, and "old men": a symbolic interactionist ethnography of the social construction of hegmonic masculinity. Paper presented at the SCOS conference, UCLA, Los Angeles, CA.

Cohen, E. (1989). "Primitive and remote" hill tribe trekking, Thailand. *Annals of Tourism Research*, **16**, 30–61.

Deci, E.L. (1980). *The Psychology of Self-determination*. Toronto: Lexington Books.

Dimaggio, P.J. & Powell, W.W. (1983). The iron cage revisited: institutional isomorphism and collective rationality in organizational fields. *American Sociological Review*, **48**, 147–60.

Dutton, J.E. & Dukerich, J.M. (1991). Keeping an eye on the mirror: image and identity in organizational adaptation. *Academy of Management Journal*, **34**(3), 517–54.

Everett, P.B., Pieters, R. & Titus, P.A. (1994). The consumer–environment interaction. *International Journal of Research in Marketing*, **11**, 97–105.

Freidson, E. (1960), Client control and medical practice. *American Journal of Sociology*, **65**, 374–82.

Friedman, R.A. & Podolny, J. (1992). Differentiation of boundary spanning roles: labor negotiations and implications for role conflict. *Administrative Science Quarterly*, **37**, 28–47.

Gagliardi, P. (1990). *Symbols and Artifacts: Views of the Corporate Landscape*. New York: Aldine de Gruyter.

Gordon, G.G. (1991). Industry determinants of organizational culture. *Academy of Management Review*, **16**(2), 396–415.

Gouldner, A.W. (1957). Cosmopolitans and locals. *Administrative Science Quarterly*, **2**(3), 281–306.

Greenberg, J. & Baron, R.A. (1995). *Behavior in Organizations: Understanding and Managing the Human Side of Work*. London: Prentice-Hall.

Hamper, B. (1991). *The Rivethead: Tales from the Assembly Line*. New York: Warner Books.

Jensen, M.C. & Meckling, W.H. (1976). Theory of the firm: managerial behavior, agency costs and ownership structure. *Journal of Financial Economics*, **3**, 305–60.

Jones, M.O., Moore, M.D. & Snyder, R.C. (1988). *Inside Organizations*. Beverly Hills, CA: Sage.

Katz, D. & Kahn, R.L. (1973). *The Social Psychology of Organizations*. New York: Wiley.

Keller, R.T. & Holland, W.E. (1975). Boundary-spanning roles in a research and development organization. *Academy of Management Journal*, **18**(2), 388–92.

Koslowsky, M., Kluger, A.N. & Reich, M. (1995). *Commuting Stress: Causes, Effects, and Methods of Coping*. New York: Plenum.

Lawrence, P. & Lorsch, J. (1967). *Organization and Environment*. Boston: Harvard University Press.

Leflaive, X. (1996). Organizations as structures domination. *Organization Studies*, **17**(1), 23–47.

Lele, M. (1986). How service needs influence product strategy. *Sloan Management Review*, **28**(1), 63–70.

Lysonski, S. & Woodside, A.G. (1989). Boundary role spanning and performance of industrial product managers. *Journal of Production and Innovative Management*, **6**, 157–68.

Marks, M.L. & Mirvis, P.H. (1981). Environmental influences on the performance of a professional baseball team. *Human Organization*, **40**(4), 355–60.

Mars, G. & Nicod, M. (1984). *The World of Waiters*. London: George Allen & Unwin.

Martin, J. (1992). *Cultures in Organizations*. New York: Oxford University Press.

Meindel, J.R., Ehrlich, S.B. & Dukerich, J.M. (1985). The romance of leadership. *Administrative Science Quarterly*, **30**, 78–102.

Mills, P.K. & Morris, J.H. (1986). Clients as "partial" employees of service organizations: role development in client participation. *Academy of Management Review*, **11**(4), 726–35.

Morgan, G. (1986). *Images of Organization*. Beverly Hills, CA: Sage.

Oldham, G.R., Cummings, A. & Zhou, J. (1995). The spatial configuration of organizations: a review of the literature and some new research directions. *Research in Personnel and Human Resources Management*, **13**, 1–37.

Organ, D.W. (1971). Some variables affecting boundary role behavior. *Sociometry*, **34**(4), 524–37.

Organ, D.W. (1990). The motivational basis of organizational citizenship behavior. In B.M. Staw & L.L. Cummings (eds), *Research in Organizational Behavior*. Greenwich, vol. 12 (pp. 43–73). CT: JAI Press.

Perry, J.L. & Angle, H.L. (1979). The politics of organizational boundary roles in collective bargaining. *Academy of Management Review*, **4**(4), 487–96.

Pfeffer, J. (1977). The ambiguity of leadership. *Academy of Management Review*, **2**, 104–12.

Pfeffer, J. (1982). *Organizations and Organization Theory*. Boston, MA: Pitman.

Pfeffer, J. & Baron, J.N. (1988). Taking the workers back out: recent trends in the structuring of employment. In B.M. Staw & L.L. Cummings (eds), *Research in Organizational Behavior*, vol. 10, (pp. 257–303). Greenwich, CT: JAI Press.

Rafaeli, A. (1989a). When cashiers meet customers: an analysis of the role of supermarket cashiers. *Academy of Management Journal*, **32**(2), 245–73.

Rafaeli, A. (1989b). When clerks meet customers: a test of variables related to emotional expressions on the job. *Journal of Applied Psychology*, **7**(4), 385–93.

Rafaeli. A. (1996). Motivation at the point of departure: evidence from employment advertising. In M. Erez, (ed.), *Employee Motivation at Multiple Levels of Analysis*. Hillsdale, NJ: Erlbaum.

Rafaeli, A. Dutton, J.E., Harquail C.V. & Lewis, S. (1997). Navigating by attire: the use of dress by female administrative employees. *Academy of Management Journal*, **40**(1), 9–46.

Rafaeli, A. & Sutton, R.I. (1991). Emotional contrast strategies as social influence tools: lessons from bill collectors and criminal interrogators. *Academy of Management Journal*, **34**(4), 749–75.

Rheingold, H. (1994). *The Virtual Community*. London: Secker & Warburg.

Rousseau, D.M. & Parks, J. (1993). The contracts of individuals and organizations. In B.M. Staw & L.L. Cummings (eds), *Research in Organizational Behavior*, vol. 15 (pp. 1–35). Greenwich, CT: JAI Press.

Schein, E.H. (1980). *Organizational Psychology*. Englewood Cliffs, NJ: Prentice-Hall.

Schneider, B., Hanges, P.J., Goldstein, H.W. & Braverman, E.P. (1994). Do customer service perceptions generalize? The case of student and chair ratings of faculty effectiveness. *Journal of Applied Psychology*, **79**(5), 685–90.

Shamir, B. & Solomon, I. (1985). Work at home and the quality of working life. *Academy of Management Review*, **10**, 455-64.

Shanteau, J. & Harrison, P. (1991). The perceived strength of an implied contract: can it withstand financial temptation? *Organizational Behavior and Human Decision Processes*, **49**, 1–21.

Simons, T. (1994). Expanding the Boundaries of Employment: Professional Work at Home. Unpublished doctoral dissertation, Cornell University.

Singh, J., Goolsby, J.R. & Rhoads, G.K. (1994). Behavioral and psychological consequences of boundary spanning burnout for customer service representatives. *Journal of Marketing Research*, **31**, 558–69.

Smirchich, L. (1983). Concept of culture and organizational analysis. *Administrative Science Quarterly*, **28**, 339–58.

Smirchich, L. & Morgan, G. (1982). Leadership: the management of meaning. *Journal of Applied Behavioral Science*, **18**(3), 257–73.

Spekman, R.E. (1979). Influence and information: an exploratory investigation of the boundary role person's basis of power. *Academy of Management Journal*, **22**(1), 104–17.

Sutton & Rafaeli. (1988). Untangling the relationship between displayed emotions and organizational sales. *Academy of Management Journal*, **31**(3), 461–87.

Tajfel, H. & Turner, J.C. (1985). The social identity theory of inter group behavior. In S. Worchel & W.G. Austin (eds), *Psychology of Inter-group Relations* (pp. 7–25). Chicago: Nelson–Hall.

Trice, H.M. (1993). *Occupational Subcultures in the Workplace*. Ithaca, NY: ILR Press.

Tushman, M.L. (1977). Special boundary roles in the innovation process. *Administrative Science Quarterly*, **22**, 587–605.

Weber, M. (1947). *The Theory of Social and Economic Organizations*. New York: Free Press.

Weick, K.E. & Roberts, K.H. (1993). Collective minds in organizations: heedful interrelating on flight decks. *Administrative Science Quarterly*, **38**(3), 357–81.

Weick, K.E. (1976). Educational organizations as loosely coupled systems. *Administrative Science Quarterly*, **21**, 1–19.

Chapter 8

Dyadic Interaction in Organizations

Barbara A. Gutek
University of Arizona Tucson, AZ, USA

In this chapter, I focus on interactions in organizational life with the intention of encouraging more scholars to study this basic social process. Within the broad topic of interactions, I want to focus in particular on dyadic interactions on the boundary of organizations, more specifically, interactions between customers and service providers, and interactions between one organization and another organization. In so doing, I will concentrate on similarities and differences between interactions that take place between two strangers vs. interactions between two people known to each other. I call the former "encounters" and the latter "relationships". Organizations design interactions between a customer and a service provider or between themselves and a customer or supplier organization as either relationships or encounters. I will also describe a hybrid form of interaction I call a "pseudo-relationship", that is, an encounter designed to emulate a relationship.

This chapter is based on a perspective I have recently developed, especially as it concerns interactions between a provider of services and a customer (Gutek, 1995). In the chapter, I will define my terms and be consistent in my use of them; however, the way I define some terms departs from common usage. In particular, I use a more specific definition of "relationship" and a somewhat different definition of "encounter" than is often found in the extensive literature on services management, services marketing or "relationship" marketing (for some examples of these perspectives, see Berry, Parasuraman & Zeithaml, 1994; Bitner, Booms & Tetrault, 1990; Bowen & Jones, 1986; Bowen et al., 1990; Chase & Tansik, 1983; Czepiel, 1990; Czepiel, Solomon & Suprenant, 1985; Grönroos, 1990; Heskett, 1986; Kotler, 1994; Sasser, Hart & Heskett, 1991). I believe the definitions I use are helpful in understanding similarities and differences in

Creating Tomorrow's Organizations. Edited by C.L. Cooper and S.E. Jackson.
© 1997 John Wiley & Sons Ltd.

several areas, for example, "relationships" between two individuals and between an individual customer and a whole organization. I hope this new perspective will generate research, because increasingly social commerce is organized around two strangers interacting (for example, at fast-food restaurants, in emergency rooms, ordering merchandise from a catalog, or buying stocks from a discount brokerage) and I believe that a substantial proportion of interactions with strangers represents a relatively new phenomenon in modern history. This trend is a direct outgrowth of the increasing presence of formal organizations in all aspects of people's lives. Furthermore, while *individuals* are probably more likely than ever to engage in encounters in transactions, many *organizations* are seeking to establish relationships with each other. The long-term implications of such a trend, should it be demonstrated empirically, merit examination.

RELATIONSHIPS AND ENCOUNTERS

Two people who interact either have had some previous interactions and are therefore known to each other or they have never before interacted and they are therefore strangers. For researchers interested in human interaction, interactions between strangers may seem much less rich and interesting than interactions between people known to each other. It is not surprising that there are large bodies of research on dyads known to each other (e.g. dating couples, spouses, parent and child, supervisor and subordinate), but interactions between strangers have not attracted as much attention. Yet in the business world, customers often obtain goods or services from strangers. Thus, unlike many other kinds of social interaction, when a service provider interacts with a customer, the two may already know each other or they may be strangers. In short, a customer and provider can interact in relationships or in encounters.

Relationships occur when a customer has repeated contact with a particular provider. Customer and provider get to know each other, both as individuals and as role occupants. They expect and anticipate future interaction and, over time, they develop a history of shared interaction that they can draw on whenever they interact to complete some transaction. People who have a regular dentist, family physician, housekeeper, hairstylist, travel agent or full-time secretary, for example, have relationships with their providers.

Encounters, in contrast to relationships, typically consist of single episodes involving interaction between a particular customer and provider. Over time, the customer's successive contacts involve different providers rather than the same provider. As each provider is expected to be functionally equivalent, a customer should be able to complete a satisfactory service transaction with any of a number of interchangeable providers. Buying a hamburger at McDonald's is a classic encounter, but so is getting a driver's license, ordering airline tickets from an airlines reservation center, buying stocks from a discount brokerage, going to the emergency room or some HMOs to receive medical care, or going to some SuperCuts for a haircut. Each time the customer get a different service provider, but in principle, it doesn't make any difference which one the customer get because all are supposedly trained to provide the same service.

Relationships and encounters are both mechanisms for completing *transactions* involving the receipt of goods or services, and are both instances of the broader category of *dyadic social interaction*. Relationships consist of a series of *episodes* (see Liljander & Strandvik, 1995, on service episodes; Katz & Kahn, 1978, on role episodes), whereas encounters are one-time occurrences, i.e. single episodes. It may take more than one encounter to complete a transaction, however, as when one first stands in one line to place an order and in another to pick up the order.

Simply by virtue of the definition of relationships and encounters, one can infer many of their characteristics (although empirical study is needed to see if all of these inferences are correct as well as to reveal other non-obvious characteristics). In the next sections, I describe some of the characteristics of relationships (i.e. features that derive from a history of interaction between two people who anticipate interacting again in the future) and characteristics of encounters (i.e. features that derive from one-time interaction between two strangers), followed by similarities and differences between interactions between individuals and interactions between organizations. Throughout, I pose a number of research questions that follow from the relationship–encounter perspective.

Relationships

While we often reserve the term relationship for close or intimate relationships, continuing interaction between a provider–customer pair is also a relationship, a connection, although not as important to most people as the relationships formed by friendship, kinship or marriage. In fact, relationships seem like a natural way for customers and providers to act: relationships can exist in non-industrial societies, do not depend on a monetary system, and probably predate the full-blown development of markets for transactions. Table 8.1 below shows some of the characteristics of relationships and contrasts them with encounters.

In a relationship, a customer seeks out a particular person who can provide service or goods, and keeps going back to the same person, assuming the customer is satisfied with the service. Providers are motivated to deliver good service because they need customers to stay in business. Thus, relationships foster a close coupling of provider and customer. There is an inherent feedback loop between the two—and both can make adjustments to keep the relationship on track.

Over time the provider–customer pair build up a history of interaction that they can draw upon in each subsequent interaction. Because each knows the other, they can develop shortcuts in their interactions. And because each can draw on the store of shared knowledge, over time relationships can become more efficient and effective, especially where a customer and provider interact frequently. The efficiency in well-developed relationships is one of their strengths as

Table 8.1 Some characteristics of relationships and encounters

Relationships	Encounters
Provider and customer are known to each other	Provider and customer are strangers; can be anonymous
All providers not equivalent	Providers interchangeable, functionally equivalent
Based on trust	Based on rules
Elitist: customers can be treated differently	Egalitarian: customers all treated alike
Customized service	Standardized service
Difficult to start	Easy to enter
Difficult to end; loyalty is a factor	No obligation to repeat interaction
Fosters knowledge of other	Fosters stereotyping of other
Creates weak ties, networks	Does not foster networks
Does not need infrastructure	Is embedded in infrastructure
Fosters emotional involvement	Often requires emotional expressions not felt
Inherent feedback loop	Feedback loop through management, not between customer and provider
Become more effective over time	Designed to be operationally efficient

a service delivery mechanism. Comparing the efficiency and effectiveness of relationships and encounters is one worthwhile research agenda.

Relationships are based on trust. Specifically, the customer trusts the provider. In good relationships, both provider and customer are committed to the relationship and may be willing to expend energy and resources to preserve the relationship, e.g. drive an extra distance to retain a relationship or work late or come in early to accommodate a long-term customer. They both may value good relationships and the customer typically believes that his/her provider is special, has special expertise or know-how, and does not believe all providers are equal.

Relationships acquire asset specificity, that is, some of the knowledge that a provider and customer gain about each other is specific to the particular dyad and is not transferable to other customers or providers. In addition, relationships are relatively labor-intensive, as generally a provider interacts with one customer at a time. Even if many peripheral tasks are delegated to others (for example, receptionists and dental hygienists in the case of dentists; receptionists and shampoo "girls" in the case of hairstylists), the provider can handle only a certain number of customers at a time and labor costs are typically high where service is provided in relationships. In relationships, customers receive customized service if providers choose. Customers able to bring more business to the provider may be treated with more care, for example, and such customers may expect special or individualized treatment reflective of their own needs and interests. In that sense, they are elitist; not all customers are equal, neither are all providers.

Over time relationship providers build up a reputation as a good service provider and with an excess of customers can raise their fees to whatever the market will bear. I call especially successful and well-known providers "star providers". I define star providers as those who add prestige to their organization (if they work for an organization) rather than derive prestige from it. Star providers generate more transactions than average and they generate transactions based on their own name rather than the name of their organization (if they work for an organization). Star providers are expensive (for clients and for organizations that hire them) and sometimes they are fairly arrogant, too. One research issue is whether stars actually generate sufficient revenue to more than justify their own high price tag. When and under what circumstances do organizations seek out stars? And how many stars relative to other providers are desirable?

One of the more difficult aspects of relationships is getting started. How does one go about finding a family physician, a broker or financial planner, a housekeeper, a baby-sitter or a gardener? How many customers would prefer to a establish a relationship with a provider but either do not know how to find one or do not have the time/energy to do so? On the other end, it is often difficult to get out of a relationship. Both may feel bound to the other and feel guilty for severing a relationship.

Relationships have many other features (see Gutek, 1995, Chapters 2, 4, 5, 6, 7 & 10), but I'll mention just two more. Despite what I have said about a rocky beginning and ending, relationships can be quite enjoyable and satisfying to both participants, especially well-established, efficient and effective ones. Customer–provider pairs can become friends as well as parties to transactions. Furthermore, relationships create networks of contacts for both parties that can be used for instrumental as well as expressive ends. Thus, relationships provide ties to the community; they embed the person in a rich network of loose ties. And while the importance of formal organizations in providing weak ties and networks has been studied (e.g. Granovetter, 1973; 1974; Ibarra, 1993), the role of relationships as I have described them has not.

Encounters

Encounters constitute a relatively new form of service delivery and a distinctive alternative to relationships (see Table 8.1). Encounters constitute a social mechanism for delivering goods and services that is analogous to mass production in the manufacture of goods—with a reliance on standardized procedures, management of the process and interchangeable parts (the provider and customer in this case). Although the mass-production of goods has been around for over a century, the mass-production approach to service that is characteristic of encounters is much newer (see Levitt, 1972), albeit already common. In a typical encounter, a customer seeks some good or service from an organization. The customer has probably never interacted with the particular provider of the service and does not expect to interact with him/her again. The next encounter will be with a different, functionally equivalent, representative of the company. Furthermore, customers, like providers, are often just as functionally equivalent and interchangeable. It does not matter if one specific individual stops going to McDonald's, for example, as long as plenty of others do.

New domains for offering encounter services keep developing, and tracking such developments provides an interesting way to examine services. For example, New York City-based "The Great American Backrub" *Tucson Citizen* (1993) provides encounter-style $8^1/_2$-minute backrubs for $7.95 to a walk-in clientele. Similarly, Seattle-based "The Massage Bar" (McCarthy, 1995), whose name and offerings borrow the language of the popular coffee bars in the Pacific Northwest, provides backrubs at Seattle airport and at the convention center, with cheaper rates during "happy hour" (4–5 p.m.).

In encounter-style service, a sufficient number of providers can be deployed so that customers typically can obtain the service at their convenience, often 24 hours a day, and sometimes from any place where there is a telephone. For example, having a relationship with a travel agent means confining travel planning to the times one's agent is available. A person who calls the airlines directly can call literally any time, although the scope of service is typically limited, entailing separate calls to an airline, a car rental service, and a hotel, for example.

An encounter poses no requirements on a customer to return for another interaction. As a customer, one can try out some service without incurring any obligation at all. And one can quit, too. A person may go to McDonald's every week for years and then quit without anyone questioning his/her decision to do so. The departure of that customer may not be noticed in some encounter systems unless the person is unusual in some way or a very frequent user of the company's goods or services. It follows that encounters are characterized by anonymity, which sometimes is desired by customers. Providers too are anonymous but sometimes are identified by a name tag or on the telephone they often provide their first name.

If relationships are elitist, encounters are egalitarian. All customers are treated alike; they are not differentiated on the basis of status, wealth, clothing, age, sex or race, but all are expected to be treated to the same routine. Thus, although good relationships may be highly satisfying to both customer and provider, encounters, too, have many positive features, especially for the customer, so it is not clear that customers will necessarily be more satisfied with relationships than encounters.

Paradoxically, although encounters encourage equal treatment of all customers, they would appear to foster stereotyping because the two parties to the interaction have only the visible social characteristics of the other and a very limited sampling of behavior on which to base judgments. Do encounters, in fact, foster stereotyping, and if so, does the encounter environment—structured to treat everyone alike—prevent that stereotyping from leading to discriminatory treatment? Or is training necessary?

In encounters, providers may be evaluated primarily on their delivery style, on the interaction itself. Is the provider friendly, prompt, courteous? Does he/she smile, greet the customer, act attentively? When service is provided in encounters, do management(and customers) pay more attention to delivery style than when service is provided in relationships where delivery style may play a secondary role to the expertise the provider has? Much of the research on customer satisfaction seems to refer primarily to encounter-style service rather than relationship-style service (see, for example, Berry, Parasuraman & Zeithaml, 1994).

In an encounter, not only are providers assumed to be interchangeable, but the person may be eliminated altogether. This can be accomplished in several ways. First, interaction between customer and provider may be mediated by some organizational procedure like an in-basket. Second, the provider may be a machine rather than a person. Automated tellers and their kin, automated check-in services at hotels or point-of-sale debit machines, are becoming commonplace. So are the ubiquitous telephone encounters with machines that allow customers to learn everything from their bank balance to the train schedule. In principle, if the process can be standardized, it can be automated, and encounters with machines are likely to become more common in the future.

Whereas relationships are relatively self-regulating and do not require an organizational infrastructure to support them, encounters occur within *encounter systems*, human creations for delivering goods or services in encounters. They are designed and managed to be operationally efficient and re-designed and managed to be more efficient. A lot of work goes into designing a discount brokerage, for example, so that a customer, having opened an account through a telephone encounter with a person, can then buy or sell stocks by having an encounter with a voice mail system. The people who do the work of designing such an encounter system may or may not be stockbrokers, but a knowledge of production scheduling and computers is definitely required. Encounter systems thus require an infrastructure composed of providers, managers to manage them, designers to design and re-design the system to be ever more operationally efficient, and replacement specialists to see that enough providers (who typically have high turnover rates in many encounter systems) are available to meet customer demand. Comparing the workforces of relationship and encounter-style service delivery operations would provide specific information on the nature of their differences and suggest areas of job growth (e.g. technical and managerial support positions in encounter-style systems).

In contrast, a relationship may survive with only a provider and his/her customers. It is also worth noting that of the various roles in an encounter system, the provider role may be the lowest paid and lowest status, as well as having the highest turnover rate, a point that needs empirical verification. In general, it seems likely that customers who receive services in encounters typically interact with a relatively low-paid, low-prestige person, whereas in relationships the customer interacts with either the only person in the operation or with the higher status people in the operation. (As already noted, if a relationship provider delegates some tasks to others—like the "shampoo girl", dental hygienist or receptionist—those others are there to support the provider and are generally lower paid and subordinate to the provider.)

Some Differences between Relationships and Encounters

As the above discussion implies, relationships and encounters have very different characteristics. In this section, I would like to review three additional areas in which they differ. (For a longer treatment of this material, see Gutek, 1995, Chapter 4). They differ in the expression of emotional labor, patterns of attribution, and the links between customer and provider.

Emotional Labor

Hochschild (1983) called attention to the fact that an increasing proportion of workers is expected to display certain emotions as part of the job. She defined "emotional labor", a topic that has engendered a considerable amount of research and theorizing in recent years (e.g. Ashforth & Humphrey, 1993; Rafaeli & Sutton, 1987; Rafaeli, 1989a,b), as the "management of feeling to create a publicly observable facial and bodily display" (Hochschild, 1983, p. 7).

In relationships, the provider not only displays appropriate emotions, but also gradually develops real feelings about the customer, these feelings may be either positive or negative. Providers may strongly dislike certain customers but mask those feelings to maintain the relationship. The customer likewise develops real feelings about the provider over time. In therapy, for example, the provider (therapist) can become the most important person to a patient. In fact, having strong emotions about a therapist is so common the Freudian therapists gave it a name—transference. Regardless of the strength or direction of emotions, both customer and provider are expected to manage the emotional aspect of their relationship and refrain from displaying certain felt emotions that might not be appropriate. In relationships, emotional labor sometimes means putting aside real feelings and displaying other, sometimes less intense or blander, emotions.

In encounters, the situation is usually the opposite. Providers generally have very little feeling about customers, whether positive or negative, yet they may be expected to display more feeling and more caring than they actually feel. Exhibiting a customer orientation typically involves displaying caring emotions. It is an empirical question whether customers are always convinced by these emotional displays or even desire them from encounter providers. Perhaps customers who really want a relationship would seek out relationship-style service where it is available, rather than engage in encounters. While the provider is often expected to display positive emotions, and may be evaluated by management on that criterion, the customer typically has no feeling one way or another about the provider and may feel little need to be more than civil; this point has been documented in the literature (see, for example, Hochschild, 1983; Leidner,1993; Rafaeli,1989b). In some cases, the customer may ignore the provider or use the provider to vent anger. In the face of such behavior, the provider is often still expected to behave in a caring manner. More often, both provider and customer act reasonably friendly and courteously, in part because social life is simply more pleasant when everyone is pleasant. But when a person does not feel like being pleasant, the customer can act on her feelings but the provider cannot.

Patterns of Attributions

People in relationships and encounters, like people in general, tend to engage in the "fundamental attribution error" (Ross, 1977),that is, other things being equal, they attribute behavior to the actor. Thus, customers will tend to attribute the provider's behavior to the provider and providers will attribute customers' behavior to the customers. But the nature of the major difference between encounters and relationships—namely, whether or not there is a history of shared interaction—affects the pattern of attributions. In general, in relationships, especially those where interaction is frequent, both persons have a sufficiently large sampling of the other's behavior to know when the other is behaving true to nature. Any departure from "ordinary" behavior (e.g. an unusual tardiness, an unusual abruptness) is likely to get a situational attribution rather than an actor attribution. Furthermore, there is little room for making stereotypical attributions in relationships because both customer and provider have witnessed a large sampling of the other's behavior. If one party's behavior changes, the other party will tolerate several instances of the change before altering an attribution. Both persons may also tell the other if they are behaving differently for some reason (e.g. "I'm not in a very good mood today because I was up all night with a sick baby").

In encounters, the two strangers are, other things being equal, likely to attribute behavior to the actor. Thus, customers and providers who behave less than ideally will probably be seen by the other as inherently rude or uncivil. A customer who is rude is a rude person (see Leidner, 1993, for a discussion of how McDonald's workers view customers) and a provider who is detached is a cold person. It is also easy to stereotype people since both persons have only the single interaction with the other. But providers face another hurdle in encounters. Pleasant behavior may *not* be automatically attributed to them if the customer knows the organization has strong norms about providers behaving in a pleasant and courteous manner. If a checkout clerk is wearing a badge that reads, "If I fail to wish you a good day, you will receive a dollar" (as clerks in some southern California grocery stores do), the customer who is wished a good day may well attribute the comment to the store's policy rather than the inherent courtesy of the clerk. Just as standards are set for goods and services, provider behavior can be standardized and controlled. And just as the taste of a McDonald's hamburger may be attributed by customers to McDonald's standards for hamburgers, the hamburger server's behavior may be attributed to McDonald's standards for server behavior. In short, providers in encounters may be faced with a lose–lose situation. If they are rude, they are viewed as rude persons, but if they are nice, that niceness may be attributed to company norms. If this is, in fact, empirically demonstrable, it may account for the relatively high turnover rate among encounter-style providers.

Links between Customer and Provider

In relationships, customers and providers are interdependent; the fate of each depends in part on the other. In encounters, there are weak links between customer and provider. The transaction between the two can be reduced to a phone message, making the parties to the transaction quite remote from each other. For some kinds of encounters, more customers do not necessarily translate into higher wages or more prestige; processing more motor vehicle registrations, or making more hamburgers do not necessarily yield higher paychecks or more prestige (although they typically do translate into more work). A job can be as, or more, satisfying with relatively few customers for many encounter providers.

The differences in the way encounters and relationships link providers and customers furnish another fruitful area for research. For example, they can be compared to the differences in single-episode vs. repeated-play games in two-person games from game theory. For example, in a single-episode, Prisoner's Dilemma game, both players typically defect and lose points; mutual cooperation will not develop without some central authority to police the actions of the players (Axelrod, 1984). The single-episode game is like an encounter, in that neither the provider nor the customer in an encounter expects to interact with the other in the future. Because there is no expectation of future dealings, there is no reason (intrinsic to the interaction between the two parties) to cooperate with the other. Each has the potential to gain the most by cooperating as little as possible. Neither goes out of the way to help the other because they do not expect to interact again.

According to game theory, cooperation between the players can emerge if (and only if) they expect to play an infinite number of games: they establish a relationship (see Axelrod, 1984). While the provider and customer know they will not interact an infinite number of times, they do not know when their last interaction will be. Each has some reason to cooperate because if he/she defects or competes, the other party may retaliate in the next interaction. If one or the other defects, the other can try to mend the relationship and forgive the defector, or he/she can retaliate. Successive retaliations lead to the demise of the relationship.

The extent to which one believes the other will retaliate serves to keep the actor in line. Axelrod's (1984) work suggests that cooperation between customer and provider is most likely to be sustained if a relationship lasts long enough for retaliation by one party to counteract the temptation to defect. He refers to this as the "shadow of the future". If the future casts a sufficiently large shadow on the present, the two parties will continue to cooperate. Assuming that the relationship is perceived by both players to continue indefinitely, the two will cooperate with each other in general, as Axelrod has found, if one of them is nice (i.e.

cooperates until the other defects), is provokable (i.e. retaliates whenever the other defects), is forgiving (i.e. cooperates again as soon as the other cooperates), and is clear about using the strategy, called "tit-for-tat" (Axelrod, 1984; Axelrod & Dion, 1988). Under these circumstances, no oversight is required to maintain a relationship; high quality delivery of service can be maintained simply by the dynamics of the relationship.

Encounters, on the other hand, do not elicit cooperative behavior between customer and provider without some central authority to police their actions. This may involve multiple layers of management. Thus, it is the anticipation of an indefinite number of future interactions that ultimately creates a qualitative difference between relationships and encounters.

PSEUDORELATIONSHIPS

The fact that encounters are probably becoming more common does not imply that relationships will disappear of even necessarily diminish in number. While it needs empirical verification, it appears that relationships often serve as the model for encounter providers, that is, encounter providers are expected to act *as if* they had a relationship with the customers, customers they have never before seen and do not expect to see again. This is one of the things typically meant by having a customer orientation—treating the encounter customer like a relationship customer. Relationships may serve as a model for encounters in part because relationships have many positive features. It may also be the case that customers to not want to believe they are interchangeable and organizations do not want customers to think they are interchangeable. So they go to great lengths to personalize encounters, starting with having providers address customers by name and tell them to "Have a good day". Heskett (1986) summed up the issue this way: ". . . the objective of many service strategies being created today is to limit people-to-people contact to the minimum required to 'personalize' a service" (1986, p. 2).

But what does it take to personalize a service and how much time does it take? Elsewhere (Gutek, 1995, chap. 8), I describe two different hybrid forms that I call pseudo-relationships; both are encounters made to look like relationships. One kind of pseudo-relationship uses databases, typically computerized, that provide information about particular customers. Providers access this information when they interact with a customer, creating a kind of instant intimacy with the customer. Airlines have a pseudorelationship with their frequent flyers whose preferences for food and seating they have available on a database. Mail order operations often have the names and addresses of previous customers but some, like Peet's Coffee of San Francisco, also know frequent customers' previous orders and can ask them if they want the same order as last time. Some hotels, too, keep information on frequent customers that allows them to anticipate preferences.

Regardless of what information is available on customers, these pseudo-relationships, although sometimes preferable to other encounters, cannot be real relationships. First, all the information accumulated is about the customer; the customer has no corresponding information about the provider. Even more importantly, in a relationship the history of interaction is shared between a *particular* customer and provider. In a pseudo-relationship, the database which the provider accesses is available to all providers. Much of the personal information one might divulge to one's "own" secretary, physician or hairstylist would be perceived as an invasion of privacy should it come from a stranger.

The second kind of pseudo-relationship is a "relationship" with an organization rather than an individual provider. One feature of the late twentieth century is an increasing propensity for organizations to encourage people to have a "relationship" with them, the organization, rather than with individuals. Having repeat contact with the same organization is not the same as having repeat contact with the same individual, despite the common use of the term "relationship" to describe both. Any information that goes into a history of interaction must be made available to every potential provider in the organization, rather than a single individual. This fact alone is likely to limit the kind of information the customer gives and the kind of information the organization's representative either wants or is allowed to enter into the organizational record on the particular customer. Furthermore, increased usage of the organization may or may not result in better treatment, and in any event it will not lead to customized treatment. For example, just because a customer has visited McDonald's a thousand times does not mean that McDonald's will look out for that customer or will side with that customer in a disagreement with McDonald's. On any given visit, a person who has visited McDonald's hundreds of times runs the same risk of getting sick from the food or receiving poor service as a person who has never before visited McDonald's: That is both one of the virtues of encounter systems and one of their weaknesses. In addition, no matter how loyal and regular the customer, McDonald's will not provide table service or cloth napkins or otherwise customize service for its customers. Furthermore, McDonald's or any other organization providing encounter service could close their operations if they did not have enough customers; they are unlikely to continue to provide service to especially loyal and faithful customers the way a relationship provider might. There is a limited amount any customer can do to influence a provider organization. In short, customers can only have pseudo-relationships with organizations, not real relationships as I have defined them. Whether the differences I have observed between pseudo-relationships and relationships are important or meaningful to customers remains to be seen. Nor is it clear under which circumstances, if any, customers prefer pseudo-relationships to other encounters.

RELATIONSHIPS BETWEEN ORGANIZATIONS

At this point, I would like to focus on the fact that the customer as well as the provider can be an agent of an organization. Most of the discussion thus far has focused on cases in which the customer is acting as an individual whereas the provider may be acting as his/her own agent or an agent of an organization. When both customer and provider are acting as agents of the organization, we can consider this an interaction between organizations. In this respect, organizations can have both relationships and encounters with other organizations, in that an organization can go back to the same organization every time it seeks some kinds of service or goods, or it can go to any organization that could provide the relevant goods or services. In the latter case, customer organizations often choose to have an encounter with the provider organization that is least expensive or submits the lowest bid. (This may be one area where encounters are similar at the organizational and individual level; in all encounters cost may be the over-riding factor in choice of provider.)

Following the rules I have used so far, an organization would strictly speaking, have a relationship with another organization *only if* both organizations had specified a particular person to act as their agent. Otherwise, the two organizations could be considered, strictly speaking, to have encounters with each other. However, because under these circumstances, the providers in both organizations would probably understand the practices and procedures of the other, i.e. they would be familiar with the other, these might be considered another type of pseudo-relationship.

For a variety of reasons, organizations might well establish relationships (i.e. a specified individual from the provider organization always interacts with the same person from the customer organization) as well as pseudo-relationships (an organization always interacts with the same provider or customer organization but the interaction is not limited to the same two organizational agents). Relationships and pseudo-relationships between organizations are especially interesting because they seem to differ in subtle but important ways from relationships in which one or both parties are acting as individual agents. Both relationships and pseudo-relationships are established through shared organizational self-interest (Kanter, 1989), just as relationships between individual agents are established through shared individual self-interest. But the individuals occupying customer and provider roles act not for themselves but for the organizations they represent. That is, they occupy not only a customer (or provider) role but also work roles. They are also boundary-spanners; they are the means by which the two organizations communicate with each other. And sometimes the individual's own self-interest does not coincide with the organization's "self-interest", a feature that may distinguish relationships between organizations from relationships between individuals.

Organizational customers have some advantages over individual customers. For example, individuals are rarely able to compete—in volume of business, in time devoted to an issue, in the expenditure of resources—with organizational customers. Customers acting on behalf of an organization are generally seeking service an order of magnitude or more greater than any individual. And organizations are typically more able to pay a premium if that is required for relationship service. Not surprisingly, many organizations offering services or goods to both organizations and individuals—for example, telephone companies—have separate operations for the two, based in part on differences in expected volume of business. Individual customers seeking services from a telephone company typically engage in encounters, whereas business customers (acting as agents of organizations) may be assigned a particular representative with whom to develop a relationship (for which they typically pay a premium).

In addition, there are typically fewer organizational customers than individual customers; thus, it may be feasible to establish a relationship with a small set of organizational customers, whereas there are so many individual customers of large organizations, that it only makes sense to treat them as a mass market.

Organizational customers have yet another advantage over individual customers. Because the provider and customer are both acting in their organizational roles as well as customer and provider roles, they have records of previous interactions with each other. If one of the specific individuals leaves the job, it is relatively easy for a new employee to step in and take that person's place. With the help of accumulated documentation and the person in the other role, the new person can come up to speed relatively quickly. Because it is so easy to replace a particular individual, organizational relationships and pseudo-relationships can, in theory, last longer than a human lifetime. Thus, a provider might be more motivated to develop a relationship with an organizational customer than an individual customer for a whole variety of reasons, including the fact that individual customers may be more likely to end the relationship (whether through dissatisfaction, by moving to another location, or by dying). There are some countering tendencies: for example, relative to organizations, individuals may exhibit greater guilt for quitting a relationship and, relative to individuals, organizations that are dissatisfied with service providers are typically able to mobilize more resources toward exploring the possibility of finding a new provider for their goods or services. The similarities and differences between relationships between individuals and organizations, while the subject of some research (e.g. Kanter, 1989), present many possibilities for future research.

SOME CONCLUDING THOUGHTS

Toward the end of the nineteenth century, Ferdinand Toennies (1957 [1887]) contended that industrial societies were undergoing a major shift. Toennies observed that traditional societies had been characterized by *Gemeinschaft*, meaning they were held together by feelings and a sense of community, while industrial societies were characterized by *Gesellschaft*, meaning that they were held together by instrumental objectives. Under *Gemeinschaft*, people interact with each other as personalities, not just as role occupants. To offer contemporary examples, a college fraternity, religious order or mutual aid society illustrate *Gemeinschaft*, whereas most businesses are characterized by *Gesellschaft*.

Toennies wrote that:

Gesellschaft deals with the artificial construction of an aggregate of human beings which superficially resembles the *Gemeinschaft* in so far as the individuals live and dwell together peacefully. However, in the *Gemeinschaft* they remain essentially united in spite of all separating factors, whereas in *Gesellschaft* they are essentially separated in spite of all uniting factors (pp. 64–65).

The development of encounters as mechanisms for delivering goods and services, and the extent to which they replace or coexist with relationships, represents a further step away from *Gemeinschaft* and toward *Gesellschaft* and is consistent with Toennies' view of *Gemeinschaft* as representing the childhood of social order and *Gesellschaft* as its adulthood (p. 3). Although both relationships and encounters are characterized by instrumental objectives and role behavior, relationships provide leeway for the development of feelings and a sense of community and for the revelation, over time, of the individual personalities. Relationships do not exist just for their own sake—a condition of *Gemeinschaft* as defined by Toennies—but communal and mutually enjoyable aspects of relationships may help sustain them in conjunction with instrumental objectives. In comparison to relationships, encounters have no leeway for the properties of *Gemeinschaft* to emerge; they are characterized entirely by instrumental behavior on the part of both parties.

It is not surprising that the development of the service economy is being accompanied by a new form of delivering services, just as industrial economies were accompanied by new forms for producing goods. That the mass production of goods and the mass production of services involve similar processes—standardization of procedures, interchangeable parts, and the management of the process, among others—is also not all that unexpected. It makes sense to think that relationships prevailed as the prime mechanism for delivering goods and services to customers as long as there were relatively few individual customers for one's services. That is likely to be the case (but requires empirical verification) where there are relatively few customers (e.g. in rural areas) or where service is used by only a subset of society, typically the elite. Many kinds of service providers (e.g. attorneys, stockbrokers, tax analysts, nannies, gardeners, fitness trainers) traditionally have been used primarily by elites. Urbanization and the growing use of services by the middle class helps to make it productive for organizations to offer services in a mass production mode. If this is the case, then increased use of some service area should lead to the development of encounter-style operations (or, conversely, the development of encounter-style operations may lead to increased use of that service area by a broad segment of society).

The globalization of the economy has also brought additional changes. Chief among them is restructuring and downsizing. If organizations continue to shed their permanent employees, opting instead for contract workers, temporary workers and part-time workers, the interaction between employees, which historically has been in relationships, may increasingly be in encounters. What will this mean for organizations, for workers and for society? These same multinational and global organizations have too many individual customers to treat each as a true individual (rather than as a member of some customer class, e.g.

frequent flyers). True elites (e.g. the executives of the multi-national companies) may continue to get services in relationships if they so wish, and other individuals may have relationships with providers in smaller organizations or with independent practice providers. But if services follow the trend of manufacturing, it will mean that in the future most people will get most of their services in encounters, many of them with machines.

On the other hand, organizations have enough muscle, especially the multinationals, to expect that they can have relationships with supplier or customer organizations if they so choose. This brings up an intriguing possibility. Are we creating a society of organizations for organizations? If spending power is what is required to receive custom treatment, then it may be harder and harder to be a major player as an individual. In the global economy, are individuals too small, too poor and too interchangeable to be treated "as individuals"? This is another issue that can be explored empirically.

A Research Agenda

The perspective briefly described here lends itself to a variety of research methods—as well as topics. For example, modeling relationships and encounters in computer simulations would allow us to see changes over time. What happens to people's social networks when they engage in fewer relationships and more encounters? Various aspects of this topic also lend themselves to exploration through laboratory experiments. Research on attributions about both customers and providers is one example. Survey research, too, would be useful for describing the attitudes of relationship and encounter providers as well as the reactions of customers who engage in either type of service transaction. Survey research or laboratory research could be used to explore the issue of which form is less likely to lead to discriminatory treatment vs. stereotyped attitudes (see Gutek, 1995, pp. 253–7). Descriptive case studies of new encounter systems—backrubs via encounter, for example—can also be done. Several research methods might also be used to explore changes in various areas of service delivery. For example, one way of describing many of the changes in the delivery of health care is to view them as a shift from delivering health care via relationships to providing it via encounters. Other areas of professional service, e.g. higher education, may also increasingly exhibit encounter-style characteristics; case studies would either support or fail to support such a claim.

REFERENCES

Axelrod, R. (1984). *The Evolution of Cooperation*. New York: Basic Books.
Axelrod, R. & Dion, D. (1988). The further evolution of cooperation. *Science*, **242**, 1385–90.
Ashforth, B.E. & Humphrey, R.H. (1993). Emotional labor in service roles: the influence of identity. *Academy of Management Review*, **18**(1), 88–115.

Berry, L.L., Parasuraman, A. & Zeithaml, V.A. (1994). Improved service quality in America: lessons learned. *Academy of Management Executive*, **8**(2), 32–44.

Bitner, M.J., Booms, B.H. & Tetrault, M.S. (1990). The service encounter: diagnosing favorable and unfavorable incidents. *Journal of Marketing*, **54**, 71–84.

Bowen, D.E. & Jones, G.R. (1986). Transaction cost analysis of service organization–customer exchange. *Academy of Management Review*, **11**(4), 428–41.

Bowen, D.E., Chase, R.B., Cummings, T.G. & Associates (1990). *Service Management Effectiveness: Balancing Strategy, Organization and Human Resources, Operations, and Marketing*. San Francisco, CA: Jossey-Bass.

Chase, R. & Tansik, D. (1983). The customer contact model for organization design. *Management Science*, **49**, 1937–50.

Czepiel, J.A. (1990). Service encounters and service relationships: implications for research. *Journal of Business Research*, **20**, 13–21.

Czepiel, J.A., Solomon, M.R. & Suprenant, C.F. (eds) (1985). *The Service Encounter*. Lexington, MA: Lexington Books.

Granovetter, M. (1973). The strength of weak ties. *American Journal of Sociology*, **78**, 1360–80.

Granovetter, M. (1974). *Getting a Job: a Study of Contacts and Careers*. Cambridge, MA: Harvard University Press.

Grönroos, C. (1990). *Service Marketing and Management*, Toronto: Lexington Books.

Gutek, B.A. (1995). *The Dynamics of Service: Reflections on the Changing Nature of Customer Provider Interaction*. San Francisco, CA: Jossey-Bass.

Heskitt, J. (1986). *Managing in the Service Economy*. Cambridge, MA: Harvard Business School Press.

Hochschild, A. (1983). *The Managed Heart*. Berkeley, CA: University of California Press.

Ibarra, H. (1993). Personal networks of women and minorities in management: a conceptual framework. *Academy of Management Review*, **18**(1), 56–87.

Kanter, R. (1989). *When Giants Learn to Dance: Mastering the Challenge of Strategy, Management and Careers in the 1990s*. New York: Simon & Schuster.

Katz, D. & Kahn, R.L. (1978). *The Social Psychology of Organizations*. New York: Wiley.

Kotler, P. (1994). *Marketing Management* (8th edn). Englewood Cliffs, NJ: Prentice-Hall.

Leidner, R. (1993). *Fast Food, Fast Talk: Service Work and the Routinization of Everyday Life*. Berkeley, CA: University of California Press.

Levitt, T. (1972). Production line approach to service. *Harvard Business Review*, **50**, 41–52.

Liljander, V. & Strandvik, T. (1995). The nature of customer relationships in services. *Advances in Services Marketing and Management*, vol. 4 (pp. 141–67). Greenwich, CT: JAI Press.

McCarthy, M.J. (1995, June 1). Stranded at O'Hare? Well, you can drink or leave the airport. *Wall St. Journal*, A1, A6.

Rafaeli, A. (1989a). When cashiers meet customers: an analysis of the role of supermarket cashiers. *Academy of Management Journal*, **32**(2), 245–73.

Rafaeli, A. (1989b). When clerks meet customers: a test of variables related to emotional expression on the job. *Journal of Applied Psychology*, **74**(3), 28–47.

Rafaeli, A. & Sutton, R. (1987). Expression of emotion as part of the work role. *Academy of Management Review*, **12**(1), 23–37.

Ross, L. (1977). The intuitive psychologist and his shortcomings. In L. Berkowitz (ed.). *Advances in Experimental Social Psychology*, vol. 10 (pp. 173–220). San Diego, CA: Academic Press.

Sasser, W.E., Hart, C.W.L. & Heskett, J.L. (eds) (1991). *The Service Management Course: Cases and Readings*. New York: Macmillan.

Tucson Citizen (1993, November 18). They rub customers just the right way, 3B.

Toennies, F. (1957). *Community and Society* (C. Loomis, Trans.). East Lansing, MI: Michigan State University Press (original work published in 1887).

Chapter 9

Work and Family: In Search of a Relevant Research Agenda

Julian Barling
and
Deidre Sorensen
Queen's University, Kingston, Ontario, Canada

Research on the interdependence between work and family has a long and interesting history. A careful search of the literature will reveal some research activity on work and family in the 1930s and 1940s (see Barling, 1990). To some extent, this early research peaked in the 1950s, with the prevailing conclusion that work and family roles and function were interdependent, and that it was work that influenced family functioning, with maternal employment being inconsistent with effective or responsible mothering. At that point, Parsons (1959) challenged this prevailing perspective. He assumed the existence of a rigid structural differentiation between work and family, suggesting that balancing work and family demands was quite impossible.

By the early 1970s, the consensus seemed to be that work and family were indeed interdependent. However, it was assumed that men and women experienced their work and family roles differently (Hall, 1972): society expected women to enact these roles (e.g. worker, spouse, parent, self) simultaneously, while men were accorded the luxury of performing these same roles sequentially. Consistent with this assumption, perhaps the most frequent issue investigated was the presumed negative effects of maternal employment on children, on the spouse and only lastly on the mother herself.

Even though research on work and the family was firmly entrenched by the 1970s, it would be true to say that it exploded in the late 1970s and has continued unabated through the 1980s and into the 1990s. This surge of interest may have

Creating Tomorrow's Organizations. Edited by C.L. Cooper and S.E. Jackson.
© 1997 John Wiley & Sons Ltd.

been caused by, and was certainly paralleled by, the massive increase in the number of employed mothers and dual-income couples. Kanter's (1977) influential book, *Work and Family in the United States: a Critical Review and Agenda for Research and Policy*, further legitimized the area of work and family as a justifiable topic for study. During this period, several books and conceptual articles appeared (e.g. Barling, 1990, 1992a; Greenhaus & Beutell, 1985; Piotrkowski, 1979; Voydanoff, 1987) which helped to consolidate the field and stimulate research even further. In general, the research findings that followed investigated and challenged the prevailing notions (see Barling, 1990), and we now know that (a) work and family affect other; and (b) work need not exert negative effects on the family. Instead, when work is experienced positively, beneficial effects emerge on the family.

THE CHANGING WORKPLACE

For the times, they are a-changing (Bob Dylan)

While both interesting and invaluable, all this research was conducted within a context of relatively stable work organizations (at least stable in retrospect!) during a relatively quiescent social period. However, these conditions simply no longer prevail. Instead, organizations and the nature of jobs have undergone fundamental changes in the past few years, while social events have resulted in major changes to family structure. We argue that these changes have rendered much of our knowledge of the interdependence on work and family outdated, and that a new research agenda is urgently needed. We present a brief examination of some of these major changes (see Figure 9.1 for a summary) to assist in understanding the research questions that we will pose.

Perhaps the single most important organizational event of the past decade has been the headlong rush of major organizations to downsize their workforces, a phenomenon that followed major changes to the process of production, which were themselves made possible largely by the introduction and increased sophistication of computerized technology since the early 1980s. This has allowed major corporations to achieve greater levels of efficiency and productivity with fewer and fewer employees, which is now being termed, somewhat oxymoronically, a "jobless recovery". However, this downsizing phenomenon has not been limited to private organizations. Instead, government organizations are trying to cope with accumulated deficits by laying off massive numbers of civil servants, which exacerbates the rush to downsizing.

A major consequence of this is that organizations have moved from having full-time employees as their core to a "shamrock" structure (Handy, 1985), which has three "leaves", namely permanent core employees, subcontractors and part-time and temporary workers. Importantly, it is the last group that reflects the fastest growing segment of the economy (Hartley, 1995).

Several psychological consequences of this trend must be considered. First,

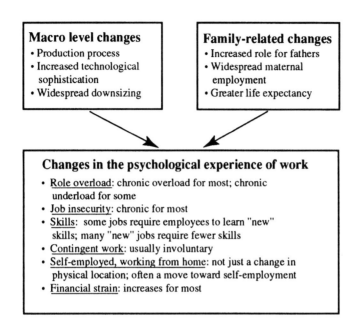

Figure 9.1 Summary of the effects of social changes on the experience of work

because there are fewer people employed, but there is the same or more work to be completed, role overload has increased for many. Second, perhaps not surprisingly, levels of job insecurity are increasing dramatically. While layoffs are by no means a recent phenomenon for blue collar workers, the extent of layoffs amongst middle and senior managers has led to more pervasive job insecurity. Third, jobs have tended to be "reskilled" or "deskilled", resulting in more challenging work for large groups of individuals, but more mundane work for many others. Fourth, the growth of contingent and key time work (Barker, 1995) has resulted in many contract employees—particularly those who would rather be employed on a full-time basis—to experience a decrease in perceived control in the workplace. Fifth, many laid-off employees are creating their own jobs, often working from home. As a result of these changes, many employees are now working harder for no more pay, with fewer resources available to them. Others no longer have as much work as they would want, or the work in which they are now involved results in "underemployment" (Feldman & Turnley, 1995). Lastly, several factors are combining together to result in increased financial strain. Quite simply, we are now engaged in a "new, ruthless economy" (Head, 1996), in which work has become more stressful for many people.

At the same time, three fundamental demographic shifts have continued, each of which will exert substantial effects on how people balance their work and family responsibilities. First, changes to the structure of the nuclear family are not recent. There are increasing numbers of single-parent and reconstituted families, and prior research on work and the family almost always assumed, erroneously as we now know, that all families were nuclear families. Second, life expectancy in the industrialized world has been increasing steadily throughout the twentieth century (e.g. Hartley, 1995; Rosenwaike, 1985). Today, the fastest growing age group in any developed country is people over the age of 85 years old. As a result of this, there may already be more adults involved in elder-care than child-care. Third, as noted elsewhere (Barling, 1990), the influx of women into the workforce has continued steadily over the past 50 years.

Clearly, there have been numerous and significant changes within both the work and family contexts. As a result, findings from research conducted in earlier, more tranquil eras may no longer be generalizable. We now turn our attention to outlining some alternative directions and questions for research on work and the family.

CHANGING WORKPLACES, CHANGING QUESTIONS

As already suggested, the changing workplace has exerted its most pronounced psychological effects on role overload, job insecurity, reskilling and deskilling of work, contingent work, and the increase in people working from their own homes, whether for themselves or for others. We will consider each of these in turn.

Role Overload

Ever since the publication of Kahn et al.'s (1964) seminal work on role stressors, a considerable body of data has been generated on the nature and consequences of role stressors (e.g. ambiguity and conflict; Jackson & Schuler, 1985). Within the work/family context, the role stressor that received the most empirical attention was *inter*-role conflict (i.e. the conflict experienced *between* salient roles such as parent and employee). As a result, the negative consequences of inter-role conflict on marital functioning and on children are now well understood. One specific aspect of inter-role conflict would be time-based conflict, where the amount of time required to fulfill one role precludes an individual from adequately fulfilling the requirements of a different role (Greenhaus & Beutell, 1985). There is some recent research on the effects on family functioning of short-term role overload. Aside from its effects on physical and mental health (Lang & Markowitz, 1986), short-term role overload affects family functioning indirectly, through its effects on negative mood and withdrawal from the relationship (MacEwen, Barling & Kelloway, 1992; Repetti, 1989).

However, these studies focused on short-term role overload, and as such their findings may no longer be generalizable. Instead of short-term role overload, chronic or long-term role overload now appears to be the norm. For example, it is estimated that in the USA, employees now accomplish 1.3 times the amount of work that they used to a few years ago (Hancock et al., 1995). Also in the USA, 34% of a random sample reported that they or someone in their families took on an extra job in the past 3 years (Uchitelle & Kleinfield, 1996), and 54% had to work more hours (i.e. overtime; Kleinfield, 1996). In Canada in December 1995, 65% of employed respondents in a nationally representative sample reported working more now than they did a few years ago (only 16% of whom received a salary increase for the additional work; Angus Reid Group, 1995).

There may well be important differences in how people cope with acute and chronic stressors in general (Pratt & Barling, 1988), and short-term and long-term role overload in particular. With short-term role overload, individuals would experience periods during which they were not overloaded when they could recover, a critical factor in coping with stress arising from overload (Sauter, Murphy & Hurrell, 1990). In addition, individuals could compensate in their interactions with the families during these periods. This would be markedly different from the unrelenting nature of long-term, chronic overload, as can be readily understood from interview data. One individual involved in downsizings reflected that "When I came back from this two years of hell and really looked at my house and started to do things . . . I couldn't believe some of the stuff that hadn't got done. Where was I? Like this took five minutes to do, why did I never have five minutes?" (Wright & Barling, 1996).

One question is whether with chronic overload, employees' abilities to cope with more mundane daily stressors could be threatened; these mundane daily work stressors may then serve as the "straw that breaks the camel's back" (Caspi, Bolger & Eckenrode, 1987). In this sense, chronic and daily stressors, which were formerly seen as distinct (Pratt & Barling, 1988), may now combine multiplicatively.

Job Insecurity

Given the frequency and extent of downsizings, it is not surprising that feelings of job insecurity are widespread. For example, in Canada, data from a nationally representative sample in December, 1995, showed that 24% of households were directly affected by a job loss or lay-off during 1995, and an additional 13% experienced an involuntary reduction in their work hours (Angus Reid Group, 1995). In the USA, close to 50% of a randomly selected sample of 1265 people were concerned that they or someone in their family may be without a job in the next year (Uchitelle & Kleinfield, 1996). Job insecurity is certainly a chronic stressor: In the same survey, 72% believed that layoffs reflect a permanent rather than a temporary problem. Added to this is the fact that most people who are laid off do not acquire an equivalent job in terms of responsibility and pay (Uchitelle & Kleinfield, 1996). There are already data showing that job insecurity exerts significant indirect effects on marital satisfaction, sexual satisfaction and psychological aggression (Barling & MacEwen, 1992). Compounding this, job insecurity will affect marital and family functioning in the same way as other chronic work stressors, i.e. through its effects on negative mood and reduced concentration (e.g. Barling, 1992a; MacEwen & Barling, 1991).

Children learn about the world of work from watching their parents; indeed, children's work beliefs are formed well before they embark on their first, full-time job (Barling, Kelloway & Bremermann, 1991; Hamper, 1991). Likewise, children learn about the experience of unemployment from observing their unemployed parents (Pautler & Lewko, 1987) and as adults learn about the nature and quality of retirement from viewing their retired parents.

Given this, what lessons might children learn from watching their parents' experiencing involuntary layoffs and reduced work hours, chronic job insecurity and simultaneously increased work loads? We suggest that children may well view the world of work with more cynicism and less trust if they perceive their parents as being insecure and overloaded. Similarly, if they see their parents as powerless to overcome this situation, they may begin to develop positive union attitudes and Marxist work beliefs (Barling, Kelloway & Bremermann, 1991). Two further questions can be raised. First, with heightened levels of youth unemployment, could children and adolescents delay thinking about their career plans and options, or worse still, implicitly or explicitly diminish their career aspirations and goals? Second, if indeed good jobs are more difficult to find, presumably teenagers might increase their chances of gaining access to good jobs by working harder? Ironically, this need to work harder might well emerge at the very time that their beliefs about work in general and their own motivation to work harder is negatively affected by watching their parents experience layoffs and job insecurity.

Reskilling and Deskilling

With downsizings and layoffs, a small group of surviving employees find themselves in an opportunistic situation: they now have access to jobs with increased scope and responsibility. In contrast, the norm for layoff victims is to find jobs with diminished scope, responsibility and pay. In the peculiar language of the 1990s, the former group find themselves "re-skilled", the latter "de-skilled". One study sheds some light on what the possible consequences of the "re-skilling" and "de-skilling" might be.

Crouter (1984) investigated the effects of an increase in participative decision-making on 55 blue-collar workers and supervisors. Despite the increased workload that is consistent with increased participation, some participants reported that they explicitly transferred what they had learned on the job (e.g. participative decision-making) to decision-making at home. This raises the question of what the effects of "de-skilling" might be on family functioning? While there is no empirical research on this issue, anecdotal evidence suggests that the de-skilled partner may lose respect in the eyes of other family members (Bragg, 1996). Intriguingly, there may be some support for this: Komarovsky's (1940) early research showed that sexual activity within the marriage decreased when male breadwinners lost their jobs, often because their spouses lost respect for them. The question of how laid-off individuals are perceived by their families could be addressed, because jobs help provide individuals with an identity and self-esteem (Jahoda, 1982).

Contingent Work

Together with the changing nature of organizations has come a change in the nature of jobs and work. Whereas full-time, core jobs were the norm for much of the twentieth century, the growing trend as we enter the twenty-first century is toward contingent work (Barker, 1995), which is also referred to as key-time work (Hartley, 1995). The central element here is for the provision and availability of work to be determined by the need for work; hence, employees would be offered work when and if it became available. Thus, contingent work is invariably offered on a part-time basis, with variable schedules, few if any benefits and lower wages than those accorded to full-time workers. Clearly, employees involved in contingent work do so out of necessity rather than choice. Just how common is contingent work? The largest single private sector employer in the USA is now Manpower Inc., with 767 000 contingent workers for hire (Uchitelle & Kleinfield, 1996).

Positive effects accrue when employees voluntarily choose their work schedule, including part-time employment (Barling & Gallagher, 1996). In this respect, the involuntary involvement of employees is one of the more troublesome aspects of contingent work from a psychological perspective. For example, negative effects accrue to the children and mothers employed on a full-time basis who would rather be employed part-time, or mothers employed on a part-time basis who would prefer to be employed on a full-time basis, compared to their counterparts whose employment status and employment volition are congruent (Barling, Fullagar & Marchl-Dingl, 1987; Hock & DeMeis, 1990).

Self-Employment, Working from Home

One question that should not escape our empirical attention is what job alternatives exist for people who have been laid off? There are several alternatives. Some become unemployed, while others may view this as an opportunity and go on to find better jobs, for example jobs with greater responsibilities (Cascio, 1993). However, we will not discuss these two alternatives further. First, there is already a large literature on unemployment and family functioning (e.g. Barling, 1990). Second, we know that jobs loaded with responsibility (whether in large or small organizations) are more likely to produce healthy and productive employees (e.g. Sauter, Murphy & Hurrell, 1990).

Many individuals who have been laid off find themselves moving from being employees in large organizations to owners of small businesses working from

their homes. Likewise, having employees working from home is becoming increasingly popular amongst larger organizations: many individuals who retain
their employment are being encouraged to work from home, or "telecommute".
What are the possible consequences of this trend? We argue that several outcomes of working from home could exert important effects on family functioning.
First, work provides more to workers than simply pay (Jahoda, 1982). Instead,
the workplace can also be a place where people fulfill social needs and a find a
source of social support. While the *amount* of social support might remain constant when working from home (as is the case with unemployed individuals), the
type of support changes (Jackson, 1988). The interactions between family members become more intense and emotionally charged. Consequently, the possible
stress-buffering nature of social support is reduced, making it more likely that
"reverse buffering" will occur, i.e. the greater the amount of support received, the
worse any effects of stress (MacEwen & Barling, 1988).

Second, working from home might increase the inter-role conflict and family
overload, especially for individuals with child-rearing or elder-care responsibilities. Despite the fact that individuals with family responsibilities are often
advised to accept part-time work to increase their availability for family
responsibilities (Heins et al., 1983), there is no evidence to suggest that this
reduces inter-role conflict or role overload (Barling & Gallagher, 1996). Instead,
we ask whether working from home would increase inter-role conflict and role
overload.

Financial Strain

Individuals have perhaps always expressed concerns about financial strain. However, various factors occasioned by the social, organizational and demographic
changes have undoubtedly increased levels of financial strain. First, as already
noted, after a layoff, most people see substantial pay reductions in their next jobs;
this is exacerbated because contingent work typically offers few if any benefits.
Objectively, therefore, many people either have or may soon experience financial
strain. Second, the psychological effects of this are made worse as most governments throughout the industrialized world are either reducing previous levels of
income support, or publicly toying with the idea. Third, increasing life expectancy
also combines with decreased income support from governments to cause even
greater financial pressures and anxieties. Fourth, financial insecurity and strain is
elevated in most single-parent families. Such an increase in perceived financial
strain should be of some concern: research has consistently linked both objective
and subjective financial strain with negative outcomes. For example, subjectively
perceived financial hardship predicts the quality of parental functioning (Simons
et al., 1992) and marital functioning (Conger et al., 1990).

In winding up this section on changes in workplace conditions, several issues
warrant discussion. First, the nature of financial strain raises an important conceptual and practical issue. The workplace factors described here do not neces-

sarily act in isolation. Indeed, if anything, they probably interact. For example, becoming a contingent worker against one's wishes after holding a full-time job would probably also be associated with financial strain. From a research perspective, ignoring these interactions would result in a truncated perspective of the effects of work on the family. Practically, these interactions help understand why work may be experienced as so stressful. Second, any increase in overall work-related stress would be important, as Greenhaus & Beutell (1985) note the potential for strain-based inter-role conflict: Specifically, when the strain in one role domain (e.g. work) exceeds an individual's abilities to cope, the likelihood decreases that the same individual can function effectively in other roles (e.g. family-related roles). Third, the cross-national generalizability of any research results should be tested rather than assumed. This is especially important given differing cultural perspectives, for example on the role of women in the family, and the vigour with which public policy solutions to work–family issues are pursued in different countries (Richter, 1992). Similarly, countries' differing experiences with industrialization make it essential that the issue of cross-national generalizability is confronted (Lewis, 1992).

Lastly, a comment about the role of perceived control is justified. A major common factor underlying the perceived stressfulness of all these workplace factors is the felt lack of personal control. In fact, the very basis of job insecurity is a feeling of powerlessness (Ashford, Lee & Bobko, 1989). Many of these shifts in the workplace environment are occurring at the expense of personal control: employees are working longer hours because they have to, rather than because they want to; contingent work invariably occurs at the behest of the employer, not the employee; and the financial strain is a result of external factors. While there has been considerable previous research on the role of perceived control in organizations, the role of perceived control has not received as much scrutiny in investigating work and family linkages. Our knowledge of work and family might benefit from attention to the following questions: first, is perceived control a common underlying causal factor in the current experience of workplace stress?; second, if perceived control is indeed a major causal factor, does this assist in any way in helping people balance work and family issues?

CHANGES IN FAMILY DEMOGRAPHICS

Not only has the workplace environment changed in recent years, but so has our idea of the family unit. This leads to a fundamental question: what is our conceptualization of "family"when we write about and study work and family? With few exceptions (Barling, 1990; Futoran, 1992), an examination of the current literature on work and family could leave a reader with the erroneous assumption that all families are "nuclear" families! Demographic changes (e.g. the continuing increase in the number of single-parent families, homosexual partners and parents, or children returning home to a formerly "empty nest" because of financial pressures) demand that we now extend our focus beyond the formerly normative or traditional "nuclear" family. As we move into the twenty-first century, relying on outdated stereotypes of the nature of the family will surely result in an irrelevant body of knowledge.

As one example, if single parents experience less social support, more financial strain and greater overload, the pressures they experience are potentially considerable. Despite the fact that the effects of both social support and financial strain have received considerable attention in studies on work and family (see Barling, 1990), this literature deals almost exclusive with traditional families. It would be critical to include single fathers in any future research focusing on single parents. This group is growing in size, and while there is a huge body of research on employed mothers, there is precious little research on employed fathers (Barling, 1992b)

While changes away from the "nuclear" family have been occurring for some time, a more recent demographic shift has been toward increased life expectancy (Scharlach, Lowe & Schneider, 1991). This might increase the stress on employees who may now be more likely to provide elder-care as well as fulfilling other roles and responsibilities. This stress is exacerbated by the fact that increased life expectancy does not guarantee good health (Hepburn & Barling, 1996), and social services to assist the elderly may be decreasing with government downsizing and budget deficits. Initial research findings show that eldercare responsibilities affect partial absenteeism (e.g. arriving late, leaving early; Hepburn & Barling, 1996). Two issues emerge from these findings: First, given the increasing number of employees likely to be involved in elder-care in the future, just how organizations as well as individuals confront the growing need for elder-care will be critical. Second, while most of the research on work and family focus on the way in which work affects family, this finding reminds us that family responsibilities also influence work. If successful enactment of family roles becomes more stressful, the question of how family responsibilities and strains influence work will gain in importance.

As noted earlier, there has been a steady increase in the number of employed mothers in the workforce in the past 50 years. One major lesson with both conceptual and practical implications has been learned from research on maternal employment. Despite social stereotypes to the contrary, maternal employment need not be negative for children (Barling, 1990); instead, where work role experiences are positive, positive effects accrue to the family. Other questions, however, can be raised. For example, there is a considerable body of research showing that sons' career choices are influenced by their fathers, although similar effects do not emerge for mothers and daughters (see Barling, 1992b). One positive possibility is that the limited number of employed mothers, combined with the limited range of jobs they held, mitigated against any statistical effects emerging. In addition, why would "modern" daughters want to follow mothers into "segregated" jobs? Now that mothers are not only entering the workforce but expanding the range and quality of jobs they are taking, do similar effects exist for daughters and their mothers as well? (Steele & Barling, 1996). In understanding how such values are transmitted across generations, it is also possible that it not merely the gender of the parent and child that makes a difference, but also the psychological identification with the parent, irrespective of gender (Barling, Kelloway & Bremermann, 1991).

In closing this discussing on the changing structure of the family, perhaps the most important consideration for future research would be to start off with a consideration of precisely what is meant by "the family". Undoubtedly, the consequences of such a discussion could exert a huge effect on a future agenda for research on work and the family.

CONCLUSION

Major changes affecting organizations and their employees, and demographic changes that influence the family, suggest that we need to reconsider the research questions relevant to an understanding of the interdependence of work and family. We make no pretense to having provided a complete agenda for research. Rather, our goal in this chapter has been to initiate thinking about such a research agenda, and to offer some initial directions.

Acknowledgments

Financial assistance from the Imperial Oil Charitable Foundation and the Social Sciences and Humanities Research Council of Canada to the first author is gratefully acknowledged.

REFERENCES

Angus Reid Group (1995). *The Public's Agenda, Assessment of 1995, the Death of the Middle Class, and Charities/Luxuries*, December 26.

Ashford, S.J., Lee, C. & Bobko, P. (1989). Content, causes and consequences of job insecurity: a theory-based measure and substantive test. *Academy of Management Journal*, **32**, 803–29.

Barker, K. (1995). Contingent work: research issues and the lens of moral exclusion. In L.E. Tetrick & J. Barling (eds), *Changing Employment Relations: Behavioral and Social Perspectives* (pp. 31–60). Washington, DC: American Psychological Association.

Barling, J. (1990). *Employment, Stress and Family Functioning*. Chichester: Wiley.

Barling, J. (1992a). Work and family: in search of the missing links. *Journal of Employee Assistance Research*, **1**, 271–85.

Barling, J. (1992b). Fathers' employment: a neglected influence on children. In J.V. Lerner & N.L. Galambos (eds), *Employed Mothers and Their Children* (pp. 181–210). New York: Garland Publishing.

Barling, J., Fullagar, C. & Marchl-Dingle, J. (1987). Employment commitment as a moderator of the maternal employment status/child behavior relationship. *Journal of Occupational Behaviour*, **9**, 113–22.

Barling, J. & Gallagher, D.G. (1996). Part-time work. In C.L. Cooper & I.T. Robertson (eds), *International Review or Applied and Organizational Psychology*, vol. 11 (pp. 243–77). Chichester: Wiley.

Barling, J., Kelloway, E.K. & Bremermann, E.H. (1991). Pre-employment predictors of union attitudes: the role of family socialization and work beliefs. *Journal of Applied Psychology*, **76**, 725–31.

Barling, J. & MacEwen, K.E. (1992). Linking work experiences to facets of marital functioning. *Journal of Organizational Behavior*, **13**, 573–83.

Bragg, R. (1996, March 5). Big holes where the dignity used to be. *New York Times*, pp. 1, 16–18.

Cascio, W. (1993). Downsizing. What do we know? What have we learned? *Academy of Management Executive*, **7**(1), 95–104.

Caspi, A., Bolger, N. & Eckenrode, J. (1987). Linking person and context in the daily stress process. *Journal of Personality and Social Psychology*, **52**, 184–95.

Conger, R., Elder, G., Lorenz, F., Conger, C., Simons, R., Whitbeck, L., Huck, S. & Melby, J. (1990). Linking economic hardship to marital quality and stability. *Journal of Marriage and the Family*, **52**, 643–56.

Crouter, A.C. (1984). Participative work as an influence in human development. *Journal of Applied Developmental Psychology*, **5**, 71–90.

Feldman, D.C. & Turnley, W.H. (1995). Underemployment among recent business college graduates. *Journal of Organizational Behavior*, **16**, 691–706.

Futoran, G.C. (1992). Work, family and stress. *Contemporary Psychology*, **37**, 1090–91.

Greenhaus, J.H. & Beutell, N.K. (1985). Sources of conflict between work and family roles. *Academy of Management Review*, **10**, 76–85.

Hall, D.T. (1972). A model of coping with role conflict. *Administrative Science Quarterly*, **4**, 471–86.

Hamper, B. (1991). *Rivethead: Tales from the assembly Line*. New York: Time-Warner.

Handy, C. (1985). *The Future of Work*. Oxford: Basil Blackwell.

Hartley, J. (1995). Challenge and change in employment relations: issues for psychology, trade unions and managers. In L.E. Tetrick & J. Barling (eds), *Changing Employment Relations: Behavioral and Social Perspectives* (pp. 3–30). Washington, DC: American Psychological Association.

Head, S. (1996). The new, ruthless economy. *New York Review of Books*, February 29, 47–52.

Hancock, L., Rosenberg, D., Springen, K., King, P., Rogers, P., Brane, M., Kaeb, C. & Gegax, T.T. (1995). Breaking point. *Newsweek*, March 6, 56–62.

Heins, M., Stillman, P., Sabers, D. & Mazzeo, J. (1983). Attitudes of pediatricians toward maternal employment. *Pediatrics*, **72**, 283–90.

Hepburn, C.G. & Barling, J. (1996). Eldercare responsibilities, interrole conflict and employee absence: a daily study. *Journal of Occupational Health Psychology*, **1**, 311–18.

Hock, E. & DeMeis, D.K. (1990). Depression in mothers of infants: the role of maternal employment. *Developmental Psychology*, **26**, 285–91.

Jackson, P.R. (1988). Personal networks, support mobilization and unemployment. *Psychological Medicine*, **18**, 397–404.

Jackson, S.E. & Schuler, R.S. (1985). A meta-analysis and conceptual critique of research on role ambiguity and role conflict in work settings. *Organizational Behavior and Human Decision Processes*, **36**, 16–78.

Jahoda, M. (1982). *Employment and unemployment: a social psychological analysis*. New York: Cambridge University Press.

Kahn, R.L., Wolfe, D.M., Quinn, R., Snoek, J.D. & Rosenthal, R.A. (1964). *Organizational Stress: Studies in Role Conflict and Ambiguity*. New York: Wiley.

Kanter, R.M. (1977). *Work and Family in the USA: a Critical Review and Agenda for Research and Policy*. New York: Sage Foundation.

Kleinfield, N.R. (1996). The company as family no more. *New York Times*, March 4, pp. 1, 12–14.

Komarovsky, M. (1940). *The Unemployed Man and His Family: the Effect of Unemployment upon the Status of Men in 59 Families*. New York: Arno Press.

Lang, D. & Markowitz, M. (1986). Coping, individual differences and strain: a longitudinal study of short-term role overload. *Journal of Occupational Behaviour*, **7**, 195–206.

Lewis, S. (1992). Work and families in the United Kingdom. In S. Zedeck (ed), *Work, Families and Organizations* (pp. 395–431). San Francisco, CA: Jossey-Bass.

MacEwen, K.E. & Barling, J. (1988). Inter-role conflict, family support and marital adjustment of employed mothers: a short-term, longitudinal study. *Journal of Organizational Behavior*, **9**, 241–50.

MacEwen, K.E. & Barling, J. (1991). Maternal employment experiences affect children's behavior via mood, cognitive difficulties and parenting behavior. *Journal of Marriage and the Family*, **53**, 635–644.

MacEwen, K.E., Barling, J. & Kelloway, E.K. (1992). Effects of short-term role overload on marital interactions. *Work and Stress*, **6**, 117–126.

Parsons, T. (1959). The social structure of the family. In R.N. Amshen (ed), *The Family: Its Function and Destiny* (pp. 241–74). New York: Harper & Brothers.

Pautler, K.J. & Lewko, J.H. (1987). Children's and adolescents' views of the work world in times of economic uncertainty. In J.J. Lewko (ed), *How Children and Adolescents View the World of Work*. San Francisco, CA. Jossey-Bass.

Piotrkowski, C.S. (1979). *Work and the Family System*. New York: Macmillan.

Pratt, L.I. & Barling, J. (1988). Differentiating between daily events, acute and chronic stressors: a framework and its implications. In J.R. Hurrell, L.R. Murphy, S.L. Sauter & C.L. Cooper (eds), *Occupational Stress: Issues and Developments in Research* (pp. 41–53). London: Taylor & Francis.

Repetti, R.L. (1989). Effects on daily workload on subsequent behavior during marital interaction: the roles of social withdrawal and spouse support. *Journal of Personality and Social Psychology*, **57**, 651–9.

Richter, J. (1992). Balancing work and family in Israel. In S. Zedeck (ed), *Work, Families and Organizations* (pp. 362–94). San Francisco, CA: Jossey-Bass.

Rosenwaike, I.A. (1985). Demographic portrait of the oldest son. *Milbank Memorial Fund Quarterly*, **63**, 187–205.

Sauter, S.L., Murphy, L.R. & Hurrell, J.J. (1990). Prevention of work-related psychological disorders: a national strategy proposed by the National Institute for Occupational Safety and Health. *American Psychologist*, **45**, 1146–58.

Scharlach, A.E., Lowe, B.F. & Schneider, E.L. (1991). *Eldercare and the Workforce: Blueprint for Action*. Lexington, MA: Lexington Books.

Simons, R.L., Lorenz, F.O., Conger, R.D. & Wu, C-I. (1992). Support from spouse and mediators and moderators of the disruptive influence of economic strain on parenting. *Child Development*, **63**, 1282–1301.

Steele, J. & Barling, J. (1996). Influence of maternal sex-role beliefs and role satisfaction on daughters' vocational interests. *Sex Roles*, **34**, 637–48.

Uchitelle, L. & Kleinfield, N.R. (1996). On the battlefields of business, millions of casualties. *New York Times*, March 3, pp. 1, 26–29.

Voydanoff, P. (1987). *Work and Family Life*. Thousand Oaks, CA: Sage.

Wright, B. & Barling, J. (1996). "The executioner's song": listening to downsizers' reflectious on their experiences. Manuscript submitted for publication, School of Business, Queen's University, Kingston, Ontario K7L 3N6.

Chapter 10

Evolutionary Psychology and Organizational Behavior

Nigel Nicholson
London Business School, UK

What is being called the "new science" of evolutionary psychology offers a radically new perspective to the social sciences. My purpose in this chapter is to introduce readers of organizational behaviour to its base assumptions and key concepts, and consider how they might apply in our field. What does this view of human nature signify for organizational behavior in the information age? It argues that whatever adaptations we achieve or seek are dependent upon bio-genetic imperatives and within the limitations of what it means to be human. First, I begin by outlining the background to this emerging discipline and go on to explore how it can be integrated with an applied psychological theory of human functioning. The final section of the paper considers how these ideas reinterpet knowledge at three organizational levels; individual differences and relationships, primary groups, and communities. Implications for the future of work and organization are discussed.

THE NEW SCIENCE OF EVOLUTIONARY PSYCHOLOGY

Darwin's *Origin of Species* turned upside-down the thinking of the Victorian era about what it means to be human, social morality and the role of the deity in our affairs. Darwin was himself immensely troubled by the far-reaching implications of the theory of natural selection, although less inhibited philosophers, most notably Herbert Spencer, were eager to explore the application of the evolution-ary metaphor to social development. Note that this raises an important point about the need to distinguish evolutionary theory as ostensive and metaphorical,

Creating Tomorrow's Organizations. Edited by C.L. Cooper and S.E. Jackson.
© 1997 John Wiley & Sons Ltd.

i.e. here I am concerned with what we are learning about genetic influences on human behavior, rather than the numerous applications of the natural selection model beyond the biological sphere. Within the latter category are fast-growing and fertile fields of inquiry, such as population ecology models of organization–environment linkages (Hannan & Freeman, 1989), evolutionary computing (Koza, 1992) and models of economic and social development (von Hayek, 1988).

Direct applications of evolutionary theory to individual psychological processes and their social consequences have had a much longer and more uneven treatment in the literature. Apart from ethologically-oriented research on such issues as language development and diurnal body rhythms, individual psychology has been largely preoccupied with "protean" models of human learning, motivation and cognition,—relatively free from constraining notions about "human nature". Reactions were generally hostile to sociobiological speculations about aggression, sexuality, territoriality and status hierarchy (Morris, 1967; Ardrey, 1967; Wilson, 1975). The value these writings might have brought by focusing serious attention on reminding us of our evolutionary heritage was largely lost through their over-extension of analogy from primate observation, extravagant speculation and some demonstrably incorrect assertions.

Evolutionary psychology represents a clear break from this work, although within the same tradition, by presenting a stream of much more refined and developed concepts, drawing upon the explosion of recent knowledge about genetics, paleontology and ethology (Trivers, 1985). In this chapter I want to consider some of these ideas and how they might affect how we think about organizations and behavior within them.

The Background—Our Genetic Inheritance

Mapping the human genome and paleontological investigations are transforming our view of the origins of *Homo sapiens*, and the area is thick with fresh ideas, new data and unresolved controversies. However, several preliminary propositions can be stated to summarize key premises for the evolutionary psychology paradigm.

1. *The selfish gene.* Species' characteristics, including humankind, are constituted by the evolutionary process (see below) to favor those which best achieve the intergenerational transmission of genetic material (Dawkins, 1989).
2. *Punctuated equilibrium.* Species alter little during their evolutionary lifetimes. Rather they fine-tune to their adapted domains, until some radical environmental shift or mutation triggers species development (Eldredge & Gould, 1972).
3. *The ancestral environment.* The domains to which species characteristics are shaped to maximize fit are those in which they developed, rather than those they currently occupy (Wright, 1994).

4. *Phylogenetic development. Homo sapiens* does not sit atop an evolutionary tree of progressive refinement, but is a single branch of the primate family. This is still an area of debate and discovery, but our ancestry seems to stretch back at least four million years to the populous and successful *Australopithecus*, and runs in parallel with our closest relatives, the chimpanzees, from whom we differ genetically by a mere 1.6% (Jones, 1993).

5. *Hunter-gatherer primates.* For most of our evolution, from australopithecine to modern human, our adaptation has been to a hunter-gatherer functionality (Diamond, 1991). Our upright stance and enhanced brain capacity evolved in the service of the social complexities of clan living under these conditions.

6. *Modern existence.* There is no evidence of human species biological evolution which relates to patterns of modern living. The capacity for language facilitated social rather than biological development, such as the very recent innovation of agriculture (c. 10000 years) and large fixed community dwelling (c. 6000 years). Hunter-gatherer communities have remained a visible paradigm until very recent times.

7. *The redundancy of characteristics.* It follows, therefore, that species characteristics are not always functional or adapted to their environments. Thus do domesticated animals exhibit a range of behaviors with no current survival or reproductive value. Humans likewise, have redundant characteristics, such as toenails. Natural selection proceeds as much by the elimination of redundant characteristics as it does the creation of new ones.

8. *Exaptation.* This term was coined (Gould & Vrba, 1982) to denote the characteristics exhibited by many species which are adaptive by-products of evolution. They serve different functions in their current environment functions from those for which they originally evolved (e.g. some storks use their wings to shade water in which they are fishing). In humans, much of what our brains and hands do now are divergent extensions from their original biological utility.

It would seem that our social disorders, as much as our dietary disorders (e.g. excessive sodium), are due to the distance exaptation via social evolution has removed us from the ancestral environment to which we are biologically adapted. In other words, the psychology of modern man rests on a platform of genetically-based drives and dispositions which were selected by the ancestral environment as affording the best chances of successful transmission of individual genes to the next generation.

The familiar "nature–nurture" question has generally been framed in terms of the extent to which we are able, through cognitive and experiential mediation, to transcend or contradict our biogenetic physical or mental inheritance. This is an incorrect formulation. Exaptation connotes extension, not transcendence, of human nature. It is the premise of this chapter that however functionally autonomous higher mental processes and linguistic mediation might appear, they cannot be separated from the biological purposes of the organism. How they serve these ends, though, is infinitely varied and inventive. Let us now consider more closely what this means.

The Selectionist Paradigm and Human Psychology

The evolutionary process has three elements: superfecundity, blind variation and environmental selection (Cziko, 1995). Species are driven genetically to reproduce more offspring than can be supported by the environment. Mating and random mutations generate phenotypical variation in the offspring. The environment affects the life chances of the phenotype selectively according to its characteristics and "fit" with the local domain. The most favored members have superior chances to reproduce and transmit their genes. In this manner humans developed stable characteristics for the specific domain of hunter-gatherer existence. These characteristics include bipedal locomotion, manual dexterity (opposable thumb) and language facility. Each of these has proved to be highly subject to exaptation. Thus being equipped to walk into the bush, pick berries and signal to our comrades about hazards and where to find new food supply, we are also equipped in our modern environment to ride a bike to the office, plan our next article and start tapping it out on a keyboard.

If one accepts the selectionist premise, then it would be illogical to apply it only to certain human characteristics. In other words, we should conceive of ourselves as functionally integrated organisms, in which all of our characteristics serve the common purpose of adaptation to and reproduction in the ancestral environment. This necessarily means that some of our attributes are no longer functional to our current environment, such as diurnal rhythms to modern patterns of working. Some, such as music-making, are the product of exaptation (from the ancestral utility of signalling and sound recognition), while others continue directly to serve the same ancient purposes, such as sexual attraction. In one sense, which characteristics we class as which matters little—they are all of the piece we call human nature.

Thus does this argument require us to consider our psychology—autonomic and intentional, conscious and unconscious, emotional and cognitive—as sourced by a genotype adapted to the domain and lifestyle which has predominated for all but a small fraction of our time on the planet. This is the point of resistance for some social scientists who would like to conceive of a few basic "drives" as primitive and biological, but reserve the bulk of human psychology within the almost unbounded adaptive domain of "higher mental processes". The "Standard Social Science Model" (Tooby & Cosmides, 1992) argues that our enormous synaptic power and prodigious ability to learn means that much of what is most important in our lives and behaviors is socially constructed, culturally evolved and transmitted on Lamarckian rather than Darwinist principles, thereby allowing us almost limitless opportunities to "invent" ourselves in post-industrial society.

The counter to this perspective is not to deny either learning or cultural transmission but to point out that its products are still subject to selectionist processes. If our environments are socially constructed, then it behoves us to ask the question, what forces motivated their construction? An evolutionary perspective argues that we are disposed to construct environments in which we can thrive, i.e. fulfil our biogenetic aims through the functional use of our capabilities. Additionally, for each of us, the artifacts of social life are part of our individual environment, and do not impress themselves upon us as *tabula rasa* but as adapted fully functioning organisms, i.e. we are constituted to tune in and respond selectively to information and environmental influence. In other words, if we are to understand how we function at even the most abstract or symbolic levels, we still require a model of how we are constituted.

The model to meet this need would link temperament, personality, social identity, motivation and action patterns. Here follows the outline of such a model.

AN EVOLUTIONARY PROCESS MODEL OF PSYCHOLOGICAL FUNCTIONING

The concept of temperament was used by early psychologists to hypothesize about human "instincts". This approach was largely supplanted by more sophisticated personological and cognitive theories. However, new evidence from genetics is encouraging its revival as a concept which brings an integrated view of biochemical processes and psychological dispositions (Bates & Wachs, 1994; Kagan et al., 1995). Personality theorists' use of trait concepts overlaps strongly with these ideas through two developments. First is the "Big Five" factor model of personality, which is being claimed as a universal model of the structure of dispositions (Digman, 1990). Although the factorial structure of this model is still under debate, the principle of a genetically founded universal structure is becoming accepted by personality theorists (Nicholson, 1996a). This is not undisputed, although arguments are mainly around factorial integrity rather than the principle of a universal structure. It can be argued that the Big Five has evolutionary functionality for our ancestral environment (Buss, 1991): emotionality (for security), extraversion (for sociality), openness (for exploration), agreeableness (for nurturance) and conscientiousness (for structure). Second, is the mounting evidence for a high degree of heritability in individual differences on most of these dimensions (Bouchard et al., 1990). Geneticists are currently identifying some of the specific elements in this structure (e.g. linkage between a dopamine receptor gene and novelty-seeking).

A selectionist theory of psychological functioning suggests that traits can be conceived of as desired "goal states", against which environmental conditions and effected actions are implicity and explicitly compared. Within the field of

organizational behavior, a theoretical analysis has been developed which recon-
ciles personality with goal theory in a manner entirely consistent with an evolutionary perspective (Cropanzano, James & Citera, 1993). Perceptual control
theory (Powers, 1973) identifies how goals structure attention and the formation
of behavioral routines, such that discrepancies between perceptions and goal
states trigger emotional states and new behaviours. An evolutionary perspective
thus can equate temperament and traits with meta-goals, operating at the deepest
and most biologically rooted level of functioning. The expression of these stable
genetic dispositions can be activated, reinforced or dampened by neonatal and
childhood experience, but the scope for their structure and content to be revised
in adulthood to meet environmental demands is limited. The selectionist control
model allows us explain the development of social performance and identity over
the life-span in terms of how sub-goals are acquired, retained, developed or
abandoned over a person's life history. Self-identity constructs thus can be highly
variable, but tuned in to higher, more general, dispositional structures. In this
manner, Yost, Strube & Bailey (1992) argue that individuals operate multiple
possible selves at any point in time, evolving over time as a function of the
guiding intent of core identity and the selective impact of variable environmental
conditions. Similarly, behavioral routines (habits, skills, etc.) can be conceived of
as hierarchically linked with goals via control systems operating on selectionist
principles. German action theory (Frese & Zapf, 1994) essentially takes the same
position through its conception of action as goal-oriented behaviours, hierarchically nested from meta-heuristic through to sensorimotor levels, activated selectively by feedback, and control loops.

An important implication of this analysis is that goals and behavior patterns
lower in the hierarchy are more environmentally specific and modifiable through
experience. They function on the systems theory principle of equipotentiality, as
alternative paths and strategies for alignment to higher-order goals and environmental contingencies. Any of the meta-goals of personality can be served by an
enormous variety of sub-goals and behaviors—which are selected for retention
and use according to their adaptiveness, i.e. motivation and performance evolve
over the life-span within the limiting parameters of primary dispositions.

The complex relationship between psychological structure and behavior can
be modelled as operating in three principal ways.

First, is *direct impulse*. In situations of low constraint—what Mischel (1968)
called "weak situations"—we are confronted with choices. Under these low-
constraint conditions dispositions effect behaviours in a direct causal linkage, as
when we witness individuals free to follow impulses such as to do something
creative, nurture someone in need, impose order on a task, or engage a stranger
in conversation. Internal goal states are satisfied directly by behavioral
expressions.

Second is *reactivity*. When "strong" situations impact upon us, they also signal
to us the adaptiveness of our goal states, arousing emotions, needs and
cognitions. Thus does environmental change evoke individual differences in
psychological response. For example, emotionality or neuroticism connotes emo-

tional lability in the face of change, and extraversion, according to Eysenck (1953), connotes our conditionability to new stimuli.

Third is *structuration*. The sociologist Giddens (1984) coined this term to denote the impact of agency on social structures. From a psychological perspective, Staw (1991) has argued that many structural organizational phenomena are the product of choices and preferences originating in individual dispositions. The theme here is that we are motivated to construct environments or selectively choose to enter situations which are congruent with our psychological constitutions and quit or change those which are incongruent.

Much behavior is the product of a fourth process–what I shall call *chemistry*— the effect of specific interpersonal interactions. This really is an extension of the first three, since we are motivated to seek out the company of certain individuals and environments which are likely to contain congruent people (structuration), to behave towards them according to our needs and interests (impulse), and to react to their behaviors in characteristic ways (reactivity). They do exactly the same in relation to us. Each of us is the environment of the other. Social interaction is a fast-paced dance of mutual adaptation, in which the parties select and match from their repertoires of goal-related routines to optimize the mutual fulfilment of individual goal states.

The model of psychological functioning this analysis brings us to is fundamentally dialectical. Situations, and the behaviors which take place in them, are continually being moulded for mutual adaptation, under the guiding influence of striving for consistency with enduring goal states. In order to understand the implications for organizational behavior, therefore, we need to examine the nature of these goal states. The major implication of evolutionary psychology is to identify these as a number of key enduring themes in how we have evolved to prosper in our ancestral environment. So, having constructed a model of the selectionist process, let us consider what evolutionary psychology has to say about *content*—the nature of the evolved psyche and how it predisposes us to live and work.

THE MODERN HUNTER-GATHERER—THEMES FOR ORGANIZATIONAL BEHAVIOR

Three themes will be briefly considered: individual differences; primary groups; and community. Each could in itself be the subject of extended analysis, beyond the scope of this chapter, and will be developed in subsequent writings.

Individual Differences

The management of diversity in organizations connotes a wide range of differences: race, culture, disability, age and gender. Although there is much current debate about the genetics of race and intelligence, the overwhelming weight of evidence and logic is that race and culture are inseparable. The politics of race are the product of the human tendency to make discriminatory identifications with visible groups rather than genetically encoded differences in psychological make-up. Age and disability do not alter the deep structures of individuality so much as constrain how it is acted out. This is not true of gender, where evidence is continuing to mount of genetically encoded psychological differences, and hence this discussion will focus on sex differences.

There is a high degree of convergence from neurobiological, psychological, ethological and anthropological research about the pervasiveness of sex differences in brain functioning, motivation and cognition, communications and interaction styles, and social roles. Evolutionary psychology offers a unifying framework for the analysis of these in terms of how they serve the reproductive interests of our species. The interests of genetic transmission are served in species by sexual reproduction and the nurturance of young. For humans, these involve mechanisms of competitive attraction to maximize the quality of genetic stock and elaborate bonding to secure infant survival through our exceptionally long gestation and immaturity. These two goals—attraction and bonding—are present in us all, but are importantly differentiated for males and females. These centre on the nature of the investments men and women make to advance their reproductive goals (Trivers, 1972). Women, with their much more limited reproductive time and capacity, are the scarce resource and therefore are governed by a psychology of selectiveness. Their reproductive interests lie in partnerships with males who are resource-rich and committed and can add value to their genetic investment. Male parental investment is a key concept in understanding the sexual psychology of all primates, and especially humans. The intensity of care, resourcing and training are directly related to their offspring's life chances and subsequent likelihood of successfully transmitting their genetic material to the next generation. Unfortunately, the desirable attributes of male resource richness and commitment do not always go together. To achieve this conjunction requires females to develop successfully strategies of attraction and selection on the one hand, and involvement and bonding on the other. Additionally, they benefit from a high degree of social awareness and networking, to understand the market they are in, i.e. to know which males represent good bets for resource extraction and low risks of deception.

Males, as the plentiful resource, are governed by a psychology of competition. They seek to maximize their reproductive opportunities and to guarantee the security of their offspring. Their quest is for partners who are receptive and faithful, the former for fecundity, the latter for exclusive investment in their progeny. Again, these qualities are not always correlated, leading males to a mixed strategy of status acquisition and dominance. In polygynous societies (including our own, via the serial monogamy of multiple marriages), it is the high-status and resource-rich males who secure the most reproductive opportunities (although not necessarily the most offspring).

The politics of gender relations are complicated by the awareness of each sex of the other's agenda, for instance, what Darwinist writers call the "evolutionary arms race" of men's affinity for exploiting women and women's interest in detecting male deception. However, family life remains an optimum solution for both under a variety of environmental conditions, and the different patterns of gender relations and family structures to be found cross-culturally represent the local adaptations of these themes. Turn to the novels of Jane Austen for dramatic exposition of these genetic politics—characters struggling towards assortive bonding through minefields of mismatched assets.

To see this analysis as having relevance for organizational life requires the assumption that these differentials are not suspended, only reworked, through social and life-span development. Male and female motives relating to sexual selection are not just switched on in the presence of appropriate stimuli but are ever-present influences on plans and behaviour. They form the deep structures of gender-specific goal states. Despite rigorous searches for disconfirmation, sex differences in personality and social behavior are pervasive in our field, and in directions consistent with the above analysis.

This being said, there are two major qualifications to this position which caution against overdrawing gender differences in observable behaviors. First, around our genetically encoded deep goal structures there is individual variation (Tooby & Cosmides, 1990). This variety is adaptive in species through what evolutionists call "frequency-dependent selection". This is the tendency for some characteristics to have adaptive utility in inverse proportion to their frequency in a population. Conscientiousness, for example, is a source of advantage in a world of laid-back others, but as conscientiousness rises in frequency, the advantages of being an easy-going free-rider also increase. In this manner populations can settle to equilibria of diverse and complementary interacting characteristics. This variation also permits multiple opportunities for selective assortment and adaptation. This suggests that we should view gender stereotypes as points of central tendency, rather than dichotomous categories. Second, social conditions and cultural mores regulate, sometimes with extreme force, the scope for the phenotypical expression of genotypical differences. However, even when, whether for reasons of inborn temperament, social learning or situational constraints, men and women's behaviors and attitudes are similar, this does not alter the fundamental case, which is relational. Men and women are in an important sense *contexts* for each other, contexts whose meanings are non-equivalent. Similarities in orientations at any point in time do not alter the biogenetic differences between the architectures of their base psychological functioning.

By the processes outlined above, individual differences within as well as between the sexes allow men and women to pursue, selectively, life-courses congruent with their psychological make-up. Comparison of men and women in working environments is always problematic for the reason that one is seldom comparing like with like (Gutek, 1995). Women in male-dominated occupations, or pursuing careers in competition with men, are a survivor population of people willing to confront and overcome the unequal obstacles of entry and competition (Nicholson & West, 1988). Many have opted for more traditional sextyped roles.

And when we look at these, we find replicated patterns. Nowhere in the organizational literature is this spillover of the evolutionary paradigm of gender relations into working life better portrayed than in Rosabeth Kanter's brilliant analysis of the role of secretaries in *Men and Women of the Corporation* (1977), although it must be stressed that this was not the author's intent.

The persistence and ubiquity of gender role-typing in work organizations (Schein & Mueller, 1996), (male) sexual harassment (of women) (Bargh & Raymond, 1995), and female occupational and career disadvantage (Humphries & Rubery, 1995), suggest that the genetic politics underlying these phenomena will require more than just ideological opposition to be eliminated. Those who give primacy to the social construction of gender would no doubt say that we have not done enough to eliminate the hegemony of patriarchal values. This is partially correct—the values are deep-rooted but how they are acted out can be regulated, i.e. the hegemony can be addressed, although perhaps only by radical means, such as rebalancing organizational demography (Ely, 1995). An increasingly common strategy for women persistently hitting "the glass ceiling" is to start their own businesses (Davidson, 1996).

In short, this analysis leads to the conclusion that the liberation of women in organizations from the problems I have described is most likely to come from truly feminized organizations, i.e. where organizational structures, cultures and processes are conceived around a female value set (Eagly & Johnson, 1990). Certainly some Western organizations (especially professional firms) have moved significantly and successfully towards this position. However, it is arguable that they have done so by depending upon self-selection into and out of them by women and men with congruent orientations, more than by means of resocialization. If so, this implies that such organizations are unlikely to come to represent a dominant paradigm in society. Many men and women will continue to prefer traditional forms.

Primary Groups

The family unit is a universal paradigm among humans for the successful reproduction of genetic material, although family forms are historically and locally adapted to conditions of life expectancy, food supply and environmental hazard. Evolutionary psychology's interest in the family concerns the kinds of dependence, cooperation and conflict repeatedly manifest among siblings and parents. Cooperation is an evolutionary imperative among family members, "kin selection" in the language of evolutionary psychology. It is the disposition of individuals to seek to advance the interests of those who are presumed to share a portion of their genes, especially relative to non-kin rivals. However, within families the same forces are a source of conflict. First, these is conflict between siblings; a simple product of the individual's desire to maximize his/her life chances relative to others competing for the same primary source of resource supply. Sibling relations thus involve symmetrical dualities, although these may be moderated by age, birth order and gender effects, and by the relative strengths and attributes of the offspring. Parents are likely to favor "gifted" siblings, in whom investment will stand a better chance of further genetic reproduction, especially in conditions of resource scarcity. A second source of conflict exists in parent–offspring relations (Trivers, 1974), which also have a duality, but without the same symmetry. Here, the parents' interest is in engendering cooperation among siblings, with whom they share equal amounts of genetic material. This is achieved through intensive socialization of the child, who in early life is entirely resource-dependent on the parent and is normally receptive to influence. However, the child's interests are not the parents', and growing independence brings the possibility of rebellion against a parental authority which has diminished resource value. The asymmetry extends beyond parents to other kin. In the extended family, Uncles and aunts, for example, have more common genetic interest with the parents than the children, creating the possibility of extended family conflicts arising from parental injunctions for family loyalty vs. the offsprings' more autonomous motivations. Turn to Shakespeare rather than Jane Austen for dramatic expositions of these themes (patricide, usurpation, plotting, etc.).

The most visible examples of the genetic politics of the family in organizational behavior are to be found in the family firm, and the frequent struggles for succession (Goffee & Scase, 1985). In some parts of the world, especially in Asia, family relations are heavily regulated by cultural norms to repress these conflicts. Not just in Asia but throughout the world family firms can achieve tremendous strength and market power when the chemistry of family members' values and skills gel successfully. The relevance of the kinship model has been insufficiently studied within the field of organizational behavior.

Now let us assume that the patterns of family relationships to which our psychology is attuned is a model for other relationships, i.e. our motive structures continue to operate "as if" other relationships contained similar sets of divergent and convergent interests. Note, this is similar to the psychoanalytic assertion of the generalizability of parent–child models in other social relations (e.g. the parent–adult–child schema of transactional analysis). Within organizational behavior the study of primary groups outside the laboratory has been relatively neglected until the recent growth of interest in teams (West, 1996a). Many of the kinship themes of shared and divergent interests are visible in this literature, for whose effective management a number of conditions are necessary, including a size no larger than the normal range of family groupings and processes for the open exploration and resolution of conflict. Effective group processes follow the selectionist paradigm of generation, variation and selection. An important consequence of this "reflexivity", the evolution of new task and environmental adaptations via introspective exchange (West, 1996b), is the generation of new shared social representations which have a lasting effect upon the motives and cognitions of individual members (Moscovici & Doise, 1994). These clearly have adaptive advantage, and constitute a vital building block for the culture of community. Organizations which are able to activate this dynamic have significant advantage over more bureaucratic forms for their capacity to survive in changeful environments (Goffee & Jones, 1996).

A second area where the evolutionary logic of kinship applies is leadership. Most management books on leadership are recipes for effective parenting—how to socialize, engender cooperative relations and commitment among subordinates (Meindl, 1990). The reality of this model looks very different from its two sides. The legitimacy of managerial authority and submission to its values is not unproblematic in most organizations. Immediate subordinates are more sceptical of these values than their bosses care to imagine. Respect is often greater for leaders among subordinates at multiple levels removed from the leader whilst at the executive level the threat of patricide (and more rarely, matricide) is an ever-present danger. Sibling rivalry is enacted in many ways, most commonly through impression management tactics—managing upwards for advantage over one's peers (Giacolone & Rosenfeld, 1989).

Of course there are other models of leadership, which emphasize self-management and empowerment. These too are often viewed with scepticism as a commitment-binding device and, where they do work more successfully, arguably do not remove the politics of competition and envy. Moreover, they lack the stability of the more unequal power relations of traditional forms, and seem to work best in temporary or intermittent forms, e.g. project teams, task forces. However, an evolutionary perspective does not leave us with the squabbling family as the sole model of relating. There is a countervailing cooperative logic from non-kinship relations.

Community

Family life in the ancestral environment was embedded within the network of the clan, which in most hunter-gatherer communities probably rarely exceeded a size of 150 (Dunbar, 1996). Our primate sociability is instrumental to the enormous personal advantages from deal-making under conditions of trust with non-kin with whom we are likely to have repeated interactions (Ridley, 1996). However, the non-zero sum gains from cooperation needed to be balanced with prudence against exploitation. Reciprocal altruism, it is argued, is the individual genetic disposition which achieves this balance parsimoniously (Trivers, 1971). Applications of game theory have explicated the logic of this strategy, and in a classic experimental simulation of a community of repeatedly interacting dyads, found one strategy to be a consistent winner of an evolutionary contest (Axelord, 1984). "Tit-for-tat", as it is called, argues for cooperation on the first interaction, and thereafter punishes defection with one's own defection, and rewards cooperation conversely. Indeed, it has been argued (Frank, 1988) that altruism in situations where cheating would be undetectable, is a practised value with hard-wired origins, in order to equip us with self-concepts favorable to the successful performance of trustworthy appearance across a wide range of situations. However, as research on negotiation shows, reciprocal altruism is highly sensitive to context and role (Neale & Bazerman, 1991). Consistent with evolutionary theory, defection becomes increasingly likely among those who are resource-poor or in circumstances of low trust. In the arena of risk-taking, behavioral decision theory predictions readily fit as well—risk aversion under conditions of gain, and risk-seeking under conditions of loss (Kahneman & Tversky, 1979) make adaptive sense to the organism motivated to survive at all costs, and to secure its wealth against hazard.

The significance of the reciprocal altruism concept is that it is an individual strategy which creates a community by "training" other players to cooperate (Murnighan, 1991). The character of community relations can be seen as the result of individual differences in the motives people bring to exchange relations, e.g. in the propensity to defect. Much writing on the theme is concerned with these consequences: the politics of deception, impression management, guilt and shame. These are all seriously problematic in many modern organizations and society more widely (Scheff, 1995). Current interest in organizational citizenship clearly points to the necessity of communities interacting on a high-trust basis for these behaviors to be resolved through self-regulation (Wood, 1991)—in short, on qualities of organizational culture.

The radical view evolutionary psychology brings to the concept of culture is that culture is the adapted product of individual psychological architecture (Tooby & Cosmides, 1992). The surface content may be perceived as infinitely varied but it rests upon forms which are regular and universal. Reviews of the vast literature on organizational culture identify several competing perspectives (Martin, 1992). An evolutionary perspective can help to resolve these by drawing attention to how organizational forms relate to our ancestral paradigms. It would suggest, for example, that integrated cultures, i.e. corporate "clans", require kinship or quasi-kinship linkages within units of moderate size (Ouchi, 1981, has argued along similar lines). In larger units, sub-cultures become the focus of identification, but only under conditions of relative stability, otherwise cultural fragmentation can be expected. The bureaucratic paradigm is one of the chief means by which cultural stability is preserved. Bureaucracies do so by trading on one of the key themes in evolutionary psychology: status hierarchy.

The historical universality of hierarchy in societies (Murdock, 1945) and their ubiquity in primate and other species is, according to evolutionary psychology, a direct consequence of individual differences, gender relations and the reproductive imperative. Opportunities to reproduce one's genes accrue unequally according to the adaptive advantage of one's characteristics. For humans, physical attributes (strength, attractiveness), cognitive abilities (intelligence, language facility), and personality (stability, conscientiousness) are all bases for discrimination and the ability to accrue resources and reproductive opportunities. This in itself is sufficient to create hierarchy, but at the cost of continual contest for advancement as abilities mature or decay, or as the selective impact of the environmental context shifts. Clearly this incurs costs in efficiency and well-being. Institutionalized status hierarchies resolve this problem by individuals accepting a relatively stable status allocation, including submission to the higher authority of others, in exchange for security and freedom from contest. This creates a non-zero sum exchange in which status is a resource (Wright, 1994), which means that although anarchistic conflict is avoided, individuals remain highly motivated to improve their status position, given the opportunity. Hence, in organizational life we see institutionalized hierarchy everywhere, alongside, to an equal degree, office politics. The success of bureaucracy is due to its ability to solve one problem, the desire for ordered status arrangements; its weakness is its inability to solve the other, the desire for self-advancement.

The field of careers exemplifies this duality. Individuals' desire for both security and status advancement have traditionally been provided by hierarchical managed career systems. The "new" model of career self-management in delayered and decentralized organizations threatens both these needs, and the psychological contract now being advocated offers an unconvincing trade of "employability" for job security and portfolio development in place of status enhancement (Nicholson, 1996b). Evidence from our large multi-company employee attitude survey data base at London Business School shows that desires for promotion remain at persistently high levels in all types of firm, including those making major investments in non-hierarchical career systems. Job insecurity, likewise, can be seen to have pervasively corrosive effects on morale and loyalty, i.e. breaking human evolution's preferred social contract dissolves the glue of community. Even more extreme effects spring from unemployment. Jahoda's classic study showed how the workless Austrian community of Marienthal in the 1930s suffered an acute disorientation and depression through deprivation of experiences essential to personal and social identity (Jahoda, 1982). However, we are also witnessing increasing numbers of individuals who pursue the career paths of self-employment or contracted-out professional work. In a sense these *are* the hunter-gatherers of the modern era, and it would be mistaken to assume that they lack either community or status orientation. It is simply that these characteristics of their networks are less immediately visible than in institutional settings.

The conclusions to be drawn from these arguments are various. First, they suggest that small- to medium-sized organizations will be most successful in generating a communitarian culture. Second, many large organizations will continue to use the architecture of hierarchical status ordering to satisfy the interests of their members or to predict and control their behaviour. Third, large organizations which decentralize invite local rather than corporate identifications to prevail. Fourth, in conditions of insecurity, individuals will seek and create alternative identifications. Fifth, the information technology revolution may transform the nature of the tasks we do and the settings in which we work, but it will also be used as a new tool for achieving the time-honored human purposes we have been considering. Nor will it ever eliminate many forms of social intercourse, such as face-to-face communication and group meetings. Even the promised virtual organization will be more "organization" than "virtual", i.e. exhibiting familiar and ancient forms, experiences and behaviors. None of these observations is novel. However, what is less recognized is that these are not simply descriptive generalizations about contemporary industrialized society, but consequences of ineradicable themes in human nature.

CONCLUSION

We are organisms adapted for life on this planet. The radical insight that evolutionary psychology proposes is that everything we think, make or do comes from the source of our common psychological heritage, and that all the structures and symbols of our social world are creations to serve the ends of our human nature. For the reasons explored in this chapter, some do so better than others. This new discipline therefore provides some specific answers to questions about the pathologies of life in industrial and post-industrial society, about the origins of many of our problems, and some indications of how they might be addressed.

We should, however, also consider how this view may be criticized. A chief difficulty it presents is level of specificity. Although the paradigm generates powerful, parsimonious and testable propositions, these are often at a high level of generality. It is easy to fit specific observable phenomena and research data into the frame, but this is legitimately open to criticism as *ex post* reasoning. The applications discussed in this chapter are open to this charge. They have been offered as a stimulus rather than a solution, to encourage more deductive hypothesis generation and testing within our field of a potentially important set of ideas. The specificity problem can never be fully resolved, since many of the phenomena of interest in our field are highly local adaptations to very specific occupational and organizational circumstances. The evolutionary perspective may prove incapable of producing novel propositions about some of these, but it should help us to see linkages between areas currently treated as unrelated, and between levels of analysis. At the very least it forces us to reframe our thinking about the basic assumptions of our field.

A second possible criticism is that the thrust of the paradigm is fundamentally conservative. Clearly it shows the functionality of many traditional forms and social relations, but that does not equate with their advocacy. The distance we have travelled from our ancestral origins has yielded a vast variety of social forms, and each brings its own tensions and fulfilments. Which we prefer is a matter of moral and practical choice. The practical choice is to do with how they serve our purposes. The moral choice is not about our purposes, but about how they are expressed and resolved in thought and action. Ethics, in this context, are which outcomes we prefer to deal with from the imperfect match between what we are and how we live. However, we should note that these are not free choices—the logic of the paradigm compels us to apply it to them equally. Ethical systems may be socially constructed, but they are also willed psychological environments, springing form the same source of deeply embedded inclinations.

This perspective is uncompromising. The logical integrity of evolutionary psychology's thesis makes it an all-or-nothing paradigm. It is not possible to buy only some of its propositions, although many require further explication and test, or to limit its applicability to certain areas of human life and experience. If one accepts its central premise, then even the most symbolic and socially constructed phenomena are subject to its interpretive frame. By this means it offers nothing less than a frame for integrating the social sciences with each other, and with the natural sciences (Tooby & Cosmides, 1992).

The question of how it relates to organizational behavior therefore suggests the need for a completely fresh look at every area of the field, of which only a few have been touched upon here. The same challenge can be offered to all other applied social science topics such as the design of work environments, the behaviour of consumers and the operation of markets. The effect of this is not to invalidate current theory or established knowledge, but to recontextualize them in ways which integrate their insights and point ways forward for research and application.

Acknowledgments

The author is grateful for the comments on this chapter of John Hunt, Roy Payne and Michael West.

REFERENCES

Ardrey, R. (1967). *The Territorial Imperative*. London: Collins.

Axelrod, R. (1984). *The Evolution of Cooperation*. New York: Basic Books.

Bargh, J.A. & Raymond, P. (1995). The naive misuse of power: Non-conscious sources of sexual harrassment. *Journal of Social Issues*, **51**, 85–96.

Bates, J.E. & Wachs, T.D. (eds) (1994). *Temperament: Individual Differences at the Interface of Biology and Behavior*. Washington, DC: American Psychological Association.

Bouchard, T., Lykken, D., McGue, M., Segal, N. & Tellegen, A. (1990). Sources of human psychological differences: the Minnesota study of twins reared apart. *Science*, **250**, 223–8.

Buss, D.M. (1991). Evolutionary personality psychology. *Annual Review of Psychology*, **42**, 459–92.

Changeux, J.-P. & Chavaillon, J. (1995). *Origins of the Human Brain*. Oxford: Clarendon.

Cropanzano, R., James, K. & Citera, M. (1993). A goal hierarchy model of personality, motivation, and leadership. In B.M. Staw & L.L. Cummings (eds), *Research in Organizational Behavior*, vol. 15 (pp. 267–322). Greenwich, CT: JAI Press.

Cziko, G. (1995). *Without Miracles: Universal Selection Theory and the Second Darwinian Revolution*. Cambridge, MA: MIT Press.

Davidson, M.J. (1996). Women and employment. In P.B. Warr (ed.), *Psychology at Work*, 4th edn. Harmondsworth: Penguin.

Diamond, J. (1991). *The Rise and Fall of the Third Chimpanzee*. London: Radius.

Digman, J.M. (1990). Personality structure: emergence of the five-factor model. *Annual Review of Psychology*, **41**, 417–40.

Dawkins, R. (1989). *The Selfish Gene*. Oxford: Oxford University Press.

Dunbar, R. (1996). *Gossip, Grooming and Evolution of Language*. London: Faber & Faber.

Eagley, A.H. & Johnson, B.T. (1990). Gender and leadership style: a meta-analysis. *Psychological Bulletin*, **108**, 233–56.

Eldredge, N. & Gould, S.J. (1972). Punctuated equlibria: an alternative to phyletic gradualism. In T.J. Schopf (ed.), *Models in Paleobiology*. San Francisco, CA: Freeman, Cooper.

Ely, R. (1995). The power in demography: women's social constructions of gender identity at work. *Academy of Management Journal*, **38**, 589–634.

Eysenck, H.J. (1953). *The Structure of Personality*. London: Methuen.

Frank, R. (1988). *Passions Within Reason*. New York: Norton.

Frese, M. & Zapf, D. (1994). Action as the core of work psychology: a German approach. In H.C. Triandi, M.D. Dunnette & L.M. Hough (eds), *Handbook of Industrial and Organizational Psychology*, vol. 4. Palo Alto, CA: Consulting Psychologists Press.

Giacolone, R.A. & Rosenfeldl, P. (eds) (1989). *Impression Management in the Organization*. Hillsdale, NJ: Sage.

Giddens, A. (1984). *The Constitution of Society*. Berkeley, CA: University of California Press.

Goffee, R. & Jones, G. (1996). The social integration of the modern corporation: an exploration of community concepts. Paper presented to the Academy of Management Conference, Cincinnati, August 1996.

Goffee, R. & Scase, R. (1985). Proprietorial control in family firms: some functions of quasi-organic management systems. *Journal of Management Studies*, **22**, 53–68.

Gould, S.J. & Vrba, E.S. (1982). Exaptation—a missing term in the science of form. *Paleobiology*, **8**, 4–15.

Gutek, B.A. (1995). Sex differences. In N. Nicholson (ed.), *Encyclopedic Dictionary of Organizational Behaviour*. Oxford: Blackwell.

Hannan, M.T. & Freeman, J. (1989). *Organizational Ecology*. Cambridge, MA: Harvard University Press.

Humphries, J. & Rubery, J. (1995). *The Economics of Equal Opportunities*. London: Equal Opportunities Commission.

Jahoda, M. (1982). *Employment and Unemployment: a Social-psychological Analysis*. Cambridge: Cambridge University Press.

Jones, S. (1993). *The Language of the Genes*. London: Harper Collins.

Kagan, J., Nidman, N., Arcus, D. & Reznick, J.S. (1995). *Galen's Prophesy: Temperament in Human Nature*. New York: Free Association Books.

Kahneman, D. & Tversky, A. (1979). Prospect theory: an analysis of decision under risk. *Econometrica*, **47**, 263–91.

Kanter, R.M. (1977). *Men and Women of the Corporation*. New York: Basic Books.

Koza, J.R. (1992). *Genetic Programming: On the Programming of Computers by Means of Natural Selection*. Cambridge, MA: MIT Press.

Martin, J. (1992). *Cultures in Organizations: Three perspectives*. New York: Oxford University Press.

Meindl, J.R. (1990). On leadership: an alternative to the conventional wisdom. In B.M. Staw & L.L. Cummings (eds), *Research in Organizational Behavior* vol. 12 (pp. 159–204). Greenwich, CT: JAI Press.

Mischel, W. (1968). *Personality and Assessment*. New York: Wiley.

Morris, D. (1967). *The Naked Ape*. New York: McGraw-Hill.

Moscovici, S. & Doise, S. (1994). *Conflict and Consensus*. London: Sage.

Murdock, G.P. (1945). The common denominator of cultures. In G.P. Murdock (ed.), *Culture and Society*. Pittsburgh: University of Pittsburgh Press, 1965.

Murnighan, J.K. (1991). *The Dynamics of Bargaining Games*. Englewood Cliffs, NJ: Prentice-Hall.

Neale, M.A. & Bazerman, M.H. (1991). *Cognition and Rationality in Negotiation*. New York: Free Press.

Nicholson, N. (ed.) (1996a). Work and personality. *Applied Psychology: an International Review*, **45**(3), whole issue.

Nicholson, N. (1996b). Career systems in crisis: change and opportunity in the information age. *Academy of Management Executive*, **10**, 40–51.

Nicholson, N. & West, M.A. (1988). *Managerial Job Change: Men and Women in Transition*. Cambridge, MA: Cambridge University Press.

Ouchi, W.G. (1981). *Theory Z: How American Business Can Meet the Japanese Challenge*. New York: Addison-Wesley.

Powers, W.T. (1973). *Behavior: the Control of Perception*. Greenwood, NY: Aldine/de Gruyter.

Ridley, M. (1996). *The Origins of Virtue*. London: Viking.

Scheff, T.J. (ed.) (1995). Shame and related emotions: an interdisciplinary approach. Special issue of *American Behavioral Scientist*, **38**(8).

Schein, V.E. & Mueller, R. (1996). Think manager–think male: a global phenomenon? *Journal of Organizational Behavior*, **17**, 33–41.

Staw, B.M. (1991). Dressing up like an organization: when psychological theories can explain organizational action. *Journal of Management*, **17**, 805–19.

Von Hayek, F.A. (1988). *The Fatal Conceit*. Chicago: University of Chicago Press.

Tooby, J. & Cosmides, L. (1990). On the unversality of human nature and the uniqueness of the individual: the role of genetics and adaptation. *Journal of Personality*, **58**, 17–67.

Tooby, J. & Cosmides, L. (1992). The psychological foundations of culture. In J.H. Barkow, L. Cosmides & J. Tooby, *The Adapted Mind: Evolutionary Psychology and the Generation of Culture*. Oxford: Oxford University Press.

Trivers, R.L. (1971). The evolution of reciprocal altruism. *Quarterly Review of Biology*, **46**, 35–56.

Trivers, R.L. (1972). Parental investment and sexual selection. In B. Campbell (ed.), *Sexual Selection and the Descent of Man*. Chicago: Aldine.

Trivers, R.L. (1974). Parent–offspring conflict. *American Zoologist*, **14**, 249–64.

Trivers, R.L. (1985). *Social Evolution*. Menlo Park, CA: Benjamin/Cummings.

West, M.A. (ed.) (1996a). *Handbook of Work Group Psychology*. Chichester: Wiley.

West, M.A. (1996b). Reflexivity and work group effectiveness. In M.A. West (ed.), *Handbook of Work Group Psychology*. Chichester: Wiley.

Wilson, E.O. (1975). *Sociobiology: the New Synthesis*. Cambridge: Harvard University Press.

Wood, D.J. (1991). Corporate social performance revisited. *Academy of Management Review*, **16**, 691–718.

Wright, R. (1994). *The Moral Animal: Evolutionary Psychology and Everyday Life*. New York: Little, Brown.

Yost, J.H., Strube, M.J. & Bailey, J.R. (1992). The construction of self: an evolutionary view. *Current Psychology: Research and Reviews*. **11**, 110–21.

Part III

New Forms and New Processes for Organizing

Chapter 11

The Discipline of Organization Design

Susan Albers Mohrman
Allan M. Mohrman Jr
and
Ramkrishnan Tenkasi
Center for Effective Organizations, University of Southern California, Los Angeles, CA, USA

Organization designs are increasingly being managed as competitive tools (Pfeffer, 1994; Lewin & Stephens, 1993; Galbraith & Lawler, 1993; Nadler et al., 1992). New organization forms are emerging, required competitively and enabled by telecommunications technology that permits almost instantaneous transfer of information anywhere in the world (Huber, 1990). For example, companies have removed layers of management (Lawler, Mohrman & Ledford, 1995); have unbundled the vertically integrated organization, blurred the boundaries between organizations, and created complex network structures (Galbraith, 1995); and are replacing their "line and box" hierarchical organizations with various configurations of self-contained and cross-cutting teams and networks (Mohrman, Cohen & Mohrman, 1995). Companies house a variety of idiosyncratic organizational approaches. New organizational forms embody changing logics: lateral capabilities are emphasized, often at the expense of hierarchical control; structures are conceived as dynamic and malleable rather than stable. These new organization designs create a changing landscape upon which organizational behavior occurs.

Although these new forms are responses to environmental forces, they are created by the people involved in the process of their design. The viewpoint put forth in this chapter is that the academic field of organizational studies must seriously grapple with the reality that, since organizations are purposefully designed by people, they are *artificial* (Simon, 1969). We argue that it is time for organization design to be treated as a discipline, and for increased academic attention to generating theory and technique to underpin it. The interplay between design, designing and organizational behavior must become a critical focus of study. Organization design bridges macro and micro, and designing is a fundamental ongoing organizational process that has to be understood in its own right.

This requires changes in the way we go about doing organizational science. A large body of knowledge exists, much of it useful in informing design, but it often requires reconceptualization in light of new organizational forms, and translation to the perspectives and language of designers. In addition, a large amount of new work is required to extend our models and theoretical understanding.

ORGANIZATION DESIGN: THE CASE FOR A DISCIPLINE

An organization's design is its configuration of technologies, processes and structures (Huber & Glick, 1993). Its importance derives from its role in shaping the distribution of resources, authority and information. It provides a context that shapes behavior in the organization. In turn, the behavior of people shapes the design of the organization. Increasingly, design is being recognized as a major determinant of organizational capability and a potential competitive advantage. Galbraith (1994) has noted that as organizations grow and evolve, and as they adopt changing strategies, they have to develop new capabilities. To do this they put in place a consistent set of structures, management processes, rewards and incentives, people and human resource practices to support new performances.

Organization design research has explored the relationships of various organizational configurations to organizational outcomes, most typically to indicators of organizational effectiveness (Lewin & Huber, 1986). A systems perspective has underpinned much of the academic work on organizational theory (e.g. Katz and Kahn, 1978) and design. It has stressed that organizational effectiveness is related to the fit between the various aspects of the design of the organization and between the design of the organization and its environment and strategy (e.g. Beer, 1980; Miles & Snow, 1978; Galbraith, 1973; Lawrence & Lorsch, 1967).

Most designs, and for that matter most organizational theory, have been within the framework of bureaucratic theory, and have accepted its premises (Lewin & Stephens, 1993). Organizational change and redesign occur through time—primarily in an incremental or routine fashion, as organizations put in place changes to bridge a gap between current or desired performance, to adopt up-to date practices, or to adjust to demographic, economic and social trends (March, 1981). Recent changes, however, have often been discontinuous. Unstable environmental conditions and competitor capabilities have made it necessary to find new ways of operating to achieve a quantum change in levels of performance in such areas as flexibility, innovativeness in products and services, service responsiveness, cycle time, cost, quality, and financial performance. Organizations are having to search for designs that eliminate the dysfunctional aspects of the bureaucratic form itself—the slowness, segmentation, sub-optimization, and risk aversion that it fosters. New approaches represent re-interpretations of the assumptions of bureaucracy, such as hierarchical control, specialization, routinization and formalization. New organizational forms are created. New patterns of organizational behavior are evoked.

It is increasingly being understood in today's world that organizational redesigning is an ongoing process, made possible through the self-designing capabilities within the organization (Weick, 1993). Organizations work continually to bring various aspects into alignment with the requirements of their context, generating an ongoing stream of designing activity (Monge, 1993). Studies of organizational redesign have found that entire industries—including electronics, healthcare, telecommunications, utilities and financial services—have been in a state of hyperturbulence. The demands placed on them by the environment "exceed the adaptive capacities of members sharing an environment" (McCann & Selsky, 1984, 460), leading to revolutionary change. This situation unfolds through time and may lead to a succession of radically new strategies for survival that entail redesigns that redraw the industry, the organization and interorganizational networks in fundamental ways ((Meyer, Goes & Brooks, 1993).

In addition to ongoing changes in the environment triggering ongoing redesign activities, the new forms of organization that are emerging have as their essence dynamic configurations of organizational units and relationships. As once vertically integrated organizations increasingly reconfigure themselves as networks (Nohria & Eccles, 1992), they increasingly accomplish work through a dynamic configuration of temporary project teams and alliances (Mohrman, Cohen & Mohrman, 1995), and the need to redesign the organization to fit today's tasks and strategies is continual.

Organizations also have to become capable of ongoing self-improvement; they exist in a competitive race to see which companies can learn and implement improved approaches quickly enough to be industry leaders and survivors. Today's organizations often house a stream of process improvement teams and redesign teams, frequently referred to as collateral structures (Stein & Kanter, 1980). As organizations become based on flexibility rather than stability, and as parts of organizations become more diverse, responsibility for initiating redesign is dispersed throughout the organization (Weick, 1993). Performance improvement activities have become part of the expected behavior within organizations.

In summary, designing is a fundamental process in today's organizational world, and designs are becoming more varied and fundamentally different than in the past. Because of this, there is a need for a discipline of organizational design. A discipline is a body of theory and technique that must be studied and mastered to be put into practice (Senge, 1990, p. 10). Effective designing, whether of small units or large corporations, will be a key organizational competency in the future (Mohrman & Cummings, 1989). To underpin this competency, frameworks for design and designing are required.

Currently, managers have not been trained in organizational design, neither have students of organizational behavior. In part this is because the research and frameworks that have been produced by scholars have not been particularly useful for this purpose. Our claim is not that most existing research is irrelevant to design; rather, that design has been irrelevant to much academic work. Organizational studies have generally not been cast in a manner that makes the results useful for design. Academic work on the network organization, for example, is currently primarily descriptive, focuses on abstract properties, and is aimed at theoretical understanding. Practitioners, on the other hand, want to know how to build a network and what it contributes to the outcomes that they seek (Kanter & Eccles, 1992). They are going about their business finding these things out by experimenting with new forms and learning from their own experiences. The emergence of new organizational forms affords an opportunity for management and organization theory to become highly relevant to practice (Lewin & Stephens, 1993). If academia is to contribute a body of knowledge upon which to base a design discipline, however, organizational studies will have to address a number of key issues of methodology and focus.

KEY ISSUES IN DEVELOPING A DISCIPLINE OF ORGANIZATION DESIGN

Let us first address an overarching philosophical issue: should organizational studies be concerned with design? Isn't that the purview of consultants and practitioners? While this can be, and has been, debated at length, the point of view in this chapter is that design and designing are part of the essence of organizations. Organizations are "artifacts"—created by people for their instrumental purposes. They are designed when they start up, redesigned as they go through life-cycles and change their strategy, and transformed when they encounter major societal and environmental upheavals. At the micro level, ongoing self-designing is part of the activities of effective units as they go about carrying out their missions in the organization. Thus, design and designing are important focuses for organizational studies; the blurring of the lines between the student of organizations and the practitioner is inevitable.

Laying the foundation for a discipline of organizational design has two aspects. First, a base of content knowledge about the organization as a system that can be designed must be generated and presented in a way that can guide action. Second, and perhaps more important, knowledge about the designing process is required. A thorough treatment of these two requirements for a discipline is not possible in a chapter of this length. Rather, we will use the remainder of the chapter to lay out several of the key issues that must be addressed.

An overarching issue is the need to take seriously the open systems nature of organization. A classic definition is that an organizational system is an organized, cohesive complex of elements standing in interaction with each other and with the environment (Evered, 1980). Another definition stresses the processual aspect of the system as a "set of coherent, evolving, interactive processes which temporarily manifest in globally stable structures" (Jantsch, 1980, p. 6). This latter definition is perhaps more helpful in understanding organizations today, since it acknowledges the dynamic nature of the system and focuses on organizing as a process that yields structures, a perspective that has also been taken by Weick (1979).

The second related issue is that organizational systems are populated by human beings and are the product of human beings and their interactions. The design of the organization is intended to shape the behavior within it. In a sense, however, the organization exists through the meaning attributed to it by human beings (Taylor, 1987). Design is the product of the behavior of the people in the organization. This reality needs to be central to the discipline of organization design.

These two issues, in combination, define a number of challenges that are particularly important to inform design and designing, particularly in an era when new organizational forms are emerging. Examples will be provided below.

The Implications of Organizations as Open Systems

Much organizational redesign has been conceptualized and initiated at the macro level of the overarching structure, including its units, sub-units and lateral integrating mechanisms. For example, a typical scenario in today's world is that organizations are becoming global; creating focused, decentralized business units that are integrated by a series of lateral linking structures that plan and coordinate across business units around the world. Work is being done in focused business units, in a series of flexibly configured teams that deal with a whole piece of work, and in integrating teams whose function is to make sure lateral interdependencies are addressed. Often these units are largely self-directing; lateral and self-management replace many of the functions of the hierarchy.

While this flexible, lateral organization has been described conceptually (e.g. Galbraith, 1994), it is less easily designed as an operational entity; behavior does not automatically assume the new patterns anticipated by the designers of a new macro structure, neither do organizational processes automatically shift. The shift in macro design away from a vertical hierarchical logic carries with it a shift in almost all of the key organizational processes, including decision-making, information-sharing, goal-setting and planning. The systems that support these processes must fit with the way work is intended to be performed, and each to some extent provides the context for the others. For example, the information systems provide the distributed information required to support lateral decision-making, and the lateral goal-setting process provides the support for lateral planning.

These organizational systems have traditionally been designed to support managing work vertically. A great deal of the organizational behavior literature has focused on the resultant behavioral dynamics. In new organization designs, the vertical dimension does not disappear, but becomes attenuated through the reduction of levels and declines in its relative prominence. A hierarchy of systemic levels remains—individuals, teams or groups, business units and businesses—with more inclusive levels providing a context for less inclusive elements (Mohrman, Cohen & Mohrman, 1995). Organizational processes need to support simultaneous vertical and horizontal activities.

Structure and the systems that support work provide the context in which people behave. Changes in the design of these aspects of the organizational system is intended to alter behavior within the organization. People have to engage in new activities, develop new competencies, relate in new ways to an expanded network of people, and direct their actions towards new objectives. The human resources systems have as their objective securing, developing and motivating the employees necessary to carry out the strategy of the organization. While historically directed toward individuals and individual performance, these systems now have to address group and business unit levels as well. In team-based organizations, for example, the team is the primary performing unit, and it makes most sense to address individual performance within the context of the interdependent team of which the individual is a part (Mohrman, Cohen & Mohrman, 1995).

In a flexible, lateral organization, the concept of well-defined jobs, and of human resource systems that prepare people for these, is no longer relevant. Responsibilities change fluidly as the set of tasks to be accomplished and the configuration of people available change. The management of competencies and capabilities—developing them and making sure they are where they are needed—is becoming the core principle of these new systems (see Lawler & Ledford, this volume). The notion of career is changing, also in a fundamental way. Careers will for the most part no longer consist of progression through a series of upward job moves that carry with them increased breadth of responsibility for a vertical segment of the organization. The new career will consist of continual broad and deep competency development through a series of work assignments that may span organizations (Hall & Associates, 1996).

This image of how the organization operates draws into question the learnings from a huge amount of research that has been done within hierarchical job-based contexts. In the arena of human resource practices, where research has traditionally been tightly connected to practice, the new organizational landscape is calling for new approaches. The design prescriptions for human resource systems that fit the new organization and new social reality are in their infancy.

Achieving a design fit among the macro-structural design of the organization, its work and other systems is not automatic nor trivial. Designers of the macro system often assume more malleability of organizational behavior than is actually the case. There is a great deal of evidence, for example, that reconfiguring work into cross-functional teams does not result in the intended collaborative behavior unless other aspects of the organization also change: behavior at the higher levels of the organization must also become collaborative, goal-setting and rewards of team members must be aligned, and other organizational systems must be reconfigured to fit a new collaborative way of doing work. At the very micro level, even the language used by people in teams where the context does not change continues to reflect the segmentation, competition and hierarchical orientation of the old order (Donnellon, 1996).

Likewise, the designers can seriously underestimate and misread the ripple effect of structural change. For example, a number of organizations we have studied have implemented internal markets by creating expert service and support groups that have to pay for their own existence through contracts with business units. The purpose of the changes was to generate increased responsiveness to business requirments. These organizations have not anticipated the collapse of sharing of information and resources and the subsequent demise of cross-unit learning that can result from a design that puts units in overt or perceived competition with one another for limited resources.

An important ramification for researchers of the systemic nature of organizations has to do with the dimension of time. Organizations existing as open systems in a rapidly evolving environment are continually introducing change. Furthermore, systemic change is of necessity iterative, particularly because, given the current condition of organizational science knowledge, it is based on spotty design knowledge (Mohrman & Cummings, 1989). Organizations are forced to learn as they implement, and to iterate as they learn. A snapshot in time provides little information about what design configurations contribute to outcomes and to subsequent change and learning. Organizational behavior occurs within ever-shifting designs. An important focus for research is how employees orientate their actions, given the fluidity of the context in which they perform; likewise, how does the organization attend to issues of motivation and commitment when it itself is such a shifting phenomenon? Another research implication is that methdology to understand and inform organizational design and designing has to reflect the complexity, interactivity and dynamic nature of the phenomena (Monge, 1993).

To inform the discipline of organization design, the kinds of knowledge that will be useful include exemplars and principles to guide designing. Given that the present focus is on organizations in a turbulent environment when new organizational forms are emerging, researchers can contribute by creating typologies that capture new organizational forms, and describe the attributes of new organizational forms and their relationship to one another, to behavior, and to organizational outcomes (Lewin & Stephens, 1993). Concrete depictions of ideal types and general and form-specific principles to guide the designing process can be derived. Depictions of the way in which organizations reconfigure themselves—principles and practical guidelines for self-organization—will be equally important.

Building the knowledge foundation for the discipline of organizational design will require organizational science to change its prevailing approaches in the following ways:

- More attention will have to be given to cross-level phenomena and to emergent phenomena. This will require a bridging of the traditionally separate domains of macro and micro organizational science. Methodologies for studying phenomena that have cross-level impact and manifestation will become more commonplace (Klein, Dansereau & Hall, 1994; Rousseau, 1985). Relational analyses, such as form–context relationships and network relationships, are critical to understanding the problems of organizational design (Monge, 1993). Organizational behavior will have to become understood in light of the requirements of the context in which it unfolds. Knowledge is also needed about how relationships among elements at lower systemic levels result in emergent phenomena at higher levels, so we can understand better the macro ramifications of micro behavior and design decisions.
- More attention will have to be given to interdisciplinary phenomena. Human resource systems, information systems, and financial measurement and valuation systems are key organizational sub-systems that directly influence behavior and have to be aligned as organizations change form. Adequately understanding their interactions will require approaches that integrate the social–psychological, cybernetic and economic disciplines.
- Focus will be increasingly on process aspects of organization, rather than the preoccupation on structures. As structures are increasingly ephemeral and virtual, methodologies for studying and designing processes will become increasingly important. Systems for supporting processes, such as information systems to support communication, will also be key focuses.
- Longitudinal and action-based designs will be required to investigate iterative and evolutionary design and design processes.
- Increasingly, researchers will focus on issues and problems confronting organizations, since it is these that yield self-organizing activity. Researchers will have to provide a bridge between the language and perspectives of practitioners and their own perspectives and language.
- Because of the emerging diversity of form (Galbraith, 1994) and the idiosyncratic nature and timing of the evolution of organizational form in different industries and organizations, rich case studies will be a useful theory-building methodology (Cameron, Freeman & Mishra, 1993).
- Modeling mythodologies, which have often been thought of as attempts to analogize "natural" organization behavior for descriptive purposes, are also inherently methodologies of design. Computer-based modeling of organization designs can not only suggest potentially emergent phenomena but can also function as an integral part of the designing process.
- Because the majority of research in organizational science has been conducted in bureaucratic organizations, researchers will have to consciously

scrutinize what we think we know to determine whether it is based on faulty assumptions about the nature of the human organization. Thus, much theory may have to be recast, and research results re-interpreted in light of a new range of forms and expanded assumptions.

The open systems nature of organizations and the importance of organizational fit have long been acknowledged by organizational scholars; however, organizational science has been primarily analytical, focusing on the piece parts. The differentiation between organizational behavior and organizational theory is itself a manifestation of this orientation. Design, on the other hand, focuses on synthesizing piece parts into wholes that perform in larger contexts. The discipline of design calls for a more concerted focus on the whole system in defining, executing and interpreting research. In particular, more attention will have to be given to understanding the whole system, and to processes and relationships that define the system.

The Implications of Organizations as Human Creations

Because organizations are artificial creations of human beings, they embody the values, interests and purposes of their designers (Weick, 1993; McWhinney, 1980). Organizations have a wide variety of stakeholders; consequently, designs often represent compromises or reflect widely shared belief structures and values that may characterize a society. Purpose is a key element of an organization's design, and determining purpose is a key aspect of organizational designing.

Purpose also relates directly to another element of the discipline of organizational design: the determination of the definition of effectiveness. Most current organizational theorists subscribe to the notion that effectiveness is subject to multiple definitions, and that true effectiveness may require the simultaneous accomplishment of several goals. For example, the competing values model of effectiveness (Quinn & Rohrbaugh, 1983) enumerates four goals: eonomic efficiency; internal integration and coordination; adaptiveness and responsiveness to the external environment; and utilization of human capital. According to this model, collectively achieving these can result in the achievement of economic profit.

During a period of turbulence and fundamental change, agreement about cause–effect and shared preferences for outcomes erode. The compromise of values and beliefs that underpinned the old order falls apart, and designing requires that a new set of understandings be created that can serve as the basis for a design that embodies a new compromise or that a novel design emerges that inspires commitment from everyone (Weick, 1993).

This issue is central to the methodological component of the discipline of designing. Various approaches to design are possible (McWhinney, 1980). In one approach, the set of goals is given, perhaps by top management or by experts, and the designing task is a technical one of finding the most direct path to the goals.

Alternatively, multiple stakeholders may participate in the selection of a design that cannot fully meet their multiple and conflicting sets of purposes. They search for a solution that addresses a set of goals that people are able to agree to. A third approach is also a participative one, and begins by stepping back to more fundamental levels and searching for core meanings to guide the design process. It is a process by which a group can create a new social reality—perhaps a unique organizational configuration capable of attaining a newly defined set of goals.

The organizational redesign activity of the past decade has been carried out with a somewhat limited mix of outcome focuses: economic and market perform-ance to ensure survival; and improvement of organizational coordination and integration in the service of efficiency, innovation and environmental responsive-ness. The changes have been in service of the organization's strategic direction and objectives, generally set by top management. Interestingly, although organi-zations are human creations, very little of the redesign activity has been guided by workforce preferences. Downsizing, increases in the gap between the outcomes of those at the highest and lowest levels of the organization, the increased use of outsourcing and contract labor rather than full-time employees, and the breach-ing of the implicit employment contract between employees and their organiza-tions, are manifestations of this. A backlash is beginning to occur, in the form of increasing societal attention to the issue and pressures on employers to address the concerns of employees. The next iteration of the ongoing transition for many organizations may be to seriously incorporate an expanded set of purposes in their designs.

From an organizational science perspective, critical issues arise that are central to the resolution of this tension, and that reinforce the need for cross-level perspectives to guide research to inform design. As examples: What impact do the emerging organizational forms have on employee commitment, effort and behavior? Cynicism and distrust? Perceived opportunity? How do these em-ployee impacts affect subsequent organizational performance? What human re-source practices provide the foundation for excellent performance in an organization that does not provide job security or a career?

The solutions to many of the human problems caused by the emergence of new organizational forms may lie beyond the realm of one organization. People are only partially included in the organizational system (Rousseau, 1985)—they also have identities as members of families, communities and other organizational systems. The design solution to the problems caused by the transient nature of organizational attachments may lie in interorganizational or community-based approaches. People may seek certain outcomes, such as opportunities for growth and development, and attainment of benefits through alternative routes, such as community-based insurance pools or employability and placement centers. To fully understand individual behavior in organizations may require the organiza-tional researcher to take a broader, interorganizational, community and societal perspective.

The tight connection of purposes and values to design means that the discipline of design will have to include methodologies and principles for determining purpose and creating a workable agreement among organizational stakeholders.

- Researchers will have to be much more explicit about the values underpinning their research, and be explicitly cognizant of the values underpinning the designs that they study.
- Research will have to take into account the purposes that different stakeholders have in their interaction with organizations. Employees with different employment relationships (e.g. core "careerists", temporary contract workers, etc.) may have different preferred outcomes (Rousseau & Wade-Benzoni, 1995), and may respond quite differently to different designs.
- Research examining design will have to take into account the designing process, the impact of different approaches to designing on the creation of shared meaning and agreement in the organization, and the ramifications of that for the effectiveness of designs in eliciting intended organizational behavior and outcomes.

Because organizations are designed by human beings and their behavior determines whether an organization will be effective, the integration of a phenomenological perspective is critical to a deep understanding of the discipline of design. Based on the work of Edmund Husserl, a fundamental premise of the phenomenological approach is that when we try to understand any phenomenon we project our intentions and attribute meaning. In trying to understand the organizational world, we can only deal with interpretations, and as researchers we are in many cases interpreting interpretations (Rabinow & Sullivan, 1987).

When we try to understand and change an organization, there will be no clear and consensual account of how it is currently operating and the problems it is encountering, let alone agreement about the desired state (Schon, 1987). Designs embody meaning. Designing is a meaning-creating activity and, in a time of uncertainty and fundamental change, the best designs may be those that enable meaning to emerge, by establishing processes that work toward a shared interpretation (Weick, 1993). Meaning may be the most potent shaper of behavior, and may allow the organization to continually self-organize and deal with increasing amounts of uncertainty and complexity (Wheatley, 1992). Designs that provide rich feedback about multiple outcomes and provide opportunity for collective interpretation and action planning are examples. Designing that provides for rich interaction, that shares divergent viewpoints and provides a forum for progression toward shared interpretations also addresses the phenomenological reality.

New designs, once implemented, imply new understandings and meaning. For example, one of the hardest transitions for people to make in the flexible organization is to develop a new understanding of career (Hall & Associates, 1996). Even if people can accurately describe the changed organizational landscape, they may hold on tenaciously to their definition of career as movement through a now pitifully scarce succession of hierarchical jobs. An important research question is, what processes help people develop new understandings that fit the changing organizational designs that are being created?

More broadly, our current research has found that within the same organization, people in different units attach quite different meaning to new designs, yielding differences in their behavior and in the outcome effectiveness of the design (Tenkasi, Mohrman & Mohrman, 1996). For example, across the hall from each other, one customer service unit might see their new cross-functional unit as an exploitative way to exact more work with the same pay; another may see it as a way to broaden knowledge and skills and take on more responsibility that will ultimately lead to even more opportunities. People's mental maps are of great import in shaping their behavior: important aspects of the mental maps are one's own position of centrality and influence, as well as how one images power, influence, support and activity flows in the new organization (Massarik, 1980).

Researchers may find that they have difficulty studying new organizational forms because they have difficulty finding a language that fits the varieties of meaning that exist in the organization. Questions asked of organizational members often have built into them a framework for understanding the organization that may not resonate with the new reality. As an example, in our own research looking at organizations in transition, we have found that it is difficult to identify the organizational unit to which an organizational member belongs. Even when local management has presented us with membership lists for teams that have formal responsibilities that are measured and rewarded, "team members" often don't think of themselves as belonging to that team because they see themselves as existing in a dynamic set of activities that often extend beyond the team. They may not even think of that team as existing: their own understanding of the composition of the team is quite different than the formal documents would indicate. This raises fundamental questions for researchers. How many of the core framework concepts that we employ make sense in the new organization? What kind of language can be used to elicit meaningful data in a changing situation?

For researchers contributing to the building of the discipline of design, the implications are profound.

- Designs can not be understood in the absence of understanding the meaning that is attached to them by various participants. Researchers need to be cognizant of the meanings of organizational members as well as their own meaning that frames the designing of research, interpreting of results, and drawing of implications. Particularly during a time of rapid transition, analysis of design effectiveness requires that this phenomenological perspective be taken into account.
- Methodological knowledge about designing has to have as a premise the assumption that organizational members will attribute meaning to the design, and that the effectiveness of an organizational design depends on creating sufficient shared meaning to provide the foundation for coordinated action.

- Since language is a critical carrier of meaning, the translation of theory-based research into useful design knowledge requires a translation process from the abstract, theoretical language of the researcher to the practical, action-oriented world of the designer. The language used in the framing and conduct of research must track to the phenomena being studied.

IMPLICATIONS FOR THE ORGANIZATIONAL SCIENCES: AGENDA FOR THE FUTURE

We have argued that designing is a fundamental organizational process and that research that provides the knowledge to underpin a discipline of organizational design is an appropriate arena of focus for organizational scientists. The discipline should include both the theory and guidelines to underpin the design process, and methodology to guide the practice of design. The importance of designing as an organizational process has been made salient by the ubiquitous redesigning that is occurring in organizations throughout the world. Designing has become a key competence for organizational managers.

Taking this mission seriously would, in our view, require some fundamental redirection of organizational science. It would require that disciplinary boundaries be blurred, and much more research be cross-level. Organizational design is systemic—it requires a simultaneous consideration of multiple goals, sub-systems and levels. Designs unfold through time; more longitudinal and action-oriented case studies will be necessary to understand the dynamics that are inherent. Serious design-oriented work would require that the values be made explicit and become part of the underpinnings of design and designing knowledge. Furthermore, it would require a serious treatment of the phenomenological nature of organizations, and a willingness to insert meaning into theoretical models.

These changes may demand a change in the meaning of organizational sciences for many researchers. Although at a general level we all recognize that organizations are human creations, we often act as though they have a permanent and real nature that can be understood solely through rigorously controlled scientific method. Taken seriously, the artificial nature of organizations means that we should open ourselves up to the fact that what we are studying is ephemeral, subject to change by the very knowledge our studies yield, and that principles, models and methodologies for design are perhaps the most useful contribution we can make from the understandings we gain from our research.

REFERENCES

Beer, M. (1980). A social systems model for organization development. In T. Cummings (ed.), *Systems Theory for Organization Development* (pp. 73–115). Chichester: Wiley.
Cameron, K.S., Freeman, S.J. & Mishra, A.K. (1993). Downsizing and redesigning organizations. In G.P. Huber & W.H. Glick (eds), *Organizational Change and Redesign: Ideas*

and Insights for Improving Performance (pp. 19–65). New York: Oxford University Press.

Donnellon, A. (1996). *The Paradoxes and Contradictions of Team Work*. Cambridge, MA: Harvard Business School Press.

Evered, R. (1980). Consequences of and prospects for systems thinking in organizational change. In T. Cummings (ed.), *Systems Theory for Organization Development* (pp. 5–15). Chichester: Wiley.

Galbraith, J.R. (1994). *Competing with Flexible Lateral Organizations*, 2nd edn. Reading, MA: Addison-Wesley.

Galbraith, J.R. (1995). *Designing Organizations*. San Francisco, CA: Jossey-Bass.

Galbraith, J.R. & Lawler, E.E. III (1993). Introduction: challenges to the established order. In J.R. Galbraith, E.E. Lawler II & Associates, *Organizing for the Future: the New Logic for Managing Complex Organizations* (pp. 1–12). San Francisco, CA: Jossey-Bass.

Galbraith, J.R. (1973). *Designing Complex Organizations*. Reading, MA: Addison-Wesley.

Hall, D.T. & Associates (1996). *The Career Is Dead. Long Live the Career: a Relational Approach to Careers*. San Francisco, CA: Jossey-Bass.

Huber, G. (1990). A theory of the effects of advanced information technologies on organizational design intelligence and decision making. *Academy of Management Review*, **15**, 47–71.

Huber, G. & Glick (eds) (1993). *Organizational Change and Redesign: Ideas and Insights for Improving Performance*. New York: Oxford University Press.

Jantsch, E. (1980). *The Self-organizing Universe*. Oxford: Pergamon Press.

Kanter, R.M. & Eccles, R.G. (1992). Making network research relevant to practice. In N. Nohria & R.G. Eccles (eds), *Networks and Organizations: Structure, Form and Action* (pp. 521–7). Boston, MA: Harvard Business School Press.

Katz, D. & Kahn R.L. (1978). *The Social Psychology of Organizations*, 2nd edn. New York: Wiley.

Klein, K.J., Dansereau, F. & Hall, R.J. (1994). Levels issues in theory development, data collection, and analysis. *Academy of Management Review*, **19**(2), 195–230.

Lawler, E.E. III, Mohrman, S.A. & Ledford, G.E. Jr (1995). *Creating High Performance Organizations: Practices and Results of Employee Involvement and Total Quality Management in Fortune 1000 Companies*. San Francisco, CA: Jossey-Bass.

Lawrence, P.R. & Lorsch, J.W. (1967). *Organization and Environment: Managing Differentiation and Integration*. Boston, MA: Harvard University, Graduate School of Business Administration.

Lewin, A.Y. & Stephens, C.U. (1993). Designing post-industrial organizations. In G.P. Huber & W.H. Glick (eds), *Organizational Change and Redesign: Ideas and Insights for Improving Performance* (pp. 393–410). New York: Oxford University Press.

Lewin, A.Y. & Huber, G.P. (1986). Organization design: introduction to the focused issue. *Management Science*, **32**, 513.

March, J.B. (1981). Footnotes to organizational change. *Administrative Science Quarterly*, **27**, 515–37.

Massarik, F. (1980). Mental systems: towards a practical agenda for a phenomenology of systems. In T.G. Cummings (ed.), *Systems Theory for Organization Development* (pp. 61–72). Chichester: Wiley.

McCann, J.E. & Selsky, J. (1984). Hyperturbulence and the emergence of type 5 environments. *Academy of Management Review*, **9**, 460–70.

McWhinney, W. (1980). Paedogenesis and other modes of design. In T.G. Cummings (ed.), *Systems Theory for Organization Development* (pp. 273–306). Chichester: Wiley Sons.

Meyer, A.D., Goes, J.B. & Brooks, G.R. (1993). Organizations reacting ro hyperturbulence. In G.P. Huber & W.H. Glick (eds), *Organizational Change and*

Redesign: Ideas and Insights for Improving Performance (pp. 66–112). New York: Oxford University Press.

Miles, R.E. & Snow, C.C. (1978). *Organizational Strategy, Structure, and Process*. New York: McGraw-Hill.

Mohrman, S.A., Cohen, S.G. & Mohrman, A.M. Jr (1995). *Designing Team-based Organizations: New Forms for Knowledge Work*. San Francisco, CA: Jossey-Bass.

Mohrman, S.A. & Cummings, T.G. (1989). *Self-designing Organizations: Learning How to Create High Performance*. Reading, MA: Addison-Wesley.

Monge, P. (1993). (Re)designing dynamic organizations. In G.P. Huber & W.H. Glick (eds), *Organizational Change and Redesign: Ideas and Insights for Improving Performance* (pp. 323–45). New York: Oxford University Press.

Nadler, D.A., Gerstein, M.A., Shaw, R.B. & Associates (1992). *Organizational Architecture: Designs for Changing Organizations*. San Francisco, CA: Jossey-Bass.

Nohria, N. & Eccles, R.C. (1992). *Networks and Organization: Structure, Form and Action*. Boston, MA: Harvard Business School Press.

Pfeffer, J. (1994). *Competitive Advantage Through People*. Boston, MA: Harvard Business School Press.

Quinn, R.E. & Rohrbaugh, J. (1983). A spatial model of effectiveness criteria: towards a competing values approach to organizational analysis. *Management Science*, **29**, 363–77.

Rabinow, P. & Sullivan, W.M. (eds) (1987). *Interpretive Social Science: a Second Look*. Berkeley, CA: University of California Press.

Rousseau, D.M. & Wade-Benzoni, R.A. (1995). Changing individual–organization attachments: a two-way street. In A. Howard (ed.), *The Changing Nature of Work* (pp. 290–322). San Francisco, CA: Jossey-Bass.

Rousseau, D.M. (1985). Issues of level in organizational research: multi-level and cross-level perspectives. In L.L. Cummings & B.M. Staw (eds), *Research in Organizational Behavior*, vol. 7 (pp. 1–37). Greenwich, CT: JAI Press.

Senge, P.M. (1990). *The Fifth Discipline: the Art and Practice of the Learning Organization*. New York: Doubleday Currency.

Schon, D. (1987). The art of managing: reflection and action within an organizational learning system. In Ravinow, P. & Sullivan, W.M. (eds), *Interpretive Social Science: a Second Look* (pp. 302–326). Berkeley, CA: University of California Press.

Simon, H.A. (1969). *The Sciences of the Artificial*. Cambridge, MA: MIT Press.

Stein, B.A. & Kanter, R.M. (1980). Building the parallel organization: creating mechanisms for permanent quality of work life. *Journal of Applied Behavioral Science*, **16**, 371–86.

Taylor, C. (1987). Interpretation and the sciences of man. In Rabinow, P. & Sullivan, W.M. (eds), *Interpretive Social Science: a Second Look* (pp. 33–81). Berkeley, CA: University of California Press.

Tenkasi, R., Mohrman, S. & Mohrman, A.M. Jr (1996). Organizational learning for transition. Working paper, Center for Effective Organizations, University of Southern California, Los Angeles, CA.

Weick, K.E. (1993). Organizational redesign as improvisation. In G.P. Huber & W.H. Glick (eds), *Organizational Change and Redesign: Ideas and Insights for Improving Performance* (pp. 346–82). New York: Oxford University Press.

Weick, K.E. (1979). *The Social Psychology of Organizing*. New York: Random House.

Wheatley, M.J. (1992). *Leadership and the New Science: Learning About Organization From an Orderly Universe*. San Francisco, CA: Berrett-Koehler.

Chapter 12

Perspectives on Process Management: Implications for Research on Twenty-First Century Organizations

Kathleen M. Sutcliffe
The University of Michigan Business School, Ann Arbor, MI, USA
Sim B. Sitkin
Fuqua School of Business, Duke University, Durham, NC, USA
and
Larry D. Browning
College of Communication, University of Texas, Austin, TX, USA

This chapter was developed with the charge of the editors of this handbook in mind: "to stimulate new and exciting research, not to simply replough old territory". Thus, we wanted to go beyond simply assessing the current state of contemporary process management theory and practice as others have recently done (for examples, see recent work by Denison, 1996; Hackman & Wageman, 1995; Wruck & Jensen, 1994). One way to approach the task was to think forward from the present to the future by identifying evolving current trends and making predictions about the future. An alternative was to "historicize an outcome" (Weick, 1979)—to imagine that a future event has already happened, think about the consequences, and then work backward toward the possible causes. We chose the latter approach, imagining the world of twenty-first century organizations, asking ourselves three questions:

- What are the key attributes of organizational processes that will have been most influential for organizational adaptation and survival?
- To what organizational and individual outcomes will process management practices have made significant contributions?

Creating Tomorrow's Organizations. Edited by C.L. Cooper and S.E. Jackson.
© 1997 John Wiley & Sons Ltd.

- What streams of organizational research will have been most influential for advancing our knowledge of the above?

In our previous work (Sitkin, 1992; Sitkin, Sutcliffe & Schroeder, 1994), we proposed that the essence of process management (e.g. TQM and related change efforts) involves dual core goals (reliability and learning) and distinct types of processes related to each of those goals. We also argued that these fundamentally distinct goals were not antithetical, but jointly necessary to organizational effectiveness. Thus, we argued, these two goals could be simultaneously pursued under the rubric of a more general and integrated approach, so long as that approach incorporated the two processes associated with each goal (i.e. control processes that are associated with reliability enhancement, and exploration processes that are associated with learning enhancement).

In this chapter, we build on this idea to examine the more general implications of recent theoretical formulations of process management for how effective organizations will function under conditions likely to emerge in the twenty-first century. Although our perspective on process management, which forms the conceptual underpinning of this chapter, is not widespread, it is shared by others in part due to the sudden emergence of a similar set of ideas in several parts of the field at about the same time. To reflect these related ideas, we also draw upon recent research by Eisenhardt (1993) and her colleagues (e.g. Brown & Eisenhardt, 1995; Eisenhardt & Tabrizi, 1995), March and Tamuz (March, 1991, 1995; March, Sproull & Tamuz, 1991; Tamuz, 1987, 1994), and others, whose work speaks to issues of process management and includes distinctions similar to ours.

ANTICIPATING THE ORGANIZATIONAL CONTEXT OF THE TWENTY-FIRST CENTURY

Managers and management scholars agree that the world of organizations is changing and that organizations in the twenty-first century will have to adapt to those changes to remain effective (e.g. D'Aveni, 1994; Fombrun, 1992; Bartlett & Ghoshal, 1989). Organizational survival is increasingly challenged by rising global competitiveness combined with increased interfirm cooperation, rapid technological breakthroughs, a demographically transformed workforce, and intensifying customer demands.

Tolerance for organizational shortcomings has dropped, as individual and corporate customers "vote with their feet" by switching to new suppliers if they cannot get what they want at a good price. These sophisticated and demanding customers, coupled with willingly responsive competitors, make it increasingly essential for organizations to provide remarkably consistent levels of service and product excellence. The need for dramatically improved reliability has driven the recent interest in process improvement programs, such as total quality management (e.g. Dean & Bowen, 1994; Garvin, 1987; Wruck & Jensen, 1994) and high reliability organizations (LaPorte & Consolini, 1991; Weick & Roberts, 1993)—and a generally conservative drive to avoid products or processes which are riskier and thus might damage the firm's reputation (Albert & Whetten, 1985; Fombrun, 1996) or stimulate legal action (Bies & Tyler, 1993).

While the demands for reliability rise, the world confronting organizations is increasingly characterized as "unreasonable", "discontinuous", "volatile", "uncertain" and "chaotic" (Drucker, 1969; Peters, 1987; Nonaka & Takeuchi, 1995; Handy, 1989). To respond to the demands of an unpredictable world, organizations must make faster, more integrative decisions (e.g. see Brown & Eisenhardt, 1995; Tamuz, 1987) that draw on the knowledge embedded in its systems and practices, its employees, and extra-organizational collaborators (Brown & Duguid, 1991; Lave & Wenger, 1991; Leonard-Barton, 1995; Nonaka & Takeuchi, 1995). Moreover, they must become more adept at learning and innovating, in terms of both new products and services and new administrative structures and processes (Galbraith, Lawler & Associates, 1993; Kodama, 1991; Senge, 1990).

Today, in the late twentieth century, much of the literature still suggests that organizations face a choice: to compete by being highly reliable in exploiting that which they already know and are known for, or to compete by being a leader in exploring new, breakthrough technologies or systems. Most existing work focuses *either* on the enhanced delivery of product, service or performance reliability *or* on the enhancement of organizational learning capacity—in essence viewing the pursuit of reliability or learning as a trade-off. Many organizations reflect this either/or view.

Yet a recently emergent theme in the literature (e.g. March, 1991; Sitkin, 1992; Weick, 1984) concerns the notion that what organizations need is to break through the idea that they can effectively frame their choice as an either/or proposition. Instead, unwavering short-term demands for quality performance coupled with rapidly changing capability requirements make it an impossible luxury for organizations to be able to focus on only one of the two goals. Specifically with respect to organizational effectiveness, we believe that dominant twenty-first century conditions will *require* the *simultaneous* pursuit of two meta-processes—reliability-focused control processes and learning-focused exploration processes—or, at a minimum, will favor those organizations that are able to master the apparent inconsistency suggested by their simultaneous pursuit. Thus, organizational survival will increasingly hinge on the capacity to balance control-based performance reliability and exploration-based resilience[1] (Brown & Eisenhardt, 1995; March, 1995; Miller, 1993; Sitkin, Sutcliffe & Schroeder, 1994).

---

[1] In this paper, we use two primary forms of terminology that need to be clearly distinguished at the outset. Throughout, we are contrasting the use of control-based processes to achieve reliability as a goal, with the use of exploration-based processes to achieve resilience as a goal. When we are focusing on processes, we will contrast reliability-focused *control processes* and resilience-focused *exploration processes*. When we are focusing on goals, we will contrast control-based *reliability* and exploration-based *resilience*.

FOCUS AND STRUCTURE OF THE CHAPTER

The chapter contains three parts. First, we discuss our use of the term "process" and what we see as critical conceptual issues concerning organizational process research and management. Second, we assess the implications of our conceptualization of organizational processes for organizations in the twenty-first century by considering the effect of increasingly uncertain and changing twenty-first century conditions and requirements on organizational outcomes such as capability utilization, capability development and trust. Finally, we consider the implications of our ideas for current/future organizational research and conclude with a discussion suggesting that a focus on process management may have critical implications for the conduct of significant organizational research in the twenty-first century.

CRITICAL THEORETICAL ISSUES IN PROCESS MANAGEMENT RESEARCH

To deal with the challenges posed in the late 20th century, organizations have adopted a number of process-oriented programs such as total quality management (TQM), organizational re-engineering, and business process re-engineering (BPR). The differences between these process improvement approaches can be striking. For example, TQM is focused on enhancing products and services to customers and suppliers through incremental improvements that reduce defect rates of existing parts and products and remove waste and inefficiency. In contrast, organizational and business process re-engineering attempts to achieve the same ends, but by implementing more extensive, systemic, almost radical changes in operations, productivity and quality. While TQM and BPR differ significantly in their orientation toward incremental vs. radical change, they both have focused in practice on enhancing the reliability of organizational operations using similar techniques, such as non-hierarchical organizing practices that involve the coordination of a chain of events taking place both inside and outside the boundaries of a formal organization (e.g. Garvin, 1984; Hammer, 1990).

Despite their distinctions, process management approaches share certain fundamental core principles and practices which are likely to continue into the twenty-first century. According to a Conference Board (1991) report, the most commonly used practices (in order of prevalence) include: (a) the use of teams for problem-solving, to simplify and streamline work practices, and to facilitate cooperation by breaking down barriers between organizational constituents (e.g. departments, customers, suppliers) (Deming, 1986; Ishikawa, 1985); (b) training and education related to a myriad of topics, but most frequently aimed at enhancing interpersonal skills, problem-solving and quality-improvement processes, team leading and building, running meetings, supplier qualification, and benchmarking (Hackman & Wageman, 1995; Olian & Rynes, 1991); (c) use of scientific methods and statistical tools to monitor performance and identify areas for performance improvement and use of problem solving and other process-related techniques to facilitate group processes (Hackman & Wageman, 1995); (d) developing improved relationships with suppliers (Lawler, Mohrman & Ledford, 1992); and (e) better determining customer requirements (Deming, 1986). Two additional practices, benchmarking (Camp, 1989) and employee involvement (Lawler, Mohrman & Ledford, 1992), have also become strongly associated with the process perspective. We highlight these typical practices because knowing the generic practices and activities that are associated with a process management perspective is crucial for understanding how process management can positively affect future organizational competencies—a topic that will be discussed later in this chapter.

The hypothesized benefits of the earlier-mentioned process management practices in routine or certain situations is relatively straightforward and there are numerous empirical examples of how such approaches have improved process accuracy (i.e. reduced error rates), process efficiency (i.e. reduced costs) and process cycle time (i.e. reduced time to complete a process) (Hackman & Wageman, 1995). In contrast, there is little data cited in this literature to support the idea that process management practices lead to improvements under less certain, non-routine situations. In fact, organizational theory traditionally links organic processes and uncertain situations (Burns & Stalker, 1961; Lawrence & Lorsch, 1967) and it has been generally accepted that "organic situations" lack structure: the implication being that process management is futile under such conditions.

Contrary to this received wisdom, in our earlier work we realized that actively implementing structure can be helpful in carrying out work in uncertain and non-routine conditions, and that this idea had been missed in mainstream process management thinking (Sitkin, Sutcliffe & Schroeder, 1994). Thus, we hypothesized about how process management practices *can be* designed and tailored to uncertain situations to enhance performance. There are at least two benefits of using process management tactics in uncertain situations. First, process management tactics may help people cope with an unclear and changing environment because such practices help them to rapidly build intuition and flexibility (Eisenhardt & Tabrizi, 1995; Sitkin, 1992, 1995; Weick, 1984, 1985). Second, process management tactics may simultaneously "provid[e] enough structure so that people will create sense-making, avoid procrastination, and be confident enough to act in these highly uncertain situations, which easily lead to paralyzing anxiety and conflict" (Eisenhardt & Tabrizi, 1995: 88).

Process management is concerned with redefining organizations as a collection of processes. In this chapter we conceptualize "process management" very broadly and more generally than it is usually conceptualized by researchers examining process management techniques. To begin to refine the construct, it is necessary first to identify critical process-related issues. Three such issues will be discussed here: the invisibility of process, the classification of process, and the role of uncertainty in understanding process.

Processes as Low Salience Features

Serious work on organizational processes has been scant compared with other forms of organizational study. Further, over the past 20 years, organizational research has been dominated by a focus on structure and function, rather than process. Because processes tend to be harder to perceive than other organizational structures such as departments, functions, or tasks, for example, it is only recently that firms (and scholars) have begun to pay attention to them—a condition that reduces the available data base and thus reduces the detail and reliability of any attempt at categorization. Organizational processes have tended to be unnoticed, unnamed and unmanaged because our attention has been focused on individual departments and their goals, rather than on sets of inter-related work activities which cross formal boundaries and involve various organizational members.

Classifying Organizational Processes

Classifying organizational processes is complex. Still, organizational scholars during the past 30 years have proposed several simple classification schemes. Early examples include the work by March and his colleagues (Cyert & March, 1963; March & Simon, 1958) and their distinction between problem-driven and slack search, Quinn's (1980) distinction between synoptic and incremental strategic decision-making, Burns & Stalker's (1961) contrast between mechanistic and organic organizational processes, or Ouchi's (1977, 1979, 1981) studies of input, behavioral and output control processes.

In a study of the differences in processes associated with information flows in organizations, Daft & Lengel (1984) distinguished vertical and horizontal organizational information processes. They found that vertical processes relate to the interpretation of the environment and the reducation of equivocality in order to determine what to do and where to head. In contrast, they found that the horizontal process relates to the reduction of uncertainty to enable internal coordination and task performance. Finally, they noted that organizations must both interpret the environment and coordinate tasks internally to be effective.

In a recent review of process management perspectives and implications for organizational design, Denison (1996) builds a hierarchical framework that distinguishes three fundamental organizational process modalities. His scheme is much like Daft & Lengel's, but splits internal coordination and task performance into two separate elements. Denison's first modality involves *designing* strategic and operational goals, the second involves *managing* (e.g. middle management processes concerned with organizing work), and the third is concerned with *implementing* (e.g. lower-level processes concerned with task activity).

Combining our meta-process distinction and Denison's framework provides a 3 × 2 categorization scheme for looking at organizational processes (see Table 12.1). This is a useful way to distinguish organizational processes for a discussion

Table 12.1 Differences between control and exploration across process modes

Meta processes	Process mode		
	Designing	Managing	Implementing
Control	Develop shared goals, schedules and criteria	Coordinate across units	Work to specs: test and tighten
Exploration	Articulate distinct goals and missions Independent units	Parallel activity tracks Encourage development of outliers	Push boundaries Pursue opportunities Search for novelty

related to twenty first century organizations because it allows us to ask about specific managerial and employee action sets that might be associated-with differing conditions. That is, it allows us to distinguish between processes concerned with the improvement of existing production processes and stable value chains (reliability enhancing processes) and processes concerned with defining or redefining real or potential value chains (innovation/learning enhancing processes) (Denison, 1996; Sitkin, Sutcliffe & Schroeder, 1994).

Denison's framework is helpful in terms of translating reliability-focused control and resilience-focused exploration goals into types of actions available to organizational managers and other members. Specifically, Denison usefully distinguishes the need to *design* a facilitating infrastructure, *manage* the interaction among units and individuals, and *implement* the designs through practices that accomplish the work to be done. By parsing the processes into three modes—designing, managing and implementing—Denison's scheme helps to clarify how actions taken in pursuit of control or exploration can be distinguished.

There are two key distinctions between control and exploration that are manifest throughout Table 12.1. First, control emphasizes clarifying that which is shared or convergent, whereas exploration emphasizes independence and divergence. Second, control stresses the clear, the articulated, the specific. In contrast, exploration stresses the emergent, the suggestive, the general.

Designing for control involves the pursuit of reliability by articulating clear, specific shared understandings that will govern activities. If reliability is to be achieved it is crucial that goals not be divergent, responsibilities not be fuzzy, and criteria to be met in products or services be unequivocal. The role of designers of control-oriented processes is to be sure that goals and responsibilities are clear and shared, schedules and criteria for performance are specific and understood, and that any general understandings about the purpose, tasks or roles are as concrete as possible. Design for exploration, in contrast, emphasizes the opposite: distinct and independently defined goals, fuzzy expectations and performance criteria carried out by independent operating units.

Managing for control and exploration exhibit equally distinctive practices. Given a well-defined set of goals, plans and performance expectations, a control orientation stresses tightly coupled action plans and close coordination across operating units and individuals. Since the thrust of control-oriented processes is to more carefully home in on established targets, systems and procedures to reduce needless variation are an essential part of managing for control. In contrast, the pursuit of the fuzzier goals and emergent expectations associated with an exploration orientation fosters the use of parallel processes and the development of innovative ideas (Bendor, 1985; Cohen, March & Olsen, 1972; George, 1981). The management of exploration processes, in other words, involves the active generation of greater variance, as this is the only route to discovery and capacity-building.

Implementing refers to doing work in a way that supports the underlying goals for which a process is being used. The implementation practices that support control include conforming to work, product and service specifications—and even tightening those specifications as a result of experience gained. Research on learning curves illustrates this approach (Epple, Argote & Devadas, 1991). In contrast, when practices are implemented that support exploration, these efforts involve challenging accepted standards and specifications, rather than conforming to them, looking for new and novel opportunities rather than avoiding or minimizing risky activities.

Uncertainty and Organizational Processes

Uncertainty figures strongly in a discussion of process management just as it has in many other areas of organizational inquiry, including organizational design (Burns & Stalker, 1961; Galbraith, 1973; Lawrence & Lorsch, 1967), organizational decision-making (Argote, 1982; March, 1988; Sutcliffe & Zaheer, 1998) and organizational control (Perrow, 1967; Thompson, 1967; Ouchi, 1981). In these works, a central distinction is made between situations described as certain, analyzable, routine or predictable and those situations described as uncertain, unanalyzable, non-routine and unpredictable. For example, Thompson (1967) discusses the much more complex and open-ended coordination requirements involved when action interdependencies cannot be specified *a priori*. Similarly, Williamson (1975) describes the difficulties associated with contractually specifying transaction expectations under uncertain conditions. Scholars from this wide variety of disciplinary perspectives have long recognized that technical transformation processes that are well understood present organizational members with a fundamentally different challenge than processes that are poorly understood (Perrow, 1967, 1984). An implication of this distinction is that while more certain activities can be accomplished through the use of systematic, routine, rational, bureaucratic procedures, uncertain conditions require a more flexible, experimental and improvisational approach.

We developed this same distinction in our theorizing about the total quality management perspective, its practices and related outcomes (Sitkin, Sutcliffe & Schroeder, 1994). As noted earlier, we were concerned that most process management programs had been advocated as universally applicable to all organizational activities, with virtually no attention to the nature of situational or task uncertainty. Our thinking was based on the familiar contingency theory notion that asserts that when organizational systems are poorly attuned to contextual requirements, a number of problematic outcomes may follow (Lawrence & Lorsch, 1967; Perrow, 1967; Thompson, 1967). We hypothesized that conditions of high uncertainty would require an alternative to standard process management practices (i.e. standard TQM practices), and also hypothesized that matching different operating practices to situational requirements would enhance the effectiveness of the process management techniques. With this in mind, we developed a contingency-based model and suggested that the specific process management practices adopted by an organization will enhance effectiveness only to the extent that they are matched to the level of situational uncertainty. An implication of our thinking was that rational cybernetic control (e.g. engineering) approaches fit best in certain situations, whereas experiential, learning-oriented, improvisational approaches fit best in uncertain situations. Thus, the central thrust of our examination of TQM was that process management programs cannot be effectively designed or used without taking situational uncertainty into account.

CRITICAL PROCESS COMPETENCIES FOR TWENTY-FIRST CENTURY ORGANIZATIONS

It is generally acknowledged that conditions of uncertainty are likely to be intensified in the twenty-first century. To adapt continuously in times of turbulence, uncertainty and complexity, organizations will be required to balance reliability-enhancing control processes and resilience-enhancing exploration processes in order to deal more quickly and effectively with the multiple challenges. Practices associated with each of the processes (provided they are tailored to the level of situational uncertainty) will be the dual cornerstones of adaptiveness in the twenty-first century, because such practices are designed to: (a) facilitate accuracy, efficiency and speed in routine situations; and also (b) bring a certain level of control and order to uncertain situations, thereby contributing to more rapid adaptation to continuously changing marketplace conditions (March, 1995; Sitkin, Sutcliffe & Schroeder, 1994).

What does it mean in a concrete sense for organizations to "balance" or "integrate" utilization of the two process approaches, as we and previous authors (e.g. March, 1991; Sitkin, Sutcliffe & Schroeder, 1994) have stressed? One approach, which we have explored elsewhere (Sitkin & Sutcliffe, 1994), examines the conditions under which control and exploration are related as a trade-off, are orthogonally related, or are synthetic and result in mutually greater gains. Another approach, which we will introduce here, concerns the similarities and differences between the two process approaches in terms of the classical "ITO" (i.e. input, transformation and output) process model.

Table 12.2 Differences between control and exploration across process foci

Meta processes	Process focus		
	Input	Transformation	Output
Control	Homogeneity of people, materials, etc.	Tight coupling Exploitation Cybernetic control First-order learning	Reliability enhancement Short-term-performance enhancement Trust
Exploration	Heterogeneity of people, materials, etc.	Loose coupling Exploration Interactive control Second-order learning	Resilience enhancement Long-term capability enhancement Trust

To explore the ITO formulation, we draw on Ouchi's research on organizational process to assess the implications of the control/exploration distinction. Drawing on the classical process formulation, Ouchi published a series of papers (1977, 1979, 1981) that examined how organizations manage process inputs (i.e. resources), process transformations (i.e. activity), and process outputs. Surprisingly, Ouchi's work has not been linked with efforts to understand recent developments in organizational processes (e.g. TQM, BPR) and thus the potential value of distinguishing input management processes, transformation management processes and output management processes has remained unrealized.

As shown is Table 12.2, Ouchi's framework helps to distinguish more clearly process attributes that will be applicable to control enhancement and those that will be more appropriate for exploration enhancement for each component.

Focusing on Inputs

Input management—which involves determining the desired mix of people, materials, equipment and other resources—would stress homogeneity and meeting pre-specified criteria if the goal were control; but would emphasize heterogeneity if the goal were exploration.

Several lines of research help to illustrate how inputs might vary in terms of human inputs (e.g. hiring, socialization, etc.). March (1991) conducted a series of simulations to examine the effect of hiring unsocialized newcomers on the degree of knowledge and the degree of "exploration" in organizational systems. He inferred from his results that homogeneous hiring practices ensure high average levels of knowledge of organization work practices, but at the expense of fostering low levels of code-breaking exploratory behavior.

A second way that human inputs can be varied to match the control vs. exploration dichotomy is to look at whether work teams should be formed to maximize homogeneity or heterogeneity, a theme which has received considerable attention. One example of a recent empirical study is Eisenhardt & Tabrizi's study (1995) of how team composition (among other factors) influenced the speed and innovativeness of product development. They found that the more heterogeneous the team, the faster, more innovative, and ultimately more pragmatic they were.

Of course, there are a large number of inputs that can be studied in terms of the control/exploration distinction. We have used human inputs to illustrate and have been illustrative rather than exhaustive in citing relevant work. Furthermore, while we have discussed input process management in terms of a bifurcation of control and exploration, in fact, much of the recent work on these issues is more consistent with our general thesis that organizations will increasingly need to integrate the approaches rather than select between them. March (1991), for example, found that moderate levels of homo-/heterogeneity were optimal. Cardinal (1995) drew on Ouchi's work to examine how pharmaceutical companies attempted to influence the development of routine, incremental product improvements as opposed to more disjunctive, radical product innovations, and found that the highest levels of effectiveness rested on the capacity to combine high levels of diversity with deep specialization in hiring and retention practices.

Focusing on Transformations

The attributes associated with managing transformations also differ depending on the dominant process logic being applied (i.e. whether the goal is the pursuit of control vs. exploration). As shown in Table 12.2, the characteristics associated with managing transformations from a control perspective are derived from cybernetic theories of control that require regulatory standards and activities that are sufficiently routine to be well understood (Green & Welsh, 1988). There is an emphasis on tight-coupling, repetition and standardization that implies a certain degree of task routineness and a moderate to high amount of certainty to understand cause—effect relationships. Further, managing transformations from a logic of control involves first-order rather than second-order learning, in that it involves more effectively exploiting familiar skills in addressing known problems (Sitkin, Sutcliffe & Schroeder, 1994).

In contrast, from an exploration logic, the attributes associated with managing transformations are embedded in the improvisational, experiential and iterative. There is an emphasis on loose-coupling, experimentation and interaction. Managing transformations from a logic of exploration often means that the context is fundamentally uncertain, and uncertain transformation processes are likely to promote second-order rather than first-order learning because second-order learning entails an increasing ability to explore the unknown and to identify and pursue novel solutions.

Focusing on Outputs

Finally, output process management can be seen as the central driver of the original distinction, since the goal is to foster outcomes appropriate to the situation at hand (i.e. high or low uncertainty). Nonetheless, drawing upon the Ouchi typology allows us to place outcome-related features more clearly into a broader framework. As shown in Table 12.2, we highlight three output factors as critical in clarifying the process distinction drawn in this chapter: reliability vs. resilience, performance enhancement vs. capability enhancement, and situation-specific trust.

Reliability is a primary output of control-oriented processes (Sitkin, Sutcliffe & Schroedor, 1994). Reliability can be thought of as a particular form of specialization that can be a very effective organizational strategy for organizations operating in a stable environment. This is because enhancing reliability in stable conditions accelerates first-order learning and, under stable conditions, rapid learning (associated with learning-curve advantages) can lead to strategic advantages for firms further along the learning curve (Epple, Argote & Devadas, 1991). Adhering to current products/services in familiar domains, fine-tuning well established methods and increasing the efficiency in using resources will contribute to sustained, predictable outcomes and short-term performance enhancements. When an organization achieves reliability, a number of things are working smoothly: reliability implies there is an effective culture, a high degree of agreement on goals and values, that the structure of the organization is contributing to close coordination of tasks, and that personnel are well trained and motivated.

As noted throughout this chapter, reliability and its accompanying short-term performance enhancements are important in the short term, particularly in more stable environments. Yet, the relentless pace of change and unending variety of challenges will require organizations and their members to also cultivate resilience if they are to weather the barrage of storms on the horizon in the twenty-first century and persist in their actions (Starbuck & Nystrom, 1981). According to *Webster's Third New International Dictionary*, resilience is defined as "the capability of a strained body to withstand a shock without permanent deformation or rupture", or "an act of springing back". Resilience in organizational members, units, and for the organization as a whole is essential for effective coping under conditions of rapid change.

At the individual level, resilience is enhanced by experiences that allow for the exercise of imagination, judgment and discretion (Kobasa, 1979; Kobasa, Maddi & Kahn, 1982), by the ability to make and recover from mistakes (Kobasa, Maddi & Kahn, 1982; Sternberg & Kolligian, 1990) and by observing role models who demonstrate these behaviors. The attributes of exploratory processes coupled with process management practices are likely to instantiate the conditions necessary to bring about resilience. For example, in theory, effective process management collocates decision-making authority with those who are most likely to have the relevant specific knowledge necessary to make a decision (Wruck & Jensen,

1994). Resilience is likely to develop as individuals are able to exercise their discretion and judgment, thereby effectively utilizing their specific knowledge. At the same time, individuals may develop resilience resources as a consequence of training and the development of specialized knowledge. In general, process management practices (e.g. training, innovation incentives, leadership support for independent thinking) may inadvertently contribute to the development of hardier individuals that are better able to withstand ambiguous and changing organizational conditions (Sutcliffe, 1995; Weick, 1985).

At the team and organizational levels, resilience is likely to develop as these units come to understand better their collective capabilities, competencies and identities. Although little is known about how team (and organizational) performance is influenced by collective beliefs, scholars increasingly acknowledge that collective beliefs can have a very positive effect on performance (Klimoski & Mohammed, 1994; Lindsley, Brass & Thomas, 1995; Sutcliffe & Bunderson, 1996; Wood & Bandura, 1989). Collective beliefs about the efficacy of the team (Sutcliffe & Bunderson, 1996; Wood & Bandura, 1989) and beliefs about the team's capacity for action (response repertoire) (Sutcliffe & Bunderson, 1996; Weick, 1988) may be particularly important for cultivating resilience and for enhancing long-term capabilities.

As Weick (1988, 1995, p. 34) and others have argued, it takes a complex sensing system *to register and regulate* complexity. Specially trained, multifunctional teams may develop better sensing and coping capabilities—especially if they perceive they have the ability to act (Westrum, 1991). Teams who believe they have a lot of expertise and who perceive many possibilities for action may be better able to grasp variations in their environments (Sutcliffe & Bunderson, 1996). And the more a team sees in any situation, the greater the likelihood that team members will see specific changes that need to be made. As Weick (1988, p. 311) notes, "[i]f people think they can do lots of things, then they can afford to pay attention to a wider variety of inputs because, whatever they see, they will have some way to cope with it". Jointly believing that the team has capacity and that capacity makes a difference reduces defensive perception, allows the team to see more and, as they see more, increases the likelihood that team members will see where they can intervene to make a difference (Weick, 1988). Exploratory processes build resilience, and also enhance longer-term capabilities through their effects on motivation and persistence in handling obstacles and adversities, and through their effects on registering and handling the complexity in dynamic and complex decision environments (Sutcliffe & Bunderson, 1996; Sitkin, 1992).

Finally, resilience and capacity are linked positively with identity. Organizations that perform well and out-perform their counterparts in the long term, will secure positive reputations and images (Fombrun, 1996). The attractiveness of an organization's image may strongly affect the extent to which organizational members identify with their organization (Dutton & Dukerich, 1991; Dutton, Dukerich & Harquail, 1994). This, in turn, is likely to influence internal interpersonal dynamics such as trust and cooperation between internal units (Ashforth &

Mael, 1989), which is a critical component for managing uncertain processes (Sitkin & Stickel, 1996). Strong member identification is also hypothesized to influence the extent of organizational citizenship behaviors which preserve, support and improve the organization (Dutton, Dukerich & Harquail, 1994). These extra-role contributions may be an alternative source of flexibility under rapidly changing conditions.

Trust will also be an output of the two overarching processes we have discussed. Trust is becoming increasingly important to organizational researchers as scholars recognize the role trust plays in facilitating cooperative relationships within and among organizations and in contributing to organizational performance (Ghoshal & Bartlett, 1994; Kramer, 1993; Ring & Van de Ven, 1992). Some antecedents of trust include a broad level of involvement in core organizational activities, an increase in the overall level of personal competence at all levels of the organization, and perceptions of fair and equitable decision processes. The practices associated with the implementation of control and exploratory processes, such as the use of multifunctional teams, the dissemination of decision-making authority to the lowest level possible, training for specific skills and training more generally, as well as rationalized decision procedures based on objective data and an awareness of business priorities, are likely to be instrumental in creating trust and facilitating the contextual conditions necessary for good performance.

There is a danger, however, that is highlighted by our distinction between control and exploration. Sometimes, processes and practices are forced on wary "resisters" while ignoring the possibility that the root of employee's resistance is an accurate perception of misfit rather than fear of change. Trust is likely to be established and sustained only when organizational processes in use match the requirements and expectations of those involved. When procedures and practices used by an organization do not match prevailing norms and expectations, task requirements or other situational constraints, trust is likely to be seriously and negatively affected. In two studies of mismatches between organizational processes and practices and the technical or social needs of organizational members (Sitkin & Roth, 1993; Sitkin & Stickel, 1996), the mismatch led to high levels of distrust. In contrast, when matches occurred trust was enhanced.

To this point we've discussed how control and exploration differ with respect to the issues of inputs, transformations and outputs. Before we move on, we want to return to our initial point that control and exploration need to be integrated and that organizations of the future cannot simply make trade-offs between the two. For example, one problem with enhancing reliability under conditions of uncertainty or rapid change is that it can put fast-learning firms at a disadvantage by foreclosing opportunities to discover other good alternatives (Levinthal & March, 1981; March, 1988: 10, 1995). As routines and systems become more focused on amplifying and developing a single strength, several things can result: flexibility decreases, myopia increases, and learning and adaptation are curtailed (Miller, 1993)—a deadly combination in times of turbulence, uncertainty and complexity.

If, as we argue above, the two apparently conflicting processes must be simultaneously pursued, how can organizations achieve this? Although there is little research examining the competencies, investments and performance trade-offs of trying to balance the pursuit of both types of processes (March, 1991, 1995), several studies merit closer attention. Recently, researchers have found that an integrated control/exploration approach to innovation-enhancing processes may be critical for fast and flexible adaptation (Cardinal, 1995; Eisenhardt & Tabrizi, 1995; Henderson & Clark, 1990; Simon, 1995). We believe the resilience of organizations and their members for withstanding change and ambiguity will be facilitated by the simple pursuit and balancing of the two overarching processes and associated practices described herein. Ultimately, success in the twenty-first century may be a consequence of developing coping skills and competencies that allow people to see better how they can intervene in small ways (Sutcliffe & Bunderson, 1996). Thus, firms in the twenty-first century must pursue reliability while simultaneously paying attention to the development of new competencies (i.e. innovation-enhancing processes) if they are to remain viable over time.

We have focused on several outcomes of process management that will enable future organizations to attain and sustain their viability. There are other implications for organizational research that we wish to consider in the next section. More specifically, we consider theoretical links to several existing streams of organizational research and also the implications of the process perspective for the conduct of significant research.

LINKS TO CURRENT ORGANIZATIONAL RESEARCH

We have suggested that to survive the twenty-first century, organizations of the future will have to pay particular attention to two processes: reliability-focused control processes and resilience-focused exploration processes. Much of the research on process management to date has been more broadly focused on detailing the achievement of reliability (Wruck & Jensen, 1994), and it is only recently that researchers have turned their attention to exploratory, innovation-enhancing processes and their underlying practices (e.g. Eisenhardt & Tabrizi, 1995; March, 1991, 1995; Sitkin, Sutcliffe & Schroeder, 1994). Still, more work remains to be done and there are several existing streams of organizational research that may inform our thinking in both areas. These links are discussed more fully in the following sections.

Links to Research on High Reliability Organizations

For some time, researchers have been concerned with high reliability organizations (HROs)—"organizations that require nearly error-free operations all the time because otherwise they are capable of experiencing catastrophes" (Weick & Roberts, 1993, p. 357). Even though all organizations make errors, HROs are distinguished by their quest to prevent failures (i.e. adverse outcomes) assumed to result from the amplification of errors (i.e. faulty processes) when they have little experience or information and compressed time within which to make high-consequence decisions (March, Sproull & Tamuz, 1991; Tamuz, 1987; Weick & Roberts, 1993).

With respect to errors and failures, traditional organizations have much more in common with HROs than is readily apparent—especially since the process management movement has brought the elimination of errors and enhancement of reliability to the forefront in traditional organizations (Obstfeld & Sutcliffe, 1996). For example, financial institutions, high status hotels, hospitals, and other high-performing total quality organizations with extensive environmental inter-action, increasingly operate with extraordinary concern for reliability and the elimination of error to prevent problems, to manage the real or potential conse-quences of risks, and to create a competitive advantage. As organizations are driven to squeeze slack out of their operations through downsizing and other resource constraints, they come to exhibit the tightly-coupled, closed system profile of many HROs (Weick, 1990, pp. 29–34). This is likely to continue as environments become more competitive, uncertain, turbulent and complex. Thus, the need to optimize processes and eradicate errors that may potentially lead to significant failure outcomes is crucial. With this in mind, one interesting avenue for future research could be to systematically compare the similarities and differences between traditional organizational practices designed to enhance reliability and the effective approaches used by "high reliability" organizations (Obstfeld & Sutcliffe, 1996).

There are several potential areas for future researchers to investigate. One fruitful area concerns the importance of conceptual slack (i.e. divergence in analytical perspectives) in enhancing reliability. High efficiency operating envi-ronments (i.e. just-in-time) tend to reduce conceptual slack, which means that alternative perspectives for analysis and adaptation are restricted. HROs develop sophisticated forms of redundancy (i.e. conceptual slack) that enhance mindfulness through overlapping responsibility for complex processes (Obstfeld & Sutcliffe, 1996).

A second possible area concerns structural and operational flexibility. Studies of HROs have shown that these systems shift their decision dynamics, authority structures and functional patterns in response to the level of organizational demands (LaPorte & Consolini, 1991). Flexibility in the HRO literature is often discussed in the context of the advantages generated by different combinations of loose and tight coupling among subgroups (Obstfeld & Sutcliffe, 1996). As we noted earlier, organizations in the twenty-first century will require the same potential for flexible response (Wruck & Jensen, 1994) if they are to cope with diverse competitive circumstances.

Two additional overlaps between research on high reliability and traditional organizations concern the interaction among subsystems and their impact on the system's overall performance (Grabowski & Roberts, 1996) and vigilance and mindfulness under stress (Weick, 1985). First, reliability issues generated by an organizational subpart may trigger additional reliability issues for others. Second, as organizations increasingly adopt more demanding operating standards in order to remain competitive, they increase the risk that stressful circumstances may impair judgment and lead to small- and large-scale failures (Staw, Sandelands & Dutton, 1981). Twenty-first century organizations can benefit from an increased understanding of how HROs continuously address these perpetual challenges.

Links to Research on Innovation

As noted earlier, organizational theorists have long accepted the idea that uncertain situations require an organic approach and have assumed that organic approach means a lack of structure (Burns & Stalker, 1961; Lawrence & Lorsch, 1967). Yet a growing body of work is challenging this received wisdom (Jelinek & Schoonhoven, 1990; Weick, 1993). For example, Eisenhardt (1993) and her colleagues (Brown & Eisenhardt, 1995; Eisenhardt & Tabrizi, 1995) have focused on trying to understand the fine-grained adaptive practices of firms operating in high rates of contextual change (e.g. rapid product life cycles or highly interdependent and shifting strategies of competitors). Work on small failures (Sitkin, 1992; Tamuz, 1994) and work on new product development (e.g. Cardinal, 1995; Eisenhardt, 1993) identifies a set of conditions—including decentralization, allowing mistakes and actively "processing" these errors, allowing for practice in anticipating, recognizing and resolving problems—that facilitate the effectiveness of innovation-enhancing processes under uncertain conditions. Most recently, Eisenhardt & Tabrizi (1995, p. 108) found that the speed and quality of innovation-enhancing processes in uncertain conditions is unpredictable, experiential and iterative, and a consequence of: (a) the use of multifunctional teams; (b) real-time learning through design iterations and frequent testing; (c) frequent milestones; and (d) powerful leaders. In sum, this work reaffirms the central notion that practices that build on a rational control perspective seem to fit best in more certain situations, while tactics that build on ideas about intuition and improvisation fit best in uncertain situations. Continued work in this area will help to build a clearer understanding of the specific innovation-enhancing practices that can facilitate speed and flexibility in future competitive and fast-paced conditions.

CONCLUSION

We have argued that organizational survival in the twenty-first century will require the capacity to balance the conflicting goals of control-based reliability with those of exploration-based resilience. In this chapter, we have distinguished two types of meta-processes—control and exploration—and examined their mediating role with respect to capability utilization (i.e. reliability and short-term performance enhancement), capability development (i.e. resilience and longer-term capability enhancement), and trust, which we argued will become increasingly crucial for survival in the twenty-first century. In addition to exploring the theoretical and empirical underpinnings of the proposed linkages, we considered the linkages with current research on organizations. Taking the kind of approach to studying organizational processes that we have proposed may have an additional more general benefit—enhancing the significance of future organizational research more broadly.

A focus on process may serve as an important springboard for the conduct of significant research in the twenty-first century for several reasons. Organizational scholars strive to conduct significant research. Our socialization into the academy instills a clear sense that the primary goal of academic research is the pursuit of incremental contributions to knowledge. As students, we are exposed to Davis' (1971) proposition that research contributions are judged significant because they are "interesting", Webb's (1961) proposition that the choice of a problem contributes to significant research, and Thomas & Tymon's (1984) ideas that relevance makes research significant. While some research projects yield significant outcomes, other research projects yield dull, routine outcomes. What contributes to the difference?

Although significance is a nebulous construct, hard to define and measure, and undoubtedly multidimensional, all of us judge some research as more favorable, more positive, more insightful and more practical than other research. Notwithstanding its nebulous aspects, significant research can be differentiated from less significant research along a number of other dimensions.

Daft, Griffin & Yates' (1987, p. 782) elegant study of the factors associated with significant and not-so-significant research outcomes indicated that while significant research sometimes can be distinguished by factors related to research outcomes, factors antecedent to the conduct of the study and to the process of doing research are far more important in contributing to the significance of the project. More specifically, factors pertaining to certain antecedent conditions—such as researchers' interactions with others, the integration of ideas and methods from different fields, and taking advantage of chance opportunities—were important in differentiating significant and less significant research. In addition, significant research was characterized by less clarity and more uncertainty during the beginning stages, high levels of excitement and commitment through the life of the project, as well as considerable and intense intellectual effort necessary to reduce equivocality during the research process (Daft, Griffin & Yates, 1987). In significant research "investigators expended effort thinking through the theory, and they had to figure things out as they went along" (Daft, Griffin & Yates, 1987, p. 782). On the other hand, the early stages of not-so-significant research projects were characterized as orderly, methodical projects where researchers knew exactly what to do from the beginning (Daft, Griffin & Yates, 1987, p. 782).

Using process management as an organizing concept around which to build interdisciplinary research programs, in fact, may induce the kind of antecedent research conditions that Daft and his colleagues found to differentiate significant from not-so-significant research, in that the study of process crosses disciplinary boundaries, and efforts to design and implement research in these areas is likely to intensify interdisciplinary interactions (Sutcliffe, 1995). Second, interdisciplinary discussions may serve as a "chance opportunity" (Daft, Griffin & Yates, 1987, p. 782) that highlights a number of possible interdisciplinary research avenues, and also fuels a sense of excitement and commitment that can help facilitate significant from no-so-significant projects. Finally, as we (Sitkin & Sutcliffe, 1994) have noted in our earlier work, if the field is to avoid the "faddish" elements of process management perspectives, the time has come for researchers to do some deep theoretical thinking about process management, its implementation, and the particular domains in which it can contribute to organizational theory and managerial practice.

Perhaps as scholars we can more systematically pursue the duality of control and exploration. For example, the mandate and editorial practices of the journal *Organization Science* include the conscious effort to take risks on some manuscripts that appear to be exceptionally generative (i.e. congruent with principles of exploration), while remaining cognizant of control-based criteria for top-tier publications.

With a few exceptions, research on organizational process management has historically followed a fairly lock-step incremental approach. If exploration processes are moved to center stage in terms of both the nomenclature and the conceptualization of process management, then our thinking about and understanding of process will be more well suited to our vision of twenty-first century contexts. Furthermore, the implication of the research of Daft, Griffin & Yates (1987) is that the very act of thinking more deeply about process is likely to stimulate increasingly significant research efforts on the topic.

Acknowledgments

The authors gratefully acknowledge support from the National Science Foundation (Grant No. SBR-94-96229 and SBR-94-20461) for the research on which this chapter is based.

REFERENCES

Albert, S. & Whetten, D. (1985). Organizational identity. In L.L. Cummings & B.M. Staw (eds), *Research in Organizational Behavior*, vol. 7 (pp. 263–95). Greenwich, CT: JAI Press.

Argote, L. (1982). Input uncertainty and organizational coordination in hospital emergency units. *Administrative Science Quarterly*, **27**, 420–34.

Ashforth, B.E. & Mael, F. (1989). Social identity theory and the organization. *Academy of Management Review*, **14**, 20–39.

Bartlett, C.A. & Ghoshal, S. (1989). *Managing Across borders: the Transnational Solution*. Boston, MA: Harvard Business School Press.

Bendor, J.B. (1985). *Parallel Systems*. Berkeley, CA: University of California Press.

Bies, R.J. & Tyler, T.R. (1993). The "litigation mentality" in organizations. *Organization Science*, **4**, 352–66.

Brown, J.S. & Duguid, P. (1991). Communities of practice. *Organization Science*, **2**, 40–58.

Brown, S.L. & Eisenhardt, K.M. (1995). Product development: past research, present findings, and future directions. *Academy of Management Review*, **20**, 343–78.

Burns, T. & Stalker, G.M. (1961). *The Management of Innovation*. London: Tavistock.

Camp, R.C. (1989). *Benchmarking: the Search for Industry Best Practices that Lead to Superior Performance*. Milwaukee, WI: Quality Press.

Cardinal, L.B. (1995). *Technological Innovation in the Pharmaceutical Industry: Managing Research and Development Using Input, Behavior, and Output Controls*. Manuscript under review.

Cohen, M.D., March, J.G. & Olsen, J.P. (1972). A garbage can model of organizational choice. *Administrative Science Quarterly*, **17**, 1–25.

Conference Board (1991). *Employee Buy-in to Total Quality*. New York: Conference Board.

Cyert, R.M. & March, J.G. (1963). *A Behavioral Theory of the Firm*. Englewood Cliffs, NJ: Prentice-Hall.

D'Aveni, R.A. (1994). *Hypercompetition: Managing the Dynamics of Strategic maneuvering*. New York: Free Press.

Daft, R.L., Griffin, R.W. & Yates, V. (1987). Retrospective accounts of research factors associated with significant and not-so-significant outcomes. *Academy of Management Journal*, **30**, 763–85.

Daft, R.L. & Lengel, R.H. (1984). Information richness: a new approach to managerial behavior and organization design. In B.M. Staw & L.L. Cummings (eds), *Research in Organizational Behavior*, vol. 6 (pp. 193–233). Greenwich, CT: JAI Press.

Davis, M.S. (1971). That's interesting! Towards a phenomenology of sociology and a sociology of phenomenology. *Philosophy of Social Sciences*, **1**, 309–44.

Dean, J.W. & Bowen, D.E. (1994). Management theory and total quality: improving research and practice through theory development. *Academy of Management Review*, **19**, 392–418.

Deming, W.E. (1986). *Out of the Crisis*. Cambridge, MA: MIT Center for Advanced Engineering Study.

Denison, D.R. (1996). Toward a process-based theory of organizational design: can organizations be designed around value chains and networks? In J. Walsh & A. Huff (eds), *Advances in Strategic Management*. Greenwich, CT: JAI Press, in press.

Drucker, P. (1969). *The Age of Discontinuity: Guidelines to our Changing Society*. New York: Harper & Row.

Dutton, J.E. & Dukerich, J.M. (1991). Keeping an eye on the mirror: the role of image and identity in organizational adaptation. *Academy of Management Journal*, **34**, 517–54.

Dutton, J.E., Dukerich, J.M. & Harquail, C.V. (1994). Organizational images and member identification. *Administrative Science Quarterly*, **39**, 239–63.

Eisenhardt, K.M. (1993). High reliability organizations meet high velocity environments: common dilemmas in nuclear power plants. In K.H. Roberts (ed.), *New Challenges to Understanding Organizations* (pp. 117–36). New York: Macmillan.

Eisenhardt, K.M. & Tabrizi, B.N. (1995). Accelerating adaptive processes: product innovation in the global computer industry. *Administrative Science Quarterly*, **40**, 84–110.

Epple, D.E., Argote, L. & Devadas, R. (1991). Organizational learning curves: a method for investigating intra-plant transfer of knowledge acquired through learning by doing. *Organization Science*, **2**, 58–70.

Fombrun, C.J. (1992). *Turning Points: Creating Strategic Change in Corporations*. New York: McGraw-Hill.

Fombrun, C.J. (1996). *Reputation*. Boston, MA: Harvard Business Press.

Galbraith, J.R. (1973). *Designing Complex Organizations.* Reading, MA: Addison-Wesley.

Galbraith, J.R., Lawler, E.E. & Associates (1993). *Organization for the Future: the New Logic of Managing Complex Organizing.* San Francisco, CA: Jossey-Bass.

Garvin, D.A. (1984). What does "product quality" really mean? *Sloan Management Review*, **26**, 25–42.

Garvin, D.A. (1987). Competing on the eight dimensions of quality. *Harvard Business Review*, **65**, 101–9.

George, A. (1981). *Presidential Decision-making in Foreign Policy.* Boulder, CO: Westview Press.

Ghoshal, S. & Bartlett, C.A. (1994). Linking organizational context and managerial action: the dimensions of quality of management. *Strategic Management Journal*, **15**, 91–112.

Grabowski, M. & Roberts, K.H. (1996). Human and organizational error in large scale systems. *IEEE Transactions on Systems, Man, and Cybernetics*, **26**, 1–15.

Green, S.G. & Welsh, M.A. (1988). Cybernetics and dependence: reframing the control concept. *Academy of Management Review*, **13**, 287–301.

Hackman, J.R. & Wageman, R. (1995). Total quality management: empirical, conceptual, and practical issues. *Administrative Science Quarterly*, **40**, 309–42.

Hammer, M. (1990). Re-engineering work: don't automate, obliterate. *Harvard Business Review*, **68**, 104–12.

Handy, C. (1989). *The Age of Unreason.* Boston, MA: Harvard Business School Press.

Henderson, R.M. & Clark, K.B. (1990). Architectural innovation: the reconfiguration of existing product technologies and the failure of established firms. *Administrative Science Quarterly*, **35**, 9–30.

Ishikawa, K. (1985). *What Is Total Quality Control? The Japanese Way.* Englewood Cliffs, NJ: Prentice-Hall.

Jelinek, M. & Schoonhoven, C.B. (1990). *The Innovation Marathon.* London: Basil Blackwell.

Klimoski, R. & Mohammed, S. (1994). Team mental model: construct or metaphor? *Journal of Management*, **20**, 403–37.

Kobasa, S.C. (1979). Stressful life events, personality, and health: an inquiry into hardiness. *Personality and Social Psychology*, **37**, 1–11.

Kobasa, S.C., Maddi, S.R. & Kahn, S. (1982). Hardiness and health: a prospective study. *Journal of Personality and Social Psychology*, **42**, 168–77.

Kodama, F. (1991). *Emerging Patterns of Innovation.* Boston, MA: Harvard Business School Press.

Kramer, R. (1993). Cooperation and organizational identification. In K. Murnighan (ed.), *Social Psychology in Organizations: Advances in Theory and Research.* Englewood Cliffs, NJ: Prentice-Hall.

LaPorte, T. & Consolini, P. (1991). Working in theory, but not in practice: theoretical challenges of high reliability organizations. *Journal of Public Administration Research and Theory*, **1**, 19–47.

Lave, J. & Wenger, E. (1991). *Situated Learning: Legitimate Peripheral Participation.* New York: Cambridge University Press.

Lawler, E.E., Mohrman, S.A. & Ledford, G.E. (1992). *Employee Involvement and Total Quality Management: Practices and Results in Fortune 1000 Companies.* San Francisco, CA: Jossey-Bass.

Lawrence, P.R. & Lorsch, J.W. (1967). *Organization and Environment.* Homewood, IL: Irwin.

Leonard-Barton, D. (1995). *Wellsprings of Knowledge.* Boston, MA: Harvard Business School Press.

Levinthal, D. & March, J.G. (1981). A model of adaptive organizational search. *Journal of Economic Behavior and Organization*, **2**, 307–33.

Lindsley, D.H., Brass, D.J. & Thomas, J.B. (1995). Efficacy-performance spirals: a multilevel perspective. *Academy of Management Review*, **20**, 645–78.

March, J.G. (1988). *Decisions and Organizations*. New York: Blackwell.

March, J.G. (1991). Exploration and exploitation in organizational learning. *Organization Science*, **2**, 71–87.

March, J.G. (1995). The future, disposable organizations, and the rigidities of imagination, *Organization*, **2**(3/4), 427–40.

March, J.G. & Simon, H.A. (1958). *Organizations*. New York: Wiley.

March, J.G., Sproull, L.S. & Tamuz, M. (1991). Learning from samples of one or fewer. *Organization Science*, **2**, 1–13.

Miller, D. (1993). The architecture of simplicity. *Academy of Management Review*, **18**, 116–38.

Nonaka, I. & Takeuchi, H. (1995). *The Knowledge-creating Company*. New York: Oxford University Press.

Obstfeld, D. & Sutcliffe, K.M. (1996). Everyday reliability in traditional organizations: learning from high reliability organizations. Working paper, University of Michigan.

Olian, J.D. & Rynes, S.L. (1991). Making Total Quality work: aligning organizational processes, performance measures, and stakeholders. *Human Resource Management*, **30**, 303–33.

Ouchi, W.G. (1977). The relationship between organizational structure and organizational control. *Administrative Science Quarterly*, **22**, 95–113.

Ouchi, W.G. (1979). A conceptual framework for the design of organizational control mechanisms. *Management Science*, **25**, 833–48.

Ouchi, W.G. (1981). Markets, bureaucracies, and clans. *Administrative Science Quarterly*, **25**, 129–41.

Perrow, C. (1967). A framework for the comparative analysis of organizations. *American Sociological Review*, **32**, 194–208.

Perrow, C. (1984). *Normal Accidents: Living with High Risk Technologies*. New York: Basic Books.

Peters, T. (1987). *Thriving on Chaos*. New York: Harper & Row.

Quinn, J.B. (1980). *Strategies for Changes: Logical Incrementalism*. Homewood, IL: Irwin-Dorsey Press.

Ring, P. & Van de Ven, A. (1992). Structuring cooperative relationships between organizations. *Strategic Management Journal*, **13**, 483–98.

Senge, P. (1990). *The Fifth Discipline: the Art and Practice of the Learning Organization*. New York: Doubleday.

Simon, R. (1995). *Levers of Control*. Boston, MA: Harvard Business Press.

Sitkin, S.B. (1992). Learning through failure: the strategy of small losses. In B.M. Staw & L.L. Cummings (eds), *Research in Organizational Behavior*, vol. 14 (pp. 231–66). Greenwich, CT: JAI Press.

Sitkin, S.B. (1995). On the positive effects of legalization on trust. In R. Bies, R. Lewicki & B. Sheppard (eds), *Research on Negotiation in Organizations*, vol. 5 (pp. 185–217). Greenwich, CT: JAI Press.

Sitkin, S.B. & Roth, N.L. (1993). Explaining the limited effectiveness of legalistic "remedies" for trust/distrust. *Organization Science*, **4**, 367–92.

Sitkin, S.B. & Stickel, D. (1996). The road to hell: the dynamics of distrust in an era of quality. In R.M. Kramer & T.R. Tyler (eds), *Trust in Organizations: Frontiers of Theory and Research* (pp. 196–215). Thousand Oaks, CA: Sage.

Sitkin, S.B., Sutcliffe, K.M. & Schroeder, R.G. (1994). Distinguishing control from learning in total quality management: a contingency perspective. *Academy of Management Review*, **19**, 537–64.

Sitkin, S.B. & Sutcliffe, K.M. (1994). *Strategy as Control versus Strategy as Learning*. ORSA/TMS Conference—College of Organizations Program on Organizational Learning, Detroit, MI.

Starbuck, W.H. & Nystrom, P.C. (1981). Why the world needs organizational design. *Journal of General Management*, **6**, 3–17.

Staw, B.M., Sandelands, L.E. & Dutton, J.E. (1981). Threat-rigidity effects in organizational behavior: a multilevel analysis. *Administrative Science Quarterly*, **26**, 501–24.

Sternberg, R.J. & Kolligian, J. (1990). *Competence Considered*. New Haven, CT: Yale University Press.

Sutcliffe, K.M. (1995). TQM as an organizing construct for the conduct of significant research. Paper presented at the Annual Meetings of the Academy of Management, Vancouver, B.C.

Sutcliffe, K.M. & Bunderson, J.S. (1996). Competence learned: developmental processes in organizational teams. Paper presented at the Annual Meetings of the Academy of Management, Cincinnati, OH.

Sufcliffe, K.M. & Zaheer, A. (1998). Uncertainty in the transaction environment: an empirical test. *Strategic Management Journal*, in press.

Tamuz, M. (1987). The impact of computer surveillance on air safety reporting. *Columbia Journal of World Business*, **22**(1), 69–77.

Tamuz, M. (1994). Developing organizational safety information systems for monitoring potential dangers. In G.E. Apostolakis & T.S. Win (eds), *Proceedings of PSAM II*, vol. 2 (section 71) pp. 7–12. Los Angeles, CA: University of California.

Thomas, K.W. & Tymon, W.G. (1984). Necessary properties of relevant research: lessons from recent criticisms of the organizational sciences. *Academy of Management Review*, **7**, 345–52.

Thompson, J.D. (1967). *Organizations in Action*. New York: McGraw-Hill.

Webb, W. (1961). The choice of a problem. *American Psychologist*, **16**(5), 223–7.

Weick, K.W. (1979). *The Social Psychology of Organizing*, 2nd edn. Reading. MA: Addison-Wesley.

Weick, K.E. (1984). Small wins: redefining the scale of social problems. *American Psychologist*, **39**(1), 40–49.

Weick, K.E. (1985). A stress analysis of future battlefields. In J.G. Hunt & J.D. Blair (eds), *Leadership on the Future Battlefield* (pp. 32–46). McLean, VA: Pergamon.

Weick, K.E. (1988). Enacted sensemaking in crisis situations. *Journal of Management Studies*, **25**, 305–17.

Weick, K.E. (1990). Technology as equivoque: sensemaking in new technologies. In P.S. Goodman (ed.), *Technologies in Organizations* (pp. 1–44). San Francisco, CA: Jossey-Bass.

Weick, K.E. (1993). The collapse of sensemaking in organizations: the Mann Gulch disaster. *Administrative Science Quarterly*, **38**, 628–52.

Weick, K.E. (1995). *Sensemaking in Organizations*. Newbury Park, CA: Sage.

Weick, K.E. & Roberts, K. (1993). Collective mind in organizations: heedful interrelating on flight decks. *Administrative Science Quarterly*, **38**, 357–81.

Westrum, R. (1991). *Technologies and Society: the Shaping of People and Things*. Belmont, CA: Wadsworth.

Williamson, O.E. (1975). *Markets and Hierarchies*. New York: Free Press.

Wood, R. & Bandura, A. (1989). Social cognitive theory of organizational management. *Academy of Management Review*, **14**, 361–84.

Wruck, K. & Jensen, M. (1994). Science, specific knowledge, and total quality management. *Journal of Accounting and Economics*, **18**, 247–87.

Chapter 13

New Approaches to Organizing: Competencies, Capabilities and the Decline of the Bureaucratic Model

Edward E. Lawler III
and
Gerald E. Ledford Jr
Center for Effective Organizations, University of Southern California, Los Angeles, CA, USA

The academic literature and the business press regularly stress the challenges that contemporary organizations face. Increasingly, organizations find themselves in global business competitions that demand ever higher levels of performance. Scholars and managers are arguing for innovations in organization design as a potential way to achieve higher and higher levels of performance (e.g. Lawler, 1996; Ulrich & Lake, 1990). The 1970s and 1980s saw considerable interest in total quality management and employee involvement. The 1990s have seen a fascination with re-engineering, downsizing and delayering.

As the focus on organization design has increased, the traditional bureaucratic approach to organizing has come under heavy criticism. According to its critics, it does not produce the high levels of speed, quality and productivity that are needed in highly competitive global businesses. Nor does it create organizations that can change rapidly and adapt easily to the increasingly turbulent business environment. The key principles of the bureaucratic model include a high degree of specialization, the division of labor down to the level of the job, the use of a hierarchical authority, and a reliance on formal rules and standard operating

Creating Tomorrow's Organizations. Edited by C.L. Cooper and S.E. Jackson.
© 1997 John Wiley & Sons Ltd.

procedures. These design elements create and maintain top-down management control and organizational stability. In an era of constant change and demands for ever higher levels of performance, bureaucratic designs appear clumsy and lethargic.

It is one thing to say that organizations can be a source of competitive advantage, and that the bureaucratic approach is ineffective; it is another to identify and implement a superior organizational approach. At this point, it is not clear that any one approach has emerged as the clear successor to the bureaucratic model. Most organizations still embrace such key features of the traditional bureaucratic model as individual jobs, hierarchical relationships, and individual accountabilities.

One alternative approach to organizing that is gaining popularity calls for a focus on the competencies and capabilities of organizations and individuals. The idea of looking at the competencies and capabilities of individuals clearly is not new. Indeed, the bureaucratic model calls for selecting individuals who have the ability and skills to do carefully prescribed jobs (Lawler, 1994). Industrial psychology has focused on doing just this from its beginnings as a discipline. What is new is the elevation of competencies and capabilities to a central role in the organization's strategy, structure and human resource practices.

There is an increasing body of research and theory in the areas of business strategy, organization design, and human resource management that focuses on how organizations can be designed using a competency approach. Although this thinking has not coalesced into a coherent, integrated body of work, a critical mass has developed. The discussion that follows gives a brief overview of the existing literature. We next discuss issues that have yet to be resolved. Finally, we discuss where this approach appears to be headed.

COMPETENCIES, CAPABILITIES AND STRATEGY

Competencies are a major focus of the human resources management literature and of the business strategy literature. In the former, Spencer & Spencer (1993) argue that the job performance of individuals is strongly influenced by a set of competencies upon which the skills and knowledge that are necessary for successful job performance rest. They go on to argue that organizations should focus on identifying individuals with the right competencies and on developing the competencies of individuals.

In the strategy literature, the "core competencies" approach is highly influential. C.K. Prahalad and Gary Hamel describe this approach in an article that, at one point, was the most requested reprint in the history of the *Harvard Business Review* (Prahalad & Hamel, 1990). They argue that corporations can identify a relatively small number of competencies that give them competitive advantage in the marketplace. For example, Sony's core competencies in miniaturization and precision manufacturing provide competitive advantages across a large number of product lines and markets.

Stalk, Evans & Schulman (1992) of the Boston Consulting Group have presented a variation on this approach that focuses on "strategic capabilities" that are organizational and operational rather than technical in nature. For example, Wal-Mart's strategic capabilities in distribution, marketing and information systems provide important competitive advantages. Later writings of Prahalad & Hamel have absorbed this approach into the core competencies stream (e.g. Hamel & Prahlad, 1994). Two important collections of papers that are based on European conferences (Hamel & Heene, 1994; Sanchez, Heene, & Thomas, 1996) have added depth to the core competencies approach.

There are several key characteristics of core competencies (Hamel, 1994; Rumelt, 1994). First, competencies represent a complex "bundle" of skills and technologies that span multiple business and products (for example, precision manufacturing). Second, competencies are more stable and evolve more slowly than the products and markets that have been the traditional focus of strategy. Third, core competencies are difficult to imitate; witness the unsuccessful attempts of auto makers around the world to match the productivity and quality of the Toyota production system during the past two decades. Finally, core competencies are the true battleground for interfirm competition.

Lado & Wilson (1994) provide a view of the link between strategy and competencies, derived from a resource-based view of the firm. They distinguish among four types of competencies. Managerial competencies include articulating a strategic vision and enacting the environment. Input-based competencies include exploiting imperfections in the labor market, creating an internal labor market, and investing in firm-specific human capital. Transformational competencies include harnessing innovation and entrepreneurship, fostering organizational learning, and promoting organizational culture. Finally, output-based competencies include building a corporate reputation, product or service quality, and customer loyalty.

Ulrich & Lake (1990) as well as Lawler (1992, 1996) argue for the importance of organizational capabilities. According to them, organizational capabilities allow organizations to perform in particular ways that are critical to business performance. Quality, speed, low-cost operation, learning, innovation and customer focus are examples of the kinds of capabilities that are mentioned in these writings. According to Lawler, these capabilities do not rest with any one individual, or for that matter in an area of technological excellence. Instead, they rest in the systems, structures, cumulative knowledge and mindset of the organization. As a result, they are hard to develop and hard to duplicate, but potentially a significant source of competitive advantage. In essence, they are the key to allowing organizations to turn their important technological and operational core competencies into products and services that are superior to those offered by other organizations. In the case of Wal-Mart, for example, the organizational capabilities argument is that its competitive advantage is not just in its distribution, marketing and information system capabilities; it is in its ability to operate a customer-focused organization, a capability that rests in its communication, involvement and training practices.

The strategy-based view of core competencies and organizational capabilities is different from the competency approaches, which are rooted in the human resource tradition. For example, competency-based pay systems commonly reward individuals for such competencies as communication, team orientation and flexibility (Zingheim, Ledford & Schuster, 1996). Strategists might see individual competencies as necessary for business success, but would not recognize these as "core organizational competencies". They identify core competencies through intensive analysis and conceptualization of a business. The common practice of human resource consultants, which involves shopping a prepackaged list of competencies to potential clients and letting clients pick those that they like, is anathema to the strategic approach because it negates the entire idea of an organization developing competencies and capabilities that provide a unique competitive advantage.

ORGANIZATIONAL DESIGN AND EFFECTIVENESS

The literature on competencies and capabilities leads to some rather straightforward predictions about when an organization will be effective. Essentially, it argues that an organization will be effective when it has the competencies and capabilities to implement a well-developed business strategy, that is, when the organization can execute the kind of behaviors that are necessary for it to deal effectively with its business environment. It is also worth noting here that the resources available to an organization may come into play as well in determining the effectiveness of the organization.

Figure 13.1 presents a model which captures the relationship between organizational effectiveness and strategy. It shows that organizational effectiveness is the result of an organization having a good fit among its strategy, competencies,

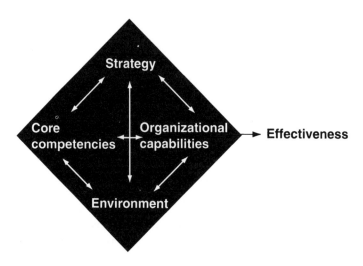

Figure 13.1 Organizational effectiveness model

capabilities and environment. It shows the environment as an important part of the relationship for two reasons. First, an organization may do a wonderful job of executing its strategy but the strategy may not fit the business environment. Second, as the environment changes, the organization may need to change its strategies, capabilities and competencies. In this respect the environment, like the existing competencies, capabilities and resources of the organization, should be an important input to the strategy development process.

The business strategy literature on core competencies is relatively silent with respect to how organizations can be designed in order to create the right mix of core competencies. The literature on organizational capabilities is much more concerned with how organizations should be designed. In many respects this is hardly surprising, since organizational capabilities tend to rest more in an organization's design and in its systems than do core competencies. In order for either of these approaches to be useful and testable, they must ultimately be tied to how organizations can be designed to produce particular competencies and capabilities. This topic has the potential for stimulating research that focuses not only on how competencies and capabilities are developed, but also on how they are related to organizational success in the marketplace. As will be discussed next, organizational behavior research does provide some useful theory and valuable ideas about how organizations can be designed to produce particular competencies and capabilities.

DESIGNING ORGANIZATION FOR COMPETENCIES AND CAPABILITIES

A key determinant of the usefulness of the competencies and capabilities approach lies in determining whether it leads to different thinking about the design of an organization. The classic star model which is presented in Figure 13.2 argues

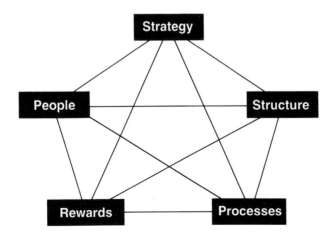

Figure 13.2   The star model

for a fit among an organization's strategy, structure, processes, people and rewards (Galbraith, 1973). The star model (and similar models, such as the Leavitt diamond and the McKinsey Seven S model) can be a helpful way of thinking about how competencies and capabilities can be developed in an organization. Once the strategy has been defined and the competencies and capabilities needed to implement the strategy identified, it becomes a matter of identifying and developing the structures, processes, reward systems and human resources management practices that will produce the needed competencies and capabilities. It is worth looking at the points of the star and examining the implication of the competencies and capabilities approach for how they might be conceptualized and operationalized.

Structure

The structural component of the star model addresses structure at the micro or job design level as well as at the macro or organizational architecture level. Perhaps the most interesting and potentially radical implication of the competencies and capabilities approach concerns its implications for job design. The job is the organizational atom in bureaucratic designs. It is the lowest level of organizational structure, the point at which the division of labor stops. The entire organization is built on the basis of job descriptions and individual accountability for job performance. Job descriptions are also the basis for the design of all major human resource systems, including selection, training, pay, career development and performance management (Ash, Levine & Sistrunk, 1983).

Currently, the rate of organizational change is so great that the well-defined stable job appears to be an historical anachronism (Bridges, 1994; Lawler, 1996; Lawler & Ledford, 1992). The focus on speed to market, quality and lateral processes, and the use of downsizing, re-engineering, work redesign, team-based designs, and other changes have made the conventional job obsolete in many companies. Increasingly, employees do not have a discrete, stable job; instead, they have a constantly changing mix of tasks to perform. These changes are especially common and significant in the case of managers and professionals, whose work has always been the most difficult to capture in a job description. Even where the job continues to be a relevant concept, the downsized human resource function may be unable to administer job-based systems that include extensive job descriptions. Thus, firms are increasingly abandoning job descriptions and careful job analysis because they lack the personnel to create and maintain them.

A number of authors have argued that the focus should be on the skills and knowledge of individuals rather than on the nature of their jobs (e.g. Lawler, 1994). This leads directly to the idea of replacing a job description with a skills and knowledge description. To be useful, this skills and knowledge description needs to identify what technical and organizational skills and knowledge an individual needs. It also needs to identify how to determine whether an individual actually possesses them. As we will discuss later, this is a critical element for any reward system that is focused on rewarding individuals for developing skills and knowledge.

It has been argued in the literature on teams that it may not make sense for organizations to focus on and measure individual performance in team-based environments (Mohrman, Cohen & Mohrman, 1995). Instead, the argument is that performance is best measured at the team or business-unit level, because this is where performance can be most objectively measured, and where performance is best measured to create key lateral processes. In this approach, it is often argued that tasks should be assigned to groups, teams or parts of an organization. For this assignment process to be an informed one, the organization must be able to identify the skills and knowledge of each individual. And, of course, for the organization to be adequately staffed, it must insure that individuals develop the right sets of skills and knowledge for the organization to be able to perform its key business tasks.

The competency and capability argument also has some interesting implications for macro organization design. Indeed, it is at this level of structure that it may already be having its greatest impact. Some current trends in organization design, for example the trend away from unrelated, multi-business corporations, may be the result of this trend. Unrelated multi-business corporations typically find it difficult to develop any particular distinguishing competencies and capabilities. As a result, their effectiveness and reason for being (as contrasted to a single business corporation) is hard to defend. Thus, it may be a less preferred approach to organizing in the future (Galbraith, Lawler and Associates, 1993). On the other hand, approaches such as front–back and process organizing seem to be growing in popularity, partly because they allow the organization to develop capabilities in quality, speed to market and customer focus (Galbraith, 1994).

A good guess is that focusing on the kind of competencies and capabilities a particular organization structure generates will, over time, lead to some innovative approaches to organization design. The bureaucratic approach to thinking about macro organization focuses on functional expertise, achieving organizational growth, and control. Focusing on developing competencies and capabilities provides a significantly different starting point for organization design. In essence, it provides a new set of lenses through which to view the world of organization design. Thus is seems inevitable that it will lead not just to a movement away from the functional bureaucratic organization, but to the invention of a number of macro organization structures which provide competitive advantage through the creation of new and different capabilities.

Processes

Perhaps the most direct implications of the competencies and capabilities approach for organizational effectiveness concern measurement. In the bureaucratic model, measurement processes are focused on measuring operational and financial results in ways that fit an individually-oriented bureaucratic approach to control. The alternative is to focus on measuring the level of organizational performance around such capabilities and competencies as speed to market, technical expertise, quality and whatever other competencies and capabilities are critical to the organization's effectiveness.

The competencies and capabilities approach also suggests that, as was discussed in the structure section, the organization needs to be very aware of the skills and knowledge of each individual employee. It needs to be able to develop an information system that includes data on both what individuals need to know and their current knowledge. This approach fits well with a human resources information system that is keyed to the performance capabilities of each individual. There already are a few organizations with information systems in which managers throughout the organization can enter a database and determine the skills and knowledge of individuals in the organization. This not only enables them to make staffing decisions, it also allows them to obtain an overall sense of how capable an organization is to staff particular projects and to perform in particular ways.

Organizations that have adopted total quality management thinking provide an interesting example of how the focus on developing a particular capability leads to changes in information processes. Almost without exception, these organizations have changed their measurement systems to focus more on product quality and customer satisfaction. The re-engineering approach is different, with its emphasis on cycle time and, of course, on staffing levels. Still, it too often has changed the nature of the information and communication processes in organizations because it asks different questions about organizational performance (e.g. process cycle time).

Reward Systems

The approaches to structure and processes that are suggested by competencies and capabilities thinking have significant implications for the design of reward systems. They argue strongly for the use of skill- or competency-based pay and for pay-for-performance systems that focus on collective rather than individual performance. Both of these follow directly from the types of structures and the kind of information and measurement processes that fit the competencies and capabilities approach.

The argument for paying individuals for their skills and competencies rather than for the job they are doing follows directly from the argument that individuals no longer have fixed jobs. Further, the key to organizational effectiveness is developing the right mix of skills and knowledge to support the organization's needed competencies and capabilities. The use of skill-based pay is one way to accomplish this (Ledford, 1991, 1995).

There already is a significant increase in the use of skill- and competency-based pay (Lawler, Mohrman & Ledford, 1995). In most cases, it is being used in manufacturing and non-exempt white collar work, because it is there that teams are being introduced and where the competencies needed to do specific tasks are most easily identified and measured. There is, however, increasing interest in using competency-based pay for knowledge workers and managers (Ledford, 1995; O'Neal, 1993/94; Tucker & Cofsky, 1994). This trend follows from the movement away from jobs. It is the logical way to support the development of particular competencies and capabilities in an organization. It encourages employees to develop the skills and knowledge that create the organization's competencies and capabilities.

Competency-based pay also may be the best way to determine the actual market value of individuals. As organizations increasingly look out for individuals with particular performance capabilities, it follows that the market value of individuals is likely to be determined by what they can do, not by what job they are doing (Lawler, 1990). Thus a logical alternative to job-based pay is to pay individuals for what they can do by assessing and by determining the market value of their skills, knowledge and competencies.

Individual performance-based pay or merit pay is a staple of the traditional bureaucratic approach to organizing. It fits the logic of the bureaucratic approach because it targets individual performance effectiveness as the key behavior. The fit with most of the capabilities and competencies that organizations wish to develop, however, is poor. Competencies and capabilities often involve complex behavior on the part of multiple individuals and the effectiveness of these is often only visible at the collective level. Thus it is not surprising that over the last decade there has been an increased use of profit-sharing, gain-sharing and other reward systems which pay for collective behaviors (Lawler, Mohrman & Ledford, 1995). Often these collective reward systems focus on performance measures that reflect capabilities such as speed to market, customer satisfaction, and innovation.

People

The competencies and capabilities approach to organizing suggests a very different approach to thinking about the human resources management systems of an organization. The absence of jobs makes most traditional human resources management systems unusable because they rest on the foundation of a good job description. They pay individuals based on job size and job performance, select individuals for particular jobs, and train and develop individuals to do jobs or a series of jobs during their careers. Earlier it was suggested that a person description needs to be substituted for a job description in the competencies and capabilities approach. This person description needs to form the basis for the human resources management systems of the organization. It needs to be used as a basis for the selection process as well as for training and development and pay purposes.

Looking first at the organization's hiring decisions, the competence and capability approach suggests a different starting point from the one that is traditionally used. Instead of hiring somebody to fill a job, the organization needs to view itself as hiring a new organizational employee (Bowen, Ledford & Nathan, 1991). One way to state this is than individuals are hired for organizational membership, not to fill a job. It needs to look at the kinds of skills and capabilities it needs as an organization and determine whether a job applicant's skills and knowledge contribute to the organization's capabilities and competencies. This suggests using approaches such as realistic job (work and organization) previews, team-based selection processes, extensive hiring and entry processes and, perhaps most importantly, a focus on an individual's ability to develop new skills and competencies.

The selection process needs to be supported by the kind of human resources information system that carefully catalogues and enables the skill and knowledge development of individuals, and that links it to kinds of competencies and capabilities called for by the organization's strategy. It also suggests a career management system in which individuals make career moves in order to develop the skills and knowledge they need in order to contribute to the organization's key capabilities. For example, if operating lateral processes is a key capability, then cross-functional career moves need to be an important part of the human resources management system (Galbraith, 1994). These moves need to be built into the career management, reward and information systems. This suggests making available to individuals extensive information about the career opportunities as well as directly rewarding them for cross-functional moves.

Finally, the competencies and capabilities approach has some interesting implications for employment stability and security. Many of the competencies and capabilities that provide competitive advantage (e.g. quality, speed to market) require effective relationships among many individuals. This suggests that relatively permanent employees are needed because employment stability is a necessary precondition to the development of effective working relationships. It does not, however, necessarily argue that everyone should be "guaranteed" a job for life. Quite the contrary. The needed organizational competencies and capabilities may change as the environment changes and the business strategy changes. Under these conditions, it is important that organizations either be able to develop existing employees so that they have the needed new skills and knowledge or hire replacement employees with the kinds of skills and capabilities that are needed to support the new competencies and capabilities.

There already exists some research on the relationship between competencies and employment stability. For example, Capelli & Crocker-Hefter (1996) compared several pairs of competitors. One member of each pair pursued flexible, entrepreneurial, "prospector" strategies (for example, Pepsi), while the other pursued "defender" strategies aimed at protecting established market niches (for example, Coca-Cola). The former consistently emphasize hiring employees who bring advanced skills to the organization, while the latter devote far more resources to employee development and emphasize employment stability to a greater degree.

The competencies and capabilities approach is compatible with a ring-of-defense or core employee approach to employment stability (Handy, 1990, 1994). This strategy involves establishing a core group of employees who are relatively permanent members of the organization. Individuals outside the core have less job security and at the extreme may be temporary employees or consultants. If an organization is going to compete on its technical competencies or organizational capabilities, it needs to protect the individuals who are most important to them. A clear implication is that individuals ought to be laid off or terminated based on how important they are to the organization's competencies and capabilities, not based on seniority or hierarchical position.

The challenge in implementing a ring-of-defense approach is to identify individuals who are critical to the competencies and capabilities that the organization has identified as its competitive advantage. It also requires decisions about which knowledge is best provided by members of the organization and which is best purchased from consulting firms or individuals. As a general rule, the more important a competency or capability is to an organization's competitive advantage, the less sense it makes to purchase it from a vendor. It is risky to depend on a vendor, since in most cases they are free to sell the same services and resources to business competitors.

UNRESOLVED ISSUES IN HUMAN RESOURCES MANAGEMENT

The rise of competency-based systems raises many researchable questions that are important for practice as well as theory. As will be discussed next, many of these questions concern the impact of competency management systems on the human resources management practices of organizations.

What Types of Competency-Based Management Systems Are There, and to What Extent Do Different Systems Have Different Effects?

It is important to answer these questions to develop theory that is grounded in organization reality. At this point, there are few data with which to construct a meaningful typology, or even to address the issue of whether there are differences. The only study of any scope is a survey of 217 companies using 148 different competency models (American Compensation Association, 1996). It did not attempt to categorize the different models empirically or theoretically. Thus, it provided no information on the dimensions among which competency-based management systems differ.

Ledford (1995) has argued that most competency-based pay system designs make a set of conservative design choices. They are based on a logic and set of practices that are analogous to job-based systems and are not based on business strategy. The methodology of the McBer consulting firm is the most widely used in the USA. It involves studying high performers and attempting to identify characteristics that distinguish them from average and low performers. This procedure focuses on existing individual competencies, uses a bottom-up analysis procedure analogous to job analysis, tends to be very complex and precise, and focuses on the competencies of successful individuals rather than focusing on the pattern of individual competencies that are needed to make an organization successful.

While this methodology is applicable in many situations, it could be disastrous in others. In environments that are rapidly changing, a much more nimble, anticipatory, temporary structure may be more appropriate. For example, some firms use a "learning contracts" approach, in which employees redefine learning objectives each year in performance appraisal sessions with supervisors. These learning contracts marry individual needs and interests with organizational needs and strategic directions.

Another possible dimension concerns the extent to which firms use internally generated "home-grown" approaches to competency management, as opposed to relying on external consultants. Many consulting firms have extensive product offerings in the competency arena. These products have been important in popularizing competencies and providing the area with increased legitimacy. But do home-grown systems have different effects than "store-bought" systems? How different are the approaches fostered by different consultants? Organizational change theory suggests that these approaches might be quite different in their effects, due to the level of customization to the firm's needs and to the level of employee commitment that might be associated with an internally generated system.

How and Why Have Competency-Based Management Systems Originated and Evolved in Organizations?

What are the goals of these systems? Why were they adopted? How integrated are competency plans with business strategies? Some systems are very elaborate and are developed through painstaking analysis of extensive data, while others are relatively simple and are based on limited data analysis. Do different design and implementation processes produce significantly different competencies, and do the resulting competency management systems have different effects?

Employee responses to competency management are also important. Do employees understand and endorse the approach? Do they see it as significantly different from job-based human resources management? How do different design characteristics influence employee attitudes, such as the simplicity of the system or whether competencies in the model are abstract or observable? How do different design processes affect employee attitudes?

Of special theoretical interest are sense-making (e.g. Weick, 1995) and institutional (e.g. Scott, 1995) processes during implementation. The competency approach represents a challenge to the highly institutionalized concept of the job, as well as a response to the decline in the utility of the job as the basis for organizing work and human resource practices. To what extent are these considerations explicit in the deliberations of managers who implement systems? What strategies do they use to help employees confront the shift from job to competency? How do managers make use of such institutional agents as consulting firms to establish the legitimacy of the effort?

What Human Resource Subsystems Are Typically Used to Manage Competencies?

Do organizations favor using one human resource subsystem or several? Are there any patterns in how different human resource systems tend to become involved?

Of particular theoretical interest is the extent to which different firms make use of emotionally "cool" vs. "hot" human resource systems in managing competencies. Selection systems are relatively "cool" in that they most affect people who are not currently members of the organization. Pay tends to be a "hot" system in that it affects all employees throughout their employment and it tends to generate strong emotions. Training and development, personnel planning, performance appraisal, and other human resource systems fall at various points in between.

Why do some firms first emphasize competency management using emotionally "cool" human resource systems such as selection (which primarily affect people not currently part of the organization), while others move first into emotionally "hot" areas such as pay? Do employees respond differently when "hot" systems like pay are involved in competency management? Does the use of either type of system increase the odds of sustaining a competency-based system? This represents an extension of past work on emotion in organizations, which has focused primarily on the norms governing the expression of emotions by individuals (e.g. Sutton, 1991) and on affect evoked by the organization as a whole (e.g. Sutton & Callahan, 1987).

How Effective is the Competency Management Approach?

Practitioners rightly are especially interested in effectiveness. How do different constituencies (senior managers, the HR function, employees on the system, etc.) assess the effectiveness of competency management? What criteria do they use, and what is their conclusion? To what extent do they believe that they have adequate information to reach a conclusion? To what extent is there any hard evidence of the effectiveness of competency management systems?

Again, there are virtually no data with which to answer these questions. The American Compensation Association (1996) study of 217 plans found that a majority of competency-based plans for staffing, training and development, performance management and compensation had been in place for less than a year or were in development. Of the few firms using competency-based programs for more than a year, most organizations reported positive effects in such areas as communicating valued behaviors, raising the competency level of employees, emphasizing person-based characteristics and reinforcing new values. Clearly, these data are preliminary. Much research is needed to discover how effective competency and capability management systems are.

Most of the research on competency effectiveness to date has taken the form of validity studies in the industrial psychology tradition (for example, Boyatzis, 1982; Spencer & Spencer, 1993; Ulrich et al., 1995). The effectiveness criteria in these studies typically are individual-level effectiveness measures, attempting to distinguish high and low performers on particular jobs. For example, Boyatzis (1982) identified 21 competencies (such as conceptualization, memory, objectivity and self-confidence) that distinguished high- from low-performing managers. Similarly, Ulrich et al. (1995) found that the colleagues, supervisors and clients of human resource managers rate the performance of the human resources managers more favorably to the extent that they displayed competencies in business knowledge, delivery of human resources services and management of change. Such studies typically assume, but do not demonstrate, that organizational effectiveness is enhanced by fostering the individual competencies identified in this way.

Role of Environmental Agents

Government policy-makers and industry associations may be interested in promoting competency- and capability-based approaches for a variety of reasons. To the extent that these approaches are associated with better performance, they may offer advantages for nations that do a better job of developing the competencies of their work forces. Governments and industry associations can play a unique role in legitimizing the competency concept and in helping to create competency certification efforts that have generality beyond the bounds of a particular firm. This may help create more efficient labor markets, because firms know that certified candidates possess certain general competencies.

These considerations have led to extensive collaboration between government ministries in UK and certain industry associations, aimed at developing national competency certifications that are relevant throughout an industry (Burke, 1995). This work began at the level of factory employees, but is migrating to the level of managerial and professional employees in many industries. At present, little is known about the value of government and industry association involvement in the certification process. For example, it is not clear whether it truly leads to portable certifications, as proponents hope.

From Individual Competencies to Organizational Competencies and Capabilities

One of the most difficult linkages between strategy and human resource management involves the translation of general organization strategy to the kinds of people that are needed in an organization. Capabilities and competencies thinking can be of help here since there are some obvious links between the development of core competencies and the kind of skills and knowledge individuals need. This is perhaps most clear in the case of such technical core competencies as understanding adhesive processes or the refining of crude oil. These translate very directly to having some individuals with technical knowledge in these areas.

The same easy translation is not always possible with respect to more complex core competencies such as miniaturization, or with respect to organizational capabilities such as innovation and quality. The challenge here is to define the mix of skills that individuals need to have to produce these organizational capabilities. In many cases, it likely is a matter of developing a pattern of skills throughout the workforce that in total gives the organization the competencies and capabilities it needs. There is little research to guide the design process in part because it is a new research area and in part because the questions are so extraordinarily complex.

For example, in the case of quality, does everyone need to know statistical process control or does only a percentage of the workforce need to know it so that when needed, there is someone available who can perform it? This is just one small example of the overall staffing challenge that an organization faces when it wishes to develop relatively complex organizational capabilities. It is no longer a matter of finding an individual who fits a particular job; rather it is a matter of determining how many individuals in each part of the organization need to be able to do certain things for the organization to be able to operate in a particular way. Some of the organizational change efforts, such as re-engineering and total quality management, do offer answers that specify the kind of training and skills individuals need. Most of these answers, however, are not based on any research evidence to show the kind and number of skills that individuals need in order for the organization to have a particular capability.

CONCLUSION

The many questions that are raised by the movement to a competency-based human resource management system leads to an obvious conclusion: it represents nothing short of a re-invention of the practice of human resource management. As such, it requires the development of new human resources systems as well as new research to support their development and determine their effectiveness.

With respect to an overall move to competency-based organizations and competency-based organizing, human resource management is just one of the elements of an organization that need to be developed and studied. Similar questions can be raised and research needs identified with respect to organization design, information and measurement processes, and reward systems. Their design rests on concepts and research that is tied to the traditional bureaucratic approach to organizing. The competency-based approach to organizing raises different questions. New research is needed to provide answers to questions concerning how organizational competencies and capabilities can be built, what the best mix of competencies and capabilities is for success in different industries, how quickly competencies and capabilities deteriorate in an organization, what organizational structure leads to the development of capabilities such as quality, speed to market, operating globally and organizational learning.

THE FUTURE OF COMPETENCIES AND CAPABILITIES

We expect to see much more emphasis on the management of competencies and capabilities in the future. The forces that have led to the current interest will not abate for the foreseeable future. Global competition, downsizing, delayering, a less hierarchical division of labor, the decline of the bureaucratic form, the shrinking of the human resource function, and other forces will continue to increase interest in the management of competencies and capabilities. Further, as examples of competency management become more prominent in the corporate world, the approach is likely to become more legitimate, encouraging further diffusion. The available evidence suggests that employees tend to prefer organizational practices such as skill-based pay that embody the competency management perspective (e.g. Jenkins et al., 1992). This argues that employees may be a positive force for adoption of such approaches.

New information technology is likely to play an especially important role in the development of new approaches to competency management. Especially in the case of large-scale implementation, as in adoption at the division or corporate level, a great deal of information is needed to manage these systems. There must be some method of tracking skills, competencies and capabilities at the individual level and matching them with the strategic needs of the organization. New information technology makes this much more practical. For example, one firm we have worked with has used competencies in their performance management process. The design of their system uses "360 degree" appraisals (that is, appraisals by peers and customers as well as supervisors) to assess competencies. This firm found two dozen vendors that sell automated systems for conducting "360 degree" appraisals. The firm can have all employees complete the appraisals on a given day using networked personal computers, and receive compiled results almost instantly.

In summary, we see the increased use of competency-based systems as an important development, and in general we see it as positive. However, we have some concerns.

First, many organizations may be setting themselves up for legal challenges by the use of competency management systems that have not been validated. This is especially a problem where competency systems lead to the introduction of personality testing. Many proponents of competency-based approaches argue that personality characteristics are a type of person-based competency that should be the basis for selection, career development, compensation and so on. Personality testing in organizations almost vanished about two decades ago, because personality tests often have an adverse impact on women and minorities, and organizations could not prove that differences in test scores were related to job performance. Personality tests are especially likely to be challenged in court because the tests often do not have face validity for employees. There appears to be very little recognition in the current literature of the problems with testing.

A second concern is the relationship between competency management and employment stability. Many organizations that look closely at the mix of competencies currently in the organization vs. those needed in the future may conclude that their current employees do not have the right skills. Those that do face difficult choices concerning keeping current employees and retooling their skills, hiring new permanent employees, or hiring outside contractors with specialized skills that the organization may not need permanently. Organizations facing rapid change in the profile of needed skills will be tempted to buy rather than develop new skills. This raises larger social issues about the nature of the employment contract between employees and organizations. It also raises interesting questions concerning the extent to which the organization has a responsibility for employee development and whether employees should be primarily responsible for their own development.

Finally, there is the ultimate question of whether the competency-based approach is a useful paradigm, that is, an adequate replacement for the bureaucratic model. Undoubtedly, the answer will partly depend on the ability of organizations to develop structures and systems that support the development of key capabilities and on research which measures the effectiveness of organizations that adopt them. However, the perception of its usefulness is likely to be only partly influenced by the research evidence. It is also likely to be influenced by whether it helps managers understand their increasingly difficult roles in complex organizations, and whether it helps them understand and direct organizational change; in short, whether it helps them make sense of their business environment.

Our guess is that competency and capability-based management thinking will grow in popularity because it is a useful way to think about organizational effectiveness. It is a potentially powerful way to help with an age-old problem in organizations: translating strategy into organization design, information processes, reward systems and human resource management systems. It has the potential to develop a more integrated and complete sense of what constitutes fit among the key elements of an organization.

REFERENCES

American Compensation Association (1996). *Raising the Bar: Using Competencies to Enhance Employee Performance*. Scottsdale, AZ: American Compensation Association.

Ash, R.A., Levine, E.L. & Sistrunk, F. (1983). The role of jobs and job-based methods in personnel and human resources management. In K. Rowland & G. Ferris (eds), *Research in Personnel and Huamn Resources Management* (pp. 45–84). Greenwich, CT: JAI Press.

Bowen, D.E., Ledford, G.E. Jr & Nathan, B.R. (1991). Hiring for the organization, not the job. *Academy of Management Executive*, **5**(4), 35–51.

Boyatzis, R.E. (1982). *The Competent Manager: a Model of Effective Performance*. New York: Wiley.

Bridges, W. (1994). *JobShift: How to Prosper in a Workplace without Jobs*. Reading, MA: Addison-Wesley.

Burke, J. (1995). *Outcomes Learning and the Curriculum: Implicatons for NVQs, GNVQs, and Other Qualifications*. London: Falmer.

Capelli, P. & Crocker-Hefter, A. (1996). Distinctive human resources as firms' core competencies. *Organizational Dynamics*, **24**(3), 7–22.

Galbraith, J.R. (1973). *Designing Complex Organizations*. Reading, MA: Addison-Wesley.

Galbraith, J.R., Lawler, E.E. & Associates (1993). *Organizing for the Future: the New Logic for Managing Complex Organizations*. San Francisco, CA: Jossey-Bass.

Galbraith, J.R. (1994). *Competing with Flexible Lateral Organizations*, 2nd edn. Reading, MA: Addison-Wesley.

Hamel, G. (1994). The concept of core competence. In G. Hamel & A. Heene, *Competence-based Competition*. New York: Wiley.

Hamel, G. & Heene, A. (1994). *Competence-based Competition*. New York: Wiley.

Hamel, G. & Prahalad, C.K. (1994). *Competing for the Future*. Boston, MA: Harvard Business School Press.

Handy, C. (1990). *The Age of Unreason*. Boston, MA: Harvard Business School Press.

Handy, C. (1994). *The Age of Paradox*. Boston, MA: Harvard Business School Press.

Jenkins, G.D. Jr, Ledford, G.E. Jr, Gupta, N. & Doty, D.H. (1992). *Skill-based Pay: Practices, Payoffs, Pitfalls, and Prospects*. Scottsdale, AZ: American Compensation Association.

Lado, A.A. & Wilson, M.C. (1994). Human resource systems and sustained competitive advantage: a competency-based perspective. *Academy of Management Review*, **19**(4), 699–727.

Lawler, E.E. III (1990). *Strategic Pay*. San Francisco, CA: Jossey-Bass.

Lawler, E.E. III (1992). *The Ultimate Advantage: Creating the High-Involvement Organization*. San Francisco, CA: Jossey-Bass.

Lawler, E.E. & Ledford, G.E. (1992). A Skill-based Approach to Human Resource Management. *European Management Journal*, **10**, 383–91.

Lawler, E.E. III. (1994). From Job-based to competency-based organizations. *Journal of Organizational Behavior*, **15**, 3–15.

Lawler, E.E., Mohrman, S.A. & Ledford, G.E. (1995). *Creating High Performance Organizations: Practices and Results of Employee Involvement and Total Quality Management in Fortune 1000 Companies.* San Francisco, CA: Jossey-Bass.

Lawler, E.E. III. (1996). *From the Ground Up: Six Principles for Creating the New Logic Corporation.* San Francisco, CA: Jossey-Bass.

Ledford, G.E. Jr (1991). The design of skill-based pay plans. In M. Rock & L. Berger (eds), *Handbook of Compensation*, 3rd edn. New York: McGraw-Hill.

Ledford, G.E. Jr (1995). Paying for the skills, knowledge, and competencies of knowledge workers. *Compensation and Benefits Review*, **27**(4), 55–62.

Mohrman, S.A., Cohen, S.G. & Mohrman, A.M. (1995). *Designing Team-based Organizations: New Forms for Knowledge Work.* San Francisco, CA: Jossey-Bass.

O'Neal, S. (1993/94). Competencies: the DNA of the corporation. *ACA Journal*, **2**(3), 6–13.

Prahalad, C.K. & Hamel, G. (1990). The core competence of the corporation. *Harvard Business Review*, **68**(3), 79–93.

Rumelt, R.P. (1994). Foreword. In G. Hamel & A. Heene, *Competence-based Competition.* New York: Wiley.

Sanchez, R., Heene, A. & Thomas, H. (1996). *Dynamics of Competence-based Competition.* Tarrytown, NY: Elsevier Science/Pergamon.

Scott, W.R. (1995). *Institutions and Organizations.* Thousand Oaks, CA: Sage.

Spencer, L.M. & Spencer, S.M. (1993). *Competence at Work.* New York: Wiley.

Stalk, G., Evans, P.E. & Shulman, L.E. (1992). Competing on capabilities: the new rules of corporate strategy. *Harvard Business Review*, **70**(2), 57–69.

Sutton, R.I. (1991). Maintaining organizational norms about expressed emotions: the case of bill collectors. *Administrative Science Quarterly*, **36**, 245–68.

Sutton, R.I. & Callahan, A.L. (1987). The stigma of bankruptcy: spoiled organizational image and its management. *Academy of Management Journal*, **30**, 405–36.

Tucker, S.A. & Cofsky, K.M. (1994). Competency-based pay on a banding platform. *ACA Journal*, **3**(1), 30–45.

Ulrich, D., Brockbank, W., Yeung, A.K. & Lake, D. (1995). Human resource competencies: an empirical assessment. *Human Resource Management*, **34**(4), 473–95.

Ulrich, D. & Lake, D. (1990). *Organizational Capability.* New York: Wiley.

Weick, K.E. (1995). *Sensemaking in Organizations.* Thousand Oaks, CA: Sage.

Zingheim, P., Ledford, G.E. Jr & Schuster, J. (1996). Competencies and competency models: one size fits all? *ACA Journal*, **5**(1), 56–65.

Chapter 14

Organizational Partnerships: The Role of Human Factors in Mergers, Acquisitions and Strategic Alliances

Sue Cartwright
Manchester School of Management, UMIST, Manchester, UK

INTRODUCTION

The build up and aftermath of the recession, major social economic and political changes within Europe and the demands of an increasingly global market have collectively transformed the ownership, shape and structure of many organizations. During the last decade, there has been substantial growth in the number of mergers, acquisitions, joint ventures and other forms of strategic alliance, both domestically and internationally (Cartwright & Cooper, 1994, 1996). The total global value of mergers and acquisitions (M & As) in 1995 was $229 868 million (KPMG Dealwatch No. 1 1996). This represents an increase over the previous year's figure of just over 10%. In particular, there has been a growing trend towards cross-border partnerships and a high concentration of M & A activity within the pharmaceutical, banking and insurance sectors.

A strategic alliance has been defined (Hall, 1995) as: "a strategic tool, useful for both offensive and defensive situations, where one or more legal entities actively co-operate in order to attain competitive advantage, and where each party has the option to withdraw from the alliance if it is not working out to their satisfaction". M & As differ from joint ventures and strategic alliances in that they can be motivated by a variety of reasons other than the purely strategic (Cartwright & Cooper, 1996). Napier (1989) distinguishes between financial or

Creating Tomorrow's Organizations. Edited by C.L. Cooper and S.E. Jackson.
© 1997 John Wiley & Sons Ltd.

value-maximizing motives, driven by financial considerations, and managerial or non-value-maximizing motives, driven by strategic considerations. Levinson (1970) draws attention to the underlying, often unstated, psychological motives, such as fear of obsolescence.

Furthermore, organizations merge or acquire with the intention of forming a more permanent and binding entity, usually between two parties of unequal status and without the potential comfort of any exit or co-operation clause if things do not work out satisfactorily. The Oxford dictionary defines merger as "the joining or gradual blending of two previously discrete entities". Legal definitions describe the event in more brutal terms as "an amalgamation of two organizations pursuant to statutory provisions in which one corporation survives and the other disappears". An acquisition is defined as "an outright gain. . . . property, including a firm that is procured" (Hogan & Overmeyer-Day, 1994). Consequently, realizing the synergistic potential of a combination is recognized to be more problematic in circumstances of M & A than joint venture, although many of the elements, processes and potential sources of dissatisfaction and conflict are somewhat similar.

M & As, as major change events, are an interesting human as well as economic phenomenon. They have come to be associated with a range of negative outcomes, including high labour turnover (Unger, 1986), low morale (Sinetar, 1981), high absenteeism (Davy et al., 1988) reduced job satisfaction and organizational commitment and employee stress (Schweiger & Ivancevich, 1985). The disappointing financial performance of M & As has long been a source of concern and considerable research attention within the financial and strategic literature. M & A gains are difficult to assess (Hogan & Overmyer-Day, 1994), but typically overall success rates, quoted by even the more optimistic sources, rarely exceed 50% (Cartwright & Cooper, 1996; Marks, 1988; British Institute of Management, 1986; Kitching, 1967). Similarly, studies of joint ventures and strategic alliances indicate failure and dissolution rates in the region of 40% (*Industry Week*, 3 October, 1988; Kogut, 1988; Killing, 1982). Within the financial literature, poor M & A performance is typically attributed to the factors outlined in Table 14.1 below. The emphasis which has been placed on rational economic explanations has often obscured or ignored the underlying human factors which are required to make a combination successful.

The impact of M & A on individuals and the contribution of human factors to merger performance still remains a challenging and relatively under-researched area. Over the years, an extensive range of variables have been advanced (Hogan & Overmyer-Day, 1994), and more often discussed than researched, as possible reasons for M & A underperformance. Although often inter-related, these can generally be considered to fall into three areas: factors relating to partner selection and lack of cultural fit; the way in which the integration process is (mis)managed; and the negative response of employees to widescale organizational change (Table 14.1).

The lack of empirical contribution from the behavioural sciences has been the source of some ongoing criticism within the M & A literature. It has been

Table 14.1 Factors commonly cited as responsible for M & A underperformance

Financial and strategic literature	OB literature
Poor selection decisions • Lack of strategic fit	Poor selection decisions • Lack of organizational/cultural fit
Price considerations • Overinflated price paid • Poor exchange rates	Integration problems • Power, size and culture differences • Insensitive or poor management of the integration process, e.g. particularly poor communication
Market changes	The generalized and widescale disruptive, demotivating and stressful nature of "change"
Financial mismanagement and/or incompetence in achieving economies of scale	

variously described as being fragmented, eclectic and lacking in any developed merger paradigm (Humpal, 1971; Hunt, 1988). There is encouraging evidence to suggest that the OB literature is becoming more research/theory-driven and less speculative and anecdotal in its approach to M & As.

Since the 1980s, M & A activity has been dominated by combinations between organizations in similar rather than unrelated activities. This has two important effects. First, as the success of related M & As is more dependent upon the wider integration of people and cultures, at both organizational and national level, it has served to raise the profile of human factors. And, secondly, it has emphasized the outdatedness of much of the earlier M & A literature, based mainly on the conglomerate model of the 1960s. Historical developments in the human M & A literature from the 1960s onwards are well documented in several comprehensive review articles (e.g., Hogan & Overmyer-Day, 1994; Cartwright & Cooper, 1990; Napier, 1989). As the aim of this chapter is to stimulate future research and so is concerned with looking forward rather than looking back, it is not the intention to provide yet a further review here. Instead, it is proposed to focus on selected key issues and themes of relevance to the 1990s and beyond, and discuss these within the framework of an agenda for future research.

In developing this agenda, a major focus of this chapter will be devoted to:

1. The issue of cultural compatibility and the choice of appropriate methods of cultural enquiry at both corporate and national level.
2. Specific problems related to research design and outcome measures associated with M & As.

It will also consider the application of other potentially useful psychological theories and models to our understanding of the M & A event and process, at a more micro level of analysis, in the form of a number of short research topics and ideas. The research topics which have been selected are not exhaustive, but are presented as "food for thought".

THE CULTURAL DIMENSION

Poor cultural fit or lack of cultural compatibility has increasingly been cited by the financial press and experienced M & A managers as a source of M & A underperformance. A growing number of OB researchers (Cartwright & Cooper, 1996; Ashkanasy & Holmes, 1995; Nahavandi & Malekzadeh, 1988) have also emphasized the importance of organizational culture to the merger process.

There are many definitions of organizational culture within the management literature (Rousseau, 1990; Schein, 1985; Martin, 1985; Harrison, 1972, 1987). However, they all reflect the classic sociological/anthropological definition of the concept as concerning the internalization of a shared set of beliefs, values, feelings, attitudes, assumptions and expectations about the internal and external environment which guide and influence the behaviour of organizational members. According to Morgan (1986), culture is the mechanism by which groups socially construct reality. The culture of an organization is reflected in many ways and influences not only its structure and managerial style, but also the way in which an organization conducts its business in the widest sense. This includes the market strategy it adopts; the type and quality of the service it offers its customers (Harrison, 1987); its HRM systems and practices (Holt & Kabanoff, 1995); and the kind of psychological environment it creates for its employees (Cartwright & Cooper, 1996).

M & As are considered to represent a major organizational event to employees because they threaten and disturb the taken-for-granted values and norms of one's familiar organizational culture and often force the integration of two culturally different groups who do not share the same "reality". According to this perspective, because cultural differences challenge basic assumptions, and influence perceptions and expectations of M & A, they can create tension and conflict between the two combining parties which inhibits the merger process. Hall & Norburn (1987) hypothesized that the degree of cultural fit between merging organizations would be directly correlated to merger success. Empirical data based on isolated case studies indicate that M & A can result in cultural integration and the creation of a new culture (Graves, 1981) or the cultural displacement of the acquired or smaller and/or less powerful partner (Buono, Bowditch & Lewis, 1985). Graves (1981), in a study of the merger of two small-medium sized firms, concluded that success, in this case measured by the subjective assessments of those involved, was related to the ability to integrate and create a new and different culture. Buono, Bowditch & Lewis (1985), in a study of a banking merger, where one culture effectively took over the other, found that this had adverse outcomes. They report that initial positive attitudes towards the combination were not sustained and comparative levels of organizational commitment and job satisfaction reduced amongst the employee group, whose culture was subsequently displaced. Studies have also observed (Altendorf, 1989; Cartwright & Cooper, 1996) that M & As tend to make cultures more cohesive and ethnocentric and hence more resistant to change. Furthermore, from the outset, organizational members tend to automatically focus on the perceived differences between the cultures and fail to recognize any similarities which clearly exist (Weber, 1989). Cross-cultural research (Trompenaars, 1993) suggests that "different" tends to be equated with "wrong".

There is a developing body of research studies which have attempted to utilize cultural dimensions as a means of understanding the dynamics of M & As and so more precisely define what constitutes cultural compatibility or fit. This requires the answer to two research questions: what happens when two cultures come together; and what types or aspects of culture influence whether or not the combination will result in a successful M & A outcome? The acculturation model proposed by Nahavandi & Malekzadeh (1988) has been particularly useful in providing a much-needed framework for the more systematic study of the merger process. Acculturation is an anthropological term defined as "the process whereby two groups (cultures) that have come into direct contact resolve the conflicts and problems that inevitably arise as a result of that contact". According to this model there are four possible modes of acculturation, dependent upon the willingness of organizational members to abandon their own culture and their perceptions of the attractiveness of the other organization's culture. These modes are: assimilation, integration, separation and deculturation. Although it is implied that one mode is likely to be optimal, with the exception of deculturation, all three modes can result in satisfactory outcomes provided both parties are in agreement as to the preferred mode. There is a high degree of correspondence between this model and that of Buono & Bowditch (1989), which suggests that merger outcomes can take three forms; cultural pluralism (separation), cultural blending (integration) or cultural takeover (assimilation).

Cartwright & Cooper (1996) successfully tested this model by examining the organizational and individual outcomes of a sample of European mergers and acquisitions over time. In attempting to ascertain the blend of cultural characteristics or types which are likely to combine successfully, they utilized the typology developed by Harrison (1972). This involved the collection of qualitative (i.e. archival material, observations and interviews) and quantitative (i.e. questionnaire) data on the pre-existing and post-integration cultures of the combining organizations. It was found that M & A success was significantly related to the degree of constraint that organizational members were accustomed to in their pre-existing cultures, and needed to acclimatize to in the new merged organization. Success was based on managerial assessments and employee attitudes and behaviours, which in some cases was supplemented by financial data.

Disagreements as to the preferred mode of acculturation were found to be the outcome of misunderstanding or non-acceptance of the implicit terms of the organizational marriage and the direction of cultural change. Characteristically, such circumstances resulted in cultural ambiguity and collisions. Culture change was found to be more readily accepted by organizational members if it increased autonomy rather than reduced it.

The process of merger is often likened to marriage (Humpal, 1971), with culture analogous to personality. This analogy is useful provided that it is recognized that any inference of choice is likely to be false as most organizational marriages, even "friendly' ones, are often "arranged". According to Cartwright & Cooper (1996), there are three types of organizational marriages which have different partner requirements in terms of cultural compatibility:

1. The *traditional* marriage, in which there is dominance or perceived superiority of one partner who seeks to take over and assimilate the other's culture.
2. The *open* marriage, in which each party retains a high degree of independence and freedom and operates essentially as a culturally separate unit.
3. The *modern* or *collaborative* marriage, characterized by an acceptance of each partner's equality and desire to combine their strengths to maximum value by cultural integration.

Two further empirical studies (Ashkanasy, 1995) have subsequently built on this work and, in the main, supported its findings in emphasizing employee discretion as an important cultural dimension in M & As. However, this research also suggests that employee support and consideration may be another salient and independent dimension which influences M & A outcomes.

THE METHODOLOGICAL ISSUES

Although the findings discussed above have contributed to move the literature on, they are still very much pioneer studies and need to be developed by future research. In particular, there has been surprisingly little research conducted in the area of international M & As, where the dynamics of any combinations are likely to be further complicated by national cultural stereotypes and perceived differences in ideologies and managerial style.

Methodologically, M & As constitute a researcher's nightmare. As highly sensitive and essentially private organizational events, M & As are difficult for both access and conducting research. Because M & A is a dynamic process, the choice of appropriate methods of data collection, instruments and outcome measures are critical; both in terms of *which* ones to use and *when* to apply them. When opportunities to research M & As arise, they have to be responded to quickly. Consequently, researchers have considerably less time to plan their research design than in most other circumstances. Some researchers (Berney, 1986) have attempted to control for extraneous variables by conducting simulated studies involving MBA students as subjects. However, because of the artificiality, particularly concerning the level of commitment of the participants, there are recognized limitations with such studies.

The situation becomes further complicated when the focus of the study concerns a concept like culture. While there may be consensus as to definition, there are multiple and potentially conflicting interpretations of the concept and continuing debate amongst researchers as to the appropriate methods of assessment and scientific enquiry.

Present practice indicates that strategic logic almost always over-rides cultural fit in partner selection decisions. There is a strand of research (Jemison & Sitkin,

1986) which asserts that the success of M & As would be significantly improved if the status of cultural fit was elevated from being desirable to being a necessary attribute for organizational marriage, the implication being that the issue of culture fit should become part of the selection criteria and form part of the due diligence procedure. To be influential, this assertion needs to be adequately substantiated. More research studies are required which more directly link culture and cultural incompatibility with merger performance, which is measured in "hard" monetary terms as well as the more traditional "softer" indices associated with OB research, e.g. job satisfaction, employee trust and organizational commitment. In this respect a multi-disciplinary approach, perhaps with economists collaborating with OB researchers, might be helpful in establishing a range of measures indicative of organizational performance, competitiveness or capacity.

Individual measures alone are likely to be insufficient to reflect adequately the complex circumstances in which M & As take place. Some researchers have indirectly attempted to quantify negative M & A outcomes in economic terms, by focusing on voluntary attrition rates. For many organizations, high attrition may be considered as inevitable, or even desirable, as a cost-effective means of reducing headcount and achieving economics of scale. Performance measures are likely to be less problematic and more easy to establish if studies focus on the impact of M & A on productivity and performance at departmental or work group level, rather than at organizational level. In a manufacturing concern, this might involve monitoring the impact of M & A on departmental wastage and error rates, through-put time, etc.

In deciding the type and form these measures might take, research practice in other areas may be a useful stimulus for ideas. For example, economic measures have been increasingly discussed and successfully applied within the occupational stress literature (Cooper, Liukkonen & Cartwright, 1996) and may provide useful models in this regard, particularly in addressing the issue of merger stress. It is also interesting to note that external assessments of M & A outcomes have not included customer satisfaction measures, particularly given the high concentration of activity in the service sector.

In order to understand fully the relationship between culture and individual and organizational M & A outcomes, there is clearly a need for not only more research studies but more studies of a longitudinal rather than cross-sectional design. This is particularly important given that merger is considered to be temporally a four- or five-stage process (Gill & Foulder, 1978; Cartwright & Cooper, 1996). Existing longitudinal studies have investigated the merger process up to a maximum period of 30 months post-merger (Ashkanasy, 1995), whereas the time-scale for culture change is generally recognised as being 2–3 years or more. This would suggest that 3 years may be a more appropriate period over which to collect data. From an organizational perspective, co-operation and support for research over such a long time period is likely to be more forthcoming if an action research approach is adopted.

From a researcher's viewpoint, in order to be able to investigate the cultural dynamics of a combination, the research design needs to incorporate pre- as well as post-measures. Purity of measurement can only be achieved if data on the pre-existing cultures is collected on a speculative basis and in more stable circumstances. This would necessitate identifying organizations with a high probability of merging or acquiring in the future. Although there is one occasion reported in the literature where due to a fortuitous "accident" this happened in part (Mirvis, 1985), this approach is clearly impractical. Therefore, at best, any assessment or measures have to be introduced immediately after the deal has been agreed and ideally prior to any physical, procedural and socio-cultural integration. Although cultural retrospection is considered to be less of a problem in the context of M & As, these assessments may still be contaminated by the merger process, which has effectively already begun. Altendorf (1986), in describing the Getty–Texaco combination, intimates that the resultant increase in intra-organizational cohesiveness which develops in an M & A situation may cause members to describe their culture in a more positive way than they would in more usual and hence less threatening circumstances.

EXPLORING AND REPRESENTING CULTURAL DIFFERENCES

By far the most important challenge for future M & A researchers concerns the way in which culture is represented and measured. The more popularist management literature has tended to reduce the concept of culture to its behavioural elements, i.e. "the way things are done around here". This reflects a pragmatic view of culture (Bright & Cooper, 1993) as being something an organization *has*. Implicit in this approach is the notion that culture is a property or attribute of an organization and hence amenable to quantitative measurement. In contrast, cultural purists, in emphasizing that culture is a collective, socially constructed phenomenon, regard culture as something an organization *is*. According to this viewpoint, culture cannot be broken down into neat, measurable constituent parts or dimensions, but rather it has to be understood in its own unique terms and so requires an ethnographic investigative approach. Fedor & Werther (1995) suggest that organizational culture can be studied from three perspectives: integration, differentiation and fragmentation. The integration perspective focuses on the consistencies within a culture, whereas differentiation and fragmentation are concerned with identifying the ambiguities and inconsistencies within a culture and its subcultures. Although all three perspectives can be used effectively in the study of cultural compatibility in M & As, Fedor & Werther (1995) found that the integration perspective was the most useful when executives had to evaluate the potential fit amongst international alliances. This approach is consistent with other research studies (Ashkanasy & Holmes 1995; Cartwright & Cooper 1996).

Some M & A researchers who have attempted to conceptualize and represent cultural differences between combining organizations have found it useful to draw upon type theories of organizational culture. Characteristically, such typologies conceive organizational culture as falling into four broad or ideal types. Harrison (1972) has drawn the distinction between power, role, task/achievement and person/support cultures. Kabanoff (1991, 1993) has proposed a value-based organizational typology utilizing the categories elite, meritocratic, leadership and collegial. Austin & Ashkanasy (1995), in a merger study of academic libraries, used the four-type classification of Weber (1989): obedience, loyalty, empowerment and laissez-faire cultures. There are numerous other typologies which have been proposed in the literature (e.g. see Trompenaars 1993; Hall 1995); whilst different descriptive labels are applied to these types, there are considerable similarities amongst the typologies as to the cluster of features commonly associated with each type. Other researchers, working mainly at national level (Hofstede, 1991) have advocated a dimensional approach, whereby different cultures can be compared in terms of their relative position on a number of key dimensions or factors, e.g. orientation towards individualism vs. collectivism; the extent to which they seek to avoid uncertainty or risk.

Therefore, there is no shortage of available culture measures (Harrison & Stokes 1990; Saville & Holdsworth 1993; Tucker, McCoy & Evans 1990; Trompenaars 1993; Sashkin 1984; Cooke & Lafferty 1989) which focus on behaviours, and to a lesser extent values. In a recent correlational and factor-analytic study of four major self-report measures (Xenikou & Furnham, 1996), there was found to be considerable overlap and inter-correlations between subscales both within and between measures. Of the measures compared in this study, the Organizational Culture Inventory (OCI) (Cooke & Lafferty, 1989) was found to have the best internal reliability and appeared to most adequately tap the fundamental dimensions of culture.

Research into cultural aspects of M & As has adopted a variety of approaches. Generally, it has involved the use of individual in-depth interviews, questionnaires, observation and archival information, frequently in combination as a means of triangulation. Smit, Schabracq & Smit (1996) have used artificial intelligence (i.e. neural networks) to compare and map basic elements of team cultures which they assert can be usefully applied to M & A situations. Cartwright (1995) has suggested that cultural differences between combining organizations could be explored by adapting certain techniques from the selection and organizational socialization literature (Anderson & Thomas, 1995), where there are some useful parallels.

In the context of future M & A research, there is considerable scope for more innovative ways of combining qualitative and quantitative methods of data collection. As certain methods of cultural enquiry may be more appropriate for studying and explaining certain aspects of culture (Rousseau, 1990), or be more appropriate for different employee groups or populations, both qualitative and quantitative methods are likely to be inadequate unless used in combination.

Questionnaire measures have the advantage of being more cost-effective and less labour-intensive means of collecting data from large samples. They also

enable systematic comparisons to be made between organizations and/or departmental cultures and provide a baseline by which to monitor post-integration time.
Compared with qualitative methods, standardized questionnaires address a defined and possibly more confined domain of cultural enquiry which may not
necessarily reflect cultural priorities. Furthermore, further research is needed to
establish the psychometric properties of many of these instruments (Xenikou &
Furnham, 1996).

Questionnaire measures may be a useful means of comparing the pre-existing
organizations to establish cultural similarities and differences. However, they are
less useful in identifying and addressing the perceptions that one employee group
has of "the other". These perceptions are important, as often they are negative
and obstructive to integration. These perceptions cannot be meaningfully elicited
by questionnaires as employees would be unable to rate "the other" culture and
differentiate in the detail expected by such instruments.

It has been suggested (Schneider, 1989) that culture determines the types and
sources of information which its members selectively attend to, and the way in
which this information is interpreted and evaluated. For example, French,
Japanese and Asian cultures tend to be more intuitive and philosophical in their
reasoning than Anglo-American cultures, which are perceived to oversimplify
reality. Consequently, Japanese organizations make greater use of qualitative
information in decision making than US–UK organizations, which place more
emphasis on quantitative information—empirical evidence, "hard" facts and linear deductive reasoning models. Therefore, the methods employed to study M &
As need to be carefully considered, particularly in the context of international
combinations.

MERGER STRESS

According to Marks (1988), M & As differ from any other process of major
organizational change in terms of the speed of change, the scale of change and the
critical mass of the unknown they present for both parties. In broad terms, the
fundamental causal factors underlying the stress response are increasingly recognized to be change, lack of control and high workload (Cartwright & Cooper,
1996), all of which are characteristic of the M & A environment. Consequently,
an important, but less developed, theme of research within the M & A literature
has sought to address the impact of M & As on employee health and well-being
and its performance implications.

There are a number of research studies which have examined the relationship
between stress and major intra-organizational change and restructuring
(Ashford, 1988; Nelson, Jackson & Cooper 1995). Such studies have demonstrated that organizational transitions tend to be universally stressful and little
moderated by personality characteristics. There are still comparatively
few studies which have been undertaken in the specific context of M & As

(Schweiger, Ivancevich & Power, 1987; Cartwright & Cooper, 1993, 1996; McHugh, 1995).

A recent study of middle managers involved in a merger between two savings and loan institutions (Cartwright & Cooper, 1993) demonstrated that merger adversely affected mental health for some appreciable time post-merger and had a significantly more pronounced effect on employees of the target company or smaller merger partner. As stress would seem to arise more from the uncertainty and the perceptions which employees have as to the likely changes which may result, rather than the actual changes themselves, the period before and immediately after the event is considered to be critical (Schweiger, Ivancevich & Power, 1987). Cultural transitions which result in ambiguous or fragmented cultures are likely to further heighten experienced stress. McHugh (1995) examined the impact of merger on teacher stress in Northern Ireland with similar conclusions. Based on a sample size of 76, she found that many teachers achieved scores on the General Health Questionnaire (Goldberg, 1972) which were indicative of moderate to severe psychological disturbance. Mean scores on the GHQ were found to be significantly poorer for teachers within merger-threatened schools than non-merger-threatened schools.

Whilst these studies have highlighted the potentially stressful nature of M & As, the findings are based on relatively small sample sizes. Furthermore, comparative to more mainstream occupational stress research, they have been less sophisticated in their approach in isolating causal relationships between specific stressor variables and health outcomes. Further research is needed to identify what specific aspects of the merger process are most stressful and the extent to which these change over time. For example, job insecurity is likely to be an immediate and significant source of stress in the early stages of M & A; however, post-rationalization, does this stressor disappear to be replaced by others? More systematic research in this area would provide a useful basis for implementing and evaluating intervention strategies to improve M & A management and performance. This would perhaps require the development of specific merger stress audit instruments.

THE CONTROL ISSUE

The issue of control features strongly in the current literature as a factor in determining both the initial response of employees to the event itself and as a key area of potential conflict between the combining cultures post-integration. M & As are considered to be negatively appraised by employees because they invoke a sense of loss and create uncertainty. Furthermore, they are perceived to be significant and consequential events over which the vast majority of employees have no control. According to Mirvis (1985), the psychological response to merger can be understood within the framework of the Kubler–Ross model of personal bereavement. In coming to terms with the event, employee emotions will progress through four discrete stages: (a) disbelief and denial; (b) anger through rage and resentment; (c) emotional bargaining, and finally (d) acceptance. The validity of this model does not appear to have been systematically applied and tested by empirical research. It would therefore be interesting to try to establish whether the intensity and duration of the bereavement is related to variables such as age, tenure or degree of organizational attachment or citizenship behaviours. As already discussed, employee discretion and control has been identified as an important cultural dimension in determining employee decisions as to whether to accept or reject a change in culture.

Control is an area which is well worthy of further investigation in the context of M & As. This might involve investigating the ways in which the individual restores and regains control of these situations, or focusing on the impact and effectiveness of various types of organizational initiatives to increase employee involvement.

Although there is some evidence to suggest that merger stress is indiscriminate and little moderated by personality, the concept of locus of control (LOC) (Rotter, 1966) has rather been neglected. The LOC variable concerns the individual's perceived rather than actual control over their lives and is considered an important factor in the stress process. There is some debate as to whether LOC is a stable trait or is situationally influenced. Rodin (1986) found that externality, a belief that the individual is controlled by external forces such as luck or chance, increases with age. O'Brien & Kabanoff (1979) suggest that external beliefs may come about through certain life experiences such as unemployment. This may also apply to M & A events. M & As provide an ideal naturalistic setting to develop our understanding of LOC, its stability vs. its variability and the impact which it may have in moderating experienced stress.

COMMUNICATION

The role of communication is emphasized throughout the M & A literature, although again there has been little systematic research in this area. A highly commendable study was conducted by Schweiger & DeNisi (1991) which demonstrated that the provision of realistic merger previews (RMPs) and merger-related communication had a significant impact on employee perceptions of organizational honesty, caring and trustworthiness and job satisfaction, compared with more typical situations when such information was absent or minimal. Many more enlightened organizations are investing in extensive multimedia methods of communication to provide employees with merger-related information. In the recent Glaxo–Wellcome merger, which doubled the size of the workforce, the organization disseminated information via the World Wide Web and satellite broadcasts throughout the USA and Europe, as part of its communication strategy. Yet, still the organization considered that it could have done more in this area (Hume, 1996). Such initiatives offer considerable research opportunities to investigate the effectiveness of the content, form and type of various merger communication strategies on employee attitudes and behaviours.

PSYCHOLOGICAL CONTRACT

In recent years, there has been a growing interest in the psychological contract as an explanatory framework in the employment relationship (McFarlane, Shore & Tetrick, 1994). According to Rousseau (1990), the psychological contract is the employee's perception of the reciprocal obligations and expectations that employer and employee have of each other, the violation of which has potentially important negative consequences (Rousseau & Aquino, 1993). M & As represent a major change and violation in the psychological contract. It has increasingly become the practice for merged organizations to cut jobs and terminate permanent employment contracts, only to then re-employ many employees on short-term working contracts. The extent to which the psychological contract is subsequently successfully re-established and re-negotiated is likely to have a significant impact on M & A outcomes and again presents an interesting research opportunity.

CONCLUSIONS

M & As still constitute a relatively "virgin" and untouched territory for research activity. In this respect, they provide tremendous opportunities for imaginative research into a wide range of OB topics and issues, some of which have been discussed in this chapter. In particular, they provide an ideal research setting in which to explore further the concept of culture. On the other hand, they are methodologically "messy" areas in which to work and do not easily lend themselves to systematic study. The research studies that have been conducted are interesting and, hopefully, will provide a stimulus for further much-needed research. This research needs to be more focused and less "broad-brush" in its approach. Because it is likely to be easier to gain access to joint ventures and strategic alliances than M & As, they may provide a good opportunity to develop a more robust methodology, which can be subsequently transferred to M & A situations.

Finally, as M & As look set to remain a relatively enduring feature of organizational evolution, as the same time, there is a developing trend toward divestment and the reverse process of de-merger. Recent examples include companies such as ICI, AT & T and Hanson. Evidence based on the ICI experience (Donaldson, 1994) would suggest that in common with mergers, demergers are clothed with secrecy and adversely affect employee morale. As a new and possibly important phenomenon of the future, demerger may also present interesting research opportunities.

REFERENCES

Altendorf, D.M. (1986). When cultures clash: a case study of the Texaco takeover of Getty Oil and the impact of acculturation on the acquired firm. August 1986, PhD Dissertation, Faculty of Graduate School of Business Administrator, University of Southern California.

Anderson, N. & Thomas, H.D.C. (1995). Work group socialization. In M.A. West (ed.), *Handbook of Work Group Psychology* (pp. 423–50). Chichester: Wiley.

Ashkanasy, N.M. (1995). Organizational mergers and acquisitions: a natural crucible for research in organizational culture. Paper presented at the Inaugural Conference on Industrial and Organizational Psychology, Sydney, 15–16 July.

Ashkanasy, N.M. & Holmes, S.J. (1995). Perceptions of organizational ideology following merger: a longitudinal study of merging accounting firms. *Accounting, Organizations and Society*, **20**, 19–34.

Ashford, S.J. (1988). Individual strategies for coping with stress during organizational transitions. *Journal of Applied Behavioural Science*, **24**(1), 19–26.

Austin, G. & Ashkanasy, N.M. (in press). Merging tertiary education libraries: case studies in cultural change. Australian Academic Research Libraries.

Berney, E.J. (1986). Management decision-making in acquisitions—an intergroup analysis. PhD Thesis, *Abstracts International, No. 86-14199*, Ann Arbor, MI.

Bright, K. & Cooper, C.L. (1993). Organizational culture and the management of quality: towards a new framework. *Journal of Managerial Psychology*, **8**(6), 21–7.

British Institute of Management (1986). *The Management of Acquisitions and Mergers*. Discussion Paper No. 8, Economics Department, September.

Buono, A.F. & Bowditch, J.L. (1989). *The Human Side of Mergers and Acquisitions*. San Francisco, CA: Jossey-Bass.

Buono, A.F., Bowditch, J.L. & Lewis, J.W. III (1985). When cultures collide: the anatomy of a merger. *Human Relations*, **38**(5), 477–500.

Cartwright, S. (1995). Integrating people and cultures: combining the bear with the fish. Paper presented at the Inaugural Australian Industrial and Organizational Psychology Conference, Sydney, July.

Cartwright, S. & Cooper, C.L. (1990). The impact of mergers and acquisitions on people at work: existing research and issues. *British Journal of Management*, **1**, 65–76.

Cartwright, S. & Cooper, C.L. (1993). The psychological impact of merger and acquisition on the individual: a study of building society managers. *Human Relations*, **56**(3). 327–47.

Cartwright, S. & Cooper, C.L. (1994). The human effects of mergers and acquisitions. In C.L.Cooper & D.M.Rousseau (eds), *Trends in Organizational Behaviour*. Chichester: Wiley.

Cartwright, S. & Cooper, C.L. (1996). *Mergers, Acquisitions and Strategic Alliances: Integrating People and Cultures*. Oxford: Butterworth-Heinemann.

Cooke, R.A. & Lafferty, J.C. (1989). *Organizational Culture Inventory*. Plymouth, MI: Human Synergistics.

Cooper, C.L., Liukkonen, P. & Cartwright, S. (1996). Stress prevention in the workplace: assessing the costs and benefits to organizations. Luxembourg Office for Official Publications of the European Communities, *European Foundation for the Improvement and Living and Working Conditions*, Ref. EF/96/09/EN.

Davy, J.A., Kinicki, A., Kilroy, J. & Scheck, C. (1988). After the merger: dealing with people's uncertainty. *Training & Development Journal*, **November**, 57–61.

Donaldson, H. (1994). Under the microscope: personnel's role in demerger. *Personnel Management*, **February**, 34–8.

Fedor, K.J. & Werther, W.B. Jr (1995). Making sense of cultural factors in international alliances. *Organizational Dynamics*, **23**(4), 33–47.

Gill, J. & Foulder, I. (1978). Managing a merger: the acquisition and the aftermath. *Personnel Management*, **10**, 14–17.

Goldberg, D. (1972). *The Detection of Psychiatric Illness by Questionnaire*. London: Oxford University Press.

Graves, R. (1981). Individual reactions to a merger of two small firms of brokers in the re-insurance industry: A total population survey. *Journal of Management Studies*, **18**(1), 89–113.

Hall, W. (1995). *Managing Cultures: Making Strategic Relationships Work*. Chichester: Wiley.

Hall, P.D. & Norburn, D. (1987). The management factor in acquisition performance. *Journal of Management Development*, **8**(3), 23–30.

Harrison, R. (1972). How to describe your organization. *Harvard Business Review*, **5**(1), 119–28.

Harrison, R. (1987). *Organizational Culture and the Quality of Service*, London: Association for Management Education and Development.

Harrison, R. & Stokes, H. (1990). *Diagnosing Your Organization's Culture*. Berkeley, CA: Harrison & Associates Inc.

Hogan, E. & Overmyer-Day, L. (1994). The psychology of mergers and acquisitions. In C.L. Cooper & I.T. Robertson (eds), *International Review of Industrial and Organizational Psychology*, vol 9 (pp 247–79). Chichester: Wiley.

Holt, J. & Kabanoff, B. (1995). The relationship between organisational value systems and HRM systems: a configurational approach. Paper presented at the Inaugural Conference on Industrial and Organizational Psychology, Sydney, July.

Hume, J. (1996). Maintaining business and industrial performance during the world's largest pharmaceutical merger. Paper presented at International Communications for Management Conference "Mergers and Aquisitions: the Human Impact". The Selfridge Hotel, London, January.

Hofstede, G. (1991). *Cultures and Organizations*. London: McGraw-Hill.

Hunt, J. (1988). Managing the successful acquisition: a people question. *London Business School Journal*, **Summer**, 2–15.

Humpal, J.J. (1971). Organizational marriage counselling: a first step. *Journal of Industrial and Organizational Psychology* **9**, 247–79.

Industry Week, 3 October 1988.

Jemison, D. & Sitkin, S.B. (1986). Corporate acquisitions: a process perspective. *Academy of Management Review*, **11**(1), 145–63.

Kabanoff, B. (1991). Equity, equality, power and conflict. *Academy of Management Review*, **16**, 416–41.

Kabanoff, B. (1993). An exploration of espoused culture in Australian organizations. *Asia Pacific Journal of Human Resources*, **31**, 1–29.

Kitching, J. (1967). Why do mergers miscarry? *Harvard Business Review*, **Nov/Dec**.

Killing, J. (1982). How to make a global joint venture work. *Harvard Business Review*, **Nov/Dec**.

Kogut, B. (1988). The merger syndrome: the human side of corporate combinations. *Journal of Buyouts and Acquisitions*, **Jan/Feb**, 18–23.

Levinson, H. (1970). A psychologist diagnoses merger failures. *Harvard Business Review*, **March/April**, 84–101.

McFarlane Shore, L. & Tetrick, L. (1994). The psychological contract as an explanatory framework in the employment relationships. In C.L. Cooper & D.M. Rousseau (eds), *Trends in Organizational Behaviour*. Chichester: Wiley.

McHugh, M. (1995). Organizational merger: a stressful challenge. *Review of Employment Topics*, **3**(1), August. Belfast: Labour Relations Agency.

Marks, M.L. (1988). The merger syndrome: the human side of corporate combinations. *Journal of Buyouts and Acquisitions*, **Jan/Feb**, 18–23.

Martin, J. (1985). Culture collisions in mergers and acquisitions. In P.J. Frost, L.F. Moore, M.R. Louis et al. (eds), *Organizational Culture*. Sage: Beverly Hills.

Mirvis, P.H. (1985). Negotiations after the sale: the roots and ramifications of conflict in an acquisition. *Journal of Occupational Behaviour*, **6**, 65–84.

Morgan, G. (1986). *Images of Organizations*. London: Sage.

Nahavandi, A. & Malekzadeh, A.R. (1988). Acculturation in mergers and acquisitions. *Academy of Management Review*, **13**(1), 79–90.

Napier, N.K. (1989). Mergers and acquisitions: human resource issues and outcomes: a review and suggested typology. *Journal of Management Studies*, **26**, 3 May.

Nelson, A., Cooper, C.L. & Jackson, P.R. (1995). Uncertainty amidst change: the umpact of privatization of employee job satisfaction and well-being. *Journal of Occupational and Organizational Psychology*, **68**, 57–71.

O'Brien, G.E. & Kabanoff, B. (1979). Comparison of unemployed and employed workers on work values, locus of control and health variables. *Australian Psychologist*, **14**, 143–54.

Rodin, J. (1986). Health control and ageing. In M.M. Baltes & P.B. Baltes (eds), *Ageing and the Psychology of Control*. Hillsdale, NJ: Erlbaum.

Rotter, J.B. (1966). Generalised expectancies for internal vs. external control of reinforcement. *Psychological Monographs*, **80**, 1–28.

Rousseau, D.M. (1990). Assessing organizational culture: the case for multiple methods. In B. Schneider (ed.), *Organizational Climate and Culture*. San Francisco, CA: Jossey-Bass.

Rousseau, D.M. & Aquino, K. (1993). Fairness and implied contract obligations in job terminations: the role of remedies, social accounts and procedural justice. *Human Performance*, **6**, 135–49.

Sashkin, M. (1984). Pillars of excellence: organizational beliefs questionnaire. Bryn Mawr, PA: *Organizational Design & Development*.

Saville & Holdsworth (1993). *Corporate Culture Questionnaire*. Thames Ditton: Surrey.

Schein, E.H. (1985). *Organizational Culture and Leadership*. San Francisco, CA: Jossey-Bass.

Schneider, S.C. (1989). Strategy formulation: the impact of national culture. *Organizational Studies*, **10**(2), 149–68.

Schweiger, D.M. & Ivancevich, J.M. (1985). Human resources: the forgotten factor in mergers and acquisitions. *Personal Administrator*, **November**, 47–61.

Schweiger, D.M., Ivancevich, J.M. & Power, F.R. (1987). Executive action for managing human resources before and after acquisition. *Academy of Management Executive*, **2**, 127–38.

Schweiger, D.M. & DeNisi, A.S. (1991). Communication with employees following a merger: a longitudinal field experiment. *Academy of Management Journal*, **34**(1), 110–35.

Sinetar, M. (1981). Mergers, morale and productivity. *Personnel Journal*, **60**, 863–7.

Smit, I.T., Schabracq, M. & Smit, W. (1996). Investigative team cultures: problem solving assisted by neural networks. Paper presented at Society of Industrial and Organizational Psychology, San Diego, CA, April.

Trompenaars, F. (1993). *Riding the Waves of Culture: Understanding Cultural Diversity in Business*. London: Nicholas Brealey Publishing.

Tucker, R.W., McCoy, W.J. & Evans, L.C. (1990). Can questionnaires objectively assess organizational culture? *Journal of Managerial Psychology*, **5**(4), 4–11.

Unger, H. (1986). The people trauma of major mergers. *Journal of Industrial Management*, (Canada), **10**, 17 April.

Weber, Y. (1989). The effects of top management culture clash on the implementation of mergers and acquisitions. Unpublished doctoral dissertation, University of South Carolina.

Xenikou, A. & Furnham, A. (1996). A correlation and factor analytic study of four questionnaire measures of organizational culture. *Human Relations*, **49**(3), 349–71.

Chapter 15

Mining for Innovation: The Conceptual Underpinnings, History and Diffusion of Self-Directed Work Teams

Karin B. Evans
Bell Atlantic, Richmond, VA, USA
and
Henry P. Sims Jr
University of Maryland, College Park, MD, USA

Thumb through any popular business publication, talk to employees in almost any organization, or ask a slew of management consultants what they have been up to, and the word "team" will resurface again and again. The use of the word may vary—"we've been doing a little team-building", "he's a team player", "if we're going to beat the competition, we'd better fire up the team",—but many people involved with organizations are glad to share their commitment to the team philosophy. Perhaps it was the popularization of what appears to be such a basic concept that led Manz & Sims (1993, p. 7) to lament that "teams" have perhaps "reached the stage of recurring management fads that occasionally sweep the United States".

In this paper, we examine the self-directed work team as an important organizational innovation for the business community. We use Rogers' (1983, 1995) theory of diffusion of innovations as a foundation to trace the conceptual underpinnings, history, implications and diffusion of the self-directed work team in the USA.

Creating Tomorrow's Organizations. Edited by C.L. Cooper and S.E. Jackson.
© 1997 John Wiley & Sons Ltd.

WHAT IS A SELF-DIRECTED WORK TEAM?

Self-directed work teams operate under a variety of labels: "self-managed teams", "autonomous work groups", and "self-managing work groups" (Sims & Dean, 1985, p. 26). The names differ and the specifics of the implementation vary widely. Nevertheless, the definition, philosophy, and function of these self-regulating groups are essentially the same (Gordon, 1992; Sims & Dean, 1985). Self-directed work teams are groups of 6–18 employees that share the responsibility for completing a collection of inter-related tasks (Dumaine, 1990; Jessup, 1990; Manz & Sims, 1993; Orsburn et al., 1990; Wellins, 1992). The key defining element is a high degree of judgment and decision-making discretion. Members of self-directed teams run one segment of the business as if it were their own. They plan, perform and measure whole operations. The teams typically have a keen awareness of their specific responsibilities, internal clients (possibly other teams) and external customers.

Cummings (1977) identified three primary conditions which define a self-directed work team: task differentiation, boundary control and task control. Task differentiation is the extent to which a groups' primary tasks form an interdependent whole which can be differentiated from the other tasks of the organization. The inter-related tasks foster cooperation within the group while reducing the dependence on external resources. Often, team members rotate through the different tasks associated with their team (Lee, 1990; Manz & Sims, 1993; Orsburn et al, 1990). This cross-training makes it easy for team members to understand and assist one another with their work. Team members are often "paid for knowledge", i.e. pay is based on competence in performing each of the team's jobs.

The next defining characteristic of a self-directed work team, boundary control, is the extent to which the team has control over their physical and symbolic territory (Cummings, 1977; Manz & Sims, 1993). Examples of boundary control include the following: a designated work area which team members can claim as their own; group members with the skills necessary to handle their work without reliance on external resources; and group members who are in charge of "boundary control decisions" that reduce external intervention such as quality control (Cummings, 1977, p. 628).

The last condition for self-directed work teams is task control (Cummings, 1977). Examples of task control include the following: choice of and ability to adjust work methods; ability to modify production goals as new situations are encountered; and feedback to group members. Self-directed work teams are typically held accountable for their work in much the same way that managers are typically accountable for the work of their employees. Teams are evaluated on traditional measures of performance such as quality, meeting deadlines, productivity rate and cost control (Hoerr, 1988; Manz & Sims, 1993; Jessup, 1990; Versteeg, 1990).

Team leadership responsibilities are traditionally vested to an internal, elected team leader, or divided among group members based on their strengths (Jessup, 1990; Manz & Sims, 1993; Orsburn et al., 1990; Sims & Manz, 1994). Many self-directed work teams maintain responsibility for personnel decisions such as time recording, training, performance reviews, and selection and dismissal of team members. The teams typically have access to some external coaching through team facilitators.

There appears to be a good deal of consistency as to the roles of self-directed work teams across organizations (Gordon, 1992; Orsburn et al., 1990; Manz & Sims, 1993). Tasks range from setting work schedules to setting goals and evaluating performance. According to a 1992 survey published in *Training* magazine (Industry Report, 1992), self-directed work teams are most involved in the following tasks: setting work schedules (69%); working directly with external customers (59%); setting production quotas or performance targets (57%); and training (55%).[1]

THE DIFFUSION OF INNOVATIONS— A THEORETICAL PERSPECTIVE

The most widely recognized theoretical statement of the diffusion of innovations is the work of Rogers, initially in 1962, then Rogers & Shoemaker (1971), and most recently Rogers (1983, 1995). Overall, the theory addresses the phenomenon of how the use of an invention or discovery expands as a function of time. In this theory, "innovation" means a discovery or invention. This discovery may be a physical entity, such as a personal computer, or a social invention, such as a self-directed work team. The term "diffusion" refers to the spread of the invention within a larger social system or society.

The fundamentals of the theory are typically expressed through a graphical representation called a "diffusion curve". Typically, this curve has time on the x-axis, often in months or years, and frequency of use on the y-axis. Later in this paper, we show an inferred diffusion curve to represent the spread of self-directed teams.

The theory of diffusion of innovations centers around the "adopters" of an innovation. An adopter does not invent the innovation, but is one who becomes aware of the innovation and makes a decision to use or adopt the innovation. The notion of "early adopter" is of particular interest to diffusion theorists, because this person plays a critical role in the rate of diffusion. In the case of self-directed

---

[1] The survey was conducted by Lakewood Publications of Minneapolis. The survey was sent to 12 000 organizations from the Dun & Bradstreet Directory and Subscribers to *Training* magazine with a response rate of 13.4%. Survey results may reflect somewhat of a pro-innovation bias, as subscribers to *Training* may be more knowledgeable and interested in new training and work techniques than the average manager.

work teams, the adopter is likely to be an organization or organizational sub-unit, and the key decision-maker is likely to be an executive or group of executives that have the power to implement teams.

In addition, the theory identifies several characteristics that typically influence the rate of diffusion. For example, the circumstances in which an innovation is invented or "discovered" can have an important impact on the rate of diffusion. Other important innovative attributes that influence the rate and quality of the diffusion include the perceptions potential adopters have of an innovation's perceived relative advantage, compatibility, complexity, trialability and observability.

The theory also discusses the important roles of change agents and opinion leaders. Change agents are individuals external to the actual community of adopters who implement the innovation. Change agents serve as a communication link between resource systems (i.e. consulting firms, school systems, public health agencies) and potential adopters.

Opinion leaders are highly respected individuals with similar backgrounds to potential adopters who serve as role models as they adopt and talk about an innovation. Opinion leaders have the ability to informally and consistently influence the adoption behavior of others. Change agents often work to gain the support of opinion leaders, so that they have peer advocates to assist them with their diffusion effort.

In this paper, the target innovation of interest is the self-directed work team, a social innovation. We use Rogers' theory to explore how this innovation originated and diffused through organizational systems in the USA.

THE "DISCOVERY" OF SELF-DIRECTED WORK TEAMS

Although the current attention to self-directed work teams could easily lead one to believe that they are a relatively new phenomenon, many believe they were actually "discovered" in 1949 in a coal mine in Yorkshire, UK (Orsburn et al., 1990, p. v; Trist & Bamforth, 1951; Fox, 1990). Eric Trist, a researcher from the Tavistock Institute of Human Relations in London, was working with several graduate students to study the inter-relationships between human resources, technology and work environments. As Trist reported, he went into the coal mines with Ken Bamforth and "came up a different man (Fox, 1990, p. 260)". What was lurking in the depths of the coal mines were several self-directing work teams which Trist described as follows.

> In single place systems, the miner possesses the necessary range of skills to undertake all facework tasks in a self-contained work place. His role is that of a multi-skilled, self-supervising workman towards whom the deputy stands in a service rather than a supervisory relation. Groups of up to six men share a place, the men selecting their own mates. Since all members do all jobs, either on the same or on different shifts, they share equally in the same paynote (Trist et al. 1951, p. 289).

Trist's original coal mine research led to the development of socio-technical systems theory. The main premise of this theory is that any production system involves both technology and work structure (Cummings, 1978). The design of the work structure is important to the success of the organization because it ties the people to the technology, and thus will impact both of these important ingredients of organizational success. The main purpose of research based on socio-technical theory is to design work structures that create the "best match", between organizations and technology (Cummings, 1978, p. 627; Sussman, 1976).

In a recent interview, Trist explained that his contribution to the development of socio-technical systems theory and self-directed work teams was to conceptualize the process, explicate a model, and articulate the major concepts: focusing on the entire work process; the importance of work groups over individual workers; internal group regulation and discretion; and redundancy of functions (Fox, 1990). Trist and his colleagues continued to experiment with the socio-technical systems theory and self-directed work teams in India, Norway, Australia and Sweden (Fox, 1990; Orsburn et al., 1990).

THE INNOVATIVE ATTRIBUTES OF SELF-DIRECTED WORK TEAMS

Rogers (1983) identified a number of attributes of innovations which have been found to influence the rate of diffusion: relative advantage, compatibility, complexity, trialability and observability. Rogers writes that "innovations exist only in the eye of the beholder (p. 212)". In other words, what matters is how the innovation is perceived by the potential adopters.

Relative Advantage

Rogers (1983, p. 213) described the "relative advantage" of an innovation as the extent to which potential adopters perceive the innovation as better than the idea it supersedes. Rogers explained that the perceived relative advantage of an innovation is important because diffusion is very much an uncertainty-reduction process. People will be more likely to adopt a new idea like self-directed work teams when they are more convinced that the consequences will be positive.

From the success stories that are being told about self-directed work teams, it appears that some adopters perceive self-directed work teams to offer a clear relative advantage over more traditional work styles. Sims & Dean (1985, p. 26) wrote that the "general consensus" was that self-directed work teams provide a 20–40% increase in productivity over more traditional systems. Managers perceived these savings to come about because of a reduction in required surveillance which results in less overhead, wasted time and higher quality control.

In addition, the perceived relative advantage may be high because of the success stories popularized by the media. Popular business media tend to have what Rogers (1983, p. 92) refers to as a "pro-innovation bias", as they tend to publicize the companies which have successfully implemented self-directed work teams. Companies may be enticed by the lure of increased productivity described in case studies published in periodicals such as *Business Week* (Hoerr, 1989), and *Fortune* (Dumaine, 1990). Of course, the companies that have had negative experiences are not likely to want their name associated with failure; and thus, there is an obvious absence of self-directed disaster stories printed in the media. This silencing of failure increases the projection of a positive relative advantage.

Rogers (1983) also discussed relative advantage in terms of the status benefits that the innovation could potentially bring to adopters. As the concept of self-directed work teams continues to be diffused throughout the business network, companies may begin to feel a need to implement them in order to appear to be on top of the latest trend. Managers may fear appearing old-fashioned or power-hungry, and thus perceive a benefit to parting with the traditional way of doing business.

Compatibility

Although the perceived relative advantage of self-directed work teams may be high, there are a number of reasons why potential innovators may not see the new work design as compatible with their current way of doing business. Rogers (1983) described "compatibility" as the extent to which potential adopters perceive an innovation to be consistent with their values, previous ideas and needs. The more compatible an innovation appears to a potential adopter, the more likely they are to implement it.

First, on the surface, the concept of self-directed work teams seems inconsistent with the traditional American values of individual achievement and accountability (Asgar, 1992; Carson, 1992; Manz & Sims, 1993). The implementation of self-directed work teams requires a fundamental change in values on the part of both management and workers. Team members are recognized for their group performance, rather than as individuals. A highly motivated and productive worker may receive the same recognition and rewards as a lazy and less productive teammate.

Jack Asgar, president of a management consulting firm called Practical Management Inc., illustrated this value compatibility problem when he argued that if employees are not held accountable, important work will fall through the cracks because workers are not accustomed to such a system. He suggested that anyone who believes in team accountability should test the philosophy in the following manner. The next time a manager holds a meeting of eight or more people, he/she should announce that they share the "team responsibility" for locking the door after the meeting. He writes, "I assure you that nine times out of ten, the door will remain unlocked (Asgar, 1992, p. 21)".

Similarly, self-directed work teams are also incompatible with many previous work systems, such as the traditional reward systems and the traditional management structure. Most reward systems and pay-scales are based on individual performance. Some companies that have adopted self-directed work teams have found that one method of making their pay-scale more compatible with the team concept is to pay employees for the skills they are able to bring to the team effort (Lee, 1990; Orsburn et al., 1990). Employees are paid for what they know, rather than for their individual contribution at a given point in time.

Such team-based reward systems again bring up the issue of accountability. If workers know that their pay is based on passing a number of skills tests on a variety of team tasks, or if they will automatically receive a percentage of the team's profits, no matter what their contribution, their desire to work hard day after day may be minimized.

Another reason why some potential adopters may feel that the self-directed work team concept is incompatible with their current way of doing business is the threat to the established management structure. In most cases, it will be the responsibility of a company's managers to decide whether or not to implement self-directed work teams; and yet, they are the group that seemingly has the most to lose from this innovation.

There are several reasons why many managers are reluctant to implement self-directed work teams. First, managers may feel threatened because they believe it will reduce their power and influence (Sims & Dean, 1985; Manz, Keating & Donnellon, 1990). However, Sims & Dean (1985) and Manz, Keating & Donnellon (1990) wrote that this concern is unfounded because, although direct authority is lessened, indirect power resulting from influence and achievement is increased.

Second, managers will need to adopt a whole new set of skills as they learn to become coaches and facilitators, rather than traditional managers who do whatever it takes to get the job done (Manz, Keating & Donnellon, 1990; Manz & Sims, 1993; Orsburn et al., 1990). It may also be difficult for employees to accept their new self-management role. Some workers prefer being told what to do. They may not want to assume management responsibility, and may resent having to do what they perceive as the manager's job (Hoerr, 1988; Manz & Sims, 1993).

Third, and perhaps most importantly, is management's fear that they will coach themselves out of a job. If teams truly are more efficient, and can do much of what managers have done in the past, then many management jobs may be eliminated. This compatibility problem may be the most difficult obstacle to the diffusion of self-directed work teams. Some former managers may choose to use their influence to sabotage the performance of the newly formed teams (Orsburn et al., 1990).

Although the concept of work teams appears to be incompatible with some of the current values and practices of managers, it does appear to be consistent with their needs. American business continues to become more competitive, and the absence of competitive standing equates to reduced job security. Some potential adopters may agree with Tom Peters, one of America's most acclaimed management consultants (and change agent for self-directed work teams), that work teams will give American businesses an advantage as they compete against other world economic powers (Peters, 1987).

One final issue related to compatibility is what Rogers referred to as a "technology cluster (1983, p. 236)". Rogers explained that the boundaries around innovations are often fuzzy, and that potential adopters often perceive one innovation to be closely related to another. This is clearly the case with self-directed work teams and an earlier related innovation, quality circles.

Sims & Dean (1985) proposed that self-directed work groups could be a natural evolution, or outgrowth of quality circles. They wrote that organizations that have utilized quality circles should consider taking the more aggressive step toward employee participation by implementing self-directed work teams. They refer to quality circles as the "structural and procedural midway point" between the traditional forms of management and self-management for three reasons (Sims & Dean, 1985, p. 30). First, quality circles begin to foster a different approach to problem-solving. In traditional management systems, employees wait for their supervisors to solve problems. Through quality circles, they begin to see that they share the responsibility of organizational problem-solving, and that it feels good. Self-directed work teams take this a step further and ask teams of workers to assume responsibility for certain tasks and the related problems. Second, quality circles begin to foster a sense of trust between employees and management. Quality circles give all employees a forum in which to work toward the common good of the organization. And third, quality circles begin to get employees to work as a team, through collaboration. In essence Sims & Dean are calling for the reinvention of quality circles into self-directed work teams.

In a special status report on the spread of work teams in *Training* magazine, Gordon (1992) described the adoption of self-directed work teams as an evolution of the quality circle. Similarly, Cheney, Sims & Manz (1993, p. 156) argued that quality circles provided the original "paradigm shift" to employee empowerment.

Complexity

Rogers (1983) wrote that the "complexity" of an innovation will negatively impact the rate of adoption. The fundamental elements involved in the implementation of self-directed work teams are somewhat complex. It seems likely that the moderate complexity of self-directed work teams may impact the quality of diffusion as well as the speed. Cummings (1978) wrote that when managers don't understand the self-managing designs, they may apply them inappropriately, which results in confusion and other unintended consequences.

Another concern regarding the complexity of self-directed work teams is that the quality of the diffusion effort may suffer if potential adopters perceive them to be more simple than they are in actuality (Manz & Sims, 1993). Managers may feel that they already know what a team is. After all, many of them have participated on teams from the time they were very small.

If potential adopters underestimate the complexity of the self-directed concept, they may get carried away by their intuitive appeal and implement them without regard to the philosophy or structure. One example is the company who merely removed supervisors from work groups, arbitrarily pronounced that the groups were now "self-managing teams", but provided no resources or training to support this change. Such a simplistic approach is a sure recipe for disaster. Perhaps it is the oversimplification of the concept that has led some adopters to reinvent the self-directed work team concept and strengthened the perception that they are just another management fad.

Trialability

Rogers (1983, p. 231) defined "trialability" as the extent to which a potential adopter can experiment with an innovation on a limited basis. In one sense, self-directed work teams are very difficult to implement on a trial basis. The two main reasons for this difficulty are related to what Zaltman & Duncan (1977) refer to as two additional critical innovation attributes: time and reversibility.

The implementation of self-directed work teams requires a strong commitment by members at all levels of the organization (Manz & Sims, 1993; Orsburn et al., 1990; Versteeg, 1990). And, self-directed work teams can be very time-consuming and expensive. Consultants estimate that they can take anywhere from 18–24 months (Sims & Dean, 1985) to 5 years (Orsburn et al., 1990) until they are running smoothly. Cummings (1978) explained that one reason it is so difficult to try out the team concept is that it takes so much time and effort to develop the social aspects of a work group, such as group decision-making, task iteration and other internal dynamics. He wrote that "these social conditions are not created by design fiat, but through careful attention to the processes by which group members develop their own ways of working together and of adjusting their internal activities to changing task and environmental circumstances (Cummings, 1978, p. 630)."

For these reasons, the self-directed work team concept is not easily tried but then discarded (Manz & Sims, 1993; Orsburn et al., 1990; Versteeg, 1990). The adoption of self-directed work teams requires asking workers to make a complete shift in the way they approach their work. When accompanied by restructuring, jobs are often lost. Although it is not prudent to "try" self-directed work teams for a short period of time, some companies are attempting to do this.

There are a number of companies, however, which have found a way to test how self-directed work teams will work on a trial basis at a limited number of sites. Although this partial adoption would seem like a logical way to test the concept, in some companies there appears to be reluctance to diffuse the innovation throughout the organization even after success at the initial sites (Orsburn et al., 1990; Manz & Sims, 1993; Walton, 1975). Procter & Gamble and General

Motors are examples of companies where success in some plants has not led to company-wide diffusion.

Observability

What Rogers (1983, p. 232) dubs "observability" and Zaltman & Duncan (1977) refer to as "communicability" appear to have made quite a positive impact on the diffusion of self-directed work teams. When the coal miners were utilizing self-directed work teams in the late 1940s, they literally needed to be dug up before they could be observed. Even then, the only people really paying any attention to them were academics, and the communication was taking place in the form of scholarly work rather than being written to an applied audience. As companies like Procter & Gamble began to implement this innovation, there was very little public discussion. Information about self-directed work teams was considered proprietary, and employees were forbidden to discuss their implementation with anyone outside the company (Manz & Sims, 1993; Orsburn et al., 1990).

It appears that this secretive approach to self-directed work teams continued for many years, despite a widely distributed interview of Sims in *US News and World Report* in 1981. In 1985, Sims & Dean wrote that one of the reasons for the slow diffusion of the self-managed work team concept is that the concept has received little media attention. They speculated that many companies were quite secretive about their efforts.

Not long after Sims & Dean's article, the media eventually began to describe the successful efforts of companies utilizing self-directed work teams. *Business Week* ran a story on General Motors (Bernstein, 1987) and on Aid Association For Lutherans (Hoerr, 1988). In 1990, *Fortune* published an article entitled, "Who needs a boss?" (Dumaine, 1990), which Manz & Sims (1993) credited for having brought much popular attention to the subject. Since then, there has been a surge of media attention, and the rate of diffusion has increased dramatically. In fact, Katzenbach & Smith's (1994) recent book, *The Wisdom of Teams*, is a national best-seller, and executives can even listen to the highlights in their cars, because it has recently been released as a book on tape. It seems that once some people started talking about self-directed work teams, others started to as well. In the late 1980s, talking about self-directed work teams shifted from being a taboo release of a proprietary secret to good public relations.

Two Additional Attributes: Routine vs. Radical and Durability

In addition to Roger's innovation attributes outlined above, Zaltman & Duncan (1977) described two additional attributes which are worth brief exploration: routine vs. radical; and durability. First, as is clear from the above discussion, correctly implemented self-directed work teams require a radical change in organizational structure and philosophy (Manz & Sims, 1993; Orsburn et al., 1990).

Orsburn and his colleagues wrote, "Self-directed work teams are revolutionary in a very literal sense. At bottom, self-direction is a return to the place we started from to the simple, natural, satisfying way that people did business in the early light of the modern era (p. 6)".

Another concern evident from the above discussion is the level of durability. Self-directed work teams have been enduring in many of the companies that have implemented them strategically and carefully. For example, Procter & Gamble has been profiting from them for over 20 years (Orsburn et al., 1990). The question that remains, however, is how durable they will be in companies that have implemented them simply because it is "the thing to do" (Manz & Sims, 1993, p. 7).

THE RATE OF DIFFUSION

There has been little research about the rate of adoption of self-directed work teams in the USA. The limited data available, however, illustrate a very slow adoption rate for the first 20-odd years, with the diffusion rate quickly picking up momentum after 1990 (see Figure 15.1). In fact, the diffusion curve seems to be quite similar to the earlier stages of Rogers' (1983) classic diffusion curve.

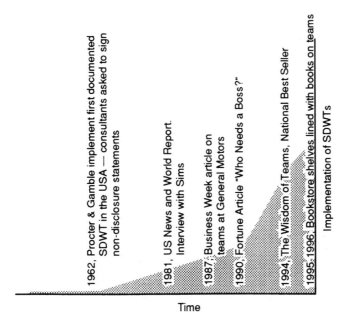

Figure 15.1 Estimated self-directed work team diffusion curve

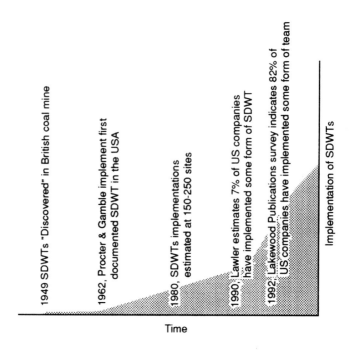

Figure 15.2 Timing of key SDWT publications relative to the diffusion curve

There is no publicly documented evidence of any US company adopting self-directed work teams before 1962, the year Proctor & Gamble first began implementing them in some plants. For the next 20 years, a number of other companies explored them on an experimental basis, but by 1980 it is estimated that only about 150–250 work sites had implemented self-directed work teams (Manz & Sims, 1993).

By 1990, Edward Lawler, Director of the Center for Organizational Effectiveness at the University of Southern California, estimated that 7% of all US companies had implemented some form of self-directed work team (Manz & Sims, 1993). But after 1990, the self-directed work team concept really gained wide-spread attention. Companies began to implement self-directed work teams and share their successes with the media (see Figure 15.2). According to a 1992 survey conducted by Lakewood Publications, it is estimated that 82% of all US companies with 100 employees or more had groups which they classified as a team, and 35% had implemented self-directed work teams (Gordon, 1992). The rate is even higher in companies with more than 10 000 employees (42%). Of the organizations that had implemented self-directed work teams, the average respondent said that one-third of the employees in the organization belonged to a self-directed team. However, a recent study conducted by the Center for Effective Organizations (Lawler, Mohrman & Ledford, 1995) reported that in 1993, although 68% of the Fortune 1000 companies studied had some form of self-directed team, 49% reported having "almost no" employees actually participating on a team, and only 5% indicated that they had at least half of their employees directly involved in self-directed teams (Lawler, Mohrman & Ledford, 1994). So, although most companies may indicate, "sure, we do teams", the extent to which the innovation has spread throughout the organization may, in fact, be quite small.

ADOPTER CHARACTERISTICS

Rogers (1983) explained that there are some innovations that individuals cannot adopt until their organization makes a decision to implement the innovation. The truth of this statement is quite evident when analyzing the diffusion of self-directed work teams. It would be a rare organization that would allow a group of workers to get together, restructure the company, and start managing themselves. However, once an organization makes the decision to adopt self-directed work teams, management then has the task of diffusing the idea to employees and persuading them that the innovation is to their benefit (Orsburn et al., 1990). Orsburn and his colleagues (1990) have created a checklist for diffusion within an organization which includes such items as holding information meetings, transferring members from successful teams to newly formed teams, and bringing in mature teams (opinion leaders) to make presentations. Certainly, organizations could benefit from more research in the area on intraorganizational diffusion of self-directed work teams. This paper focuses, however, on the characteristics of whole organizations as adopters, rather than on the individual members of the organization.

Rogers (1983) described three groups of variables which have been found to influence organizational innovativeness: individual characteristics of the leader; internal structural characteristics of the organization; and external characteristics of the organization. Rogers wrote that there is a positive relationship between the organizational leader's attitude toward change and organizational innovativeness. Much of the research on self-directed work teams also considers this an essential ingredient for successful adoption. Dumaine (1990, p. 58) is one writer who emphatically emphasized the importance of managerial commitment to the team effort: "I guarantee that if you come across someone who says teams didn't work at his company, it's because management didn't take an interest in them".

Over the years, a supportive climate continues to be one of the main organizational characteristics necessary for the successful implementation of self-directed work teams (Manz & Sims, 1993; Orsburn et al., 1990). Manz & Sims (1993) described the visionary leadership of W.L. Gore from W.L. Gore and Associates who has such a high commitment to change that he allows his employees to create their own jobs, and encourages the whole company to function as one, highly integrated, self-directed team.[2] In other companies, it appears to be the change-orientation of individual plant leadership rather than of the entire organization that nurtures the growth of self-directed work teams (Orsburn et al., 1990). Perhaps this scattered diffusion indicates that in larger companies the CEO is too far removed to have a dramatic impact on the diffusion of this type of innovation. He/she must depend on the vision and insights of his/her site mangers to decide whether diffusion makes sense in their plants. Further research will need to be done to test this hypothesis.

Rogers' (1983) next category of variables is the structural characteristics of the organization. Rogers highlights six key elements of organizational structure which have been found to influence the innovativeness of an organization: centralization, formality, size, organizational slack, complexity and interconnectedness.

The limited research that has been done on organizational innovativeness has shown that the level of centralization is negatively related to innovativeness, as is the level of formality of the organization. This research is consistent with the above discussion of decentralized organizations that have partially implemented self-directed work teams. The Yorkshire coal mine was not a highly centralized or formal organization (Trist & Bamforth, 1951). The miners were down there in the dark, away from management control. It is difficult for management to maintain strict adherence to rules and regulations under these circumstances.

Similarly, Procter & Gamble maintains a world-wide collection of sites that essentially run as individual organizations (Orsburn et al., 1990). David Hanna, a Procter & Gamble employee, describes a 1983 international meeting where self-directed teams were suggested as a means of managing organizational change. After hearing the presentation, one technician stood up and said, "Why has it taken the rest of the company so long to get excited about high commitment team systems when we've been using them in our plant since 1968?" (Orsburn, 1990, p. iv). There are many possible answers to that very important question; one of which may be that the top management of the organization didn't really know how that particular plant was being run.

Perhaps it is the high degree of centralization and formality that have made self-directed work teams so difficult to implement in the government. Manz & Sims (1993) describe the conspicuous absence of self-directed work teams in the government sector. However, our personal observation is that the recent Gore initiative toward "re-inventing government" has suddenly and surprisingly unleashed a significant movement toward teams in the public sector. Whether this burgeoning interest will create some real change remains to be seen.

---

[2] The company as team approach is actually a re-invention or related innovation to the self-directed work teams discussed in this paper, as it does not meet the traditional definition of a small group with closely related tasks. Still, the visionary leadership provides a good example of the leadership necessary to foster a participative environment.

On a related note, much research on self-directed work teams has indicated that they are most easily implemented in new sites, or "greenfield" operations, where there is not a pre-established way of doing business (Dumaine, 1990; Manz & Sims, 1993; Orsburn, 1990; Lee, 1990). In greenfield sites there are no established rules; teams can become the norm from the very beginning.

Rogers (1983) reported that another related structural characteristic, size, would have a positive impact on organizational effectiveness. Although size does not seem to have helped the government, in general, this prediction seems to be valid. As mentioned previously, more organizations with over 10 000 employees are currently utilizing self-directed work teams than smaller organizations (Gordon, 1992). One reason for this difference is that these large organizations are finding it difficult to remain centralized. There are necessarily subdivisions in a group of this size, and teams are one way to give workers a sense of community and autonomy in what otherwise might be an impersonal organization. Another reason is that the larger organizations have the resources necessary to invest in the restructuring of the work force, what Rogers (1983, p. 361) refers to as "organizational slack". They can afford to hire consultants, and they may have more cosmopolitan human resource professionals than the smaller firms.

Rogers (1983) also indicated that the level of complexity, defined as the level of knowledge and expertise possessed by organizational members, and the level of interconnectedness, would have a positive impact on organizational innovativeness. This prediction seems to have proved true for the adoption of self-directed work teams. Again, there is much about the philosophy behind self-directed work teams which is consistent with these structural characteristics.

Self-directed work teams are most common in the manufacturing sector where work processes are inter-related (Manz & Sims, 1993). Manz and Sims (1993, p. 12) wrote, "in the manufacturing sector, it's no longer a question of whether or why to use teams, but of fine turning to specific sites". In manufacturing, the workers tend to be the best experts on their specific tasks. Generally, management is too far removed to understand the finer details. In addition, manufacturing processes often involve a series of highly inter-related tasks.

Although self-directed work teams are less common in white collar organizations, they seem to have spread in organizations that have highly specialized, inter-related tasks, such the insurance industry (Dumaine, 1990; Hoerr, 1988; Manz & Sims, 1993). All considered, it is most likely the interconnectedness of the task and the complexity of the job, rather than the collar of the worker, that impacts the success of self-directed work teams. Dumaine (1990) described the importance of analyzing these characteristics when deciding whether to implement self-directed work teams.

In addition to leader characteristics and structural characteristics, Rogers (1983) also wrote that external characteristics of the organization, such as system openness, will influence organizational innovativeness. There has been little written about the influence of this characteristic on the diffusion of self-directed work teams, but intuitively it makes sense. As new employees who have been exposed to the self-directed work team concept enter the organization, or more employees have contact with members of other organizations, as at professional conferences, the more knowledgeable they will be about the team concept.

ORGANIZATIONAL CONSULTANTS AS CHANGE AGENTS

Rogers defined a change agent as an individual who "influences client's innovation decisions in a direction deemed desirable by the change agency" (Rogers, 1983, p. 312). It can be argued that in many ways, external and internal organizational development consultants have filled this role.

External Consultants

From the very early stages of this innovation, external consultants seem to be driving its spread in the USA. As has been discussed earlier, Procter & Gamble had tried to keep their team implementations quiet. Consultants who worked with P & G were required to sign non-disclosure statements (Manz & Sims, 1993). But after a while, a small group of consultants (many of whom were former employees) "spread the word" through an informal network. This grapevine information was a strong influence on the early diffusion of the innovation in the USA.

Consultants appear to be using two primary methods for diffusing self-directed work teams: directly working with clients to implements self-directed work teams, and writing about these experiences and publishing them in the form of books or popular articles or magazines. Two of the main resources for this chapter, Manz and Sims' (1993) *Business Without Bosses* and Orsburn et al.'s *Self-Directed Work Teams: The New American Challenge (1990)* rely on consulting and research experiences as a primary source of information about self-directed work teams. Naturally, each of these books promotes the use of a consultant as an integral part of the implementation process. One chapter of *Business Without Bosses* documents this consulting/recording/diffusion process of one of the chapter's co-authors, Keating, as follows.

> He analyzed the existing operating approach, proposed a self-managed work team design, and then worked directly with the core management team during its transition toward a self-management philosophy. Detailed documentation was kept in a journal during this process (Manz & Sims, 1993, p. 26).

It is clear from their writing that Manz & Sims genuinely believe in the value of self-directed work teams for their readers, and the clients and potential clients of their contributing authors. However, there is also a benefit to them in their role as change agents as they write this practitioner-oriented book, which may exaggerate their pro-innovation bias. This writing is a form of public relations that is contributing to the rapid spread of self-directed work teams. To be fair, Manz &

Sims make it clear that launching self-directed work teams is likely to be accompanied by "bumps and warts", and does not always go as smoothly as one would want.

In addition to the case studies published in the popular media, in the last 3 years there has been a barrage of consultants advertising their assistance in implementing self-directed work teams. Some advertise methods to improve already implemented teams. For example, Development Dimensions International (DDI) (1992) ran an advertisement with the headline, "How to make your team efforts sizzle rather than fizzle". In the body of the advertisement, they promise "techniques for an empowered workforce", which are presented in 20 comprehensive learning units. According to DDI, the diffusion efforts of this packaged approach have been quite successful, with 500 organizations utilizing the approach.

Other organizations focus on the quality improvement benefits of teams. An advertisement for Joiner Associates (1992), in the same issue of *Training* read, "If you are driving quality, we're selling maps". They promise teams as a method of improving quality throughout the organization. The popular magazines are also filled with self-directed work team seminars, such as the one offered by Zenger-Miller, Inc., "Self-directed work teams: from feasibility to implementation (*Training*, **28** January, 1991)." Also, Wentworth Publishing is now publishing a newsletter just for organizations to purchase for their team members, called "Today's Team".

In the past several years, it appears that consultants have been successful in their efforts as change agents to promote the spread of self-directed work teams. The media, education efforts, and personal contact have worked both to introduce and reinforce the self-directed team concept.

There is something a bit unusual, however, about consultants fulfilling the role of change agents. There are so many consultants working to implement the same, or very similar concept, and yet they are all working for different change agencies, or perhaps working independently. The actual goals and values of the various change agencies and agents may vary. Some may be quite client-focused and only diffuse the innovation to those organizations that can truly benefit from the new organizational structure, and others may create a need in the client system, even though they know the implementation might actually be destructive to that organization. And yet, all of these independent change agents are in a sense working together to diffuse the same concept. For example, an article heralding the success of a self-directed work team implementation may be good public relations for the consultant who writes it, but also assists the diffusion efforts of other consultants as well.

Internal Consultants

It has been our experience that in addition to external consultants, some larger organizations have internal consultants who serve as change agents, spreading the self-directed concept throughout the organization. The exact role of such internal consultants varies from organization to organization, and may even vary among business units within the same organization. Such internal consultants sometimes partner with external consultants in their strategic team development and training efforts.

The role of an internal consultant often looks quite similar to the work of an external consultant: conducting intensive needs analysis and feasibility studies; developing teaming strategies and implementation plans; communicating the benefits of self-directed teams to employees and customers; developing and delivering team training programs; and developing processes to select, develop and reward team leaders and members at various levels of the organization. As with external consultants, one critical aspect of the internal consultant's job is selling the benefits of moving to a self-directed work team arrangement. This involves constant stakeholdering with senior managers and formal and informal communication to employees at all levels of the organization. Also similar to the external consultant, the widespread diffusion of teams within the organization can mean job security for the internal consultant.

Many organizations find that the advantage of having an internal consultant(s) dedicated to the diffusion and development of teams is, as employees, that they have the ability to "talk trucks" with team members, and thus truly customize the team structure to ensure that it meets the needs of employees, customers and shareholders. It has been our experience that the consultant-to-team ratio also contributes to the success of the internal consultant. Generally, if this ratio is too high, it is difficult for the consultant to be in touch with the development of individual leaders and teams. If this ratio is too low, the consultant may end up intervening too much, and taking on a leadership, rather than a consultative role. Such over-intervention can actually retard lasting team growth as team members and leaders become overly dependent on an outside facilitator.

We have also found that internal consultants who have the appropriate mix of organizational development knowledge and experience and a solid understanding of the bottom-line business goals and processes are the most respected as change agents within the organization. When organizations assign employees to the role without this appropriate balance of "soft" and "hard" skills and knowledge, employees often question management's commitment to the development of teams as a true enabler to accomplishing bottom line results.

Finally, the issue of credibility can work both for or against an internal consultant. On the one hand, internal consultants are sometimes not given equal standing with external consultants for "expertness". However, this is frequently counterbalanced by the superior knowledge of the internal consultant to the unique parameters of the change situation within this particular organization.

TEAM MEMBERS AS OPINION LEADERS

Rogers (1983) defines opinion leaders as individuals who are able to informally influence other people's attitudes or behavior. In general, opinion leaders are somewhat homophilous to other members of the potential client system, and are highly linked into the interpersonal communication network.

In the diffusion of self-directed work teams, the strongest opinion leaders appear to be individuals who have participated in other self-directed work teams. Trist found this to be true in the coal mines: "Many of the workmen concerned in the early stages have contributed substantially to the understanding of the issues" (Trist et al., 1951, p. 4). Similarly, consultants today know the importance of bringing in members of successful teams to share their experiences with potential adopters. (Manz & Sims, 1993; Orsburn et al., 1990). Consultants also understand the importance of convincing the most senior, or well respected, workers about the value of self-directed work teams (Orsburn et al., 1990). They know that resistance by the informal leaders in the organization could be fatal to the diffusion effort.

Professional associations also offer a forum to help facilitate discussion among current and future team members (and in such circumstances may also function as change agencies). For example, the Association for Quality and Participation held a session which brought together different companies who were implementing or had implemented self-directed work teams (Orsburn et al., 1990). Workers from different companies were able to share their ideas.

THE CONSEQUENCES

There is a great deal of evidence of positive consequences of self-directed work teams. Employees seem to be more satisfied with their jobs (Cummings, 1978; Gordon, 1992; Manz & Sims, 1993; Sims & Manz, 1996; Orsburn et al., 1990). Many companies have shown increases in productivity and profits of as much as 40% (Dumaine, 1990; Gordon, 1992; Hoerr, 1988; Manz & Sims, 1993; Orsburn et al., 1990). In addition, companies have found that self-directed work teams increase the quality of products and customer service (Hoerr, 1988; Gordon, 1992; Manz & Sims, 1993; Orsburn et al., 1990.) Two recent scientific studies of team performance and/or high involvement systems are a recent paper from Barry Macy and associates at the Texas Center for Productivity and Quality of Work Life (1991), and a study published by Lawler, Mohrman & Ledford (1995) at the Center for Effective Organizations. Very strong effects, especially in terms of financial outcomes, were observed with team applications. In general, there is a good deal of evidence to suggest that when implemented correctly, and in the right type of companies, self-directed work teams can lead to serious improvements. Perhaps the advantages of self-directed teams were articulated best by Charles Eberle, a former vice president at Procter & Gamble, who spoke with the advantage of years of practical experience:[3]

---

[3] Quoted by Kim Fisher in "Are you serious about self-management?", a paper delivered at the International Conference on Self-managed Work Teams, Dallas, Texas, October, 1991.

> At P & G there are well over two decades of comparisons of results—side by side— between enlightened work systems and those I call traditional. It is absolutely clear that the new work systems work better—a lot better—for example, with 30–50% lower manufacturing costs. Not only are the tangible, measurable, bottom-line indicators such as cost, quality, customer service and reliability better, but also the harder-to-measure attributes such as quickness, decisiveness, toughness and just plain resourcefulness of these organizations.

There are also, however, some potentially negative consequences that also need to be considered. Perhaps the most obvious potential negative consequence is one that often follows any innovation that increases efficiency and productivity, downsizing (Manz & Sims, 1993; Orsburn et al., 1990). As teams assume the responsibilities of middle managers, there will be a need for fewer of them. This may result in the elimination or demotion of many middle managers, a group which is already at the top of businesses' endangered species list.

Middle managers are not the only employees who may feel the negative consequences of self-directed work teams. Older workers who cannot adjust to the team concept may also be displaced (Manz & Sims, 1993). Experienced workers sometimes become frustrated because they are forced to do a variety of tasks, many of which they feel they've outgrown. They may feel threatened by the rapid pay advancement of less experienced workers who are able to learn new tasks quickly. Also, the Manz & Sims (1993) research has shown that some "high status" employees may initially "feel like losers" because their relative sense of privilege seems to diminish when other employees become empowered.

In addition, there may be workers who do not want to be empowered (Hoerr, 1988). They may like being told what to do, or like having the ability to do what they feel they are best at, without worrying about the intricacies of running a team. If self-directed work teams become widespread, there may not be jobs available for workers who just want to sweep the floor or assemble machinery, or who prefer to work by themselves.

There is also some concern that teams will be actually used to disempower or exploit employees (Barker, 1993; Manz & Angle, 1993). Management may see teams as a way to create peer pressure for employees to comply with management's established rules and procedures. Barker (1993) found that employees in a self-directed environment developed a concertive system of control that was more restrictive on organizational members than the traditional management structure had been.

Pfeffer (1982, p. 246) wrote that "once an innovation is institutionalized, it is adopted and accepted not because it has rational or technical properties but because social expectations are that good, well-managed organizations will do so". There is a possibility that the team concept may become so widespread that employees may perceive it as the normal way of doing business. The philosophical and practical reasons for the existence of teams may fade away as teams become integrated into the organizational structure, and they may lose their utility as an empowerment tool.

FINAL REMARKS

Has the diffusion of self-directed work teams been a success? Well, it had a slow start, but that may be because for a long time no-one was trying to diffuse it. In the last few years, however, concentrated efforts to diffuse this innovation have led to more rapid adoption. And yet, the integrity of the self-directed work team philosophy has generally remained intact. When people talk about self-directed work teams, they are still focusing on many of the same issues that Trist identified in the 1940s.

The success of organizational innovations depends a great deal on timing. Perhaps the change agents were strategic about when they began encouraging their clients to implement. Perhaps these organizational change agents knew that the quality circle phase would help prepare clients to implement this innovation. Perhaps they knew that managers first needed to experience a philosophical shift to the acceptance of employee empowerment.

Or perhaps this is giving the change agents too much credit. Maybe it's more of a bandwagon effect. Some companies and consultants produced successful self-directed work team implementations; they shared the good news, so others implemented. At any rate, it appears that since a concerted, and somewhat collective, effort has been made by change agents to diffuse this innovation, the results have been quite successful.

What should be done differently in the future diffusion of this innovation? If speed is the key goal, nothing at all. The diffusion efforts of the consultants and writers, along with an increasing network of team members as opinion leaders, seem to be doing the job quite nicely. But if this innovation is to be durable, we need to take a step back and analyze what is actually happening in these self-directed work teams. Research needs to be done to examine the long-term impact of these teams on the organization. Does the role of the self-directed work team change over time in a given organization? Do workers feel that they truly have autonomy in their work, or in name only? Do workers actually prefer the self-directed team as a long-term way of organizational life? How do students training to be future organizational leaders feel about the limited leadership positions of the team structure? Do teams "plateau" as a learning device? As the diffusion becomes more widespread, it should also be easier to examine the consequences of this innovation.

Despite the fact that this innovation was originally "discovered" by academics, the academic community has really played the role of "laggards" in relation to this innovation. Organizational scholars need to "adopt" self-directed work teams in the sense that they recognize their potential impact and devote the energy and resources necessary to the understanding of this important innovation.

REFERENCES

Asgar, J. (1992). Teams and accountability. *Training*, **29**, 21.

Barker, J.R. (1993). Tightening the iron cage: concertive control in self-managing teams. *Administrative Science Quarterly*, **38**, 408–37.

Bernstein, A. (1987). GM may be off the hook. *Business Week*, **September 28**, 26–7.

Carson, N. (1992). The trouble with teams. *Training*, **29**, 38–40.

Cheney, A.B., Sims, H.P. & Manz, C.C. (1993). Teams and total quality management: an international application. In C.C. Manz & H.P. Sims (eds), *Business Without Bosses: How Self-managing Teams are Building High-performance Companies*. New York: Wiley.

Cummings, T.G. (1978). Self-regulating work groups: a socio-technical synthesis. *Academy of Management Review*, **3**, 625–33.

Development Dimensions International (advertisement for) (1992). How to make your team efforts sizzle rather than fizzle. Advertisement, *Training*, **29**, 5.

Dumaine, B. (1990). Who needs a boss? *Fortune*, **121**, 52–60.

Fisher, K. (1991). Are you serious about self-management? Paper delivered at the International Conference on Self-managed Work Teams, Dallas, October.

Fox, W.M. (1990). An interview with Eric Trist, father of the sociotechnical systems approach. *The Journal of Applied Behavioral Science*, **26**, 259–79.

Gordon, J. (1992). Work teams—how far have they come. *Training*, **29**, 59–65.

Hoerr, J. (1988). Work teams can rev up paper pushers, too. *Business Week*, **November 28**, 64, 68, 72.

Hoerr, J. (1989). The payoff from teamwork. *Business Week*, **July 10**, 55–62.

Joiner Associates Inc (advertisement for) (1992). If you're driving quality, we're selling maps. *Training Magazine*, **29**, 28.

Industry Report (1992). *Training*, **29**, 25–8.

Jessup, H.R. (1990). New roles in team leadership. *Training and Development Journal*, **44**, 79–83.

Katzenbach, J.R. & Smith, D.K. (1994). *The Wisdom of Teams: Creating the High-performance Organization*. New York: Harper Business.

Lawler, E.E., Mohrman, S.A. & Ledford, G.E. (1994). *Power-sharing Involving Work Design*. Los Angeles, CA: The Center for Effective Organizations, University of Southern California.

Lawler, E.E., Mohrman, S.A. & Ledford, G.E. (1995). *Creating High Performance Organizations: Practices and Results of Employee Involvement and Total Quality Management in Fortune 1000 Companies*. San Francisco, CA: Jossey-Bass.

Lee, C. (1990). Beyond teamwork. *Training*, **6**, 25–32.

Macy, B.M., Bliese, P.D. & Norton, J.J. (1991). Organizational change and work innovation: a meta-analysis of 131 North American field experiments, 1961–1990. Working paper, Texas Tech University.

Manz, C.C. & Angle, H.L. (1993). The illusion of self-management: using teams to disempower. In C.C. Manz & H.P. Sims Jr (eds), *Business Without Bosses: How Self-managing Teams are Building High-performance Companies*. New York: Wiley.

Manz, C.C., Keating, D.E. & Donnellon, A. (1990). Preparing for an organizational change to employee self-management: the managerial transition. *Organizational Dynamics*, **19**, 15–26.

Manz, C.C. & Sims, H.P. Jr (1993). *Business Without Bosses: How Self-managing Teams are Building High-performing Companies*. New York: Wiley.

Orsburn, J.D., Moran, L., Musselwhite, E. & Zenger, J. (1990). *Self-directed Work Teams: the New American Challenge*. Homewood, IL: Business One Irwin.

Pfeffer, J. (1982). *Organizations and Organization Theory*. Boston, MA: Pitman.

Peters, T. (1987). *Thriving on Chaos*. New York: Harper and Row.

Rogers, E.M. (1962). *Diffusion of Innovations*. New York: Free Press.

Rogers, E.M. (1983). *Diffusion of Innovations*. 3rd edn. New York: Free Press.

Rogers, E.M. (1995). *Diffusion of Innovations*. 4th edn. New York: Free Press.

Rogers, E.M. & F.F. Shoemaker (1971). *Communication of Innovations: a Cross-cultural Approach*. New York: Free Press.

Sims, H.P. Jr (1981) How to get what you want from your job. Featured interview in *U.S. News and World Report*, August 31 (pp. 66–7).

Sims, H.P. & Dean, J.W. (1985). Beyond quality circles: self-managing teams. *Personnel*, **62**, 25–32.

Sims, H.P. & Manz, C.C. (1994). The leadership of self managing teams. In *Interdisciplinary Studies of Work Teams*, vol. 1 (pp. 187–221).

Sims, H.P. Jr & Manz, C.C. (1996) *Company of Heroes: Unleashing the Power of Self-leadership*. New York: Wiley.

Sussman, Gerald I. (1976). *Autonomy at Work: a Sociotechnical Analysis of Management*. New York: Prager.

Trist, E.L. & Bamforth, K.W. (1951). Some social and psychological consequences of the longwall method of coal-getting. *Human Relations*, **4**, 3–38.

Trist, E.L., Higgin, G.W., Murray, H. & Pollock, A.B. (1951). *Organizational Choice: Capabilities of Groups at the Coal Face under Changing Technologies*: London: Tavistock.

Versteeg, A. (1990). Self-directed work teams yield long-term benefits. *The Journal of Business Strategy*, **11**, 9–12.

Walton, R.E. (1975). The diffusion of new work structures: explaining why success didn't take. *Organizational Dynamics*, **Winter**, 3–22.

Wellins, R.S. (1992). Building a self-directed work team. *Training and Development*, **46**, 24–8.

Zaltman, G. & Duncan, R. (1977). *Strategies for Planned Change*. New York: Wiley.

Zenger-Muler, Inc. (advertisement for) (1991). Self-directed work teams from feasibility to implementation. *Training*, **28**.

Chapter 16

Group Decision-Making and Effectiveness: Unexplored Boundaries

Michael A. West
Institute of Work Psychology, University of Sheffield, UK
Simon Garrod
University of Glasgow, UK
and
Jean Carletta
Human Communication Research Centre, University of Edinburgh, UK

INTRODUCTION

Teams will be increasingly the functional unit of organizations in the twenty-first century in response to the challenges of new forms of organization and increasingly complex environments. The information technology and communication revolutions now occurring will, at the same time, pose new challenges and opportunities for group decision-making and communication. This chapter directly addresses these themes. As organizations become more complex and the need for laterality increases, teams are being deployed. Self-managing teams are also being created to foster empowerment. The requirement to develop products and services quickly and to respond promptly and personally to customer needs also favours the adoption of teamwork. Teams enable organizational learning, cross-functional communication and more effective quality management (Mohrman, Cohen & Mohrman, 1995). Moreover, teamwork is associated with the high levels of innovation and adaptability organizations of the future require. However, we believe that researchers' consideration of how these teams can best

Creating Tomorrow's Organizations. Edited by C.L. Cooper and S.E. Jackson.
© 1997 John Wiley & Sons Ltd.

function has not yet deeply probed their potential. Given the challenges they will face, the requirement to translate theory into potent prescription in this area has never been greater. Moreover, teams face the challenges of managing new technologies of information exchange and communication which must affect their decision-making capacity. Mobile telephones, e-mail, video and telephone conferencing are all relatively new forms of information exchange, the impact of which on team functioning and effectiveness is little understood. Will these new technologies aid teams of the future, or present challenges so great that their decision-making ability will be reduced? This chapter is about what makes teams and team decision-making effective or otherwise. The principal claim is that effective decision-making groups will be those that are what we shall term "reflexive" and the first section of the chapter will address this basic claim. In the second part of the chapter we examine how the micro-processes of communication underlying decisions tend to a conspire against a group acting reflexively. Out of this discussion will emerge some general principles for effective group discussion and functioning which promote reflexivity and prepare groups for the challenges of their organizational futures.

BACKGROUND

Psychologists have traditionally taken what might be termed a "technical-rational" approach to understanding how groups operate (Schôn, 1983). Yet the complexity of teams and their environments suggests that such an orientation is unlikely to produce valid and powerful explanatory frameworks. As Schôn (1994) argues, technical-rational and hence mechanical manipulations of work group design and functioning can affect particular consequences, e.g. clarifying goals for groups will, in most circumstances, lead to greater effectiveness. However, such formulations ignore the fact that groups and their environments change over time and that their goals are likely to be multiple and competing. In some circumstances it is valuable for groups to be unclear about their objectives. A hospital management team which has to begin generating income rather than relying on central government funding will require a period of goal orientation characterized by consideration and uncertainty. In such circumstances, having clear goals may be counter-productive and contribute to ineffectiveness rather than effectiveness. Moreover, the concept of effectiveness itself is political rather than empirical (or technical-rational) in the sense that there are multiple constituents of most complex decision-making teams in modern organizations. Effectiveness in relation to one stakeholder group will spell ineffectiveness for another (e.g. saving money for a local health organization may not be in the best interests of patients who want the best quality of care).

According to the technical-rational approach, professional activity consists in instrumental problem-solving made rigorous by the application of scientific theory and technique. Schôn describes an alternative approach, which he terms "reflection-in-action": ". . . both ordinary people and professional practitioners often think about what they are doing, sometimes even while doing it. Stimulated by surprise, they turn thought back on action and on the knowing which is implicit in action" (Schôn, 1983, p. 50). He goes on, "It is this entire process of reflection-in-action which is central to the 'art' by which practitioners sometimes deal with situations of uncertainty, instability, uniqueness and value conflict" (Schôn, 1983, p. 50). In the approach described below we adopt this reflection-in-action orientation to understanding group effectiveness, which is referred to as "reflexivity".

But first we need to distinguish between complex decision-making (CDM) and simple decision-making (SDM) groups. There is good reason to believe that CDM groups will dominate the organizational landscape of the next 40 years and that they should therefore demand high priority in our theorizing. There is a clear qualitative difference between groups operating with relatively low control and discretion (SDM groups—e.g. in a shop floor environment which is relatively certain and predictable) and those with high autonomy, in unpredictable environments, where achieving desired outputs is a relatively complex and unclear process (CDM groups). Examples of CDM groups are: top management teams, primary health care teams, social services teams, community psychiatric teams, project teams in commercial settings, nursing teams and research teams. Characteristic of these groups is that:

- They operate in uncertain, unpredictable environments.
- They often work with complex and unpredictable technology.
- Task performance requirements can change daily.
- They have high team member interdependence.
- They have autonomy over their day-to-day work.
- The nature of the tasks they are required to perform is complex, i.e. there are multiple elements and multiple interactions between elements
- The components of effectiveness are multiple and the team is responsible to multiple constituents.

Existing models of group performance tend to represent static rather than dynamic processes. Group variables such as participation in decision-making are assumed to have a consistent relationship with productivity. However, such models are less and less appropriate for CDM groups of professionals from diverse backgrounds (an increasingly common form) working in challenging and changing environments. The groups themselves often change rapidly as a result of experience and member turnover, requiring repeated adaptation of communication and decision-making processes (McGrath & O'Connor, 1996). Groups even change their environments as a result of their own work via processes of innovation, political pressure of simply their own effectiveness. Any model of team decision-making, communication and effectiveness must be able to account for these dynamic characteristics of groups. The conceptual approach offered here focuses on group communication, decision-making and effectiveness, and proposes that what may best predict group effectiveness is an overarching factor which potentially will influence all aspects of group performance—group task reflexivity.

In discussing group task reflexivity we consider how real CDM groups actually operate. The examples we draw on come from decision-making meetings which were recorded from four teams in UK manufacturing companies and one UK primary health care team. The teams involved were chosen to provide a range of informal meeting types. The meetings lasted anywhere from 15 minutes to all day but were usually just under an hour long. For each team a series of six meetings was recorded, except for one team where three long meetings were recorded instead. The number of participants in a meeting varied between four and a dozen. Some teams were reasonably homogenous and met as a matter of routine; other teams were attempting to solve particular problems which their companies were facing, and were composed of people representing a wide range of skills and expertise. So the collection was designed to cover a range of meeting types among CDM groups and give a good indication of the range of things which go into such decision-making. Two of the manufacturing teams proved to be particularly reflexive, where reflexiveness was assessed in relation to the goals and activities of the teams and the extent to which the meetings fulfilled these goals (see below). One of these firms (henceforth, "the auto-parts firm") manufactures automobile components using a printing process; the other (henceforth, "the lighting firm"), makes lighting equipment. In contrast, examples from a primary health care team are used to show unreflexive behaviour. Extracts from the meetings will be used to illustrate group task reflexivity in the rest of the chapter.

GROUP TASK REFLEXIVITY

Group task reflexivity is defined as the extent to which group members overtly reflect upon, and communicate about, the group's objectives, strategies (e.g. decision-making) and processes (e.g. communication), and adapt them to current or anticipated circumstances.

There are two central elements to this concept of reflexivity—literally "bend back"—which are reflection and adaptation. Rennie (1992) describes the concept in the following way:

> Throughout the history of philosophy and psychology, this quality has been described as consciousness, will, thinking, reason, judgement, reflection, agency, self-monitoring, recursion, meta cognition, and reflexivity among others (pp. 224–5).

Reflexivity has also been described as "a turning back on the self" and can encompass both self-awareness and agency. The reflection component of group task reflexivity parallels Kahn's (1992) concept of psychological presence, but at the group level and manifested in intragroup communication. Non-reflexivity, according to Rennie (1992), is "... the state of acting ... without awareness of the action". Group members are not aware of decision-making or communication processes in any reflexive sense—they are just deciding and communicating. A reflexive model of group processes incorporates the idea that group task processes are "circular" or "spiralling". The group's reality is continually renegotiated during group decision-making and communication. Understandings negotiated in one exchange between group members may be drawn upon in a variety of ways in order to inform subsequent discussions, and offer the possibility of helpful and creative transformations in meaning. The meanings of particular representations of the group's circumstances are not stable, but depend on context of use and group members' reactions to them. Reflection involves behaviours such as questioning, planning, exploratory learning, analysis, diversive exploration, making use of knowledge explicitly, planfulness, learning at a meta level, reviewing past events with self-awareness, digestion, and coming to terms over time with a new awareness.

How does reflection change into action or adaptation? It is through reflection in communication that intentions are formed and the potential for carrying them out is built up. During group reflection, courses of action can be discussed and decisions may be reached about contemplated actions. Subsequently a decision may be converted into action. During reflection there is indeterminacy and the group has choices and hence the possibility of control over change. Some groups may reflect in their discussions without subsequently taking action while others may adapt and make decisions (whether appropriate or inappropriate) without reflection. The decisions and actions of reflexive groups need not always be "right", "appropriate" or "adaptive", since group actions will lead to new information, further reflection and action, continuing in a spiral, until group members are satisfied with the outcome. However, the result of continuous cycles of reflexive communication and decision-making will be group task effectiveness.

Indicators of Group Task Reflexivity

What are the domains of reflection and action which characterize reflexive groups? Broadly reflexive groups are likely to communicate about and effect change in relation to objectives, strategies, group events, processes and environments. Reflection might therefore be upon the topics discussed below.

Group Objectives

We have found that reflexive teams in our sample explicitly considered their objectives as an introduction to each meeting, and in many cases they discussed and evaluated alternatives before proceeding. For example, here is an extract from the opening discussion at a lighting firm management meeting where they are considering whether to float the company on the stock exchange. Speaker 1 is the accountant advising the board and speaker 2 is a member of the board:

Speaker 1: "I've written down a couple of things because I think it's important to . . . I'm sure this has come up in a number of your internal discussions, but the question is slightly formalising it, so that we all know what you're aiming at. It's to understand what each of the shareholders' aspirations are, bearing in mind that there is some difference in ages and, no doubt, personal circumstances. Er, so therefore it would be useful just to, each of you to give a little speech, pre-prepared or otherwise, as to what you would actually like out of life or out of [this firm]. And, since [Speaker 2] has finished eating, I'll let him speak first."

Speaker 2: "Sorry, can you repeat the question?"

(general laughter)

Speaker 1: "Yes."

Speaker 2: "What is my aspiration?"

Speaker 1: "Basically, your short-viewed aspirations, as in, er, how long you will carry on working, how long you will carry on working for [this firm], when would you like to cash in your chips, and those sort of issues."

In general, reflexive teams check the appropriateness, clarity and value of their objectives and ensure that the members of the team are committed to them before proceeding.

Group Strategies or Plans for Achieving Goals

Again reflexive teams are careful to specify their strategies and plans in detail including the time-span and effectiveness of alternatives. Part of this involves setting up sensible goals. Thus, in this first meeting of a middle management team in an auto-parts firm, they have been considering delays in throughput of new products between order and delivery, but the team itself has not specified how long it usually takes and how much they need to cut that back. The facilitator then takes up this issue in the following:

Facilitator: "How long does that take approximately?"

Team member 1: "Four to six weeks on a good uninterrupted bit."

Facilitator: "Four to six weeks?"

Team member 1: "We've seen it come to the likes of eight to ten. And then, really serious cases . . ."

Facilitator: "What do customers expect?"

Team member 1: "Customers would really like these parts within two to three weeks."

Facilitator: "Two or three weeks?"

Team member 1: "To be honest with you, and that's what we've got to drive at, but, at the moment, we're not set up to be anything better than four weeks at the moment. But we can improve on it, there's no reason why, as [team member 2] said, we've got plenty of capacity . . ."

Facilitator: "We're just not using it properly."

Team member 1: "... It's maybe how we plan it."

Here the facilitator is concentrating the team's decision-making onto more specific goals, such as in this case, defining a realistic time for throughput of new products. In general, reflexive groups concentrate on the detailedness, clarity, value, alternatives, time-span and effectiveness of strategies and plans.

Group Events

Reflexive teams show awareness of what is happening in their group. Thus they note group successes or errors, are aware of changes in group membership and intra-group conflicts. To take another example from the auto-parts firm meetings, the following extract illustrates a recognition that they have to overcome intra-group conflicts to solve their production problems and stop treating any of their members as scapegoats for past failures:

Team member 4: "... When [Person Y] asks, 'who gave those dates?' you can say 'we did'" (laughs).

(team members all laugh)

Team member 4: "I nearly said 'I did.' 'We did'."

Team member 5: "No, you nearly said '[Speaker 2] did'."

Team member 4: "Rock my socks, okay? But we've gotta do this as a team thing, we've gotta really be seen to be supporting each other. I mean, yesterday it could have been down to one of these old meetings, where it was ... remember the old meeting? 'Who gave these dates? Was it you, Speccy?'"

(team members all laugh again)

Team member 4: "Yes."

Team member 5: "It's your fault, then."

Team member 4: "Don't blame the champion, you know the champion is only part of the team."

Group Processes

Reflexive teams will also concentrate on and be aware of group processes such as their decision-making, communication, frequency of interaction, self-appraisal and so on. As an example of sensitivity to the communication process, here is a short extract from near the beginning of another one of the auto-parts firm meetings. Speaker 1 is about to review what has been covered at previous meetings to bring a new team member up to date, and so he apologises to those who are already aware of what has happened in the previous meetings:

Speaker 1: "Well, basically, before I start I should like to apologise to [Speaker 2] and [Speaker 4], ..."

Speaker 4: "That's alright."

Speaker 1: "... because they've already been part of this meeting. I'll work it through with you because we've got new additions to the team."

Other examples of concentrating on processes might be reflected in support for innovations in the team and monitoring effectiveness.

Environment

Finally, reflexive groups will tend to be aware of the environment in which they operate. For example they will recognize such things as the impact of technology, reward systems, inter-group relations, organizational objectives and the wider social impact (e.g. ecological issues) in what they do. A short example taken from a later point in the lighting firm's flotation meeting shows how well aware the management team is of the technical limitations of their company:

> *Speaker 2*: "Yes, yes. And then sort of rolled up with this aspiration is, is also the fundamental belief that, with the technology where it is today, that we are all pushing our luck a little bit to depend on [this firm] and its current technology to provide an ongoing both interesting work environment and quite good remuneration package for another 10, 15 years or so, or however long the three of us wish to keep on, on, on, working as well."

Thus non-reflexive groups can be identified by their failure to discuss objectives, strategies, events, processes and environments, and by a tendency to react to the situation that exists at the moment. This is in contrast to reflexive groups, which plan strategies ahead and actively structure the situation, including potential feedback. Reflexive groups will have a more comprehensive and penetrating intellectual representation of their work, a longer time-frame, a larger inventory of environmental cues to which they respond, a better knowledge and anticipation of errors and a more active orientation towards their work. Non-reflexive groups will exhibit defensiveness against discussion of group processes, strategy planning and change, and be recalcitrant in their willingness to review and reflect on their experience and objectives.

Between reflection or awareness and action there has to be some degree of group planning, and Action Theory (Frese & Zapf, 1994) provides a very helpful deconstruction of this process. Frese & Zapf (1994) describe four dimensions of plans, which can be used to gauge the extent of reflexivity. Detailedness is simply the extent to which a plan is worked out in detail before, as opposed to during, action. Inclusiveness of potential problems relates to the extent to which a group develops alternative plans in case of inadvertent circumstance. *A priori* hierarchical ordering of plans reflects the extent to which plans are broken up into subplans before action begins. Long- vs. short-range plans is self-evident, although in uncertain environments both may be necessary to sustain effectiveness. High reflexivity is evidenced when groups plan in greater detail. This is indicated by recognizing potential problems, hierarchical ordering of plans, and engaging in long- as well as short-range planning.

How a group reacts to and seeks feedback is also an indicator of reflexivity. Groups which discuss performance feedback in a self-serving manner, rather than reflecting on performances issues, are likely to be low in reflexivity and consequently low in performance. Feedback search rate is another useful indicator of reflexivity, since it suggests that a group is sufficiently open in its interpretation of its world and functioning, to value external feedback.

In relation to the wider organizational environment, such non-reflexive groups will tend to comply unquestioningly with organizational demands and expectancies; accept organizations' limitations; fail to discuss or challenge organizational incompetence; communicate indebtedness and dependence on the organization; and rely heavily on organizational direction and reassurance. Reflexive groups, in contrast, will be more likely to reflect on and discuss the relationship with the organization and other organizational groups, and be prepared to challenge the appropriateness of organizational objectives. They are more likely to be minority influence groups (see Nemeth & Owens, 1996) within the organization, generating conflict and innovation.

Empirical Support for the Reflexivity–Effectiveness Relationship

There is good support for the proposition that task reflexivity will predict group task effectiveness in both social psychological and organizational research. Hackman & Morris (1975) found that in 100 laboratory groups (three persons per group, working on a 15-minute task) only 142 comments were made about the performance strategy of the group (less than 2 comments per group). However, process discussions following these comments turned out to facilitate group performance. The judged creativity of group products was related to the number of comments made about performance strategy. Previous work also suggests that task orientation (a conceptually similar factor) is associated with team innovation and effectiveness (West & Anderson, 1996). Tjosvold (1990) described constructive controversy within groups as the extent of open exploration of opposing opinions. He argued for a direct causal relationship with effectiveness, and offered empirical support for this proposition.

Group problem-solving, especially early on, is significantly improved when members examine the way in which they have defined the situation and considered whether or not they are solving the "right" problem. Evidence has accumulated in this area as a result of the coherent and major body of research developed by Maier and colleagues (Maier, 1970). Maier's work suggested that cognitive stimulation in groups may produce novel ideas, a unique combination of sub-ideas, or a complex solution whose total value is "greater than the sum of its parts". The group product might be improved, Maier found, if groups were encouraged to be "problem-minded" rather than "solution-minded", i.e. to question and communicate about its current approach or to consider other aspects of the problem. Maier also found that group productivity was improved when the group analysed problem facets as sub-tasks, and if members separated and re-combined problem-solving strategies. Similar effects on productivity were found when groups were encouraged to produce two different solutions to a problem, so that the better of the two might be adopted (Maier, 1970). Particularly for CDM groups, more planning enhances group performance (Hackman, Brousseau & Weiss, 1976; Smith, Locke & Barry, 1990).

Another line of supportive findings for this general proposition comes form research on problem identification by groups (Moreland & Levine, 1992). For example, a group that detects problems too slowly or misdiagnoses them will probably fail, whatever solutions it develops for those. Indeed, misdiagnosis of problems is a major threat to group effectiveness. Attributing problems to the wrong causes, or not communicating about potential consequences, are common failings which can undermine group effectiveness, especially when group members refuse to reflect on the possibility of error. A major factor determining group task effectiveness is group norms regarding problem-solving. Non-reflexive groups regard problems as threats to morale and discourage identification of problems by their members. Those who become aware of problems is such groups are reluctant to talk about them because they expect to be censored. When problems are brought into the awareness of non-reflexive groups, the tension produced can prevent appropriate planning and action. Reflexive groups that engage in more extensive scanning and discussion of their environments are also better than non-reflexive groups at identifying problems. Moreover, as the environment of groups becomes more uncertain, problem identification becomes more difficult. Non-reflexive groups will tend to deny, distort or hide problems and wait and watch to see what occurs with them (Moreland & Levine 1992). In non-reflexive groups, identifying a problem is more likely to be seen as harmful, by threatening morale or creating conflict over such issues as who caused the problem and who should solve it.

In a somewhat different vein, recent research on how scientific teams operate also highlights the importance of reflexivity. Dunbar (1996) carried out a detailed analysis of meetings in top rank science laboratories in order to document the discovery process. He noted that in many cases breakthroughs arose through distributed problem-solving in groups, and the effective groups were those which concentrated their discussion on negative and surprising findings. Whereas individual scientists out of a group context tend to attribute inconsistent evidence to error of some sort, the other scientists in a group focus on the inconsistency and dissect it. As often as not this will lead to proposing alternative and novel hypotheses and explanations. In fact, Dunbar found that one of the best indicators of effectiveness among his science teams was the amount of time they spent dissecting these negative and inconsistent findings.

Research designed to improve group decision-making also provides further support for the general position adopted here. For example, Rogelberg, Barnes-Farrell & Lowe (1992) had groups use a technique of structured decision-making to solve complex and novel problems, which produced higher quality decisions than groups using conventional methods. The "stepladder" technique employed by Rogelberg et al. involved each group member presenting his/her perceptions of the problem and potential solutions to the group in turn, without having heard the input of other members. One consequence was the constant reiteration and verbalization of group members' ideas in discussion, to the types of processes the theory would predict in highly reflexive groups. Because each group member had an opportunity to present his/her views, there was less pressure to conform, which may have enabled groups to freely evaluate ideas rather than actively avoiding disagreements and promoting conformity. Group members also tended to work very hard and to fully understand the group outcome. The "stepladder" groups were in effect continually discussion and re-making their decisions.

Other research on the remaking of group decisions has also indicated beneficial effects on group output (Maier & Hoffman, 1960). For complex tasks, a higher rate of communication is clearly and positively related to group performance (Foushee, 1984; Williges, Johnson & Briggs, 1986). Moreover, the act of communication itself reveals knowledge, so that the most knowledgeable members on particular issues in stepladder groups could reveal their knowledge to the group, thus making individual expertise known. Better ideas were more likely to be expressed, and were more likely to be attended to and recognized as better. Johnson & Johnson (1987) also showed that verbalization and reiteration increased comprehension, understanding and retention of information within groups, which together are likely to promote greater effectiveness. Rogelberg et al. comment that, "An entering member maybe acted as a consultant or reviewer with all other members curious and active listeners. It was a common anecdotal report by participants that, while an entering member was presenting options, the core group would constantly ask 'Why do you say that?' This questioning of views may have led to more viable and effective information, which the group could use when making a final decision" (p. 736).

In fact, we will argue below that the effectiveness of this technique comes from how it overcomes some of the constraints inherent in spontaneous face-to-face communication.

What Initiates Task Reflexive Processes?

When groups "turn back on themselves" and discuss their objectives, group processes, strategies and their environments, it is likely that discrepancies between actual and desired circumstances are revealed and that this may be aversive. "Every symptom embodies a contrast between realism and idealism: members realize that conditions within the group are not what they ought to be" (Moreland & Levine, 1992, p. 19). As a consequence of reflection or problem identification, the group experiences anxiety and uncertainty, members become increasingly aroused and thus the motivation to reflect may be reduced (although above a certain threshold of arousal, problem-solving activity will take place). Because reflection often involves recognizing discrepancies between real and ideal circumstances, then it is unlikely to arise spontaneously within the group. Moreover, reflection may demand change in action and much organizational and psychological research has indicated that individuals in organizations are chronically resistant to change.

The kinds of factors which are likely to induce reflexivity are interruptions and particularly conflicts, crises, shocks, surprises, obstacles and changes. When intra-group task conflicts occur, groups characterized by high levels of task reflexivity are more likely to respond by discussing the underlying processes associated with the conflict as well as the causes of them. Similarly, interruptions to the group's work by senior managers or other groups are likely to lead to reflection and action. Unpredictable outside events could interfere with the group's functioning and offer another opportunity for reflection, discussion and action. Technical interruptions due to machine breakdown or malfunction, and organizational problems such as lack of supplies, can cause further reflection. Errors and failures in group functioning in particular can stimulate groups to reflect on the processes or assumptions which led to them. Task-reflexive groups are more likely to respond to errors, failures and crises by reflecting upon and discussing underlying assumptions, as well as strategies and processes. Non-reflexive groups, in contrast, will tend to deny errors or give up on long-term planning and fall back upon short-term strategies at times of crises (cf. Schultz, 1980).

Group member changes are another example of interruptions which provide an opportunity for reflection. As Katz (1982) has argued, project newcomers represent a novelty-enhancing condition, challenging and improving the scope of existing methods and accumulated knowledge. Interestingly, the longer groups have been together, the less they communicate with key information sources (Katz claims), scan the environment, and communicate within the group and with other organizational divisions and external professions. Group longevity is associated with a tendency to ignore and become increasingly isolated from sources that provide the most critical kinds of feedback, evaluation and information (Katz, 1982). This suggests that without optimal changes in membership and function, groups may become less reflexive over time.

Difficulties over time allocation and synchronization of time use present further opportunities for reflection (see McGrath & O'Connor, 1996). Gersick's (1988, 1989) notion of punctuated equilibrium suggests that there are critical temporal points in the lives of teams which also have the potential to stimulate reflection and action. Other examples include group successes—non-reflexive groups are likely to accept successes unquestioningly; groups high in reflexivity are more likely to analyse and consider the causes of success. Similarly, organizational change can trigger a group to reconsider its objectives, strategies, processes, its organizational environment and its relationship with the wider social environment.

Other factors which may impact upon the group's propensity to reflect or take action and adapt include the characteristics of team members. Jackson's (1996) review of the work on the composition of work groups suggests that group heterogeneity or diversity may stimulate many opportunities for reflexivity, while in homogeneous group such opportunities would be more rare. Group cultural heterogeneity may operate in a similar way. However, diversity in status and power will tend to reduce open discussion and reflection.

Now we consider these processes at a more micro level—a level generally neglected by organizational scientists and I/O psychologists. At the same time we consider some of the ways the micro-analysis of communication and decision-making processes can explain the effectiveness of reflexive groups.

COMMUNICATIVE CONSTRAINTS AND REFLEXIVITY

At the outset we argued that complex decision-making is increasingly becoming a group activity. In many, if not most, situations, the knowledge and skills which feed into an effective decision are distributed among a number of people. Also it is often the case that we require others to elicit the knowledge relevant for the decision. As Dunbar (1996) has demonstrated, innovative decisions often only arise out of group interaction and communication. Of course, the hallmark of group and distributed decision-making is consensus and this can only be achieved efficiently through face-to-face communication; consider how many letters would have to be exchanged to reach consensus from a group of eight people on a controversial topic. Whatever the individual contributions to the decision may be, the decision itself has to reflect consensus within the group.

Thus, in order for decisions to be made in a group, the participants need to communicate their ideas and thoughts to each other effectively. Group decision-making has largely been studied without reference to communication, assuming that it places no constraints on decision-making and therefore has no impact on the decisions that are made. In fact, research on face-to-face communication has shown that the transfer of information and ideas between people is highly constrained by both the physical facts of how people communicate and by the need for the communicators to come to a mutual understanding of what the communication means. Although these constraints have been studied primarily in the context of two-person dialogue, they have an even larger impact on group meetings and hence on group decision-making. We argue that in order to understand group decision-making, it is important to take communicative constraints into account, and demonstrate that a number of commonsense recommendations about how to run meetings can be accounted for by these constraints.

We describe three major communication constraints: linearity, relevance and consensus.

Constraint 1: Linearity of discussion. The first and most basic communication constraint is what we call linearity. Taking part in a discussion is in certain respects like taking part in a football game. In football only one player can control the ball at any time irrespective of the number of players in the team, while in group discussion only one person at a time can hold the floor. In football, who gets to control the ball next is not randomly determined but to a great extent influenced by the current player. Similarly, in conversation the current speaker exerts considerable control over who is likely to speak next. For example, the next person to speak at a meeting is disproportionately likely to be a recent speaker—someone directly engaged in conversation with the current speaker— or sitting across the table from the current speaker—someone who can catch the current speaker's eye (Dabbs & Ruback, 1987; Parker, 1988; Steinzor, 1955). This means that the opportunity to contribute to a meeting is limited by factors which may be irrelevant to the importance of the contribution at that point.

Constraint 2: Relevance.   Not only are turn-taking patterns constrained in face-to-face communication, but also what may be said next is constrained. Because successful communication depends on establishing mutual understanding, speakers have to respect various relevance constraints in what they say. Locally, any contribution has to be conditionally relevant to its predecessor. Thus utterances in a discussion typically fall into what are called adjacency pairs: questions elicit answers, greetings elicit reciprocal greetings and statements elicit either affirmation or objection (Schegloff & Sacks, 1973). This means that any contribution to a discussion, however important it may be, is going to have to be designed to fit into these local constraints of conditional relevance.

At a more global level, utterances also have to contribute to the current topic of discussion if they are to be understood. This means that it may be difficult to introduce an important point if it cannot easily be related to the current topic of discussion. One might think that this would not be a serious problem because speakers should be able to close the current topic and introduce a new one to make their point. But topic management is also subject to the important constraint of consensus.

Constraint 3: Consensus.   Even a cursory analysis of dialogue reveals that it is basically organized around establishing consensus (Clark & Schaefer, 1989; Garrod, in press). This is why utterances never stand alone in a dialogue. For information to contribute to the common understanding, it has to be accepted and often negotiated between participants. Thus, issues remain open until resolved in some way to the mutual satisfaction of the participants. This does not mean that everyone has to be in complete agreement before a topic is resolved, but at least they have to agree to disagree about it.

At first glance, the need for consensus does not appear to constrain group decision-making very much. However, the ways in which people communicate their agreement with a decision are quite limited. Clark & Schaefer argue that people show acceptance of information or agreement with some plan mostly by means of behaviours which are only available in face-to-face communication: nodding, eye contact, and backchannel utterances. In addition, it is difficult to make sure that the people involved with a decision understand what their partners mean by their proposals or the information that they give, unless the decision is discussed face-to-face. Face-to-face discussion allows people presenting information to know when their partners are puzzled and starts a more interactive and complete discussion process than, for instance, making decisions by exchanging a series of memoranda or e-mail messages.

How the Constraints Affect Decision-making

The effects of communication constraints on two-person dialogue have been widely studied, partly because they must be taken into account when developing computer systems which engage in dialogue with human users. The effects on group communication are less well known, but have implications for both face-to-face group decision-making in meetings and software tools which aid decision-making. We suggest that they also tend to work against group task reflexivity.

Group Size and Opportunity to Contribute

Meeting convenors are commonly advised to keep groups small because the more people there are present in a meeting, the more difficult it is to make good decisions. Although other phenomena are also at work here (such as *social loafing*, and *groupthink*), a major problem with large groups is that the more people present, the greater the competition to take the floor at any one time. By the relevance constraint, a contribution is most apt at the time that the person thinks of it and wishes to make it, but by the linearity constraint, only one person can contribute to the meeting at any one time. This means that in a large group, there are many good contributions which will not make the floor at all, and the contributions that do get heard are likely to be said at the wrong time and as a consequence be interpreted incorrectly. Large groups simply run into a communication bottleneck because too many people are using one communication channel.

Although special interventions such as adopting the step-ladder technique mentioned above may help circumvent some of these problems, they also tend to interfere with the spontaneity and efficiency of the discussion for other reasons.

Contributional Inertia and a Tendency toward "Adhocracy"

As we noted in discussing the linearity constraint, turn-taking at meetings is not random. The next speaker is likely to be someone who has made a recent contribution, and is often the previous speaker. There are a number of reasons for this, ranging from their being more likely to have attracted the current speaker's gaze to the fact that only those directly participating in (as opposed to overhearing) the current conversational exchange are in a strong position to give the kind of feedback that would make the current speaker pass the initiative over (see, for example, Schober & Clark, 1989). The net effect is that discussion tends to cycle around only a small group of contributors in any stretch of a meeting. This will often work against the kind of reflexivity discussed earlier. People who have spoken most recently are exactly those who are unlikely to shed new light on a problem, or introduce a new perspective. Just as limiting is the fact that the speakers who are most likely to be introduced into the current discussion are often those simply sitting opposite the current speaker. Again this is probably due to the fact that they have a greater chance of giving the right kind of feedback to be selected by the current speaker.

The social structure of meetings therefore tends toward "adhocracy" rather than democracy (Boden, 1994). However, in circumstances where there is a marked status discrepancy between participants, it is higher status members that will tend to dominate the floor (Dabbs & Ruback 1987) and this may also get in the way of allowing the most appropriate information to enter the decision process.

How to Avoid the Communication Constraints

We have argued that in complex decision-making, acting reflexively is likely to make the team more effective, but the way in which people communicate in small groups conspires against reflexive action. One solution to this problem is to intervene in the communication process in order to counteract the communication constraints; the stepladder technique is one drastic form of intervention which completely changes the character of the interaction so that lower status people are not blocked from contributing. There are three basic approaches to such interventions. The first is not to interfere with the course of the discussion, but to make participation rates more equal by removing advantages to participants in taking over the floor. This is the motivation behind recommendations such as using round tables with the chairs equal distances apart, seating talkative/high-status people across from non-talkative/low-status people, and so on. These techniques can help, but they still leave who gets the floor to chance; they are a very weak form of intervention. The second approach is to try to keep the size of the meeting down. As we have already argued, large meetings fall foul of a number of basic communication constraints. In addition, small meetings tend to de-emphasize status differences; it is easier to notice when someone is being blocked from gaining the floor and do something about it.

The third approach is to make sure that some member of the meeting is there to facilitate the interaction, monitoring the detrimental effects of communication constraints in order to correct for them. This is a stronger method, simply because such activity can directly affect who gets the floor next as well as guiding a meeting to more reflexive actions. The facilitating actions we have observed from our corpus include:

1. *Introducing explicit goals, objectives, and targets, so that it is easier for members of the meeting to share understanding of what was agreed.*

This is illustrated below in the meetings of the auto-parts firm, where members of the team have had specific training in holding such meetings and where there is always a facilitator present. Each meeting begins with a few sentences of review summarizing the last meeting and setting out the objectives for the current meeting—this is important because it means that the meetings start out on the right track. Meeting One is just intended as a briefing:

> *Team member 4*: "Okay. What we'd like to do today for the kick-off of this exercise is really update everyone where we are at the moment. We've got one or two new team members, and we want to update them on how the project team on New Orders has developed."

The second meeting was about what the function of the New Order Timing Coordinator should be:

> *Team member 3*: "I don't know if it was the same matter. It was just to let you know that but also I think today maybe we could establish what [Speaker 2]'s job requirement's gotta be from all of us, what do we all need from him? . . ."
>
> *Team member 4*: ". . . Yeah, that's fair . . ."
>
> *Team member 3*: ". . . And maybe a second part of that is to, actually, maybe come up with some sort of contingency plan if the funding's rejected . . ."
>
> *Team member 4*: ". . . Mm . . ."
>
> *Team member 3*: ". . . So that if it is rejected us people on this table can maybe still complete the actions. And basically it's really just about a brainstorming for [Speaker 2]'s job. What do you need, [Speaker 5], people like that, for [Speaker 2], really just . . ."
>
> *Team member 6*: ". . . Yeah . . ."
>
> *Team member 3*: ". . . solid information, isn't it?"

The fourth meeting was a review of current new orders, demonstrating how the new system would work to some affected outsiders.

> *Team member 4*: "Okay, you want me to introduce you, yeah?"
>
> *Team member 8*: "Mmhmm."
>
> *Team member 4*: "Okay, this is [Speaker 8], er, who works in the automotive sales department, [Speaker 10] works in automotive sales. The purpose of this meeting is to review all the new orders that we have in place at the moment and give a status against each one and advise the customer, er, we're using this as a vehicle to demonstrate where we are just now regarding communications between each other on the, where the new orders are, so it's basically we'll go to the meeting."

Other cases where the facilitator played an important role in this group were:

2. *Bringing the meeting back to the point (which, in the case of an error or failure, probably means making them reflect when they were being dragged off-track by excuses).*
3. *Drawing out people who aren't speaking.*

4. *Summarizing the meeting so far so that the context is open enough for important contributions which were missed previously to be aired.*

The series of meetings from the auto-parts firm also suggests that the facilitator rarely intervenes, but when she does it is to organize the meeting in various ways. It may be to ensure that a proper record is taken:

Facilitator: "You'll take the minutes next week?"

Offer support for the meeting:

Facilitator: "I've got it typed up for you. Okay?"

and

Facilitator: "And I'll get you a room."

Make responsibilities clear:

Facilitator: "It's surely up to you to make sure it doesn't slip."

Suggest agendas:

Facilitator: "Right. So will that do us for this week then? You can give us an update next week on how you got on."

and

Facilitator: "So what're we gonna do at our next meeting, then? Just everybody? Gather information and report back."

and

Facilitator: "So are we gonna do that today or are we leaving it till next week's meeting?"

Raise the issue of whether they need to meet and arrange submeetings:

Facilitator: "Are we gonna meet again?"

and

Facilitator: "So that's youse two'll sit down for that?"

and

Facilitator: "Are youse gonna do this outwith the meeting?"

Set deadlines:

Facilitator: "Right, then we'll have a copy by next week?"

or praise people to make the team feel that they are doing something:

Facilitator: "So we've definitely seen improvements since you've taken over."

and

Facilitator: "Congratulations, [Speaker 2]."

Although these interventions may seem to be of little consequence, it is interesting to note that the facilitator says very little in the meetings yet the kind of issues she is resolving can, in less well-organized settings, be extremely disruptive. Here is an example of the opening of a meeting recorded from a health care team who are trying to negotiate the issue of who takes minutes (apart from the particular issue of minutes, it is interesting to note how different the discussion is with a large team of 10 speakers):

Speaker 2: "I reckon we've got everybody. We don't . . ."

Speaker 1: ". . . The only thing, the only thing that I think we're lacking, whether we want to do it on a rota thing or whether we need somebody, is, minutes, or, . . ."

Speaker 2: ". . . everybody that needs to work, as a team."

Speaker 2: ". . . What, more secretarial."

Speaker 1: "Yeah. That's the only thing that we haven't got, I mean if, . . ."

Speaker 2: ". . . Yeah. . . ."

Speaker 1: ". . . if you, . . ."

Speaker 2: ". . . Well why don't just one of us . . ."

Speaker 1: ". . . agree to do it. . . ."

Speaker 1: ". . . do it as a ro. . . ."

All speakers: ". . . Hmmmm . . ."

Speaker 1: "Or one person do it,"

Speaker 5: "I don't think you participate properly then, do you?"

Speaker 2: "Well that's the trouble, yeah. Yeah. I can't. . . ."

Speaker 1: ". . . Which which the other option is do it on a rotation basis."

Speaker 5: "I can't. . . ."

Speaker 2: ". . . Yeah . . ."

Speaker 5: ". . . spell."

Speaker 3: "Nor can I."

Speaker 1: "Sorry?"

Speaker 5: "I can't spell."

(laughter from all speakers)

Speaker 1: "Well, I mean it doesn't matter, does it? I mean . . ."

Speaker 2: ". . . 'Cos perhaps we just need to get the, ya know, key points that . . ."

Speaker 5: ". . . Hmm. Yeah . . ."

Speaker 2: ". . . are, that are made at the meeting . . ."

Speaker 5: ". . . Yeah, yeah . . ."

Speaker 2: ". . . down."

Speaker 1: ". . . We can just get some . . ."

Speaker 2: ". . . And things that we need to have action on."

Speaker 1: "Yeah, so you think, so should we do it on a rotation basis then?"

Speaker 5: "Yeah."

Speaker 2: "Yeah."

Speaker 4: "Do you want me to do it today then, with both [Speaker 7] and myself being here?"

Speaker 1: "Right."

Speaker 4: "'Cos at the next, one [Speaker 7] won't be here. . . ."

Speaker 2: ". . . Well volunteered! . . ."

Speaker 4: ". . . will she? . . ."

Speaker 1: ". . . Well volunteered. Yes. We've. . . ."

Speaker 4: ". . . Well, it looks like we're both on the same. . . ."

Speaker 2: ". . . Well, I'll second that, yeah. . . ."

Speaker 3: ". . . Yeah, definitely."

All speakers: "Passed."

Speaker 1: "I've got a pad, have you got, oh you've got . . ."

Speaker 4: "Thank you."

Speaker 2: ". . . Do it on another . . ."

Speaker 9: "Do we not need a receptionist or something? . . . receptionists, don't they come into it? . . ."

Speaker 1: "No, what we decided with the practice manager and the receptionist is that we'd bring them in to specific meetings if necessary. Erm, . . ."

If we were considering individual decision-making, an extra one and a half minutes spent working out how to get going would not be unreasonable, but in a group of 12 this represents 18 person-minutes! For group decision-making to be worthwhile, the process does need to be effectively managed, and this is where facilitators seem to play a very important role.

Much of the activity of the facilitators corrects for the effects of the communication constraints; in summarizing and taking care of organizational details, the facilitator stunts branches of the discussion which both waste time and detract from the important points. In addition, facilitators boost effectiveness by making contributions which start periods of reflection in the meetings.

CONCLUSIONS

The propositions relating group task reflexivity, communication and decision-making to group tasks are not meant simply to describe the current pattern of group processes in organizational settings. Many "groups" in organizations do not have sufficient member interdependence, clear objectives, and appropriate group task performance feedback necessary for minimally effective CDM group performance (Guzzo & Shea, 1992). Indeed, group or team functioning in a wide variety of organizational settings appears to be rather primitive. Consequently, it is suggested that processes of task reflexivity in group functioning require considerable practical development if the potential of work groups is to be realized.

For example, in relation to reflexivity towards wider organizational and social environments, teams in modern organizations seem generally non-reflexive. Group members behave as though organizational objectives and wider social issues are givens and not for consideration. We argue that group members display high reflexivity not just when they focus on group objectives, strategies, events and processes, but also when they consider the appropriateness of their organization's objectives in the wider society.

These ideas about reflexivity, communication and decision-making challenge researchers and practitioners to reflect on, and change, how we work with groups, because (according to the propositions) so few are functioning optimally. An important implication of the ideas outlined here is that interventions, facilitators and group leadership in CDM groups should be based on enabling groups and individuals to be reflexive over time, rather than on static technical-rational "fixes" of group processes. Indeed, it is suggested that practitioners should be giving processes of team self-development and functioning away—reflexivity interventions involve enabling group members themselves to nurture reflexivity over time, so that it is truly group development rather than indoctrination. It is also suggested that practitioners train teams to consider specifically how they communicate within the group so that they can overcome the natural tendency of group communication to work against reflexive action.

However, even in relation to reflexivity on group objectives, strategies, events and processes, only rarely do groups possess a high degree of reflexivity. This is not to argue that the propositions described above are not generalizable. The fact that group functioning in many organizational settings is somewhat primitive, is no reason for abandoning the propositions. Rather, they can provide a stimulus for those involved in working with groups to consider how levels of reflexivity could be raised and maintained.

Our research results are couched in terms of the decision-making structure of firms as they operate at the moment—in teams of individuals, often of long-standing, which meet face-to-face both informally as part of an office structure and during pre-arranged meetings. We have shown that in this arrangement, the constraints placed on decision-making by the facts of communication work against reflexive behaviour and therefore against effective and innovative activity. Although these results have implications for how decisions are currently made, communication constraints will become even more important for decision-making in the future. Two major changes are occurring in business organizations which impinge on communication and decison-making.

The first is a tendency for employees to be in any particular job for only a short time, with teams and companies being reconstituted to fit current needs. This means that decision-making groups interacting within a business are likely to be flexible in terms of membership, and as often as not short-lived. Consequently, the development of shared meanings, behavioural norms and effective communication and decison-making strategies will be more limited.

The second is a move away from static occupation of offices and the promotion of open office arrangements, teleworking and working from home. This means that a greater proportion of our interaction occurs without the kinds of face-to-face cues which make it easier to judge the reaction of one's interlocutors to one's utterances and to break in with an important contribution. Most people would agree that having a telephone conversation with someone is more cumbersome and not as informative as meeting with them face-to-face, especially, as will increasingly be the case, when the interlocutors do not already know each other well. The same is certainly true of teleconferences. What is not so well known is that it is also true to a degree in videoconferences, both now and probably under every conceivable improvement of the current technology. In face-to-face meetings, participants rely heavily on visual cues in their turn-taking as well as in establishing consensus. This is why each participant's volubility is affected by seating arrangement, as Steinzor (1955) discovered. People talk more if they are sitting across from a talkative member of the group and less if they are sitting next to them. This is because they can see people across from them more easily and so are more likely to pick up the crucial cues involved. Video conferences are not just visually impoverished, making these cues more difficult to read; they encourage greater concentration on the image of the person currently speaking, making the cues less likely to be noticed in any competition to get the floor next. This is important in that it further randomizes the order of utterances; at least in a face-to-face meeting one can often give an important contribution if one is sufficiently determined. In addition to shifting in their chairs and gesturing, people quite often use "uh-huh" and other backchannel utterances just before they take over the floor of a meeting, possibly because this will attract the attention of the other participants and make them more likely to cede the turn. Such utterances are more difficult to hear in videoconferencing than in face-to-face meetings, especially since sounds are decoupled from their sources. People also relate to video images of other people differently than they do to the people themselves, even when those images are presented in such a way as to most naturally simulate real face-to-face encounters. Beattie & Hughes (1987) claim that there is less emotional arousal in people talking to a video and that is why speech production isn't as hesitant when talking to a video as when talking face-to-face. This could mean people feel more left out of videoconferences and social loafing increases; possibly they just can't be bothered responding because they don't have enough energy invested in the discussion. Other researchers have ascribed the difference to cognitive overload because of the amount of visual processing going on, so that, even in two-party dialogues mediated with videotunnels that enable effective eye-contact, it seems to take more speech to convey the same amount of information (Anderson et al., in press).

What this indicates is that the same communication constraints which adversely affect companies at present by working against reflexive behaviour will still have an important (and possibly stronger) effect on the companies of the future.

These two strands of group reflexivity and communication are rich for texturing our understanding of how to promote the effectiveness of teams as functional units in organizations in the twenty-first century. The ideas explored in this chapter also suggest that we may take too much for granted the assumptions that team effectiveness and good team communication can simply be achieved. On the contrary, our consideration of the barriers to reflexivity and the real difficulties of team communication, compounded by the use of new technologies, suggest researchers, theorists and practitioners have much work to do to ensure the effective functioning of teams in organizational settings.

Acknowledgments

The first author would like to thank the staff of the Graduate School of Management, University of Queensland, Brisbane, Australia, for hospitably providing facilities enabling the preparation of this manuscript during his sabbatical. Some of this work was supported by a grant from the UK Economic and Social Research Council (ESRC).

REFERENCES

Anderson, A.H., O'Malley, C., Doherty-Sneddon. G., Langton, S., Newlands, A., Mullin, J., Flemming, A.M. & Van der Velden, J. (in press). The impact of VMC on collaborative problem-solving: an analysis of task performance, communicative process and user satisfaction. In K. Finn, A. Sellen & S. Wilbur (eds), *Video-mediated Communication*. Hillsdale, NJ: Erlbaum.

Beattie, G.W. & Hughes, M. (1987). Planning spontaneous speech and concurrent visual monitoring of a televised face: is there interference? *Semiotica*, **65**(1–2), 97–105.

Boden, D. (1994). *The Business of Talk: Organizations in Action*. Oxford: Blackwell.

Clark, H. & Schaefer, E. (1989). Contributing to discourse. *Cognitive Science*, **13**, 259–294.

Dabbs, J.M. Jr & Ruback, R.B. (1987). Dimensions of group process: amount and structure of vocal interaction. *Advances in Experimental Social Psychology*, **20**, 123–169.

Dunbar, K. (1996). How scientists really reason: scientific reasoning in real-world laboratories. In R.J. Sternberg & J.E. Davidson (eds), *The Nature of Insight* (pp. 365–95). Cambridge, MA: MIT Press.

Foushee, M.C. (1984). Dyads and triads at 35 000 feet: factors affecting group process and aircrew performance. *American Psychologist*, **39**, 885–93.

Frese, M. & Zapf, D. (1994). Action as the core of work psychology: a German approach. In H.C. Triandis, M.D. Dunnette & L.M. Hough (eds), *Handbook of Industrial and Organizational Psychology* 2nd edn, vol. 4 (pp. 271–340). Palo Alto, CA: Consulting Psychologists Press.

Garrod, S. (in press). The challenge of dialogue for theories of language processing. In S. Garrod & M. Pickering (eds), *Language Processing*. London: UCL.

Gersick, C.J.G. (1988). Time and transition in work teams: toward a new model of group development. *Academy of Management Journal*, **31**, 9–41.

Gersick, C.J.G. (1989). Marking time: predictable transitions in task groups. *Academy of Management Journal*, **32**, 274–309.

Guzzo, R.A. & Shea, G.P. (1992). Group performance and intergroup relations in organizations. In M.D. Dunnette & L.M. Hough (eds), *Handbook of industrial and organizational psychology*, vol. 3 (pp. 269–313). Palo Alto, CA: Consulting Psychologists' Press.

Hackman, R.J., Brousseau, K. & Weiss, J.A. (1976). The interaction of task design and group performance strategies in determining group effectiveness. *Organizational Behavior and Human Performance*, **16**, 350–65.

Hackman, R.J. & Morris, C.G. (1975). Group tasks, group interaction process, and group performance effectiveness: a review and proposed integration. In L. Berkowitz (ed), *Advances in Experimental Social Psychology*, vol. 8 (pp. 47–97). New York: Academic Press.

Jackson, S.E. (1996). The consequences of diversity in multidisciplinary groups. In M.A. West (ed), *Handbook of Work Group Psychology* (pp. 53–76). Chichester, UK: Wiley.

Johnson, D. & Johnson, F. (1987). *Joining Together: Group Theory and Group Skills*. Englewood Cliffs, NJ: Prentice-Hall.

Kahn, W.A. (1992). To be fully there: psychological presence at work. *Human Relations*, **45**, 321–49.

Katz, R. (1982). The effects of group longevity on project communication and performance. *Administrative Science Quarterly*, **27**, 81–104.

Maier, N.R.F. (1970). Problem-solving and creativity in individuals and groups. Belmont, CA: Brooks/Cole.

Maier, N.R.F. & Hoffman, L.R. (1960). Quality of first and second solutions in group problem-solving. *Journal of Applied Psychology*, **44**, 278–83.

McGrath, J.E. & O'Connor, K.M. (1996). Temporal issues in work groups. In M.A. West (ed.), *Handbook of Work Group Psychology* (pp. 25–52). Chichester, UK: Wiley.

Mohrman, S.A., Cohen, S.G. & Mohrman, A.M. (1995). *Designing Team-based Organizations: New Forms for Knowledge Work*. San Francisco, CA: Jossey-Bass.

Moreland, R.L. & Levine, J.M. (1992). Problem identification by groups. In S. Worchel, W. Wood & J.A. Simpson (eds), *Group Process and Productivity* (pp. 17–47). Newbury Park, CA: Sage.

Nemeth, C. & Owens, P. (1996) Making work groups more effective: the value of minority dissent. In M.A. West (ed.), *Handbook of Work Group Psychology* (pp. 125–42). Chichester, UK: Wiley.

Parker, Kevin C.H. (1988). Speaking turns in small group interaction: a context-sensitive event sequence model. *Journal of Personality and Social Psychology*, **54**(6), 965–71.

Rennie, D.L. (1992). Qualitative analysis of the client's experience of psychotherapy. In S.G. Toukmanian & D.L. Rennie (eds), *Psychotherapy Process Research* (pp. 211–34). Newbury Park, CA: Sage.

Rogelberg, S.G., Barnes-Farrell, J.L. & Lower, C.A. (1992). The stepladder technique: an alternative group structure facilitating effective group decision-making. *Journal of Applied Psychology*, **77**, 730–7.

Schegloff, E.A. & Sacks, H. (1973). Opening up closings. *Semiotica*, **3/4**, 289–327.

Schober, M.F. & Clark, H.H. (1989). Understanding by addressees and overhearers. *Cognitive Psychology*, **21**, 211–32.

Schön, D.A. (1983). *The Reflective Practitioner: How Professionals Think in Action*. New York: Basic Books.

Schön, D.A. (1994). Teaching artistry through reflection-in-action. In H. Tsoukas (ed.), *New Thinking in Organizational Behaviour* (pp. 235–49). Oxford: Butterworth-Heinemann.

Schultz, P. (1980). Regulation und Feldregulation in Verhalten, V: die wechseleitige Beeinflussung von mentaler und emotionaler Beawpruchung. *Psychologische Beiträge*, **22**, 633–56.

Smith, K.G., Locke, E.A. & Barry, D. (1990). Goal setting, planning and organizational performance: an experimental simulation. *Organizational Behavior and Human Decision Process*, **46**, 118–34.

Steinzor, B. (1955). The spatial factor in face to face discussion groups. In A. Paul Hare, E.F. Borgatta & R.F. Bales (eds), *Small Groups: Studies in Social Interaction* (pp. 348–53). New York: Knopf.

Tjosvold, D. (1990). *Team Organization: an Enduring Competitive Advantage*, Chichester, UK: Wiley.

West, M.A. & Anderson, N.R. (1996). Innovation in top management teams. *Journal of Applied Psychology*, **81**, 680–93.

Williges, R.C., Johnston, W.A. & Briggs, G.E. (1966). Role of verbal communication in teamwork. *Journal of Applied Psychology*, **50**, 473–8.

Part IV

Future Careers

Chapter 17

Identity, Values and Learning in the Protean Career

Douglas T. Hall
Jon P. Briscoe
and
Kathy E. Kram
School of Management, Boston University, MA, USA

"The career is dead—long live the career!" Such is the paradoxical state of career experience in contemporary organizations. What does it mean?

On the one hand, the career as we have traditionally known it is dead. That is, the long-service-in-one-organization career, the career based on personal loyalty and identification, the career based on a series of moves around and through one firm—this career is dead. On the other hand, people still have careers. If we think of the career as the series of work-related activities, experiences and personal learnings the person has over the course of her/his work life (Hall, 1976), then people still have careers.

THE NEW CAREER ENVIRONMENT: THE PROTEAN CAREER AND IDENTITY SHIFTS

Our opening statement also suggests that not only has the career itself changed, but our understanding of the factors that shape the career is fundamentally different as well. In the past the focus was more on what has been called the *external career*, the series of positions or jobs that the person holds over the course of the career. Perhaps related to the fact that the external opportunity structure has become more constrained, the focus has shifted to the *internal career*, which describes the individual's perceptions and self-constructions of career phenomena (Hall, 1976; McAdams & Ochberg, 1988).

Creating Tomorrow's Organizations. Edited by C.L. Cooper and S.E. Jackson.
© 1997 John Wiley & Sons Ltd.

Related to the shift from external to internal career is the shift in the nature of the models used to explain career processes and outcomes (Hall & Mirvis, 1995). In the early years of research on careers (1950s and 1960s), the focus was on models which would predict the choice of a broad occupational field (e.g. teacher, nurse), as well as on the processes of success within an occupation (see, for example, Super, 1957, in psychology; Becker, 1963, in sociology). In the 1970s, career models arose to predict what specific job position, within an occupational field, an individual would choose and what job would be a good (i.e. satisfying, productive, involving) fit for that individual (Schein, 1978; Hall, 1976). In the 1980s the focus shifted to the individual in the organization as a system. Research looked at career stages, life cycles, and organizational career ladders and timetables (Hall & Associates, 1986). In their literature review, Chartrand & Camp (1991) reported that the most frequently studied construct in career research reported in the *Journal of Vocational Behavior* between 1986 and 1990 was organizational commitment.

We would argue that the central focus of careers as we move into the twenty-first century is increasingly the *self*. As the business environment has become more turbulent, complex and demanding, with organizations taking less responsibility for employee career development, individuals have had to view the career as one of self-employment. This is what we have called the *protean career* (Hall, 1996). Key to the protean career is one's ability to reinvent oneself and one's career, to change one's personal identity, and to learn continuously throughout the career. What this means, then, is that whereas the old career contract was with the organization, the new contract is with the self. Thus, another way to express our career paradox is as follows: the *organizational* career is dead—long live the *protean* career!

The central question of this chapter is, what facilitates the development of the protean career? Why are so many individuals unable to enter the "new economy", being relegated to a bleak life of constant job-hunting or minimum-wage jobs and insecure life-styles, with little in the way of satisfaction, meaning, and future? Our answer focuses on four factors: identity, learning, values and relationships.

PERSONAL IDENTITY AS A KEY TO THE PROTEAN CAREER

We will use the term *personal identity* (or simply, identity, for short) to describe the person's image of him/herself in relation to the environment (Erikson, 1966; Hall, 1971). We are using identity synonymously with related terms, such as self-concept, self-image and sense of self.

Our use of "identity" is different from the concept of *social identity*, which is used to describe the way the person sees her/himself as a member of a demographic group (e.g. gender, race, age) (Thomas & Alderfer, 1989). Personal identity can include social identity, if feeling part of a particular group is central to one's overall view of the self; indeed, some people may see their social identity as the same as their personal identity.

The personal identity is made up of a number of *sub-identities*, each of which is the person's view of the part of the self which is engaged in the enactment of a particular *role* (e.g. employee, parent). One's identity growth is promoted by *psychological success*. Success in valued work tasks leads to intrinsic satisfaction and increased career involvement, which means a larger portion of the identity is invested in the career role (Hall, 1976).

In the following sections we will examine in detail what forces lead to identity learning. First, we will consider the traditional sources of identity learning, found in the extant literature. Then we turn to what we are proposing as two newer forms of identity development: values and relationships.

TRADITIONAL SOURCES OF IDENTITY LEARNING

Identity Growth through Adult Development and Work Experience

Traditional models of careers have consistently taken a developmental view of individuals' work-related experiences (Dalton, 1989), suggesting that identity— and for our purposes here, the career sub-identity—would evolve in predictable ways over the life course and/or over the course of an organizational career (Hall, 1976; Super, 1957).

Similarly, studies of adult development by Levinson et al. (1978; Levinson, 1996) have illuminated the concept of the "life structure" and associated structure-building and structure-changing periods over the life course. They demonstrated in successive studies—first of men and then of women—how fundamental questions about identity predictably resurfaced during structure-changing periods as individuals altered external circumstances, reoriented their internal relationship to particular facets of the life structure, or experienced major events over which they had little or no control (such as the loss of a job). These same developmental perspectives consistently suggest that personal values become increasingly central to the definition of self, and thus identity, over time.

However, the pace at which external circumstances change and individuals are called upon to adapt and revise their self-concept is substantially greater today than in the 1980s or earlier. Indeed, Robert Kegan (1994) argues that the current occupational and social environment demands an identity capacity ("stage 4") that is greater than most people now possess ("stage 3"). It seems to us, therefore, that stable and transitional periods are necessarily of shorter duration, and questions about identity and competence are likely to resurface more often than traditional models would predict. In addition, we can no longer assume that those with 15 years of experience in a career will achieve the clear sense of identity and security in a work role that are generally defined as prerequisites for mentoring others.

There are two important consequences of these new trends. First, identity—and in particular the career sub-identity—will not only have to be revised more often due to regular and rapid changes in the environment, but individuals at all stages of life and career are no longer able to count on a stable job or set of role expectations for definition of the self. Second, in the absence of such stability in a work role, individuals at every stage are necessarily more dependent on relational help as a vehicle for developing a sense of identity and for learning new skills and competencies (Kaplan, 1990).

Social Identity and Diversity Learning

Although we have pointed out the distinction between personal identity and social identity, learning related to one can facilitate the other. For members of non-dominant groups in a given culture, developing a sense of personal identity necessarily entails developing a strong sense of one's social identity in that culture as well (Erikson, 1966); Thomas & Alderfer, 1989; Cox, 1993). In fact, having a strong sense of social group identification appears to mediate some negative effects of prejudice and discrimination on personal outcomes, such as health (James, Lovato & Khoo, 1994).

As a society becomes more subject to turbulent change, even those members of dominant groups will experience challenges related to their social identity (e.g. White males in contemporary US culture) and will thus have to grow in their personal identities as well (Kram & Hall, 1996). Thus, one can argue that for any individual, exploration of one's social identity can promote personal identity learning.

More concretely, Walker (1996) has argued that *the skills developed as part of learning related to valuing differences (i.e. valuing diversity) are precisely the career skills associated with learning how to learn.* Walker describes the core tasks in learning to value differences as being learning about oneself, learning about others, and learning how to work with others. The personal and career abilities which these core tasks promote are: learning how to learn; self-discovery; interdependent relationships; effective communication; and personal coping.

Feedback-Seeking

As a social psychological construct, identity by definition requires interchanges with the environment, particularly if it is to be "accurate" (i.e. congruent with the perceptions of significant others). And again, as with relational influences, there is another relatively low-cost form of identity learning: feedback-seeking. Feedback can be viewed as a self-regulation activity that helps the person set standards for desired behavior, detect discrepancies, and reduce discrepancies (Ashford & Tsui, 1991).

Personality Factors

Related to the person's behaviors is a set of personality characteristics that appear to predispose a person to be better able to learn about him/herself as a result of experience. These include *personality hardiness*, flexibility, tolerance of ambiguity, tolerance of uncertainty, dominance and independence (Hall, 1986). In a similar vein, Staw's (1984) notion of a *positive basic personality predisposition* would also likely empower an individual to seek negative feedback and be more open to change. Research on learning how to learn by Bunker & Webb (1992) also identified many of these personality constructs as critical to what we are calling identity learning. And Driver's (1994) concept of the *spiral career concept*, an orientation favoring novelty and frequent change, is also useful here.

Changes in Personal Life, Organizational and Work Roles

We know from a vast literature on adult development and job stress that changes in one's personal life (family, personal health, friendships) can trigger significant changes in personal identity (Levinson, 1996; Levinson et al., 1978).

Perhaps the most powerful source of identity change in today's environment is coming from traumatic changes in the work role, through restructuring and downsizing. Job loss represents the removal of what is in the US culture the most important element of a person's identity (Hall, 1976; Hall et al., 1996). The impact of the career role on the identity is especially strong if the career work is fulfilling to the individual (Brockner, 1988). Thus, being laid off, or even the fear of being laid off (which seems endemic in the 1990s) can alter one's self-perceptions in numerous negative ways. There is much concern that these negative identity effects will be so devastating that many workers will not be able to adapt successfully to the demands of the new work environment, especially those who are older and poorly educated (Kleinfield, 1996). However, it does appear that the negativity of the effects on victims and survivors of job loss is ameliorated in part by two aspects of procedural justice: advance notice and "interactional justice" (having reasons for an action clearly and adequately explained, and being treated with dignity and respect) (Brockner et al., 1994).

Of course, there can be positive experiences in the organizational and work role, and these can enhance one's personal identity. Hall (1986) has developed a model of a mid-career change process in which career routines can be altered so that new sub-identities are explored, resulting in new kinds of mastery and psychological success.

As we have seen, then, there are many factors in the person's behavior, in the basic personality, in one's personal life and in the work environment that affects one's personal identity. However, there appears to be a certain *identity paradox* here. A person needs to be able to adapt his/her identity independently in order to adapt to new environmental conditions. Yet certain kinds of people find it more comfortable than others to engage in self-directed identity change (those who are hardy, flexible, tolerant of ambiguity and uncertainty, and career-resilient). It seems to be precisely those individuals who most need to adapt their identities may who find it the most difficult to change.

What else can be done to promote identity learning? In the following sections we will examine two new arenas in an attempt to get better leverage on this difficult matter of identity growth. Our view is that, ironically, much of the answer lies. "close to home": inside ourselves (i.e. our values) and in our connections with other people. First we turn to values.

LEARNING FROM SELF: VALUES

Values symbolize our "enduring beliefs" about specific modes of conduct and "end-states" of existence (Rokeach, 1973). Values or "standards" (Carver & Scheier, 1982) are thought to both anchor integration of personality and the governance of expressing that personality to others. A major research interest in values is aimed at understanding the consequences for individuals and organizations resulting from the "fit" between individual values and the organization's values (e.g. Chatman, 1989). The general assumption has been that personal satisfaction and organizational productivity will be positively correlated with higher or "better" person–organization fit. Empirical research (Posner, Kouzes & Schmidt, 1985) and common sense bolster that claim.

In those situations of great challenge that the protean career generates, one of the few things that will still make sense to individuals is their values. Values are usually taken for granted, only reflected upon when they are seriously challenged and when life roles cause people to assess or redefine their values. As rapid and continuous change come to dominate the career landscape, we believe that values will become more salient to people in awareness and importance, and that they will become more key to initiating identity growth.

Values are especially important in the protean career, since they provide principles that can be applied across diverse work situations and challenges. They provide for the individual a sense of stability that allows the "self" to persevere and grow in an uncertain and turbulent environment.

Protean careerists grow in their identities through practicing and *expressing* their values. Katz & Kahn (1978, p. 362) argued that the expression of values increases the clarity of one's self-image but, more importantly, "brings the self image closer to the ... self-ideal". But while value expression is an important part of affirming one's identity, research indicates how working contexts and individuals themselves heavily influence whether a given person fully expresses or filters out key motivating values (Briscoe, 1996). For example, strongly independent individuals are more likely than less independent people to express their values, even in the face of strong organizational socialization not to do so.

Often values not customarily expressed at work and which are linked to other sub-identities (e.g. spiritual) are expressed "off-line" in informal settings, with trusted colleagues and toward people in personal crisis. Familiarity and trust, which need time and exposure to be nurtured, are conditions that draw out personal values not always expressed in more routine, open and visible work role performances.

As individuals move into the protean career, where and how they find opportunities to express their personal values will vary. And while value expression within the work role is key to motivation, most attention has been given not to the values the individual brings to the organization, but the values the organization brings to the individual. The emphasis among most scholars and organizational practitioners as well has been (and currently remains) on how organizations can select recruits that match their values, and socialize such recruits to accept and enact their values (Schein, 1978).

The protean career realities challenge the notion that organizations should emphasize their own values so much at the expense of exploring, learning form, and providing a stage for individual values. Consider that employees are working more independently and at greater distances from one another. They are more likely to have several mini-careers and work for several organizations at once or over a career. Working relationships are more ephemeral. Reputations, work sub-identities and relationships are established not on a single stage but across various, sometimes shifting, settings. This has consequences for individuals and organizations.

We would speculate that among protean careerists a psychological shift will take place away from the organization's values and more toward one's own. With so much ongoing change with work activity and its associated relationships, the individual's own core values will surface as more of a constant than organizational values. Greater independence and role breadth granted to knowledge workers and others in the new economy should also increase the emphasis upon personal values, as expressed values are subject to fewer role constraints.

Ironically, while personal values may be expressed and emphasized more on a personal level, their reflected expression toward the employing organization may be muted. First of all, as already mentioned, instead of being a "one-company" employee, many are and will be working across several organizations. Secondly, downsizing, rapid technological shifts and the many other factors fueling the protean career will undermine many of the factors that support the expression of more core personal values, such as having trusted, familiar and time-tested colleagues.

Certainly one possible response could be the diminishment of the work sub-identity as a prime source of value expression. They may pour themselves more into their other subidentities within their families, groups of friends, and community and religious groups. For such people, the job may come to be seen more strictly in terms of its economic utility. Already we are seeing some high-performing managers deciding to opt out of a "high potential" designation, to get balance between their work and non-work subidentities (Derr and Briscoe, forthcoming).

Individuals with a strong need to develop their identity through value expression at work will have to adapt. They may seek out "solo" careers that allow expression, such as artistic careers, independent consulting or teaching. On the other hand, they may seek out institutions less vulnerable to shifting global markets or technological change, such as religious or non-profit institutions. Individuals so intent on finding opportunities to express their values will almost by definition be leaders. And intelligent, adaptive organizations will find ways to be clear in communicating their core values and recruit employees with similar values. In this way, attention to the needs and values of employees would become more strategic, as it is now in focusing on customers. The result is a two-way relationship, with qualities of reciprocity and mutual respect.

Years ago Harry Levinson (1962) argued that this was the best way to maintain the psychological contract: a process of mutual employer–employee coping and adaptation to changing environmental conditions. A critical part of the social connective tissue between an individual and his/her work environment is the person's web of relationships. Through relational connection we can see the environment promote the growth of the person's identity, at the same time as the individual is expressing her/his values and thereby influencing the environment. In the following section, we will elaborate on how these relational influences can contribute to the individual's identity development.

LEARNING FROM OTHERS: THE NEW RELATIONAL APPROACH

The Need for Relational Learning in a Turbulent, Uncertain Environment

In the absence of organizational career paths and corporate career development programs, the developmental tasks of early and middle adulthood are dramatically different from what they were when the prevailing adult development theories of Levinson et al. (1978) and others were developed. As a result of this turbulence, people need to look toward new sources of esteem, identity and psychological well-being (Handy, 1996).

One of the most available sources of identity growth is relational learning. By "relational" we mean the forms of connections the person has with other people, which might occur through work assignments, formal and informal relationships at work, networks of various kinds, as well as social, family, community and other relationships (Hall et al., 1996). Such an approach assumes that relationships are a primary site for learning—both short-term and long-term, both task learning and personal learning. It also assumes that individuals at *all* stages of life and career can benefit from relationships that foster learning; and one of the strengths of such relationships is that they can be reciprocal (Kram, 1988, 1996).

Relational Qualities and Competencies

In contrast to traditional mentoring, where the primary focus is on the junior's learning, developmental relationships are necessarily transformed into alliances characterized by *mutuality, interdependence* and *co-learning* (Kram & Hall, 1996). This is consistent with relational models of growth and development derived from studies of women's development, which conceptualize growth as movement through increasingly complex states of interdependence rather than individuation (Miller, 1986; Jordan et al., 1991; Fletcher, 1994).

In order for individuals to benefit from connections with others at work, they will need capacities for self-reflection, empathy and active listening, as well as the willingness to be vulnerable and self-disclosing (Kram, 1996). While there is some evidence to suggest that women are historically socialized to acquire these capacities, a recent study of successful executives (mostly male) indicates that such relational skills are characteristic of those who are able to learn from challenging assignments (McCall, Lombardo & Morrison, 1988). There is already data to suggest that reflection may soon be defined as a core managerial competence (Seibert, 1996).

With an increasingly diverse workforce, individuals of all demographic backgrounds face new challenges: non-dominant groups (people of color, foreign nationals), women, parents trying to juggle job demands and family, White men now facing unpredictable career paths, organizational uncertainty, and new roles at work and at home. A relational approach suggests that individuals who face such ambiguity and conflict in their personal identity can benefit from multiple alliances with others in which they have the opportunity to learn through reflection and dialogue (Isaacs, 1993). From individuals who are similar to them, they may find models of whom they may become as well as assistance (through coaching and counseling) with the dilemmas that they currently face. From those who are different, they may find new perspectives that help them to enhance their understanding of an increasingly complex and volatile workplace (Walker, 1996).

The highly turbulent career context that we have described can have adverse impacts on the availability of relational assistance, as greater work stress reduces colleagues' time and energy for helping others. Intentional efforts are required to encourage relationship building and relational assistance. Less obvious, however, is the potential work synergy that is available in flattened, team-based organizations where, in the course of collaborating on important work, continuous task and personal learning occurs. In high-output teams, members are expected to help each other learn new skills and may also serve as coaches and mentors to each other, as each must continuously re-invent his/her identity and career. This will only come about as organizations create rewards and recognition for taking the time to coach and mentor, offer education and training on relevant interpersonal skills, and create systems that foster personal learning. Such systems might include 360-degree feedback processes, internal and external coaching opportunities, mentoring programs and dialogue groups (Kram & Hall, 1996; Kram, 1996).

PARADOXES OF IDENTITY: PERSONAL AND ORGANIZATIONAL

As we think back over these influences on personal identity in the contemporary work environment, we are struck by several paradoxes. While we do not claim to have the resolutions to these paradoxes, we do feel strongly that new directions for research would go a long way toward doing so.

Paradox #1: The career is being driven increasingly by identity and values at a time when opportunities to express identity and values through work are diminishing

David Campbell has made this observation for career planners, "If you don't know where you want to go, you'll probably end up somewhere else". (Campbell, 1974). When Campbell wrote those words in the pre-downsizing era of the 1970s, there was a sense of great opportunity, and the main career task for many people was to figure out where they wanted to go—i.e. what their identities and values were. The paradox is that, now that people are more in touch with identity, values, and where they want to go, as the saying goes, there's no "there" there.

Research is needed to help us understand more fully what "there" means in the post-organizational society. One area to pursue is the notion of *career as one's chosen work in life*. By "work" we mean an area of protean endeavor guided by personal values and seen as a "path with a heart" (Shepard, 1984), not as a "career path" external to the individual.

A second direction for self-expression that we have discussed is the *search beyond the organization for identity and values expression*. Since the energy for career direction is coming more from inside the person than from the organization, the search for fulfillment is no longer contained primarily within the boundaries of the organization. Thus, we offer two ideas for future research:

Proposition 1: A growing influence on life and career satisfaction will be the congruence among identity, values, and one's chosen work. Traditional predictors, such as satisfaction with the job, with the employing organization, and with pay and other rewards, will decrease in importance.

Proposition 2: Individuals who search outside the organization for support in their development will be more likely to experience success than those who search only inside the organization.

Paradox #2: Relational sources of identity development are more needed than ever, just as they are becoming less accessible

As we have been saying, a major source of identity development in today's work environment can be found in various forms of supportive relationships. And, even though there are still many people in one's role set, even after downsizing (since organizations are still human systems), those others have less time to be helpful, less energy, and often less desire or motivation. This reduced accessibility of help from others is due largely to the zero-sum, competitive dynamics that are created with the uncertainties and stresses of downsizing.

This paradox is especially troubling, as it is not necessary that the process of organizational learning and adaptation become a zero sum situation. Organizations that provide a leadership style and a culture that promotes development (i.e. human capital) will be both more effective and more secure for employees. We need case research that is rich in descriptive detail on organizations that manage to go counter to the current norm and provide a culture that supports relational development.

Proposition 3: The following types of organizations are more likey than others to have a culture that contains high levels of relational development: values-driven leadership; investments in human capital; and a change process characterized by high levels of procedural justice.

Paradox #3: Learning from experience is becoming more critical but, with a more turbulent environment, past experience has less relevance to current experience

As we have said elsewhere, people see more value today in mentoring and other forms of learning from other people's experience, but as the rate of change accelerates, a senior mentor's experience bears little resemblance to what a protegé might expect to encounter in her/his career. So people may be seeking mentors more, but it is ever harder to find a mentor that one can identify with and who has relevant wisdom to share.

And since a big part of mentoring has traditionally been identification (an identity-ideal, someone the person would like to be like in the future), what other ways are there of seeking an identity-ideal? We would argue that increasingly the basis of mentoring and identification within the mentoring relationship will not be role experience but rather personal qualities. What qualities as a person does this potential mentor have that I would like to emulate (as opposed to what career role or status has this person achieved)? (Note again the theme of looking inside, to the self.)

Since the search is not for someone who has taken a particular path to a particular role, this means that there could be a wide variety of types of people, representing collectively a set of personal qualities one values, from whom one might learn. Thus, mentoring may be done more in *groups* in the future, as opposed to happening in the traditional dyadic mentor–protegé relationship; and as we have been saying, these groups will exist to an increasing extent outside of the employing organization. Examples would be self-created support groups, professional networks, group activities initiated by professional associations, and the like. For example, the Academy of Management now has several pre-convention workshops that address the career development needs of members: doctoral consortia, junior faculty workshops, senior faculty development seminars, etc.

Thus, we propose some testable ideas that may help resolve this third dilemma.

> *Proposition 4*: Consistent with the idea of protean careers and turbulent environments, mentors' personal identities are becoming more important to protegés than are the mentors' roles and status attainments.

> *Proposition 5*: As the availability of traditional mentoring decreases inside organizations, people will turn increasingly to group forms of developmental assistance (support groups, networks, affinity groups—often outside the employing organization).

Paradox #4: The career is dead. Long live the career

And now we are back where we started. Just as it appears that career opportunities in today's global economy are becoming increasingly bleak, as illustrated by many years of newspaper headlines and magazine cover stories with titles such as "The end of the job", "Economic anxiety" and "The age of downsizing", there is renewed interest in career development and continuous learning.

We have already given away our punch line on our idea for resolving this dilemma: the organizational career is dying, but the protean career is thriving. Increasingly, one's career work is becoming an arena for expressing one's identity and values, and one's membership in a particular organization is becoming less central to one's overall identity.

> *Proposition 6*: Organizational factors are becoming less important in determining individual career outcomes; intrapersonal (especially identity and values) and interpersonal (especially relational connection) factors are becoming more important in shaping career directions and rewards.

With pcoplc working across organizational boundaries in a variety of ways (sometimes self-employed, or working part-time for an organization, or as independent sontractors for an organization, etc.), sub-identities and roles are not as distinct as they were in the past. There is more value attached to being a "whole person" in one's work and personal life. Thus, as people strive for balance and psychological success in their lives, fewer salient rewards are controlled by the organization, and more by the individual—with a little help from his/her friends!

Acknowledgments

The authors would like to thank Barbara Walker and Susan E. Jackson for their helpful comments on this paper.

REFERENCES

Ashford, S.J. & Tsui, A.S. (1991). Self-regulation for managerial effectiveness: the role of active feedback seeking. *Academy of Management Journal*, **34**, 251–80.

Becker, H.S. (1963). Careers in a deviant occupational group. In *Outsiders* (pp. 59–78). Glencoe, IL: Free Press.

Briscoe, J.P. (1996). Influences upon personal "value expression" at work: an empirical study. Paper presented at the 3rd Biennial International Conference on Advances in Management, June 26–29, 1996, Boston, MA.

Brockner, J. (1988). *Self-esteem at Work*. Lexington, MA: Lexington Books.

Brockner, J., Konovsky, M., Cooper-Schneider, R., Folger, R., Martin, C. & Bies, R.J. (1994). Interactive effects of procedural justice and outcome negativity on victims and surivivors of job Loss. *Academy of Management Journal*, **37**, 397–409.

Bunker, K.A. & Webb, A.D. (1992). *Learning How to Learn From Experience: Impact of Stress and Coping*. Greensboro, NC: Center for Creative Leadership, Report No. 154.

Campbell, D. (1974). *If You Don't Know Where You're Going, You'll Probably End up Somewhere Else*. Allen, TX: Tabor Publishing.

Carver, C.S. & Scheier, M.F. (1982). *Attention and Self-regulation: a Control Theory Approach*. New York: Springer-Verlag.

Chartrand, J.M. & Camp, C.C. (1991). Advances in the measurement of career development constructs: a 20-year review. *Journal of Vocational Behavior*, **39**, 1–39.

Chatman, J. (1989). Improving interactional organizational research: a model of person–organization fit. *Academy of Management Review*, **14**, 333–49.

Cox, T. Jr (1993). *Cultural Diversity in Organizations: Theory, Research and Practice*. San Francisco, CA: Berrett-Koehler.

Dalton, G. (1989). Developmental views of careers in organizations. In M.B. Arthur, D.T. Hall & B.S. Lawrence (eds), *Handbook of Career Theory* (pp. 89–109). New York: Cambridge University Press.

Derr, C.B. & Briscoe, J.P. (forthcoming, 1997). Managing high potentials: practices in the United States. In F. Bournois & S. Rousillon (eds), *Managing High Potentials: Theoretical and International Perspective*. London: Prentice-Hall.

Driver, M.J. (1994). Workforce personality and the new information age workplace. In J.A. Auerbach & J.C. Welsh (eds), *Aging and Competition: Rebuilding the US Workforce* (pp. 185–204). Washington, DC: The National Council on the Aging, Inc., and the National Planning Association.

Erikson, E.H. (1966). The concept of identity in race relations: notes and queries. *Daedalus*, **95**, 145–71.

Fletcher, J. (1994). Toward a theory of relational practice in organizations: a feminist reconstruction of "real" work. Doctoral dissertation, Boston University School of Management, Boston, MA.

Hall D.T. (1971). A theoretical model of career subidentity development in organizational settings. *Organizational Behavior and Human Performance*, **6**, 50–76.

Hall, D.T. (1976). *Careers in Organizations*. Glenview, IL: Scott, Foresman.

Hall, D.T. (1986). Breaking career routines: midcareer choice and identity development. In D.T. Hall & Associates, *Career Development in Organizations* (pp. 120–59). San Francisco, CA: Jossey-Bass.

Hall, D.T. & Associates (1996). *The Career is Dead—Long Live the Career*. San Francisco, CA: Jossey-Bass.

Hall, D.T. & Associates (1986). *Career Development in Organizations*. San Francisco, CA: Jossey-Bass.

Hall, D.T. & Mirvis, P.H. (1995). Careers as lifelong learning. In A. Howard (ed.), *The Changing Nature of Work* (pp. 323–61). San Francisco, CA: Jossey-Bass.

Handy, C. (1996). *The Age of Uncertainty*. Boston, MA: Harvard Business School Press.

Isaacs, W.N. (1993) Taking flight: dialogue, collective thinking and organizational learning. *Organizational Dynamics*, **Autumn**, 24–39.

James, K., Lovato, C. & Khoo, G. (1994). Social identity correlates of minority workers' health. *Academy of Management Journal*, **37**, 383–96.

Jordan, J.V., Kaplan, A.G., Baker-Miller, J., Striver, I.P. & Surrey, J.L. (eds) (1991). *Women's Growth In Connection*. New York: Guilford.

Kaplan, R.E. (1990). Character change in executives as "re-form" in the pursuit of self-worth. *Journal of Applied Behavioral Science*, **26**(4), 461–81.

Katz, D. & Kahn, R.L. (1978). *The Social Psychology of Organizations*, 2nd edn. New York: Wiley.

Kegan, R. (1994). *In Over Our Heads: the Mental Demands of Modern Life*. Cambridge, MA: Harvard University Press.

Kleinfield, N.R. (1996). The company as family, no more. *The New York Times*, **March 4**, A1, A12.

Kram, K.E. (1996). A relational approach to career development. In D.T. Hall (ed.), *The Careet is Dead—Long Live the Career* (pp. 132–57). San Francisco, CA: Jossey-Bass.

Kram, K.E. (1988). *Mentoring at Work: Developmental Relationships in Organizational Life*. Lanham, MD: University Press of America.

Kram, K.E. & Hall, D.T. (1996). Mentoring in a context of diversity and turbulence. In E. Kossek & S. Lobel (eds), *Human Resource Strategies for Managing Diversity*. London: Blackwell.

Levinson, D.J., Darrow, D., Levinson, M. & McKee, B. (1978). *Seasons of a Man's Life*. New York: Knopf.

Levinson, D.J. (1996). *Seasons of a Woman's Life*. New York: Knopf (in collaboration with Judy D. Levinson).

Levinson, H. (1962). *Men, Management, and Mental Health*. Cambridge, MA: Harvard University Press.

McAdams, Dan P. & Ochberg, R.L. (eds)(1988). *Psychobiography and Life Narratives*. Durham, NC: Duke University Press.

McCall, M.W. Jr, Lombardo, M.M. & Morrison, A.M. (1988). *The Lessons of Experience*. Lexington, MA: Lexington Press.

Miller, J.B. (1986). *Toward a New Psychology of Women*. Boston, MA: Beacon Press.

Posner, B.Z., Kouzes, J.M. & Schmidt, W.H. (1985). Shared values make a difference: an empirical test of corporate culture. *Human Resource Management*, **24**, 293–309.

Rokeach, M. (1973). *The Nature of Human Values*. New York: Free Press.

Schein, E.H. (1978). *Career Dynamics*. Reading, MA: Addison-Wesley.

Seibert, K. (1996). Experience in the Real Teacher if You Can Learn From It. In D.T. Hall (ed), *The Career is Dead—Long Live the Career* (pp. 246–64). San Francisco, CA: Jossey-Bass.

Shepard, H.A. (1984). On the realization of human potential: a path with a heart. In M.B. Arthur, L. Bailyn, D.J. Levinson & H.A. Shepard (eds), *Working with Careers*. New York: Center for Research on Careers, Graduate School of Business, Columbia University.

Staw, B.M. (1984). Organizational behavior: a review and reformulation of the field's outcome variables. *Annual Review of Psychology*, **35**, 627–66.

Super D.E. (1957). *The Psychology of Careers*. New York, NY: Harper & Row.

Thomas, D.A. & Alderfer, C.P. (1989). The influence of race on career dynamics: theory and research on minority career experiences. In M.B. Arthur, D.T. Hall & B.S. Lawrence (eds), *Handbook of Career Theory* (pp. 133–58). New York: Cambridge University Press.

Walker, B. (1996). The Value of Diversity in Career Self-Development. In D.T. Hall (ed.), *The Career is Dead—Long Live the Career* (pp. 265–77). San Francisco, CA: Jossey-Bass.

Chapter 18

Career Issues Facing Contingent and Self-Employed Workers: Prospects and Problems for the Twenty-First Century

Daniel C. Feldman
University of South Carolina, Columbia, SC, USA

It is becoming increasingly clear that the major employment trend begun over the past quarter-century will continue into the next quarter-century as well: fewer and fewer people will be working full-time on a permanent basis for large, established firms. Whether these new firms are called "shamrock firms", "boundaryless firms", "virtual organizations", or by some other name, the attribute which they all share in common is the assumption that much of the work will be done by employees who are only working for the organization limited hours per week (e.g. part-time workers), for limited periods of time (e.g. temporary workers and subcontractors), in stop-gap jobs as prelude or postscript to more permanent positions (e.g. underemployed college graduates and "bridge employment" early retirees), geographically separate from the organization's operations (e.g. telecommuters and "home workers") or as independent service providers (e.g. entrepreneurs and consultants).

Unfortunately, the main impact of shrinking organization size on career development has been to decrease the number of employees organizations feel responsible to develop and the staff resources available to develop the remaining employees—not a reconceptualization of career development in the context of a major share of the firm's work being done by employees who are not permanent,

Creating Tomorrow's Organizations. Edited by C.L. Cooper and S.E. Jackson.
© 1997 John Wiley & Sons Ltd.

full-time or even physically present at the organization. This chapter, then, explores the future prospects and problems associated with managing careers outside traditional organizational boundaries in the century ahead.

In the first section, we explore the three career development issues most salient to contingent, transitional, and self-employed workers themselves: creating opportunities for skill development outside of traditional organizations, generating opportunities for career advancement in non-traditional career paths, and managing transitions into and out of the core workforce. In the second section, we examine the three career issues most salient to organizations: increasing productivity of non-core employees, sustaining the motivation of non-core employees, and generating a team-oriented work environment with a sizeable contingent workforce. In the third and final section of the chapter, we highlight the implications these changes in traditional career patterns have for future theory development, research methodology and management practice.

The literature on this topic has used a wide variety of terms to describe workers managing careers outside traditional organizational boundaries, depending on their type of work arrangement: "contingent workers", "part-timers",

Table18.1   Factors influencing career self-management of non-core employees

Opportunities for skill development
    Frequency of contact with core employees
    Duration of contact with core employees
    Concerns about safety and liability
    Age and career stage
    Diversity of clients served
    Diversity of services provided
    Recognizability of occupational group
    Number of non-core workers employed
    Routineness of work

Opportunities for career advancement
    Criticality of services provided
    Replaceability of non-core workers
    Industry and firm growth
    Flexibility of opportunity structures in labor markets
    Ability to practice occupation outside core organizations
    Career stage

Transitions into and out of the core workforce
    Amount and duration of contact with core employees
    Employment gaps
    Work–family conflict
    Career anchors
    Age and career stage
    Income
    Opportunities for bridge employment
    Opportunities for satisfactory employment
    Free choice about career transition

"temporary workers", "subcontractors", and so forth. As we will see below, there are major differences among these types of non-traditional employees. For our purposes here, we will use the term "core employees" to refer to those workers who are employed full-time by one organization on a permanent, continuous basis. The term "non-core employees" will be used to refer to those employees who work limited hours per week, for limited or irregular periods of time, or on a non-continuous basis, for one or more employing firms.

NON-TRADITIONAL CAREERS: THE INDIVIDUAL'S PERSPECTIVE

For individuals who are pursuing careers outside traditional organizational boundaries, either by choice or by necessity, three challenges are particularly daunting: generating opportunities for additional skill development; creating opportunities for further career advancement; and managing transitions into and out of the core workforce. Below, we examine the factors which are most likely to facilitate or impede career self-management in these non-traditional career paths; these factors are summarized in graphic form in Table 18.1. For ease of presentation, the propositions for this section appear in Table 18.2.

Opportunities for Skill Development

Even for contingent workers, consultants, telecommuters, and entrepreneurs, there may be considerable opportunities for additional skill development outside traditional career paths. However, the availability of these skill development opportunities and/or the likelihood that individuals will avail themselves of these developmental opportunities will vary significantly across groups of non-traditional employees.

Frequency and Duration of Contact with Core Employees

Non-core employees should have more opportunities for skill development *within* traditional organizational settings the more frequent their contact with core employees and the longer the duration of that contact. Previous research suggests, for example, that within the hierarchy of contingent jobs, employees who work longer hours per week and who have longer job tenure are more likely to receive increased work responsibilities and more in-house training (Feldman & Doerpinghaus, 1992; Feldman, Doerpinghaus & Turnley, 1995). Thus, we would expect year-round, permanent, part-time workers both to have more opportunities for organizational training and to be more likely to avail themselves of that training than temporary workers and "home workers" (*Proposition 1*).

Table 18.2 Propositions on career self-management of non-core employees

Opportunities for skill development

P1: Non-core employees will have greater opportunities for skill development within core organizations and will be more likely to avail themselves of that training: (a) the more frequent their contact with core employees; (b) the longer the duration of contact with core employees.

P2: Non-core employees will have greater opportunities for skill development within core organizations and will be more likely to avail themselves of that training the greater the core organization's concerns about safety and liability regulations.

P3: Non-core employees will have greater opportunities for skill development within core organizations: (a) the younger their age; and (b) the earlier their career stage.

P4: Non-core older workers and mid- and late-career employees are more likely to obtain skill development outside core organizations.

P5: The greater the diversity of clients serviced and the greater the diversity of services provided, the greater the opportunities for non-core employees to obtain skill development outside core organizations will be.

P6: Non-core employees will be able to obtain skill development outside core organizations to the extent that they are members of recognizable occupational/ trade groups with supporting professional associations.

P7: Non-core employees working for employment agencies, consulting firms and subcontractors will be more likely to receive training from their emploers: (a) the greater the number of workers employed; and (b) the more routine and repetitive the employees' tasks.

Opportunities for career advancement

P8: Opportunities for career advancement for non-core workers will be: (a) positively related to criticality of the services they provide; (b) negatively related to their replaceability and substitutability.

P9: Opportunities for career advancement for non-core workers will be: (a) positively associated with industry growth; and (b) negatively associated with firm or sub-unit decline.

P10: Opportunities for career advancement for non-core employees will be: (a) negatively associated with rigidity of opportunity structures in an occupation; and (b) positively associated with ability to practice an occupation outside formal organizational boundaries.

P11: Loss of subsequent career advancement opportunities due to non-core employment will be greater for individuals in early-career stages.

Transitions into and out of the core workforce

P12: Ease of transition from non-core to core positions will be positively associated with: (a) frequency of prior interaction with core employees; and (b) duration of prior interactions with core employees.

P13: Ease of transition from non-core to core positions will be negatively associated with: (a) time out of the core workforce; and (b) level of work–family conflict.

P14: Non-core workers with security, stability, and managerial competence career anchors will transition into core organizations more readily than non-core workers with autonomy, creativity, and entrepreneurial career anchors.

P15: Ease of transition from core to non-core positions will be positively associated with: (a) age; (b) career stage; and (c) employees' accumulated capital.

P16: Ease of transition from core to non-core positions will be positively associated with: (a) availability of non-core employment in the same occupation or organization; (b) free choice about movement out of core positions; and (c) satisfactory employment in non-core positions which utilize their education and previous work experience.

Concern with Safety and Liability Regulations

Governmental safety and liability regulations should also influence the availability of skill development opportunities to non-core employees. As Davis-Blake & Uzzi (1993) found, the use of "external" workers raises significant concerns about ensuring safety regulation compliance. In addition, the courts have taken a rather broad interpretation of the liabilities employing organizations have for these external workers. Employing organizations are likely to be held liable for damages generated by external workers if they work under the core organization's daily supervision and perform their jobs at the core organization's work site (Feldman & Klaas, 1996). Thus, we propose here that non-core employees will have greater opportunities to upgrade training within core organizations and are more likely to avail themselves of that training the greater the core organization's concerns about safety and liability regulations (*Proposition 2*).

Age and Career Stage

Both age and career stage of non-core employees may influence the availability of opportunities for skill development within core organizations. As *Proposition 3* suggests, core organizations are more likely to provide some type of structured skill development for young, early-career employees. In part, this may be due to organizations' traditional inclination to provide some training and orientation to all new workers on the assumption they have not had sufficient training elsewhere. In part, too, this may be due to the lower "per unit" cost of training large numbers of young, early-career employees relative to training small batches of middle-aged, mid-career employees.

In contrast, different individual and organizational factors are likely to influence non-core employees' opportunities to obtain skill development and to avail themselves of those opportunities *outside* core organizations. For example, mid- and late-career employees should be *more* likely to obtain further skill development outside traditional core organizations (*Proposition 4*). Here we suggest that older workers and those in later career stages are more likely to be knowledgeable about the variety of training programs, institutes, and workshops externally available to them. In addition, mid- and late-career employees are more likely to have accrued the capital (or are more likely to be able to afford the time off work) to take advantage of these opportunities.

Diversity of Clients Serviced and Services Provided

So far, we have been discussing skill development largely in the context of formal training. However, there are often significant opportunities for non-core employees to obtain skill development through informal means, such as interactions with clients and peers. Non-core workers should have greater opportunities for skill development outside core organizations the greater the diversity of clients they serve and the greater the diversity of services they provide (*Proposi-*

tion 5). The greater the variety of clients served and the greater the variety of services provided, the more opportunities non-core workers will have to observe different constellations of problems and problem solutions. Thus, consultants providing a wide array of services to a broad spectrum of clients (e.g. general management consultants) may have much greater opportunities to learn from their clients than contingent workers providing limited, routinized services to a small number of clients (e.g. electrical subcontractors in residential construction).

Recognizable Occupational Group

Along the same lines, both the mentoring literature (e.g. Kram, 1985) and the socialization literature (e.g. Louis, Posner & Powell, 1983) suggest that peers can provide a viable alternative to top-down formal training. Opportunities for further skill development outside core organizations should be greater when non-core workers are members of a recognizable occupational or trade group (*Proposition 6*). For instance, while often working only tangentially or sporadically for hospitals, nurses still have professional associations and peer support networks to tap into for technical advice, training programs, and professional support. In contrast, with the exception of insurance and real estate agents, most sales staff have no recognizable trade association or organized peer network to provide such support services.

Number of Non-Core Workers Employed/Job Routine

While it may not be common, some providers of contingent employment may also make available skill development opportunities to non-core employees. For example, temporary agencies may provide computer training for clerical workers sent out to client firms, or consulting firms may provide sales and service training to their employees. These human resource intermediary firms will be more likely to provide such skill development the greater the number of employees and the more routinized and repetitive the employees' tasks (*Proposition 7*). Under these circumstances, both the limited scope of the training and the large number of employees receiving the training make the cost of providing such skill development relatively low.

Opportunities for Career Advancement

The nomenclature typically used to describe non-core employees certainly has suggested that these workers do not have much interest in, or much hope for, career advancement: "peripheral workers", "contingent workers", "disposable workers" (Rotchford & Roberts, 1982). However, as the non-core workforce has become more diverse and more heavily composed of individuals with high career investment, the issue of career advancement opportunities for non-core employees becomes more significant (Feldman, 1990, 1995). Career advancement can be broadly defined here in a variety of ways, depending upon the circumstances of the employees themselves: promotions, acquisition of permanent positions, salary growth, positions of greater responsibility, and so forth. In this next section, we examine the factors which both facilitate and impede the career advancement of non-core employees.

Criticality of Service Provided/Replaceability of Non-Core Workers

The criticality of the service provided by non-core workers will be positively related to their career advancement, while employee replaceability and substitutability will be negatively related to career advancement (*Proposition 8*). To the extent that non-core workers provide a valuable service in a niche market, they will have significantly more opportunities to increase the scope of their business and their revenue (Pfeffer, 1982). For example, entrepreneurs who provide critical services in markets with very little competition will have ample opportunities to expand their main business, enter into other client services, and create wealth. In contrast, non-core workers who are easily replaceable and substitutable will have considerably fewer opportunities for career advancement. It is for this reason that many clerical workers, unskilled blue-collar workers, and retail salespeople have difficulty exiting low-level non-core jobs.

Industry and Firm Growth

Macro-economic conditions can also influence the ability of non-core workers to achieve career advancement. The growth of the industry in which non-core workers are employed and the growth of the main firms or subunits non-core workers service will both influence advancement opportunities (*Proposition 9*). When their industry is growing quickly, part-time and temporary workers have many more opportunities to obtain higher pay and/or full-time employment; we saw this, for example, in the career patterns of contingent school teachers in the 1960s and contingent nurses in the 1970s.

In contrast, when the major firms or subunits where non-core workers are employed face business declines, non-core employees are especially hard hit because the use of non-core employees is highly cyclical. For instance, contingent construction workers see their job opportunities decline along with those of local contractors, and subcontractors to defense firms see their job opportunities fall with the elimination of major defense contracts.

Flexibility in Opportunity Structures in Labor Markets

The opportunity structures for individuals in non-core positions will also influence their career advancement potential (Doeringer, 1990). Labor markets in various occupations differ in the extent to which career paths are rigid in nature (i.e. whether there is a clear progression of career moves to be taken in a certain order at certain time intervals). In labor markets where there is high rigidity, there also tend to be high penalties for "career disorderliness" (Kilty & Behling, 1985); individuals lose significant opportunities for advancement if they drop in and out of the core labor force or get out of sync with the traditional career path. For example, the career path for corporate law is much more rigid than the career path in sales, and thus the penalties for career disorderliness in corporate law are substantially greater than for workforce exits or part-time employment in retailing.

Along the same lines, labor markets differ in the extent to which an occupation or trade can be practiced outside formal, core organizations. For instance, nurses have more opportunities to practice their profession outside established core organizations than dentists do; the service is more portable and the equipment costs are considerable less.

Thus, rigidity of opportunity structures will be negatively related to career advancement opportunities for non-core employees, while ability to practice one's trade outside formal organizational boundaries will be positively related to career advancement opportunities (*Proposition 10*). While rigid opportunity structures penalize non-core workers for non-traditional career patterns, the ability to readily practice one's trade outside traditional core organizations should facilitate career advancement opportunities.

Career Stage

Finally here, the loss of career advancement opportunities associated with non-core employment will be greater for individuals in the early stages of their careers (*Proposition 11*). First, the penalties for career disorderliness are generally greater earlier in one's career; across occupations, there is greater formality of career progression steps and greater penalties for lack of full-time organizational commitment at early career stages. Second, there may be some long-term positive benefits of participating in large organizations' formal training programs early in one's career; such training may serve as a market signal of the employee's level of competence and expertise. Third, it may be very difficult to launch non-core career paths in fields like entrepreneurship and consulting without the external validation provided by previous full-time work experience in large, established firms.

Transitions into and out of the Core Workforce

From the individual's perspective, another major career issue surrounding non-core employment is transitioning into and out of the core workforce. While the "people-processing strategies" used to socialize full-time newcomers are fairly well documented (see Van Maanen & Schein, 1979), the career transitions of contingent and self-employed workers have received substantially less attention. Moreover, the factors which ease transition from non-core employment to core employment are quite different from those influencing the transition from core employment to non-core employment.

Amount and Duration of Previous Contact

In examining the factors which influence the transition from non-core employment to core employment, it appears that amount of prior contact with core employees and duration of contact with core employees will be positively associated with ease of transition into the core workforce (Brett, 1984). Analogous to Proposition 1, here we suggest that the lower the dissimilarity of job content and job context between two successive jobs, the easier the transition should be (*Proposition 12*). Thus, non-core employees with high levels of prior contact with the core organization will have more realistic expectations of their new jobs, will suffer less entry shock, and should have less trouble learning the organization's procedures and adjusting to social norms.

Employment Gaps and Work–Family Conflict

In contrast, ease of transition from non-core to core positions will be negatively associated with time out of the core work force and amount of work–family conflict (*Proposition 13*). The longer workers have been out of the core workforce, the more difficulty they are likely to have dealing with the greater levels of structure, regulation, and bureaucracy in core organizations. For these workers, the transition from having high control over their work schedules to having low control may be particularly unsettling. In addition, many employees enter non-core employment as a way of balancing work–family life conflicts (Feldman, 1990; Feldman & Doerpinghaus, 1992). To the extent that movement back into the core workforce regenerates work–family conflicts, the transition will be more difficult.

Career Anchors

Along the same lines, the literature on career anchors suggests there may be important differences across individuals in their adaptation to core work organizations (*Proposition 14*). Individuals with security and stability career anchors will appreciate the greater structure and routine associated with core employment; likewise, those with managerial competence career anchors will find greater opportunities for advancement and status in core organizational settings (see Schein, 1978). In contrast, individuals with autonomy, creativity, and entrepreneurial career anchors will find core organizations more constraining, more difficult to adapt to, and less satisfying of their personal needs and interests.

Age, Career Stage, and Income

In terms of transitioning out of the core workforce into non-core positions, older workers and those in later career stages should have an easier time adjusting

(*Proposition 15*). It is not uncommon for older workers and those in later career stages to start decelerating and to look for less taxing job situations (Dalton, Thompson & Price, 1977). Consequently, non-core positions are often quite attractive to individuals who want to keep on working but not at the same level of intensity (Doeringer, 1990). Moreover, with age and later career stage often comes greater financial independence; older workers making the transition into non-core positions are often financially more able to absorb the loss of short-term regular income associated with various forms of contingent work and self-employment (Rothberg & Cook, 1985).

"Bridge Employment" and "Satisfactory Employment"

The research on career transitions suggests some other factors that might influence the ease of transition out of core positions into non-core career paths. In investigations of how individuals adjust to retirement, for example, a variety of outside interests (e.g. leisure pursuits, church involvement, family involvement, etc.) have been studied. The logic has been that individuals with greater outside interests will be more willing to retire and will adjust more readily to retirement. Most of these studies have yielded non-significant or small magnitude results. In contrast, Feldman (1994a) argues that it is an employee's *certainty* about his/her plans after leaving core employment (rather than the content of those plans) that leads to ease of transition.

Because there is some anxiety associated with any job transition, the greater an individual's certainty about what the next job will hold, the easier his/her transition into that position will be (Brett, 1984; Louis, 1980). For this reason, opportunities for non-core employment *in the same occupation or organization* should ease transitions into non-core positions as well (*Proposition 16*). This "bridge employment" (Doeringer, 1990) should generate both less content change and context change in these kinds of career transitions.

Voluntariness of the transition into non-core employment and "satisfactory employment" in non-core jobs using their skills and experience should also be positively associated with ease of transition out of the core workforce. As previous research on contingent workers suggests, when workers are voluntarily taking non-core positions to achieve work–family balance, they adjust more easily than when they are forced into these positions by layoffs (Feldman & Doerpinghaus, 1992; Feldman, Doerpinghaus & Turnley, 1995). Similarly, when workers entering non-core positions are also entering underemployment, they, too, will be more resistant to non-core jobs (Kaufman, 1982). In these cases, workers are facing not only less steady work but also work which is significantly less challenging. Thus, senior accountants voluntarily moving into part-time jobs in financial consulting prior to full-time retirement are likely to adjust more easily to non-core employment than senior accountants laid off from their jobs and forced into part-time jobs as accounts payable clerks.

Table 18.3 Factors influencing organizational career management of non-core employees

---

Productivity of non-core employees
    Frequency and duration of contact with non-core
        employees
    Similarity of compensation
    Professional identification
    Financial independence of non-core employees

Motivation of non-core employees
    Peer support
    Pro-rated benefits
    Opportunities for repeat business
    Motivating potential of jobs

Teamwork and team orientation
    Divisibility of work
    Amount of cross-unit coordination required
    Schedule flexibility of non-core employees
    Level of cross-training among group members
    Number of non-core employees in group
    Demographic dissimilarity among group members
    Type of non-core employment contract

NON-TRADITIONAL CAREERS:
THE ORGANIZATION'S PERSPECTIVE

Managing significant numbers of non-core workers has presented special challenges to employing organizations as well. Here, we consider the three most salient organizational challenges facing firms reliant on non-core or transitional workers: increasing the productivity of non-core employees; sustaining the motivation of non-core employees; and generating a team-oriented work environment with a sizeable contingent workforce. The factors most central to managing non-traditional careers from the organization's perspective are summarized in Table 18.3, while the propositions for this section appear in Table 18.4.

Productivity of Non-Core Employees

Surprisingly, there has been very little empirical research on the productivity of non-core workers. Across different types of transitional workers, we would generally expect there to be modest performance decrements relative to full-time core workers performing the same tasks. There are at least two reasons for this proposed performance deficit. First, as noted earlier, non-core workers may receive less formal training and have fewer opportunities to upgrade training. Second, because non-core employees may work irregular hours (either per day or

Table 18.4   Propositions on organizational career management of non-core employees

Productivity of non-core employees
  P17: The productivity of non-core employees will be higher: (a) the more frequent
       the contact with core emplorees; and (b) the longer the duration of contact
       between non-core and core employees.
  P18: The productivity of non-core employees will be higher: (a) the more frequent
       the contact between non-core and core employees; (b) the longer the duration
       of contact between non-core and core employees; and (c) the more equivalent
       non-core salary is to core employee salary.
  P19: Non-core workers will engage in more organizational citizenship behaviors: (a)
       the greater their professional identification; and (b) the greater their financial
       dependence upon a client firm.

Motivation of non-core employees
  P20: Peer support from co-workers will be positively associated with the motivation
       level of non-core employees.
  P21: For part-time and temporary workers primarily employed by one organization,
       pro-rated benefits and seniority-based pay raises will be positively associated
       with the motivation levels of employees.
  P22: For consultants and subcontractors, opportunities for repeat or expanded
       business will be positively associated with work motivation.
  P23: The motivating potential of non-core jobs will be positively associated with the
       motivation levels of non-core employees.

Teamwork and team orientation
  P24: Integration of non-core employees into group projects will be more successful
       when: (a) the group project is easily divisible into individual tasks; and (b) the
       project requires little cross-unit coordination.
  P25: Integration of non-core employees into group projects will be more successful
       when: (a) there are high levels of cross-training among group members; and (b)
       non-core employees have high levels of flexibility in scheduling their work.
  P26: Integration of non-core employees into ongoing work groups will be: (a)
       inversely related to the number of non-core employees who are joining the
       work group; and (b) positively related to the demographic similarity of non-core
       employees to core employees.
  P27: Team contributions of non-core employees will be highest among: (a)
       permanent part-time employees; (b) long-term consultants and subcontractors;
       and (c) bridge-employed early retirees.
  P28: Team contributions of non-core employees will be lowest among: (a) temporary
       employees; (b) seasonal workers; and (c) moonlighters.

per week), they may have less time to peak in their performance. However, there
are several characteristics of the job and work environment which might mitigate
against this hypothesized performance decrement.

Frequency and Duration of Contact

The more frequent and the longer the duration of contact between non-core and
core employees, the more likely non-core employees' performance will be higher.
As noted earlier, frequency and duration of contact should increase opportunities for learning within the core organization (*Proposition 17*). In addition, fre-

quency and duration of contact should lead to greater normative control of non-core employees. Moreover, extensive contact should decrease the start-up time and transaction costs often associated with contingent workers, thereby facilitating transitional workers' reaching peak performance more quickly.

Similarity of Compensation

In addition, the more similar the salary (compensation excluding benefits) of non-core and core employees performing the same tasks, the greater non-core employees' productivity is likely to be (*Proposition 18*). Consistent with equity theory (Lawler, 1981), non-core employees should be more likely to perform high quality and/or high quantity work when their salary approximates that of full-time, permanent employees. In contrast, non-core workers who are paid significantly less than their core counterparts might reduce their productivity to come into equity with their colleagues.

Professional Identification and Financial Independence

An area of employee performance which has received increased attention in the organizational sciences literature over the past decade is organizational citizenship behavior, namely, the willingness of employees to help out above and beyond normal job requirements (Graham, 1991). Again, this is a topic which has received very little attention in terms of transitional workers, largely because most researchers have assumed that non-core workers would have insufficient organizational identification or commitment to make such additional efforts worthwhile. Here we propose that transitional workers will engage in organizational citizenship behaviors when: (a) their occupational/professional identification is high; and (b) when they are heavily financially dependent upon a core organization (*Proposition 19*).

In the case of part-time nurses or part-time professors, for example, the norms of professionalism are likely to prevail even if there are insufficient organizational inducements to go above and beyond the call of duty. For many non-core workers, the norms of the profession about providing high-quality service across situations may override local organizations' less stringent demands.

Along the same lines, non-core workers who are heavily financially dependent upon a core organization (e.g. the organization accounts for a major percentage of their business or the organization is a critical reference for future clients) are also more likely to engage in organizational citizenship behaviors. For these workers, too, the prospects of future economic gain may create incentives to help out beyond what the dictates of the present employment contract require.

Motivation of Non-Core Employees

Another challenging task for core organizations is motivating transitional workers who may not be legally (or psychologically) their employees. Previous research on the satisfactions and dissatisfactions of contingent employees in their jobs suggests some avenues to pursue here, both in terms of extrinsic and intrinsic motivation.

Peer Support

In terms of extrinsic rewards, it appears as if peer support from non-core workers may be the most significant motivator (Feldman & Doerpinghaus, 1992; Feldman, Doerpinghaus & Turnley, 1995). Particularly for part-time and temporary employees engaged in clerical and sales positions (roughly half the US contingent workforce), the opportunities for social contact outside the household are important incentives to participate in the workforce. This social support induces contingent workers to show up at work and compensates non-core workers (in part) for sometimes unchallenging work assignments. In addition, peer support can create normative pressure on contingent workers to follow organizational policies and procedures. Thus, the motivation of non-core employees should be positively associated with peer support in the workplace (*Proposition 20*).

Pro-Rated Benefits

In terms of monetary incentives for non-core workers, two different patterns seem to emerge. For workers engaged in regular part-time employment with one organization and temporary workers regularly employed by one agency, pro-rated benefits and seniority-based pay raises appear to be significant motivators (*Proposition 21*). While most contingent workers recognize their compensation packages will be less than those of their core colleagues, they resent not receiving at least some pro-rated benefits based on hours worked per week (in the case of sick leave) or based on years worked (in the case of pay increases). Without at least some additional economic incentives, part-time and temporary employees soon begin to resent the compensation practices of their current employers and start looking for employment elsewhere (Feldman & Doerpinghaus, 1992; Feldman, Doerpinghaus & Turnley, 1995). Moreover, there is at least some observational data that the absence of these kinds of economic incentives leads to decreases in on-the-job performance of non-core employees as well (Greenberger & Steinberg, 1986).

Opportunities for Repeat Business

The economic incentives of consultants and subcontractors appear to be somewhat different. These workers are employed by a variety of firms over the course of a year, and thus are not dependent upon incremental increases in pension or health insurance benefits offered by specific clients. In contrast, continuance incentives (e.g. opportunities for further contract work or opportunities to provide related services) should be more significant motivators of their job performance. For subcontractors and consultants, then, motivation to perform well will be more closely tied to opportunities for repeat or expanded business (*Proposition 22*).

Motivating Potential of Jobs

Probably the most important intrinsic incentive for non-core employees is the motivating potential of the work itself (Hackman & Oldham, 1980). Non-core workers who are engaged in important activities requiring higher-level skills should be much more motivated to perform well than transitional workers engaged in unchallenging, repetitive jobs (*Proposition 23*). Thus, we would expect the motivation levels of temporarily-employed technical consultants to be higher than those of temporary filing clerks, and the motivation levels of part-time nurses to be significantly higher than those of part-time typists.

Teamwork and Team Orientation

Yet another problem facing managers of transitional workers is creating a team-oriented work environment. The obstacles to creating teamwork even among full-time, permanent employees are daunting enough; the potential problems associated with generating team orientation among non-core employees may be even more difficult to overcome. The nature of the work itself, the relational demography of the work group, and differences in patterns of non-core employment can all influence the development of effective group behavior.

Structure of the Group Task

Pearce's work (1993), as well as the work of Davis-Blake & Uzzi (1993), suggests that the addition of non-core employees to intact work groups changes the dynamics of groups. In general, the addition of these "external" workers often shifts the tasks which require the most coordination (and which are subject to the most governmental regulation) to core employees. Because transitional workers, by definition, are not regularly present in the core organization, the integration of non-core employees and core employees into the production of goods and services may also be harder to accomplish.

As *Proposition 24* suggests, this integration of non-core and core employees will be more readily accomplished when: (a) the group project is easily divisible into individual tasks; and (b) the group project requires little cross-unit coordination. When the group project is easily divisible into individual tasks, the absence of non-core workers does not impede the ability of core workers to make progress on their own contributions to the group. Moreover, one of the greatest impediments to group effectiveness is "coordination decrements" involved in trying to schedule meetings around various members' idiosyncratic preferences and constraints (Steiner, 1966). Those coordination decrements should be lower when the group project requires little cross-unit coordination.

Cross-Training and Flexibility of Non-Core Workers

High levels of cross-training among group members should also mitigate against problems created by the absence of specific non-core workers at critical junctures in the group project. Along similar lines, coordination decrements are typically higher among groups using contingent workers because their presence in the workplace is less frequent and/or less predictable. Thus, the more flexibility non-core workers have in the days and times they can be at work, the smaller those coordination decrements should be (*Proposition 25*).

Demographic Composition of the Group

The composition of the work group also plays a role in influencing the effectiveness of non-core employees. In general, it should be easier to integrate non-core employees into ongoing groups the smaller the number of non-core employees within the group (*Proposition 26*). In large part, this is because the coordination problems multiply the greater the number of non-core employees who have to be scheduled for work or for meetings; the logistics of scheduling can become as time-consuming as performing the work itself. In addition, integrating newcomers to a work group can take significant amounts of energy from veteran employees (Feldman, 1994b). The fewer non-core employees who have to be integrated, the less overloaded veteran employees will feel in terms of bringing these transitional workers up to speed.

Along the same lines, the socialization literature suggests that demographic dissimilarity between newcomers to a group and veteran workers can influence how readily newcomers are integrated into the group (Jackson, Stone & Alvarez, 1993). When there is demographic dissimilarity between core employees and non-core employees, non-core employees may receive less information, less accurate information, and less social support from their peers; in addition, they may have more negative attributions drawn about their performance. Thus, the greater the demographic similarity between core employees and non-core employees, the more easily non-core employees may be integrated into ongoing team projects.

Type of Non-Core Employment Contract

As noted above, there are significant differences in the types of contingent employment relationships non-core workers have with their employers. Some contingent workers are employed regularly by one firm, while others are employed by multiple firms. Some contingent workers are voluntarily contingent workers, while others are involuntarily forced out of core positions. Some contingent workers are underemployed in positions which do not utilize their skills and experience, while others are satisfactorily employed in non-core positions which do utilize their talents. These differences in patterns of contingent work can have major consequences for non-core employees' investments in work teams (Feldman, 1990).

We would generally expect team contributions to be highest among permanent part-time employees, long-term subcontractors and consultants, and bridge employees (e.g. older employees working part-time before full retirement). In all these cases, the non-core employees have a longer history with the firm which cements their interpersonal relationships with core employees, increases their organizational commitment, and decreases the time needed to get up to speed on job assignments (*Proposition 27*).

In contrast, team contributions of non-core workers will be lower among temporary workers, seasonal workers, and "moonlighters" (*Proposition 28*). In the case of temporary workers, most of these employees are involuntarily out of the core workforce and underemployed (Feldman, Doerpinghaus & Turnley, 1995). Consequently, their main focus is on getting new jobs or new careers, not in investing more heavily in transient employers. For much the same reasons, seasonal workers and moonlighters may have lower team orientations as well. In the case of seasonal workers, non-core employees are simply not going to be employed long enough by a firm to become deeply involved in its business. In the case of "moonlighters" (e.g. those working in contingent positions as second jobs), employees have too many conflicting investments in their main jobs to take on unnecessary additional burdens from a second employer.

CONCLUSIONS AND IMPLICATIONS

In this final section, we explore avenues for future research on careers outside traditional organizational boundaries in terms of both theory development and research methodology. In addition, we consider the implications this important career trend has not only for the management of contingent and transitional workers by core organizations but also for the self-development of these workers themselves.

Theory Development

One particularly fruitful research paradigm which might be used to understand the career patterns of self-employed, contingent, and transitional workers is Nicholson and West's (1989) theory of work transitions. Nicholson & West suggest that most job transitions take place in four consecutive stages: preparation, encounter, adjustment, and stabilization. In addition, Nicholson and West (1989) suggest that job transitions vary along a series of dimensions, such as speed of movement, continuity between consecutive assignments, and propulsion (the extent to which the transition cycle is initiated by the person him/herself or external forces).

In the context of non-core employment, these transition cycles are both abbreviated and compressed. Workers often have little advance notice of entry (preparation) and less time to settle in and master new jobs (stabilization); moreover, workers are under greater pressure to "hit the ground running" and adjust quickly to transitional assignments (encounter and adjustment). In addition, non-core workers often have little control over the rate at which they change jobs and how much time is spent in the transition process. Using Nicholson and West's framework might be instrumental in understanding exactly which ways career transitions of non-core workers are different from those of core employees and, in so doing, also shed some light on how these career transitions could be better managed.

A second major avenue for future theoretical work is the institutional or organizational issues involved in managing the careers of non-core employees. Agency theory might be particularly helpful here. Whose interests do contingent workers serve—their own, the human resource intermediary firm which placed them, or the client organization—and how do those interests change across contingent employment relationships? Perhaps more importantly, how do different types of agency relationships influence the productivity and job effectiveness of transitional workers? As the patterns of contingent employment become more complicated than the traditional two patterns (part-time workers employed by one firm on a continuous basis and temporary workers employed by one temporary agency), these agency issues will come more to the forefront of the research agenda.

Yet another avenue for future theory development is the interrelationships between non-core employment and innovative practices of organizing, such as flextime, job-sharing, and home-working (Feldman, 1995). For example, the original conception of flextime allowed essentially full-time employees to allocate their hours at work at their convenience. However, it is less clear today whether flextime is a scheduling innovation or an alternative form of part-time work. Similarly, it is sometimes unclear whether job-sharing is a scheduling innovation or a hybrid form of contingent employment. Is "home-working" simply a shift in place of job performance or a change in the psychological contract between organizations and employees?

A fourth, and related, theoretical issue deserving future attention here is identity theory. Implicit in the discussion above is the notion that "contingentness" may be both objectively and subjectively determined. At some level, there have to be objective indices that point to some type of organizational detachment; on the other hand, there appear to be significant differences across individuals in how they perceive the peripherality of their work arrangements. How do contingent workers make sense of the surprises and contrasts they find in new job settings (Louis, 1980)? Who do contingent workers take as their referent others in making sense of their new environments and in making equity assessments? How does past job history influence workers' sense of relative deprivation or frustrated entitlements in contingent employment? In short, how workers define themselves as contingent, the meanings they attach to that definition, and whether "contingent-ness" is self-perceived as an attractive or aversive career state are critical issues to examine in the years ahead.

Research Methodology

There are three areas in terms of research methodology which are especially deserving of further attention. The first involves sampling. On the positive side, there has been extensive, well-executed research on part-time and temporary workers (see Jackofsky & Peters, 1987). On the other hand, there has been little empirical work on the smaller segments of the contingent workforce, namely, self-employed consultants, bridge-employed early retirees, "home-workers," subcontractors and free-lance employees.

As a result, we know much more about contingent employment relationships between employees and one firm to which they are fairly regularly attached, but considerably less about contingent employment relationships which are tangential to any one specific core organization. Consistent with our earlier discussion, then, greater sampling across types of contingent employment is critical to understanding the different meanings of "contingentness" to employees themselves, the different referent groups transitional workers utilize, the varying degrees of relative deprivation (or advantage) non-core employees experience, and the evolving forms of agency relationships which may be emerging.

The second direction for future methodology improvement is expansion of the set of dependent variables used. Previous research has documented fairly well the attitudinal differences both between full-time employees and contingent workers (e.g. Jackofsky & Peters, 1987) and among different groups of contingent workers (Feldman & Doerpinghaus, 1992; Feldman, Doerpinghaus & Turnley, 1995). With few exceptions, however (e.g. Davis-Blake & Uzzi, 1993; Pearce, 1993), what has been conspicuously absent in this research area is careful consideration of job performance and job effectiveness.

Part of the problem, of course, is that contingent workers are often not at any one organization long enough to be assessed. Another problem is that evaluations of contingent workers are often perfunctorily done by the providers of contingent workers rather than by the client organizations. Nonetheless, since the main reason advanced for the use of contingent and transitional workers is their cost-effectiveness, it is vital to examine whether the savings generated by lower benefit and salary costs are counterbalanced by losses in job performance.

Third, while previous research has focused on the *job* experiences of contingent workers, we know considerably less about the *career* patterns and experiences of contingent workers. As the propositions presented in the earlier sections of this chapter suggest, we need to know much more about how workers transition into and out of contingent and self-employment, the impact of contingent and self-employment on skill development and career advancement, and the influence of contingent and self-employment on self-perceived career success. Ironically, then, while we know quite a bit about how contingent workers experience their jobs, we know much less about how they experience their *careers*. Given the nature of these emergent forms of employment, that is a significant gap indeed.

Institutional Practice

While the description of contingent employment patterns has proceeded at a steady pace, prescriptive writing on the management of non-core employees has lagged significantly. With few exceptions, there has been little written on the human resource issues involved in managing contingent, transitional, and self-employed workers. As the propositions presented earlier suggest, managing these workers may require new or innovative practices in job redesign, compensation and socialization.

Perhaps the first, and foremost, issue needing additional research is the organizational decision to use contingent workers. During the wave of downsizing in the late 1980s and early 1990s, the driving force behind this decision was eliminating permanent positions and decreasing escalating benefit costs. However, as we head into the next century, there may well be other forces driving this decision, such as strategic decisions to shift core businesses, decrease the number of regular services provided for customers, increase the hours of business operation, establish strategic alliances with new ventures, and so forth. Why organizations decide to use contingent workers, then, may have important implications for how core workers are reorganized, as well as for what expectations transitional workers bring with them to their jobs.

A related issue here is the selection of contingent workers themselves. In the case of part-time and seasonal workers, most organizations have hired these employees through their own human resource departments. However, in the case of temporary workers, organizations have the option of establishing their own temp pools or choosing from a wide variety of temporary agencies. In the case of selecting consultants, subcontractors and free-lancers, the linking-up process between core organizations and service providers (or human resource intermediary firms such as executive search firms) can be even more complex. Which agency relationships are most effective for end-users is a managerial issue of paramount importance in the years ahead.

At a broader societal level, the increased use of contingent workers and self-employed workers has tremendous implications for social protections guaranteed to employees in the workplace (Feldman, 1995; Feldman & Klaas 1996). Unfortunately, the financial safety nets and protections of employee rights mandated by federal legislation frequently provide relief only for full-time permanent employees and not for their more transitional co-workers. As what it means to be an "employee" changes in the decades ahead, so, too, must legislation protecting employees change to accurately reflect the new workplace realities.

Individual Career Planning

Finally, as we head into the next century, we need to learn much more about the role of contingent employment and self-employment in terms of individuals' own career planning. As some of the earlier propositions suggest, there appear to be both organizational factors (such as the opportunity structures for an occupation and industry growth) and individual factors (such as age, career stage and marital status) that facilitate or impede the career progression of contingent and self-employed workers.

The main message from large, established firms to employees over the past decade has been: don't rely on us for continued employment. As a result, more and more employees have entered some kind of contingent or self-employment relationship, voluntarily or involuntarily, to cope with widespread downsizing. However, the nature of contingent employment and self-employment present substantial obstacles to workers in terms of creating opportunities for further skill development, generating opportunities for further career advancement, and managing transitions both between contingent work arrangements and between contingent and core employment.

Given the lack of institutional career support currently provided to these workers, how they plan and manage their own careers will largely determine both the financial and psychological success they derive from workforce participation. Given that contingent and self-employment already accounts for roughly 33% of US jobs today, how to manage careers outside traditional organizational boundaries may well become the dominant career issue in the century ahead.

REFERENCES

Brett, J.M. (1984). Job transitions and personal and role development. In K.M. Rowland & G.R. Ferris (eds), *Research in Personnel and Human Resources Management*, vol. 12 (pp. 155–85). Greenwich, CT: JAI Press.

Dalton, G.W., Thompson, P.H. & Price, R.L. (1977). The four stages of professional careers: a new look at performance by professionals. *Organizational Dynamics*, **6**, 19–42.

Davis-Blake, A. & Uzzi, B. (1993). Determinants of employment externalization: the case of temporary workers and independent contractors. *Administrative Science Quarterly*, **29**, 195–223.

Doeringer, P.B. (1990). *Bridges to Retirement*. Ithaca, NY: Cornell University Press.

Feldman, D.C. (1990). Reconceptualizing the nature and consequences of part-time work. *Academy of Management Review*, **15**, 103–12.

Feldman, D.C. (1994a). The decision to retire early: a review and conceptualization. *Academy of Management Review*, **19**, 285–311.

Feldman, D.C. (1994b). Who's socializing whom? The impact of the socialization of newcomers on insiders, work groups, and organizations. *Human Resource Management Review*, **4**, 213–33.

Feldman, D.C. (1995). Part-time and temporary employment relationships: achieving fit between individual needs and organizational demands. In M. London (ed.), *Employees, Careers, and Job Creation* (pp. 121–41). San Francisco, CA: Jossey-Bass.

Feldman, D.C. & Doerpinghaus, H.I. (1992). Patterns of part-time employment. *Journal of Vocational Behavior*, **41**, 282–94.

Feldman, D.C., Doerpinghaus, H.I. & Turnley, W.H. (1995). Employee reactions to temporary jobs. *Journal of Managerial Issues*, **7**, 125–41.

Feldman, D.C. & Klaas, B.S. (1996). Temporary workers: employee rights and employer responsibilities. *Employee Rights and Responsibilities Journal*, **9**, 1–21.

Graham, J.W. (1991). An essay on organizational citizenship behavior. *Employee Rights and Responsibilities Journal*, **4**, 249–70.

Greenberger, E. & Steinberg, L. (1986). *When Teenagers Work*. New York: Basic Books.

Hackman, J.R. & Oldham, G.R. (1980). *The Design of Work*. Reading, MA: Addison-Wesley.

Jackofsky, E.F. & Peters. L.H. (1987). Part-time versus full-time employment status differences: a replication and extension. *Journal of Occupational Behavior*, **8**, 1–9.

Jackson, S.E., Stone, V.K. & Alvarez, E.B. (1993). Socialization amidst diversity: the impact of demographics on work team oldtimers and newcomers. In B.M. Staw & L.L. Cummings (eds), *Research in Organizational Behavior*, vol. 15 (pp. 45–109). Greenwich, CT: JAI Press.

Kaufman, H. (1982). *Professionals in Search of Work*. New York: Wiley.

Kilty, K.M. & Behling, J.H. (1985). Predicting the retirement intentions and attitudes of professional workers. *Journal of Gerontology*, **40**, 219–27.

Kram, K.E. (1985). *Mentoring at Work*. Glenview, IL: Scott Foresman.

Lawler, E.E. III (1981). *Pay and Organization Development*. Reading, MA: Addison-Wesley.

Louis, M.R. (1980). Surprise and sense making: what newcomers experience in entering unfamiliar organizational settings. *Administrative Science Ouarterly*, **25**, 225–51.

Louis, M.R., Posner, B.Z. & Powell, G.N. (1983). The availability and helpfulness of socialization practices. *Personnel Psychology*, **26**, 857–66.

Nicholson, N. & West, M. (1989). Transitions, work histories, and careers. In M.B. Arthur, D.T. Hall & B.S. Lawrence (eds), *Handbook of Career Theory* (pp. 181–201). Cambridge: Cambridge University Press.

Pearce, J. (1993). Toward an organizational behavior of contract laborers: their psychological involvement and effects on employee co-workers. *Academy of Management Journal*, **36**, 1082–96.

Pfeffer, J. (1982). *Organizations and Organization Theory*. Marshfield, MA: Pittman.

Rotchford, N. & Roberts, K. (1982). Part-time workers as missing persons in organizational research. *Academy of Management Review*, **7**, 228–34.

Rothberg, D.S. & Cook, B.E. (1985). *Part-time Professionals*. Washington, DC: Acropolis Books.

Schein, E.H. (1978). *Career Dynamics: Matching Individual and Organizational Needs*. Reading, MA: Addison-Wesley.

Steiner, I.D. (1966). Models for inferring relationships between group size and potential group productivity. *Behavioral Science*, 11 273–83.

Van Maanen, J. & Schein, E.H. (1979). Toward a theory of organizational socialization. In L.L. Cummings & B.M. Staw (eds), *Research in Organizational Behavior*, vol. 1 (pp. 209–64). Greenwich, CT: JAI Press.

Chapter 19

New Directions in Social Network Research on Gender and Organizational Careers

Herminia Ibarra
Harvard University, Boston, MA, USA
and
Lynn Smith-Lovin
University of Arizona, Tucson, AZ, USA

Networks of relationships play a central role in the career development process. Networks directly shape the course of careers by regulating access to jobs, providing mentoring and sponsorship, channeling the flow of information and referrals, augmenting power and reputations, and increasing the likelihood and speed of promotion (e.g. Brass, 1984; Burt, 1992; Granovetter, 1973; Kram, 1988; Ibarra, 1995). Fueled by persistent evidence of labor market inequalities in the distribution of income, power and status to men and women in the workplace (see Baron & Pfeffer, 1994, for a review), a growing stream of research has investigated differences between men's and women's networks and the effects of such differences on career-related outcomes (Burt, 1992; Brass, 1985; Ibarra, 1992). To date, however, no comprehensive perspective on networks and women's careers has been offered. Given the trend toward more flexible forms of organization, in which managers must increasingly rely on networks to get things done (Kanter, 1995) and the frequently suggested link between networks and women's inability to crack the glass ceiling (Morrison, White & Velsor, 1987), an understanding of gender and career networks is of both theoretical and practical importance.

This chapter focuses on the processes through which gender and networks

Creating Tomorrow's Organizations. Edited by C.L. Cooper and S.E. Jackson.
© 1997 John Wiley & Sons Ltd.

shape professional and managerial careers. We have three primary objectives: we review the current state of knowledge on gender, networks and careers; we argue in favor of a "social interactionist" theoretical perspective; and we suggest three areas for future research.

First, we summarize the current state of knowledge on networks, gender and careers. Although situational factors such as formal position (Ibarra, 1992), work-group affiliation (Brass, 1985) or occupation (Aldrich, Reese & Dubini, 1989; Moore, 1990) account for most of the variance in features of men's and women's networks, the existing evidence suggests that different network configurations appear to be effective in promoting the careers of men and women. We attempt to explain the contingent effects and suggest that future research should shift focus from comparing men's and women's networks towards exploring why different networks work for women and men, and what factors affect the formation of networks with such characteristics.

Second, we propose that the relationship between gender and career outcomes must be understood from a *social* structural perspective. A social structural perspective underscores the embeddedness of social relationships within structural contexts that govern the availability and ease of developing various kinds of social contacts (Pfeffer, 1983). We depart from a strictly structural approach, which focuses on formal positions and their distributions across organizations, industries and occupations but ignores their effect on emergent, i.e. non-prescribed, interaction patterns (see Baron & Pfeffer, 1994, for a review). We also take a different view from that of researchers concerned with one-on-one career relationships such as mentoring ties (Kram, 1988), who do not study the broader informal structures in which those specific ties are embedded. The perspective we adopt, therefore, is *interactional*: in this chapter, we attempt to bridge the gap between causal processes at the macro-structural level of socio-economic organization and those operating at the individual level.

The point of view we adopt also departs from current views on the formation of network ties in organizational settings that rest on conceptions of rational actors striving to maximize the economic utility of their networks by competing with others for scarce instrumental resources. As noted by DiMaggio (1992, p. 122), prevailing models:

> often treat network membership and the access of each member to relations with others as fixed, actors as having a keen sense of their utility functions, and information as either abundant or a resource to which access is constrained by existing relational networks . . . [Such assumptions have] greatest applicability to stable networks under conditions of relatively low uncertainty.

We argue below that such assumptions are no longer widely valid. Work careers and the organizations in which they occur have changed in the past decades. Yet network studies are conducted largely as though the old assumptions of institutional stability still hold: they have not explored in much depth the social processes that affect network formation and produce career outcomes, have failed to account for network change, and have studied networks only within relatively narrow organizational boundaries. Therefore, we suggest that future research on gender and careers would benefit from a network perspective that shifts emphasis from linking outcomes and static structures to exploring dynamic processes and interaction strategies, and from research conducted within organizational boundaries to studies that span the boundaries of work, family and community. We argue that combining structural, social psychological and social constructionist perspectives (e.g. Baron & Pfeffer, 1994; Kilduff & Krackhardt, 1994) has the potential for offering insights that cannot be understood from any single perspective.

Our third and final objective is to suggest three areas—social identity, impression management and cumulative processes—for further research and theory development. The relationship between social identity and social networks has been remarkably under-investigated. Yet, social psychological processes such as social comparison, categorization and attraction, which shape social identity, provide the conceptual underpinning for prevalent network theories. We argue that social identity theory provides a theoretical framework for understanding the processes of network formation and change, given structural constraints such as organizational demography. Further, although the empirical evidence points to the effects of social networks on the interpretation of one's social environment, this body of knowledge has not been applied to career-relevant phenomena, including the development of reputation and signaling or impression management processes. The ability to display role-appropriate attributes to decision-makers significantly affects the course of careers. Drawing from symbolic interaction theories, we suggest that social networks affect the extent to which individuals learn, comply with and internalize organizational and occupational norms regarding the presentation of self. Finally, the dynamic processes that shape both networks and careers are often mentioned but infrequently investigated. Differences in the starting points of careers explain much of the variance in the positions achieved by men and women later in their careers. We argue that longitudinal network research is needed to investigate how interaction processes produce differential rates of return on credentials, achieved positions and social resources for men and women. Additionally, only dynamic analyses can take into account the effects of life-course factors on careers.

The chapter is organized into four sections. The first section briefly reviews social network theory and research on gender and careers to date. The second section elaborates on the three research themes noted above. A brief third section highlights some of the methodological implications of these new directions. The final section of the chapter considers our suggestions in light of the changing nature of organizations and organizational careers (e.g. Hall, 1996), in particular, the suggested demise of the internal labor market, increasing workforce diversity, and changing organizational forms.

RESEARCH TO DATE ON SOCIAL NETWORKS AND CAREERS

Networks of relationships are social resources. While some resources, such as sponsorship or career advice, derive directly from particular one-on-one relationships, social network theory argues that it is the structural or aggregate features of any set of relationships that most critically affect the flow of information and the distribution of opportunities. Networks not only provide direct and indirect access to resources, they also serve as signals of the current or likely future status of an individual. Being perceived to have connections to the "right people", for example, has a positive effect on individuals' reputations as effective performers (Kilduff anpersand Krackhardt, 1994).

Two types of network research may be distinguished. Research at the system or organizational level aims to discern the structure of relations among all actors who co-exist within defined boundaries, such as an organization or department. Research in this domain has focused on the determinants and consequences of holding more or less central positions, or on the incidence and structure of cliques, i.e. subgroups of dense interaction, and blocks of structurally equivalent individuals. By contrast, research at the "egocentric" or personal network level examines the set of relationships defined by a focal individual and his/her contacts with others, without collecting comprehensive data on the network relationships of the contacts. Egocentric research has focused on the types of people and types of relationships that the focal individual's network comprises. These affect the ability of contacts to offer useful resources as well as their propensity to offer them to the focal individual (see Marsden, 1990; Smith-Lovin & McPherson, 1992, for a more detailed review of types of network research). As we discuss in more detail below, we argue that future research will need to rely increasingly on egocentric rather than system-based methods because boundary definition has become more difficult in today's organizations (Hall, 1996). The boundary definition problem is exacerbated in research on women's careers. Because of the relative scarcity of professional and managerial women in certain sectors, different boundaries may be relevant for men and women working in the same jobs and firms.

Network Centrality

People who are centrally located within organization-wide webs of interaction have greater control over scarce resources and enjoy a broad array of benefits and opportunities unavailable to those on the periphery of the network (Burt, 1992; Brass, 1984; Ibarra, 1993). Network centrality is correlated with perceived power, promotion (Brass, 1984), and ability to diagnose the "political landscape" (Krackhardt, 1992). A broad range of research also suggests that centrality has a powerful effect on attitudes and perceptions predicting a range of career-related phenomena, including job satisfaction, perceptions of ability to take risks, feelings of belonging or acceptance, and organizational commitment (see Rice, 1993; Ibarra & Andrews, 1993, for reviews).

Network Composition

The literature on "egocentric" networks emphasizes the career benefits of personal networks characterized by weak ties, non-redundant relationships, and high range. Tie strength is a function of the amount of time, the emotional closeness, and the frequency of interaction that characterize a relationship (Granovetter, 1973, p. 1361). Weak ties derive their power from serving as bridges through which socially distant ideas, influences or information reach the individual (Granovetter, 1973) and as means for contact with people of higher status (Lin, 1982). Strong ties, by contrast, tend to connect people to similar others, and thus, a network high in strong ties is more likely to link the individual to interconnected parties and redundant resources, and to confine interaction to people of similar social and occupational status.

Most empirical support for the "strength of weak ties" argument has been confined to studies of finding a job (Boxman, DeGraaf & Flap, 1991; Lin, Ensel & Vaughn, 1981; Granovetter, 1982). Burt (1992), however, argues that the relevant measure is not the "weakness" of a tie but non-redundance—the absence of interconnection among the focal individual's network contacts. In a study of managerial careers, he finds that those managers with non-redundant networks advanced more quickly in their careers. Strong ties of trust and loyalty, however, ensure reliability under conditions of uncertainty (Kanter, 1977; Krackhardt, 1992). Access to career resources such as coaching and advocacy for promotion may require stronger ties than other types of instrumental resources (Kram, 1988; Podolny & Baron, 1996). Appropriate balancing and usage of strong and weak ties, however, has not yet been investigated.

Range refers directly to the diversity of group affiliations contained within a personal network. For the same reasons cited above, a broad range of network relationships provides greater access to instrumental resources than contacts drawn from a restricted group. People whose network contacts extend beyond their required workflow interactions, immediate workgroups or work units tend to be perceived as more powerful (Brass, 1984). But the status of those contacts is also key (Lin, 1982). Having contacts within an organization's "dominant coalition" tends to be correlated with power and future promotion (Brass, 1984). External contacts may be particularly critical. Professional association or club memberships and informal interaction with managers in other firms predicted managerial income attainment, net of education, work experience and hierarchical level (Boxman, DeGraaf & Flap, 1991), and intra-organizational centrality (Ibarra, 1992; Miller, 1986).

Gender Differences in Networks

A social structural perspective on gender and attainment calls attention to two broad categories of factors that significantly shape social networks: sex stratification and cognitive bias. In the USA, women are under-represented in high-level managerial positions, particularly in Fortune 500 firms (O'Leary & Ickovics, 1992). Men and women are segregated into different jobs, occupations, firms and industries, such that women are over-represented in lower prestige and lower-paying jobs (see Baron & Pfeffer, 1994, for a review). Consequently, relative to their male counterparts, women usually have a smaller pool of high-status, same-gender contacts available to them for informal interaction (Ibarra, 1992). As well, the structure of sex roles outside the workplace often contributes additional constraints on interaction patterns for women (Ross, 1987).

A second category of contextual influences that shape networks encompasses a range of phenomena including categorization, cognitive and attribution processes. These processes are both cause and consequence of stratification patterns (Baron & Pfeffer, 1994). Perceptions of who is trustworthy, powerful (i.e. has valued resources available for exchange) and upwardly mobile—which are highly subject to gender bias (O'Leary & Ickovics, 1992)—directly shape networks by affecting an individual's currency for informal exchange (Kilduff & Krackhardt, 1994). These perceptions can pose significant network development barriers for women, as cognitive processes interact with structural features of the organizational context to perpetuate patterns of advantage and disadvantage (Baron & Pfeffer, 1994; Ridgeway, 1991). As discussed below, although the impact of macrostructural phenomena on network interaction patterns and their consequences is relatively well understood, the role of cognitive and interaction processes in shaping women's social networks has been under-investigated.

Structural Factors

The empirical evidence to date suggests that three factors—formal position, organizational demography and life-course factors—account for most gender differences in networks. Most effects of gender on networks appear to be mediated by the effects of position. Men and women in similar jobs, occupations and hierarchical levels attain similarly central positions (Brass, 1985; Ibarra, 1992; Miller, 1986) and have similar egocentric networks (Burt, 1992; Aldrich, Reese & Dubini, 1989; Moore, 1990). But since men and women, on average, tend to attain different levels and hold different jobs, organizational demography constrains the pool of potential network contacts who are both "homophilous" (i.e. similar on the basis of gender) and influential (Ibarra, 1992). Consequently, women who work in male-dominated industries, firms or jobs tend to differ from men in similar settings in the homophily of workplace ties (i.e. the extent of same-gender relationships). Accordingly, McPherson & Smith-Lovin (1987) distinguish between induced homophily, which is the result of availability of different types of contacts, and choice homophily, resulting from preferences for interaction with like-others, which can only be ascertained after considering organizationally-induced homophily. In highly segregated environments, induced homophily is likely to dominate, with little variance in network composition explained by choice within groups.

Finally, a range of family and life-course factors seem to account for significant gender differences in networks. In particular, kinship ties tend to account for a greater proportion of women's ties and this effect is heightened with child-rearing, even when the effects of occupation are held constant (Campbell, 1988; Fischer & Oliker, 1983; Moore, 1990). Kinship ties create diversity in age, educational background and sex, but limit the range and status of network ties on other dimensions (Marsden, 1987) and, thus, their career instrumentality. Men and women in professional and managerial jobs, however, do not differ significantly in their non-kinship networks (Moore, 1990).

Alternative Routes

Other evidence suggests that women's career outcomes are not necessarily hampered by their inability to develop useful networks, but instead indicates that women have to use different network means to achieve the same career goals as men. Many studies, reviewed in more detailed below, find that an interaction between gender and human capital or structural position—rather than main effects for either—explains network characteristics. Similarly, the empirical evidence to date suggests that gender interacts with network characteristics to account for career outcomes.

A series of studies designed to explore the relationships between gender and centrality in intra-organizational networks found no gender differences in centrality—once the effects of formal position and human capital were held constant—but did find significant differences in the ability of men and women to convert positional and human capital resources into network centrality (Ibarra, 1992; Miller, 1986; Miller, Lincoln & Olson, 1981). In particular, attributes such as hierarchical rank, educational attainment and external professional contacts earned men greater access to more central positions than they did women.

More recently, Burt (1992) found that men and women managers did not differ in network structure but in the relationship between network structure and speed of career mobility. While men's mobility was fostered by "bridging ties" to people who were not directly connected to one another, women required strong ties to strategic partners to signal their legitimacy and, thus, contribute to their advancement. Burt hypothesized that networks dominated by strong ties, while potentially detrimental for men, are beneficial for women by serving to compensate for women's lower status and legitimacy in the managerial world. This interpretation is consistent with Ibarra's (1997) findings of a gender by opportunity interaction effect in predicting the strength of network ties: while men and women in middle management jobs did not differ in the strength of their information and career network relationships, gender differences emerged within the subgroup of those managers that had been slotted for their organizations' fast-tracks. The fast-track men reported networks much like those of Burt's highly mobile managers, while the fast-track women built networks that were higher in both the tie strength and range of contacts. These organizational findings bolster Granovetter's (1982) conclusion that weak ties are less advantageous for people in insecure positions, whether economically or socially; they are also consistent with findings from the mentoring literature which suggest that close mentoring relationships are particularly critical for women's careers (Noe, 1988).

Another reason why women appear to use different network routes than men may be the limits on availability of women in the workplace. Men's workplace ties are primarily with men, regardless of the type of relationship involved; women, by contrast, tend to have "functionally differentiated" networks, in which ties to men provide certain types of instrumental access, while relationships with a mix of men and women provide social support and friendship (Ibarra, 1992; Lincoln & Miller, 1979). Although few have studied the career consequences of homophily, Brass (1985) found that homophilous networks were more detrimental for women than for men because the firm's dominant coalition, which controlled the promotion process, was male. In a study of middle managers, Ibarra (1997), by contrast, found a significant correlation between advancement opportunity and same-gender ties for women. She concludes that, when women are under-represented in managerial and professional ranks, homophilous ties play a key role in gaining advice from others who have experienced similar obstacles and psychosocial supports such as role-modeling (Kram, 1988). Thus, women may respond to limited availability of homophilous contacts by reaching beyond the immediate work-groups or functional areas to establish informal contact with other women. Similarly, minorities have support networks that span a broader range of groups than whites, as a result of their relationships with other minorities outside their departments and firms (Ibarra, 1995; Thomas, 1990).

In sum, in most business contexts, not only do men and women differ in their opportunity for informal interaction with high-status, same-gender others (Ibarra, 1992), but "female" is a lower ascribed status than "male" (Ridgeway, 1991), women's power positions are less legitimate (Burt, 1992), different expectations concerning appropriate behavior are communicated to men and women (O'Leary & Ickovics, 1992), and men and women are subject to different role demands outside the workplace (Hochschild, 1989). Consequently, men and women holding structurally equivalent formal positions may be viewed as operating in different social contexts that require different network configurations to accomplish similar career objectives.

In our view, this pattern of findings raises critical questions for future research on gender and careers. First, what are the processes by which men and women come to develop different types of networks? Beyond contextual factors, what are the key determinants of network formation? Second, what are the interactional and social construction processes by which social capital like status and legitimacy accrues to some individuals at higher rates than others? Finally, are there significant divergences, obstacles and opportunities that occur at particular junctures in men's and women's career paths? What facilitates the course of network change to meet new career requirements? These questions are the subject of the following section, which outlines new directions for theory and research.

NEW THEORETICAL DIRECTIONS: FROM STRUCTURES TO PROCESSES

Social Identity and Networks

The development of a professional identity has been a central theme in the careers literature (Schein, 1978). Although identity development occurs in the context of a network of relationships, little empirical research has investigated the relationship between identity and networks. Social identity, which may encompass professional identity, refers to "the perception of oneness with or belongingness to some human aggregate" (Ashforth & Mael, 1989, p. 21). Below we argue that network development may be viewed fruitfully as the enactment of social identity. Conversely, social identities are shaped by the social contexts in which they develop.

Effects of Identity on Network Formation

Most network research has focused on outcomes of social networks, paying relatively little attention to their antecedents. Perhaps this is because most organizational network research has operated under a strong assumption that people seek to maximize instrumental value from their contacts. Social identity theory suggests that network behavior is not only driven by instrumental motives, but that it is also an expression of social identity (Foote, 1951). However, the simple existence of homophily on some trait is not sufficient motive for tie formation: because ascribed categories such as gender acquire their meaning in the context of social interaction, we argue below that social identity precedes homophily. Following Wharton (1992), we emphasize the importance of developing frameworks for understanding how demographic characteristics such as gender become social categories that shape interaction patterns. Further, people may be similar on a wide range of dimensions, not simply gender. Social identity theory, therefore, may be used to predict when and how different dimensions of similarity and difference are activated to shape network patterns.

Social identity theory (Tajfel & Turner, 1985; Turner & Oakes, 1989) suggests that people classify themselves and others in terms of social categories such as gender, racial or ethnic group, organizational membership or religious affiliation, and in terms that define themselves and others relative to individuals in other categories. Individuals participate in activities and institutions that are congruent with valued aspects of their identities (Stryker & Serpe, 1982; O'Reilly & Chatman, 1986). From a network development perspective, therefore, identity affects the choice of social contexts within which potential network contacts are available (induced homophily), as well as the discretionary contacts that are developed within those contexts (choice homophily). People are "selective" in forming their networks. They "create self-confirmatory structures—social environments that foster the survival of their self-views—by choosing interaction partners and social settings that assist them in confirming their self concepts" (Swann, 1987). Thus, one may expect a predominance of network ties to people who are members of a group with which the individual is identified. As such, social identity theory provides a fundamentally different perspective on the motivation underlying individuals' explicit or implicit network behaviors. Instead of acting only to maximize instrumental resources, people seek to enact their identities.

One important way in which this perspective is relevant for research on gender and careers concerns how gender identity affects the homophily of women's networks. In work environments in which the distribution of power and status favors men numerically, the extent to which gender is a salient identity will affect women's interaction choices. These choices affect their networks on a variety of structural dimensions (Ibarra, 1993). A social identity perspective may also help to explain why large within-gender and within-race group differences in homophily have been found in previous studies (Ibarra, 1997). Women and minorities vary in the strength of their identification with these categorizations in systematic ways; this fact may explain their network formation.

A key question for future research, therefore, is what factors moderate the relationship between organizational demography and network structure? Although the pool of available, prescribed and useful relationships will be constrained by job requirements, management structure and organizational demography (Blau, 1977; Pfeffer, 1983), we argue that the formation of discretionary relationships and the definition of the boundaries within which people construct their networks may be affected systematically by social identity processes. This perspective is consistent with a broader body of research that highlights the relationship between demography and social identity, and their effects on the nature of social interactions. Thomas (1993) found that minorities holding similar formal positions differed with regard to racial identity, and that their identities influenced the nature of the relationships they established. In particular, identities shaped the demographic and cognitive attributes of the mentors they sought out. Ely (1994) discovered a significant correlation between organizational demography and constructions of gender identity, which, in turn, affected the nature of peer and hierarchical relationships among women in law firms. Chatman & Brown (1996), in a study of network formation among MBA students, found that social identity mediated the effects of demographic similarity at the dyadic level on friendship formation: identification with one's gender or race group explained variance in the development of friendship ties over and above that explained by demography.

Another way in which social identity theory can enhance research on gender and career network structures is by directing attention to a previously unresearched problem. Much social network theory and research is premised on the researcher's ability to determine the appropriate boundaries of a social network (Marsden, 1990) and on the availability of contacts within particular organizational groups (Blau, 1977). A social identity perspective, however, suggests that the categorizations that are salient to individuals influence the pools from which they draw their network contacts. Therefore, the choice of the scope of a network becomes a theoretically interesting question, rather than a methodological decision made for the researcher's convenience.

The Effects of Network on Identity

Social identity theory also provides a framework within which to explore competing bases for homophily and their effect on aggregate network characteristics, which in turn, affect social identity. People have multiple identities (e.g. consultant, wife, mother, tennis player, Protestant), but these are viewed as hierarchically organized by their degree of *commitment* or network-embeddedness (Stryker & Serpe, 1982). Commitment is a function of the number, affective importance, and multiplexity of network ties that are formed by the person when enacting the identity (Thoits, 1983). To the extent that an individual has many valued relationships that are premised on her social identity as a lawyer, for example, and the nature of the interaction is multidimensional (e.g. the ties are both professional and friendship ties), then commitment to that identity is high. Increased commitment heightens the prominence of the identity, increasing the probability that it will be invoked across a variety of situations and that new network ties will be formed on the basis of homophily on this dimension. Rewarding experiences in a role identity increase the salience of the role; alternatively, investments in a role may decrease as commitment to alternatives increases (Stryker & Serpe, 1982). Within the self-structure, one's various identities compete for the time and energy that it takes to maintain network ties.

Different environments offer different opportunities for maintaining or developing identities. For example, identities are much more likely to become salient in environments where there is intergroup differentiation (Tajfel & Turner, 1985). Skewed patterns of minority and majority representation at the workgroup and organizational level are especially likely to make identities perceptually and behaviorally prominent in social interaction (Kanter, 1977; Wharton, 1992). In this way, organizational demography has a profound effect on the identities that are salient at work. Within a given environment, the relationship between a person's network and social identity is dynamically self-reinforcing, as identities that are frequently enacted lead to the development of network ties that increase identity commitment. As those ties provide positive social support or information on how to deal with organizational tasks effectively, commitment leads to greater prominence of the identity.

Because gender is not the only basis for identification, research is needed to investigate whether and when sex-based homophily is a more important basis for perceived similarity than, for example, sharing a similar educational background or occupation, as well as to explore potential interaction effects among varying forms of homophily (Brass, 1985). Of interest, therefore, would be research designs aimed at uncovering those factors that have the greatest impact on social and professional identity. These may include socialization and career development practices, and organizational and occupational cultures (Barley, 1989). Job characteristics, such as degree of professionalization, are also likely to affect both identity and network by affecting the number of organizational contexts in which "like-others" may be found. Similarly, exploring how cosmopolitan and local identities may shape women's networks may be particularly fruitful, because a key distinction between cosmopolitans and locals involves the boundaries within which they construct their lives and careers (Merton, 1968; Kanter, 1995). We will want to explore how relationships formed in different contexts (e.g. within the work organization, across similar work organizations, within the community outside work, etc.) affect identities that are enacted at work.

Networks and Impression Management

As reflections of social identity, networks also serve as signals to others about the current status or probable future of an individual. Spence (1974) argued that human capital influences job and promotion decisions only to the extent that these assets can be observed by decision-makers. Since managerial abilities of interest to decision-makers are not easy to observe accurately (Kanter, 1977), alternative indicators often are used as proxies. The ability to signal desirable traits, such as competence and career advancement potential, affects an individual's ability to attract influential actors to his/her network circle. Personal networks both influence others' perceptions of the status of an individual, while simultaneously influencing the individual's capacity to acquire tacit knowledge concerning role requirements and to internalize those requirements. Again, network structures work in a dynamically self-reinforcing manner, influencing both perceptions and real resources that will, over time, serve to confirm perceptions.

Two sets of research questions in this domain may be particularly productive. The first concerns the effect of social networks on reputational processes. The second area pertains to the processes by which individuals actively signal the identities they want to achieve. Such impression management efforts affect individuals' abilities to develop certain types of ties; yet, the relationships in which people are embedded constrain the availability of models for an effective and appropriate presentation of self. As discussed below, gender intervenes in both processes in ways that are not yet well understood.

Networks and Reputation

Kilduff & Krackhardt (1994) conceptualized the development of reputation in internal labor markets as a cognitive process that unfolds within a social context, but is distinct from structural characteristics of that context. They found that both job performance measures and co-workers' perceptions that individuals had strong friendship ties to prominent actors contributed positively to reputation, but actually having ties to prominent individuals had no effect. More generally, social information processing plays a particularly important role in shaping perceptions under conditions of uncertainty or ambiguity. When judgments are problematic, people are more likely to arrive at socially derived interpretations of events (Salancik & Pfeffer, 1978). In cross-gender relationships, however, it has been well documented that strong ties between a prominent man and junior woman are often viewed with suspicion (Kram, 1988). Further, if effective networks for men and women differ, then whether they establish reputations by different means is a question that merits inquiry.

A recent study by Burt & Knez (1996) begins to answer that question. Building on Burt's (1992) previous finding that the correlation between network structure and speed of mobility varies by gender, Burt & Knez (1996) explore the ways in which network structure affects the development of trust. They find that indirect connections to third parties amplify trust, increasing the effects of trust within strong relations, while at the same time they significantly increase distrust within weak relations. They also find a third-party interaction effect with gender: trust between men and women is as likely as between people of the same sex, but is more affected by third parties. Networks associated with mobility for women— networks based on strong ties to sponsors who "lend" their contacts to the protege—however, are found to be especially prone to amplifying distrust. The findings suggest that the relationship between network structure and career mobility may be moderated by the extent to which gaining the trust of key others is problematic.

Thus, network ties may serve as signals of status, playing a formative role in the development of reputation. Yet, particularly in early career, when a person's professional network is in the formative stages, the question remains of what it is that allows an individual to attract the attention of prominent players to his/her network. To answer this question, we turn to the role of impression management processes and their relationship to social networks.

Networks and Self-Presentation

Although few studies have made direct linkages between networks and the presentation of self, a broad body of research indicates that the interpretation of behavior and the extent to which norms regarding the presentation of self are learned, internalized and viewed as legitimate role requirements may be a function of the social network in which the individual is embedded (Ashforth & Humphrey, 1993). This has direct applicability to the social identity issues highlighted above, as well as the study of cumulative processes, which we recommend in the next section.

While previous researchers have emphasized the social context in which individuals learn the "rules" about what constitutes an appropriate presentation of self, context has been largely examined at the dyadic level (e.g. status differences between service provider and client, Hochschild, 1983) or the organizational level (e.g. occupational norms and socialization mechanisms; Van Maanen & Barley, 1984). The informal network context in which display rules are learned has been relatively overlooked. Strong network relationships facilitate the learning of tacit knowledge (March & Olsen, 1975), foster personal and group identification (Kram, 1988) and, as noted above, affect the salience and time commitment that people accord to their multiple-role identities (Stryker & Serpe, 1982). But having a broad range of ties to different types of people is also important, as this affects the likelihood of finding appropriate role models (Ibarra, 1996).

Impression management is also highly relevant to the study of factors that affect the course of women's careers. In most organizations, men and women face different burdens of proof in establishing their competence. In research on the glass ceiling (Morrison, White & Velsor, 1987), an "inappropriate image" was found to be a key derailment factor for women but not for men. The perspective suggested here calls attention, not to traits such as "competitiveness" or "cooperativeness" which are attributed by some psychologists to gender differences in sex-role socialization (e.g. Gilligan, 1982), but to the relationship context, in which people come to understand and view as legitimate the more tacit elements of a role's success requirements and to identify with their firm, profession, senior role-models and peers.

We are especially interested in ways that the composition of a person's network affect their success in learning an appropriate presentation of self. With progression to higher career levels, role performances become more individualized and more difficult to prescribe on technical grounds. Finding a successful personal style for accomplishing interactions with others is a key component of success at these levels. Having a larger and broader array of network contacts as role models may enhance one's ability to find a workable pattern of behavioral interaction (Ibarra, 1996). For those in a minority position, finding a contact that has successfully addressed the legitimacy problems that come with that identity may be key to finding an effective style in the new, more prestigious positions.

Networks and the Career Cycle over Time

As noted by Doreian (1990, p. 245), "any serious analysis of social processes must include time, as processes are realized through time". Network research has focused, conceptually and methodologically, on stability rather than change. Although a few organizational researchers have documented the dynamic nature of networks, particularly as they affect and are affected by organizational and technological changes (e.g. Barley, 1989), the dominant focus has been on the endurance of social structure and its dependence on slowly changing organizational characteristics such as demography. A compelling argument for such an emphasis is that, while the specific actors comprising the network will change over time, the patterns of interaction and structural features of networks tend to remain stable (McPherson, Popielarz & Drobnic, 1992).

Both of the sections above—on differential bases of social identification and on the impression-management implications of networks—argue for a more dynamic research strategy. We suggest three reasons why the dynamic study of networks is essential to understanding relationships among gender, networks and careers. First, at the macro-level, differential patterns of hiring, promotion and attrition for men and women in managerial and professional careers (Baron & Pfeffer, 1994) are likely to affect the accumulation of social capital over time. Cumulative advantage and disadvantage processes at the informal level are also important, but have not been studied extensively. Second, at the micro-level, careers develop in passage through transitions. Although career transitions have been conceptualized as requiring major changes in role relationships and networks, these transitions typically have not been studied with network methods. Finally, research on the balance of work and family has not only lacked the benefit of a network perspective but, as we argue below, requires attention to changes over time in the social contexts in which work and family arrangements are negotiated.

Cumulative Processes

Research to date on careers supports the theories of cumulative advantage or disadvantage. Rosenbaum (1984) found that small differences in starting salaries accumulate to produce large salary differentials by mid-career. The promotion process is a tournament, where winning earlier rounds is necessary for competition in subsequent ones. Scant research, however, has examined cumulative informal processes. Small informal network differences in early career can culminate to create positions at the center or periphery of elite informal circles in later career. Further, while early career promotions are more likely to be based on technical skills and knowledge, at mid-career more subjective factors play a more important role. At these later career stages, all the candidates will be competent technical performers, and success potential becomes more ambiguous (Kanter, 1977).

The empirical evidence indicates that the types of ties that may be most useful in early career, in getting a job, or at lower status levels (Lin, 1982; Lin, Ensel anpersand Vaughn, 1981) may be quite different than those that those that become important over the long term. Evidence suggests that business school networks, which develop in a context in which the proportions of men and women are more balanced than in the workplace, and in which friendship may be expected to play a stronger role in tie formation, are nevertheless strongly stratified by gender (Chatman & Brown, 1996). Even earlier, college networks have a significant impact on starting salaries, which, in turn, significantly affect later salaries: Belliveau (1996) found that women graduating from elite women's colleges received lower starting salaries than women from elite co-educational institutions. Their human capital was the same but their social capital differed significantly. The coeds were able to compare notes on current market rates with the undergraduate men in their social networks; the women from the women's colleges had lesser access to such information. How small differences in informal networks in early career may cumulate to produce a position on the periphery of elite informal circles in later-career merits empirical investigation.

Further, the intervening processes that produce this cumulative advantage need to be studied. We do not know much, for example, about processes of tie formation and tie loss, although they appear to be different processes (McPherson, Popielarz & Drobnic, 1992). Do the "old" weak ties become stronger over time for those who are more successful, or does attainment follow a "replacement" model, whereby less useful "social capital" is, over time, traded in for superior social capital? Podolny & Baron (1997) noted the importance for mobility of dissolving ties that cease to be instrumentally useful. They found that women were particularly prone to retaining ties beyond their ability to contribute to career advancement and take longer to add new ties subsequent to a promotion. Because organizational demography constrains the availability to women of same-gender network contacts that are useful instrumentally (e.g. high status), they argued that women incur greater "switching costs", which in turn, shape their network strategies and produce observed gender differences in loyalty. Is taking into account ties that cease to exist as important as understanding the new ties that come into existence? Is the process of professional development one of steady expansion from a core of network contacts, or one of unsteady or discontinuous change? How do changes in the work environment, such as downsizing, affect these patterns? Such questions can only be addressed by examining networks over time.

Career Transitions

Just as few studies have examined networks over time, few attempts have been made to explore the role of networks of relationships in transporting an individual from one role to the next. Career transitions not only require the learning of new skills and competencies but also the development of new or altering of old relationships. Thus, the transition process is facilitated or hindered by the relational context—the set of relationships with peers, seniors and juniors inside and outside the firm—in which it takes place (Hall, 1996; Kram, 1988).

At the heart of the transition process, and status passage, more generally, is the phenomenon of anticipatory socialization (Merton, 1968), whereby the focal individual begins to take on the identity, attitudes and relationships of the next role, before he/she has actually attained it. There is evidence to suggest that one reason women may have a more difficult time with career transitions is that men are more likely to undergo anticipatory socialization, with greater and frequent opportunities to observe role models and to practice in small doses the behaviors that will be required of them in the next role (Ibarra, 1996). Even when they are positioned in equivalent positions and career paths, women report that they are given different training, development opportunities, promotional criteria and supervision than men (Ohlott, Ruderman & McCanley, 1994; Morrison, White & Velsor, 1987). Do network ties commensurate with a role (e.g. the next managerial level) precede the transitions, thus "pulling" the individual into the new role informally, or are they formed only later as a function of the new role requirements? Observing change in development in networks prior to and following major career transitions is likely to be fertile ground for understanding basic network change processes. As we discuss below, one major kind of transition concerns the adjustments women make in response to pressures associated with the balance of work and family.

Work and Family Balance

As we redirect our attention to network dynamics over the full span of careers, and to critical career transitions, work and family balance will appear as one of the significant issues facing professional women. Research designs and conceptual models that focus on the confluence of social network and identity phenomena that shape work–family decisions may be especially productive. While a mounting body of research has documented the formal and institutional arrangements that make it difficult for women to manage career requirements and family responsibilities simultaneously (Bailyn, 1993), scant attention has been to the interaction context in which work–family decisions are made. The concepts of commitment and salience (discussed above) will help to explain how women manage the negotiations with significant others about the relative importance of family and work identities (Hochschild, 1989), and the resulting balance of time and effort allocated to each.

Factors including women's higher incidence of career interruptions (Ragins & Sundstrom, 1989) and the exodus of women from corporate America (Morrison & Von Glinow, 1990) suggest that women's work-related networks may be more subject to disruption, possibly making alternative networks and identities (e.g. kin, neighborhood) more salient and attractive. The attrition of homophilous ties inside the employing firm over time may decrease not only the level of instrumental support that strong homophilous ties can provide but, following the identity perspective suggested above, may lower the position of one's professional identity within ones' identity hierarchy. Tsui, Egan & O'Reilly (1992) found that "being different" reduces organizational commitment. Simultaneously, ties to non-employed women outside the domain of work may exert a pull in the direction of a more traditional female role. Combining the social identity and cumulative advantage perspectives, therefore, yields a different conceptual and methodological lens for exploring work–family issues at both micro and macro interaction levels.

A life-course perspective (Elder & O'Rand, 1995) may be particularly useful in explaining discontinuous shifts in networks as family and work are coordinated in individuals' lives. Gender interacts statistically with major family transitions to change network patterns. Munch, McPherson & Smith-Lovin (1994), found that childbirth leads women to drop work-related ties in order to limit the overall size of their networks, while men substitute family ties for male social friends, but without losing work contacts. Changes in family status, therefore, are associated with patterns of social relations which shape and give meaning to women's and men's experiences both in the family and at work. Following the arguments developed above, the network configurations created by major family transitions, in turn, will shape the hierarchical ordering of social identities and the cultural assumptions that women and men make about the appropriate balance of work and family. We suspect that changes in network characteristics associated with family transitions may explain cohort and individual differences in women's responses to work–family pressure. Research on networks and turnover may also be helpful since the evidence indicates that attrition follows informal network patterns (Krackhardt & Porter, 1986). In research on work–family decisions, shifts in the structure of women's friendship ties brought on by turnover patterns may explain differences in women's responses to work–family pressure.

METHODOLOGICAL ISSUES

The social identity perspective, attention to impression management, and dynamic approaches suggested above dictate a somewhat different methodological approach than has been common in organizational network research. In particular, we suggest a need for greater attention to the definition of the boundaries within which network data are collected and greater attention to solving the methodological problems of investigating networks longitudinally. To answer the types of questions we have raised, traditional network surveys will also need to be combined with in-depth observational, interview data other types of instruments which tap social identities and reference groups.

Network Boundaries

Most earlier organizational studies assess the structural form of complete networks by locating all ties within the firm or department. Our emphasis on the composition, boundaries and content of an individual's network environment requires information on egocentric networks—the set of relationships that are relevant for a particular individual regardless of the social context in which they are maintained (see Marsden, 1990, for a systematic discussion of different research strategies). Studying egocentric networks has a number of advantages for our purposes. First, it allows standard survey technology of measurement and inference: data on egocentric networks are collected through survey questions that are administered to individuals in a standard manner. Second, rather than having a bounded system defined by the researcher, the study of egocentric networks allows the respondent to define the boundary of the relevant social world. The range and boundaries of the network then become interesting variables in their own right, rather than an operationally defined limiting factor.

Longitudinal Network Analysis

Developments in the directions that we have outlined also require greater attention to both theoretical and methodological issues pertaining to networks over time (McPherson, Popielarz & Drobnic, 1992). Marsden & Podolny (1990) and Burt & Ronchi (1990) are excellent examples of a new trend toward dynamic studies of work networks. As we move toward study of network dynamics over time, however, several difficult methodological problems arise. As with any over-time measurement, we must determine whether observed changes in networks are real or instead attributable to measurement reliability issues (Doreian, 1990). Since the reliability of the egocentric network measures that we advocate can be determined in a manner parallel to that of any survey measure, this problem is not insurmountable. A more difficult conceptual issue is what constitutes the beginning and end of a tie. While formal work relations and concrete exchange patterns may be easy to define, it is more difficult to say when a friendship or a mentoring relationship begins. It is even more difficult to say when such relationships are effectively dissolved, since they tend to gradually decrease in their contact volume (Marsden, 1990). A related problem is the need for theoretical guidance in specifying the appropriate time window within which changes in networks are to be expected. It is in this domain where career theory, with its long history of investigating career cycles and stages may be most fruitfully combined with a network approach to yield new insights.

Even when theoretical and measurement problems are resolved, data problems are significant. Burt & Ronchi (1990) demonstrate how archival records may be used to trace some types of network connections back over considerable periods of time. Concentrating on egocentric networks allows the application of normal survey methods like panel designs and event history analysis to the study of networks over time. The study of more informal, ephemeral ties through which information, reputation and impression management flow in organizations, however, may require more in-depth observational or interview methods until they are better understood. Life history data (McPherson, Popielarz & Drobnic, 1992) allow more powerful event history analyses, but measurement properties of retrospective network data are not well understood at this point. Clearly, more theoretical and methodological work will be necessary before we achieve an understanding of structural dynamics.

SOCIAL NETWORK RESEARCH AND CHANGES IN ORGANIZATIONAL CAREERS

The new directions outlined above are particularly germane given the changing nature of organizations and organizational careers. Of the many developments changing the career landscape today (see Hall, 1996, for a review), three are especially relevant for social network research on gender and careers: changing workforce demographics, the rise of "boundary-less" careers and organizations, and the breaking down of boundaries between work and non-work spheres. In the sections below, we conclude that these imply significant changes in the research questions that we ask, the methodologies we use, and most importantly, the theoretical perspectives we draw upon.

First, and most obvious, is the changing demographic composition of the workforce. Most of our current theories, however, are based on research conducted with fairly homogeneous populations and in contexts where professional and managerial women are in the minority. At the present time, it is fair to say that we have yet to unravel the effects of gender from those of demography. To understand the portion of variance that is currently unaccounted for by structural theories, however, we need theories about what motivates human behavior (Foote, 1951). We have argued above that social identity theory has particular potential to shed light on network formation and change processes that cannot be explained alone by demographic and stratification theories.

Second, managers, until recently, were assumed to develop and advance within a single organization. New developments have dramatically altered this model. As increased competition and downsizing unravel the myth of life-long job security with one firm, managers have found that career development involves moving from firm to firm in search of opportunities, thus increasing the value of external relationships. Many have even begun to develop careers independent of formal organizations as self-employed professionals. Within the firm, a shift from a hierarchical structure to the flat "re-engineered" organization has placed an increased priority on developing relationships beyond those proscribed by organizational charts. Also, the expanding role of global business highlights the new role of trans-national relationships in career development (Kanter, 1995). These developments place a premium on individuals' abilities to create, change and dissolve networks as the requirements of their situations change, and on our ability as researchers to study and conceptualize dynamic processes. While the network methods most familiar to organizational behavior researchers are premised on closed organizational boundaries within which network data are collected, boundary-less careers and organizations require measurement techniques and conceptual frameworks that do not impose superficial boundaries.

Third and last, career theorists predict that the assumption of a clear division between work and family domains will be untenable increasingly, as "work and non-work roles overlap and shape jointly a person's identity" (Hall, 1996:21). As employees are less tied to any particular work organization, or even to one developmental career path, their movement from one venue to another may make work-related network ties less stable and close than family, professional or community ties. Lower geographic mobility, induced by the increasing prevalence of dual-career families, would reinforce this trend by allowing longer-term ties to community organizations and to neighborhood friends. If the commitment-salience argument in social identity theory is correct, this shifting of tie stability toward increased instability at work and increased stability in the community may be reflected in a shift of identity salience that de-emphasizes work identities. Alternatively, people increasingly may expand the scope of their professional networks beyond their local organization to create ties that will survive movement from one employer to another. We hypothesize that professions and jobs that have a more developed structure for creating such extra-organizational ties (e.g. national or regional associations) will retain greater commitment than jobs that typically have been centered in the organizational unit. Jobs that allow work and family to be integrated to a larger degree (e.g. where work is done at home or couple-based entrepreneurial acitivites) will create multiplex network ties that will simultaneously reinforce several identities. These complex relationships will have the potential to create role conflicts, however, that may produce mixed emotions and difficult coordination tasks. Both women and men may begin to experience both the rewards and pressures of combining family and work involvement.

CONCLUSION

This chapter presents a view of women's careers as significantly affected by interaction processes that mediate the relationship between the structural features of organization contexts and outcomes such as mobility and professional development. This perspective represents a counter-argument to currently influential theories of gender differences, which argue that men and women exhibit different interpersonal preferences as a result of socialization to their respective gender roles, and that these orientations explain different paths and choices. In focusing on informal interaction, we also propose theoretical alternatives to network theories that are premised on economic models of human behavior. Inquiry along the lines suggested here may be used to further our understanding of the role of identity, strategic action and cumulative processes in shaping the course of women's careers.

REFERENCES

Aldrich, H., Reese, P.R. & Dubini, P. (1989). Women on the verge of a breakthrough: networking among entrepreneurs in the United States and Italy. *Entrepreneurship and Regional Development*, **1**, 339–56.

Ashford, B.E. & Humphrey, R.H. (1993). Emotional labor in service roles: the influence of identity. *Academy of Management Review*, **18**, 88–115.

Ashford, B.E. & Mael, F. (1989). Social identity theory and the organizations. *Academy of Management Review*, **14**, 20–39.

Bailyn, L. (1993). *Breaking the Mold*. New York: Free Press.

Barley, S.R. (1989). Careers, identities and institutions: the legacy of the Chicago School of Sociology. In M.B. Arthur, D.T. Hall & B.S. Lawrence (eds), *Handbook of Career Theory* (pp. 41–65). Cambridge: Cambridge University Press.

Baron, J. & Pfeffer, J. (1994). The social psychology of organizations and inequality. *Social Psychology Quarterly*, **57**, 190–209.

Belliveau, M. (1996). Blind ambition?: the effects of social networks and institutional segregation on the compensation of elite coeducational and women's colleges graduates. Working paper, Fuqua Business School.

Blau, P.M. (1977). Inequality and heterogeneity: a primitive theory of social structure. New York: Free Press.

Boxman, E.A.W., De Graaf, P.A. & Flap, H.E. (1991). The impact of social and human capital on the income attainment of Dutch managers. *Social Networks*, **13**, 51–73.

Brass, D.J. (1984). Being in the right place: a structural analysis of individual influence in organization. *Administrative Science Quarterly*, **29**, 518–39.

Brass, D.J. (1985). Men's and women's networks: a study of interaction patterns and influence in an organization. *Academy of Management Journal*, **28**, 327–43.

Burt, R.S. (1992). *Structural Holes*. Cambridge, MA: Harvard University Press.

Burt, R.S. & Ronchi, D. (1990). Contested control in a large manufacturing plant. In J. Weesie & H. Flap (eds), *Social Networks Through Time* (pp. 121–58). Utrecht, The Netherlands: ISOR.

Burt, R.S. & Knez, M. (1996). Trust and third party gossip. In R.M. Kramer & T.R. Tyler (eds), *Trust in Organizations* (pp. 68–89). Thousand Oaks, CA: Sage.

Campbell, K.E. (1988). Gender differences in job-related networks. In *Work and Occupations* (pp. 179–200). Beverly Hills, CA: Sage.

Chatman J.A. & Brown, R.A. (1996). It takes two to tango: demographic similarity, social identity and friendship. Working paper, Haas School of Business, University of California, Berkeley.

DiMaggio, P. (1992). Nadel's paradox revisited: relational and cultural aspects of organizational structure. In N. Nohria & R.G. Eccles (eds), *Networks and Organizations: Structure, Form and Action* (pp. 118–42). Cambridge, MA: Harvard Business School Press.

Doreian, P. (1990). Mapping networks through time. In J. Weesie & H. Flap (eds), *Social Networks Through Time* (pp. 245–64). Utrecht, The Netherlands: ISOR.

Elder, G.H. Jr & O'Rand, A. (1995). Adult lives in a changing society. In K.S. Cook, G.A. Fine & J.S. House (eds), *Sociological Perspectives on Social Psychology* (pp. 452–75). Boston: Allyn and Bacon.

Ely, R.J. (1994). The effects of organizational demographics and social identity on relationships among professional women. *Administrative Science Quarterly*, **39**, 203–38.

Fischer, C. & Oliker, S. (1983). A research note on friendship, gender, and the life cycle. *Social Forces*, **62**, 124–32.

Foote, N.N. (1951). Identification as the basis for a theory of motivation. *American Sociological Review*, **16**, 14–21.

Gilligan, C. (1982). *In a Different Voice*. Cambridge, MA: Harvard University Press.

Granovetter, M. (1973). The strength of weak ties. *American Journal of Sociology*, **6**, 1360–80.

Granovetter, M. (1982). The strength of weak ties: a network theory revisited. In P.V. Marsden & N. Lin (eds), *Social Structure and Network Analysis* (pp. 105–30). Beverly Hills, CA: Sage.

Hall, D.T. (1996). *The Career is Dead. Long Live the Career*. San Francisco, CA: Jossey-Bass.

Hochschild, A. (1983). *The Managed Heart*. Los Angeles, CA: University of California Press.

Hochschild, A. (1989). *The Second Shift: Working Parents and the Revolution at Home*. New York: Viking.

Ibarra, H. (1992). Homophily and differential returns: sex differences in network structure and access in an advertising firm. *Administrative Science Quarterly*, **37**, 422–47.

Ibarra, H. (1993). Personal networks of women and minorities in management: a conceptual framework. *Academy of Management Review*, **18**(1), 56–87.

Ibarra, H. (1995). Race, opportunity, and diversity of social circles in managerial networks. *Academy of Management Journal*, **38**(3), 673–703.

Ibarra, H. (1996). Inauthentic selves: surface acting, social identity and professional networks. Harvard Business School working paper.

Ibarra, H. (1997). Paving an alternate route: gender differences in managerial networks for career development. *Social Psychology Quarterly*, **60**(1), 91–102.

Ibarra, H. & Andrews, S.B. (1993). Power, social influence, and sense making: effects of network centrality and proximity on employee perceptions. *Administrative Science Quarterly*, **38**, 277–303.

Kanter, R.M. (1977). *Men and Women of the Corporation*. New York: Basic Books.

Kanter, R.M. (1995). *World Class: Thriving Locally in the Global Economy*. New York: Simar & Schurter.

Krackhardt, D. & Porter, L.W. (1986). The snowball effect: turnover embedded in communication networks. *Journal of Applied Psychology*, **71**, 50–55.

Krackhardt, D. (1992). The strength of strong ties: the importance of philos in organizations. In N. Nohria & R.G. Eccles (eds), *Networks and Organizations: Structure, Form and Action* (pp. 216–39). Cambridge, MA: Harvard Business School Press.

Kilduff, M. & Krackhardt, D. (1994). Bringing the individual back in: a structural analysis of the internal market for reputation in organizations. *Academy of Management Journal*, **37**, 87–108.

Kram, K.E. (1988). *Mentoring at Work. Developmental Relationships in Organizational Life*. New York: University Press of America.

Lin, N. (1982). Social resources and instrumental action. In P.V. Marsden & N. Lin (eds), *Social Structure and Network Analysis* (pp. 131–45). Beverly Hills, CA: Sage.

Lin, E., Ensel, W.M. & Vaughn, J.C. (1981). Social resources and strength of ties: structural factors in occupational status attainment. *American Sociological Review*, **46**, 393–405.

Lincoln, R. Jr & Miller, J. (1979). Work and friendship ties in organizations: a comparative analysis of relational networks. *Administrative Science Quarterly*, **24**, 181–99.

March, J.G. & Olsen, J.P. (1975). The uncertainty of the past: organizational learning under ambiguity. *European Journal of Political Research*, **3**, 147–71.

Marsden, P.V. (1990). Network data and measurement. *Annual Review of Sociology*, **16**, 435–63.

Marsden, P.V. (1987). Core discussion networks of Americans. *American Sociological Review*, **52**, 122–31.

Marsden, P.V. & Podolny, J. (1990). Dynamic analysis of network diffusion processes. In J. Weesie & H. Flap (eds), *Social Networks Through Time* (pp. 197–214). Utrecht, The Netherlands: ISOR.

McPherson, J.M. & Smith-Lovin, L. (1987). Homophily in voluntary organizations: status distance and the composition of face-to-face groups. *American Journal of Sociology*, **52**, 370–79.

McPherson, J.M., Popielarz, P.A. & Drobnic, S. (1992). Social networks and organizational dynamics. *American Sociological Review*, **57**, 153–70.

Merton, R. (1947). *Social Theory and Social Structure*. New York: Free Press.

Miller, J. (1986). *Pathways in the Workplace*. Cambridge: Cambridge University Press.

Miller, J., Lincoln, J.R. & Olsen, J.P. (1981). Rationality and equity in professional networks: gender and tace as factors in the stratification of interorganizational systems. *American Journal of Sociology*, **87**, 308–35.

Moore, G. (1990). Structural determinants of men's and women's personal networks. *American Sociological Review*, **55**, 726–35.

Morrison, A.M., White, R.P. & Velsor, E. (1987). Breaking the glass ceiling: can women reach the top of america's largest corporations? Reading, MA: Addison-Wesley.

Morrison, A.M. & Von Glinow, M. (1990). Women and minorities in management. *American Psychologist,* **45**, 200–8.

Munch, A., Miller McPherson, J. & Smith-Lovin, J. (1994). Gender, children and social context: a research note on the effects of childrearing for men and women. Paper presented at the American Sociological Association meetings.

Noe, R.A. (1988). Women and mentoring: a review and research agenda. *Academy of Management Review,* **13**(1), 65–78.

Ohlott, P., Ruderman, M.A. & McCauley, C.D. (1994). Gender differences in managers' developmental job experiences. *Academy of Management Review,* **37**(1), 46–67.

O'Leary, V.E. & Ickovics, J.R. (1992). Cracking the glass ceiling: overcoming isolation and alienation. In U. Sekeran & F. Leong (eds), *Womanpower: Managing in Times of Demographic Turbulence* (pp. 7–30). Beverly Hills, CA: Sage.

O'Reilly, C. & Chatman, J. (1986). Organizational commitment and psychological attachment: the effects of compliance, identification, and internalization on prosocial behavior. *Journal of Applied Psychology,* **71**, 492–9.

Pfeffer, J. (1983). Organizational demography. In L.L. Cummings & B.M. Staw (eds), *Research in Organizational Behavior,* vol. 5 (pp. 299–357). Greenwich, CO: JAI Press.

Podolny, J.M. & Baron, J.N. (forthcoming). Resources and relationships: social networks, mobility and satisfaction in the workplace. *American Sociological Review.*

Ragins, B.R. & Sundstrom, E. (1989). Gender and power in organizations: a longitudinal perspective. *Psychological Bulletin,* **105**(1), 51–88.

Rice, R.E. (1993). Using network concepts to clarify sources and mechanisms of social influence. In G. Barnett & W. Richards Jr (eds), *Advances in Communication Network Analysis.* Norwood, NJ: Ablex.

Ridgeway, C. (1991). The social construction of status value: gender and other nominal characteristics. *Social Forces,* **70**, 367–86.

Rosenbaum, J.E. (1984). *Career Mobility in a Corporate Hierarchy.* New York: Academic Press.

Ross, C.E. (1987). The division of labor at home. *Social Forces,* **65**, 816–33.

Salancik, G. & Pfeffer, J. (1978). A social information processing approach to job attitudes and task design. *Administrative Science Quarterly,* **23**, 224–53.

Schein, E. (1978). *Career Dynamics: Matching Individual and Organizational Needs.* Reading, MA: Addison-Wesley.

Smith-Lovin, L. & McPherson, M.J. (1992). You are who you know: a network approach to gender. In P. England (ed), *Theory on Gender/Feminism on Theory* (pp. 223–51). New York: Aldine.

Spence, A.M. (1974). *Market signaling: informational transfer in hiring and related screening processes.* Cambridge, MA: Harvard University Press.

Stryker, S. & Serpe, R.T. (1982). Commitment, identity salience and role behavior. In W. Ickes & E. Knowles (eds), *Personality, Roles and Social Behavior* (pp. 199–218). New York: Springer-Verlag.

Swann, W.B. Jr (1987). Identity negotiation: where two roads meet. *Journal of Personality and Social Psychology,* **53**, 1038–51.

Tajfel, H. & Turner, J.C. (1985). The social identity theory of intergroup behavior. In S. Worchel & W.G. Austin (eds), *Psychology of intergroup relations,* 2nd edn (pp. 7–24). Chicago: Nelson-Hall.

Thoits, P.A. (1983). Multiple identities and psychological well-being: a reformulation and test of the social isolation hypothesis. *American Sociological Review,* **48**, 174–87.

Thomas, D.A. (1990). The impact of race on managers' experiences of developmental relationships (mentoring and sponsorship): an intra-organizational study. *Journal of Organizational Behavior,* **2**, 479–92.

Thomas, D.A. (1993). The dynamics of managing racial diversity in developmental relationships. *Administrative Science Quarterly,* **38**, 169–94.

Tsui, A.S., Egan, T.D. & O'Reilly, C.A. III (1992). Being different: relational demography and organizational attachment. *Administrative Science Quarterly*, **37**, 549–79.
Turner, J.C. & Oakes, P.J. (1989). Self-categorization theory and social influence. In P.B. Paulus (ed), *Psychology of group influence*, 2nd edn (pp. 233–75). Hillsdale, NJ: Erlbaum.
Van Maanen, J. & Barley, S.R. (1984). Occupational Communities. In B. Staw & L.L. Cummings (eds), *Research in Organizational Behavior*, vol. 6 (pp. 287–365). Greenwich, CT: JAI Press.
Wharton, A.S. (1992). The social construction of gender and race in organizations: a social identity and group mobilization perspective. In P. Tolbert & S. Bacharach (eds), *Research in the Sociology of Organizations*, vol. 10 (pp. 55–84). Greenwich, CT: JAI Press.

Chapter 20

Employee Transfer: So Much Activity, So Little Information

Dan R. Dalton
and
James C. Wimbush
Indiana University, Bloomington, IN, USA

It has been estimated that organization-sponsored transfers account for some 500 000 relocations per year at the cost of some $20 billion (Fisher & Shaw, 1994; Lawson and Angle, 1994). Moreover, it has been estimated that the cost of relocating one employee and his/her family is some $37 000 (Galer, 1991). It may be notable that this level of activity is not unique to the USA. Consider, for example, that Munton and West (1995) recently recounted a British manpower study indicating that some 250 000 employees in the UK relocate every year at their employers' request. These levels of activity may not be surprising. It has been suggested, for example, that to meet the demands of rapid changes in both market conditions and technology, firms need flexibility in terms of employee skills for assignment to different tasks and *flexibility in terms of mobility for assignment to different geographical locations* (Tsui et al., 1995; emphasis added). At the same time, there is an inherent conflict in moves of this sort. Pinder (1989) has suggested that transfers cause the interests of the organizations to invade the personal life of the employee more directly and substantially than virtually any other organizational intervention. Curiously, however, there is virtually no empirical attention to the consequences of employee transfer behaviors.

Creating Tomorrow's Organizations. Edited by C.L. Cooper and S.E. Jackson.
© 1997 John Wiley & Sons Ltd.

CONTEMPORARY SNAPSHOTS OF THE RELOCATION DILEMMA

Perhaps the following will help to illustrate how difficult such personnel relocations and their policies can be.

Consider. One could imagine any number of reasons why employees might not elect to transfer job locations when they currently have a job. That is, a choice not to accept a transfer does not, at least in the immediate term, jeopardize their current employment. Notably, however, *Business Week* (1995) recently reported that unemployed executives will not relocate for a *new* position. Indeed, while the percentage of executives who would relocate for such purposes has varied from less than 20% to some 35% over a 4-year period, the current percentage of unemployed executives so inclined is only some 16%.

Consider. A recent front page article in the *Wall Street Journal* (Blumenthal & McCartney, 1996) described a fascinating trend in the relocation of high-level corporate executives—their families are not relocating with them. For many such executives these relocations—largely as a function of promotions in these cases—amount to an extensive commuting arrangement for the transferred party. According to Coldwell Banker Relocation Services, Inc., a firm that handled some 34000 corporate transfers in 1995, spouses did not accompany the relocating partner in 8% of the domestic transfers and 5% of the international.

Consider. A recent discussion in the *Wall Street Journal* (Templin & White, 1994, B6, p. 3) may provide yet another illustration of the pressing nature of the "transfer" issue:

> General Motors Corp. is hiring temporary workers to staff some factories because it is unable to move 8300 idled workers who are receiving virtually full wages for staying put. GM is so desperate for extra hands at five plants that it is raffling off a $10 000 voucher toward a new car to entice some 1100 idled employees . . . to attend a "jobs fair" . . . that will showcase transfer opportunities. So far, these workers, laid off since August 1992, have turned down lucrative offers elsewhere . . .

The promise that GM's most recent 3-year contract with the United Auto Workers would provide the flexibility to move laid-off workers to plants where additional personnel were needed has not materialized. The corporation is paying overtime to on-site workers and hiring temporary workers—GM has declined to disclose how many temporary workers are involved—because idled workers are declining transfer opportunities. It has been estimated that GM is paying more to idled workers than the entire payroll of other corporate members of the *Fortune 500*. While the situation at GM represents an extreme case, it does underscore the potential gravity of transfer-related concerns (Dalton et al., 1995).

TRANSFER

> An employee transfer has been defined as a relatively permanent job reassignment that entails the movement of an employee within an organization from one of its operating sites to another (Pinder & Walter, 1984, p. 188).

Others have argued that employee transfer includes an additional element beyond that of change of geographical location (e.g. Dalton & Todor, 1993). Under that categorization an employee would have transferred under three conditions:

- An employee has relocated from one geographical location to another within the same company but retains essentially the same job.
- An employee transfers from one job responsibility to another but within essentially the same location.
- An employee has relocated from one geographical location to another and moves from one job responsibility to another.

The distinction between these categories is largely one of the level of the individual who has made the transfer. When a manager or executive moves from one location to another within the same company, we generally refer to that as a "relocation". Such a transfer could have been made at the request of the individual or the company. We should note here that a managerial/executive promotion often has much the same character. It is not at all unusual for a managerial/executive promotion to have a concomitant change in location as well (the third category).

Often, the expression "transfer" refers to non-managerial/non-executive personnel. Under a collective bargaining agreement, for example, an employee could routinely transfer between jobs, between locations, or both. Having noted these distinctions, we are aware that the extant literature often does not differentiate between the levels of employees involved and whether changes in locations also include changes in job responsibilities. We will use the terms "transfer" and "relocation" interchangeably.

As we think about our review of the literature in the general area of employee transfer, we are surprised by several aspects of what we perceive as a potentially important imbalance in this work. First, while there has been some attention to some individual level antecedents and correlates of employee transfer (e.g. Brett, Stroh & Reilly, 1992, 1993; Fisher & Shaw, 1994), we notice that there has been no attention to individual level *outcomes* associated with employee transfer. Second, there has been no attention to this phenomenon at either the group or the organization level. Third, with modest exception, we see no integration with other forms of employee withdrawal or opportunistic behavior (e.g. turnover, absenteeism).

Employee Transfer: What Do We Know?

Fisher and Shaw (1994) remind us that much of the research on employee relocation has taken two forms. One approach is to examine adjustment to a past transfer using retrospective surveys in which respondents are asked to answer a series of questions about their recent relocation. While retrospective surveys may be problematic on a number of levels, their interpretation may be especially suspect as the time lapse between the event (in this case a transfer) and the recollection increases. Time lapses for studies of this sort can average 2 years or more.

Another approach does not include actual employee transfer at all; rather the variable of interest has been respondent reports of willingness to relocate or their mobility intentions. These studies do not address a specific transfer of job or location (e.g. Brett, Stroh & Reilly, 1993; Noe, Steffy & Barber, 1988; for a notable exception, see Turban, Campion & Eyring, 1992). About such studies, Fisher and Shaw (1994, p. 210) suggest that:

> Because nearly all actual decisions to relocate are made with a specific place/job in mind, it is unclear how relevant these studies are to the affect that would be aroused at the prospect of a *particular* relocation assignment (emphasis in the original).

Even so, there is a body of research, while not always consistent, which has examined a number of factors which have been hypothesized to be related with a person's general willingness to relocate (for outstanding compendia, see Brett, Stroh & Reilly, 1992, 1993; Fisher & Shaw, 1994). There is evidence, for example, that (a) potential relocation is facilitated when individuals' spouses are willing to relocate; (b) unmarried individuals are more likely to relocate; (3) women are less willing to consider a potential relocation; (d) employees in certain functional areas (e.g. sales, operations; marketing) may be more likely to consider relocation; and, (e) those with higher career ambitions are more likely to accept a potential relocation. There is no consensus, however, regarding whether employee age, number of children, income level, company or job tenure, and prior relocation are factors in the relocation decision. The research does suggest that employee attitudes (e.g. company identification, organizational commitment and loyalty, job involvement, job satisfaction) are not related to employees' reported willingness to relocate.

More notable in our view is the conspicuous absence of studies examining the consequences of transfer on the performance—or other outcome measures—for those who have transferred. Also, we know of no research which has examined the consequences of the transfer phenomenon on groups, subunits and organizations.

At some risk of understatement, research programs which are designed to examine behavioral and/or group or organization-level dependent variables are likely to make an important contribution to the academic as well as business community. Perhaps we can initiate some discussion by viewing transfer from an alternative perspective. For example, is transfer/relocation the functional equivalent of employee turnover?

TRANSFER AS UNIT-LEVEL TURNOVER?

Rather than considering transfer—as it is most often defined—as a change of job or location within the same organization, it may be productive to consider transfer as a subset of employee turnover. Indeed, we will argue that intraorganizational transfer has, in many ways, the same character as employee turnover. Further, we will argue that in some cases transfer actually may have more dysfunctional elements than employee turnover.

Consider an example from current policies in the US military services. An individual in the service will be transferred from post to post every 3 years or so. From the point of view of the military service, this is not a recurring turnover statistic. After all, this individual has not left the employ of the USA. He/she remains, irrespective of the number of transfers (of which there might be 10 or so in a career to retirement), a member in good standing of the armed forces of the USA.

But, when considered from the point of view of the officer in charge, the transferred employee, a trained person familiar with the local equipment, local work group and so forth, is no longer present. The officer will probably receive replacement personnel, but there is certainly no guarantee that the replacement will be of the quality and experience of the transferred employee. Even if he/she were so qualified, there would still be the matter of socialization with the current officers, location, work group and so forth.

From the armed services point of view, no turnover occurred. From the local point of view, it certainly did. Clearly, these disparate points are mirrored in the private sector as well. There is no question than an individual instance of transfer is local turnover. From the view of the local supervisor, that employee may as well have quit. This point can be persuasively made by considering the consequences at the limit.

Suppose a manager's entire workforce has been transferred—an admittedly unlikely scenario—and replaced altogether with a new group of employees. Surely, no manager would be indifferent to this movement of personnel. We do not believe that any manager would be especially calmed by the realization that "turnover" did not actually occur. It could be persuasively argued that any transfer is the equivalent of turnover from the local perspective.

This may be notable because of what appears to be a diametrically different view of employee transfer as compared to employee turnover. Much of the literature addressing employee relocation and transfer underscores its positive aspects, including organizational flexibility and employee development (e.g. Anderson, Milkovich & Tsui, 1981; Brett, 1984; Brett, Stroh & Reilly, 1993; Noe, Steffy & Barber, 1988; Pinder & Walter, 1984; Tsui et al., 1995). Interestingly, regarding non-management employees, the question of the advisability of employee transfer programs is apparently a potential platform of agreement between the sometimes adversarial camps of management and labor. Fossum (1987, p. 294), for example, has observed that:

> Employers have adapted in the short run to changing competitive conditions through lower wages and fewer permanent employees. Labor has countered by attempting to enhance employment security. Vehicles to achieve this have included restrictions on subcontracting, *between-facility transfer rights*, and retraining programs (emphasis added).

Others (e.g. Noe, Steffy & Barber, 1988:559), too, have noted the importance of lateral transfer policy: . . . organizations *are utilizing lateral transfers* and downward movement as alternatives to layoffs, to meet employee development needs, and to adapt to the demands created by voluntary and involuntary turnover (emphasis added).

Conversely, employee turnover is not normally viewed with favor in the business community. The preponderance of research and conceptualization in this area has a common thread: as turnover is a dysfunctional element in most organizations, efforts and resources should be marshaled to minimize its occurrence. At a general level, employee turnover is associated with a host of costs including loss of productivity, recruitment and training (see Cascio, 1991 for an excellent treatment of these issues and others; see also Dalton & Todor, 1993). It is interesting that, while employee turnover is considered a problem by many, employee transfer is viewed positively, especially since transfer can be understood as an instance of turnover at the local level.

In fact, an argument can be made that iterative transfer—what we will refer to as the "domino effect"—may render transfer to be far the more serious organizational disruption, particularly for non-managerial employees. Compare the following scenarios, the first concerning turnover, the others addressing transfer.

Scenario 1. An employee quits or is terminated; for the domino effect, whether the separation was voluntary is not at issue. A decision is made to replace the departing employee. Hopefully, a suitable candidate (or several) is identified and a person hired. This course of events reflects a rather unimaginative scenario, routinely observed in every manner of organization.

The impact of this separation is probably modest. An experienced employee was lost and replaced with a new-hire. While there are costs involved in such an exchange, these costs are not of immediate interest. The point is that *one* person was lost, and *one* person gained. Accordingly, only one person will require training, socialization, and whatever other processes take place so that the new employee is able to contribute to the organization.

Scenario 2. Our hypothetical employee still quits. At this point, however, this scenario departs fundamentally from the first. For this case, no attempt is made to secure a new hire. Rather, the now available job is "up for bid". In many organizations, other employees have the right to be considered for this recently available job. An employee who would bid for this job is actually requesting an intraorganizational transfer. Such a bidding procedure is routine, commonly part of a collective bargaining agreement. In agreements of this type, before a new-hire could be hired, current employees have the right to bid for the newly opened job.

In any case, since the collective bargaining agreement contains language which provides for such transfers, the recently open job is put to bid. Consider the simplest case, one with only a single bid iteration. Ms A quits; Mr B bids and is transferred to Ms A's prior job. Obviously, there is still a personnel problem: someone must still be identified to assume the responsibilities of Mr B—the successful bidder. For this case, let us assume that a new-hire is obtained to fill the job vacated by B, this because none of the current employees elected to request a transfer to this position. This scenario differs from the first in one important element. Instead of one inexperienced person as in the first scenario, there are two. Mr B is not yet familiar with his new job, the job into which he just transferred, and of course the new-hire who took B's old job will require some time to contribute at a reasonable level.

Scenario 3. The last scenario (one iteration) is the most benign of transfer processes, and, frankly, unrealistically elementary. What is far more likely in a collective bargaining context is on the order of Ms A quits, Mr B transfers into A's slot, Ms C transfers into B's slot, Mr D successfully transfers into C's job, and then a new-hire is generated to take D's now open position. This is the nature of the "domino" effect of employee transfer. Here, one employee is not lost and replaced by another one. In many ways, at least at the local level, we have the equivalent of four turnovers. There are four people (B, C, D—all transfers—and the new-hire) who are unfamiliar with their new job, work group, supervisor, location and so forth. It is curious that the organizational literature provides no recognition of this phenomenon and certainly no assessment of its costs and benefits for the contemporary organization.

There is another curious aspect of employee transfer which may unfavorably differentiate it from turnover. There has been some discussion that turnover is not invariably dysfunctional to the organization (e.g. Abelson, 1987; Abelson & Baysinger, 1984; Dalton, Krackhardt & Todor, 1981; Dalton, Todor & Krackhardt, 1982; Dalton & Todor, 1979, 1982, 1993; Hollenbeck & Williams, 1986; Lucas et al., 1987; Staw, 1980; Staw & Oldham, 1978). One of the arguments often made is that some employee turnover is beneficial, clearly in the interests of the organization. It has been suggested that "it may not be how many, but who is leaving" (Dalton & Todor, 1993, p. 202) that in some part allows us to determine whether turnover is dysfunctional. There has been some research indicating that a large portion of employee turnover is, in fact, functional, that is, some 40–50% of employee turnover involves the departure of persons whose leaving is in the interests of the organization (Dalton, Krackhardt & Todor, 1981; Hollenbeck & Williams, 1986; Lucas et al., 1987).

Notably, transfer does not have this benefit. We should remember that, at the local level, a group, or unit, or location may greatly benefit from a person leaving through transfer to another unit. Of course, this presumably only visits the low productivity or whatever other factor renders this employee unsatisfactory to another unit.

Rather than considering transfer/relocation as the equivalent of turnover at the local level, there may be yet another perspective. May transfer be reasonably considered as a substitute for other behaviors?

IS TRANSFER A SUBSTITUTE FOR TURNOVER OR ABSENTEEISM?

Some 40 years ago, March and Simon (1958) speculated that there should be a relationship between internal mobility (transfer) and turnover. They suggested that the perceived opportunity for employees to request and receive intraorganizational transfers would reduce their propensity for leaving the organization. For many employees, then, the availability of intraorganizational transfer (the local turnover to which we have referred) can serve the same purpose as leaving the organization. Changing jobs (transferring) within organizations may resolve dissatisfaction with one's work as readily as changing organizations (quitting). Simply put, many employees may prefer to move within an organization (transferring) to moving outside it (quitting).

Others, too, have endorsed that view. Gustafson (1982, p. 168), for example, noted the potential positive impact of transfers of subsequent employee turnover: "In addition to their other merits, mobility programs (transfers) also may have a favorable long-term effect on resignations". Jackofsky (1984; see also Jackofsky & Peters, 1983) has argued that both transfer (job turnover) and quitting (organizational turnover) should be elements in the overall examination and assessment of turnover and that such an approach will provide a more complete representation of the turnover phenomenon.

Dalton & Todor (1987), consistent with these general principles, reasoned that employees presumably attempt to transfer for some reason. Accordingly, if the employees are able to reduce their problem—whatever its nature—through transfer, they would be correspondingly less likely to quit. On the other hand, employees who attempt to use the transfer option but are not successful will evince much higher levels of turnover. They examined the relevant records for employee transfer and turnover over a 4-year period for two separate companies in the same industry. The results for the two companies compare favorably. In both cases, the highest turnover rates (company 1, 60%; company 2, 59%) were associated with those individuals who requested transfers and were not accommodated. Conversely, the more modest levels of turnover (company 1, 18%; company 2, 12%) were evident when employees were able to enjoy the transfer process.

It would appear, then, that individuals who wish to leave their current position (transfer) and are able to move within the organization are much less likely to leave the organization than those who wish to move but can not. An individual with the ability to "withdraw" from an otherwise unacceptable situation would prefer to move within the organization (transfer) than leave it entirely (quit).

It seems reasonable that a similar logic may also operate with respect to employee absenteeism. In fact, Anderson, Milkovich and Tsui (1981) argued that levels of both turnover and absenteeism may depend in part on the internal mobility (including lateral transfers) of employees. Dalton and Mesch (1990) provided a direct test of this proposition. Relying on two separate organizations over a 4-year period, they reported that in both cases the absence rates are about twice as great for those employees who had not received a transfer (company 1, 5.88%; company 2, 5.16%) over the period compared to those who had received a transfer (company 1, 3.24%; company 2, 2.44%).

It appears, then, that both employee turnover and employee absenteeism may be importantly related to transfer behavior. Employees who have received a transfer are apparently far less likely to quit than those who have requested a transfer, but have not received it. Beyond that, there is evidence that those who have received transfers have a far lower incidence of absenteeism than those who do not receive transfers.

We should note an important qualification for these results. In both of these studies, transfers are requested, i.e. initiated by the employee. In no case were any of the transfers initiated by either of the two separate companies involved. We suspect that this is an important distinction. We are aware of no evidence addressing whether subsequent levels of turnover, absenteeism, or any behavior for that matter, are impacted by *company-initiated* transfers.

Other Outcomes about Which We Know Nothing

We are not aware of any other empirical work which addresses any additional aspects of *behavior* which may be related to those who have transferred. Is their performance better or worse in the post-transfer period as compared to their prior levels of performance? We would add that it is not immediately apparent what one would expect. Related to this uncertainty is that we do not know who transfers. By "who", we refer not to their identity, but rather to their profile. What, for example, is the quality of those employees who accept transfers as some function of plant closings or reorganizations? Are these employees transferring because of their perception that their skills assure a continuing high-quality relationship with the firm? Or are some of these employees accepting the transfer because they have little realistic probability of finding comparable employment in the same region at a parallel wage? Derivatively, are the better employees less likely to accept transfer as they are relatively certain that they can secure comparable employment and remain in the region?

We should also mention that the existing literature does not reflect any distinction—or frankly much recognition—between transfers which are employee-initiated and those which are employer-initiated. While it is true that we know very little about employee-initiated transfers, we know virtually *nothing* about behaviors (e.g. performance, turnover, absenteeism, grievances) in the post-transfer period for individuals who have relocated at the request of the employer.

Is it true, for example, that employees who have accepted a company-initiated transfer are more likely to be promoted? Have their careers been accelerated? What is the impact, if any, on their work-related income? Perhaps a more interesting question concerns the impact of such transfers on *household* income. Are such employees as productive? Is it true that employees who have accepted relocation are more/less likely to quit subsequently than a comparable group of employees who did not relocate? It would seem that these questions are fundamental and potentially critical factors in firms' decisions about transfer—company initiated or otherwise—and the policies which would govern such employee movement. To our knowledge, there are no empirical data available which have been brought to bear on these questions.

Beyond the issue of employee *behavior* which may be affected by transfer are the *consequences* of such activity at different levels of analysis. Many—we suspect the overwhelming majority—of persons accepting transfers are members of groups, which are part of a subunit, which is part of the company.

What about the Company, the Subunit or the Group?

Obviously, the relocation of any individual who was part of a work group will affect not one but two intact work groups. The group from which the individual departs is now operating with one less member or is operating with a "new" member; the group to which the relocated employee now reports will certainly have one "new" member, perhaps one more member, and possibly both. An issue, of course, is what impact this has on both intact work groups. Will these groups be more productive or less? Will the "new" member be, in the language of network analysis, an isolate? If so, for how long? What difference does this make?

Similar questions can be fairly raised at the subunit and organizational levels as well. Is it true that organizations with lower/higher levels of relocation have a competitive advantage within their industry with regard to productivity and profitability? Are larger or smaller subunits/organizations more or less robust to these effects? Are impacts, if any, more notable for service-type organizations wherein face-to-face interactions with clients/customers might be more essential than in the manufacturing sectors?

SUMMARY

As we previously noted, it is estimated that 500000 employees are relocated annually in the USA at a cost of some $20 billion. Given that, we have to be surprised by how little we actually know about the phenomenon. Strikingly, there has been virtually no attention to employee *behavior* or to the consequences of employee transfers of individuals (e.g. productivity) or to the productivity of groups, units or the organization level.

Lawson and Angle (1994) remind us of an interesting, and increasingly common, corporate phenomenon wherein the issue is not the relocation of a few, or even many, employees. Rather, the issue is the relocation of entire organizational units. Typical rationales in favor of individual relocation may be absent in relocations of this type:

> From the employees' perspective, the career advancement traditionally associated with individual transfers is typically absent in group relocations. Rather than moving to accept promotions or to increase their skills, employees moving with a business unit will simply be following their jobs (Lawson & Angle, 1994, pp. 35–6).

As is the case with individual transfer, we are aware of no research which has examined the performance consequences of organizational unit relocations. While there has been some acknowledgment that productivity can be expected to decline during the period surrounding individual relocations (Pinder & Schroeder, 1987), there is no information regarding either the magnitude or the duration of such productivity losses at the group or the organizational unit level. Interestingly, there is one report of a facility relocation in which *no* employees who were offered lateral transfers accepted the reassignment (Summers & Holcombe, 1990).

We should reiterate that the existing literature rarely reflects any distinction between transfers which are employee-initiated and those which are employer initiated. Moreover, there seems to be little attention to the differences, if any, between executive/managerial relocation and transfers of non-executive/non-managerial employees. While we are aware of no data on which to base our estimate, we would be confident that the number of non-managerial transfers in any given year in the USA would be far greater than those estimated for the managerial group. Indeed, with transfer rights a fundamental element of most collective bargaining agreements, and the operation of the "domino effect" to which we have referred, we would be surprised if millions of employees were not involved in the transfer of jobs, locations or both.

We also wonder about the common refrain that an employee's willingness to accept relocation assignments is an important element of his/her career development and subsequent opportunity. As has become our refrain, we are aware of no research which directly addresses this question. We do find it interesting, however, that both *Business Week* (Weinstein, 1995) and the *Wall Street Journal* (Capell, 1996) have recently featured articles which essentially debunk that proposition.

We join others in their criticism that "withdrawal" behaviors (principally turnover and absenteeism) are typically examined independently (e.g. Dalton & Mesch, 1990; Dalton & Todor, 1993; see also Gupta & Jenkins 1991; Hulin, 1991; Mitra; Jenkins & Gupta, 1992). There is some evidence—not nearly enough— that transfer, absenteeism and turnover may be alternatives to one another. An approach, referred to as a "meta-construct", which would include the simultaneous study of several behaviors as adaptive responses to the work environment (e.g. Hulin, 1991) has been strongly advocated. Given the apparent similarities in the potential consequences of transfer and turnover, such an approach might be welcomed in both the academic and business communities. We would hope that the "transfers as local turnover", "domino effect", limited attention to the *behavior* of transferred employees, and no attention to consequences at the group, subunit or organizational level to which we have referred would stimulate some discussion as well as empirical attention.

We concur completely with Munton and West (1995, p. 374) in their sentiment that:

> Understanding patterns of adjustment to job change and relocation is of enormous practical and theoretical importance, both because of the ubiquity of the change in people's lives and because of the increasing requirement for employees to relocate both nationally and internationally.

Even so, the organizational literature provides little guidance—indeed little recognition—with respect to the dynamics of transfer/relocation. More critically, it provides no assessment of the costs and benefits of these dynamics for the contemporary organization. One could presume that firms adopting policies to encourage (or not actively discourage) employee-initiated transfers do so with the belief that, on balance, the benefits of such activity are greater than the costs. Further, one could presume that firms aggressively pursuing policies of employer-initiated transfers do so with a similar logic. In fairness, however, we would also have to add that this perspective is only an article of faith. There is simply no evidence to support such a view. We are reminded of an element of our title, "So Much Activity, So Little Information".

REFERENCES

Abelson, M. (1987). Examination of avoidable and unavoidable turnover. *Journal of Applied Psychology*, **72**, 382–6.

Abelson, M. & Baysinger, B.D. (1984). Optimal and dysfunctional turnover: toward an organizational level model. *Academy of Management Review*, **9**, 331–41.

Anderson, J.C., Milkovich, G.T. & Tsui, A. (1981). A model of intra-organizational mobility. *Academy of Management Review*, **6**, 529–38.

Blumenthal, K. & McCartney, S. (1996). To some commuters, going home means a long plane ride. *Wall Street Journal*, **March 7**, A1, 4; A6, 1.

Brett, J.M. (1984). Job transitions and personal and role development. In K.M. Rowland & G.R. Ferris (eds), *Research in Personnel and Human Resources Management* (pp. 155–85). Greenwich, CT: JAI Press.

Brett, J.M., Stroh, L.K. & Reilly, A.H. (1992). Job transfer. In C.L. Cooper & I.T. Robertson (eds), *International Review of Industrial and Organizational Psychology*. Washington, DC: Employee Relocation Council.

Brett, J.M., Stroh, L.K. & Reilly, A.H. (1993). Pulling up roots in the 1990s: who's willing to relocate? *Journal of Organizational Behavior*, **14**, 49–60.

Business Week (1995). Job left, I didn't. November 27, p. 6.

Capell, P. (1996). The right move? Relocation often seems like it should be the perfect solution to a stagnant career. It isn't. *Wall Street Journal*, **February 26**: R7, 1.

Cascio, W.F. (1991). *Costing Human Resources: the Financial Impact of Behavior in Organizations*, 3rd edn. Boston, MA: PWS-Kent Publishing Company.

Dalton, D.R., Cairns, D.A., Canavan, J.M., Downey, J.L., Fowler, A., Freiwald, G.M., Johnson, P., King, H.R. & Lincoln, R.W. (1995). Human resource management and employee turnover and transfer: what we know is not always what we need. In G.R.

Ferris, S.D. Rosen & D.T. Barnum (eds), *Handbook of Human Resource Management* (pp. 615–29). Cambridge, MA: Blackwell.

Dalton, D.R., Krackhardt, D.M. & Todor, W.D. (1981). Functional turnover: an empirical assessment. *Journal of Applied Psychology*, **66**, 716–21.

Dalton, D.R. & Mesch, D.J. (1990). The impact of flexible scheduling on employee attendance and turnover. *Administrative Science Quarterly*, **35**, 370–87.

Dalton, D.R. & Todor, W.D. (1979). Turnover turned over: an expanded and positive perspective. *Academy of Management Review*, **4**, 225–36.

Dalton, D.R. & Todor, W.D. (1982). Turnover: a lucrative hard dollar phenomenon. *Academy of Management Review*, **7**, 212–18.

Dalton, D.R. & Todor, W.D. (1987). The attenuating effects of internal mobility on employee turnover: multiple field assessments. *Journal of Management*, **13**, 705–11.

Dalton, D.R., Todor, W.D. & Krackhardt, D.M. (1982). Turnover overstated: the functional taxonomy. *Academy of Management Review*, **7**, 117–23.

Dalton, D.R. & Todor, W.D. (1993). Turnover, transfer, absenteeism: an interdependent perspective. *Journal of Management*, **19**, 193–219.

Fisher, C.D. & Shaw, J.B. (1994). Relocation attitudes and adjustment: a longitudinal study. *Journal of Organizational Behavior*, **15**, 209–24.

Fossum, J.A. (1987). Labor relations: research and practice in transition. *Journal of Management*, **13**, 281–300.

Galer, S. (1991). The cost of getting there from here. *CFO: The Magazine for Chief Financial Officers*, **6**(7), 12.

Gupta, N. & Jenkins, G.D. (1991). Rethinking dysfunctional employee behaviors. *Human Resource Management Journal*, **1**, 39–59.

Gustafson, H.W. (1982). Force-loss analysis. In W.H. Mobley (ed), *Employee Turnover: Causes. Consequences, and Control* (pp. 139–85). Reading, MA: Addison-Wesley.

Hollenbeck, J.R. & Williams, C.R. (1986). Turnover functionality VS. turnover frequency: a note on work attitudes and organizational effectiveness. *Journal of Applied Psychology*, **71**, 606–11.

Hulin, C.L. (1991). Adaptation, persistence, and commitment in organizations. In M.D. Dunnette & L.M. Hough (eds), *Handbook of Industrial and Organizational Psychology*, 2nd edn (pp. 445–505). Palo Alto, CA: Consulting Psychologists Press.

Jackofsky, E.F. (1984). Turnover and job performance: an integrated process model. *Academy of Management Review*, **9**, 74–84.

Jackofsky, E.F. & Peters, L.H. (1983). Job turnover versus company turnover: reassessment of the March and Simon participation hypothesis. *Journal of Applied Psychology*, **68**, 490–95.

Lawson, M.B. & Angle, H.L. (1994). When organizational relocation means family relocation: an emerging issue for strategic human resource management. *Human Resource Management*, **33**, 33–54.

Lucas, G.H., Parasuraman, A., Davis, R.A. & Enis, B. (1987). An empirical study of sales force turnover. *Journal of Marketing*, **51**, 34–59.

March, J.G. & Simon, H.A. (1958). *Organizations*. New York: Wiley.

Mitra, A., Jenkins, G.D. & Gupta, N. (1992). A meta-analytic review of the relationship between absence and turnover. *Journal of Applied Psychology*, **77**, 879–89.

Munton, A.G. & West, M.A. (1995). Innovations and personal change: patterns of adjustment to relocation. *Journal of Organizational Behavior*, **16**, 363–75.

Noe, R.A.; Steffy, B.D. & Barber, A.E. (1988). An investigation of the factors influencing employees' willingness to accept mobility opportunities. *Personnel Psychology*, **41**, 559–80.

Pinder, C.C. (1989). The dark side of executive relocation. *Organizational Dynamics*, **17**, 48–58.

Pinder, C.C. & Schroeder, K.G. (1987). Time to proficiency following job transfers. *Academy of Management Journal*, **30**, 336–53.

Pinder, C.C. & Walter, G.A. (1984). Personnel transfers and employee development. In K.M. Rowland & G.R. Ferris (eds), *Research in Personnel and Human Resources Management* (pp. 187–218). Greenwich, CT: JAI Press.

Staw, B.M. (1980). Consequences of turnover. *Journal of Occupational Behavior*, **1**, 53–73.

Staw, B.M. & Oldham, R.R. (1978). Reconsidering our dependent variables: a critique and empirical study. *Academy of Management Journal*, **21**, 539–59.

Summers, T.P. & Holcombe, J.S. (1990). The effect of offers to relocate on attitudes of departed employees following a merger. *Journal of Social Behavior and Personality*, **5**, 323–6.

Templin, N. & White, J.B. (1994). GM goes to great lengths to match workers and work. *Wall Street Journal*, **April 21**, B6, C3.

Tsui, A.S., Pearce, J.L., Porter, L.W. & Hite, J.P. (1995). In G.R. Ferris (ed), *Research in Personnel and Human Resources Management* (pp. 117–51). Greenwich, CT: JAI Press.

Turban, D.B., Campion, J.E. & Eyring, A.R. (1992). Factors relating to relocation decisions of research and development employees. *Journal of Vocational Behavior*, **41**, 183–99.

Weinstein, G.W. (1995). Before saying yes to going abroad. *Business Week*, **December 4**, 130–32.

Chapter 21

Dynamic Self-Reliance: An Important Concept for Work in the Twenty-First Century

Michael Frese
University of Amsterdam, The Netherlands

THE IMPORTANCE OF SELF-RELIANCE IN TOMORROW'S JOBS

Self-reliance is to depend on and trust one's knowledge, skills and efforts (motivation). The most important components are that one is able to acquire knowledge and skills by oneself (self-training) and to self-start motivational processes (initiative). Self-training is important because the environment does not stand still; it changes, and therefore one has to rely on oneself to acquire knowledge and skills. Self-reliance is dynamic if it tends towards growth and higher mastery. I want to argue in this chapter that tomorrow's jobs will require a higher degree of self-developed knowledge, skills and motivation than today's jobs. Further, I would like to explicate the implications of self-training and initiative. Finally, potential misunderstandings and research questions will be discussed.

Creating Tomorrow's Organizations. Edited by C.L. Cooper and S.E. Jackson.
© 1997 John Wiley & Sons Ltd.

Tomorrow's Jobs—Trends

The following trends of how jobs will change are reasonable predictions:

1. *Global competition.* There is no doubt that there is a more global competition today than in the past and it is highly probable that this trend will increase. In the 1960s, in the US economy 7% of companies were exposed to international competition, while in the 1980s this number climbed to above 70% (Gwynne, 1992). Global competition will not only reign on the company level but more and more also on the individual level. With better communication devices, software developers in India compete for work with software developers in Holland or Switzerland. The most forceful competitors of German construction workers are British, Portuguese, and Polish workers who work as small-scale entrepreneurs in Germany, selling their labor power.

2. *Faster rate of innovation.* There will be more pressure to innovate (Kanter, 1984) because of the global market and because the time to create new products from new knowledge becomes shorter. Hamel & Prahalad (1994) have argued that the competition between firms will be more and more on opportunity shares (shares in future markets with products that may not exist yet). This is of particular importance for the European countries, which have fallen back against the USA and Japan in terms of innovativeness and patents.

3. *Increase of complexity.* While there is little effect of new technology *per se* (Frese & Zapf, 1987), changes in work organization interacting with new technology will make work intellectually more demanding (Davis, 1995; Womack, Jones & Roos, 1990). Moreover, since the rate of change is increasing, this implies that new knowledge has to be acquired constantly.

   The factors that contribute to an increase of work complexity are production for small niches, customization and customer orientation. Most car companies already work on a principle of demand, with each car being specified individually and separately. Complexity of work also increases because of increasing environmental turbulances and ever faster-developing fashions and global changes.

   A factor that leads to higher complexity in social skills is the higher cultural diversity of workers. Immigrant, minority and women employment increases in all Western countries. In the USA,Hispanics, Asians and African-Americans will grow to about 27% and females to about 45% of the labor force by 2005 (Howard, 1995).

4. *Increase of group work.* Ever since Womack, Jones & Roos (1990) showed that in Japan 69% of all automobile workers were working in groups, while the respective percentage was 17% in the USA and not even 1% in Europe, introduction of group work has been an important aspect of productivity improvement. Group work is being introduced, particularly in Europe (Germany and Holland), often relating it to the tradition and experiences that were made 15–20 years ago with semi-autonomous groups (Antoni, 1994).

Group work will be more frequent in the future. First, if production responsibilities are put back to the shop floor (as is common to all new production concepts), it will not just be single persons who can make decisions. Since there are dependencies among shop floor workers, team decisions have to be made. This implies that group participants should know something about each other's work, therefore there is a need for job rotation. Second, new production methods (like lean production) are geared towards reducing coordination costs by reducing the number of supervisors. Coordination is then done within production units (teams). Third, increasing complexity will increase the need for coordinated effort. Since high-complexity decisions require the input from sources of different disciplines, there will be a higher need for interdisciplinary team work. Interdisciplinary work is difficult because one has to be able to talk about one's own discipline in ways that other people understand, has to learn to understand the basics of another discipline quickly, and has to learn to appreciate the different approaches taken by various disciplines (which is as difficult as cross-cultural learning at times) (Baron, 1993). In interdisciplary teams, one has to be able to rely on each person within the group (and consequently the person has to rely on him/herself as well, because he/she may be the only expert for a certain area in this group). Finally, teams will have to react to environmental turbulence, since local shop floor teams are better regulators of such turbulence (cf. the sociotechnical system approach of Emery & Trist, 1969).

One implication of a higher degree of team work is the higher need for good social and communication skills. It is interesting that the automobile companies that invested in East Germany have selected even blue collar workers by assessment centers, in order explicitly to gauge the social skills of their newly employed blue collar workers, who are working in lean, team-based production systems.

5. *Change of the job concept.* Some authors have argued that the notion of jobs as we know it will evaporate (Bridges, 1995; Rifkin, 1995). First, there is a clear reduction of jobs in the traditional production and service industries. With every re-engineering attempt, the number of blue and white collar workers is reduced tremendously. Louisville's Capital Holding reduced its back-office staff from 1900 to 1100 while increasing business by 25% after re-engineering (Bridges, 1995). Technological innovation leads to a reduction of personnel, as well. For example, cashier jobs (the third largest clerical group in the USA) will be cut by 10–15% by new scanning equipment (Rifkin, 1995); this trend will probably be increased by electronic shopping. The reduction in jobs will lead to the knowledge that one cannot stay in this type of job; therefore there is higher pressure to develop one's knowledge and to show initiative to get jobs. Second, temporary and project work increases. A symbol of this is that a fast-developing company with a very high work force in the USA is Manpower—a temporary employment agency (Bridges, 1995). More and more companies are outsourcing, employing people only on a project basis, or they are even reducing the company to a virtual company

consisting of a network of small scale entrepreneurs. Third, even in companies that still provide jobs, the job concept is also changing. People are assigned to projects and not to jobs. For example, Microsoft has no regular working hours, people are accountable to their project team, which is again accountable to the larger project. When a project ends, employees move on to another project (Bridges, 1995). "The dejobbed systems lack the normal kind of 'edges' that tell workers when they have done a normal, satisfactory job. Since they are expected to do *anything necessary* to accomplish the expected results, they are no longer protected by the boundaries of a job" (Bridges, 1995, p. 42). Finally, there will be more telework and similar forms of work. For example, at Arthur Anderson in Paris one can register for an office at any time and plug in one's computer but one does not have one's own office any longer. In other companies, employees work from home or a hotel.

6. *Reduced supervision.* With the advent of lean production (Womack, Jones & Roos, 1990), management layers are taken out and responsibility for production is being given to the shop floor again. Therefore, supervisors' functions change; they should not intervene directly into day-to-day affairs but should rather be mentors of the groups they supervise (Cascio, 1995; Emery & Trist, 1969).

The Importance of Self-Reliance in Future Work

All of the above-mentioned trends increase the importance of self-reliance. To deal with global competition, employees have to be able to keep up with new knowledge and with new ideas. Moreover, new ideas have to be advanced. Self-reliance, that is being able to rely on one's knowledge, skills and motivation, enables one to stay in this race. Whenever employees are working outside a rigid structure, they have to motivate themselves, for example in telehomework. Reduced supervision also reduces the outside structure of the job.

Tayloristic jobs have tended to take away the authority from the people; they were given to the supervisor, the bureaucracy, the assembly line, etc. To realize the opportunities that exist now, one has to show a high degree of self-reliance ("It is worth saying . . . that these changes once again put a premium on the values of self-reliance and individualism", Bridges, 1995, p. 40). For example, getting another project after the last one is a matter of having a good reputation and initiative.

Thus, all of the above changes of the work place that can be projected into the future, are related to self-reliance (knowledge, skills and motivation). A good indicator of future trends in the work place are jobs at the forefront of modern technology that can already be empirically researched. The work place of software designers is such a job. In a careful study of the work situation of this profession, we have come to the conclusion that the following aspects are of primary importance in their jobs (Brodbeck, 1994; Frese & Hesse, 1993):

- A high degree of learning by oneself (e.g. new techniques and methods, etc.).
- A high degree of communication with co-workers.
- A high degree of interdisciplinary work (e.g. with customers who are experts in another area).
- A high degree of working in groups.
- A high degree to which the people determine, themselves, how they are solving problems.

These empirical observations reinforce the above-mentioned trends and they point again to the importance of self-reliance.

THE CONCEPT OF SELF-RELIANCE

The two major components of self-reliance are to acquire knowledge and skills by oneself and to motivate oneself. These two components will be discussed under the headings of self-training and self-initiative.

Self-Training

Self-training implies that there is no training plan outside oneself but that the plan is developed by the learning person. From an action theory perspective, self-training can be described by explicating the following components (cf. Frese & Zapf, 1994): learning goals, orientation and prognosis, learning strategies, feedback processing. In order to be useful for self-training, these components have to be self-reflective, self-sufficient, adequate and action-oriented. For each component, one can discuss environmental and person support factors.

Learning Goals

If one wants to acquire new skills, one needs to develop learning goals for self-training. Dweck & Leggett (1988) have contrasted pupils with learning goals and with performance goals. Those with learning goals learn better because such goals imply that one thinks of one's ability as flexible and that ability and effort are positively related. In contrast, pupils with performance goals perceive their effort negatively, because having to exert effort means that one's ability is low. The concept of a learning goal is of paramount importance because it means that problems and difficulties are seen as chances to learn rather than as bad aspects of performance. One implications of a learning orientation is that the learner is much less dependent on other people's impression of how well one does and, therefore, more self-sufficient. Thus, this orientation fosters self-reliance to a much higher extent. In terms of environmental support factors, all factors that increase exploration and active approaches will help to develop learning goals (active approaches to training are superior, Frese et al., 1988). Of particular importance are learning organizations (Argyris, 1993).

Orientation and Prognosis

Orientation here means that one develops a good mental model of the system in which one is functioning (e.g. the sociotechnical system of one company) and that one can predict the dynamic system's future behaviors well (Dörner et al., 1983). Issues here are the need to think dynamically, synthetically, within systems and laterally, instead of along simple linear lines (e.g. extending growth curves without taking into account breakdowns and accelerations).

The resulting mental model must be holistic and action-oriented. A holistic concept implies that one knows the important parameters of a task. If the task is too complex to learn in one sitting, an overall global idea of the task should be developed (Volpert, 1971). This global picture can then be used to develop hypotheses to be tested. This stands in sharp contrast to a sequential procedure. Here one just learns each step by itself—often by a sort of drill—and then adds the other steps to it. A mental model can be more or less action-oriented. In an observational study on computer users, only those parts of the mental model that had direct relevance to actions, were useful in solving problems (Lang, 1987).

In terms of environmental supports, everything that helps people to think about other people's jobs and concepts is important for developing a good orientation, for example, many horizontal relations between departments within organizations (Kanter, 1984) and group members being exposed to different viewpoints (Andrews, 1979).

Learning Strategies

The most important, successful, learning strategy for self-training is exploration (Greif & Keller, 1990). It is successful because it is an active approach to learning and it makes best use of one's experiences in the learning process. Empirical studies have shown that exploratory learning is superior to other forms of learning that are not active (Frese et al., 1988; Greif & Janikowski, 1987). In one study (Dormann & Frese, 1994), two learning procedures were compared—one did not allow exploration (sequential training); the other one necessitated exploration. The most interesting finding was that some people in the sequential group actually showed self-reliance and deviated from the instructions: in spite of the instruction not to explore, they explored, anyhow; we found that those subjects learned more than those who followed the instructions.

In terms of environmental support, again learning organizations provide support for learning strategies.

Feedback Processing

There is a psychological truism that without knowledge of results, there can be no learning (Annett, 1969). Feedback tells a person whether or not he/she is still on the way towards a goal (thus, without an explicit goal, one cannot use feedback). Feedback connects us to the objectivity of the world and has a (self-) motivating function. However, there are certain feedback functions that are not always useful. For example, augmented feedback (that is feedback that is only used for the purpose of training, such as a buzzer for good aiming when learning to shoot) actually leads to worse real-life performance because one becomes accustomed to the feedback in training (Volpert, 1971). Most importantly, feedback interventions, for example performance evaluation, are often detrimental to performance (Kluger & DeNisi, 1996), partly because they lead to state orientation (one thinks about oneself rather than about the task) and partly because they make one dependent on other people's judgment, thus reducing one's self-reliance.

The two most important naturally occurring causes of learning are first, a new task, and second, errors. Learning because of new tasks is one reason why complex jobs lead to more intellectual flexibility and to a higher degree of self-reliance (Kohn & Schooler, 1983). The issue of learning through errors is a bit newer and may be even more important. We will therefore discuss some research findings and ideas.

The Function of Errors in Learning

Errors tell us that we did something wrong. Thus, in principle, they are negative feedback and are, therefore, learning devices and of particular importance for self-training (Frese & Zapf, 1994). Errors are ambivalent because, depending upon personal orientations or environmental conditions, they may on the one hand lead to crippling self-derogatory thoughts and defensiveness or, on the other hand, they may be the prime material that stimulates learning.

Since errors are defined by not achieving a goal and by the feeling that one "should have known better" (Frese & Zapf, 1991), the typical first reaction to errors is negative. However, the real problem of an error is the negative error consequences (loss of time, loss of material or money, maybe even loss of life). Errors get their "bad name" from these negative error consequences. However, it is possible to distinguish the error action from the error consequence. Not every slipping leads to falling or even breaking one's arm. An error prevention approach attempts to block the action error. An alternative is the error management approach, which attempts to block the negative consequences (as when one learns to fall in Jiu-Jitsu). More formally, "error management implies that error handling is supported with the goal of avoiding negative error consequences, of dealing quickly with error consequences once they occur, and of learning from the error to reduce the future occurrence of this type of error" (Frese & van Dyck, 1996). Thus, the error management concept is more positive towards errors, attempts to reduce the negative consequences rather than the error *per se*, and emphasizes learning from errors. Since errors are ubiquitous, this is a better strategy, in general, and it is of particular importance for self-training.

In an experiment, we attempted to demonstrate the positive function of errors for learning (Frese et al., 1991). The experiment used quite a radical approach: the error training group received only a list of commands to be used to solve the given tasks. Otherwise, the trainees were on their own—a situation that produced many chances for errors. In order to reduce the frustrations that result from errors, the subjects were repeatedly given a set of "heuristics". These heuristics specified that errors should not be perceived negatively but as learning opportunities. Examples were "I have made an error. Great!" or "There is always a way to leave the error situation". In contrast, the error avoidance group received a training that mimicked commercial tutoring programs—a so-called sequential training. The subjects had to solve the same tasks as the other group, but they were told precisely how to go about it. Thus, they did not have the chance to make errors. The error training group did much better in performance tasks after the training than the other group—a result replicated several times (Frese, 1995).

Thus, the argument so far has been that errors have a positive function for learning. So it is possible and even better to make errors for the learning process. However, when we are talking about self-training, we assume, of course, that people are involved in their daily stream of actions and that errors should also help them to learn in this situation. Moreover, errors should be of paramount importance for the self-training process. In the following I shall argue that errors have a particular importance for self-training because they help to instigate learning (at least under certain conditions). This leads to the following points (which are developed further below): (1) errors disrupt premature routinization of actions; (2) errors instigate new learning, exploration and creative solutions; (3) errors may lead to higher motivation; (4) additional frustrations because of errors have to be reduced by learning how to deal with errors effectively; and (5) this positive function of errors appears more frequently given certain personal and organizational antecedents.

1. People have a tendency to develop routine and automatic patterns of dealing with the world when the environment is redundant. Errors usually lead to new thinking about one's actions (see Frese & Zapf, 1994). Therefore, errors *reduce the danger of routinization* of action strategies and help to make people think again. Inventors like Edison often reported that errors have helped them in making inventions.
2. Errors can *increase exploration*. When an error occurs the person may start exploring to find a better way of doing things. Exploratory behavior and performance indicators are highly correlated (Dormann & Frese, 1994). Pfeffer (1992) suggests that there is a difference in the way exploration is done in the different training groups: the error avoidance group used exploration more in a trial-and-error sense, while the error training group used exploration more specifically in an hypothesis-driven way.
3. Errors may increase the *motivation to learn*. This was suggested by some qualitative observations in our experiments. While the participants in the error avoidance group went away after the training without waiting much longer, it was difficult to persuade the trainees of the error training group to leave the computer room. They "bombarded" us with further questions and

seemed highly interested. This may have been due to a sort of Zeigarnik effect (Ovsiankina, 1928)—if an action is interrupted, it is more frequently resumed. An error always interrupts an action; therefore one is motivated to complete it.

Another factor is that an error always signifies a discrepancy between a given state and a goal. Since we know that a high discrepancy leads to high motivation (Locke & Latham, 1990), motivation arises from making an error. Of course, if the discrepancy becomes too high, people may actually give up or an error may lead to self-oriented thoughts and, thus, divert attention from the task. Therefore, errors are always a double-edged sword from a motivational perspective.

4. Errors are *upsetting and frustrating*. Thus, in order to learn, these negative feelings must be reduced by becoming more tolerant of one's errors. Making an error always holds at least two facets; losing time and being subjected to the additional frustration about oneself that one has "made such a stupid mistake". While time loss can only be reduced by good handling strategies, the additional emotional upset can be reduced by developing a more positive attitude towards errors. This refers again back to the issue of learning goals that perceive errors as a chance to learn something (Dweck & Leggett, 1988). Such an attitude also decreases the tendency to give up in case of an error.

It seems that our use of heuristics in error training had indeed helped to defray the negative frustrations due to errors in the error training group. Thus, the emotionally toned heuristics on the positive notion of errors in the training process are important ("You have made an error. Great!"). One may actually learn better emotional strategies to deal with errors (Frese et al., 1991).

5. In order for errors to have positive effects, certain prerequisites must be met. First, making errors and learning from them has to be supported at the workplace. For this reason, Peters (1987) suggested that organizations should facilitate making errors—fast failure forward. People are encouraged to make their errors quickly. The rationale is that people will make errors anyway, therefore it would be better to speed up the error process under somewhat safer conditions, so that people can learn from their mistakes. Thus, a positive error culture is important (Frese & van Dyck, 1996). Second, error orientations contribute to learning from errors. With a newly developed Error Orientation Questionnaire (EOQ, Rybowiak et al., 1997) we have shown that people with a stronger tendency to learn from errors in work have more feelings of self-efficacy and self-esteem, are more ready to change things in their work and display more initiative. People who take more risks—even if taking risks means making more errors—are more qualified, have higher self-efficacy, take on more responsibility at work; they are also more interested to implement changes in their workplace and show more self-reported initiative. Finally, people who cover errors up have higher job uncertainty, more career stress, lower self-esteem and lower self-efficacy.

Thus, the orientation towards errors is important. Leeson, who single-handedly brought down Baring's Bank, may be a good example for a person who could not deal with errors well. For example, he was not willing and capable to anticipate errors. As a matter of fact, Rawnsley (1995) describes Leeson as being particularly harsh to employees who made errors. Moreover, the error culture of Baring's Bank was not one of allowing errors to appear and managing them adequately.

Let's come back to the issue of self-reliance. We are constantly in a stream of action: errors interrupt this stream and we become conscious of our ways, we think about them again, we explore alternatives, we come up with new solutions. But this is only true if certain prerequisites are met: the most important are that there is a positive error culture in the organization and that we believe that we can and should learn from our errors, that errors should not just lead to a feeling of catastrophe but to new learning. This then helps us to acquire new knowledge and skills in our daily work.

A Short Note on Defensiveness, Self-Reflection and Learning

A particular problem that hinders self-training is defensiveness. Defensiveness reduces the perception for an opportunity to learn something (e.g. in an error situation), because one is busy defending oneself (Argyris, 1993). According to Dörner's studies, defensiveness is one of the most important reasons why one persists in a wrong track and is not able to grasp the complexity of a system (Dörner et al., 1983; Dörner & Schaub, 1994). Defensiveness can be contrasted to self-reflection. Self-reflection in this sense should not be confused with lack of action orientation but it is related to being able to think freely about one's errors, faults and difficulties in order to overcome them. Self-reflection is necessary for knowing in which areas one has to advance one's knowledge and skills, where one has to rethink one's strategies and where one has to overcome problems due to one's personality.

Self-Motivation: Initiative

To be self-reliant, one has to be able to motivate oneself. Motivation oneself means initiative. I have studied initiative since the downfall of the East German communist republic in 1990 because I was interested to research the changes that came along with modern capitalism (Frese et al., 1996). As a matter of fact, it was this research and the concomitant research on software developers that convinced me eventually that self-reliance was of central importance in future companies. Therefore, both a questionnaire form and an interview-based "behavioral measure" of initiative have been developed (Frese et al., 1997).

The centerpiece of self-reliance and initiative is to be self-starting (Frese, in press). This means that people do not wait for orders, suggestions or ideas from other people, but develop their own ideas and start acting themselves. Since at the workplace one is usually given tasks, initiative implies that one takes on extra-task activities that were not prescribed. Examples are a secretary checking the mail of his/her boss and responding to important letters during the boss's absence without having been asked to do that.

Personal initiative is a behavior syndrome of an individual's taking a self-starting, active and persistent approach to work. Additional aspects of the concept are that this behavior is consistent with the organization's mission, goal-directed and action-oriented (see Frese et al., 1996). While self-starting is the center, initiative also implies that one does not give up when new suggestions do not work out immediately or are blocked by opposition. Initiative, therefore, implies that one will deal with these obstacles actively and persistently.

Personal Initiative and Other Constructs

Personal initiative is related but not identical to other constructs, such as entrepreneurship/intrapreneurship, organizational citizenship behavior (Organ, 1988) and achievement motive (for details, see Frese et al., 1997). It is instructive to look at the differences to organizational citizenship behavior (OCB). Both concepts are similar because they go beyond direct role requirements and contribute indirectly to organizational effectiveness (Organ, 1988). OCB is more passive, however, as shown in the compliance factor ("does not take extra breaks", adherence to rules, etc.). In contrast, the concept of initiative often implies a certain rebellious element. Supervisors often fail to support initiative and even punish active approaches. A worker with high initiative contributes to *long-range* positive outcomes for the organization, but in the short term he/she may well be a nuisance factor to the boss because he/she is constantly pushing new ideas.

A Model of Personal Initiative

In our 5 year longitudinal study on initiative in East Germany we have slowly developed a model of personal initiative that helps us understand the antecedents of initiative (Figure 21.1). We differentiate between skills, a responsive environment (environmental supports), and orientations. There are distal and proximal antecedents (Kanfer, 1992)—the distal constructs being personality factors and the proximal constructs being orientations. From an occupational socialization perspective, environmental supports should have an influence on the orientations and on initiative (Frese, 1982; Frese et al., 1996). We assume that there may be interactions between orientations and personality prerequisites and between environmental support (and skills) and orientations. Personal initiative should in turn have an influence on organizational functioning.[1]

---

[1] Actually, reverse paths are also possible; an example for the path from initiative to orientations is the path from initiative on self-efficacy.

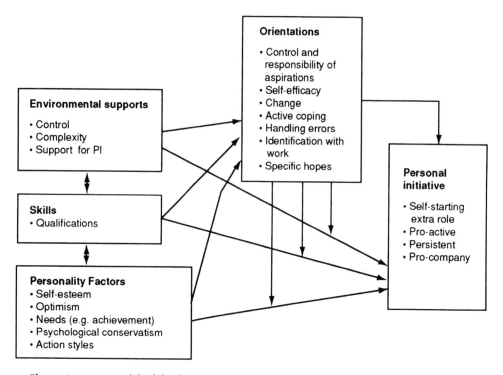

Figure 21.1 A model of the functioning of personal initiative (PI)

This model has not yet been tested in its entirety but various parts can prob-ably be upheld under empirical scrutiny. We cannot go into detail here and therefore we would like to concentrate on two antecedents: control aspirations and self-efficacy.

Initiative should be influenced by a desire to "be on top of things". Control aspirations are hypothesized to be lowered or increased by control at work. If workers do not control their environment and their own behaviors at the workplace, their aspirations for control are frustrated and reduced because help-lessness cognitions develop. Work control and complexity, indeed, influence control aspirations (Frese et al., 1994). Similarly, having higher control aspira-tions leads to job changes, because one attempts to get jobs that allow more control (Frese et al., 1994). This does not necessarily mean that one actually gets a new job formally; it may also affect informal task assignments.

Self-efficacy (Bandura, 1986) should be related to control and complexity of work, because these allow the employee to enact mastery and thus learn self-efficacy. At the same time, self-efficacy should influence initiative because one needs to be confident of one's competence to actually be self-starting and be persistent in spite of obstacles. Thus, self-efficacy should be a mediator between environmental supports (control and complexity) and initiative. This has been shown to be true (Speier & Frese, 1997). However, self-efficacy may also function as a moderator of the relationship between environmental supports and initiative leading to a compensatory relationship. Having little control at work is not so important for people with high initiative; they will still show high initiative. In contrast, control at work has a stronger effect for low self-efficacious workers (Speier & Frese, 1997).

The discussion of these two antecedents may suffice to give the gist of what one can do with this model. The general idea is that initiative does not develop in a vacuum—it is related to long-standing personality and environmental characteristics. There are direct antecedents and long-range effects. In any case, a complex behavior syndrome like initiative can fruitfully be studied empirically, and it does give meaningful results (Frese et al., 1997).

POTENTIAL MISUNDERSTANDINGS

The most important potential misunderstanding assumes that environmental factors do not play any role for self-reliance. One could argue that, after all, the person is self-reliant and is therefore independent of the environment. This view is empirically wrong. Environmental factors do play a role in the development and in upholding self-reliance. Therefore, it is no surprise that control and complexity of work actually influence initiative. However, in the case of self-reliance, the effect of the environment is not linear and not short-term. Thus, people may show a high degree of initiative in spite of lack of control at work (and they do, if their self-efficacy is high; see Speier & Frese, 1997). But in the long run, their self-efficacy is reduced when control and complexity of work is low. Moreover, the environment presents opportunities given a high degree of self-reliance. We assume that self-reliance leads to active scanning of the environment, for example, in the case of the small-scale entrepreneur who looks for opportunities to sell and innovate. Obviously, the concept of using errors as a chance to learn relates self-reliance to environmental factors (errors are partly determined by the environment, being the result of an interaction of the person and the environment; see Frese & Zapf, 1991).

Another potential misunderstanding refers to the dynamic nature of self-reliance. Self-reliance could mean that the person is self-centered and does not really grow. Opportunities are not used, goals are not changed, etc. We do not want to imply such a viewpoint. For this reason, the title of this chapter refers to *dynamic* self-reliance. Since self-reliance is related to self-training, a dynamic viewpoint is implied. Moreover, self-reliance requires a long-term orientation—this again leads to a dynamic nature of self-reliance. We assume that self-reliance scans for opportunities and reacts quickly to environmental turbulence (using them as challenges, much like errors).

Further, one could assume that self-reliance is just old wine in new bottles. From this perspective self-reliance is just an instance of internal motivation or self-actualization. We do not think so. Internal motivation is task-driven (one is motivated by playing the piano). But being task-driven does not necessarily mean that one also shows self-reliance (although we believe that internal motivation is an antecedent of self-reliance). A similar difference exists between achievement motive and self-reliance. While achievement motive is probably an antecedent (see Frese et al., 1997), it is not self-starting by itself.

RESEARCH ISSUES

Because of the future job changes, self-reliance with its concepts of self-training and initiative are of major importance for organizational psychology. Obviously, the concept of self-reliance as an umbrella term for self-training and initiative is new and needs to be explicated and researched. Thus, there are many issues that await conceptual and empirical answers. The most obvious ones are whether we can substantiate the issues raised in Figure 21.1. Which antecedents are operative? Which interactions exist? Which variables constitute the behavior syndrome?

Further questions are to look at related concepts and their correlations and causal relationships with self-reliance, concepts such as self-management, self-efficacy (Bandura, 1986), self-esteem, achievement motive, self-actualization, innovative behavior (West & Farr, 1990) and active coping (Lazarus & Folkman, 1984).

Surprisingly, we know more about how to make people *less* self-reliant, e.g. how to make them helpless (Seligman, 1975). Helplessness is the opposite of self-reliance. Recently Seligman (1991) has talked about optimism as being the opposite of helplessness. I do not agree. Helplessness is a behaviour syndrome (Seligman, 1975), similar to self-reliance. The latter may be related to optimism, but self-reliance is the better antonym for helplessness (empirically, there is also no significant correlation between Seligman's attributional style questionnaire and initiative).

Similarly, the relationship between OCB and self-reliance has to be empirically established. We assume that continuous dynamic self-reliance is often (but not always) fed by dissatisfaction with a certain situation (and possibly with the supervisor). In contrast, it is assumed that OCB should be related to a "feel-good" factor (Organ, 1988).

The relationship of group work and self-reliance is complex and interesting. In principle, group work could have a negative effect on self-reliance (diffusion of responsibility, free-riding, etc.) but we know very little of how it is actually happening when group work is introduced in industry.

Leadership issues should be related to self-learning and initiative. Thus, charismatic and transformational forms of leadership should actually foster self-reliance by increasing standards, self-efficacy and intellectual curiosity. However, as far as I know, this has not been really studied (Bass, 1990), although Manz & Sims (1989) have opened up interest in this issue with their concept of superleadership (which is probably related to self-reliance). Often, the concept of empowerment implies that organizations enhance self-reliance. However, people who show high self-reliance may be less dependent upon organizational empowerment than those who do not.

Organizations that provide degrees of freedom of action and empowerment should enhance initiative and self-training. For example, advantages of participation in decision-making have been mainly looked at from the perspective of enhancing motivation from the outside. Our thinking may reconceptualize this issue because we would assume that the major functions are to increase self-starting behaviors and self-training and exploration because people are able to participate in the error-making process. Moreover, it is useful to ask the question how certain kinds of ideal organizational designs (e.g. Mintzberg's, 1983, organizational forms) are related to self-reliance.

We know surprisingly little about self-training. While there is a fully developed literature on learning, there is little that describes the processes of self-training. There are obvious relationships to the concept of the learning organization (Argyris, 1993) that need to be explored.

An additional issue of self-reliance is how one deals with stress in terms of active coping strategies (Lazarus & Folkman, 1984). There is some evidence that initiative is related to active coping strategies and that people with high initiative are able to overcome the stressful situation of unemployment better (Frese et al., 1997).

Whatever the specifics, there is no doubt that behaviors that are called for in future workplaces will have to be studied intensely—and self-reliance will be one of them.

Acknowledgments

The thoughts discussed in this paper have been developed during the ongoing project AHUS (Aktives Handeln in einer Umbruchsituation—active actions in a radical change situation) which is supported by the Deutsche Forschungsgemeinschaft (DFG, No. Fr 638/6-5) and the European Mobility Grant (No. CHRX-CT 93-0298 (DG 12 COMA) 75/90 0611110), Prevention of human errors in systems for energy production and process industry), both of which are gratefully acknowledged. Doris Fay and Sabine Sonnentag have helped by critically reading a earlier version of this article.

REFERENCES

Andrews, F.M. (ed.) (1979). *Scientific Productivity*. Cambridge: Cambridge University Press.

Annett, J. (1969). *Feedback and Human Behaviour*. Harmondsworth: Penguin.

Antoni, C.H. (1994). Gruppenarbeit—mehr als ein Konzept: Darstellung und Vergleich unterschiedlicher Formen der Gruppenarbeit (pp. 19–48). In C.H. Antoni (ed.), *Gruppenarbeit in Unternehmen*. Weinheim: Psychologie Verlags Union.

Argyris, C. (1993). *Knowledge for Action*. San Francisco, CA: Jossey-Bass.

Bandura, A. (1986). *Social Foundations of Thought and Action*. Englewood Cliffs, NJ: Prentice-Hall.

Baron, J. (1993). Why teach thinking?—an essay. *Applied Psychology: An International Review*, **42**, 191–213.

Bass, B.M. (1990). *Bass and Stogdill's Handbook of Leadership: Theory, Research and Managerial Applications*, 3rd edn. New York: Free Press.

Bridges, W. (1995). *Jobshift*. London: Nicholas Braeley.

Brodbeck, F.C. (1994). Software-Entwicklung: ein Tätigkeitsspektrum mit vielfältigen Kommunikations- und Lernanforderungen. In F.C. Brodbeck & M. Frese (eds), *Produktivität in Software-Projekten* (pp. 13–34). München: Oldenbourg.

Cascio, W.F. (1995). Whither industrial and organizational psychology in a changing world of work? *American Psychologist*, **50**, 928–39.

Davis (1995). Form, function, and strategy in boundaryless organizations. In A. Howard (ed.), *The Changing Nature of Work* (pp. 112–38). San Francisco, CA: Jossey-Bass.

Dormann, T. & Frese, M. (1994). Error training: replication and the function of exploratory behavior. *International Journal of Human–Computer Interaction*, **6**, 365–72.

Dörner, D., Kreuzig, H.W., Reither, F. & Staeudel (eds) (1983). *Lohhausen. Vom Umgang mit Unbestimmtheit und Komplexitaet*. Bern: Huber.

Dörner, D. & Schaub, H. (1994). Errors in planning and decision-making and the nature of human information processing. *Applied Psychology: An International Review*, **43**, 433–54.

Dweck, C.S. & Leggett, E.L. (1988). A social-cognitive approach to motivation and personality. *Psychological Review*, **95** 256–73.

Emery, F.E. & Trist, E.L. (1969). Socio-technical systems. In F.E. Emery (ed.), *Systems Thinking*. London: Pergamon

Frese, M. (1982). Occupational socialization and psychological development: an underemphasized research perspective in industrial psychology. *Journal of Occupational Psychology*, **55**, 209–24.

Frese, M. (1995). Error management in training: conceptual and empirical results. In C. Zucchermaglio, S. Bagnara & S.U. Stucky (eds), *Organizational Learning and technological Change*. Berlin: Springer.

Frese, M. (in press). Personal initiative: the theoretical concept and empirical findings. Amsterdam: Manuscript prepared for a book by M. Erez, H. Thierry & U. Kleinbeck.

Frese, M., Albrecht, K., Altmann, A., Lang, J., von Papstein, P., Peyerl, R., Prümper, J., Schulte-Göcking, H., Wankmüller, I. & Wendel, R. (1988). The effects of an active development of the mental model in the training process: experimental results in a word processing system. *Behaviour and Information Technology*, **7**, 295–304.

Frese, M., Brodbeck, F., Heinbokel, T., Mooser, C., Schleiffenbaum, E. & Thiemann, P. (1991). Errors in training computer skills: on the positive function of errors. *Human Computer Interaction*, **6**, 77–92.

Frese, M., Erbe-Heinbokel, M., Grefe, J., Rybowiak, V. & Weike, A. (1994). "Mir ist es lieber, wenn ich genau gesagt bekomme, was ich zu tun habe": Probleme der Akzeptanz von Verantwortung und Handlungsspielraum in Ost und West. *Zeitschrift für Arbeits- und Organisationspsychologie*, **38**, 22–33.

Frese, M., Fay, D., Leng, K., Hilburger, T. & Tag, A. (1997). The concept of personal initiative: operationalization, reliability, and validity in two German samples. *Journal of Occupational and Organizational Psychology* (in press).

Frese, M. & Hesse, W. (1993). The work situation in software-development—results of an empirical study. ACM SIGSOFT *Software Engineering Notes*, **18**, A-65–A-72.

Frese, M., Kring, W., Soose. A. & Zempel, J. (1996). Personal initiative at work: differences between East and West Germany. *Academy of Management Journal*, **39**, 37–63.

Frese, M. & Van Dyck, C. (1996). Error management: learning from errors and organizational design. Presented at the Academy of Management Congress 1996, Cincinnati.

Frese, M. & Zapf, D. (1987). Die Einführung von neuen Techniken verändert

Qualifikationsanforderungen, Handlungsspielraum und Stressoren kaum (The introduction of new technology changes complexity, job discretion and stressors only very little). *Zeitschrift für Arbeitswissenschaft*, **41**, 7–14.

Frese, M. & Zapf, D. (1994). Action as the core of work psychology: a German approach. In H.C. Triandis, M.D. Dunnette & J.M. Hough (eds), *Handbook of Industrial and Organizational Psychology*, vol. 4, Ltd edn (pp. 271–340). Palo Alto, CA: Consulting Psychologists Press.

Frese, M. & Zapf, D. (1991). Fehlersystematik und Fehlerentstehung: Eine theoretische Einführung. In M. Frese & D. Zapf (eds), *Fehler bei der Arbeit mit dem Computer* (pp. 14–31). Bern: Huber.

Greif, S. & Keller, H. (1990). Innovation and the design of work and learning environments: the concept of exploration in human–computer interaction. In M.A. West & J.L. Farr (eds), *Innovation and Creativity at Work* (pp. 213–50). Chichester: Wiley.

Greif, S. & Janikowski, A. (1987). Aktives Lernen durch systematische Fehlerexploration oder programmiertes Lernen durch Tutorials? *Zeitschrift für Arbeits- und Organisationspsychologie*, **31**, 94–9.

Gwynne, S.C. (1992). The long haul. *Time*, **September 28**, 34–8.

Hamel, G. & Prahalad, C.K. (1994). *Competing for the Future*. Boston, MA: Harvard Business School Press.

Howard, A. (1995). Rethinking the psychology of work. In A. Howard, (ed.), *The Changing Nature of Work* (pp. 513–55). San Francisco, CA: Jossey-Bass.

Kanfer, R. (1992). Work motivation: new directions in theory and research. In C.L. Cooper & I.T. Robertson (eds), *International Review of Industrial and Organizational Psychology*, vol. 7 (pp. 1–54). Chichester: Wiley

Kanter, R.M. (1984). *The Change Masters*. London: Routledge.

Kluger, A.N. & DeNisi, A. (1996). The effects of feedback interventions on performance: a historical review, a meta-analysis and a preliminary feedback intervention theory. *Psychological Bulletin*, **119**, 254–84.

Kohn, M.L. & Schooler, C. (1983). *Work and Personality*. Norwood: Ablex.

Lang, J. (1987). Mental Modelle bei Experten. Master's Thesis, University of Munich, Department of Psychology.

Lazarus, R.S. & Folkman, S. (1984). *Stress, Appraisal, and Coping*. New York: Springer.

Locke, E.A. & Latham, G.P. (1990). *A Theory of Goal Setting and Task Performance*. Englewood Cliffs, NJ: Prentice-Hall.

Manz, C.C. & Sims, H.P. (1989). *Superleadership*. New York: Prentice-Hall.

Mintzberg, H. (1983). *Structures in Fives: Designing Effective Organizations*. Englewood Cliffs, NJ: Prentice-Hall.

Organ, D. (1988). *Organizational Citizenship Behavior: the Good Soldier Syndrome*. Lexington, MA: Lexington Books.

Ovsiankina, M. (1928). Die Wiederaufnahme unterbrochener Handlungen. *Psychologische Forschung*, **11**, 302–379.

Peters, T. (1987). *Thriving on Chaos*. New York: Knopf.

Pfeffer, S. (1992). Fehlermanagement im Computertraining. Unpublished Master's thesis, Department of Psychology, Munich.

Rawnsley, J. (1995). *Going for Broke*. London: Harper Collins.

Rifkin, J. (1995). *The End of Work*. New York: G. Putnam's Sons.

Rybowiak, V., Garst, H., Frese, M. & Batinic, B. (1997). Error Orientation Questionnaire (EOQ): reliability validity, and different language equivalence. *Journal of Organizational Behaviour* (in press).

Seligman, M.E.P. (1975). *Helplessness*. San Francisco, CA: Freeman.

Seligman, M.E.P. (1991). *Learned Optimism*. New York: Knopf.

Speier, C. & Frese, M. (1996). Generalized self-efficacy as a mediator and moderator between control and complexity at work and personal initiative: a longitudinal field study in East Germany. *Human Performance*, **10**, 171–92.

Volpert, W. (1971). *Sensumotorisches Lernen. Zur Theorie des Trainings in Industrie und Sport* (Sensori-motor learning: theory of training in industry and sports). Frankfurt-am-Main: Limpert.

West, M.A. & Farr, J.L. (eds) (1990). *Innovation and Creativity at Work*. Chichester: Wiley.

Womack, J.P. Jones, D.T. & Roos, D. (1990). *The Machine that Changed the World*. New York: Rawson.

Part V

The Nature of the Research Enterprise: New Methods and New Constructs

Chapter 22

An Aesthetic Perspective on Organizations

James W. Dean Jr
University of North Carolina, Chapel Hill, NC, USA
Edward Ottensmeyer
Clark University, Worcester, MA, USA
and
Rafael Ramirez
Groupe HEC, Paris, France

What is man before beauty cajoles from him a delight in things for their own sake, or the serenity of form tempers the savagery of life? (Schiller).

In this chapter, we make available to readers of this volume a relatively new way of seeing organizations: the aesthetic perspective. Readers are doubtless familiar with conceptions of organizations as rational economic tools, as cultures, and as social structures. In this chapter we ask the reader to consider the possibility that organizations can be seen as objects of beauty or ugliness, and that they are often perceived in this manner by the people in and around them. Furthermore, we ask readers to consider the potential of this viewpoint to shed new light on some standard questions in organizational behavior.

In the first part of this chapter, we introduce the idea of aesthetics, and discuss its roots in philosophy. In the second part, we show how our perspective generates new questions and new answers about problems in organizational behavior. In the third part, we explore the relationship of aesthetics to more familiar perspectives on organizations, and illustrate our perspective with some case examples.

We believe aesthetics will become more important to understanding organizations and their behavior as issues concerning the environment and biotechnology become higher priority items for decision-makers. When considering issues such as the value of a rare species of tropical fish whose survival might be jeopardized

Creating Tomorrow's Organizations. Edited by C.L. Cooper and S.E. Jackson.
© 1997 John Wiley & Sons Ltd.

by a construction project, aesthetics will come to be more and more accepted as a help in understanding organizations. The reason is that such issues involve aspects which cannot be reduced to views of organizational phenomena provided by other perspectives, be they discounted cash flow calculations or ethics. Aesthetics is a help in facing such issues, and it will become more important to understand what it offers.

WHAT IS AESTHETICS?

The term "aesthetics" is derived from the ancient Greek. Its original meaning related to the way we experience the world we inhabit through the senses. Aesthetics is a part of philosophy, that is, of the study of how we understand what we understand, and of how we do not understand what we believe we do not understand. The original ancient Greek meaning has evolved over time, in two main directions; the first, "purer" one, relates to the study of beauty and ugliness—regardless of their manifestation (i.e. it can entail sunsets, smiles, gestures, or whatever); the second, more "applied" one, concerns the study of art.

This history has three important implications. First, because of its Greek origins, aesthetics is a Western conceptualization of (mental) experience. While it assumes that all minds—not only Western ones—experience beauty and/or ugliness, the way in which the aesthetic mind considers both experience and mental activity itself is ineluctably Western. Confucian, Bhuddist, Mayan, Cree, Inuit, Egyptian or Taoist intellectual systems may look upon what we in the West scope out under "aesthetics" in quite different ways, and may not make the same distinctions between ethics and aesthetics, for instance, as we do.

Second, aesthetics is concerned with a way of knowing, of knowing both the world we live in and the way we know this world. Aesthetic knowledge is considered to be both universal (all minds know part of what they experience aesthetically) and specific (there is something in aesthetic experience that cannot be "explained away" through non-aesthetic explanations).

Third, the way we sense aesthetically covers experiences we qualify as "beautiful" or "ugly". Because aesthetics is considered to be universal, all experiencers are taken to have the potential, at least, to experience beauty and ugliness. This universality extends to individuals in organizations, and individuals experiencing organizational phenomena. Thus it follows from aesthetics itself, without—for the moment—extending our analysis to the field of organizational studies, that aesthetics is relevant to organizational phenomena, as it is relevant to all experienced phenomena.

A large number of philosophers in the last 200 years or so have considered aesthetics, each in a particular way. There are hundreds of books and thousands of articles in several languages (e.g. German, French, Spanish, Italian, Danish and English) arguing the merits of each perspective, and exploring the similarities and differences among them. While it is beyond the scope of this chapter to review this vast literature, in relating aesthetics to organizational studies, we have found it very helpful to use the Kantian tradition, as developed by Ernst Cassirer and Suzanne Langer.

Langerian Aesthetics

Suzanne Langer, an American philosopher, wrote a remarkable book entitled *Philosophy in a New Key* (1942), which took up a distinction originally made by Cassirer (her teacher) between "discursive" and "presentational" symbols. "Discursive" symbols have one-to-one signifiers to signified semantics, and are supported by tools such as dictionaries or legends. "Presentational" symbols do not have such semantics and are not helped by such tools—music and paintings are examples. You cannot make sense of a note in a sonata the way you can of a word in text.

Aesthetics, Cassirer and Langer argued, studies how we make sense of presentational symbols. It also studies why we use presentational symbols to start with. Presentational symbols cannot be "translated" into discursive ones—much is lost in the conversion. For example, you may read a damned good review of a theater play in the New York Times, but it can not replace experiencing the play itself. Or, as Isadore Duncan is reputed to have said regarding the meaning of her dance, "If I could tell you what it meant, there would be no point in dancing it" (Bateson, 1972, p. 137).

This distinction between presentational and discursive symbols explains why it is difficult to define aesthetics. Definition pertains to discursive symbolism, while aesthetics is concerned with presentational symbols. Both presentational and discursive symbols are means that minds use to experience both what surrounds them and the experience itself. Kantian philosophy, particularly as developed by Cassirer and Langer, shows that in fact the distinction between what is experienced and the experience itself is meaningless: we only experience what we experience. Constructivist social scientists such as Berger & Luckmann (1966) derive their conceptions from Bishop Berkeley, who supposed that our minds construct what we experience. In contrast, Langerian (and indeed Kantian) philosophy invites us to suppose that what we experience exists independently of our being there.

We take this independent-from-us existence to be "given"—and thus we consider them to be "data" (from Latin, *data*, meaning, "given"). But this (given) data is not in fact accessible to us, except through experience. It is accessible to us only when we act. We access data as facts (from the Latin *factum*, that is, what we created in acting). In the Kantian tradition, we distinguish fact (which we make in experience) from data—which is needed, in addition to our acting, to create facts. Reality is thus the actual encounter between us and data, between our minds and what we assume to exist independent of our minds. Facts are made in many different ways, including through mental activities such as perceiving and conceiving.

Facts that are aesthetically experienced are, according to Langer, facts that are symbolized presentationally. Minds use symbols to "capture" experiences: to apprehend them and share them. Presentationally symbolized experiences are experiences which minds form, be they conceptions or perceptions. Recent empirical perception psychology and neurobiology research supports Langer's views (Ramirez, 1987). That which our mind experiences aesthetically has—according to Langer—forms that our mind relates to felt life. Mind appreciates life through feeling, and this experience is also symbolized presentationally. Thus, when the form of felt life and the form of that which mind experiences and symbolizes presentationally "match", we experience beauty. As Gregory Bateson (1979, p. 17) put it, "By aesthetic, I mean responsive to the pattern that connects."

Aesthetics and Form

One of the authors of this chapter (Ramirez, e.g. 1987, 1991) has argued that an important bridge between aesthetic experience and organizational phenomena is form. Organizational studies are permeated by reference to forms, which can be understood as presentational symbols. We can not actually experience organizations, or convey our experiences of them, without form intervening. Indeed, we can not even conceive of organizations without evoking form, because the very language we use to depict organizational phenomena is full of references to form. We re*form* institutions, trans*form* work practices, enhance or measure per*form*ance, *form*alize procedures, analyze in*form*al behavior, *form*ulate strategies, have personnel wear uni*form*s, fill out *form*s (*formulaires* in French), and in*form* people.

If aesthetics is form, what about content? In French, one can talk about "*la forme*" and "*le fond*" (content) as two distinct and complementary entities. The reference to Descartes' mind/body distinction is inevitable. This distinction is not as easy to maintain in the light of modern neurobiology, perception psychology or cybernetics, and is incompatible with our view of aesthetics (see Ramirez 1987, 1991, for a full argument). Thus, form and content in aesthetics are intricately linked in, for example, a musical composition, a painting or an organization. As Scruton (1994) puts this point:

> The aesthetic interest . . . always sees more in an object than its mere appearance: if it did not, then it is difficult to see why we should place such a value on it. For example, when looking at a painting, I do not see only colors, lines, and shapes. I see the world that is represented by them; the drama which animates that world; the emotion that is expressed through it. In short, I see a meaning.

Content-less form is a "limiting case" which is useful in logic but does not actually occur in practice; the same applies to form-less content. Aesthetics is, we believe, one way of attacking such distinctions, which may have—thanks to Descartes and the many people he has inspired—become a part of everyday views on organizational phenomena in ways which distract us from much more instructive ways of looking at them.

WHAT IS THE MEANING OF AESTHETICS IN ORGANIZATIONS?

The Objects of Beauty in Organizations

Our position is that there are no "specific", pre-determined aspects of organization that are "in and of themselves" beautiful. To show how this is so, let us take two examples from the press. First, "the suffering of animals is not merely ugly but wrong" (*Economist*, 1995). If *Economist* is right, animal rights groups exist for aesthetic as well as ethical reasons. This point of view can also be extended to environmental groups, and is also pertinent both to anti-abortion (i.e. pro-life), and to pro-abortion (i.e. "pro-choice") groups. Note that in both the anti- and pro-ethical stances, the alternative is considered ugly. Ugliness, like beauty, is an aesthetic experience, or a description of something that is experienced aesthetically.

Interest groups seeking to preserve species, landmarks, historic buildings, ways of life, and cultures are often also experienced in ways which combine ethics and aesthetics. Preservation seeks to safeguard the vitality of something valued, like the animal rights groups analyzed by *Economist*, and seeks to preserve "nature" from the utilitarian abuses of domestication. Preserving aboriginal ways of life in Northern Canada or the rhinoceros in Kenya is, for some people, as aesthetic as preserving the honor of the Argentinean Army is for others.

Let us turn to the second press cutting: "This spring, Citibank members will use their cards for something priceless: the preservation of America's National Parks . . . Parks have provided the opportunity to experience the beauty of our country first hand . . ." (Advertisement, *Life* magazine, Summer 1991). The valuing of natural beauty is, a bank's PR department tells us, "priceless". It implicitly argues that if you monetize aesthetic value, you do violence to it (cf. Aglietta & Orléan, 1982). As the saying goes, monetize love and you get prostitution instead. A bank, an institution so very concerned with money, values aesthetic experience—and recognizes it to be beyond the reach of monetary valuation.

The experience of beauty, we have seen, entails an interaction between subject and object. In the Kantian tradition to which we adhere, *both* are required for the experience of beauty to take place. All kinds of objects, which can include your lover's smile, the laugh of your children, the wag of the tail of your dog, a sunrise seen from atop a mountain, the sound of a brook, a punk concert . . . and even organizations, can be experienced as beautiful.

The organizational phenomena most amenable to being experienced as beautiful are those that are relatively limited in time and in space. The temporal limit is often in hours: thus, concerts, operas, plays, and team sports are objects centered on organizational phenomena that are often experienced aesthetically. On some occasions such "beautiful" organizational phenomena have lives counted in terms of days and not hours, as is the case with music, theater, or film festivals such as Woodstock, the Festival d'Avignon, or the Cannes Film Festival;

as well as athletic events such as the Olympic Games. In business terms meetings, trade shows, market days, or take-over battles are in some instances considered aesthetically—these are also organizational phenomena limited in time to event-like proportions.

Organizational forms that are limited in space are also more easily experienced aesthetically than are those that are diffused. These are organizations "set" in stages, "held" in meeting rooms or conference halls or market squares. Organizations for which maintaining a certain type of aesthetically appreciated form is critical, such as the army or the church, have devised ways of excluding their contexts from the confines of barracks or monasteries. As technological and managerial developments capitalize on the increasing liquidity of assets (Davis, 1987, Normann & Ramirez, 1994), value creation activities can be located anytime, anywhere. Activities become dispersed in time and space. Time "out" of such dispersion is taken to form views of the whole, explaining the practice of specially held organizational events such as "corporate retreats", where management teams review ("re-view") their organization and business.

The interest in "corporate culture" can also be interpreted as a response that leaders give to this problem. Efforts to render culture explicit can be interpreted as efforts to glue together, temporally and spatially, disparate projects into a single firm to be experienced as one, coherent, form. Professional service organizations such as law practices or consultancies—which have addressed this problem for decades—work hard at addressing what Maister (1985) calls the "one-firm-firm" challenge.

Beauty may be found in very unlikely places in organizations, when one is least expecting it. One of the authors encountered such a surprise aesthetic experience while conducting research in an underground coal mine in West Virginia. It was on the way to the "hoot owl" (midnight) shift a few days before Christmas. During the trip to the coal face, the rail car carrying the miners and one researcher went through the mountain and out the other side, into a remote valley where a full moon shone on a silent snowfall. One or two of the miners had turned on their lamps, so there was a warm glow inside the car. During the brief interlude before we entered the total darkness of the next mountain, one of the miners produced a harmonica, and softly began to play *Silent Night*. The combination of the moonlight and snowfall, the loveliness of the melody, and the camaraderie reflected in the thoughtful faces of the miners in the glow from the lamp as they prepared for their night's work, produced an image of such beauty that it has stayed with this researcher for more than 15 years.

In summary, then, a wide variety of organizations and organizational phenomena can be experienced as beautiful, although those limited in time and space appear to have a greater tendency to be perceived in this manner (perhaps small *is* beautiful!). A list of such potential objects of aesthetic appreciation could include products (an automobile) and services (an airline flight), organizational settings (the ambiance of a restaurant) and processes (fabrication in a manufacturing cell). It could also include jobs (the role of a team leader), computer programs (the look and feel of a graphical user interface), "performances" (resolution of a messy conflict), and even teams (that work together "beautifully").

Certain of these phenomena—especially products and settings—are widely accepted as possessing the capability of being experienced aesthetically, while others have generally not yet been seen in this manner.

The Perceivers of Beauty in Organizations

There are no special skills needed to be able perceive organizational beauty. We believe that everyone experiences it to some degree—but perhaps an individual is unaware of such experience until he/she labels it as such in communicating it to others. An engineer heading a refinery catalytic cracker design team, a grandmother hosting a family meal, a sales executive signing a deal with a cherished corporate customer, an analyst reviewing a corporate take-over, a shareholder attending an annual general meeting, all such individuals can experience organizational phenomena aesthetically.

Unconvinced? Pick up a newspaper and take 10 articles at will. Look for organizational phenomena in them, and rank the ten from most beautiful to ugliest. You have just demonstrated that any person can experience organizations aesthetically—but you were not aware of it. Now you are—and the more you are, the more important organizational aesthetics will become to you, for it will more and more be a legitimate way of thinking about and relating to organizational objects. As David White (1996) put it, you will find an increasing interest for situations in which things are "working beautifully".

If organizations (and their components, as discussed above) can be experienced aesthetically by just about anyone, then a wide variety of people in and around organizations may perceive organizational phenomena in this manner. This would certainly include employees and managers at all levels of the organization, as well as people in other organizations (suppliers, customers, regulators) that relate to the focal organization. Perhaps potential investors are even influenced by aesthetic considerations in making investment decisions.

The fact that all people *can* experience organizational phenomena aesthetically does not mean, however, that all people do so with equal frequency or significance. Just as people differ in their use of functional or political lenses in viewing organizations, we would expect them to differ in their use of aesthetic perspectives. While some people may be quite sensitive to the aesthetic aspects of organizations, others may not notice them at all, nor put much stock in them when they do. The extent to which this is a function of—and could be changed by—experience, would be an interesting research question.

WHAT CAN AESTHETICS TELL US ABOUT ORGANIZATIONS?

Aesthetic concepts have often not been taken very seriously in the study of organizations. As Witkin (1990) puts it, "[the] exclusion of the aesthetic from conceptualizations of . . . modern organizations . . . has meant that phenomena which are clearly recognized to be aesthetic tend to be conceptually trivialized" (p. 327). This situation has begun to change, as indicated by work by Strati (1992), Gagliardi (1996) and numerous others cited in this chapter. In this section, we will explore how an aesthetic perspective may add value to the study of a variety of important organizational questions. In fact, this wide applicability is one of the strengths that an aesthetic perspective can bring to the study of organizations. The section is divided into three parts: people as perceivers of aesthetic phenomena; people as creators of aesthetic phenomena; and aesthetics and organizational effectiveness.

People in Organizations as Perceivers of Aesthetic Phenomena

We have already demonstrated how people can experience organizational phenomena aesthetically. In this section, we consider how people's aesthetic experience of organizational phenomena can influence their behavior. Our major assumption here is simply that people are attracted to things they experience as beautiful, and repulsed by those they experience as ugly. This simple idea can lead to variety of insights about the standard preoccupations of organizational behavior, each of which can only be sketched here. We should note that there does not yet exist a theory of aesthetics in organizations from which our examples can be derived; this perspective is still very much evolving. We hope that this chapter stimulates other scholars to join us in creating such theories.

The Decision to Participate

People's decisions to join and to remain in organizations, which March & Simon (1958) refer to as the "decision to participate", may be shaped by aesthetic perceptions. When considering whether to accept a job offer, people may be influenced by their perception of the beauty or ugliness of the organization, the work to be performed, the setting for the work, and so on. Ramirez (1991) discusses the case of a woman who is "smitten" with the idea of joining a social service organization in Scotland, and interprets the woman's behavior as a case of being moved by the beauty of the organization. An aesthetic perspective on the question of job choice would provide a nice complement to models that emphasize economic considerations.

Similarly, one's decision to remain in an organization may be influenced by aesthetics. In this case, however, the decision should be better informed than one concerning a new organization. Is the setting, the work process, the structure, and so on, aesthetically pleasing, ugly, or somewhere in between? If aesthetic experiences really are a strong source of attraction, as we have assumed, it will be difficult for people to leave a situation which is experienced as beautiful, especially for people who are particularly sensitive to the aesthetic dimension of organizational life. On the other hand, a preponderance of experiences perceived as ugly will make it much easier to leave.

These same arguments may be applied to absenteeism, a weaker type of withdrawal behavior that represents the "decision to participate" on a day-to-day basis. People who experience their work and organization as beautiful are likely to be much more consistent in their attendance than those who do not. In fact, the expression sometimes used by people who miss work, that they "just couldn't face it", may be understood as having aesthetic overtones. The question of the relationship between aesthetic perceptions of organizations and the decision to participate is amenable to a great deal of empirical research.

Job Satisfaction

Our understanding of this heavily-studied aspect of organizational behavior may also be enhanced by considering the aesthetic aspects of work and organizations. Gallagher (1993) cites a study by Fried indicating that—next to their marriage—people's immediate surroundings are the most powerful predictor of satisfaction with the quality of one's life. While working conditions are often included in indices of job satisfaction, perhaps a broader conception of organizational phenomena that included aesthetics would provide a more complete picture of the precursors of overall job satisfaction. For example, for the millions of office workers who spend most of their time at work looking at a computer screen, the forms, colors, balance and harmony of the elements on their screen may be significant. Even a casual inspection of most offices will show how people have endeavored to personalize their computer-mediated environments, for example by purchasing or downloading elaborate screen-savers. White (1996) makes a parallel argument regarding the beauty of the products or services provided by the organization.

Vaill (1989, p. 119) extends this argument to work processes: "Attaching importance to form also makes it possible to take pleasure in the quality of the process that one is conducting or participating in . . . [organization members] take pleasure in the sheer conduct of the process and attach great importance to proper execution . . . What an intriguing priority for a manager to consider . . . making sure that members derive some pleasure in the process". It seems a short step from the experience of pleasure through work to job satisfaction. Perhaps research on job satisfaction that incorporated an aesthetic perspective would improve our understanding of this elusive phenomenon.

Resistance to Change

One of the perennially vexing problems of management theory and practice is the tendency for organization members to prefer their current arrangements to any new ones that are proposed, however advantageous these new conditions may appear to those proposing them. While there are doubtless many reasons for this, an aesthetic perspective may provide a unique set of insights. Perhaps people resist change because they experience beauty in their current work processes or structures, which they fear will be eliminated in any change that takes place.

While a work process may look unnecessarily complex, redundant or Byzantine to a would-be re-engineer, these very features may be a source of pleasure to those enmeshed in them. ("It's very straightforward: you make six copies of the blue form, and six of the green form. One blue and two green forms go to purchasing, two blue and one green to accounting. . . .") It may be hard for a new process, with no form(s) at all, to compete with the rococo beauty of traditional work methods.

Alternatively, the change process itself, with its culture of efficiency and patois of buzzwords, may appear sterile, cold and generally unappealing. From the perspective of those being changed, change agents are thus not prophets leading the people to a better way of life, but rather philistines who are pathetically incapable of apprehending the beauty of the current organization. Seen from this perspective, the behavior of the "change resisters", far from being stubborn and irrational, is eminently rational in that they are simply trying to preserve a set of experiences that hold great aesthetic value for them, and/or to avoid a set of experiences they perceive as aesthetically unappealing. It is this aesthetic value of resisting change that is overlooked in conventional analyses of the resistance-to-change problem. There are obvious research opportunities here, for example to determine whether using an aesthetic perspective improves our ability to understand and predict people's (un)willingness to be changed.

People in Organizations as Creators of Aesthetic Phenomena

In addition to merely *reacting* to their perceptions of aesthetic phenomena in organizations, members may also be involved in the *creation* of such processes, structures, systems, etc. In fact, one might extend this observation to include the idea that people in organizations are often engaged in cycles of enactment of aesthetics, in which they contribute to the creation of environments with aesthetic elements, to which they then react (Gallagher, 1993, p. 103). The assumption used to guide our thinking in this section is simply that—all things being equal—people will generally prefer to create something of beauty, rather than something that lacks beauty, or is actually ugly. The *ceteris paribus* condition is important, because people in organizations clearly have many other items on their agenda, many of which may lead to ugly outcomes (which, of course, are also aesthetic). Given this qualification, however, the aesthetic perspective can generate a number of novel insights about familiar problems.

Decision Processes

A fundamental insight about decision-making was provided by March & Olsen (1984): that decision processes are not tightly linked to choices to which they lead, or more poetically, that decisions are "a stage for many dramas" (p. 12). This theoretical separation between decision processes and choice opens the door for aesthetic considerations to play a role in shaping decision processes, which may be seen as an aesthetic creation of the people enacting them. Rather than simply making a choice, some decision-makers may be creating a process in which they experience beauty. For example, the complexity, order and symmetry of spreadsheets and other representations of alternatives and information about them may be a source of pleasure to decision-makers (Tufte, 1990). Perhaps some decision-makers are reluctant to make a final decision not because of risk avoidance, but rather due to their reluctance to terminate a process that they enjoy, or because of a need to balance their information search, so as to preserve the form of good decision-making. The intermingled flows of choices, information and so on may be better understood by considering their aesthetic possibilities, in addition to their rational and political content. Future research on organizational decision-making could explore this possibility.

Design

A more generally-accepted context for the operation of aesthetic concerns is the design of products. Garvin (1984) identified aesthetics as one of the operational definitions of product quality, and the field of industrial design is based on the premise that form and function can and should be jointly optimized. Thus it is not particularly novel to propose that product designers and marketers are motivated by aesthetic concerns (among others) in shaping their products.

This idea, however, can be applied to other phenomena that are "designed" in organizations, particularly the organizations themselves (i.e. their structures) and organizational processes. Organization structures can be assessed using traditional aesthetic criteria, including balance, proportion, and so on, and it would be interesting to pursue how those designing organizations take such criteria into consideration, either consciously or unconsciously. White (1996) has applied aesthetic criteria to organizational design: "An organization could be said to have harmony if all its constituent elements cohered with one another in a manner equivalent to the way all the elements of a work of art cohered with one another ... To the extent that some of the elements did not ... the organization would lack harmony, and therefore be deficient in value in this respect". Such a perspective provides another way to interpret design decisions, which complements extant functional and institutional interpretations. Again, research could help to sort out how these various perspectives interact to shape organization designs.

This same logic can be applied to organizational processes, which are increasingly thought of as being consciously designed, particularly under the rubrics of total quality, continuous process improvement and re-engineering (Dean & Bowen, 1994). This approach would provide an opportunity to study how organization members design processes that not only achieve the traditional goals of quality and efficiency, but also are a source of aesthetic enjoyment to those who design and participate in them (Vaill, 1989). For example, are judgments about process design influenced by the aesthetic aspects of their appearance on flowcharts? How do balance, flow and proportion interact with efficiency as criteria for process design?

Leadership

A final topic for which our understanding may be enhanced through the idea of aesthetic creation is leadership. Many leadership frameworks emphasize the importance of leaders creating visions. As Sandelands (1995) has argued, "A leader galvanizes a group by the power of a vision or a persona that attracts by its vitality" (pp. 21–2). It may be that these visions appeal primarily to people's aesthetic capacities, and that they succeed or fail in captivating organization members on that basis. One implication of this is that the ability to understand and create visions that address members' aesthetic sensitivities would help to differentiate between successful and unsuccessful leaders. This explanation may also explain why leaders' visions are sometimes embraced so heartily in some quarters, and greeted with yawns in others. Another implication of this idea is that it would be difficult for a compelling vision to emerge from a group of people, due to the well-known difficulties in collaborating in a creative process.

Aesthetics and Organizational Effectiveness

Our third theme in linking aesthetics to standard organizational behavior topics concerns the relationship between aesthetics and organizational effectiveness. Much (although far from all) of the interest in organizational behavior stems from the desire to understand what factors and processes shape the effectiveness of organizations. Thus it should be interesting to explore whether the aesthetic perspective can shed any light on this question.

Our premise here is that a major reason for things being considered aesthetically pleasing, or beautiful, is that they are made up of elements that are different from one another, but that are brought together in a pattern or form that produces pleasure. While aesthetics is certainly a much larger category than art, Weitz's (1956) summary statement about formalist theories of art is still apposite: "Art . . . is a unique combination of certain elements". An orchestra, for example, combines the very different timbres of strings, winds, brass and percussion, as well as the sounds of high- and low-pitched instruments within each of these groups. It is the skillful combination of very different types of sounds that gives the orchestra its unique beauty. In a symphony of conventional form, key signatures and tempi will change from one movement to the next, but the work is tied together in a way that suggests continuity and balance. For example, in what is arguably the most famous symphony, Beethoven's Fifth, the familiar four-note theme forms a pattern upon which the entire symphony rests. Similar examples could be drawn from many other contexts, e.g. the colors in a painting, the words in a poem, or the steps in a dance.

If this conception of aesthetics were applied to organizations, one could say that an aesthetically pleasing organization (or organizational component) would be one that represented the careful combination, juxtaposition or integration of different elements into a coherent form or pattern (cf. White, 1996). It is therefore striking how many extant theories of organizations make this exact claim about the factors that lead to effectiveness. Such theories can be found in virtually every corner of organization studies.

In corporate strategy we find Rumeldt's (1982) well-known finding that a strategy of related diversification—combining businesses that are different from but related to one another—outperforms strategies of no diversification or unrelated diversification. In organization design we find the equally well-known findings of Lawrence & Lorsch (1967) that successful organizations are made up of differentiated elements that are well integrated. In the groups literature we find Steiner's (1972) theory that effective groups should be made up of different types of members to increase total resources, but that these members must be integrated in such a way as to maximize performance. Finally, in the organizational behavior literature, Hackman & Oldham's (1980) model holds that successful job designs are comprised of different types of activities (skill variety) that are brought together into a coherent whole (task identity).

Thus it appears that there are clear parallels between at least one conception of aesthetics and several theories of organizational effectiveness. This may be why the terms used in aesthetic analysis, such as harmony, balance and flow are so easy to fall into when discussing organizations. This is not of course to say that organizations are effective *because* they are beautiful, merely that the same criteria appear to apply to both. This may mean, however, that a keenly developed aesthetic capacity may be a useful early warning system for managers, and may represent a possible explanation for the intuition or "sixth sense" that some managers seem to possess in anticipating when things are going wrong (see, for example, Burgelman & Grove's (1996) discussion of "strategic dissonance"). It also helps to explain why purely mechanical views of management—however seductive they may be to some—never quite seem to capture its essence. There is an elusive and artistic element in the successful harmonization of the disparate elements of organizations. As Brady (1986, p. 342) has noted: "Being overly analytical, procedural and bureaucratic in business relations is similar to the fake artist who "paints by the numbers": the holistic thought processes are absent, and what is produced satisfies the rules but is awkward and stiff".

HOW AN AESTHETIC PERSPECTIVE INTERSECTS OTHER PERSPECTIVES ON ORGANIZATION

Theories of organization are based upon metaphors or images of organization that "lead us to see and understand organizations in distinctive yet partial ways" (Morgan, 1986, p. 12) Thus, those of us who think about and study organizations should be unsurprised by the number of theories and metaphors that have been put forward as offering more robust and comprehensive ways to consider organizational phenomena. By implication, Morgan seems to suggest to us that the greater the number of images, the more we move toward a fuller understanding of what organizations are about. In the following section, we discuss briefly how an aesthetic perspective on organization relates to more traditional functional, cultural and process perspectives. Our purpose here is to highlight selected relationships rather than to present a complete review, which would be far too lengthy to include in this chapter.

Functional Theories: Putting Aesthetics to Work

How does aesthetics relate to functional theories of organization? Resource dependence theory, population ecology theory, institutional theory are labels that scholars have applied to a set of theories that call attention to the need for organizations to attract various resources required for effective, long-term functioning. Viewed from such perspectives, it might be argued that "good aesthetics is good business", and therefore functional in the way that admirable ethical business practices may be seen as functional—that is, in the service of recognizable ends such as an enhanced public image, improved efficiency or enhanced profitability.

If, for example, an architecturally attractive workspace can be shown to yield greater returns in the form of more-appealing product designs, faster new product development, or reduced time-to-market, then such an investment is clearly functional and economically rational. If highly-valued human resources can be attracted to and retained by an organization because of that organization's impressive collection of artworks on display in its office building, then aesthetics becomes an element in effective personnel practices. If lively classical music, when played in an organization's offices, causes employees to work more productively, then the aesthetic experience of great music has been used toward legitimate organizational ends. If an innovative organization design, in harmony with external market realities, serves to unleash the creative talents of employees, then aesthetic principles (either explicitly or, more probably, implicitly) are being put to good use.

But do these forms of instrumental behavior on the part of managers and organizations fully define an aesthetic perspective on organizations? We think not.

Cultural Theories: Aesthetics as an Embedded Characteristic of People and Organizations

Creating art and appreciating beauty are fundamental elements of human behavior and emotion. We cannot imagine seriously describing any culture without reference to its artistic accomplishments or to its experiences of beauty.

Viewed from this theoretical platform, aesthetics helps organizational scholars develop a fuller cultural description of organizations. People carry their values with them into organizations; aesthetic values are one set of those values. Aesthetics is part of the fabric of organizational experience and organizational reality, recognized both by its presence and its absence (Ottensmeyer, 1996). For example, a firm's product designs may be dull or avant garde, its offices drab or invigorating, its organizational design stultifying or empowering. In either case, an aesthetic dimension can be observed, and aesthetic experiences are available to those who are connected to organizations as customers, employees or managers. Just as we might, for example, observe a spectrum of control behaviors on some organizational control dimension, we can likewise observe a spectrum of aesthetic behaviors and outcomes on an aesthetic dimension. One important difference is that organization theorists are on far more familiar ground with control than with aesthetics. In discussions of culture within organization theory, art, artistry and beauty have made only cameo appearances.

Geertz (1973) notes that the ethos of a culture, which includes the aesthetic element, is the "tone, character, and quality of their life . . . it is the underlying attitude toward themselves and their world that life reflects" (p. 127). More recently, White (1996) and Sandelands & Buckner (1989) have drawn attention to the essential aesthetic elements of work within corporate cultures, arguing, respectively, that worker satisfaction is linked to producing beautiful products, and that task design has inherent aesthetic features. Thus, aesthetics may have much to contribute to culture-based theories of organization, although its boundaries clearly are not identical.

Process Theories: The Aesthetics of Process and the Artistry of Managing

Chester Barnard, writing about the processes of executive management, noted that:

> The terms pertinent to it are "feeling", "judgment", "sense", "proportion", "balance", "appropriateness". It is a matter of art rather than science, and is aesthetic rather than logical (Barnard, 1938/1968, p. 235).

Barnard also believed that, with practice, managers could develop "the artistic principle" which would help them achieve balance and proportion required in managing the inherent tensions and conflicting goals embodied in managerial work, such as quality and cost, speed and caution, differentiation and integration.

Despite Barnard's eloquent plea that attention be paid to the aesthetic elements of management, it is clear that the science of management has gotten the lion's share of scholarly attention. However, recent work in organization theory has revitalized interest in the artistry of management by focusing on such topics as the Japanese aesthetics of process (Hayashi, 1988), managing as a performing art (Vaill, 1989) and artful work (Richards, 1995). From the world of practice, we have seen reflections upon the artistry of leadership (e.g. DePree, 1987). From psychology has come new work on the concept of optimal experience or "flow" (Csikszentmihalyi, 1990). From the poet Donald Hall (1993) comes the notion of "absorbedness" to describe the process of work at its most satisfying and fulfilling. Together, this collection of ideas from various realms of inquiry may help organization theorists integrate aesthetics and managerial processes in ways that Barnard might applaud.

We see this re-discovered notion of an aesthetics of process as a critical building block for the development of a broader-gauged aesthetic perspective on organizations. Along these lines, Weick (1995) has written recently about an "aesthetics of imperfection" as a requirement for fostering real creativity in organizations.

Using Aesthetic Concepts to Describe and Understand Contemporary Organizations

How might we recognize beautiful or ugly organizations? What are the characteristics that taken collectively define the beautiful or the ugly organization? Must every component part of an organization be beautiful before that organization can be called beautiful? Can ugly results come from beautiful organizations? While these fundamentally philosophical questions are important, they remain well beyond the scope of this exploratory essay. What we can do here is to note briefly how aesthetic concepts have been used to describe and make sense of organizational phenomena.

Functional Approaches

The most familiar use of the language of aesthetics arises when observers examine ways in which organizations present themselves to the external world, via their products, services, corporate identities, or advertising. Braun appliances, Jaguar automobiles, Gateway personal computers, and Herman Miller office furniture are products that draw consumers to them, in part, because of their beautiful designs. Ben & Jerry's corporate identity as a socially responsive company helps to sell ice cream. In addition, the firm's candid, self-critical performance audit included in their annual report is a far more open and publicly displayed example of Weick's concept of an aesthetics of imperfection.

Internal working environments that support the appropriate blend of creative and productive interactions among people are functional to organizational goal attainment. One of Procter & Gamble's new buildings offers wide hallways with attractive furniture to encourage informal interactions. The oriental practice of *feng shui* (meaning wind and water) is based on the notion that the physical positioning of buildings and the location of windows and doors inside those buildings is critical to establishing a form of harmony that translates directly into worker productivity.

Cultural Approaches

Apple Computer has been praised by Yale computer scientist David Gelernter for "doing more than any other company to make technology beautiful" (cited in Stross, 1996). We could certainly add other candidates to the list, but in recent years Apple has been widely seen as—do we dare say—a cultural icon of aesthetically pleasing technology. Indeed, the Apple Macintosh computer has taken on mythic properties, creating a powerful culture that binds its makers and its users. How the Macintosh works and how it has fared in the marketplace can be understood in terms of the aesthetic values that shaped the Apple culture. (The aesthetic disdain with which Apple devotees describe IBM and Microsoft offerings is also informative.) Not only has Apple's innovative and elegantly designed software served as a critical strength, but it may also have been the source of its recent weakness. Apple's failure to license the Macintosh operating system (widely viewed as a critical strategic blunder) was driven, in part, by the firm's unwillingness to compromise its "elegance" (Stross, 1996).

Process Approaches

The process aesthetics of management and leadership is often revealed in the ways managers describe their work (e.g. DePree, 1987). Much in the way that skillful politicians, famous surgeons, or renowned scientists blend technical knowledge with feeling, judgment and intuition to seek solutions to complex problems, executives draw upon this same vocabulary of aesthetics. Often that language focuses on internal organizational design and external market harmony, since these related elements are often the primary domains of executive leadership. Firms as different as Hewlett-Packard, Ben & Jerry's, 3M, Asea Brown Boveri and Herman Miller often serve as examples of harmony achieved from the skillful and arguably aesthetic judgments of artful managers.

Some leaders go beyond the normal forms of aesthetics as manifested within organizations, as discussed above, and extend themselves into the community in such a way that the organization participates actively in the making or shaping of societal culture. Marjory Jacobson, an art historian and author of the impressive volume *Art for Work* (1994), has chronicled innovative forms of managerial thinking about art and aesthetics in both workplaces and products. She uses the French term "mecenat" (after Gaius Maecenas, an enlightened Roman arts advocate and patron of the first century BC) to describe a way in which business leaders have participated in the "making of culture" and supporting the creative process attendant to it. Her work describes a variety of ways that contemporary organizations around the world—Cartier International in France, Hess Wineries in California, Wacoal in Japan—create or draw upon artistic images in an effort to blend the aesthetics and the economics of organization. In so doing, they recognize through their actions the role of organization as a full participant in aesthetic processes at the societal level.

CONCLUSION

In this chapter, we have taken a rapid trip through a broad and diverse array of material related to aesthetics and organizations. While we were unable to dwell to any great extent on any single feature, our intent was to introduce readers to the scope and potential of the aesthetic perspective on organizations. As indicated at various points in the chapter, aesthetic perspectives have the potential to help to answer a wide range of questions about organizations and organizational behavior, and also provide a bridge between our discipline and the disciplines of philosophy, ethics and the arts. The opportunity exists in the next few years for huge conceptual advances and empirical discoveries, and we invite our readers to join us in seeking them.

REFERENCES

Aglietta, M. & Orléan, A. (1982). *La Violence de la Monnaie*. Paris: PUF.
Barnard, C.I. (1938/1968). *The Functions of the Executive*. Cambridge, MA: Harvard University Press.
Bateson, G. (1972). *Steps to an Ecology of Mind*. New York: Chandler.
Bateson, G. (1979). *Mind and Nature: a Necessary Unity*. Isle of Man, UK: Fontana.
Berger, P. & Luckmann, T. (1966). *The Social Construction of Reality: a Treatise in the Sociology of Knowledge*. Garden City, NY: Doubleday.
Brady, F.N. (1986). Aesthetic components of management ethics. *Academy of Management Review*, **11**(2), 337–44.
Burgelman, R.A. & Grove, A.S. (1996). Strategic dissonance. *California Management Review*, **38**(2), 8–28.
Csikszentmihalyi, M. (1990). *Flow: the Psychology of Optimal Experience*. New York: Harper & Row.
Davis, S. (1987). *Future Perfect*. Reading, MA: Addison-Wesley.
Dean, J.W. Jr & Bowen, D.E. (1994). Management theory and total quality: improving research and practice through theory development. *Academy of Management Review*, **19**, 392–418.
DePree, M. (1987). *Leadership is an Art*. East Lansing, MI: Michigan State University Press.
Economist (1995). What humans owe to animals. August 19.
Gagliardi, P. (1996). Exploring the aesthetic side of organizational life. In S. Clegg, C. Hardy & W. Nord (eds), *The Handbook of Organization Studies*. Thousand Oaks, CA: Sage.
Gallagher, W. (1993). *The Power of Place: How Our Surroundings Shape Our Thoughts, Emotions, and Actions*. New York: Poseidon Press.
Garvin, D. (1984). What does "product quality" really mean? *Sloan Management Review*, **26**(1), 25–43.
Geertz, Clifford (1973). *The Interpretation of Cultures*. New York: Basic Books.
Hackman, J.R. & Oldham, G.R. (1980). *Work Redesign*. Reading, MA: Addison-Wesley.

Hall, D. (1993). *Life Work*. Boston, MA: Beacon Press.

Hayashi, S. (1988). *Culture and Management in Japan* (translated by Frank Baldwin). Tokyo: University of Tokyo Press.

Jacobson, M. (1994). *Art for Work*. Boston, MA: Harvard Business School Press.

Langer, S.K. (1942). *Philosophy in a New Key*. Cambridge, MA: Harvard University Press.

Lawrence, P.R. & Lorsch, J.W. (1967). *Organization and Environment: Managing Differentiation and Integration*. Boston, MA: Harvard Business School Press.

Maister, D.H. (1985). The one-firm firm. *Sloan Management Review*, **Fall**.

March, J.G. & Olsen, J.P. (1984). *Ambiguity and Choice in Organizations*. Bergen, Norway: Universitetsforlaget.

March J.G. & Simon, H.A. (1958). *Organizations*. New York: Wiley.

Morgan, G. (1986). *Images of Organization*. Beverly Hills, CA: Sage.

Normann, R. & Ramirez, R. (1994). *Designing Interactive Strategy*. Chichester: Wiley.

Ottensmeyer, E. (1996). Aesthetics and organization: too strong to stop, too sweet to lose, *Organization*, **3**(2).

Ramirez, R. (1987). Towards an aesthetic theory of social organization. Unpublished Doctoral Dissertation, Social Systems Science, Wharton School, University of Pennsylvania.

Ramirez, R. (1991). *The Beauty of Social Organization*. Munich: Accedo.

Richards, D. (1995). *Artful Work*. San Francisco, CA: Berrett-Koehler.

Rumelt, R.P. (1982). Diversification strategy and profitability. *Strategic Management Journal*, **3**, 359–69.

Sandelands, L.W. (1995). Art and the science of society. Working paper, University of Michigan.

Sandelands, L.E. & Buckner, G. (1989). Of art and work: aesthetic experience and the psychology of work feelings. In B. Staw & L.L. Cummings (eds), *Research in Organizational Behavior*, vol. 11. Greenwich, CT: JAI Press.

Scruton, R. (1994). *Modern Philosophy: an Introduction and Survey*. New York: Penguin.

Steiner, I. (1972). *Group Process and Productivity*. New York: Academic Press.

Strati, A. (1992). Aesthetic understanding of organizational life. *Academy of Management Review*, **17**, 568–81.

Stross, R. (1996). Poisoned apple: the fall of the holy computer. *The New Republic*, **April 22**, 19–21.

Tufte, E. (1990). *Envisioning Information*. Cheshire, CT: Graphics Press.

Vaill, P. (1989). *Managing as a Performing Art*. San Francisco, CA: Jossey-Bass.

Weick, K. (1995). Creativity and the aesthetics of imperfection. In C. Ford & D. Gioia (eds), *Creative Action in Organizations*. Beverly Hills, CA: Sage.

Weitz, M. (1956). The role of theory in aesthetics. *Journal of Aesthetics and Art Criticism*, **XV**.

White, D. (1996). "It's working beautifully!": philosophical reflections on aesthetics and organization theory. *Organizations*, **3**(2).

Witkin, R.W. (1990). The aesthetic imperative of a rational-technical machinery: a study in organizational control through the design of artifacts. In P. Gagliardi (ed.), *Symbols and Artifacts: Views of the Corporate Landscape* (pp. 325–38). Berlin: deGruyter.

Chapter 23

Through the Looking Glass: A Normative Manifesto for Organizational Behavior

Linda Klebe Treviño
The Pennsylvania State University, University Park, PA, USA
and
Robert J. Bies
Georgetown University, Washington, DC, USA

Do not depend on the hope of results ... You may have to face the fact that your work will be apparently worthless and even achieve no result at all ... As you get used to this idea, you start more and more to concentrate not on the results but on the value, the truth of the work itself (Thomas Merton, from *Letter to A Young Activist*).

The social landscape of organizations is being transformed in dramatic and tumultuous ways. Almost weekly, executives at firms around the world announce another round of job layoffs as part of downsizing and cost-cutting efforts, actions justified as economically necessary for corporate survival. Indeed, there is an almost mantra-like quality of the oft-heard executive justification accompanying news of more job layoffs—"remaining competitive in the global marketplace". For corporate executives, the questions and answers are first and always *instrumental* in nature—that is, in terms of how their actions are functional for them, the organization and its interests.

But, what about the thousands of managers and workers laid off, who must now search for new positions at most likely lower salaries and wages? What of the justice of what has happened to them? Those *normative* questions are rarely addressed by corporate executives (or by management researchers). In fact, Robert Allen, Chairman of AT&T, was brazen enough to say that he saw no need to apologize for firing 40 000 people, and didn't see any need to "go on TV and

Creating Tomorrow's Organizations. Edited by C.L. Cooper and S.E. Jackson.
© 1997 John Wiley & Sons Ltd.

cry" (Sloan, 1996). That statement and attitude explain, in part, the reference to executives such as Robert Allen, as corporate "hitmen" (Sloan, 1996) and "executioners" (Lacayo, 1996). These mass layoffs have brought into sharper focus the instrumental and normative aspects of corporate actions. Although those two aspects have always existed, the normative dimension looms larger in light of current events.

Despite the obvious importance of the normative in organizational life, over the years many of us have felt that the current organizational behavior paradigm does not fully support its expression. We've all heard phrases such as the following: "You can't get hired at top universities, publish in the best journals, or get tenure doing *that* kind of research". And, we all know what *that* kind of research is. It is research that ventures across paradigmatic lines to address the normative. It seems out of the mainstream both ideologically and methodologically.

On the other hand, during the last decade we have also witnessed the emergence of a normative movement in the field of organizational behavior theory and research, a movement that we believe will expand and enrich the study of organizational behavior. Evidence of this movement is found in the growing number of top-tier journal pages and special issues dedicated to topics with normative roots and implications (e.g. diversity, justice, corporate social performance, the natural environment), as well as the increasing number of symposia and papers on similar topics at the Academy of Management meetings. Additional evidence of growing attention to the normative is found in the development of new divisions and interest groups within the Academy of Management (e.g. conflict management, women in management, organizations and the natural environment) that seem more open to normative issues.

In this chapter, we outline a normative manifesto for organizational behavior theory and research in which we call for the more explicit inclusion of the normative in a way that puts individuals' rights and concerns on an equal footing with those of the organization and recognizes the importance of the normative in organizational reality. The motivation for this manifesto is twofold. The first motive is *scientific*. There is growing empirical evidence that normative considerations matter to people and to organizations and that these considerations shape social and organizational dynamics. Research has focused on normative variables in a variety of "mainstream" organizational behavior topics such as leadership and organizational change (Cobb, Wooten & Folger, 1994), punishment in organizations (Trevino & Ball, 1992; Ball, Trevino & Sims, 1994), performance appraisal (Folger & Greenberg, 1985), layoffs (Brockner & Greenberg, 1988), power dynamics (Bies & Tripp, 1995), negotiation (Tripp, Sondak & Bies, 1995), citizenship behavior (Moorman, 1991) and organizational effectiveness (Keeley, 1978). It is becoming clearer that people make decisions and organizations take actions that are difficult to explain in purely instrumental terms (Etzioni, 1988; Keeley, 1988; Lind & Tyler, 1988). A growing number of empirical studies demonstrate that *the normative matters* to people. As such, failure to include normative considerations results in underspecified and biased models of organizational behavior. Expanding our vision to include normative concerns will broaden our research focus, raise new and important research questions, and contribute to the development of more complete models for understanding organizational behavior (Jones, 1995)—ostensibly the goal of science.

The second motive is *ethical*. Inclusion of normative concerns is simply the right thing to do. The instrumental orientation and ideology that permeate so much of organizational behavior theory and research reflect the instrumentality (i.e. bottom-line orientation) of many (if not most) managers in business organizations. If we limit ourselves to this orientation, we hold up a narrow mirror that reflects what managers do and excludes moral voices and the concerns of less powerful people in organizations. Organizational scientists thus reflect a paradigm that elevates the instrumental and devalues the normative. By restricting ourselves to instrumental explanations for managerial action, we are helping to maintain a managerial myth that keeps everyone thinking that doing the right thing is necessarily good for the bottom line and that managers do good only for instrumental reasons (Scott & Hart, 1989). If we fail to include the normative in the face of obvious empirical data that the normative matters, we are excluding from our explanations important motivations for individual and organizational conduct. Further, by studying the normative only for its instrumental purpose, we suppress its value and we perpetrate a fraud on our students, who enter the business world thinking that problems can and should be solved unidimensionally—with instrumental answers. Our role as scholars demands that we hold up a much wider mirror that brings dehumanizing and exploitative management practices into the picture, adding questions about values, rights and justice to descriptions of management practice (Scott, 1985).

In essence, our manifesto is an invitation to organizational scientists to step "through the looking glass" of the normative paradigm and attend more consciously to the dual nature of organizational life—one with instrumental and normative dimensions (Zald, 1993). We see ourselves at the apex of a triangle with the instrumental and the normative as the other points. From our vantage point, we can see both and we must acknowledge their impact if the triangle is to be complete. To deny the instrumental as a means of elevating the normative is as wrong intellectually and morally as it is currently for organizational scholars to deny the normative as a means of elevating the instrumental.

Beyond the "value added" to theory and research, work that addresses normative as well as instrumental issues has additional implications for researchers, for organizations and for students of organizational behavior. Researchers are likely to be more excited and passionate about their work if they are allowed (even encouraged) to care about the people and organizations they study. Further, an organizational science that includes the normative can't help but be more relevant to the very real problems organizations and their members are facing. Finally, acknowledging the normative in organizational behavior will require inclusion of the normative in our teaching of organizational behavior, encouraging "moral inquiry" by future management practitioners. Such moral reflection is essential to the revitalization and to the relevance of organizational behavior.

THE SOUNDS OF SILENCE: WHY THE NORMATIVE DIMENSION HAS BEEN SUPPRESSED

As Etzioni (1988) noted, the normative has always been part of social life, but we are now rediscovering it. We identify two major forces that have suppressed the normative dimension in organizational behavior theory and research.

Organizational Behavior Reflects Positivist Scientific Norms

Along with other applied social sciences, organizational behavior has struggled to be recognized as "legitimate" by the academic community. The primary method of doing so has been, initially at least, to follow the norms of positivist science. One of the most important underlying assumptions of positivist science is the objectivity the scientist brings to scientific questions. The scientist is supposed to be a "neutral, value-free, truth-seeker who tries to understand the world in a totally objective manner" (Howard, 1995, p. 131). However, in recent years, scientists and philosophers of science have been more willing to acknowledge that scientists are far from value-free and the role of values in science is being discussed in more detail. The relevant question is no longer "whether" values are important, but "how" values influence science and scientists (Howard, 1995). At a minimum, scientists' values influence the questions they ask, the methods they use, and their interpretations of data.

Within organizational behavior, the assumptions and methods of positivist science ruled for many years, and some would argue that they continue to do so, at least in the major journals. The functionalist paradigm, which is characterized by the objective study of "what is" rather than more subjective or interpretive approaches that seek change, has dominated the study of organizations (Burrell & Morgan, 1979; Gioia & Pitre, 1990). However, the organizational science community has undergone changes in recent years, acknowledging links between seemingly incompatible paradigms (Gioia & Pitre, 1990; Schultz & Hatch, 1996) and being more open to research questions, methodologies and discussions that stray from a strict positivist path. Mitroff (1972) termed the objectivity of science a "myth" that has kept us from understanding how science is really done. Scientists, especially the best ones, must be passionate advocates of their own work. Such passionate advocacy actually serves the overall objectivity of science because positions that are not advocated are rarely tested, making it more difficult to challenge existing understandings. It is the testing of different, passionately held scientific ideas that contributes to finding "truth". According to Mitroff, "Objectivity results from the heated, intense, and biased confrontation and struggle between the 'somewhat' biased ideas of 'somewhat' biased individuals. That which survives the process is labelled 'objective' or 'scientifically true'" (Mitroff, 1972, p. B615).

The Ideology of the Organizational Imperative

There is another important reason why researchers in organizational behavior have avoided normative talk. Organizational behavior, particularly as it has developed in business schools, applies social science in a particular context—business. Therefore, business's norms of rationality also influence those who study it. DeTocqueville discussed American business persons' disinclination to admit acting altruistically (see Bird & Waters, 1989). Similarly, Bird & Waters argued that managers are uncomfortable using moral language to discuss what they do (even when their intentions and actions are distinctly moral), resulting in a number of negative outcomes. One of these, moral amnesia, "reinforces a caricature of management as an amoral activity" (Bird & Waters, 1989, p. 79). Right action within the context of business is generally justified in instrumental terms—"good ethics is good business"—despite theoretical and practical problems with this approach (Quinn & Jones, 1995). Business people are told (and tell themselves) that they should do "the right thing" because it will pay off, especially in the long run.

Interestingly, there is little empirical evidence to support this instrumental view. Researchers have found it difficult to document a consistent, positive relationship between an organization's ethics or social responsibility and its bottom line (see Ullman, 1985), although a recent study has actually demonstrated such a link (Waddock & Graves, 1994). The relevant question may be whether business people do and should consider doing the right thing because it is the right thing to do. Etzioni (1988), in his book *The Moral Dimension*, cited many examples of individuals engaging in behaviors that are motivated primarily by moral concerns (e.g. returning a lost wallet to a stranger, donating blood, bone marrow or an organ). At the organizational level, research has found that top management's commitment to ethics as an end it itself has a powerful impact on business organizations' approach to ethics management within the firm (Weaver, Trevino & Cochran, 1996), suggesting that moral concerns do drive business practice as well. More research is needed to uncover the likely moral motivations that underlie many business decisions and practices, despite managers' apparent reluctance to talk about them.

The norms of business are rooted in a deep ideological foundation: the organizational imperative (Scott & Hart, 1979). The organizational imperative is based on a primary and absolute proposition, "Whatever is good for the individual can only come from the modern organization", and the related secondary proposition, "Therefore, all behavior must enhance the health of such organizations" (Scott & Hart, 1979, p. 43). Indeed, as Scott & Hart concluded, "the organizational imperative is the *sine qua non* of management theory and practice ... the metaphysic of management: absolute and immutable" (Scott & Hart, 1979, p. 46).

The ideological bias of the organizational imperative in organizational behavior theory can be traced back to the seminal and influential writings of

Chester Barnard (1938) and proponents of the industrial humanism movement (e.g. Mayo, Maslow, McGregor). Barnard, the "father" of modern management theory, articulated a general theory concerning social hierarchy and the maintenance of order (Scott, 1992), which is the ideological foundation of the field and practice of management. As Scott (1992) detailed in his analysis of Barnard's writings and influence, Barnard recognized that the economic well-being of an organization depends on the voluntary efforts of employees in service of organizational goals and objectives. As such, the goal of the managerial elite who lead and govern the organization is to "engineer" employee consent to organizational objectives. This insight by Barnard has become the unquestioned ideological foundation of modern organizational behavior theory.

At the same time as Barnard was making his impact on management thought, the industrial humanism movement developed, inspired by the Hawthorne studies. Out of this movement emerged a view of normative issues not in terms of justice and morality in dealings with workers, but in terms of how to create a work environment in which individuals could maximize their human potential or "self-actualize", while achieving organizational goals. As such, the individual came to be viewed as an "instrument" not an "end". The effect was to conceptualize morality in terms of cooperation with organizational objectives. As a result, issues of justice and morality were rarely raised, or if examined, it was in the context of advancing organizational interests such as productivity and work performance (e.g. Adam's equity theory).

Today, despite great social change in the corporate landscape, where do we find organizational behavior researchers? We find most of them identifying new and more effective means to motivate more performance out of managers and workers. We find increasing amounts of research on "transformational leadership", "high performance teams" and "total quality management". One could say that most organizational scientists have become the "foot soldiers" for the organizational imperative.

TOWARD A NEW ORGANIZATIONAL BEHAVIOR PARADIGM: *HOMO ECONOMICUS* AND *HOMO MORALIS*

A theorist's assumptions about the moral nature of man shape the development of theory proposed (Scott & Hart, 1971). As we have illustrated thus far, the assumption of *homo economicus* (that self-interest alone drives human action) explicit in the instrumental paradigm, is inadequate to fully explain and understand the richness and complexities of organizational life. We do not deny the claim of the instrumental paradigm that people and organizations are motivated by self-interest; rather, we argue that the assumption is incomplete.

To address this inadequacy, we propose a companion core assumption, *homo moralis*, which recognizes that normative motivations, in addition to instrumental motivations, shape and influence organizational behavior. In other words, we propose a *dual nature assumption* as the foundation of organizational behavior theory and research. This is similar to Etzioni's (1988) communitarian assumption that I and We are both important and that a full understanding of life in organizations can only be achieved by acknowledging its instrumental *and* normative underpinnings.

To counteract the ideological bias of the organizational imperative, we propose *the individual imperative* (Scott & Hart, 1979). According to Scott & Hart, "the primary proposition of the individual imperative is: all individuals have the natural *right* (emphasis added) to realize their potentials through the stages of their lives. It thus follows that the primary purpose of any organization, public or private, is to allow for the realization of individual potentials" (Scott & Hart, 1979, p. 53). In addition, individuals are assumed to possess certain innate and inalienable rights that we ascribe them because they are human beings. In other words, each individual is assumed to have an "inviolate personality . . . (with) independence, dignity and integrity" (Bloustein, 1964, p. 971).

The values of the individual imperative suggest a variety of organizational implications. For example, an individual's personal and unique worth must be recognized by the organization, and an individual should have the right to dissent without fear of repression. The goal is to "increase the respect of all . . . for the essential values of human life" (Beaney, 1966:271). Inclusion of the individual imperative will raise new questions about the nature of governance, and the "balancing" of individual rights and organizational interests (Keeley, 1988).

Our point is that neither the traditional organizational imperative nor the individual imperative suffices by itself. Within the new organizational behavior paradigm, we must constantly work to balance the needs, rights and duties of both. Although this makes for a complex world, it is one that better reflects reality.

BENEFITS OF WIDENING THE LENS: THE "VALUE ADDED" OF THE NEW PARADIGM

Addressing the normative more directly and in ways that integrate it into our work means thinking about our motivation to study a particular topic, how that motivation may influence how we go about studying the topic, the normative implications of our research, identifying our own moral dilemmas in conducting and evaluating research, and arguing for what we think is good and right. Doing so means that we can be caring people as well as scientists. It means expanding the scope of our science to support consideration for what's good for human beings as an important part of what we do. In such a science, the scientist becomes a human being who is dedicated to learning about issues that she/he cares about. The subjects of inquiry are human beings with intrinsic value and dignity who are motivated by both instrumental and moral concerns.

We understand the hesitancy to delve into this normative territory because we have felt it ourselves. The realm of objectivity and causality seems safer and more acceptable. In fact, one of the reasons we consider the organizational justice literature to be an area that is ripe for our broader perspective is because a strong body of legitimate "science" has clearly been established over a significant period of time. For example, equity theory and the empirical research it generated, provided a strong jumping-off point for talking about organizational justice in general, for developing theories of procedural justice, and for relating justice concerns to other individual and organizational outcomes. This research has allowed us to make the instrumental case for organizational justice—that management is better off if employees believe that managers and organizations are just. Perhaps now that the organizational justice literature has achieved scientific legitimacy and the instrumental case has been made, we can step back and ask and answer questions about why people care about justice in the first place, and what our findings mean for organizations and their members? We can also focus our research on organizational justice as an end in itself, in addition to its instrumental role in achieving management's objectives. We believe that organizational behavior will be enriched if those questions are asked and answered more routinely, and are integrated into our work as more than introductory material or addenda.

There are a number of other benefits of widening the study of these areas to allow their normative nature to be discussed. First, doing so is likely to open the field of organizational behavior to identify new and important areas. Science is advanced by asking new questions as much as it is by answering questions that have already been asked (Lundberg, 1976). By allowing our passions to fly, we are more likely to ask important new questions that diverge from previous work. For example, asking questions about justice as an end in itself suggests that perhaps we should study organizational phenomena from the perspective of disenfranchised groups as well as from the perspective of management and managers. We might also ask whether and how justice can be achieved in today's new organizational structures (e.g. "virtual" organizations) and whether new conceptualizations of organizational justice will be required.

Second, shifting the paradigm to acknowledge openly the normative nature of these issues is more likely to unleash researchers' passion and produce more exciting work. We feel our own passion as we think about studying organizational justice or ethical organizational behavior for their own sakes and not only because they are instrumental to the bottom line. Phenomenal energy will be unleashed as academics acknowledge their concerns and apply these to study what they and people in organizations truly care about. Third, addressing these normative issues clearly has implications for organizations and for society. If we are willing to put ourselves "out there" about what is good, fair and just, we are more likely to be viewed as relevant to the dialogue that exists and that could exist about how organizations relate to people and to their communities. Globalization, stiff competition, demographic changes, technological advances and the restructuring of organizations are contributing to wrenching changes in work organizations that are challenging the implied contract that used to exist between workers and their employers. Companies are switching from talk of employment security to "employability". The academic community should be a part of the discussion of the normative issues that are so much a part of organizational life if it is to have any impact on the dialogue that is occurring in living rooms, on talk shows, and in political campaigns.

IMPLICATIONS OF THE NORMATIVE MANIFESTO: FROM TEAMS TO TEACHING

Teams

Perhaps the best way to explain the normative manifesto for organizational behavior and its benefits is to apply it to a particular area of study in a way that illustrates how a more explicit focus on the normative can raise new research questions. We have decided to focus our attention on teams, but we recognize that a similar process could be applied to any mainstream organizational behavior topic.

Despite the burgeoning popularity of teamwork in organizations, and increasing attention to teams in the business press, research has advanced rather slowly. We understand and acknowledge the conventional wisdom about why this is so. Researching teams is difficult to do because of the large number of subjects needed, and because of the difficulty of gaining access to teams and organizations. On the other hand, perhaps our understanding of teams is not advancing because our conceptual models are incomplete, and we aren't asking the right questions (Donnellon, 1994).

Asking New Questions

An instrumental approach to studying teams logically focuses on questions of how teams can work more, better and faster, including the study of team structure, control, reward and feedback mechanisms, goal-setting, and the effects of these on team output, efficiency and effectiveness. These are certainly useful and appropriate topics of study. However, an approach that focuses more explicitly on the normative turns the researcher's attention to human issues, such as caring and respect within teams, and value-laden issues such as fairness (e.g. of reward or appraisal systems), rights (e.g. issues of credit and blame), duties (to the team vs. to oneself or one's family) and responsibilities (to team members by the organization and to the organization by team members). The dependent variables of interest, in addition to team performance, might include trust within the team, loyalty to the team, team *esprit de corps*, individual satisfaction and enthusiasm for the team's work, and individual integrity. We thought about some of these constructs and created the following research questions as examples of the type of work this kind of thinking might generate.

Research Question 1: How can teamwork be implemented in a way that protects the integrity of the individual?

This research question is built on the assumption that individual integrity is a valuable outcome and that work in teams should support it and not compromise it. The research would have to define integrity and tackle problems of how one would measure it. The question invites the development of theory about the characteristics of teamwork that might support or compromise individual integrity, and spurs thought about how one might study the question.

Research Question 2: How can work teams become communities of mutual support, caring, respect and encouragement, as well as productive entities?

The assumption here is that community is important and that work teams can create something more than their work. The group process literature talks about process losses. How about focusing attention on process gains? What are the team attitudes and practices that will create these valued outcomes and what do the human beings who are involved gain from the experience? The construct of group cohesiveness is related to what we're talking about here, but it doesn't capture the richness of this kind of community-building experience. Again, this research challenges the researcher to define community and to address measurement and research design issues.

Research Question 3: How do work team members think about the concepts of rights and responsibilities within teams?

This question focuses on the rights and responsibilities that team members feel they have with regard to each other. In the past, studies of psychological contracts (Rousseau & Parks, 1992) have focused on the relationship between the individual and the organization. Perhaps we need to expand that notion to think about psychological contracts between team members and between the team and the organization. If team members think about their relationships in this way, the complexity of individual/organizational relations increases dramatically.

Research Question 4: What are the normatively negative outcomes of work in teams?

Teamwork is promoted broadly in the practitioner literature as a "good". However, a more critical perspective suggests that we should ask whether or when work in teams is good, when it is not good, and what the negative outcomes might be. For example, research on in-groups and out-groups suggests that creating cohesive work teams will also create problems with intergroup conflict and rivalry. Research on group decision-making also highlights problems of conformity pressures and groupthink. Also, team loyalty may come at the expense of organizational commitment as well as individual integrity (see Question 1). Researchers should identify these outcomes and trade-offs, develop theory about the factors that influence them, and develop techniques for investigating these issues.

The idea is that, by focusing on the normative more explicitly, we can create a host of new research questions that can be studied theoretically and investigated empirically. We encourage our colleagues in organizational behavior to try the exercise; simply focus more explicitly on the normative in your own areas of interest and explore the ideas that emerge. Develop research questions and consider designing research aimed at answering them.

Research Methods

One of the reasons organizational behavior researchers may have avoided the normative in the past is because of a devotion to the methods of positive science. However, this avoidance is unnecessary. All accepted empirical methodologies are appropriate candidates for use within the new paradigm (e.g. interviews, surveys, experiments, etc.). But, because we haven't asked many of the research questions before, we may need to begin with more interpretive approaches. We may need to step back and be more passive than we're comfortable being when we're in research mode. We're used to being in "control", designing the experiment, writing the survey questions, or even the structured interview protocol. Instead, we may need essentially to "eavesdrop" on teams, "listening" closely to what managers have to say about their work in teams when they're talking to each other (e.g. Donnellon, 1994). It is likely that they will say things to each other that they wouldn't say to us.

Teaching Organizational Behavior

The normative manifesto is directed not just at issues of research, but it also carries implications for how we educate students of organizational behavior. Following the argument advanced in this chapter, we want to improve the intellectual capabilities of our students, to equip them with keen analytical and critical thinking skills. But management educators have another obligation, a moral one. Not only do we need to closely scrutinize how our teaching shapes the moral attitudes of our students, but we must provide them with opportunities to grapple with the normative issues and moral dilemmas of organizational life—much like they would in the "real world"—and experience how the instrumental and normative perspectives can and should operate together.

Toward that end, the second author and his colleague at Georgetown University, Dan McAllister, created a course project for their *core* organizational behavior class for MBA students that explicitly focused on both instrumental and normative considerations. In what was called "The OB Challenge", students in each section formed "companies" whose objectives were twofold. First, each company was responsible for creating and marketing products *for profit*. Utilizing all of their business and management skills, students were expected to become a high-performance profit-making organization—an instrumental objective. But we gave the students a second objective that was clearly normative in nature. Students were also expected to engage in community service activities and contribute their profits to community betterment. What transpired in this project was amazing, as the community service projects became the "motivator" for the students, and all of their profit-making ventures were dedicated to community service. As a result, students not only witnessed the instrumental "cooperating" with the normative, but actually experienced the instrumental *in service of* the normative. The meta-learning about the importance of the normative could not be escaped and was all the more powerful because it occured within the context of a core course in organizational behavior, rather than a separate course in business ethics (Bies, 1996).

CONCLUSION

For us, writing this chapter has provided a welcome opportunity to "know what we think as we see what we say". Over the years, our own work has walked a fine line between the normative and the instrumental. We were recipients of the mythology of fear that sometimes kept us from doing all that we wanted to do. But now we have tacked our manifesto to the wall of our academic community.

This manifesto was written as an encouragement, not only to those researchers in the normative movement, but also as an invitation to those researchers firmly rooted in the instrumental paradigm. It is our hope that this latter group of our colleagues will listen and, at a minimum, be more open to the normative in papers they review. Perhaps they would even consider the normative dimension in their own work, include normative variables in their analyses, and engage in moral inquiry as they pursue their scientific work.

While we are filled with hope for the future, we anticipate the struggles that lie ahead in advancing the normative paradigm; for we have watched others' even more modest proposals run into roadblocks and dead ends over the years. Our manifesto might meet a similar fate, but we are optimistic. Why? Because we know courageous journal editors, the powerful gatekeepers of the field, who have supported high quality and rigorous research that integrates normative issues. We will need their continued support not only for the advancement of organizational science, but for the "soul" of the field, and for our relevance to the world of organizations. We plan to continue our own work, and we invite others to join us in dialogue about and embrace of the new paradigm.

REFERENCES

Ball, G., Trevino, L.K. & Sims, H.P. Jr (1994). Just and unjust punishment: influences on subordinate performance and citizenship. *Academy of Management Journal*, **37**(2), 299–322.

Barnard, C.I. (1938). *The Function of the Executive*. Cambridge, MA: Harvard University Press.

Beaney, W.M. (1966). The right to privacy and American law. *Law and Contemporary Problems*, **31**, 253–71.

Bies, R.J. (1996). Down and out in D.C.: how Georgetown MBA students learn about leadership through service to others. *Journal of Business Ethics*, **15**, 103–10.

Bies, R.J. & Tripp, T.M. (1995). The use and abuse of power: justice as social control. In R.S. Cropanzano & K.M. Kacmar (eds), *Organizational Politics, Justice, and Support* (pp. 131–45). Westport, CT: Quorum Books.

Bird, F.B. & Waters, J.A. (1989). The moral muteness of managers. *California Management Review*, **Fall**, 73–88.

Bloustein, E.J. (1964). Privacy as an aspect of human dignity: an answer to Dean Prosser. *NYU Law Review*, **39**, 962–1007.

Brockner, J. & Greenberg, J. (1988). The impact of layoffs on survivors: an organizational justice perspective. In J. Carroll (ed.), *Applied Social Psychology and Organizational Settings* (pp. 45–75). Hillsdale, NJ: Erlbaum.

Burrell, G. & Morgan, G. (1979). *Sociological Paradigms and Organizational Analysis*. London: Heinemann.

Cobb, A.T., Wooten, K. & Folger, R. (1994). Justice in the making: toward understanding the theory and practice of justice in organizational development. In W. Pasmore & R. Woodman (eds), *Research in Organizational Change and Development*. Greenwich, CT: JAI Press.

Donnellon, A. (1994). Team work: linguistic models of negotiating differences. In R.J. Lewicki, B.H. Sheppard & R.J. Bies (eds), *Research on Negotiation in Organizations*, vol. 4 (pp. 71–123). Greenwich, CT: JAI Press.

Etzioni, A. (1988). *The Moral Dimension: Toward a New Economics*. New York: Free Press.

Folger, R. & Greenberg, J. (1985). Procedural justice: an interpretive analysis of personnel systems. In K. Rowland & G. Ferris (eds), *Research in Personnel and Human Resources Management*, vol. 3 (pp. 141–83). Greenwich, CT: JAI Press.

Gioia, D. & Pitre, E. (1990). Multiparadigm perspectives in theory building. *Academy of Management Review*, **15**, 584–602.

Howard, G. (1995). *Dare We Develop a Human Science?* Notre Dame, IN: Academic Publications.

Jones, T. (1995). Instrumental stakeholder theory: a synthesis of ethics and economics. *Academy of Management Review*, **20**(2), 404–37.

Keeley, M. (1978). A social-justice approach to organizational evaluation. *Administrative Science Quarterly*, **23**, 272–92.

Keeley, M. (1988). *A Social Contract Theory of Organizations*. Notre Dame, IN: University of Notre Dame Press.

Lacayo, R. (1996). Populist blow. *Time*, **February 26**, 28–9.

Lind, E.A. & Tyler, T. (1988). *The Social Psychology of Procedural Justice*. New York: Plenum.

Lundberg, C. (1976). Hypothesis creation in organizational behavior research. *Academy of Management Review*, **1** (April), 5–11.

Mitroff, I. (1972). The myth of objectivity, or why science needs a new psychology of science. *Management Science*, **18**, B613–17.

Moorman, R.H. (1991). Relationship between organizational justice and organizational citizenship behaviors: do fairness perceptions influence employee citizenship? *Journal of Applied Psychology*, **76**, 845–55.

Quinn, D.P. & Jones, T.M. (1995). An agent morality view of business policy. *Academy of Management Review*, **20**, 22–42.

Rousseau, D.M. & Parks, J.M. (1992). The contracts of individuals and organizations. In L.L. Cummings & B.M. Staw (eds), *Research in Organizational Behavior*, vol. 15 (pp. 1–43). Greenwich, CT: JAI Press.

Schultz, M. & Hatch, M.J. (1996). Living with multiple paradigms: the case of paradigm interplay in organizational culture studies. *Academy of Management Review*, **21**(2), 529–57.

Scott, W.G. (1985). Organizational revolution: an end to managerial orthodoxy. *Administration and Society*, **17**, 149–70.

Scott, W.G. (1992). *Chester I. Barnard and the Guardians of the Managerial State*. Lawrence, KS: University Press of Kansas.

Scott, W.G. & Hart, D.K. (1971). The moral nature of man in organizations: a comparative analysis. *Academy of Management Journal*, **14**, 241–55.

Scott, W.G. & Hart, D.K. (1979). *Organizational America*. Boston, MA: Houghton Mifflin.

Scott, W.G. & Hart, D.K. (1989). *Organizational Values in America*. New Brunswick, NJ: Transaction.

Sloan, A. (1996). The hit men. *Newsweek*, **February 26**, 44–8.

Trevino, L.K. & Ball, G.A. (1992). The social implications of punishing unethical behavior: observers' cognitive and affective reactions. *Journal of Management*, **18**(4), 751–68.

Ullman, A.H. (1985). Data in search of a theory: a critical examination of the relationships among social performance, social disclosure, and economic performance of US firms. *Academy of Management Review*, **10**(3), 540–57.

Waddock, S.A. & Graves, S.B. (1994). The corporate–social performance–financial performance link. Paper presented at the Academy of Management meetings.

Weaver, G.R., Trevino, L.K. & Cochran, P.L. (1996). Coercion, fashion, and commitment: environmental and managerial legitimacy expectations in the structuring of corporate ethics programs. Unpublished manuscript.

Zald, M.N. (1993). Organization studies as a scientific and humanistic enterprise: toward a reconceptualization of the foundations of the field. *Organization Science*, **4**, 513–28

Chapter 24

OB Meets the Information Superhighway

Boris Kabanoff
*Queensland University of Technology, Brisbane,
Queensland, Australia*
and
Eric Abrahamson
Columbia University, New York, USA

Undoubtedly some readers are thinking that the information superhighway has been a bit oversold already, and we agree with this view to an extent—but it would be unwise to throw out the baby with the bathwater. Beyond the hype are two important conclusions: that vast new electronic streams of information are becoming available to researchers and decision-makers; and that those fields that find ways of harnessing these new resources will prosper in terms of both their scientific status and their relevance, while those that don't, won't (c.f. Stone, in press). Workers in some fields are discovering this already.

Under the headline "Meet the Mother of all Big Brothers", a recent newspaper story made the following observations:

> If you thought Big Brother was scary, wait until you meet his mates in Marketing. Not only can they track your every financial movement from cradle to grave, but nowadays they can even figure out what you are going to do before you've decided to do it. Better and faster technology means marketers can now sell to individual businesses or consumers based on their actual purchasing behaviour (Australian Financial Review, 1995).

The present chapter is not really about the information superhighway *per se*, rather it is about what the superhighway symbolizes—the existence of large, longitudinal, accessible and fairly immediate sources of data about a variety of aspects of people's and organizations' behaviour. Our aim is to explain how OB

Creating Tomorrow's Organizations. Edited by C.L. Cooper and S.E. Jackson.
© 1997 John Wiley & Sons Ltd.

research can enhance both its rigour and its relevance by making use of the
opportunities arising from the informational and technological developments we
are witnessing. The challenge, as Nissan & Schmidt (1995) recently observed, is
to turn all this information into knowledge.

OB and the Search for a Natural Data Source

We are probably not the only OB researchers who have been struck by the
difference between how we typically do our research and how many of our
non-OB, business school colleagues do theirs. Specifically, it is interesting to note
the reliance that many non-OB colleagues place on large, "naturally-occurring"
databases (c.f. Kabanoff, 1996). Accounting and finance researchers have
access to vast amounts of data generated by organizations and stock exchanges;
economists seem to have the whole world generating various kinds of statistical
data for them; while marketers have scanner data, TV ratings, sales figures and
so on to work with. By contrast, the typical OB researcher generally runs a
survey, conducts interviews, designs an experiment, and so on. This probably has
some advantages, but it also has a lot of disadvantages—time, cost, small samples,
limited generalizability, lack of cumulation of research findings, scarcity of
longitudinal data, reliance on intrusive forms of data-gathering, and so on.

However, OB does have a natural source of data that is useful for studying
many issues—the texts, documents and communications, in both electronic and
non-electronic form, that are generated by and about organizations. Texts such as
annual reports, analysts' reports, interviews with organizational leaders, stories
and commentaries all offer a potential data source and all are to be found these
days in an electronic form. As is often the case, the methodology for tapping into
this information source—content- or text-analysis—has been available to us but
has not been part of mainstream, OB methodology (Woodrum, 1984). The development of the information superhighway may be the watershed event that alerts
the field to the potential of text-analysis, because it comes at the confluence of a
number of other trends in the field, such as a degree of disenchantment with
survey methodology, greater interest in qualitative methods, along with a reluctance to give up the benefits of quantification, and the availability of desktop
computing power.

Plan of the Chapter

The rest of the chapter comprises three main sections. In the first we consider
issues of reliability, validity and underlying assumptions of text analysis. Following this we examine the application of text analysis to both "macro" and "micro"
issues in OB. At the micro end we consider how text analysis can contribute to
a very traditional area of industrial/organizational psychology—testing for
personnel selection. Then at the macro end we consider how text analysis can

be used to study the nature of managerial cognitions across organizations and industries.

TEXT ANALYSIS: AN INTRODUCTION

This section draws extensively upon Kabanoff (1996). While text analysis has commonly been known as content analysis, we will use the more limited and descriptively more accurate term *text analysis* (TA) because our concern here is with text, whereas content can equally refer to pictures and other features such as colour, design and so on. Stone et al. (1966, p. 5) defined content/text analysis as "any technique for making inferences by systematically and objectively identifying specified characteristics within text". Weber (1985) states that the core process of virtually all forms of TA is data reduction, by which the many words of text are classified into much fewer content categories. While virtually all forms of TA rely to some extent on this "many words into few" approach, the extent to which the process of "word classification" is very explicitly specified and oriented to producing quantitative indices of textual content varies across different methods of TA. At the highly explicit, quantitative end is word-frequency-based TA, which is where computers can at present make their major contribution. Word-frequency-based analysis of text from various kinds of documents, and the contribution that computers can make to this process, is our focus here. At the less explicit, non-quantitative end of the continuum are what have been termed more *cognitive mapping* approaches. These usually involve more qualitative, "thematic" analysis of text and often rely upon interviews rather than upon documentary sources of text. In this type of application the computer mainly plays the role of a powerful and flexible text-manager that allows the qualitative-oriented researcher to store, cross-index and access in an efficient and reliable manner the large body of interview or field-notes data he/she has collected (e.g. Kelle, 1995). Examples of various types of TA are found in the book *Mapping Strategic Thought* edited by Huff (1990), while Weber (1985) concentrates on word-frequency-based analysis using computers.

TA: The Basic Process

As already noted, virtually all forms of TA rely to some extent on classifying the words of text into a limited number of content categories. Therefore, development of a *coding scheme* is normally a central part of a TA study. A coding scheme consists of a set of content categories. Each content category contains a number of words or phrases that are presumed to have a similar, shared meaning. For example, words that a company uses when referring to employee performance would include, among others, such words as "performance", "achievement", "service", "efficiency" and so on. A coding scheme usually comprises a set of such content categories, the selection of these being based upon the issue being investigated and theory guiding the research. Frequently, especially in the context of computer-aided text analysis (CATA), a coding scheme will be called a *content analysis dictionary*.

Weber (1985, pp. 21–24) and Wolfe, Gephart & Johnson (1993) have provided detailed descriptions of the basic TA process; here we stress the following. The time that is spent on developing, refining and testing the reliability and validity of a coding scheme is central to the confidence that can be placed on the conclusions based on TA research. Just as a survey researcher needs well constructed, reliable, valid survey questions, the TA researcher needs to devote time, attention and creativity to the development of a coding scheme.

Basic Assumptions of TA

Probably *the* core assumption of TA is that language plays a major role in how people perceive and understand their world; therefore, if we can analyse language, we gain insight into how people perceive and understand their world. That is, *words* are a *window* into important features of people's "world view". Word-frequency-based TA assumes that word frequency reflects the importance or *cognitive centrality* of a concept or construct, either to the person who produced the text or to the intended audience for the text. The more frequently a word or theme occurs, the more central or important it is. As previously noted, content analysis assumes that *related* words can be grouped to identify overall themes of importance. That is, while words such as "performance" and "service" are different, they have a common, underlying concern—task achievement. The frequency of word use can change over time, and is usually interpreted as an indication of a change in the level of attention being given to an issue. Finally, juxtaposition of words can in some circumstances be interpreted as an indication of a mental connection between different themes or concerns. For example, Kabanoff, Waldersee & Cohen (1995) examined what kinds of themes were correlated with the discussion of organizational change in companies' annual reports. Thus word-frequency-based analyses can be used to explore quite complex concepts and, while seemingly simple and naive, can be quite sophisticated in providing indicators of symbolic content in text.

The Advantages of TA Research

Quality and Quantity

One of the benefits of TA is that it combines desirable characteristics from what are generally considered two separate, even inimical research traditions—qualitative and quantitative research. By allowing us to deal systematically with, and to quantify, what are normally considered qualitative data such as documents and interviews, TA helps address the criticisms of sterility and lack of relevance that are sometimes directed at quantitative research. At the same time, TA permits those of us who believe that being able to quantify constructs is desirable, to convert qualitative data to a quantitative form.

Natural and Unobtrusive

TA opens up new data sources for OB researchers. At present the most frequently studied organizational texts are companies' annual reports (AR). Clearly, however, there are other kinds of texts that can be useful, such as newspaper reports (Fombrun & Shanley, 1990), internal magazines (Kabanoff, 1993), internal memos (Huff, 1983), reports on specific organizational events such as accidents (Gephart, 1993), and even corporate slogans (Dowling & Kabanoff, 1996). A feature of all these forms of text is that they are naturally produced, in the sense of not being produced for the researcher's purpose, and they can be unobtrusively accessed. This does not mean that such texts necessarily provide valid or objective indicators of organizational processes or policies simply because they are produced by an organization, but they do represent how the organization presents itself to its natural audience, rather than to a researcher.

Longitudinal

The opportunity to carry out longitudinal research is also enhanced by the use of text analysis. For example Barr, Stimpert & Huff (1990) were able to trace the evolution of two railway companies' different strategies for dealing with a changing business environment by studying companies' ARs over 25 years. From their analysis they felt they gained insight into how the strategic focus and adaptation of the surviving company had differed from the company that failed. D'Aveni & MacMillan (1990) identified 57 large organizations that became bankrupt during a business crisis and paired them with 57 surviving firms that were similar in size and product/market environment. They then compared what the CEOs of failed and surviving firms had focused on by coding the contents of CEOs' letters to shareholders in terms of such factors as how often CEOs referred to internal vs. external organizational concerns. What is obvious about the use of TA in such studies is that it enabled researchers to study organizations over a period of time; to infer what the top managements of these different firms were focusing on in different periods, to make quantitative comparisons, and to sample strategically so as to identify organizations that confronted similar environments but had different outcomes.

By contrast, a study by Golden (1992) has demonstrated the potential limitations of using retrospective reporting for such analyses. Golden asked CEOs to report their firms' current strategies and, 2 years later, he again asked them to report their firm's strategies of 2 years earlier. Of these retrospective accounts, 58% did not agree with the previous and validated reports of past strategy. TA can produce a less biased assessment of an organization's strategic concerns than self-report.

Insight into Cognitive Processes

The use of organizational documents, such as ARs, also gives us some access to the concerns and thinking of the members of the organization's top team, to whom direct access is limited. The recent surge of interest in the characteristics of top teams and how these relate to organizational strategies (e.g. see Sparrow's (1994) review) has focused mainly upon the study of demographic characteristics of top teams, largely because such data are fairly readily accessible. As Sparrow remarked, however, that the link between top teams' demography and organizational strategies will not be fully convincing until we demonstrate the cognitive and social process linkages between these two sets of variables, and at present these linkages are merely inferred, or a "black box". TA has the potential to tell us something about the cognitive process of the top team and thus illuminate the inner workings of that black box. This is an issue to which we return later in the chapter.

Multi-methods

Text analysis also allows us to "triangulate" an issue by using different methods and sources of data. Thus we can measure organizational values by asking organizational members to describe the values of their organizations (e.g. Chatman & Jehn, 1994), and also study them by analysing the content of organizational documents (e.g. Kabanoff, 1993). Individuals' reports about organizations' values may be coloured by their own values, their position in the organization, tenure and so on, whereas annual reports may espouse values with which senior managers hope to impress shareholders. Using two different methods to measure organizational values provides a good cross-check on the results from any one method.

Other Advantages of CATA

While these are advantages of both manual and computer-aided text-analysis, CATA also has a number of unique advantages. (a) *Perfect reliability*—classification of text by multiple human coders permits the level of reliability achieved to be assessed, while classification by computer leads to perfect reliability since the coding rules are applied in the same way by the software. Reliability is of course different from validity, but it is nice to know that once you have developed a valid coding schema the computer will be your tireless, errorless clerk that does not get bored by the task of classifying large amounts of data over and over again. (b) *Standard dictionaries*—over time a number of "generic" content-analytic dictionaries have been developed which contain categories useful in many social science contexts. For example, the Harvard Psycho-Social IV Dictionary (Züll, Weber & Mohler, 1989) consists of some 80 categories developed to operationalize a "general theory of action" and, as its name suggests, the categories are based upon concepts from psychology and sociology. Table 24.1 provides examples of

Table 24.1   Examples of content categories from the Harvard IV psycho-social dictionary

Category	Definition	Examples
Active	Active orientation[a]	Develop, competitive, earn
Change	Change without the connotation of increase, decrease, beginning, or ending	Change, transition, modify, vary, process
Collectivities	All collectivities (excluding animal)	Group, public, staff
Communication	All forms and processes of communication	Communication, debate, forecast, consult
Completion	Activities directed toward completing goals	Establish, achieve
Failure	Implying goals have not been met	Fail, miss, drop, weaken
Goals	End-states toward which striving, muscular or mental, is directed	Result, reward, targeted, intention, objective
Human	Social actors, individual and collective	Employee, manager
Increase	Indicating increase	Develop, growth, expand, extend, increase
Means	Objects, acts, or methods utilized in attaining goals	Plans, operational, network, strategy
Needs	Need, wish or interest	Desire, dedicate, intend
Negative	Negative orientation[a]	Concern, poorly
Ours	All first-person pronouns	We, our
Overstate	Emphasis on speed, frequency, inevitability, causality, size, scope	Amazing, tremendous
Passive	Passive orientation[a]	Perception allow, hope
Pleasure	Indicates that the person experiencing the feeling is enjoying it	Pride, pleased, appreciate, grateful
Political	Clearly political words, political roles, collectivities, acts, ideas	Parliament, government
Positive	Positive orientation[a]	Boost, effectively
Power	Connotation of power, control, or authority	Require, pressure, legislation, government
Strong	Strength[a]	Objectives, implementation
Time	References to when events take place, and/or time taken, and to the concept of time relationships	Annual, frequent, month
Understate	Deemphasis in the same areas as "overstate"	Some, minor, small
Weak	Weakness[a]	Subordinate, borrow, less, obliged, loss, shrunk

[a]Category is derived from the Osgood semantic differential dimensions (Osgood et al., 1957).

some of the categories that have been found useful in previous research (e.g. Kabanoff, Waldersee & Cohen, 1995). The use of standard content categories from well validated, general dictionaries is efficient and can enhance both the comparability and validity of TA studies. (c) *Efficiency*—a major drawback of manual methods of text analysis is their labour-intensive nature and inflexibility, which makes them highly unsuitable for exploratory work. On the other hand, a computer-based dictionary can be fairly readily refined as the researcher's knowledge about the text increases and reapplied to the same text, or to new text that is collected. Of course like any method, CATA has its critics and limitations.

Criticisms of CATA

One drawback in the use of CATA to analyse documents, such as Presidents' letters that are available in computer-readable formats, is that neither their author nor their author's intentions are known. This drawback raises two inter-related questions. First, was the President's letter written by a top executive or by a public relations specialist communicating for this top executive? Second, does the President's letter reflect the cognition of top executives or their attempts to manage shareholders' impressions? The second question in particular is important, because it brings into question the validity of CATA measures of computer-readable documents.

Empirical research using the President's letter has been used successfully to test hypotheses about both management cognition and management impression management. On the one hand, a number of studies have used annual-report measures of top managers' cognitions (Bowman, 1978; D'Aveni & MacMillan, 1990; Fiol, 1990). Of those, two studies hypothesized that annual report measures of executive cognition would relate with other constructs measured using other types of data (Bowman, 1978; D'Aveni & MacMillan, 1990). The hypotheses in both studies were strongly supported, providing some evidence for the construct validity of annual report measures. On the other hand, a number of studies have used annual report measures of impression management (e.g. Abrahamson & Park, 1994; Staw, McKechnie & Puffer, 1983). Here too, two of these studies hypothesized and found that annual reports measures of impression management were related to other constructs measured using other types of data, providing some evidence for the construct validity of annual report measures of impression management (Abrahamson & Park, 1994; Staw, McKechnie & Puffer, 1983).

Four studies have been designed explicitly to test the validity of annual report measures of top managers' cognitions (Bowman, 1984; Clapham & Schwenk, 1991; Huff & Schwenk, 1990; Fiol, 1990). The latter two studies provided rigorous evidence that patterns of causal attribution in annual reports were better explained by information processing rather than impression management theories. These studies support the view that annual reports constitute valid measures of top managers' cognitions, when it comes to causal attributions. The study by Fiol

(1995) reinforces, but qualifies, this conclusion. She compared Presidents' letters to internal documents belonging to the same firm. She found that patterns of causal attribution were correlated across these two types of documents, supporting the conclusions of the previous two studies. She also found, however, that the positive/negative orientation of the two types of documents were not significantly correlated. She concluded tentatively that evaluative statements in Presidents' letters may be likely to reflect impression management, whereas non-evaluative statements may tend to reflect managerial cognitions.

Thus it does not seem to be instructive to ask whether CATA-based measures are valid indicators of managerial cognition or merely reflecting impression management? A more useful question is which CATA-based measures and when are indicative of managerial cognition and when are they indicators of impression management processes? Having reviewed the basic CATA process we turn to our first illustration.

PSYCHOLOGICAL ASSESSMENT IN PERSONNEL SELECTION

Most people would agree that the use of psychological testing for selection of personnel, particularly aptitude and ability testing, has been one of the field's major contributions to the improvement of individual and organizational productivity. Nevertheless, the use of cognitive-ability testing for selection purposes is at an interesting juncture in its scientific and practical evolution. There is considerable evidence that for most practical purposes the major predictor of the quantity and quality of individuals' work performance across many different types of jobs, even highly specialized ones such as military pilots (Olea & Ree, 1994), is general cognitive ability or g, with specific cognitive abilities adding relatively little to the equation (e.g. Ree, Earles & Teachout, 1994). Given this, little may be added to our power to predict performance by improving the ability measures we already have or by developing specialized ability measures for different occupations.

In recent years the interest of researchers and practitioners has switched somewhat to exploring the potential of non-cognitive or personality-oriented testing for selection purposes. However, in comparison to the strong evidence for the validity of cognitive ability measures as predictors, the evidence for our ability to use personality factors as predictors of work performance has been and, by and large, continues to be debated (e.g. Robertson, 1995). In short, the cognitive sphere, where we understand and can measure attributes quite well, may have relatively little further potential that we can readily tap to predict individual job performance. On the other hand, the non-cognitive or personality domain, where our understanding and measurement ability are more limited, may have much remaining potential which we have thus far found hard to make use of.

A number of reasons have been offered for the relative lack of impact of personality assessment in selection; however, one important cause may be the very nature of paper-and-pencil personality tests. There have been those who have claimed that the best way of tapping into the "deep structure" of personality is not via paper-and-pencil tests based upon psychometric theory, which developed around the assessment of a very different aspect of human behaviour, that is, cognitive ability. Rather, they contend that in order to tap into the underlying dimensions of personality, we should use "projectivetype" tests—we use this term broadly here to encompass all test situations that involve asking people to respond in a relatively unstructured way to an ambiguous stimulus and analysing their responses according to some set of rules (e.g. Rorschach and Thematic Apperception Test (TAT)). Because of these tests' less structured nature, it is argued that they allow subjects more opportunity to report how they perceive and structure situations (cf. Viney 1983).

CATA and Psychological Assessment

Although projective-type tests have played little or no role in personnel selection to date, at least in part because of the time and cost involved in scoring them, CATA can provide the capability for rapidly and accurately scoring such tests. Indeed, content analysis has quite a long history of use in clinical assessment. Several decades ago, Gottschalk & Gleser (1969) developed a manual scoring method for assessing a number of different psychological states and traits, such as hostility, anxiety and alienation, from the content and form of people's free speech. That is, people are simply asked to talk for a few minutes on a topic of their own choosing and this material is scored by an expert rater following a detailed scoring manual (Viney, 1983). More recently, computer-based scoring of these same mood and personality dimensions has been developed (e.g. Gottschalk & Bechtel, 1989).

One of the most powerful demonstrations of CATA's utility in an assessment context is a study by Rosenberg, Schnurr & Oxman (1990). In this study patients from four different diagnostic groups (e.g. paranoid disorder, major depression disorder) were asked to verbalize freely on any topic for 5 minutes and this free speech sample was then subjected to three different forms of content analysis. The first of these involved a single human rater skilled in the use of the Gottschalk–Gleser manual scoring method. The other two were CATA-based methods, using the Harvard IV Psycho-Social Dictionary described previously to classify words from the free speech samples into the word categories specified by the dictionary. Rosenberg, Schnurr & Oxman (1990) then compared the ability of content-category scores derived from the three methods to discriminate between subject from the four diagnostic groups and assign them to their correct, diagnostic group. The study produced two notable results. Content measures derived from all three methods were able to discriminate between different diagnostic groups and to assign people to their diagnostic groups at levels that significantly exceeded chance levels. Thus the verbal content of 5 minutes' free speech was a useful indicator of people's psychological states. Second, the content categories provided by both CATA methods proved superior to the manually derived content categories for discriminating between and classifying people.

It seems counter-intuitive to suggest that a computer program that scores text in a simple, even primitive way by counting the frequencies of words from different categories can outperform an expert, human judge who is much more able to read the text "for its sense". Rosenberg Schnurr & Oxman (1990) suggested two explanations for CATA's superiority. First, computer-based scoring is extremely, in fact perfectly, reliable—the same word is always assigned to the same content category by the computer. Thus, at the very least CATA-based measures should have the advantage of superior reliability. Second, drawing on the ideas of Spence (1980), Rosenberg and colleagues argued that many or most words contain a core, affective meaning and that speakers, and writers, find their lexical choices being shaped to some extent by their underlying emotions, needs or psychological states. In effect, underlying psychological states "leak out" in the types of words people use, even if they are not aware of this happening. While the "amount of leakage" in any particular word is small, when the many words of speech or text are aggregated into different categories that have different emotional content, patterns may become evident. Surprising as it sounds, Rosenberg, Schnurr & Oxman's (1990) findings suggest that computers may be quite adept at "reading between the lines", at least when we are quantitatively comparing different texts. We suggest there is sufficient evidence to conclude that CATA is worthy of further investigation as a method of psychological assessment and that it has particular advantages in a selection context where time and cost are primary considerations.

Applications and Implications for Personnel Selection

McBer is a company that has employed manual content analysis of in-depth interviews for selection purposes for several decades. Based originally upon the theories of psychologist David McClelland (the "Mc" in "McBer"), the approach normally involves the construction of a specific competency model for the job by interviewing outstanding and not-so-outstanding current job-holders. This information is then used to develop a competency profile for the job, which in turn forms the basis for the development of an in-depth interview schedule where people are asked to describe in a detailed way how they would deal with a number of specific, job-related events. Transcripts of these interviews, often running to a hundred pages or so, are then subjected to intensive content analysis for evidence of the key, identified competencies. Not surprisingly, given the time and cost involved in the process, it is used mainly in selection for senior or specialized jobs. The Gallup Organization, at present best known for its opinion polling has also been using text analysis for selection purposes, according to Stone (in press). However, at this stage it is not clear how much of the apparent success of these approaches is due to the text analytic element vs. the detailed competency analyses that are carried out for each job. A study in which the first author is currently involved should provide insight into this issue.

The study is being conducted in cooperation with the Royal Australian Air Force and the occupational group being studied is pilots, a group for whom, as we noted earlier, traditional cognitive ability measures seem to have plateauxed in terms of their predictive potential. As part of the current selection process, pilot applicants are given 20 minutes in which they are asked to write an essay. The task is called a "written communication skills task" and applicants are asked to respond to four general questions, such as why the applicant wishes to join the Air Force. The study is analysing the thematic content of these essays using several different content dictionaries, including the Harvard IV, so it will be possible to profile applicants in terms of the presence of active, positive, ethical, goal-oriented, affiliative, strength and negative themes in their essays (Table 24.1).

The sample comprises applicants who have already undertaken pilot training, thus one advantage of studying this group is that several different objective performance measures are available, including whether they successfully completed the course and ratings of their performance by instructors. Another is that the contribution of the content categories to the prediction of subsequent training performance can be examined in the context of a variety of other predictor variables, including applicants' scores on the standard pilot aptitude test battery. Thus, this study should permit an assessment of CATA's ability to make a significant contribution to predictive ability beyond that provided by the current testing regime. There are very significant implications for the Air Force of any significant improvement in predicting success in pilot training, since it is estimated that it costs about 1 million dollars to train a pilot.

We believe that the "zeitgeist" is right for important innovation to occur in the selection arena. We can envisage a not too distant future in which job applicants will complete a set of computer-based assessments of their cognitive ability and will also be asked to write a brief essay about themselves and their motivation for the job using a Newton type "computer pad" that will recognize their handwriting and turn it into an accurate, electronic form. This information will then be content-analysed for a number of previously validated, content dimensions, with this process occurring in the same time that it takes the computer to produce "standard" test scores. Interviewers will have a more comprehensive applicant profile than they have ever had before, while applicants will be subjected to a more varied, briefer and therefore less stressful assessment experience.

TEXT ANALYSIS: EXAMPLES AT THE MACRO LEVEL

Text analysis at individual or small-group levels of analysis has its challenges, but in some respects these may seem minor when compared to the challenges that confront a researcher wishing to carry out text analysis at an organizational and especially an interorganizational level, for example at the industry level. Much of the challenge comes from the sheer scale required of such undertakings— analysing 1 million words of text is a challenge, analysing 5 million words is a burden, analysing 10 million words . . . let's do a survey instead! At these higher levels, researchers often wish to analyse text from hundreds of organizations, across multiple industries. Collecting such texts alone represents a daunting task, analysing them stretches all but the heftiest research budget. It is, however, precisely because human-coded text analysis has been so difficult and costly at organizational and interorganizational levels of analysis that CATA may offer some of the most promising returns at these levels. This section examines the use of CATA at these higher levels of analysis as it pertains to symbolic management, management discourse, and industry cultures.

Application and Implications for Symbolic-Management Research

The symbolic-management perspective rests on the assumption that top managers use language and other symbolic codes in order to make it appear to stakeholders that their expectations are being met and that their organizations are legitimate (Daft & Wiginton, 1979). Research in the symbolic-management literature generally focuses on the various symbolic-management tactics that managers use in order to sustain the appearance of legitimacy when their organizations face problems. A number of studies of Presidents' letters in corporate annual reports to shareholders reveal, for example, that managers and directors attribute negative organizational outcomes to uncontrollable environmental causes and positive outcomes to their own actions (Salancik & Meindl, 1984; Staw, McKechnie & Puffer, 1983). Until recently there existed only a few case studies, indicating that officers may conceal negative outcomes entirely (e.g. Sutton & Calahan, 1987). Moreover, there exists virtually no research indicating whether or not these symbolic-management tactics are effective (Ashforth & Gibbs, 1990). Research in the symbolic-management literature has generally relied on human coders to code Presidents' letters. This method requires a sizable investment of time and resources and, as we noted earlier, data sets are typically analysed in terms of a relatively few themes and the coding systems developed for the task are rarely used again by other researchers. As a result, there have been few studies in the symbolic-management area and these studies typically analyse relatively small amounts of text. Recently CATA has begun to revolutionize such research. It has greatly reduced the costs of symbolic-management research, even when thousands of letters are analysed. Abrahamson & Park (1994), for example, used CATA to analyse the use of concealment tactics in over 1000 Presidents' letters, and Abrahamson & Amir (1996) used the same method with over 2000 letters in order to investigate how letter content influenced share price.

Using these very large samples provides a number of advantages. Large sample sizes endow studies with high statistical power, making it possible to detect even small effects with great certainty. They allow researchers to investigate the effect of many independent variables. Abrahamson & Park (1994), for example, were able to examine the effect of a whole range of factors on the frequency of negative words in Presidents' letters, factors such as: company and industry performance; percentage of outside directors; percentage of shares owned by officers, outsider directors and institutional funds. Their results revealed, for example, that firms with proportionately more outside directors had a greater tendency to disclose negative outcomes. Indeed, outside directors, unlike inside directors, are not managers in these companies, and therefore have an incentive to promote more candid disclosure of company results in letters. They found, however, contrary to what was anticipated, that greater share ownership by outside directors (which might be expected to promote the general shareholder interest in candor) seemed instead to have the opposite effect, evidently reflecting the directors' concern that disclosure would lower the value of their own holdings. More startling still was the finding that the disclosure of fewer negative organizational outcomes in the President's letter was associated with greater subsequent selling of the organization's stock by its top officers and outside directors in the following quarter. These results suggest that both officers and directors may withhold negative company information long enough to sell their shares and avoid a loss when this negative information is disclosed. Thus, yet another advantage of CATA is its unobtrusive nature. Indeed, imagine how difficult it would be to carry out a study of the concealment of bad news using other methods. Case studies finding evidence of concealment would be easily discounted as anomalies, whereas questionnaire surveys of managers' and directors' concealment activity would be most unlikely to reveal the truth.

Application and Implications for the Study of Management Discourse

Increasingly, research at the organizational and interorganizational levels of analysis has begun to examine not only how organizations and employees are managed, but also what both managers and non-managers write about how to manage organizations and their employees (c.f. Barley & Kunda, 1992; Guillen, 1993). Indeed, such discourse provides the ideas and vocabularies with which managers can communicate legitimate accounts of how they manage their employees.

New types of discourse may trigger the widespread diffusion of management innovations, and the persistent use of such discourse may foster the continued use of these innovations (Strang & Meyer, 1994). Also, we need to know whether or not such discourse constitutes a useful adaptation to changing environmental conditions (Abrahamson, 1991). This would help students of management techniques decide whether to attempt to enrich certain types of management discourse or go about criticizing it (Abrahamson, 1996). In sum, since management discourse may greatly influence what both students of management and managers say, write and do, an understanding of forces influencing such discourse is an important objective for research. Until recently, two main methods have been employed to study management discourse. First, researchers who use quantitative methods tend to count the number of articles on particular management topics in order to trace changes in the popularity of management discourse on particular topics. Barley & Kunda (1992), for example, theorized that the popularity of new types of management discourse relates to up- and downswings in 50-year-long waves of macro-economic activity, so that new types of management discourse emerge with a roughly 25-year periodicity. Abrahamson (in press) counted in excess of 33 000 articles in a massive archival study that found support for Barley and Kunda's (1992) thesis. Second, researchers using qualitative methods typically read many management articles written over extended periods of time in order to study shifts in the treatment of certain topics in management discourse, and provide an overall, subjective analysis of trends. Guillen (1993), read all the management articles published between 1923 and 1958 in *Harvard Business Review* and *Factory/Industrial Management* and analysed their content by hand.

Both the article count and article hand content-analysis methods are extremely labour-intensive. Perhaps as a result, there have been very few studies to date of historical changes in management discourse. Here too, however, CATA promises to revolutionize research. In a recent study, this article's second author used a CATA program, Harvard III, to trace changes in both the amount and content of discourse about quality circles (QCs) (Abrahamson & Fairchild, 1995). The Harvard III is a generic, text analysis dictionary of the kind described earlier and is in some respects a forerunner to the Harvard IV. Counts of the number of articles about QCs over time revealed a very distinct wave-like pattern, consisting of a marked upswing in the number of articles published followed by a downturn. Analysis of the thematic content of articles also revealed clear differences in content between upswing and downturn periods. During the wave's upswing, articles contained an increasing number of words denoting emotions and positive evaluations, while negative-evaluation words declined and words denoting reasoning remained low. These results support collective behaviour theories that quasi-magical, highly emotionally charged beliefs in the potency of certain techniques characterize the early stages of a fad. In the latter stage, however, faddists regain their senses and adopt a more thoughtful and critical attitude towards the object of the fad. Indeed, results indicated that as the QC wave crested and crashed, positive evaluation and emotion words declined dramatically, whereas negative evaluations and reasoning words increased drastically.

This study indicates that CATA techniques make it possible to analyse simultaneously and reliably changes in both the popularity and the content of management discourse over time. The availability of large quantities of management discourse in electronic format, therefore, opens up many possibilities for management researchers studying management discourse (Abrahamson, 1996).

Application and Implications for the Study of Industry Cultures

Executives who belong to different organizations in an industry often pay attention to the same aspects of their organizations and environments (Abrahamson & Fombrun, 1994; Porac, Thomas & Badden-Fuller, 1989; Spender, 1989). Homogeneity in what top managers pay attention to can have important consequences for industries and member firms, although authors differ over whether these consequences are beneficial or harmful.

Halberstam (1986) stressed harmful consequences by arguing that high levels of homogeneity in an industry can blind it to external challenges. He claimed that the narrow attentional focus of U.S. auto industry managers in the 1970s, caused them to overlook competitive challenges threatening their industry. Others stress beneficial consequences, stating that executives who pay attention to the same aspects of their organizations and environments will also recognize the same challenges to their industry (Abrahamson & Fombrun, 1994). When they do, they will more readily see their common interest in opposing these challenges, and have a clear motive for acting collectively to do so. Moreover, attentional homogeneity may reduce industry rivalry, because top managers can correctly interpret each other's strategic moves and counter-moves and, therefore, misunderstandings do not cause rivalry to escalate.

Homogeneity in attention patterns may either harm or help entire industries, or, perhaps, it does both. Either way, attentional homogeneity has potentially great significance for entire industries, the companies that comprise them, and their top executives.

Research on industry-level cognitive patterns has usually employed intensive interviews of managers belonging to organizations in one industry (e.g. Porac, Thomas & Badden-Fuller, 1989). Even Spender's (1989) book-length study relying on interview data only examines three industries. Clearly, a different method is required to study systematically differences in cognitive patterns across many industries.

In a recent study, Abrahamson & Hambrick (1995) used CATA to study the degree of homogeneity in what top managers attend to in 14 industries. Abrahamson & Hambrick (1995) reasoned that the degree to which two or more Presidents' letters in an industry used the same words, or did so with the same frequency, provides an indicator of homogeneity of attention patterns in that industry. For example, they found that the lexicon of the Presidents' letters of firms in the oil and gas industry varies little, indicating a high degree of attentional homogeneity, whereas it varies greatly across the Presidents' letters of firms in the software and programming industry, indicating a low degree of attentional homogeneity. They were also able to explain differences in industry-level attentional homogeneity. Hambrick & Finkelstein (1987) noted that some industries allow great variety and change in managerial actions, while others do not. They used the term "managerial discretion" to denote this greater latitude of action. Abrahamson & Hambrick (1995) reasoned that if discretion confers options, then it must logically also confer diversity in the options that managers attend to. They found, in support of this argument, that their CATA measures of attentional homogeneity were strongly and negatively correlated with industry measures of the degree of managerial discretion. Thus, low discretion industries such as oil and gas were attentionally homogeneous, whereas high discretion industries, such as software and programming, were attentionally heterogeneous.

These results raise the intriguing possibility that CATA techniques could help greatly in accelerating the pace of research on industry-level cognitive patterns. More generally, computers and related technologies have brought about a spectacular information revolution. In a technological feat inconceivable as little as a decade ago, a standard CD-ROM disk can contain 300000 pages of textual information. This deluge of textual information makes it possible to study a great variety of macro-organizational behavior topics. At this stage, however, almost none of these possibilities have been exploited. Researchers with access to a few CATA programs will find themselves confronted with an embarassment of riches. Indeed, the challenge becomes not too little data, but rather too much data; not choosing between a few ways of analysing these data, but choosing among countless ways; not too few research opportunities, but far too many.

CATA AND THE CHANGING NATURE OF WORK AND ORGANIZATIONS

One of the greatest challenges facing contemporary managers and organizations and those who study them is the need to understand and cope with unrelenting change in technology, markets, competitors and human values. It almost seems that while the dominant concern of the previous generation of managers and researchers was with understanding the nature and requirements of stability, as reflected in the structure of tasks and organizations, the concern of this generation must be with the processes of individual and organizational change, adaptation and flexibility.

At the level of individual jobs, jobs involving relatively unchanging, standardized routines, while they will continue to exist, are being replaced by jobs involving dealing with complex and unpredictable information and jobs requiring responsiveness to unpredictable, interpersonal demands. Service jobs are a good example of the latter. While cognitive ability will remain an important influence on people's performance in such jobs, it is likely that non-cognitive factors will have an increasingly important role. No longer can it be assumed that individual differences in personality can be largely "engineered" out of consideration by routinizing and standardizing tasks. Indeed, making use of individual differences in flexibility, adaptability and creativity will be a major source of organizations' competitive advantage. As we observed earlier, the problem is that our current capability to identify and measure these individual differences in an efficient manner is poor, but, as we also explained earlier, CATA may well prove to be an major source of innovation in this area in future.

Turning to the demands that change and innovation bring at the level of organizations, it is obvious that it is important for both managers and researchers to understand how decision-makers select information from the torrent of data that assails them, interpret it and integrate it into coherent plans for action. However, as the data that are used by decision-makers become more widely and immediately available in electronic form, and so does information about their interpretations of those data, the opportunities for researchers to study managerial cognition increase. Here also we believe that CATA will be an important ally.

CONCLUSION

The information revolution, as symbolized by the information superhighway is creating new opportunities in all areas of human activity, including social science research and, more particularly, organizational behaviour research broadly defined. The challenge for us as social scientists is to turn this information into useful knowledge. We hope we have shown in this chapter the range of issues central to OB to which text analysis can be applied, ranging from the most micro, psychological level of analysis to the most macro organizational, industry and indeed societal levels of analysis. When we add to this breadth of application the power of modern computer hardware and software, the opportunities become, to our minds, truly dazzling.

REFERENCES

Abrahamson, E. (in press). The emergence and prevalence of employee-management rhetoric: long-run and short-run determinants. *Academy of Management Journal.*
Abrahamson, E (1996), Management fashion. *Academy of Management Review*, **21**, 254–85.
Abrahamson, E. (1991). Managerial fads and fashion: the diffusion and rejection of management innovations. *Academy of Management Review*, **16**, 586–612.
Abrahamson, E. & Amir, E. (1996). The association between the information contained in the president's letter to shareholders and accounting market variables. *Journal of Business Finance and Accounting*, **23**, 1157–82.
Abrahamson, E. & Fairchild, G. (1995). The collective behavior of management fashions. Working paper, Graduate School of Business School, Columbia University.
Abrahamson, E. & Fombrun, C.J. (1994). Macrocultures: determinants and consequences. *Academy of Management Review*, **19**, 728–55.
Abrahamson, E. & Hambrick, D. (1995). Attentional homogeneity in industries: the effect of discretion. Working paper, Graduate School of Business School, Columbia University.
Abrahamson, E. & Park, C. (1994). The concealment of negative organizational outcomes: an agency theory perspective. *Academy of Management Journal*, **5**, 1302–34.
Ashforth, B.E. & Gibbs, B.W. (1990). The double-edge of organization legitimation. *Organization Science*, **1**, 177–94.
Australian Financial Review (1995). *Meet the Mother of All Big Brothers*, 22 August, pp. 1, 9.

Barley S.R. & Kunda, G. (1992). Design and devotion: surges of rational and normative ideologies of control in managerial discourse. *Administrative Science Quarterly*, **37**, 363–99.

Barr, P.S., Stimpert, J.L. & Huff, A.S. (1990). Cognitive change, strategic action, and organizational renewal. *Strategic Management Journal*, **13**(5), 15–36.

Bettman, J.R. Weitz, B.A. (1983). Attribution in the boardroom: causal reasoning in corporate annual reports. *Administrative Science Quarterly*, **28**, 165–83.

Bowman, E.H. (1976). Strategy and the weather. *Sloan Management Review*, **17**, 49–62.

Bowman, E.H. (1978). Strategy, annual reports, and alchemy. *California Management Review*, **Spring**, 61–71.

Bowman, E.H. (1984). Content analysis of annual reports for corporate strategy and risk. *Interfaces*, **14**, 61–71.

Chatman, J.A. & Jehn, K.A. (1994). Assessing the relationship between industry characteristics and organizational culture: how different can you be? *Academy of Management Journal*, **37**, 522-53.

Clapham, S.E. & Schwenk, C.R. (1991). Self-serving attributions, managerial cognition, and company performance. *Strategic Management Journal*, **12**, 219–29.

D'Aveni, R.A. & MacMillan, I.C. (1990). Crisis and the content of managerial communications: a study of the focus of attention of top managers in surviving and failing firms. *Administrative Science Quarterly*, **34**, 634–57.

Daft, R.L. & Wiginton, J.C. (1979). Language and organization. *Academy of Management Review*, **4**, 179–91.

Dowling, G.R. & Kabanoff, B. (1996). Computer-aided content analysis: what do 240 advertising slogans have in common? *Marketing Letters*, **7**(1), 63–75.

Fiol, C.M. (1990). Explaining strategic alliances in the chemical industry. In A. Huff (ed.), *Mapping Strategic Thought*. New York: Wiley.

Fletcher, K.E. & Huff, A.S. (1990). Strategic argument mapping: a study of strategy reformulation at AT&T. In A. Huff (ed.), *Mapping Strategic Thought*. New York: Wiley.

Fombrun, C. & Shanley, M. (1990). What's in a name? Reputation building and corporate strategy. *Academy of Management Journal*, **33**, 233–58.

Gephart, R.P. Jr (1993). The textual approach: risk and blame in disaster sensemaking. *Academy of Management Journal*, **36**, 1465–1514.

Golden, B.R. (1992). The past is the past—or is it? The use of retrospective accounts as indicators of past strategy. *Academy of Management Journal*, **35**, 848–60.

Goodman, R.S. (1988). The determinants of a bank's success and failure in a changing regulatory environment: substantive, methodological, and statistical implications for corporate strategy. Unpublished dissertation, University of Minnesota.

Gottschalk, L.A. & Bechtel, R. (1989). Artificial intelligence and the computerization of the content analysis of natural language. *Artificial Intelligence in Medicine*, **1**, 131–7.

Gottschalk, L.A. Gleser, G.C. (1969). *The Measurement of Psychological States through Content Analysis of Verbal Behavior* (pp. 228–36). Berkeley & Los Angeles: University of California Press.

Gottschalk, L.A., Lolas, F. & Viney, L.L. (1986). *Content Analysis of Verbal Behavior: Significance in Clinical Medicine and Psychiatry*. Heidelberg: Springer-Verlag.

Guillen, M.F. (1993). *Models of Management: Work, Authority, and Organization in a Comparative Perspective*. Chicago: University of Chicago Press.

Halberstam, D. (1986). *The Reckoning*. New York: Avon.

Hambrick, D. & Finkelstein, S. (1987). Managerial discretion: a bridge between polar views of organizational outcomes. *Research in Organizational Behavior*, **9**, 369–406.

Huff, A.S. (ed.) (1990). *Mapping Strategic Thought*. Chichester: Wiley.

Huff, A.S. (1983). A rhetorical examination of strategic change. In L.R. Pondy, P.J. Frost, G. Morgan & D.C. Dandridge (eds), *Organizational Symbolism*. Greenwich, CT: JAI. Press.

Huff, A.S. & Schwenk, C.R. (1990). Bias and sensemaking in good times and bad. In Huff, A. (ed.), *Mapping Strategic Thought*. New York: Wiley.

Kabanoff, B. (1996). Computers can read as well as count: how computer-aided text analysis can benefit organizational research. In C.L. Cooper & D.M. Rousseau (eds), *Trends in Organizational Behavior*, vol. 3 (pp. 1–21). Chichester: Wiley.

Kabanoff, B. (1993). An exploration of espoused culture in Australian organisations (with a closer look at the banking sector). *Asia Pacific Journal of Human Resources*, **31**, 1–29.

Kabanoff, B., Waldersee, R. & Cohen, M. (1995). Espoused values and organizational change themes. *Academy of Management Journal*, **38**, 1075–1104.

Kelle, U. (1995). Introduction: an overview of computer-aided methods in qualitative research. In U. Kelle (ed.), *Computer-aided Qualitative Data Analysis: Theory, Methods and Practice* (pp. 1–17). London, Sage.

Marcus, A. A. & Goodman, R.S. (1986). Airline deregulation: factors affecting the choice of firm political strategy. *Policy Study Journal*, **15**, 231–46.

Narayanan, V.K. & Fahey, L. (1990). Evolution of revealed causal maps during decline: a case study of Admiral. In Huff, A. (ed.), *Mapping Strategic Thought*. New York: Wiley.

Newell, S.E. (1989). An interpretive study of the public statements and strategic actions of the CEOs of US Steel and the Presidents of the USWA: 1945–1985. Unpublished dissertation, University of Massachusetts, Amherst.

Nissan, E. & Schmidt, K. (1995). *From Information to Knowledge: Conceptual and Content Analysis by Computer*. Oxford, UK: Intellect.

Olea, M.M. & Ree, M.J. (1994). Predicting pilot and navigator criteria: not much more than g. *Journal of Applied Psychology*, **79**, 845–51.

Osgood, C.E., Suci, G.J. & Tannenbaum, P.H. (1957). *The Measurement of Meaning*. Urbana IL: University of Illinois Press.

Pfeffer, J. (1981). Management as symbolic action: the creation and maintenance of organizational paradigms. In B.M. Staw & L.L. Cummings (eds), *Research in Organizational Behavior*, (pp. 1–52) Greenwich, CT: JAI Press.

Porac, J., Thomas, H. & Badden-Fuller, (1989). Competitive groups as cognitive communities: the case of the Scottish knitwear manufacturers. *Journal of Management Studies*, **26**, 397–415.

Porac, J., Thomas, H. & Badden-Fuller, J. (1989). Competitive groups as cognitive communities: the case of the Scottish knitwear manufacturers. *Journal of Management Studies*, **26**, 397–415.

Ree, M.J., Earles, J.A. & Teachout, M.S. (1994). Predicting job performance: not much more than g. *Journal of Applied Psychology*, **79**, 518–24.

Robertson, I.T. (1995). Personality and personnel selection. In C.L. Cooper & D.M. Rousseau (eds), *Trends in Organizational Behavior*, **1**, 75–89. Chichester: Wiley.

Rosenberg, S.D., Schnurr., P.P. & Oxman, T.E. (1990). Content analysis: a comparison of manual and computerised systems. *Journal of Personality Assessment*, **54**, 298–310.

Salancik, G.R. & Meindl, J.R. (1984). Corporate attributions as strategic illusions of management control. *Administrative Science Quarterly*, **29**, 238–54.

Sparrow, P.R. (1994). The psychology of strategic management: emerging themes of diversity and cognition. In C.L. Cooper & I.T. Robertson (eds), *International Review of Industrial and Organisational Psychology*. Wiley, Sussex.

Spence, D.P. (1980). Lawfulness in lexical choice: A natural experiment. *Journal of the American Psychoanalytic Association*, **28**, 115–132.

Spender, J.C. (1980). *Industry Recipes: The Nature and Source of Managerial Judgement*, Basil Blackwell, Cambridge, MA.

Staw, B.M., McKechnie, P.I. & Puffer, S.M. (1983). The justification of organizational performance. *Administrative Science Quarterly*, **28**, 582–600.

Stone, P.J., Dunphy, D.C., Smith, M.S. & Ogilvie, D.M. (1966). *The General Inquirer: A Computer Approach to Content Analysis*. Cambridge, MA: MIT Press.

Stone, P.J. (in press). Thematic text analysis: new agendas for analyzing text content. In C. Roberts (ed.), *Text Analysis for the Social Sciences: Methods for Drawing Statistical Inferences from Texts and Transcripts*. Hillsdale, NJ: Erlbaum.

Strang, D. & Meyer, J.W. (1994). Institutional conditions for diffusion. In R.W. Scott & J.W. Meyer (eds), *Institutional Environments and Organizations: Structural Complexity and Individualism* (pp. 100–112). Newbury Park, CA: Sage.

Sutton, R. & Callahan, A. (1987). The stigma of bankruptcy. *Academy of Management Journal*, **30**, 405–36.

Viney, L.L. (1983). Assessment of psychological states through content analysis of verbal behavior. *Psychological Bulletin*, **94**, 542–63.

Weber, R.P. (1985). *Basic Content Analysis*. Beverly Hills, CA: Sage.

Wolfe, R.A., Gephart, R.P. & Johnson, T.A. (1993). Computer-facilitated qualitative data analysis: potential contributions to management research. *Journal of Management*, **19**, 633–60.

Woodrum, E. (1984). Mainstreaming content analysis in social science: methodological advantages, obstacles and solutions. *Social Science Research*, **13**, 1–19.

Zull, C., Weber, P.W. & Mohler, P.P. (1989). *Computer-aided Text Classification for the Social Sciences: the General Enquirer III*. Mannheim: ZUMA, The Center for Surveys, Research and Methodology.

Chapter 25

Idiographic Research in Organizational Behavior

James Campbell Quick
The University of Texas at Arlington, Arlington, TX, USA

Research comes from *recerche*, a form of the Middle French verb *recercher*, which means to travel through or survey. Within most disciplines and sciences, research has come to mean the careful, systematic, patient study and investigation in an area of knowledge, undertaken to discover or establish facts and/or general laws and principles. During the first century of the study of management and the emerging discipline of organizational behavior, a limited number of dominant research areas have been investigated. These include motivation, leadership, group dynamics and behavior, the design of work, and power, to name a few. One of the interesting attributes of several of these areas, e.g. motivation and leadership, is the proliferation of theories which attempt to explain the phenomena (see Steers & Porter, 1991, in the area of motivation and Bass & Stogdill, 1990, in the area of leadership). Yukl (1994) expresses frustration that leadership lacks a clear, well established body of scientific knowledge after over 50 years of research. What accounts for the proliferation of theory and research, on the one hand, and the frustration embodied in Yukl's (1994) assessment of the leadership knowledge area in organizational behavior on the other hand?

The thesis of this chapter is that research in organizational behavior, at least as the science is practiced in North America, has been too unidimensional; it relies too heavily on the natural science paradigm. While natural science has power and value as a platform for research to extend knowledge in organizational behavior, it also has limitations. Epistemology suggests that any scientific paradigm has limitations; hence, the conduct of good science and research requires multiple, complementary scientific paradigms (Payne, 1978). Specifically, the strengths of one paradigm should shore up the limitations of another and *vice versa*.

Creating Tomorrow's Organizations. Edited by C.L. Cooper and S.E. Jackson.
© 1997 John Wiley & Sons Ltd.

This chapter develops the idiographic research paradigm as a complement to the established natural science research paradigm, elaborating the intellectual rationale for this approach and demonstrating the implications of the paradigm in terms of specific research possibilities. The chapter has five sections. The first section defines the nature of organizational behavior as an area of study. The second discusses knowledge and scientific inquiry, proposes a three-dimensional framework for research, with emphasis along the nomothetic–idiographic dimension within this framework. The third discusses diagnosis in the context of organizational behavior. The fourth makes a case for the scientific manager. Finally, the fifth sets forth an idiographic research agenda for individual, group and organizational case studies.

ORGANIZATIONAL BEHAVIOR AS AN AREA OF KNOWLEDGE

Organizational behavior is an applied area of knowledge and study. As such, the study of behavior in organizations is an area of interest to scientists and managers alike. Scientists are interested in organizational behavior because of the desire to explain and predict it. Why do people act and behave in the wide variety of ways that they do in organizations? How can we understand, anticipate or even influence their behavior? Managers are interested in organizational behavior because of the desire to activate, direct and/or terminate a wide range of human behaviors within organizations. How can I motivate a person to be more productive? How can I influence a group of people to follow me in the pursuit of a particular goal or mission? How can I stop a person from engaging in behavior that is apparently dysfunctional for the organization?

Much of human behavior in organizations is based on learning specific to that environment and, as such, it is artificial in contrast to naturally occurring behavior. Such behavior is socially constructed, designed, created, developed, acquired or artificially engineered. Therefore, organizational behavior may be considered a science of design, or a science of the artificial (Simon, 1969/1996). For example, individuals do not naturally acquire such behavior as driving a truck or operating a computer system. These are acquired behaviors or skills which take learning, practice, trial and success, and which often require modification to maintain in a changing task environment. Observing and modeling other people's behaviors are central processes in social learning (Bandura, 1977), although there are other processes for learning or acquiring new behaviors. One of these processes is learning from the natural consequences, both positive and negative, of specific behaviors.

KNOWLEDGE AND SCIENTIFIC INQUIRY

Knowledge advances through scientific inquiry and epistemology addresses the nature, the sources and the limits of knowledge. Payne's (1978) epistemological essay quickly discounts dogmatism and skepticism as legitimate bases for increasing and/or refining knowledge. Rather, he argues that knowledge increases through critical scientific inquiry (that is, all knowledge is doubted and then critically evaluated) and becomes refined by a process of corroboration, either corroboration of man by man or corroboration of fact with fact. Hence, critical scientific inquiry and corroboration are the legitimate bases for advancing knowledge. The bulk of his discourse addresses the pathways to knowledge, with particular attention to the four main world hypotheses—formism, mechanism, contextualism and organicism. These four are framed within the two dimensions of dispersion–integration and analysis–synthesis.

I offer a different and three-dimensional framework for scientific inquiry. The three dimensions are nomothetic–idiographic, time, and qualitative–quantitative. This three-dimensional framework is depicted in Figure 25.1. The first dimension is anchored by large-scale, multi-case research at the nomothetic end and single-case research at the idiographic end. The second dimension, time, runs from past to future, with the present as the midpoint. The third dimension is anchored by standardized, statistical research at the quantitative end and interpretative, adaptive research at the qualitative end. The three dimensions in the framework are presented on independent axes, leading to a wide variety of possible strategies for scientific inquiry. In practice, the dimensions are not quite independent, and may in fact achieve interplay. Two examples of multiple, parallel case studies illustrate

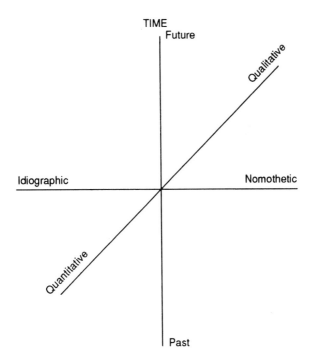

Figure 25.1 A three-dimensional framework for scientific inquiry

Table 25.1 The idiographic–nomothetic dimension in scientific inquiry

	Research paradigm	
	Nomothetic	Idiographic
World definition	Determinate	Indeterminate
World hypothesis	Mechanism	Contextualism
Core processes	Analysis	Synthesis
	Integration	Dispersion
	Reductionism	Holism
Method	Experimentation	History
Metaphor	The machine	The historical event
Interactions	Cause–effect	Reciprocal–transactional
Knowledge attribute	Positivistic–pragmatic	Hermeneutic–spiritual
Treatment of facts	Exclusive	Inclusive
Key strengths	Breadth	Depth
	Precision	Richness
	Replicability	Uniqueness
	Prediction	Comprehensive
Key limitation	Lack of richness	Lack of precision

the interconnectedness of these dimensions. The first example began with a serendipitous finding from several project groups studied for another purpose (Gersick, 1988). This study followed eight naturally-occurring teams over their life-span; hence, there is a clear time (longitudinal) dimension to the study. The research leans toward the idiographic end of the continuum because of the small number of project teams, yet it is a multiple case study so it does not anchor the idiographic end. The data sources for the study are both qualitative (e.g. meeting transcripts) and quantitative (e.g. team composition numbers, tasks and time-spans, and numbers of meetings), encompassing the range of that dimension. The second example is a study of executive team decision-making in a high-velocity environment over a period of 2 years: 1984–1985 (Eisenhardt, 1989). An inductive study of eight microcomputer organizations, this research also leans toward the idiographic, given the small number of cases. Again, data sources ranged from the quantitative (e.g. descriptive numbers on each organization, numbers of decision alternatives, and questionnaire measures of conflict, disagreement and power) to the qualitative (e.g. semistructured CEO and senior manager interviews). These two examples illustrate the blends which may play out in actual organizational behavior research.

The idiographic–nomothetic dimension forms the core of my discussion and consideration is given to the other two dimensions. The key features of the ends of this dimension are summarized in Table 25.1. Because the two other dimensions of the framework in Figure 25.1 are independent, in theory, neither of these dimensions is reflected in Table 25.1. Therefore, a biographical investigation of American general and statesman George C. Marshall exemplifies an idiographic research project which is probably also very qualitative and most likely retrospective. However, a quantitative, prospective, idiographic study is equally plausible. Such might be exemplified in the three-part Harvard case study of American Airlines (Vietor, 1984; 1987), especially if the study had been initiated in 1978 when the US Congress passed the Airline Deregulation Act. In practice, idiographic research may often be qualitative while nomothetic research is quantitative, and idiographic research may often be retrospective while nomothetic research is present or prospective.

Nomothetic Research

Natural science primarily follows a course of nomothetic research—research aimed at the establishment of general, verifiable laws. Natural science falls in the German intellectual tradition of the *Naturwissenschaften* (Bettelheim, 1983; Quick, 1988) and uses a positivist approach (Lee, 1991). Behling (1980) makes a clear case for natural science and nomothetic research in organizational behavior. The underlying method for nomothetic research is the experiment, which implicitly assumes a cause–effect relationship between the variables under study. Even with quasi-experimental designs, or correlation designs such as a cross-lagged panel design, causality is implied and inferred. Within Payne's (1978) framework, nomothetic research fits the mechanistic world hypothesis. The key characteristics of mechanism are its reliance on analysis and reductionism, and its assumption that the world and the people therein are ultimately knowable. This leads to the assumption of precision in natural science. Hence, natural science works to establish universal general laws by sequentially isolating and analyzing the human environment. In the context of organizational behavior, nomothetic research implicitly assumes a similarity among the units of study and relies on variance and covariance to generalize results across individuals, groups or organizations. Nomothetic research accounts for the inevitable variability in individuals, groups and organizations by way of its statistical analyses.

Some of the earliest research in organizational behavior was conducted by Frederick Taylor (1939) with the intention of establishing the one best way, the universal way, to lug a pig of iron, shovel coal, or any one of a variety of tasks in the American steel industry of the era. The limitations and shortcomings of this approach to the design of work gave way to at least two subsequent alternatives, job enlargement and job enrichment, both of which emerged from the nomothetic paradigm of natural science. Similar processes of unfolding theory and research in other organizational behavior topics, such as leadership, occurred as well.

The frustrations expressed by Yukl (1994) in the area of leadership are a manifestation of the limitations of nomothetic research in organizational behavior, not a statement of the bankruptcy of the paradigm. Organizational behavior is a social science, in which intersubjectively created meanings have no counterpart in the physical reality of natural science (Lee, 1991). Therefore, the limited fit of the positivist approach of natural science to the study of organizational behavior should not be surprising. A significant limitation of nomothetic research is its lack of contextual detail. The nomothetic approach has utility in organizational behavior research where robust effects may be established, such as in the area of goal-setting research (Locke & Latham, 1990) or operational selection tests using linear modeling methods (Lance, Stewart & Carretta, 1996). Hence, the strengths of nomothetic research are found in the generalizability and applicability of its findings. By design, nomothetic research is strong in both causal/predictive and descriptive/purposive explanatory power, yet its practical methods of laboratory experiments, longitudinal studies, field experiments and cross-sectional, correlational studies compromise this explanatory power (Payne, Jick & Burke, 1982). That is, there are trade-offs among the specific methods, with none being uniformly strong in both forms of explanatory power. For example, laboratory experiments yield strong causal/predictive explanatory power, while cross-sectional, correlational studies are weak in this regard.

Harrison's (1995) research on volunteer motivation and attendance decisions is an award-winning example of nomothetic research. Expanding a decision-making theory of attendance motivation for the voluntarism context, the research is conducted in a clearly specified theoretical framework of well-defined and measured constructs whose interrelationships are specified through a series of three hypotheses. Data were collected by self-report of volunteers as well as by behavioral observations by Harrison (1995), who also served as a volunteer during the course of the investigation. The data were analyzed and the hypotheses tested using correlational and regression, both logistic and hierarchical, analyses. The design included one panel ($n = 53$) and two cross-sectional ($n = 51$; $n = 53$) replications of the field study. The results supported the theory across time and samples. The research conforms well to the attributes of nomothetic research set out in Table 25.1, with the strengths which accompany the paradigm.

Idiographic Research

Humanistic or spiritual science is based on idiographic research, research aimed at understanding the particular case, be that an individual, group or organization, as a functioning whole. Idiographic research falls in the German intellectual tradition of the *Geistwissenschaften* (Bettelheim, 1983; Quick, 1988) and uses an interpretative approach (Lee, 1991). Luthans & Davis (1982) argue for idiographic research in organizational behavior from their behavioristic tradition of single case study designs. The underlying method for idiographic research is history, which implicitly assumes a hermeneutic, interpretative posture with regard to understanding causality. Within Payne's (1978) framework, idiographic research fits the contextual world hypothesis. The key characteristics of contextualism are its reliance on synthesis, or holism, and its assumption that the world and the people therein may be unknowable. This latter characteristic may lead to a lack of precision, or a fuzziness, in idiographic research. Nevertheless, idiographic research works to establish understanding of the particular individual, group, or organization under investigation.

In the context of organizational behavior, idiographic research implicitly assumes a differentness between the units of study and attempts to focus on what is unique in each individual, group or organization. Rather than attempting to account for the variance across units of study, idiographic research assumes a uniqueness in each case. By design, idiographic research is strong in both causal/predictive and descriptive/purposive explanatory power, *for the particular case* (Payne, Jick & Burke, 1982). Generalizability of idiographic case study results is weak and questionable. However, generalizability is a more appropriate criterion for nomothetic research results than for idiographic results. Rather, idiographic research aims to understand the whole and its inter-related elements, much as chaos theory attempts to understand the reproducible patterns within the context of the whole (Gleick, 1987). In the case of chaotic systems, the explanatory mechanisms for the reproducible patterns may be known perfectly, while the long-term future states are unknowable. In the case of organizational behavior in complex systems, patterns that appear unknowable at the micro level may make sense and be knowable at the macro level.

Gersick's (1994) study of a new venture, with particular attention to whether organizations are inertial or adaptable, shows the complexity that is often involved in idiographic research. This longitudinal study was initiated in June 1988 and the published research reported data collection ended in February 1990 with a follow-up feedback discussion. In the life history of organizations, or in absolute terms as Gersick notes, 1 year is a short time. However, in the context of a new venture, such as this case of M-Tech in the medical products field, 1 or 2 years constitutes a large portion of the company's early developmental history, especially when great advances are expected within a 7-year time period. In M-Tech, which was born as a new venture in June 1983, 2 years represent 33% of the organizational life history. Adapting methods she developed to study the histories of project groups, Gersick (1994) first focuses her data analysis on the company history, in skeletal and then more elaborate form. Her research conforms well to the attributes of idiographic research set out in Table 25.1 and exemplifies the strengths that accompany this paradigm.

DIAGNOSIS

Diagnosis, as a process rather than an outcome, is a good metaphor for idiographic research in organizational behavior. Diagnosis comes from *dia*, which means through, and *gnosis*, which means knowledge of. Hence, a diagnosis of a person, group or organization is made through knowledge of that particular person, group or organization. Diagnosis is appropriate to social and organizational settings because the situation and the context must be discovered (Laing, 1971). As Laing (1971) pointed out, once a diagnosis is begun in an organizational context, it never ends; rather, diagnosis becomes an ongoing process of discovery.

In addition, the observer or diagnostician becomes an integral part of the social or organizational situation being diagnosed. From a transactional–ecological world view, there is a significant connection between the elements of an event and the observer of the event and its elements (Dewey & Bentley, 1973). This is especially appropriate to idiographic research, which assumes unknowability in the limit and views precision as a myth. Knowing is a process, not a final conclusion.

Alternatively, a diagnosis is a working hypothesis for the scientific physician practicing in the medical profession (Flexner, 1910, as cited in Engel, 1987). As a working hypothesis for the particular patient, the diagnosis informs subsequent data collection from and about the patient (subject). Within the idiographic paradigm, the hypothesis (diagnosis) is modified iteratively over time as new data and new results are available. Hence, knowledge about the specific individual, group or organization advances, changes, deepens and is refined over time.

Good diagnosis may combine art with science. Most people know that a river runs downstream to the sea, but few people take the time and energy required to develop an appreciation for the undercurrents, eddies, hazards and opportunities that the river presents. In addition to time and energy, good diagnosis hinges on two characteristics embodied in the fictitious Sherlock Holmes (Doyle, 1938): careful observation and logical, deductive reasoning. Holmes appears to be especially adept at the process of careful, studious observation and attention to detail. While specific observations or facts may not be apparently meaningful when first noted, they later may become critical in the context of the larger puzzle, or whole, which Holmes is attempting to understand. Thus, Holmes couples his careful skills of observation with deductive, logical reasoning to arrive at his invariably accurate conclusions. Logical inquiry has legitimacy in the advancement of knowledge just as does scientific inquiry (Payne, 1978).

SCIENTIFIC MANAGERS

If scientific physicians can apply idiographic science in the practice of medicine, scientific managers can apply idiographic science in the practice of organizational behavior. In both cases, the application should be in the context of the wider body of knowledge established through all categories of scientific inquiry. Simon (1969/1996) places business, which includes management and organizational behavior, in the same category with medicine and engineering as sciences of design, or professions. Professions require applied or practical science, to include the appropriate application of basic scientific findings and scientific practice. Within the medical profession, George Engel at the University of Rochester's School of Medicine and Dentistry developed the parallel notions of physician scientists and scientific physicians. Engel (1987) saw a dichotomy between humanism and natural science in medicine, and believed that the medical profession needs both to be successful. Flexner (1910, as cited in Engel, 1987) was among the first to see the dynamic tension between medical practice and medical science.

Engel's argument is that natural science and nomothetic research is useful to the physician scientist interested in extending knowledge about medicine and the healing process. Idiographic research is of equal importance to the scientific physician interested in applying scientific knowledge to individual patients, while at the same time generating useful new knowledge about the particular patient. For example, the allergist concerned with people's breathing, asthma and allergies may use idiographic research in the case of an individual patient, by generating information about the person's whole life domain to understand the dynamics of the particular case. So, is there a connection between stress and an asthmatic attack? This question calls for a hypothesis (e.g. high stress in the patient's life leads to an asthma attack) and then data development (e.g. charting stressful events and asthma attacks) iteratively over time. To be more specific, the allergist may seek to understand how conflicts in the home or pressures in the work environment may be associated with an asthmatic attack for this particular individual.

When we draw the parallel to business and organizational behavior, then management scientists advance the knowledge of organizations and organizational behavior through nomothetic research, while scientific managers advance the knowledge of organizations and organizational behavior through application and idiographic research. If the scientific manager is interested in the generation of high-performance artifacts in organizations, such as healthy and productive individuals, groups and organizations, then idiographic research is useful in the scientific practice of the profession. The scientific manager is practicing a craft to design, create and develop high-performance, healthy artifacts. From an idiographic research perspective, the scientific manager generates hypotheses and then collects data for the particular case. The conceptual requirement in idiographic research is to develop data and information about the whole person, the whole group, or the whole organization. This is difficult for two reasons. First, it is encompassing and demanding. Second, it is never complete.

AN IDIOGRAPHIC RESEARCH AGENDA: INDIVIDUAL, GROUP, AND ORGANIZATION CASE STUDIES

Idiographic case studies have strong causal/predictive power for the particular case and they have strong descriptive/purposive power (Payne, Jick & Burke, 1982). The field of organizational behavior can benefit from the pursuit of idiographic case studies with an understanding that the outcome is a richer and more complete understanding of the complexity of the field, rather than a logically deduced and systematized body of knowledge. Idiographic case studies may use one of two units of analysis, or a blend of both, as their focus. One unit is the event, or act in context. The other unit is the subject, or actor, and the subject may be defined as an individual, group or organization. Regardless of which unit of analysis is used, the focus of idiographic case studies should be on outliers within a distribution, or high impact, low occurrence events or subjects. In a study of 2000 US Air Force pilot training candidates, outliers were found not to threaten the integrity of the nomothetic results, given samples large enough for correlation and regression analyses, and given tests reliable enough to be used in operational personnel selection (Lance, Stewart & Carretta, 1996). Hence, outliers may not be a particular problem for nomothetic research, on the one hand, while presenting a research opportunity for idiographic research, on the other hand.

The opening All-Academy Symposia for the 1996 Academy of Management national meetings, *Learning from Unusual Events* (Starbuck, 1996), drew attention to both events and subjects as a basis for idiographic research. For example, the 1995 Oklahoma City bombing was an extraordinary historical event which continues to transform individuals, groups and organizations throughout the USA in its aftermath. In another example, the subject case of Lincoln Electric Company draws attention to unusually effective management practices. Both event and subject case studies are important in learning about organizational behavior.

Event Case Studies

High impact events with a low frequency of occurrence create a significant or dramatic change, of either a positive or a negative nature, and are especially appropriate for idiographic research. These events create a bifurcation in life as we know it; they disrupt the continuity and predictability of experience. These events may have their primary impact on individuals, groups, organizations or a combination thereof. In the example of the 1989 razing of the Berlin Wall and ending of the Cold War, there were dramatic and immediate impacts on individual lives throughout East and West Germany, as well as around the world. These events had dramatic organizational impacts upon the US military services, to include the US Army. While the US Army lost an enemy and a mission to guide its operations, the US Air Force lost an enemy as well, leading to the dissolution of the Strategic Air Command and a dramatic reorganization of its force structure. This example is a mixed blessing, in that the event for many is characterized as positive, yet it was an important contributing factor to a significant downsizing of the US Air Force and its military installations (Adkins, in press), to the tune of a 25% reduction of force.

Learning from this event might emphasize how individuals and organizations accommodate, adapt and transform themselves in response to the event. Meyer (1982, 1992) describes how a sudden and unprecedented event created an environmental jolt to which 19 general, intermediate, San Francisco area hospitals were challenged to adapt. The Threat-Rigidity Thesis suggests that such a dramatic environmental change, or jolt, is most often experienced as a threat to which there is a response of rigidity (Staw, Sandelands & Dutton, 1981). Rigidity may well be dysfunctional if the accommodations and adaptations are radical in nature, heightening the experience of threat. Alternatively, rigidity may be functional where the accommodations and adaptations are incremental in nature, reducing the experience of threat. Meyer (1982) used a rich combination of idiographic and nomothetic, qualitative and quantitative research methods over time to examine the processes whereby the 19 hospitals adapted to the jolt in their environment.

Individual Level

There are three categories of events that are especially appropriate currently for case study analyses in organizational behavior: suicides, violent events, and individual peak performance achievements. The first two are both violent in nature. While suicides and aggressively violent events directed at people in the workplace tend to be low-frequency events in most organizations, they are high-impact events and, therefore, worthy of study in the domain of organizational behavior.

While sad, suicides create a rich opportunity for idiographic case analysis through the reconstruction of elements leading to the event. An example event case is that of Admiral Boorda, the late Chief of Naval Operations. Interviews with colleagues, family, supervisors and subordinates in the organization, and community contacts, may help to begin the process of constructing an understanding of the contributing causes for such a tragic event. The use of the deceased's archival data, records, and other evidence for his/her work and personal spaces should be added to the interview data to construct what happened prior to the event. Reconstructing the event may lead to a better understanding of the process and the system within which the event occurred, so as to identify early warnings and/or construct preventive interventions.

The analysis of violent incidents directed toward people at work is another event category in which idiographic research may be useful to the learning process, as in the case of the Oklahoma City bombing. The purpose of the case analysis is to identify elements in the individual, the organization, and the circumstances that may have contributed to the violent event. As in suicide events, the learning objective(s) centers around early warning signs and possible preventive interventions. In both suicide and violent event cases, researchers should have a dual focus on the event itself and on the possibility of a pattern of events within a larger system. A larger system analysis can help identify reproducible patterns of suicides or violent events.

Individual peak performance achievements are a third category of events at the individual level that may be fruitful for idiographic case analysis. This sort of event case analysis is done in athletics, such as for Roger Bannister's sub-4-minute mile achievement and Frank Shorter's Gold Medal performance in the Olympic Marathon. In the less known case of naval aviators, videotaped carrier landings are analyzed for performance assessment and performance improvement opportunities. This category of event case analysis is especially appropriate

for organizational positions with high success–reward and risk–failure consequences. An organizational application of individual peak performance event
analysis is entrepreneurship. The analysis of entrepreneurial successes should
consider the individual, interpersonal and environmental factors along with interactions among the factors that contributed to the success.

Group Level

The three categories of event case studies discussed at the individual level
are also rich for group level analysis. Groups, as the next level of analysis, may
be the focus for the reproducible patterns in suicides or violent events mentioned
previously. Thus, the identification of target or high-risk groups may lead to
formulation of behavioral and/or interpersonal strategies for minimizing
the target or risk profile of individuals. Interestingly, while the individual
level event case analysis may focus attention to pre-event issues, the shift of
analysis to the group level within the same event may refocus attention to
post-event issues. In the case of suicide, the impact of the event on secondary
victims should be included in the analysis, thus examining the ripple effects and
implications of the individual event for members of the person's family group,
work group and community. Similarly, in a violent event, consideration should
be given to various groups affected by the event. For example, medical personnel
may be inadvertently drawn into violent incidents, through treatment intervention for either the victim(s) or the perpetrator. Finally, in the case of individual peak performance achievements, the event case analysis might use social
learning theory for examination of the modeling effects in observers of the peak
performance.

Organization Level

Business policy and strategy has made much better use of case studies than
has organizational behavior. Organizational behavior can also benefit from
event case studies at the organizational level. Event case studies at the organizational level may be more common for post mortems on organizational crises with
an eye to preparation and prevention (Pearson & Mitroff, 1993). Two organizational level events that are rich for idiographic analysis are Union Carbide's
problem in Bhopal, India, and Johnson & Johnson's two Tylenol crises in the
1980s.

Shrivastava's (1987) *Bhopal: Anatomy of a Crisis* is an example of an event
case study, with the focus on the Union Carbide organization. This event case
study is rich along the qualitative–quantitative dimension, and rich in the exploration of the general context of the causes and characteristics of industrial crises,
and the specific context of the Bhopal crisis. The HOT (i.e. human resource,
organization, technology) analysis used in Chapter 3 of the case study allows for
the elaboration of the contributing causes to the crisis internal to Union Carbide.

The chapter also explores the Union Carbide plant's context in the environment of Bhopal. As a native of Bhopal, Shrivastava (1987) is able to use rich descriptive detail for the reader and was well positioned for the personal interviews he conducted. In addition, he employs quantitative data, such as human death and injury estimates, morbidity in affected neighborhoods as of March 23, 1985, and compensation estimates, in a detailed discussion of the controversial consequences of the crisis. This case has some richness along the time dimension, with both retrospective (for example, survivor interviews) and prospective (for example, his study spanned 2 years) elements.

In the case of Johnson & Johnson, much is made of the J&J Credo as an embodiment of the organizational culture that guided the company through the two crises. Although organizational culture is a legitimate organizational behavior topic for focusing the idiographic analysis in this case, a second organizational behavior emphasis on ethical leadership might be taken. As Chairman and CEO of Johnson & Johnson, James Burke played a pivotal role in the 1970s and 1980s in modeling ethical leadership at the company (Murphy & Enderle, 1995). He completed undergraduate education at Holy Cross, a Catholic, Jesuit college, where he received important ethical and moral education. His business education came through his graduate work at Harvard Business School. Burke called Johnson & Johnson executives to a series of Credo challenge meetings in which the significance and meaning of the Credo, at that time 30 years old, was revisited. The importance of reaffirming the ethical and moral basis for the Credo was clear a decade later, when Burke led Johnson & Johnson in facing the two Tylenol crises. Burke concluded that trust was the core value at the heart of the successes Johnson & Johnson experienced in managing these crises. For Burke, trust grows on a groundwork of moral behavior. Is this interpretation correct? One of the characteristics of idiographic case analyses is that they are also open to alternative interpretations and analyses.

Subject Case Studies

In addition to learning from event case studies, idiographic research opens the possibility of learning from subject case studies. What has Richard Hackman learned from the egalitarian culture of the Orpheus Orchestra, or what has Donald Hastings learned in leading the legendary Lincoln Electric Company (Starbuck, 1996)? In contrast to event case studies, subject case studies take the individual, the group, or the organization as the unit of analysis. Single subject case studies anchor the idiographic dimension in Figure 25.1 and require an interplay from the other two dimensions in the figure to constitute science. That is, a single subject case must be studied over time, either retrospectively or prospectively, and/or it must be studied with qualitative and quantitative methods of inquiry to acquire any scientific value. Subject case studies may overlap with event case studies; the distinction is one of emphasis and focus.

Individuals

The subject case study of leaders is one rich area for idiographic research in organizational behavior, and biographies of great leaders is not a new concept. Students of history and biography use an eclectic approach to borrowing, building and then observing and modeling to construct their own implicit model of leadership (Joplin, 1993), and the life and leadership of George C. Marshall, both as a military leader and statesman, would exemplify an individual leader worthy of biographical study. Individual case studies are especially appropriate for high-achievement, even controversial, individuals who have a significant impact during their lives or careers, such as Woodrow Wilson, Dwight David Eisenhower, and Lee Iacocca (Quick, Nelson & Quick, 1987). These individuals may set benchmarks which serve as a basis for emulation, modeling, inspiration, internalization and enhanced self-efficacy. As Levinson (1987) notes, each of us carries within us an ego-ideal of our perfected self which serves as a goal for our continued development. While many of the elements of that ideal are unconsciously internalized over our life's development, we may make conscious choices of attributes in others that we admire and choose to emulate or model. Once internalized, these become part of the ego-ideal and serve to guide behavior as well as development over time.

Groups

Groups are another important subject for idiographic research, as noted by Gersick (1994) in referring to her earlier study of project teams. The earlier research led to a new model of group development which emphasized the timing and mechanisms of change in the context of group dynamics with their context (Gersick, 1988). Subject case studies of groups might well focus on elite teams (Labich, 1996). What is needed is not a set of profiles on such elite teams, but rather a careful and in-depth idiographic study of their structure, operation and function over time. The success of such elite teams is important, as illustrated in the case of Massachusetts General Hospital's trauma team in Boston. The Mass General emergency room sees about 200 patients each day, of which about one-third are admitted. A score (20 or so) of those admitted are triaged to the trauma center because of especially traumatic, violent, often life-threatening wounds: stabbing victims and gunshot victims are routinely rolled into the trauma center on gurneys. Scotsman Alasdair Conn, chief of emergency services and head of the trauma team, prefers members with some outside interest, such as sculling or numismatics, which enable the team members to escape the mental rigors of the high-performance work demands of the trauma center.

The lynchpin of all good science is critical and rigorous evaluation. Subject case studies of groups should increase the rigor and deepen our understanding of groups and teams in organizational behavior. So, an idiographic examination of the trauma team might challenge Conn's asserted preference. Is it valid? And, what is the best composition of the trauma team in terms of doctors, nurses and technicians? Should personality assessment be used in selecting team members? Finally, might any learning about this sort of elite team be transferable or adapted for other teams in high-stress work environments?

Organizations

Idiographic case studies of organizations might take one or more of three emphases. These would be the study of high-performance organizations, highly adaptive or learning organizations, and organizations successful in innovating or creating in response to changing conditions. Steers' (1977) organizational behavior view of organizational effectiveness found adaptability–flexibility and productivity to be the top two evaluation criteria. These criteria suggest that the case study of best practice organizations may be fruitful for the study of organizational behavior.

The long history of organization case study embedded in the Harvard Business School is illustrated in the earlier noted cases of American Airlines following the deregulation of the airline industry in the USA (Vietor, 1984, 1987) and Lincoln Electric Company (Starbuck, 1996). What appears different in the 1990s and may well continue into the twenty-first century is the rate of change impacting organizations, and individuals, throughout the world (Bettis & Hill, 1995; Gowing, Kraft & Quick, in press). High-velocity environments (Eisenhardt, 1989) may become an increasingly common context within which organizations operate. Therefore, organizations engaged in downsizing, restructuring, reorganization and revitalization provide rich organization subject case studies. The craft skills essential to conduct high quality organization case analyses are somewhat idiosyncratic, as are the subjects in idiographic research, so that using a grounded theory approach may prove a fruitful path to follow in conducting these subject case studies.

FROM DICHOTOMY TO DIALOGUE

Where Engel (1987) sees dichotomy, Johnson & Hall (1996) and I see the potential for dialogue. In the alternative approaches to organizational behavior research, it often appears that there are irreconcilable differences between the opposing views (Lee, 1991). This is quite unfortunate, given that all alternative approaches to the advancement of knowledge and understanding fall under the larger umbrella of scientific inquiry. Listening to the acrimony that sometimes accompanies the debates between approaches might cause one to reflect on the Spanish Inquisition and the search for heretics, identified for execution (why not just excommunication?) for their failed beliefs. One function of Figure 25.1 is to communicate the interconnectedness of idiographic and nomothetic research; qualitative and quantitative research. The strongest debates appear to occur between the proponents of each anchor of these two continua in the figure, although there can be equal debate between retrospective, cross-sectional and prospective investigators. The potential for dialogue and learning increases with a deepening understanding and appreciation for (a) the limitations of our own preferred scientific approaches, and (b) the strengths of our less preferred approaches. The next generation of organizational behavior scholars have a rich set of tools and alternatives to plow new furrows with their own unique patterns.

Acknowledgments

The author thanks Joyce Adkins and David Harrison, David Mack and Debra L. Nelson for their critical reviews of an early draft of this chapter. He is grateful to David Harrison for the suggested three-dimensional framework presented in Figure 25.1.

REFERENCES

Adkins, J.A. (in press). Base closure: a case study in occupational stress and organizational decline. In M. Gowing, J. Kraft & J.C. Quick (eds), *The New Organizational Reality*. Washington, DC: American Psychological Assocation.

Bandura, A. (1977). *Social Learning Theory*. Englewood Cliffs, NJ: Prentice-Hall.

Bass, B.M. & Stogdill, R.M. (1990). *Handbook of Leadership, 3rd edn*. New York: Free Press.

Behling, O. (1980). The case for the natural science model for research in organizational behavior and organizational theory. *Academy of Management Review*, 5, 483–90.

Bettelheim, B. (1983). *Freud and Man's Soul*. New York: Knopf.

Bettis, R.A. & Hill, M.A. (1995). The new competitive landscape. *Strategic Management Journal*, 16, 7–19.

Doyle, Sir A.C. (1938). *The Complete Sherlock Holmes*, de luxe edn. Garden City, NY: Garden City Publishing Co.

Dewey, J. & Bentley, A. (1973). The knowing and the known. In R. Handy & E.C. Harwood (eds), *Useful Procedures of Inquiry*. Great Barrington, MA: Behavioral Research Council (originally published 1949).

Eisenhardt, K.M. (1989). Making fast strategic decisions in high-velocity environments. *Academy of Management Journal*, 32, 543–76.

Engel, G. (1987). Physician scientists and scientific physicians: resolving the humanism–science dichotomy. *American Journal of Medicine*, 82, 107–11.

Gersick, C.J.G. (1988). Time and transition in work teams: toward a new model of group development. *Academy of Management Journal*, 31, 9–41.

Gersick, C.J.G. (1994). Pacing strategic change: the case of a new venture. *Academy of Management Journal*, 37, 9–45.

Gleick, J. (1987). *Chaos: Making a New Science*. New York: Viking.

Gowing, M., Kraft, J. & Quick, J.C. (eds) (in press). *The New Organizational Reality*. Washington, DC: American Psychological Assocation.

Harrison, D.A. (1995). Volunteer motivation and attendance decisions: competitive theory testing in multiple samples from a homeless shelter. *Journal of Applied Psychology*, 80, 371–85.

Johnson, J.V. & Hall, E.M. (1996). The dialectic between conceptual and causal inquiry in psychosocial work environment research. *Journal of Occupational Health Psychology*, 1, 362–74.

Joplin, J.R. (1993). Developing effective leadership: an interview with Henry Cisneros,

Secretary, US Department of Housing and Urban Development. *Academy of Management Executive*, **7**, 84–92.

Labich, K. (1996). Elite teams get the job done. *Fortune*, **19 February**, 90–99.

Laing, R.D. (1971). Intervention in social situations. In *The Politics of the Family and Other Essays* (pp. 21–42). New York: Random House.

Lance, C.E., Stewart, A.M. & Carretta, T.R. (1996). On the treatment of outliers in cognitive and psychomotor test data. *Military Psychology*, **8**, 43–58.

Lee, A.S. (1991). Integrating positivist and interpretive approaches to organizational research. *Organizational Science*, **2**, 342–64.

Levinson, H. (1987). Psychoanalytic theory in organizational behavior. In J.W. Lorsch (ed.), *Handbook of Organizational Behavior* (pp. 51–61). Englewood Cliffs, NJ: Prentice-Hall.

Locke, E.A. & Latham, G.P. (1990). *A Theory of Goal Setting & Task Performance*. Englewood Cliffs, NJ: Prentice-Hall.

Luthans, F. & Davis, T.R.V. (1982). Idiographic approach to organizational behavior research: the use of single case experimental designs and direct measures. *Academy of Management Review*, **7**, 380–91.

Meyer, A.D. (1982). Adapting to environmental jolts. *Administrative Science Quarterly*, **27**, 515–37.

Meyer, A.D. (1992). Journey three: from loose coupling to environmental jolts. In P. Frost & R. Stablein (eds), *Doing Exemplary Research* (pp. 82–98). Newbury Park, CA: Sage.

Murphy, P.B. & Enderle, G. (1995). Managerial ethical leadership: examples do matter. *Business Ethics Quarterly*, **5**, 117–28.

Payne, R. (1978). Epistemology and the study of stress at work. In C.L. Cooper & R. Payne (eds), *Stress at Work* (pp. 259–83). Chichester: Wiley.

Payne, R., Jick, T.D. & Burke, R.J. (1982). Whither stress research? An agenda for the 1980s. *Journal of Occupational Behaviour*, **3**, 131–45.

Pearson, C.M. & Mitroff, I.I. (1993). From crisis-prone to crisis-prepared: a framework for crisis management. *Academy of Management Executive*, **7**, 48–59.

Quick, J.C. (1988). Scientific inquiry and stress. *Naturwissenschaften und Geistwissenschaften. Stress Medicine*, **4**, 137–8.

Quick, J.C., Nelson, D.L. & Quick, J.D. (1987). Successful executives: how independent? *Academy of Management Executive*, **1**, 139–46.

Shrivastava, P. (1987). *Bhopal: Anatomy of a Crisis*. Cambridge, MA: Ballinger.

Simon, H.A. (1969/1996). *The Sciences of the Artificial*, 3rd edn. Cambridge, MA: MIT Press.

Starbuck, W.H. (1996). *Learning from Unusual Events*. Briarcliff Manor, NY: Academy of Management.

Staw, B.M., Sandelands, L.E. & Dutton, J.E. (1981). Threat-rigidity effects in organizational behavior: a multilevel analysis. *Administrative Science Quarterly*, **26**, 501–24.

Steers, R.M. (1977). *Organizational Effectiveness*. Santa Monica, CA: Goodyear.

Steers, R.M. & Porter, L.W. (1991). *Motivation and Work Behavior*, 5th edn. New York: McGraw-Hill.

Taylor, F.W. (1939). *Scientific Management*. New York: Harper and Brothers. This edition of Frederick W. Taylor's work contains: (1) his paper entitled "Shop Management" presented at the 1903 national meeting of the American Society of Mechanical Engineers in Sarasota, NY; (2) his 1911 book *The Principles of Scientific Management*; and (3) the public document (Hearings Before Special Committee of the House of Representatives to Investigate the Taylor and Other Systems of Shop Management under Authority of House Resolution 90; vol. III, pp. 1377–1508) containing Dr Taylor's testimony before the committee from Thursday, 25 January 1912 through Tuesday, 30 January 1912.

Vietor, R. (1984). *American Airlines (A), (B), (C)*. Cambridge, MA: Harvard Business School.
Vietor, R. (1987). *American Airlines (A, revised)*. Cambridge, MA: Harvard Business School.
Yukl, G.A. (1994). *Leadership in Organizations*, 3rd edn. Englewood Cliffs, NJ: Prentice Hall.

Chapter 26

Toward an Explication of "Morale": In Search of the *m* Factor

Dennis W. Organ
Indiana University, Bloomington, IN, USA

This chapter argues for a reintroduction of the construct "morale" as a general factor underlying attitudinal/perceptual measures provided by members of organizations. Such a construct fits the data linking various measured antecedents to organizational citizenship behavior (OCB). Relating established measures of psychological states to an "*m*" factor would serve the interests of theoretical parsimony, as well as facilitate the communication of our knowledge to practitioners. A brief review is offered of how the term has been previously used and of pertinent speculations on what this factor might represent.

Herrnstein & Murray (1994) and Gottfredson (1996) have argued that the "*g*" factor of general intelligence will become increasingly important in an economy driven by complex technology. While *g* has been known for some years now to be a predictor of performance in almost any job, its power to predict increases with the complexity of the task. By all accounts, the jobs that will provide substantial material, social and psychological rewards in the coming years will be those steeped in complexity and drawing predominantly upon cognitive abilities.

Of course, Herrnstein & Murray and Gottfredson have reference to what we might call *task* or *technical* performance. But there is another dimension of performance, one referred to as *contextual* performance or sometimes called *organizational citizenship behavior* (OCB). This other dimension of performance includes those contributions that members render in the form of helping others, practicing courtesy in work-based transactions, and maintenance of the formal and informal structures of day-to-day governance of the workplace. Such contributions typically go beyond the formal job description (which usually emphasizes

Creating Tomorrow's Organizations. Edited by C.L. Cooper and S.E. Jackson.
© 1997 John Wiley & Sons Ltd.

task or technical performance) and enable groups to deal with many of the unforeseen episodes of interdependence upon each other. We could enumerate a lengthy list of such specific behaviors, but what they all have in common is that, however much managers or supervisors might appreciate them, they are hard pressed to "demand" or "enforce" them, neither can they often "guarantee" proportionate recompense for them in the form of pay or benefits.

I will state here two premises upon which the remainder of this chapter rests. First, while the g factor of intelligence predicts task or technical performance rather well, the more so as the task becomes complex, it generally does not predict contextual performance so well (Borman & Motowidlo, 1993). Rather, the evidence suggests that various indicators of *morale*, which is at best weakly related to technical performance, fares somewhat better in accounting for contextual performance. Second—and here I have much less in the way of hard data—contextual performance will become more important in the years ahead. I assert this premise based on the general observation that the bureaucratic forms of organization are giving way to a form of collective enterprise much less susceptible to precise formulation of job descriptions or to reliable measurement of individual task performance. Already, *Fortune* has featured a cover story predicting the end of the very concept of "job" as a finite and stable set of member requirements. As we have heard so often, the team—or, more likely, overlapping, evolving, changing sets of teams—become the important level of analysis; and teams demand much in the way of OCB. Put simply, organizations will increasingly depend more upon what people are *willing* to do, even in the most mundane forms, just as much as what they are cognitively able to do.

Putting these two premises together, then, the corollary is that morale must take its rightful place alongside cognitive ability in accounting for the effective workplaces of the future.

REVISITING MORALE

It has been quite some time now since we have read or heard much about "morale". Indeed, few of us would claim the status of construct for the term. As of 1973 the word was delisted in the *Index of Psychological Abstracts*, presumably consigning the concept to the dustbin of history. We no longer speak of morale as causing anything, and of course we make no effort to measure it. What we have rather are a host of more "precise" terms such as job satisfaction, job involvement, alienation, burnout, organizational commitment, group cohesion, trust in management, along with a separate array of "perceptions" of the workplace, i.e. dimensions of the "climate" of the organization, such as leadership styles, fairness of reward systems and procedures, supportiveness of management, organic vs. mechanistic, and the list goes on. And of course we invest herculean efforts into specifying the linkages among these various perceptions and the internal states theoretically affected by them. Like the physicist's intent to break matter down into its ever more minute constituent parts, we seem to measure our progress by our ability to multiply the number of narrower constructs associated with the cognitive/affective "set" of the person.

Perhaps it is time to question the value of such a vast smorgasbord of measures of specific attitudes and perceptions. It is not at all clear that such an approach translates into either a profounder knowledge or a more useful set of prescriptions for our consumers and constituents. James & James (1989), commenting on the unwieldy body of findings and propositions constituting the organizational climate literature, suggested that:

> The existing tendencies to compartmentalize environmental perception research by environmental domains such as jobs and leaders have resulted in a large, diffuse set of perceptual constructs that not only lacks a unifying theme, but also lacks an integrated theory regarding the substantive impact of the perceived work environment on individuals (James & James, 1989, p. 748).

The point is not to suggest that all or any of the myriad measures of member attitudes and perceptions lack "validity". In some purely technical sense, as might be borne out by confirmatory factor analysis, each of these measures might well, and probably does, tap something untapped, or not tapped as well, by alternative measures. Certainly we can distinguish between, say, satisfaction with supervision and satisfaction with pay, and it is abundantly conceivable that good leaders and good pay are not perfectly correlated. Nor is the call here to "throw out" any of these measures, which have been so laboriously developed and sometimes serve useful ends.

What I rather propose is that we consider the possibility that all such measures share, to varying degrees, some underlying general factor, insofar as they tell us anything about what goes on in the thoughts and emotions of the respondents.

An apt analogy is suggested by the g factor of intelligence (Gottfredson, 1996). There are many measures of cognitive ability, and no one has any trouble separating verbal ability from mathematical ability. Similarly, there are "valid" measures of such aptitudes as the ability to memorize lists of nonsense syllables or to interpret three-dimensional configurations from two-dimensional blueprints. Most people are better, relatively speaking, on some of these specific mental abilities than others, and the measures are found to be useful for certain ends. Still, we find that, overall, these measures are correlated, and several decades of factor-analyzing measures of mental abilities attest to an underlying factor that runs through all of them. And it happens that the more the measure taps into this general or g factor, the more useful the measure appears to be for some purposes, notably in the prediction of job performance (Gottfredson, 1996). The advantage of an underlying construct (supported, of course, by empirical data and analysis) is that it is not only meaningful, but oh so convenient, to speak of a single referent, whether that referent be regarded as a cause or effect in the matters of interest. We have an invaluable tool for summarizing and handling a lot of data— which is precisely what Kaplan (1964) fingered as one of the major functions of theory.

If we are to think of ourselves in any recognizable sense as practicing an applied science, we ultimately have to be able to state functional relationships in terms comprehensible by the non-specialist consumer of such knowledge. Arguably, we can do this much better with one term than with dozens. The only consideration that should prevent us from doing this would be the lack of empirical foundation for talking in this fashion.

So, is there such a foundation?

m AND OCB

For 15 years I have studied predictors of what I call "organizational citizenship behavior" (OCB). Early on, we found that job satisfaction related more closely to contextual performance than to productivity, technical excellence, or in-role task performance. We found appreciable correlations between respondent job satisfaction and supervisory ratings of the extent to which members helped co-workers, involved themselves in the issues of the workplace, took care of organizational property, and exhibited conscientious attendance and punctuality. Perhaps, then, job satisfaction might have much to do with the everyday mundane and discretionary contributions that are not constrained by ability or technology, while ability accounts for in-role task performance.

However, we were not content to measure only job satisfaction. We proceeded to look at leader supportiveness, perceived fairness, job scope, and organizational commitment, to name just a few perceptual/attitudinal complexes. We also examined the ability of various personality traits to predict OCB. As evidence accumulated, we sought to demonstrate that one or two of these predictors were the "real" or "direct" causes of OCB and others were 'spurious" or "indirect". In other words, we assumed that one or more psychological factors—whether it be cognitive, affective, perceptual, state or trait—"mediated" the effects of others. We wanted to get as many of those constructs in the picture as we could and somehow get them to line up in a neat, consistent, meaningful diagram of separate and distinct, direct and indirect causes.

A meta-analysis of 55 studies of OCB (Organ & Ryan, 1995) allowed us to compare the relative predictive power of satisfaction, fairness, organizational commitment and leader consideration in accounting for two types of OCB: Altruism, or forms of OCB that have as their target a specific individual (such as a co-worker); and Compliance, which pertains to the citizenship exhibited in less personal, more organizational fashion, such as exemplary conduct in following the rules, conscientiousness in use of work time, and respecting organizational property.

If we assume that each of the four predictor measures indexed a distinct psychological state, and if one (or some subset) of them acted as "direct" causes of OCB while the others represented either "indirect" causes or "spurious" relationships (by virtue of their coincidental co-variation with the "direct" causes), then we should have found one or more of the estimated population correlation coefficients much larger than the others. That is not at all what we found: to our surprise, the estimates were very similar. For Altruism, the estimated coefficients were 0.259, 0.238, 0.247 and 0.271 for satisfaction, fairness, organizational commitment, and leader consideration, respectively. For Compliance, the numbers were 0.243, 0.236, 0.255 and 0.291. Even with aggregate ns running into the thousands, the 95% confidence bands around these estimates overlap appreciably.

This rather flat profile of coefficients certainly argued against any position that some one of these constructs towered above the others in explanatory power. Furthermore, our own data in the meta-analysis, along with published results from other meta-analyses, such as that by Mathieu & Zajac (1990) of organizational commitment and one by Wofford & Liska (1993) of leader consideration, attest to the rather large correlations *between* each pair of the predictors. We therefore interpreted the data as arguing strongly for a model of OCB as a function of some more basic factor underlying the set of predictors. If those predictors overlapped to the extent of capturing something analagous to the g factor in intelligence, then perhaps this underlying common factor—call it m—was something that people had in mind when they referred to "morale".

Viswesvaran, Ones & Schmidt (1994) have argued for a "new paradigm for theory testing in the social sciences" by combining meta-analysis and path analysis. In brief, the estimates of population true score correlations between constructs are used as the co-variance input to structural equation modeling. Use of this approach allowed an exploratory test of a model positing a general morale (m) factor that leads to OCB, with measures of satisfaction, perceived fairness, organizational commitment and leader consideration intercorrelated with each other and correlated with OCB due to their loading on m.

There is some difference of opinion as to the appropriateness of inputting correlation coefficients as co-variance matrices into structural equation models (Cudeck, 1989). Also, certain problems arise when using correlations derived from meta-analysis. One such problem is the "empty cell". In our data, we had no way to estimate the true score population coefficient between fairness and leader consideration. I used the method suggested by Viswesvaran, Ones & Schmidt (1994) and estimated the true score population correlation between leader consideration and perceived fairness, by taking the average of five pairwise coefficients available from the set of predictors. Another problem was to decide on the relevant total n. I decided, arbitrarily but conservatively, to use an n of 1500 in the analysis.

I elected to treat the Altruism and Compliance measures (which generally intercorrelated in the range of 0.30–0.60) as indicators of an underlying theoretical construct akin to what Chester Barnard called "willingness of persons to contribute efforts to the cooperative system" (Barnard, 1938/1968, p. 83).

The matrix of estimated population correlations appear in Table 26.1; the model fitted to these coefficients (using the program EQS) is shown in Figure 26.1. Two estimates of fit, the Bentler–Bonnet Normed Fit Index and the Comparative Fit Index, computed at 0.935 and 0.936, respectively, and indicate a

Table 26.1 Matrix of estimates of true-score population correlations

	Satisfaction	Fairness	Organization Commitment	Leader consideration	Altruism	Compliance
Satisfaction	1.000					
Fairness	0.650	1.000				
Organization commitment	0.698	0.615	1.000			
Leader consideration	0.698	0.618*	0.437	1.000		
Altruism	0.259	0.238	0.247	0.271	1.000	
Compliance	0.243	0.236	0.255	0.291	0.656	1.000

* Coefficient estimated by average of estimates for population coefficients of other pairwise relationships among Satisfaction, Fairness, Organizational Commitment, and Leader Consideration.

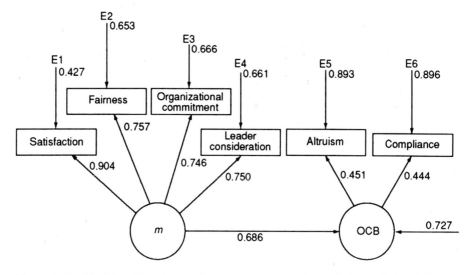

Figure 26.1 Model linking observed measures, a general morale factor (*m*) and OCB

rather good approximation of the model to the data. Of the four predictor measures, satisfaction appears to have the strongest loading on the hypothesized underlying *m* factor. However, none of the loadings, either in absolute or relative terms, can be taken too literally, because various forms of the measures (e.g. general job satisfaction, satisfaction with supervision, extrinsic and intrinsic satisfaction) were grouped together. Still, the suggestive evidence seems to support the idea that a general factor underlies contextual performance.

OTHER EVIDENCE

Two separate quasi-experiments by Skarlicki & Latham (1996a, 1996b) sought to assess the effect of training union officers in procedural fairness. The hypothesis was that such training would, by increasing the fairness perceptions of union rank-and-file, cause an increase in union-related citizenship behaviors, in comparison to holdout comparison groups in which union leaders were not so trained. The hypothesis was supported. Curiously, though, in both interventions (separated temporally, and geographically, and in very different types of union workers) the data strongly indicated that there was a direct effect of the training beyond that explained by changes in fairness perceptions. In other words, even when statistically controlling for the (supposed) mediating factor of fairness perceptions, there was still a significant effect upon OCB attributable to the training of the union leaders in procedural fairness. The lesson would seem to be that it is very difficult to change just one dimension of morale.

James & James (1989), using confirmatory factor analysis, found support for a model positing a single general second-order factor underlying 27 measures of perceptions of organization climate and four first-order factors. They drew an analogy between this factor and the g factor in intelligence, and suggested that it represents a person's general assessment of the extent to which the work environment is personally beneficial or detrimental to the well-being of the individual.

James & James found this general factor to have a very high relationship to a measure of overall job satisfaction (but little relationship to the personality measures of need for achievement, rigidity and self-esteem). Thus, the more positive this assessment, the greater the satisfaction of the participant.

Obviously, James & James' analysis preserves the distinction between *perceptions of the environment* and *descriptions of internal states*. In a theoretical sense, certainly, we can grant the plausibility of a model stating that perceptions of "what's out there" influence "what's inside". The problem, though, is that we never have access to "perceptions" as such. We have only people's reports of them. Ditto for internal states (such as attitudes, feelings, satisfactions). People's descriptions of their work environments are seldom, if ever, affectively neutral judgments. Almost every scale devised to register subjects' "perceptions" of their environment consists of some items that have widely shared meanings of "good" or "bad". The higher the "morale" of the workforce (in the general sense in which the term was historically used), the more likely it is that the workforce will describe the organization and/or its management in ways that are thought to be "good".

The point, then, is that many measures intended to provide merely *descriptions* of the work environment are quite likely to contain *evaluations* of the environment as well. It becomes quite practicable to think of a diverse set of attitudinal/perceptual indicants as sharing loadings on an underlying *m* factor.

SO, WHAT IS THIS *m* FACTOR?

One objection to the use of the term "morale" in any serious analytical discussion is the lack of consistency with which the concept has been defined. Child (1941) noted three clearly different conceptions. Two of them treated morale as an emergent characteristic of the group, i.e. a property of the group as a whole and

not as an individual's state. A third definition found in Child's review referred to
"... a condition of physical and emotional well-being in the individual that makes
it possible for him to work and live hopefully and effectively...." (Child, 1941, p.
393).

Earlier, Roethlisberger & Dickson (1939/1967), in their famed account of the
Hawthorne researches, seem to have applied the term at both the individual and
group levels. They reported that during the First Relay Assembly Test Room
studies:

> a change in morale had also been observed ... no longer were the girls isolated
> individuals ... had become participating members of a working group with all the
> psychological and social implications peculiar to such a group ... bound together by
> common sentiments and feelings of loyalty (p. 86).

Yet in *Management and the Worker* (Roethlisberger & Dickson, 1939/1967) we
also read of "a change in mental attitude or morale" (p. 190).

Scott (1967) conceived of "morale" as an "intra-organismic condition or
process", and his semantic differential measure of morale is clearly meant to
reflect the condition of the individual. Scott's analysis identified three factors in
the "me at work" scale of his instrument, one of which appears to reflect the
person's characteristic activation or energy arousal level at work. However,
the fact that Scott bracketed the term with quotation marks in the title of his
report implies that he might have been using the work in a deliberately ironic
fashion.

In recent years, only Hershey (1985) has gone on record with an attempt to
revive the concept of morale and stamp it with a distinctive referent. Hershey
takes strenuous exception to any usage that equates morale with job satisfaction.
In fact, he does not countenance the use of the word "morale" at the individual
level at all. He stresses that:

> Morale is a group phenonmenon ... a state of enthusiasm that a group has for *its*
> objectives ... *true group morale* exists when the group members and their leader
> ... wish to achieve...." the same goal for the same reason (Hershey, 1985, pp. 1,
> 21).

Hershey would not even use the term for all groups, "... because most of the
time many work groups *have no goal of their own*" (p. 27). Hershey seems to
believe that the research community began to equate morale with job satisfaction
because the latter lent itself to more straightforward measurement with attitude
scales, leading eventually to dropping morale out of the picture altogether.

My own view is that Hershey is unduly strict in his insistence that the concept
should pertain only to the group. I would compromise with him to the extent of
suggesting that we reserve the term for *group contexts* but allow it to refer to the
individual *within that context*. I also find something appealing in Hershey's emphasis on "enthusiasm" for a common goal as a defining aspect of morale. I think
I am comfortable with speaking of the morale of both individuals and the group

as a whole, so long as it is understood to imply that individuals separately, and the group as a whole, accept some (not perfect) commonality of purpose, are disposed to evaluate positively the existing collective arrangements for achieving that purpose, and have a sense of group efficacy for pursuing and realizing those ends.

However, I think it would be a mistake to construe an *m* factor as purely cognitive in its nature. It probably would not hold much interest for us if it were devoid of cognitions, but Scott's "activation" and Hershey's "enthusiasm" imply something more than pale cognitions. To qualify as *m*, perhaps we should demand that these cognitions have some potency to them.

In order to flesh out our understanding of the *m* factor, research is needed along the following lines of questioning:

1. We desire more complete knowledge of what the *effects* of morale are—much as our understanding of intelligence has developed as a function of what its effects are. What, besides OCB, are probably consequences of morale? Might not, for example, a "healthy" level of complaining be one such effect? What about the effort expended to satisfy a customer?

2. How do different measures compare in their loadings on the *m* factor? Scores of measures of affective/perceptual referents have made their way into the literature. Perhaps it could become a routine practice, whenever several such referents are used in a study, to employ them as indicants of *m* and examine their loadings on a general factor. Theoretically, this practice might well tell us something about the factor, as well as lead to an economical and practical means of indexing *m* for research and practice.

3. What is the role of personality in *m*? We have reason now to implicate disposition in accounting for a certain share of the variance in job satisfaction. Some research even suggests that this dispositional factor is genetic. But in what manner does this effect occur? Are some people just naturally more energetic, upbeat, cheerful? Or do some people just "get along" better with others? Taking the latter tack, we might expect individual differences to become more important in determining morale as tenure accumulates. Gottfredson (1996), noting that the heritability factor in *g* actually increases, rather than decreases, with age, suggests that (ironically) it is because initial differences in *g* lead to changes in one's environment and these changes accumulate. Thus, one or more personality factors might well shape the person's immediate work environment, mainly as a function of how people respond to them.

    One caveat: Given the relatively poor record of self-report measures of personality in predicting OCB, it would be nice to have other-ratings of the designated dispositional variable in future research on personality and morale.

4. As noted previously, the term "morale" seems intuitively to imply something about activation or energy arousal. With the exception of Scott (1967), we do not, to my knowledge, have any device that can be confidently regarded as

capturing variance in activation. People can be passively, even dully, satisfied. Surely morale means more than this. How can we capture this dimension of morale? Are there particular formats that would allow respondents to
express this quality in their perceptions or feelings?

5. It remains to be seen whether, empirically and logically, the construct of
    morale fits just as well at the individual or group level of analysis. Imaginative
    research designs and analytic schemes will be needed to test the explanatory
    power of the construct within and across levels of analysis.

6. One could well expect that evidence bearing on the preceding question will
    feed back into the question preceding it, i.e. if morale is a meaningful con-
    struct only at the group level, then perhaps we need to ask if work groups
    have a tendency to assort themselves into particular patterns of traits that are
    similar or, conceivably, quite different but complementary.

WHY THESE QUESTIONS ARE IMPORTANT

Our constituents who are charged with making jobless, technology-driven, team-
based organizations function and survive are looking for some answers—or, if not
answers, a few clues. It is not enough for them or us just to know that there is a
general morale factor (they probably think this way already). They look to us for,
among other things:

1. *A means of monitoring morale.* Arguably, today's managers understand bet-
    ter than their forebears that declines in morale don't show up otherwise in
    hard accounting or engineering indices until months, sometimes years, later.
    Surely we could render a signal contribution by providing a valid, reliable
    measure that includes dimensions of perceptions, affect and activation.

2. *What they can do that would affect morale.* How much of morale, for example,
    is in fact already determined by hiring decisions? Is it possible that we can
    hire for good morale, but our managing can do no better than keep the
    morale we hired, while at worst, mismanaging can cause us to lose that
    morale? If morale is to be regarded foremost as a group concept, then
    programs of team development need to address this. To what dimensions of
    the workplace is morale most sensitive? Do attributions matter—is morale
    more robust to the slings and arrows of misfortune if the latter can be
    attributed to external, unavoidable causes?

3. *Is it conceivable that morale is better left alone?* Perhaps we are dealing here
    with a phenomenon governed by its own dynamics of waxing and waning. We
    know now that mood swings have their own logic and rhythm; we have heard
    much of athletes "in a zone" or witnessed at "peak performance". Maybe
    morale, individual or group, simply cannot be sustained for long periods at
    high levels.

4. To revisit Herzberg, *are "good" and "poor" morale opposites of each other?*
    That is, are the causes of poor morale simply the opposites of whatever

causes good morale? Or does it even make sense to think of morale in traditional linear terms, let alone as a continuum? There is the possibility of several qualitatively different morale states, particularly if the underlying affective, perceptual, and arousal dimensions are imperfectly correlated with each other.

In one fashion or another, these questions have doubtless been asked before, and just as frequently by the reflective practitioner as the scholar. Essentially they all come down to the question of apportioning the proper relative importance to ability and attitude, to situation and person. If there is even a modicum of substance to what the pundits and soothsayers are telling us about the workplace of the approaching millennium, then these questions have a renewed urgency.

REFERENCES

Barnard, C.I. (1938). *The Functions of the Executive*, 30th Anniversary edn. Cambridge, MA: Harvard University Press (reprinted 1986).

Borman, W.C. & Motowidlo, S.J. (1993). Expanding the criterion domain to include elements of contextual performance. In N. Schmitt & W.C. Borman (eds), *Personality and Selection* (pp. 71–98). San Francisco, CA: Jossey-Bass.

Child, I.L. (1941). Morale: a bibliographical review. *Psychological Bulletin*, **38**, 393–420.

Cudeck, R. (1989). Analysis of correlation matrices using co-variance structure models. *Psychological Bulletin*, **105**, 317–26.

Gottfredson, L.S. (1996). What do we know about intelligence? *American Scholar*, **Winter**, 15–30.

Herrnstein, R.J. & Murray, C. (1994). *The Bell Curve: Intelligence and Class Structure in American Life*. New York: Free Press.

Hershey, R. (1985). *Organizational Morale*. Kings Point, NY: Kings Point Press.

James, L.A. & James, L.R. (1989). Integrating work environment perceptions: explorations into the measurement of meaning. *Journal of Applied Psychology*, **74**, 739–51.

Kaplan, A. (1964). *The Conduct of Inquiry*. San Francisco, CA: Chandler.

Mathieu, J.E. & Zajac, D.M. (1990). A review and meta-analysis of the antecedents, correlates, and consequences of organizational commitment. *Psychological Bulletin*, **108**, 171–94.

Organ, D.W. & Ryan, K. (1995). A meta-analytic review of attitudinal and dispositional predictors of organizational citizenship behavior. *Personnel Psychology*, **48**, 775–98.

Roethlisberger, F.J. & Dickson, W.J. (1939). *Management and the Worker*. Cambridge, MA: Harvard University Press, 1967 edn.

Scott, W.E. Jr (1967). The development of semantic differential scales as measures of "morale". *Personnel Psychology*, **20**, 179–98.

Skarlicki, D.P. & Latham, G.P. (1996a). Increasing citizenship behavior within a labor union: a test of organizational justice theory. *Journal of Applied Psychology*, **81**, 161–9.

Skarlicki, D.P. & Latham, G.P. (1996b). Organizational justice training to increase citizenship behavior within a union: a replication. Unpublished manuscript, University of Toronto.

Viswesvaran, C., Ones, D.S. & Schmidt, F.L. (1994). Combining psychometric meta-analysis and path analysis for theory testing. Paper presented at 54th Annual Meeting of the Academy of Management, Dallas, TX.

Wofford, J.C. & Liska, L.Z. (1993). Path–goal theories of leadership: a meta-analysis. *Journal of Management*, **19**, 857–76.

Epilogue: Actionability and Design Causality

Chris Argyris
Harvard University, Boston, MA, USA

Most of the chapters in this book represent very interesting ideas about developing disciplinary perspectives. Each author examines the underlying features of her/his discipline and then makes thoughtful recommendations for the future. The focus of the recommendations is understandably inward. In most chapters, little attention is given to interdisciplinary focus that connects several disciplines.

If I read the history of organizational behavior correctly, most of the push for an interdisciplinary focus usually occurs with those scholars who seek to solve critical problems of organizations. It is this respect for the challenge of understanding reality—as faced by practitioners within organizations—that leads the scholars to widen their focus.

Scholars, I believe, are becoming increasingly aware that the very methodology they use to conduct empirical research may actually reinforce their inward focus. Elsewhere, I have tried to show that normal science positivist methodology pushes social scientists to be more oriented toward the status quo (Argyris, 1980).

Some readers have interpreted this stance as being an anti-positivism and pro-subjective humanistic approach. This is only partially accurate. I believe profoundly in the importance of empirically testing our claims. This responsibility is especially important for those scholars who seek to change the status quo and to develop prescriptive knowledge. Recently, I have suggested that the humanistic research also distances itself as much from reality as humanists claim positivistic researchers have done (Argyris, 1993, 1995).

I do not think that it is possible to challenge the status quo without conducting research that questions why the status quo must be considered sacred. One way to question the status quo is to compare it with rare and perhaps non-existing universes and to study what happens when such changes are made. For example,

Creating Tomorrow's Organizations. Edited by C.L. Cooper and S.E. Jackson.
© 1997 John Wiley & Sons Ltd.

scholars of the behavior theory of the firm conducting research on organizational learning focus primarily on environmental, single-loop learning that is based on describing the universe as is (Argyris & Schön, 1996). Indeed, scholars of that view question whether universes with, for example, high trust, minimally counterproductive (to learning) coalition group behavior are even likely to be discovered (Argyris, 1996a). Such claims may be correct but surely a claim as fundamental as that deserves to be tested by these scholars through empirical research.

Recently, Van de Ven & Polley (1992) have published an empirically rigorous (from a positivistic view) study that partially did not support their own theory of organizational learning. They included some observational and interview data that described various levels of organizational defenses to explain their findings. Let us assume their qualitative data and their inferences were correct. Why did they not conduct research to reduce such organizational defenses? Would that not be a more robust test of their explanation? Although they acknowledge the existence of organizational defenses, they do not include them as part of their theoretical and empirical work.

Some scholars may counter that they leave such theorizing and empirical work to others. I suggest that such a response is questionable because it is *their* theory of learning that was disconfirmed by their own research.

There is another important issue involved. Without such research, they make it unlikely that the practitioners who cooperated by giving financial support and making themselves available for study will ever be helped to change the world so that they can be more effective. Van de Ven & Polley (1992) are not the only scholars who pull back precisely at the point that their research might be helpful to those who helped them. It is this type of stance that has led thoughtful supporters of behavioral science research in Congress to begin to feel betrayed (Johnson 1993). They are questioning the claim scholars make that they should be free to study what they wish. These claims will not survive if we choose to stop our studies when we get to the point that our most important claims may be disconfirmed.

The more I study these issues, the more I am convinced that researchers should accept actionability to be as important as validity (which I consider to be very important). I am also increasingly convinced that actionability may require a somewhat different version of causality, one that I call "design causality". My major recommendation for the future is that scholars take the production of actionable knowledge more seriously.

ACTIONABLE KNOWLEDGE

External validity is the claim that the results obtained in the research context are relevant to other contexts, especially that of the world of practice. Relevance is a necessary but not sufficient condition for actionable knowledge. For example, trust is a variable with high external validity, yet much of the research that shows its relevance rarely includes knowledge about how to *create* trust. "Create" is a key word.

Actionable knowledge is that knowledge that actors use to create consequences that they intend. In order to create (for example) trust, one must understand and predict. Understanding and prediction, however, are necessary but not sufficient features of actionable knowledge. If one asks the question, "How do you know when you know and understand phenomena like trust?" the answer, I suggest, is "When you can create or produce it in everyday life".

Most researchers state that the purpose of their research is to describe their universe as accurately as possible. They strive to produce generalizable propositions that contain the causal mechanisms related to the phenomena under study. For example, scholars of the behavioral theory of the firm observe human beings acting. The observations are organized into patterns. Some of these patterns are called key relational variables: they include limited learning, quasi-resolution of conflict, and coalition group rivalries. These concepts describe the patterns that the scholars inferred from their observations of the universe.

These descriptions do not include the causal mechanisms that the subjects used to create the patterns that the scholars observed in the first place. To my knowledge, that is not a central focus of those researchers (Argyris, 1996a). The scholars produce a set of patterns that describe the universe. They do not produce a description of the causal theories of action in the heads of the actors who produced what the scholars observed. This gap is not usually seen as a problem because the focus of most empirical research is to describe the universe. The gap is an enormous problem if the focus of the research is to describe the universe with causal propositions that explain how the universe was *created* in the first place.

An important feature of actionable knowledge is that the causal mechanisms inferred by the researchers are the same causal mechanisms that the subjects used when they were busy creating the actions that the researchers described and explained. What sense does it make to have a causal theory developed by social scientists to explain the behavior of the subjects that is different form the causal theory that the subjects used to create whatever actions the researchers are trying to explain?

ACTIONABLE KNOWLEDGE AND THE MIND/BRAIN[1]

I begin with the premise that human beings create (produce) actions. Human beings use their minds to create or produce actions. Therefore the form that actionable knowledge takes is guided and constrained by the type of knowledge that the mind can use in order to act. The mind uses designs as causal explanations and prescriptions for action. Some features of designs are:

---

[1] I refer to the mind/brain as I do to indicate that they are ultimately inter-related.

1. Designs specify (a) the action strategies required to produce (b) intended consequences and (c) the governing variables (values that form an overall framework for effective action). In order for designs to be used to produce action, the specifications are ruthlessly programmed in the human mind. The mind cannot produce actions with programs that are soft. Actions that may appear to us as ambiguous or vague are produced by designs that are unambiguous and clear. Human behavior is as "hard"—indeed probably more so—than propositions expressed in quantitative terms.

2. Designs are user-friendly. For example, they are storable, retrievable, and implementable in real life. They should not require actions which, in order to be implemented correctly, would require that life pass the actor by. For example, there exists research on frustration. It concludes that mild frustration creates creative responses. After a threshold is passed the frustration creates regression (Argyris, 1980). In order for someone to use that knowledge, let us say to create creativity in a group, it would be necessary to measure for mild frustration as well as when the frustration point is reached. How does a practitioner assess these in real life? The practitioner could use the instruments the researchers created to conduct such measures during the research. The problem is, how are these instruments going to be introduced to the group? Are the members told that the objective is to create mild frustration? Would not filling out the instruments be interrupting and frustrating? If so, does that not exacerbate the consequences? (Argyris, 1993).

3. The correct use of a design should not necessarily lead to consequences that are counter to the design. For example, the research on trust and mass communication recommends a more complex message for a "smart" audience and a less complex message for a "not so smart" audience (Argyris, 1980). In order for these strategies to succeed, they must be covered up. If one tells the audience that the reason they are getting a simplified message is that they are considered "not so smart", one could destroy the trust intended to be created in the first place.

4. Since all designs are claims about how to achieve intended consequences, they are designs about effectiveness. Designs about effectiveness are normative. If designs are to enhance effectiveness, then they must be stated in ways that are generalizable (otherwise, we would have to have millions of designs) *and* applicable in the individual case (otherwise the gap between design and action in a specific context would be large). There can be no exceptions in a design used to produce actions. How can actors use a design in order to act effectively in a given situation if it permits exceptions in such situations?

During the 1996 Academy of Management session on actionable knowledge (attended by nearly 400), several scholars said that every year they have attended similar sessions. Yet no progress has been made. I believe the first step toward progress is for social scientists to take actionability as seriously as they take validity. As I have tried to show elsewhere, the requirements of normal science methodology to generate validity may actually inhibit actionability (Argyris,

1980, 1993, 1996b). This does not mean that we must water down the standards for validity. Indeed, scholars who claim actionability must be especially concerned about validity. The challenge is to find new methods to test form validity, methods that are so robust they can be used in the everyday world where we, as social scientists, cannot be in unilateral control of events.

REFERENCES

Argyris, C. (1996a). Unrecognized defenses of scholars: impact on theory and research. *Organization Science*, **7**(1), 79–87.

Argyris, C. (1996b). On actionability. *Journal of Applied Behavioral Science*, **32**(4) (forthcoming).

Argyris, C. & Schön, D. (1996). *Organizational Learning II*. Reading, MA: Addison-Wesley.

Argyris, C. (1995). Knowledge when used in practice tests theory: the case of applied communication research. In K.N. Cissna (ed.), *Applied Communication in the 21st Century* (pp. 1–22). Mahwah, NJ: Erlbaum.

Argyris, D. (1993). *Knowledge for Action*. San Francisco, CA: Jossey-Bass.

Argyris, C. (1980). *Inner Contradictions of Rigorous Research*. New York: Academic Press.

Johnson, C. (1993). Psychology in Washington: measurement to improve scientific productivity: a reflection on the Brown report. *Psychology Science*, **4**(2), 67–9.

Van de Ven, A. & Polley, D. (1992). Learning while innovating. *Organization Science*, **3**(1), 92–115.

Index

Index compiled by Indexing Specialists, Hove, Sussex